MATERIALIST FEMINISM

MATERIALIST FEMINISM

A Reader in Class, Difference, and Women's Lives

Edited by

Rosemary Hennessy

and

Chrys Ingraham

ROUTLEDGE
New York & London

Published in 1997 by

Routledge
29 West 35th Street
New York, NY 10001

Published in Great Britain by

Routledge
11 New Fetter Lane
London EC4P 4EE

Margaret Benston, "The Political Economy of Women's Liberation," from *Monthly Review,* September 1969. Mary Alice Waters, "The Politics of Women's Liberation Today," from *The Politics of Women's Liberation,* a Merit Pamphlet from Pathfinder Press, 1970. Selma James, "Introduction" and "Women and the Subverion of the Community" from Mariarosa Dalla Costa and Selma James, *The Power of Women and the Subversion of the Community,* 1972, Bristol England: Falling Water Press. Charlotte Bunch, "Not For Lesbians Only," from *Quest: A Feminist Quarterly,* Fall 1975. Christine Delphy, "For a Materialist Feminism," originally published in *L'Arc:* 61 (1975), English tr. Mary Jo Lakeland and Susan Ellis Wolf, from *Feminist Issues 1,* no. 2 (Winter 1981). Barbara Ehrenreich, *What Is Socialist Feminism?* 1976, from International Creative Management. Martha Gimenez, "The Oppression of Women: A Structuralist Marxist View," from "Structuralist Marxism on 'The Woman Question,'" in *Science in Society* (1978) 42.3: 301–23. Annette Kuhn and Ann Marie Wolpe, "Feminism and Materialism," from *Feminism and Materialism: Women and Modes of Production,* New York: Routledge, 1978. Michèle Barret, "Ideology and the Cultural Production of Gender," from *Women's Oppression Today: Problems in Marxist Feminist Analysis,* London: Verso, 1980. Iris Young, "Social Feminism and the Limits of Dual Systems Theory," from *Socialist Review* (1980) 50/51: 169–88. Gloria Joseph, The Incompatible Ménage à Trois," from *Women and Revolution: A Discussion of the Unhappy Marriage of Marxism and Feminism,* ed. Lydia Sargent, Boston: South End Press, 1981. Hazel V. Carby, "White Women Listen!" from *The Empire Strikes Back: Race and Racism in Britain,* by the Centre for Contemporary Cultural Studies, London: Hutchinson, 1982. Frigga Haug, "The Hoechst Chemical Company and Boredom with the Economy," from *Beyond Female Masochism,* London: Verso, 1982. Lise Vogel, "From the Woman Question to Women's Liberation," from *Women Questions: Essays for a Materialist Feminism,* New York: Routledge, 1995. Lindsey German, "Theories of the Family," from *Sex, Class and Socialism,* London: Bookmarks, 1989. Swasti Mitter, "Women Working Worldwide," from *Common Fate, Common Bond,* London: Pluto Press, 1986. Maria Mies, "Colonization and Housewifization," from *Patriarchy and Accumulation on a World Scale,* London: Zed Books, 1986. Rosemary Hennessy and Rajeswari Mohan, "The Construction of Woman in Three Popular Texts of Empire," from *Textual Practice* 3.3, 1989. Nellie Wong, "Socialist Feminism: Our Bridge to Freedom," from Mohanty, Russo, and Torres, eds., *Third World Women and the Politics of Feminism,* Bloomington: Indiana University Press, 1991. Norma Chinchilla, "Marxism, Feminism, and the Struggle for Democracy in Latin America," from *Gender and Society* (1991) 5: 3. Leslie Feinberg, from *Transgender Liberation: A Movement Whose Time Has Come,* New York: World Press, 1992. Rose M. Brewer, "Theorizing Race, Class and Gender," from Stanlie M. James and Abenda P. A. Busia, eds., *Theorizing Black Feminisms: The Visionary Pragmatism of Black Women,* New York: Routledge, 1993. Barbara Smith, "Where's the Revolution?" from *The Nation,* July 5, 1993. Lillian S. Robinson, "Touring Thailand's Sex Industry," from *The Nation,* 1994. Nicola Field, "Identity and the Lifestyle Market," from *Over the Rainbow: Money, Class and Homophobia,* London: Pluto Press, 1995. Chrys Ingraham, "The Heterosexual Imaginary," from *Sociological Theory,* July 1994. Kathryn Russell, "A Value-Theoretic Approach to Childbirth and Reproductive Engineering," from *Science and Society* 58.3 (Fall). All reprinted with permission.

Library of Congress Cataloging-in-Publication Data

Materialist feminism : a reader in class, difference, and women's
    lives / edited by Rosemary Hennessy and Chrys Ingraham.
       p.   cm.
    Includes bibliographical references and index.
    ISBN 0-415-91633-X (hb). — ISBN 0-415-91634-8 (pb)
    1. Women and socialism. 2. Feminism. 3. Feminist theory.
I. Hennessy, Rosemary. II. Ingraham, Chrys, 1947–
HX546.M396   1997
335'.0082—dc21   97-12406
                                                            CIP

To all the women whose labor contributed to making these knowledges
and for those who carry them on

Contents

Archive III: Ongoing Work

Acknowledgments

Like other public events, the publication of a book often relies on invisible labor, much of it women's. Many women have helped make this book possible. From those who contributed to the text itself to those who kept the editors functioning in a daily way, we owe a debt of gratitude.

Most significant of all was the work of Mary Ellen Wogan, who labored beyond all expectations to secure permissions, assist in technological production, and provide relief and homemade jam in moments of great stress. Our thanks to Russell Sage College faculty, staff, and administration for providing significant resources toward completion of this project. We are also grateful to the Lesbian Herstory Archive in Brooklyn, NY, for giving us access to their files on socialist and marxist feminism.

In addition, we want to thank the following friends and colleagues whose material support of various kinds helped make this collection possible: Toni Blackwell, Maureen Casey, Susan Cloninger, Penny Dugan, Michelle Frempong, Corinna Genschel, Marilyn Gewacke, Marni Gillard, Layne Hamilton, Molly Hennessy-Fiske, Sue Hillery, Pam Howell, Jane Hugo, Jean Hynes, Donna Inglima, Esther Jackson, Laurie James, Deb Kelsh, Lisa Koogle, Donna Lamb, David Milford, Claudia Murphy, Sonija Neroh, Kathy Olsen, Darcel Pina, Theresa Vaughan, and Hope Wallis.

We also wish to acknowledge the life of our good friend, Ingie La Fleur, whose legacy as a marxist and feminist fighter often inspired our work on this project.

Introduction

Reclaiming Anticapitalist Feminism

Rosemary Hennessy and Chrys Ingraham

THE NEED FOR CLASS ANALYSIS OF WOMEN'S DIFFERENT LIVES

We see this reader as a timely contribution to feminist struggle for transformative social change, a struggle which is fundamentally a class war over resources, knowledge, and power. Currently the richest 20 percent of humanity garners 83 percent of global income, while the poorest 20 percent of the world's people struggles to survive on just 1 percent of the global income (Sivard 1993; World Bank 1994). During the 1990s, as capitalism triumphantly secures its global reach, anticommunist ideologies hammer home socialism's inherent failure and the Left increasingly moves into the professional middle class, many of western feminism's earlier priorities—commitment to social transformation, attention to the political economy of patriarchy, analysis of the pervasive social structures that link and divide women—have been obscured or actively dismissed. Various forms of feminist cultural politics that take as their starting point gender, race, class, sexuality, or coalitions among them have increasingly displaced a systemic perspective that links the battle against women's oppression to a fight against capitalism. The archive collected in *Materialist Feminism: A Reader in Class, Difference, and Women's Lives* is a reminder that despite this trend feminists have continued to find in historical materialism a powerful theoretical and political resource. The tradition of feminist engagement with marxism emphasizes a perspective on social life that refuses to separate the materiality of meaning, identity, the body, state, or nation from the requisite division of labor that undergirds the scramble for profits in capitalism's global system.

As the gap widens between those who own and control the world's wealth and those who do not, women's labor continues to be a primary source of capital accumulation.

Feeding and caring for children, attending to the sick and the elderly, and providing one of the main sources of cheap labor in waged work have been women's longstanding contributions to capital accumulation across the globe. Women perform most of the world's socially necessary labor, and yet they are far more vulnerable to poverty than men. Many women in the United States working inside and outside the home must provide for themselves and their families on less than two-thirds of the wages earned by men. Of all poor people over eighteen living in the United States, 63 percent are women, and women who head households bear the brunt of poverty. This disproportionate impoverishment does not affect all women, nor does it affect them to the same degree. Again, using wages as a gauge of these differences, white women earn 70 percent of white men's earnings, while black women earn only 64 percent of what white men earn (U.S. Bureau of Census 1995). It is important to remember that poverty is not mainly a function of gender or race but a permanent feature of capitalism that affects children and men too. The socially produced differences of race, gender, and nationality are not distinct from class, but they play a crucial role—both directly and indirectly—in dividing the work force, ensuring and justifying the continued availability of cheap labor, and determining that certain social groups will be profoundly exploited while others will be somewhat cushioned. In this division, it is often children who lose the most; in fact, the vast majority of the world's poor are children.

If feminism is to maintain its viability as a political movement aimed at redressing women's oppression and exploitation worldwide, the theory that underlies feminist practice cannot eclipse the material realities that bind race, gender, sexuality, and nationality to labor. And yet, these are the very connections that have been abandoned by western feminists in the past twenty years. As feminism has been absorbed into the mainstream of advanced industrial societies and incorporated into the professions, its dominant voices have grown to disparage ways of making sense of women's lives that connect the oppressive construction of difference and identity to capital's drive to accumulate. Instead, feminists have increasingly promoted knowledges and political strategies that appeal to the visible differences of sex or race. When feminists have questioned visible differences as the basis for political movement or forging coalitions, the alternatives proposed often appeal to abstract, ahistorical, or merely cultural categories like desire, matter, or performativity. In bracketing the relationship of visibility and bodies to capitalism as a class-based system, feminism has implicitly and at times even explicitly embraced capitalism—or, more commonly, ignored it. Often when feminist analysis does address class it is as one of a series of oppressions experienced by individuals. But this seeming "return to class" is in fact a retreat from class analysis. As Ellen Mieskens Wood has indicated, the retreat from class occurs not so much because class disappears from feminist analysis but because it has been transformed into another form of oppression.[1] The effect is that class is unhinged from the political economy of capitalism and class power is severed from exploitation, a power structure in which those who control collectively produced resources only do so because of the value generated by those who do not. While the concentration and global diffusion of capital has made the class possessing power more difficult to identify, it is precisely because capitalism has become ever more pervasive, insidious, and brutal that a rigorous and revitalized feminist analysis of its class dynamics is politically necessary now.

Linking women's identities and bodies, desires, and needs to class matters to feminism because capitalism is fundamentally a class system. Without the class division between those who own and those who labor, capitalism cannot exist. Women's cheap labor (guaranteed through racist and patriarchal gender systems) is fundamental to the accumulation of surplus value—the basis for capitalist profit-making and expansion. A feminism that aims to improve the lives of all women and at the same time recognizes their differential relation to one another cannot ignore the material reality of capitalism's class system in women's lives. Class objectively links all women, binding the professional to her housekeeper, the boutique shopper to the sweatshop seamstress, the battered wife in Beverly Hills to the murdered sex worker in Bangkok or the Bronx. But class also pits women against each other, dividing those allied with the private and corporate control of wealth and resources from the dispossessed.

Historically, marxist feminism has been the most theoretically developed feminist critique of the reality of class in women's lives. Because marxist feminists see the continuous historical connections between women's oppression and capitalism, theirs is a politics of social transformation that ultimately looks to the elimination of class. Many of the essays in this book reiterate the contention that a feminist politics aimed at combatting women's exploitation and oppression and eliminating the forces that divide women from one another must oppose capitalism. Against the current fashion in western feminism, the tradition of socialist and marxist feminism does not shy away from the elimination of capitalism as a long-range goal, but holds the importance of this vision as a necessary component of the fight for social justice. Granted, feminist movement in advanced industrial sectors has achieved immensely important reforms *within* capitalism, reforms that indeed have improved many women's lives. And most socialist feminists have endorsed these improvements. But if feminism is to be a social movement that aspires to meet the needs of all women, *it must also confront its own class investments in refusing to connect its analysis to a global social system whose very premise is that some women benefit at the expense of others.*

While the critical knowledges of anticapitalist, materialist feminism have been marginalized and even suppressed in the past two decades in the West, they have not disappeared. One of the objectives of this *Reader* is to make the fertile, varied archive of this work more visible and readily available to those who struggle in the ongoing collective effort to produce knowledge for transformative social change.

WHAT IS MARXIST FEMINISM?

The historical links between marxism and feminism were forged in the contradictory situation of first-world women under monopoly capitalism and played out in the insights and oversights of nineteenth-century socialists. Inspired by the historical materialism of Marx and Engels, first-wave socialist feminists—among them Clara Zetkin, Isaac Bebel, and Alexandra Kollontai—promoted the struggle for women's emancipation. Activists like Elizabeth Gurley Flynn, Mother Jones, Rose Pastor Stokes, and others took these ideas to the front lines of labor organizing. Over the course of the next century, feminists found in the theory of historical materialism concepts that could be used to explain the social structures through which women are exploited and oppressed. At the same time, feminists have not approached marxism uncritically. Indeed, the history of feminist interest in marxism has been punctuated by a great deal of critical exchange as feminists challenged marxism's limits and in the process expanded its explanatory power as a theoretical framework that might more adequately address the differential historical situation of women. This critical debate has been fundamental to what marxist feminists call political praxis—that is, the practical-theoretical struggle involved in movements for social change.

The names for the knowledges that have emerged out of the intersection of marxism and feminism in the past thirty years vary—sometimes designated as marxist feminism, socialist feminism, or materialist feminism. These signatures represent differences in emphasis and even in concepts, but all signal feminist critical engagement with historical materialism. While socialist and marxist feminist thinking was never the dominant voice of feminism in the industrialized world, during the early years of feminism's second wave and throughout the 1970s this work had a profound effect on feminist theory and practice. In the past decade or so, however, as feminism has become more absorbed into the middle-class professions, these knowledges have been increasingly discredited. As a result, many young first-world scholars and activists, whose introduction to feminism has taken place in the wake of the conservative backlash of the 1980s and '90s, are unaware of the history of socialist and marxist feminism and the knowledges it produced. It is important to remember, though, that while feminists in overdeveloped countries during this time may have ignored or consciously rejected marxism as outmoded, irrelevant, or worse, an obstacle to the emancipation of women, "two-thirds world women" activists have continued to take seriously historical materialism as a theory for social revolution (Chinchilla 1991; Dunayevskaya 1985).[2]

What has been the appeal of historical materialism for feminists? Simply put, *historical materialism is emancipatory critical knowledge.* Historical materialism offers a systemic way of making sense of social life under capitalism that simultaneously serves as an agent for changing it. It is not only interested in explaining the world but also in transforming it. In other words, as this gloss on Marx's Thesis XI on Feuerbach suggests, historical materialism argues that explaining the world (theory) and changing it (practice) are integrally connected.[3]

As emancipatory knowledge, historical materialism takes as its starting point real living individuals and what they need in order to produce their means of subsistence, that is, in order to survive. It recognizes that the continual production of life through the satisfaction of human needs is a collective undertaking involving an ensemble or system of connected productive activities. One of the key concepts of historical materialism is this recognition that the production of life is a *systemic* process, one that takes place through a system of related activities. Historically, these activities have taken the form of divisions of labor or relations of production, organizations of state and of consciousness or culture. Emancipatory change that aims to eliminate exploitation and oppression within a social system cannot take place by eradicating inequities only in one sphere of social life—whether it be the economy, state, or culture. For change to be truly emancipatory, it must include civil rights and cultural reforms and extend to the social structures that allow wealth for the few to be accumulated at the expense of the many.

Under capitalism, the production of the means to satisfy human needs has taken the form of relations of production in which resources that are collectively produced are not collectively controlled or shared. Those few who own or control the forces for producing (technology) what is needed to satisfy human needs do so because of the surplus value (profit in the form of capital) that they accrue through the unpaid labor-power of many. Knowledge-making is an integral material aspect of this arrangement because knowledges—what is considered true or the ways things are—can legitimize how labor and power are divided. For this reason, culture—the domain of knowledge production—is both a stake and a site of class struggle. Historically, the oppression of women and people of color through patriarchal and racist ideologies has been necessary to and embedded in this fundamental structure of capitalist production. While the ways of making sense that prevail in capitalist societies may serve to legitimate and reproduce divisions of labor benefiting the owning class, however, they do not always succeed in doing so and are themselves often contradictory. Moreover, oppositional knowledges that contest the ruling ideas also circulate and vie for the status of truth.

In keeping with the premises of historical materialism, marxist feminists argue that the starting point of any theory has consequences; as a way of making sense of the world, any theory helps to shape social reality. In arguing their standpoint and evaluating the usefulness of other theories, marxist feminists ask, What are the consequences of this way of thinking for transforming the inequities in women's lives? How is this way of explaining the world going to improve life for all women? Underlying these questions is marxist feminism's visionary horizon—the social transformation necessary to meet women's collective needs. In the past decade or so, however, concepts like social transformation have been disparaged by many feminists in favor of more local or contingent explanations of social life. Along with the disappearance of a vision of transformative change, class as the fundamental social structure of capitalism has also faded from most feminist analysis. Against this trend, materialist—marxist and socialist—feminism argues that social transformation is not a romantic fantasy. On the contrary, we contend that the history of social movements has shown that in times of deep cynicism it is especially important to maintain a vision of possibility on the horizon of the struggle for social change. This vision was one hallmark of the early years of feminism's second wave and is echoed throughout this book—in essays by Margaret Benston, Christine Delphy, Mary Alice Waters, Lindsey German, Barbara Smith, Nellie Wong, and others.

We have deliberately reviewed some of the premises of marxist feminism because they have been persistently misread, distorted, or buried under the weight of a flourishing postmodern cultural politics. In addition to social transformation, many other concepts that were basic to marxist feminist theory in the early 1970s—among them social structure, production, patriarchy, and class—have been dismissed by post-marxist feminists in favor of analyses that treat social life in terms of contingencies, local force relations, or discourses.[4] Post-marxist feminism rejects historical materialism's systemic view of social life, the premise that human survival is based on the existence of real living individuals who must produce the means to survive and do so under historically variant conditions. Instead, they focus almost exclusively on ideological, state, or cultural practices, anchor meaning in the body and its pleasures, or understand social change primarily in terms of the struggle over representation. While many post-marxist feminists insist that their analyses are materialist and may even present themselves as materialist feminists, post-marxist feminism is in fact cultural materialism. Cultural materialism rejects a systemic, anticapitalist analysis linking the history of culture and meaning-making to capital's class system. It is important to note that many post-marxist feminists are the very same socialist feminists whose work was once so instrumental in drafting concepts that link the production of knowledge and the formation of identities to capitalism as a global system. Among them are Michèle Barrett, Drucilla Cornell,

Nancy Fraser, Donna Haraway, Gayle Rubin, and Iris Young. Although we do include the early work of some marxist feminists who later rejected marxist feminism in this volume, we have not represented post-marxist feminism because this work is widely published internationally and readily available. However, any full understanding of feminist debates over how to understand the materiality of women's lives should attend to post-marxist feminism because it has become the dominant discourse of western academic feminism. For this reason we address its pivotal role in the historical sketch of materialist feminism that follows.

At the crest of the second wave, feminist theorists working in critical engagement with marxism and the formation of the New Left in Britain, France, Germany, Italy, and the United States developed sustained and rigorous theories of women's place in patriarchy and capitalism. Socialist feminists argued for a theoretical and political analysis that would explain the systemic intersection of capitalism and patriarchy. The lines of division between radical and socialist feminism were often blurred during this early phase of feminism's second wave. But it is clear that the theoretical frameworks feminists devised were deeply affected by the marxist theory circulating in the civil rights and Black Power movements in the United States, in first-world student and labor movements, in liberation struggles in Vietnam, China, and Cuba, and in the emergent New Left. Rejecting the "old Left" attachment to the Soviet Union and socialist parties, the New Left was an effort to acknowledge that capitalism succeeds in part because of the ways ideology permeates every aspect of daily life. And yet within New Left efforts to politicize the personal, women and women's interests were often ignored. Many of the founders of radical feminism were socialists frustrated by the refusal of men on the Left to address patriarchal systems of power. As Alice Echols's history of this period in U.S. feminism makes clear, much theoretical work in the early years of the second wave was done by feminists who wanted to elaborate and rework the New Left's analysis of global capitalism in order to explain the relationship between sex-gender structures and class.

During the early years of the second wave, socialist feminists, fortified by the burgeoning feminist movement, exerted new pressures on marxist theory and practice to reformulate the "woman question" by rethinking key categories of marxist logic, including production, reproduction, class, consciousness, and labor. They asserted that the classical marxist insights into history were gender blind and ignored women's contributions to social production, while feminist analysis—although strong regarding the systemic character of relations between the sexes—was often ahistorical and insufficiently materialist. A marriage between marxism and feminism was called for. Debate turned on the terms of the arrangement.[5] The radical force of socialist feminism over the ensuing two decades derives from its refusal simply to graft the interests of women onto classical marxism. Instead, socialist feminists worked over certain marxist concepts in order to explain women's role in social reproduction and the integral function of patriarchal structures in the smooth operation of capital accumulation and in the formation of the state and consciousness. Socialist feminists typically argued that a fundamental connection exists between women's struggle and the class struggle, and yet they also acknowledged that because capitalism is a social totality, this struggle is not confined to wage labor but is also fought out in culture.

By 1975 the systemic analysis characteristic of early radical and socialist feminism was already being displaced or recast as cultural feminism. Cultural feminism begins with the assumption that men and women are basically different. It aims to reverse patriarchal systems of value that privilege male over female, focuses on the cultural features of patriarchal oppression, and primarily aims for reforms in this area. Unlike radical and socialist feminism, cultural feminism adamantly rejects the Left's critique of capitalism, emphasizes patriarchy as the root of women's oppression, celebrates women's rituals and spaces, and veers toward separatism. Even though it does not argue for women's equality with men, cultural feminism shares an ideological affiliation with liberal feminism and with liberalism generally in that it focuses exclusively on superstructural change. Maria Mies outlines the historical background and political implications of this standpoint:

> The belief in education, cultural action, or even cultural revolution as agents of social change is a typical belief of the urban middle class. With regard to the woman's question it is based on the assumption that women's oppression has nothing to do with the basic material production relations. . . . This assumption is found more among Western, particularly American, feminists who usually do not talk of capitalism. For many Western feminists women's oppression is rooted in the culture of patriarchal civilization. For them, therefore, feminism is largely a cultural movement, a new ideology, or a new consciousness. (Mies 1986: 22)

In contrast to cultural feminists, materialist, socialist, and marxist feminists do not see culture as the whole of social life but rather as only one arena of social production and therefore as only one area for feminist struggle.

Although socialist and marxist feminism was germane to the political and theoretical development of second-wave feminism, it wasn't until the late 1970s that the term "materialist feminism" came into circulation. The development of materialist feminism in the West is linked historically to the shift to cultural politics in western marxism post-1968, and some of the unevenness in its history, in particular the growing attention to ideology, must be read in that context. Annette Kuhn, Anne Marie Wolpe, Michèle Barrett, Mary MacIntosh in Britain, and Christine Delphy in France were among the initial promoters of materialist feminism. They favored this term over "marxist feminism" in order to emphasize the point that although marxism had not adequately addressed women's exploitation and oppression, a historical materialist analysis might be developed that would account for the sexual division of labor and the gendered formation of subjectivities. More than socialist feminism, materialist feminism was the conjuncture of several discourses—historical materialism, marxist and radical feminism, as well as postmodern and psychoanalytic theories of meaning and subjectivity. In drawing on postmodern critiques of the humanist subject and neo-marxist theories of ideology, materialist feminism constituted a significant shift from the feminist debates of the early '70s, both radical and socialist alike.[6]

By the mid-80s, the general terms of debate among first-world socialist and marxist feminists had drifted so far into theorizing women's oppression in terms of culture, consciousness, and ideology that concerns over how to explain the connection between patriarchy and capitalism, or the links between women's domestic labor and ideology, had been all but abandoned. In an anthology like Judith Newton and Deborah Rosenfelt's *Feminist Criticism and Social Change* (1985), for instance, it is clear that materialist feminism was beginning to mean "more attention to ideas, language and culture than in much traditional Marxist criticism" (xix) and that, even more than its socialist and marxist feminist relatives, materialist feminism in the United States was becoming primarily an academic discourse.

While the particulars of the history of marxist feminism in advanced capitalist countries vary, the drift toward cultural feminism and away from marxist feminism has been a general transnational trend.[7] Like other members of the New Left, many U.S. feminists rallying under the banner of materialism during the '80s were critical of the role of the university in the corporate state, even as they became the bearers of the university's class privilege (Ehrenreich 1990). Like other second-wave feminists, mostly white and middle-class, many U.S. women (and men) came into feminism through a fraught relationship to the academy. As student or young faculty activists, they challenged the university's authority, tying the interests of technological experts and academic researchers to patriarchal power and to the military industrial complex driving U.S. economic and imperialist ventures globally. Yet they also stood to benefit materially from the professional credentials the university offered. The dilemma for many feminists and marxists both turned on how to make a living in this institution without betraying their radical politics. For those who found their way out of this contradictory situation by becoming oppositional intellectuals on the margins of the university, the economic recession of the 1970s exacted heavy penalties. By the '80s, however, many socialist and marxist feminists working in or near universities and colleges not only had been almost thoroughly integrated into the professional middle class, but also had abandoned historical materialism's class analysis. It is worth noting here that the relationship of the contest over knowledge in this phase of the postmodern academy's history to changes in the welfare state and in the relations of production globally remains an unwritten chapter in late feminism's class history.

If materialist feminism emerged out of western marxism, it also drew on and helped to formulate postmodernism's critique of empiricism and of the individual as an autonomous and coherent self. We understand postmodernism as a historical crisis accompanying the shifts in relations of production under late capitalism. It is symptomatic that this crisis has been most attended to in the West in terms of cultural changes, including challenges to empiricism and the Cartesian self played out primarily in avant-garde fiction and poetry, linguistics, philosophy, psychoanalysis, anthropology, and history. Understood in historical and materialist terms, however, postmodernism is not just a matter of disruptions occurring at the level of culture. Rather, these cultural changes are bound up with, and to some degree even caused by, crises in capital's divisions of labor and neoimperialist arrangements. Postmodernism, in other words, is an effect both of shifts in production from the first to the two-thirds world and of technological developments, especially microprocessing, that have made possible the rapid movement of capital and new forms of work; at the same time postmodernism is an effect of the dismantling of empire and its neoimperialist reconfiguration in the second half of the twentieth century. As the cultural logic of these late capitalist conditions, postmodernism is also deeply embedded in patriarchal structures upon which capital's multinational reach depends. For example, the recruitment of middle-class women into the newly formed service professions of overdeveloped sectors—into education and middle management—has depended upon the accompanying recruitment of two-thirds world women into the production lines in the maquilladora, the Pacific rim, and the sweat shops of the United States. The colonization of the unconscious promoted through advertising and high-tech telecommunications produces desire and sexuality, family and femininity in modalities that commodify women's bodies and labor as the property of men, even as some women are allowed more freedom to exert their "independence" in the competitive marketplace.

Marxist feminism sees in much postmodern theory a refusal to acknowledge the historical dimensions of postmodernism and a limited and partial notion of the social—in Marx's words, an effort to fight phrases only with phrases. Deconstruction's critique of western metaphysics, for instance, which has served as a matrix for much postmodern feminist cultural theory, sees the social as primarily textual and sees meaning as the effect of the radical instability of language.[8] Many cultural materialists who have critiqued or distanced themselves from deconstruction's textual analysis, however, also make use of theoretical frameworks that tend to reduce social life to representation, albeit a much more socially grounded understanding of language as discourse.[9] In contrast, historical materialist (marxist) feminists aim to make visible *the reasons why* representations of identity are changing, *why* they do not take the same forms they did a century or even fifty years ago, and how these changes in identity are connected to *historical* shifts in the production of life under late capitalism.

Marxist feminism is a critically engaged feminist standpoint, forged in part through the struggle over knowledge with other feminist perspectives. One stake in the struggle over materialism in feminist theory now is professional feminism's class alliance. If a shared commitment within feminism to the improvement of women's lives exists, there is no shared agreement that feminism necessarily involves combatting capitalism's class system. Increasingly, work that claims the signature "materialist feminism" shares much in common with cultural feminism, in that it does not set out to explain or change the material realities that link women's oppression to class. Many "materialist feminists" do not even consider themselves socialists. As the quote from Maria Mies we cited earlier suggests, however, marxist feminists do connect women's oppression to capitalism as a class system and refuse to limit feminist practice to changing forms of consciousness or discourse. We see this book as an effort to reinsert into materialist feminism—especially materialist feminism in those overdeveloped sectors where this collection will be most widely read—those (untimely) marxist feminist knowledges that the drift to cultural politics in postmodern feminism has suppressed. It is our hope that in so doing this project will contribute to the emergence of feminism's third wave and its revival as a critical force for transformative social change.

THE ARCHIVES

The book's three archives trace a rough chronology of debates from 1969 to 1996. They are not meant as a definitive collection of marxist feminism but rather as instances that convey some of the key concepts and debates from a range of sources. Several of the essays were originally published in pamphlet form, some appeared in independent Left journals, and others first appeared in books or academic collections. Many have not been readily available or widely circulated. Archive III contains mostly unpublished work. Although the essays collectively represent feminism's engagement with historical materialism during this time frame, individually they mark out a range of positions. Some speak from standpoints that veer toward radical feminism (Bunch) while others are marxist-Leninist (Waters) or revolutionary Trotskyist (Wong); others do not explicitly embrace the label marxist or socialist. At times, the points of conflict among these positions are quite overt—as in Lindsey German's critique of Christine Delphy or Meera Nanda's critical reading of Maria Mies. At other times, the critical debates extend to work outside this collection—in Lindsey German's review of feminist theories of the family, Iris Young's critical assessment of dual systems theory, or Carole Stabile's critique of postmodern feminism. We highlight these points of contention as valuable and crucial features of these archives. Against the grain of liberal feminism that sees contention over differences as threatening to sisterhood (albeit a sisterhood often premised on very undemocratic understandings of community), materialist feminism sees critique and critical exchange as a necessary aspect of articulating the collective struggle for which a social movement speaks, and in this sense as fundamental to the historical production of new knowledge.

The essays in Archive I all tackle the problem of how historical materialism might be used to explain and change women's oppression and exploitation under capitalism. We chose Margaret Benston's essay as the lead piece because it is an early, bold argument for taking the historical materialist premise that production is a fundamental necessity of human survival as the starting point for feminist theory. Even though they take varying positions on the relationship between feminism and the struggle against capitalism, most of the other essays in this archive follow Benston's lead in seeing women's labor as socially necessary and historically essential to capitalist accumulation. Some, like the essays by Mary Alice Waters and Lindsey German, contend that the struggle to abolish capitalism is a precondition for women's liberation, while others argue for a more dualistic or even unified view of the relationship between capitalism and patriarchy.

Although most of this archive sees the material as an ensemble of social practices, some of the selections endorse the classical marxist position that economic arrangements—the division of labor that is the basis for class—have a definite determining effect under capitalism. This stance is captured in a quote from socialist feminists Eleanor Marx and Edward Aveling, which Margaret Benston uses as the epigraph for her essay: "The position of women rests, as everything in our complex society, on an economic base." But not all the essays here would agree with Marx and Aveling—or with Benston. What is meant by material reality is at times vague or, especially in some of the essays in Archive II, more emphatically cultural than economic. Some writers, like Lindsey German, Martha Gimenez, or Nicola Field, endorse Benston's view, which stresses the determining material force of economic arrangements. Others, like Nellie Wong and Swasti Mitter, emphasize the global structural dimension of capitalism, while Charlotte Bunch draws attention to the ways class as economic status is affected by the institution of heterosexuality. These differences are not insignificant, nor are they merely academic. They are important points of conceptual tension that translate into action on issues like how to understand women's oppression, what sexuality, race, or gender have to do with capitalism, and how to form collective agents for change. We hope these points of difference provoke discussion and debate that further the ongoing work of feminist theory and practice.

While there is general agreement among marxist and socialist feminists on the need for analysis of capitalism and patriarchy as historically differentiated social structures (Barrett, German, Gimenez, Vogel, Young), how to theorize the relationship between them has been a vexed question. Patriarchy has been a particularly fraught concept for marxist and socialist feminists, and some of the debates about what it means, whether it is at all useful, and if so how to understand its relation to capitalism are represented here.[10] While marxist feminists are generally critical of theories of patriarchy grounded in an ahistorical understanding of power relations between men and women, much debate turns on the problem of precisely how to historicize it. Some of the early work of second-wave feminists (Delphy for instance) saw capitalism and patriarchy as dual systems of oppression for women.[11] Iris Young's essay provides a critical assessment of this dual systems approach and advances her own argument for a unified theory. Although it appears late in discussions of the relative merits of dual systems thinking, Young's alternative is not entirely new. The earlier work of marxist feminists like Annette Kuhn and Ann Marie Wolpe also called for a theoretical frame that would address the sexual division of labor and power as linked to relations between classes. In contrast, Lindsey German's critique of patriarchy theories argues that family structures within capitalism are fundamentally driven by a division of labor that patriarchal family arrangements serve.

Much of the work of materialist feminists has been to delineate how patriarchal practices have been differentiated across social groups. Hazel Carby makes this case when she challenges a feminist concept of patriarchy that ignores the fact that "racism ensures that black men do not have the same relations to patriarchal/capitalist structures as white men" (213). Carby examines how patriarchal arrangements of family, sexuality, dominance, and dependence have been historically differentiated for black men and women and how the state has made use of these structures in the service of a racialized division of labor. She highlights the ways black women are dominated differently by men of different colors (218). As the second archive makes clear, debates over whether patriarchy or some alternative concept is the more useful explanatory tool are far from resolved. In the course of her critique of western white feminists who see the family as categorically oppressive to all women, Carby recommends Gayle Rubin's notion of the sex-gender system as an alternative to the overgeneralizing concept of patriarchy. Yet Martha Gimenez takes Rubin's sex-gender theory to task as itself an ahistorical formulation of social structures.[12] Marxist feminists generally agree with Engels that patriarchal gender systems are not peculiar to capitalism. As changes in the gendered division of labor suggest, the capitalist owning class historically inherits and benefits from patriarchal social structures, but they may not all be essential to capitalism. Clearly violations of women's needs and rights as human beings by patriarchal practices like rape, battering, clitoridectomy, and other forms of sexual violence, as well as the neglect and infanticide of girls, are not exclusively bound by or peculiar to capitalism. But the historical forms these practices take and their use against many women in the world now are not independent of capitalism either.

One of the major chapters in the history of marxist and socialist feminism, and indeed one of its primary contributions to feminist theory, has been the effort to show the ways in which women's unpaid labor is necessary to social reproduction and has been a rich but often invisible source of profit for capitalism. While we have included only a few contributions to the so-called domestic labor debates in the collection, the pieces by Vogel and German review these discussions. In addition, the essays by Mariarosa Dalla Costa and Selma James, Margaret Benston, and Martha Gimenez treat the political economy of women's domestic labor. Against classical marxism, Dalla Costa and James argue that women's domestic labor is integral to the production of surplus value. They see the entire domain outside the wage market as a "social factory" that is not strictly speaking outside capitalist production at all, but is the very source of surplus labor. Women's housework—feeding, laundering, cleaning, educating—is indispensable to wage work because in doing this unpaid labor women produce the living human beings who enter the wage sector. This position is shared by Benston and Gimenez, who contend that the material base for women's oppression is their exploitation as domestic workers. As Benston explains it, women's reproductive labor in the home is necessary "if the entire system is to function," and it is therefore a crucial component in the class system. In this respect, women are potentially the central figures of subversion in the community. Swasti Mitter elaborates this point as she details the role of women's labor in the global factories of late capitalism and outlines strategies for organizing women workers internationally.

An essential feature of capitalism's gendered division of labor is gender ideology—those knowledges, beliefs, and values that present women's oppression as natural. In the 1970s, many materialist feminists in Britain and the United States especially drew upon the work of the marxist theorist Louis Althusser to explain the ideological production of gender and sexuality. In fact, some have argued that the distinguishing feature of socialist and materialist feminism is its focus on ideology (Ehrenreich). Michèle Barrett is one materialist feminist whose contributions to theorizing gender as ideology are well known. In the excerpt from her book *Women's Oppression Today,* included here, Barrett critiques the tendency of some post-Althusserian feminists to posit ideology as autonomous from class or to make it *the* materiality of social life. Unlike those feminists who were drifting into postmodern cultural feminism, Barrett argues that it is imperative to explain the connection between the materiality of ideology and the materiality outside representation. She contends that representation in itself does not effect change but it does bear a relation to things that we can know exist outside language. Unfortunately, her own later post-marxist stance abandons this position on the materiality of social life outside of language.[13]

Frigga Haug's work stands out among those feminists who have tried to make use of and extend marxism's analysis of social structures—in particular the role of ideology in reproducing women's oppression—to the material realities of women's everyday lives. Her piece included here connects the structures of affect, memory, and narrative that organize women's experiences in industrialized countries like Germany to changing relations of capitalist production and consumption. Her project on memory-work described in this essay also exemplifies the ongoing effort of marxist feminists in the West to work collectively in the critical production of knowledge.

These archives provide a collective critical challenge to an incipient racism in feminist thought that sees all women situated in the same way by patriarchal social structures. This critique applies to socialist feminists, too, for their complicity with a homogenizing Eurocentric perspective. It is represented most explicitly in the essays of Gloria Joseph and Hazel Carby.[14] Both challenge the class and race politics underlying any feminist perspective that lumps all men together as the enemy. And both contend that such a position fails to account for the lives of many first-world black women who struggle against their oppression as women but also struggle with their brothers against oppression in general. Along with other black feminists, they contend that black women's social position is compounded by racism to the degree that their relation to capitalism is historically different from white women's. In addition, because of the effects of racism, black women carry a greater burden for providing underpaid or unpaid yet socially necessary labor.

Many of the other essays in Archive II represent the efforts of materialist and marxist feminists in the past decade to explain the ways in which women and men are historically differentiated and pitted against one another through the material bonds that connect their lives across an international division of labor. Some of these essays explicitly point out the class basis of the left's increasing enchantment with identity politics (Smith, Field). One of this collection's lessons is that critical insights like these have a long history; Selma James's eloquent distinction between caste and class in Archive I is an important critique of what came to be known as identity politics. While they do not all agree on the particulars, taken together the pieces in Archive II offer a rich set of theoretical resources or the differences between women by connecting sexuality, race, and gender to capitalism as a global system. Both the historical analyses (Mies, Hennessy and Mohan, Brewer) and the more polemical essays (Wong, Smith) make clear the ways in which effective action for social change requires a theoretical "bridge to freedom" that connects the identities of women and men, black, white, queer, and straight, to capitalism as an economic system.

The third archive includes essays by a new generation of scholars who address more recent social developments—reproductive engineering, the Green Revolution, and ecofeminism—as well as longstanding issues often ignored by socialist feminists—heterosexuality and prostitution. This archive illustrates that historicizing women's lives remains a contentious concern and that debate persists over some categories of analysis like materiality and difference. While this sample of ongoing work does not present a single or even coherent standpoint, these pieces turn to historical materialism because it continues to offer feminism a useful framework for explaining and changing women's place in the world. The collection ends with Carole Stabile's strong critique of the incorporation of feminism into the academy under the mantle of postmodern dismissals of class as a category of analysis. Her critique of the class interests of postmodern academic feminism sketches the state of knowledge in an institution where many of our readers work and study. In linking postmodern feminist theory to the class interests underlying the representation of "family values" by the state and the media, her essay exemplifies a way of thinking that demystifies theoretical abstractions and connects the knowledges circulating in the academy to the growing levels of immiseration that capitalism has incurred elsewhere.

It is our hope that the three archives collected here inform readers who are new to materialist feminism of its long history and rich and vital links to historical materialism. More importantly, we hope that these archives remind readers of the intimate and necessary connection between theoretical concepts and social change. It is precisely because social change requires theoretical concepts—what we mean when we speak of the social, of power, difference, or change itself—that the legacy of materialist feminism ultimately lies with those who engage and extend its ideas for the emancipation of all people.

NOTES

1. In addition to Wood's critique of the retreat from class, see Naiman (1996).
2. We first encountered the phrase "two-thirds world women" in a note from Ann Ferguson on the materialist feminism (matfem) list on the Internet. She proposed this corrective to the

phrase "third-world women," and we find the shift in perspective it offers to be an important one, signaling less the cold war neoimperialist divisions of the globe and more the distinction between overdeveloped and peripheral sectors. The difference between one-third and two-thirds does not correlate with national boundaries so much as it signals one's historical position in relation to resources and wealth. Two-thirds world women live in parts of the United States and Europe as well as in Asia, Africa, and Latin America.

3. Marx's Thesis XI on Feuerbach is the following: "The philosophers have only *interpreted* the world, in various ways; the point is to *change* it."

4. For a more extended critique of post-marxism see Ebert (1995), Hennessy (1993), and Stabile in this volume.

5. The best source on this debate is Sargeant (1981).

6. One useful history of materialist feminism, although from a more post-marxist position than ours, can be found in chapter 1 of Landry and MacLean (1993). See also Hennessy and Mohan in this volume.

7. On this period in U.S. feminism see also Willis (1992) and Evans (1980). On French feminism see Duchen (1986, 1987). On Italian feminism see Birnbaum (1986); on British early second-wave marxist feminism in Britain see Rowbotham (1979) and Lovell (1990).

8. For examples of feminist appropriations of deconstruction see Cornell (1991), Fuss (1989), and Elam (1990).

9. This line of feminist theory has developed primarily out of the work of Michel Foucault. Examples include Braidotti (1994), Butler (1990, 1993), and Haraway (1991). See also the collections by Butler and Scott (1992), and Diamond and Quinby (1988).

10. For valuable overviews of feminist thought on patriarchy see Omvedt (1986) and Walby (1990).

11. Perhaps the most well-known discussions of the problems of dual systems theory were collected by Lydia Sargeant in the volume of responses to Heidi Hartmann's essay, "The Unhappy Marriage of Marxism and Feminism."

12. Another noteworthy critique of Rubin can be found in Hartsock (1985).

13. This shift in her thinking, already represented in the 1988 preface to the revised edition of *Women's Oppression Today,* is most fully developed in *The Politics of Truth* (1991).

14. The critique of cultural feminism by black and two-thirds world feminists constitutes an important and by now large archive in its own right. Some notable contributions include Anzaldúa (1990), Brown (1992), Davis (1983), Hooks (1984), Hull and Smith (1982), Lorde (1985), Mohanty (1991), and Ramazanoglu (1986).

ARCHIVE I

WOMEN UNDER CAPITALISM

Theorizing Patriarchy, Labor, Meaning

1

The Political Economy of Women's Liberation

Margaret Benston

The position of women rests, as everything in our complex society, on an economic basis.
—*Eleanor Marx and Edward Aveling*

The "woman question" is generally ignored in analyses of the class structure of society. This is so because, on the one hand, classes are generally defined by their relation to the means of production and, on the other hand, women are not supposed to have any unique relation to the means of production. The category seems instead to cut across all classes; one speaks of working-class women, middle-class women, etc. The status of women is clearly inferior to that of men (Dixon 1940), but analysis of this condition usually falls into discussing socialization, psychology, interpersonal relations, or the role of marriage as a social institution.[1] Are these, however, the primary factors? In arguing that the roots of the secondary status of women are in fact economic, it can be shown that women as a group do indeed have a definite relation to the means of production and that this is different from that of men. The personal and psychological factors then follow from this special relation to production, and a change in the latter will be a necessary (but not sufficient) condition for changing the former.[2] If this special relation of women to production is accepted, the analysis of the situation of women fits naturally into a class analysis of society.

The starting point for discussion of classes in a capitalist society is the distinction between those who own the means of production and those who sell their labor power for a wage. As Ernest Mandel says:

> The proletarian condition is, in a nutshell, the lack of access to the means of production or means of subsistence which, in a society of generalized commodity production, forces the proletarian to sell his labor power. In exchange for this labor

power he receives a wage which then enables him to acquire the means of consumption necessary for satisfying his own needs and those of his family.

This is the structural definition of wage earner, the proletarian. From it necessarily flows a certain relationship to his work, to the products of his work, and to his overall situation in society, which can be summarized by the catchword "alienation". But there does not follow from this structural definition any necessary conclusions as to level of his consumption . . . the extent of his needs, or the degree to which he can satisfy them. (Mandel 1967)

We lack a corresponding structural definition of women. What is needed first is not a complete examination of the symptoms of the secondary status of women, but instead a statement of the material conditions in capitalist (and other) societies which define the group "women." Upon these conditions are built the specific superstructures which we know. An interesting passage from Mandel points the way to such a definition:

The commodity . . . is a product created to be exchanged on the market, as opposed to one which has been made for direct consumption. *Every commodity must have both a use-value and an exchange-value.*

It must have a use-value or else nobody would buy it. . . . A commodity without a use-value to anyone would consequently be unsalable, would constitute useless production, would have no exchange-value precisely because it had no use-value.

On the other hand, every product which has use-value does not necessarily have exchange-value. It has an exchange-value only to the extent that the society itself, in which the commodity is produced, is founded on exchange, is a society where exchange is a common practice. . . .

In capitalist society, commodity production, the production of exchange-values, has reached its greatest development. It is the first society in human history where the major part of production consists of commodities. It is not true, however, that all production under capitalism is commodity production. Two classes of products still remain simple use-value.

The first group consists of all things produced by the peasantry for its own consumption, everything directly consumed on the farms where it is produced. . . .

The second group of products in capitalist society which are not commodities but remain simple use-value consists of all things produced in the home. Despite the fact that considerable human labor goes into this type of household production, it still remains a production of use-values and not of commodities. Every time a soup is made or a button sewn on a garment, it constitutes production, but it is not production for the market.

The appearance of commodity production and its subsequent regularization and generalization have radically transformed the way men labor and how they organize society. (Mandel 1967)

What Mandel may not have noticed is that his last paragraph is precisely correct. The appearance of commodity production has indeed transformed the way that *men* labor. As he points out, most household labor in capitalist society (and in the existing socialist societies, for that matter) remains in the pre-market stage. This is the work which is reserved for women and it is in this fact that we can find the basis for a definition of women.

In sheer quantity, household labor, including child care, constitutes a huge amount of social necessary production. Nevertheless, in a society based on commodity production, it is not usually considered "real work" since it is outside of trade and the marketplace. It is precapitalist in a very real sense. This assignment of household work as the function of a special category "women" means that this group *does* stand in a different relation to production than the group "men." We will tentatively define women, then, as that group of people who are responsible for the production of simple use-values in those activities associated with the home and family.

Since men carry no responsibility for such production, the difference between the two groups lies here. Notice that women are not excluded from commodity production. Their participation in wage labor occurs but, as a group, they have no structural responsibility in this area and such participation is ordinarily regarded as transient. Men, on the other hand, are responsible for commodity production; they are not, in principle, given any role in household labor. For example, when they do participate in household production, it is regarded as more than simply exceptional; it is demoralizing, emasculating, even harmful to health. (A story on the front page of the *Vancouver Sun* in January 1969 reported that men in Britain were having their health endangered because they had to do too much housework!)

The material basis for the inferior status of women is to be found in just this definition of women. In a society in which money determines value, women are a group who work outside the money economy. Their work is not worth money, is therefore valueless, is therefore not real work. And women themselves, who do this valueless work, can hardly be expected to be worth as much as men, who work for money. In structural terms, the closest thing to the condition of women is the condition of others who are or were also outside of commodity production, i.e., serfs and peasants. . . .

For most North Americans, domestic work as "public production" brings immediate images of a Brave New World or of a vast institution—a cross between a home for orphans and an army barracks—where we would all be forced to live. For this reason, it is probably just as well to outline here, schematically and simplistically, the nature of industrialization.

A preindustrial production unit is one in which production is small-scale and reduplicative; i.e., there are a great number of little units, each complete and just like all the others. Ordinarily such production units are in some way kin-based and multipurpose, fulfilling religious, recreational, educational, and sexual functions along with the economic function. In such a situation, desirable attributes of an individual—those which give prestige—are judged by more than purely economic criteria: for example, among approved character traits are proper behavior to kin or readiness to fulfill obligations.

Such production is originally not for exchange. But if exchange of commodities becomes important enough, then increased efficiency of production becomes necessary. Such efficiency is provided by the transition to industrialized production, which involves the elimination of the kin-based production unit. A large-scale, nonreduplicative production unit is substituted which has only one function, the economic one, and where prestige or status is attained by economic skills. Production is rationalized, made vastly more efficient, and becomes more and more public—part of an integrated social network. An enormous expansion of man's productive potential takes place. Under capitalism such social productive forces are utilized almost exclusively for private profit. These can be thought of as *capitalized* forms of production.

If we apply the above to housework and child-rearing, it is evident that each family, each household, constitutes an individual production unit, a preindustrial entity, in the same way that peasant farmers or cottage weavers constitute preindustrial production units. The main features are clear, with the reduplicative, kin-based, private nature of the work being the most important. (It is interesting to notice the other features: the multipurpose functions of the family, the fact that desirable attributes for women do not center on economic prowess, etc.) The rationalization of production effected by a transition to large-scale production has not taken place in this area.

Industrialization is, in itself, a great force for human good; exploitation and dehumanization go with capitalism and not necessarily with industrialization. To advocate the conversion of private domestic labor into a public industry under capitalism is quite a different thing from advocating such conversion in a socialist society. In the latter case the forces of production would operate for human welfare, not private profit, and the result should be liberation, not dehumanization. In this case we can speak of *socialized* forms of production.

These definitions are not meant to be technical but rather to differentiate between two important aspects of industrialization. Thus, the fear of the barracks-like result of introducing housekeeping into the public economy is most realistic under capitalism. With socialized production and the removal of the profit motive and its attendant alienated labor, there is no reason why, *in an industrialized society,* industrialization of housework should not result in better production, i.e., better food, more comfortable surroundings, more intelligent and loving child-care, than in the present nuclear family.

The argument is often advanced that, under neocapitalism, the work in the home has been much reduced. Even if this is true, it is not structurally relevant. Except for the very rich, who can hire someone to do it, there is for most women an irreducible minimum of necessary labor involved in caring for home, husband, and children. For a married woman without children this irreducible minimum of work probably takes fifteen to twenty hours a week; for a woman with small children the minimum is probably seventy or eighty hours a week.[3] (There is some resistance to regarding child-rearing as a job. That labor is involved, i.e., the production of use-value, can be clearly seen when exchange-value is also involved—when the work is done by babysitters, nurses, child-care centers, or teachers. An economist has already pointed out the paradox that if a man marries his housekeeper, he reduces the national income, since the money he gives her is no longer counted as wages.) The reduction of housework to the minimums given is also expensive; for low-income families more labor is required. In any case, household work remains structurally the same—a matter of private production.

One function of the family, the one taught to us in school and the one which is popularly accepted, is the satisfaction of emotional needs: the needs for closeness, community, and warm, secure relationships. This society provides few other ways of satisfying such needs; for example, work relationships or friendships are not expected to be nearly as important as a man-woman-with-children relationship. Even other ties of kinship are increasingly secondary. This function of the family is important in stabilizing it so that it can fulfill the second, purely economic, function discussed above. The wage earner, the husband-father whose earnings support himself, also "pays for" the labor done by the mother-wife and supports the children. The wages of a man buy the labor of two people. The crucial importance of this second function of the family can be seen when the family unit breaks down in divorce. The continuation of the economic function is the major concern where children are involved; the man must continue to pay for the labor of the woman. His wage is very often insufficient to enable him to support a second family. In this case his emotional needs are sacrificed to the necessity to support his ex-wife and children. That is, when there is a conflict the economic function of the family very often takes precedence over the emotional one. And this in a society which teaches that the major function of the family is the satisfaction of emotional needs.[4]

As an economic unit, the nuclear family is a valuable stabilizing force in a capitalist society. Since the production which is done in the home is paid for by the husband-father's earnings, his ability to withhold his labor from the market is much reduced. Even his flexibility in changing jobs is limited. The woman, denied an active place in the market, has little control over the conditions that govern her life. Her economic dependence is reflected in emotional dependence, passivity, and other "typical" female personality traits. She is conservative, fearful, supportive of the status quo.

Furthermore, the structure of this family is such that it is an ideal consumption unit. But this fact, which is widely noted in women's liberation literature, should not be taken to mean that this is its primary function. If the above analysis is correct, the family should be seen primarily as a production unit for housework and child-rearing. *Everyone* in capitalist society is a consumer; the structure of the family simply means that it is particularly well suited to encourage consumption. Women in particular are good consumers; this follows naturally from their responsibility for matters in the home. Also, the inferior status of women, their general lack of a strong sense of worth and identity, make them more exploitable than men and hence better consumers.

The history of women in the industrialized sector of the economy has depended simply on the labor needs of that sector. Women function as a massive reserve army of labor. When labor is scarce (early industrialization, the two world wars, etc.) then women form an important part of the labor force. When there is less demand for labor (as now under neocapitalism) women become a surplus labor force—but one for which their husbands, and not society, are economically responsible. The "cult of the home" makes its reappearance during times of labor surplus and is used to channel women out of the market economy. This is relatively easy since the pervading ideology ensures that no one, man or woman, takes women's participation in the labor force very seriously. Women's real work, we are taught, is in the home; this holds whether or not they are married, single, or the heads of households.

At all times household work is the responsibility of women. When they are working outside the home they must somehow manage to get both outside job and housework done (or they supervise a substitute for the housework). Women, particularly married women with children, who work outside the home simply do two jobs; their participation in the labor force is only allowed if they continue to fulfill their first responsibility in the home. This is particularly evident in countries like Russia and those of Eastern Europe where expanded opportunities for women in the labor force have not brought about a corresponding expansion in their liberty. Equal access to jobs outside the home, while one of the preconditions for women's liberation, will not in itself be sufficient to give equality to women; as long as work in the home remains a matter of private production and is the responsibility of women, they will simply carry a double work-load.

A second prerequisite for women's liberation, which follows from the above analysis, is the conversion of the work now done in the home as private production into work to be done in the public economy.[5] To be more specific, this means that child-rearing should no longer solely be the responsibility of the parents. Society must begin to take responsibility for children; the economic dependence of women and children on the husband-father must be ended. The other work that goes on in the home must also be changed—communal eating places and laundries for example. When such work is moved into the public sector, then the material basis for discrimination against women will be gone.

These are only preconditions. The idea of the inferior status of women is deeply rooted in the society and will take a great deal of effort to eradicate. But once the structures that produce and support that idea are changed then, and only then, can we hope to make progress. It is possible, for example, that a change to communal eating places would simply mean that women are moved from a home kitchen to a communal one. This would be an advance, to be sure, particularly in a socialist society where work would not have the inherently exploitative nature it does now. Once women are freed from private production in the home, it will probably be very difficult to maintain for any long period of time a rigid definition of jobs by sex. This illustrates the interrelation between the two preconditions given above: true equality in job opportunity is probably impossible without freedom from housework, and the industrialization of housework is unlikely unless women are leaving the home for jobs.

The changes in production necessary to get women out of the home might seem to be, in theory, possible under capitalism. One of the sources of women's liberation movements may be the fact that alternative capitalized forms of home production now exist. Day care is available, even if inadequate and perhaps expensive; convenience foods, home delivery of meals, and take-out meals are widespread; laundries and cleaners offer bulk rates. However, cost usually prohibits a complete dependence on such facilities, and they are not available everywhere, even in North America. These should probably then be regarded as embryonic forms rather than complete structures. However, they clearly stand as alternatives to the present system of getting such work done. Particularly in North America, where the growth of "service industries" is important in maintaining the growth of the economy, the contradictions between these alternatives and the need to keep women in the home will grow.

The need to keep women in the home arises from two major aspects of the present system. First, the amount of unpaid labor performed by women is very large and very profitable to those who own the means of production. To pay women for their work, even at minimum-wage scales, would imply a massive redistribution of wealth. At present, the support of a family is a hidden tax on the wage earner—his wage buys the labor power of two people. And second, there is the problem of whether the economy can expand enough to put all women to work as part of the normally employed labor force. The war economy has been adequate to draw women partially into the economy but not adequate to establish a need for all or most of them. If it is argued that the jobs created by the industrialization of housework will create this need, then one can counter by pointing to (1) the strong economic forces operating for the status quo and against capitalization discussed above, and (2) the fact that the present service industries, which somewhat counter these forces, have not been able to keep up with the growth of the labor force as presently constituted. The present trends in the service industries simply create underemployment in the home; they do not create new jobs for women. So long as this situation exists, women remain a very convenient and elastic part of the industrial reserve army. Their incorporation into the labor force on terms of equality—which would create pressure for capitalization of housework—is possible only with an economic expansion so far achieved by neocapitalism only under conditions of full-scale war mobilization.

In addition, such structural changes imply the complete breakdown of the present nuclear family. The stabilizing consuming functions of the family, plus the ability of the cult of the home to keep women out of the labor market, serve neocapitalism too well to be easily dispensed with. And, on a less fundamental level, even if these necessary changes in the nature of household production were achieved under capitalism, it would have the unpleasant consequence of including all human relations in the cash nexus. The atomization and isolation of people in western society is already sufficiently advanced to make it doubtful if such complete psychic isolation could be tolerated. It is likely in fact that one of the major negative emotional responses to women's liberation movements may be exactly such a fear. If this is the case, then possible alternatives—cooperatives, the kibbutz, etc.—can be cited to show that the psychic needs for community and warmth can in fact be better satisfied if other structures are substituted for the nuclear family.

At best the change to the capitalization of housework would only give women the same limited freedom given most men in capitalist society. This does not mean, however, that women should wait to demand freedom from discrimination. There is a material basis for women's status; we are not merely discriminated against, we are exploited. At present, our unpaid labor in the home is necessary if the entire system is to function. Pressure created by women who challenge their role will reduce the effectiveness of this exploitation. In addition, such challenges will impede the functioning of the family and may make the channeling of women out of the labor force less effective. All of these will hopefully make quicker the transition to a society in which the necessary structural changes in production can actually be made. That such a transition will require a revolution I have no doubt; our task is to make sure that revolutionary changes in the society do in fact end women's oppression.

NOTES

1. The biological argument is, of course, the first one used, but it is not usually taken seriously by socialist writers. Margaret Mead's *Sex and Temperament* is an early statement of the importance of culture over biology.

2. This applies to the group or category as a whole. Women as individuals can and do free themselves from their socialization to a great degree (and they can even come to terms with the economic situation in favorable cases), but the majority of women have no chance to do so.

3. Such figures can easily be estimated. For example, a married woman without children is expected each week to cook and wash up (ten hours), clean house (four hours), do laundry (one hour), and shop for food (one hour). The figures are *minimum* times required each week for such work. The total, sixteen hours, is probably unrealistically low; even so, it is close to half of a regular work week. A mother with young children must spend at least six or seven days a week working close to twelve hours.

4. For evidence of such teaching, see any high school text on the family.

5. This is stated clearly by early Marxist writers besides Engels. Relevant quotes from Engels have been given in the text.

2

The Politics of Women's Liberation Today

Mary Alice Waters

The most important basic characteristic of the emerging women's liberation movement, the key factor which gives it such revolutionary implications, is its independence. The movement, of course, is related to and interconnected with other struggles—youth, Black and Brown liberation, antiwar, working class—but it has its own dynamic, its own demands, its own organizational forms. It is not simply the women's wing of an antiwar committee, a union, or a Black organization, and its fate is not directly dependent on the evolution of other struggles. For the first time in decades, women are saying they are not willing to wait for anyone else to take up their struggle; they will do it now, in their own way, and they are not willing to subordinate their demands to the needs of any other struggle.

The second aspect of the independence of the women's liberation movement is its development outside the framework of the two capitalist parties. At this initial stage, independence from the capitalist parties is almost assumed by the large majority of the activists, and this has not yet emerged as a crucial issue within the movement. But we can be confident that as the movement grows, there will be a wing of the liberal Democrats and Republicans who will try to adapt to some of the demands of the movement, to capture its resources and energies, and divert the movement from an independent, mass-action, nonexclusionary direction.

We can be sure, for instance, that the Communist Party will try to turn the movement in this direction. One of the things they stress is the election of women to political office, and they point to the election of Shirley Chisolm, a Democrat and the first Black woman in the House, as a prime example of the kind of goal women should be fighting for. Organizations like NOW (the National Organization for Women) are also oriented toward involving women in liberal·Democratic politics.

In the future, as the movement broadens and deepens and develops a real mass base, the fight to maintain independence from the capitalist parties will be increasingly important. But the demands raised by the women's liberation movement—for control over their own lives, for economic, social, and physical liberation—are basically anticapitalist in their thrust. Although some demands can be met in their totality, the goals of women's liberation cannot be won under capitalism or embraced by the capitalist parties. The struggle to attain these goals will lead many to the realization of the need for a socialist revolution.

There have been some significant changes in the women's liberation movement in the last six months, changes we should all be fully aware of.

First has been the proliferation of organized women's liberation groups. It would be impossible to establish an exact count, but hundreds of new groups have been formed. There are now more than 100 organizations in New York alone!

Many of the new groups have been campus-based organizations, which emerged for the first time last fall. But more surprising has been the formation of dozens of groups composed of young women, mainly with college backgrounds, whose common bond is the fact that they are young women trying to deal with the problems of finding jobs and/or raising families.

There have also been numerous professional organizations like the Media Women in New York and caucuses organized within almost every academic association and in different university departments.

Black and other Third World women's liberation groups have also begun to emerge. In New York, for instance, a few women in SNCC are initiating an organization for Black women. Some of the women in the Young Lords are very militant about the need to wage a fight for women's liberation within the Puerto Rican community, and the program of the Young Lords includes a point committing the Young Lords to support the fight for women's liberation. Debate on women's liberation is coming more and more to the fore within the Chicano movement as well.

The second big development in the last six months has been the emergence of action-oriented coalitions and united fronts to work on specific projects.

In the earliest stages of the women's liberation movement, the small groups of ten to twelve women who met to discuss their own concerns and problems—what is known in the movement as consciousness-raising—such small groups were virtually the only form of organization that existed. The small groups have played a positive function insofar as they help women gain confidence in themselves, educate themselves, and realize that their problems are not individual but are shared almost universally with other women. Some small groups have, of course, gotten bogged down in a self-devouring type of group therapy, but it would be a mistake to dismiss most of the small groups as belonging in this category. They play a vital role in helping many women understand the sources and causes of their oppression.

At the same time that these small groups are important, it is also crucial for the women's liberation movement to unite in common actions, to turn outward, and this has begun to happen in the last six months. The demonstration in New Haven demanding freedom for the Connecticut Panther women, the numerous teach-ins, the broad meetings like the Congress to Unite Women in New York, the antiabortion law demonstrations scheduled in several places, and similar actions are indications of the direction in which the movement is developing.

As the movement gains confidence in itself, it is beginning to search for those demands and activities that have the potential for mass support.

Third, there has been significant growth in the movement's organizational and political capacities. For instance, arguments over whether or not a meeting needs a chairman and similar elementary questions are less frequent now than several months ago.

The political growth of the movement is reflected in the deepening search for answers to all the questions posed by the issue of women's liberation—which is, in the most fundamental sense, the problem of humanity itself. This growth is reflected in the way revolutionary ideas are received. There is a tremendous hunger for knowledge within the women's liberation movement, a search for full truths, not partial answers.

A large proportion of the activists in women's liberation are developing an anticapitalist consciousness, a realization that no basic solution can be found short of revolution. The anticapitalism is in many respects similar to the level of consciousness that developed in SDS before its demise: it lacks any real perspective for the road to be traveled from here to the revolution, but it is at least the beginning of revolutionary consciousness for many.

Fourth, the movement has broadened its base considerably in recent months. Initially, most of the women's liberation activists were women who had been radicalized around a whole series of issues, who had been members of SDS, Resistance, and various other political groupings. They came to the women's liberation movement out of disillusionment with the male chauvinist attitudes and actions so prevalent in organizations like SDS.

But the movement has arrived at a new stage now, and the recent growth of the women's liberation movement has come largely from women who have not previously been political activists. They are coming directly to the women's liberation movement and have been radicalized on that issue.

The recent numerical growth and political development of the women's liberation movement has been extremely important, but a word of caution is also in order. It is not yet a mass movement in the sense that the antiwar or Black liberation movement has a mass character and reflects the level of consciousness of the masses. The potential exists for the development of a mass women's liberation movement though, and one of our key responsibilities to the movement is to contribute to the process of formulating a program and organizing actions that will lead toward a mass struggle for women's liberation.

In this respect, it is important to call attention to the fact that some of the earliest and most militant women's actions have been those organized by welfare mothers. Their actions, in essence, have demanded that society recognize its collective obligation for raising children and providing for them adequately. Such actions, and those organized by women workers fighting for equal pay and decent working conditions, may not be called women's liberation activities, but they are dealing with the exact same issues as the campus-based and other women's liberation organizations. They are natural allies.

Our job is to be part of the vanguard of the women's liberation struggle, to work with the radicalizing young women and the organizations they are creating on the campuses and elsewhere, and to help build a movement that will struggle to win the basic democratic and transitional demands that are being raised. We want the women's liberation movement to fight for basic demands such as free abortion on demand, free child care, and equal pay, and to consciously lead the fight by involving the broad masses of women in whose interests these demands are raised. When that happens it will signify a qualitatively new stage in the development of the struggle.

A number of key questions have emerged as the focal points of political and ideological debate within the growing women's liberation movement. Although there are many which are worth discussing, four questions are of particular importance at this stage.

The first question is whether or not women should form their own organizations for struggle, raise their own demands, develop their own leadership, and organize their own actions. And our answer to this question is an unequivocal YES. Not only is there a need for separate women's organizations, but this is one of the most progressive aspects of the current women's liberation movement. The separate organizations are a reflection of the independent character of the movement that is so important. We support these organizations and we help to build them. We are in favor of restricting their membership to women only since this plays a key role in helping women to develop their own self-confidence, identity, and dignity and to realize their full abilities.

It is a progressive step for women to want to get men off their backs so they can develop their abilities freely and fully.

The logic of such organization does not lead, as some contend, to introversion and a narrowing of the concerns of women. On the contrary, it will lay the basis for women as a group, with their own special problems, to establish alliances in struggle with other oppressed sectors of the population. Far from narrowing women's horizons, it will enable them to develop a broader comprehension of the relationship between their struggles and struggles by other layers of society.

For example, one need hardly be worried that Black women who form their own organizations will forget about their struggle as Afro-Americans. On the contrary, such organizations will strengthen and help deepen both struggles.

Of course, there are some women who try to prevent the women's liberation movement from building bridges to other struggles. They usually argue that women have too many problems of their own to worry about and should not get involved in other problems to boot. This is one of the tendencies we disagree with and argue against within the movement, and our experience—on the question of the war, for example—has been that it is not difficult to convince women of the obvious need for them to join the fight against the war, as women; that there are numerous and compelling reasons why the fight to bring the troops home now is their fight.

We orient our work toward the independent forces in the movement, those who are representative of the newly radicalizing layers, who are not yet attached to any of the different political tendencies but are gravitating toward one or another. We try to reach them at their present level of comprehension and understanding. We participate in the developing struggle in a nonfactional way, in a collaborative manner, and we contribute to the struggle, trying to deepen the level of understanding of the capitalist system and what is necessary to abolish the system. In this respect our orientation to the women's liberation movement represents nothing new for us. It is guided by the same concepts that are fundamental to our work in every developing arena of struggle.

The second question around which there has been considerable debate is whether women's oppression is rooted in the development and needs of class society, or in the physical, sexual, and psychological differences between men and women. And ultimately this comes down to the key question of whether the struggle is to abolish capitalism as a precondition to women's liberation or whether the goal is to reform men.

The other major radical tendencies—those which consider themselves socialist—will agree, if cornered, that the oppression of women is rooted in class society. That is, they formally agree with the basic analysis developed by Marx and Engels. However, despite their formal positions, none of them take the step from the premise that women's oppression is rooted in class society to the only possible conclusion—i.e., the need to develop a program to lead women's struggles in an anticapitalist direction.

There is also a wing of the women's liberation movement that does not accept a historical materialist approach to the oppression of women. It adopts the basic position that the oppression of women by men is more basic and antedates the emergence of class society. A clear expression of this general tendency is found in the Redstockings Manifesto, the basic statement of principles on which one of the small group formations in New York is based. The manifesto reads, "We identify the agents of our oppression as men. Male supremacy is the oldest, most basic form of domination. All other forms of exploitation and oppression (racism, capitalism, imperialism, etc.) are extensions of male supremacy: men dominate women, a few men dominate the rest . . ."

Among the women who hold the position that men are the primary enemy, however, it is important to make some distinctions. Some are very conscious about it, have a well-worked-out position, and can defend it with very serious and elaborate arguments.

For others, such a position often simply reflects a positive desire to escape men's domination, and their ideas get twisted into a rejection of *all* men, an identification of men with the root causes of women's oppression.

The distinction is important because many women in the latter category can be convinced that men are also the victims of class society, and that women's liberation will bring men's liberation with it. The identification of men as the primary enemy is often simply an initial reaction, a first step toward deepening radicalization.

The tendency within the women's liberation movement that rejects a basic historical materialist approach is not necessarily antisocialist. Many would say that class society at least contributes to the oppression of women, but they disagree that the elimination of private property in the means of production will establish the material foundation for eliminating sexual oppression. In their minds, the fight against men is primary; the fight against the system is secondary.

And one of the most powerful "proofs" for this position, in the eyes of many radical women, is the status of women in the workers' states. As on so many other questions, Stalinism has become equated with socialism. Many women respond quite understandably by saying if that's socialism they want no part of it, and they will keep looking until they find some other solution.

We disagree with this general tendency, which rejects a materialist approach to the question of women's oppression. Just as with racism, male chauvinism and the oppression of women have very deep historical roots that are nurtured and sustained by the capitalist system. The abolition of capitalism is a precondition for the total emancipation of women. That in no way means the fight for women's liberation should be postponed, but the realization that capitalism must be abolished does determine the basic strategy for the struggle.

At the same time, however, we agree that male chauvinism and all the myriad forms of women's oppression will not suddenly disappear on the morrow of the revolution. The oppression of women is older than virtually every other form of exploitation and bondage. It is older than slavery, racism, national oppression. It has existed throughout man's entire recorded history. It permeates every aspect of human life and is so thoroughly ingrained in every human being that the average person is largely unconscious of its pernicious effects. Even within the radical movement the attitudes of male supremacy are widespread and many women are bitterly resentful of this—rightfully so.

However, while it will take time to eradicate attitudes and patterns of behavior with such deep historical roots, the socialist revolution will eliminate the material basis of women's oppression, its roots in class society and capitalist exploitation, and the causes of man's inhumanity to men and women.

One of the favorite targets of the conscious anti-Marxists and anti-Leninists within women's liberation is the "male-dominated left." It is often an attempt to capitalize on the healthy distrust and skepticism of radicalizing women who have been disillusioned by those organizations which, for all their radical verbiage, relegate women to running mimeograph machines, typing, and similar work, while men make the political decisions, act as public spokesmen, write articles, and do the other "important" work.

But it would be a mistake to ignore the fact that pressure from the extreme "feminist" point of view is reflected inside our party at times as well. For example, it is occasionally reflected in the idea that men should be excluded from women's liberation work factions on principle.

We don't want to make any concessions to this pressure in our own organization. We must understand the objective reasons for it, but at the same time, if and when it arises, we should use it as an opportunity to explain the basic principles on which a Leninist combat party is built. It unites within its ranks the most conscious elements of all oppressed sectors of the population and welds them into a unified fighting party. The party must do everything possible within its ranks to destroy the divisions and antagonisms created by class society in an advanced state of decay. We are not a federation of oppressed groups, representing different and conflicting interests, but a democratic centralist party in which all members participate in developing a program for and helping to lead a multifaceted struggle for the abolition of capitalism.

There is absolutely no contradiction between fighting to build independent women's liberation organizations with all-women leadership and at the same time recognizing that it is not just women members of the party, but our party as a whole, which is responsible for and must lead our work in the women's liberation movement.

We should also be clear on how to deal with the question of the "male-dominated left."

First of all, our party is genuinely unique among left-wing organizations. Our party has a better understanding of the issues involved in the struggle for women's liberation than any other radical group. Women play a greater leadership role in our movement than in any other left organization.

We sometimes take this for granted, but a good gauge of how different we are has been the surprised reaction of many women's liberation activists as they see how our movement functions, and the general level of understanding within our movement on the question of women's liberation.

Yet, even though we may be more advanced on the question of women's liberation than other organizations, it is still obvious that even in our party more than 50 percent of the membership and leadership is male.

In the coming few years, those percentages will become much more equal than they are now. And in the coming American revolution, women will probably play a more central role than in any previous revolution in history. But it is still quite possible that well over the majority of the central leaders of the American revolution may be men. If that happened, it would not be because we or anyone else wanted it that way, or thought it should be that way, nor would it reflect a lack of sensitivity on our part to the importance of the struggle for women's liberation.

Rather it would reflect the fact that the composition of our party and its leadership cannot be artificially modeled after our vision of the future or what is abstractly good. Unfortunately, our party will reflect much more the society we are trying to destroy than the one we are trying to establish—and it must if we are not to become utopian socialists. We are developing an instrument to be used in the fight to destroy the most powerful ruling class the world has ever known, not a microcosm of the future.

The problem of leadership and the composition of the vanguard is not something that can be artificially established, the way that RYM has tried to do it, for example.[1] It can be a healthy sign when the majority of the central leadership of a revolutionary organization is composed of women—as the majority of the YSA[2] National Executive Committee has been at times. It says a great deal about the organization. But unless it truly represents the leadership, the result can only be hypocrisy, a mockery of democratic forms, and cynical disrespect for both the formal and real leadership. While women may be the elected leadership, unless it is genuine the real leadership will simply maneuver around the elected bodies and do what they want without being subject to the control of the organization or responsible to it.

As with every other question, it is our program that is decisive, and we are the only organization that can put forward a genuinely revolutionary program and perspective for women's liberation. We are the revolutionary party of women's liberation, and to build that party, we must make use of the human material that capitalism has provided, constructing the strongest party we can.

One final word on the question of men as the enemy. We also reject the proposition that only women will gain from women's liberation. It will be a tremendous advance for men as well, as they too will be liberated from the reactionary shackles of the family institution. If anyone has any doubts on this, they need only read *Portnoy's Complaint.*

Women's liberation touches on the most fundamental questions of human existence. When it is attained, it will mean the liberation of men, women, and children from the deepest forms of sexual, psychological, social, and economic oppression. It will mean humanity has reached an entirely new historical level—classless society.

The third question around which there has been considerable discussion within the women's liberation movement is whether women's oppression affects *all* women to one degree or another or whether it is basically only a subcategory of the exploitation of women as workers. Related to this is the question of whether or not the revolt of women as women is a revolutionary development, or whether only those struggles by women workers are progressive.

On this question, our main disagreements are with Progressive Labor, because PL takes exactly the same approach to women's liberation that they do to Black nationalism. As far as they are concerned, the oppression of women is a subcategory of the exploitation of workers. Only struggles by women as *workers* are progressive; anything else can be harmful and the main danger to be avoided is the destruction of the working class only.

In the resolution on women's liberation presented to the December 1969 National Council meeting of the Worker-Student Alliance, a resolution which basically reflects

PL's line, the authors put forward the proposition that "the real basis of male chauvinism is the profits made off the double exploitation of women workers." With such a position it is hard to explain the oppression of women for thousands of years before the working class or the capitalist system came on the scene! And it fails to account for the many additional forms of oppression which must be fought and which provide the objective basis for the struggle, for the emergence of a women's liberation movement that involves women from different economic and social backgrounds.

Abortion, birth control, education, equal pay, child care, preferential hiring, and other demands are all issues that are relevant not only to working-class women but to all women. Of course, there are class differences. But the women's liberation movement as a whole, involving women from all class backgrounds, can and will be an ally of the working class in the struggle to abolish the capitalist system. In other words, it is through the battle for women's liberation, as through the battle for the liberation of oppressed nationalities, that the working class will win crucial allies.

The fourth major question being debated within the women's liberation movement is whether or not the family is a reactionary institution under capitalism, and on this question we have major disagreements with the Communist Party and Progressive Labor. Our major ally has been the most radical wing of the women's liberation movement.

Many of the radical women have educated themselves on Engels. That is, the movement's founders largely began by accepting a class analysis and a Marxist perspective on the question of the family—and this became the basic yardstick by which every other position was measured.

It was our unequivocal agreement with the basic position elaborated by Marx and Engels that won us wide respect within the women's liberation movement—as opposed to the CP and PL, for instance, which reject the Marxist analysis in practice. They try to convince people not only that the nuclear family under capitalism can be reformed, but that under socialism it will—and should—continue to exist as the basic social unit.

Women's liberation is a question shrouded in the most irrational and emotional attitudes because it cuts so deeply into the personal lives of every individual. And of all the touchy issues surrounding women's liberation, the question of the family is probably the most explosive.

Everyone is a mother, father, brother, sister, husband, wife, son, or daughter to someone or some set of people. Every individual is personally involved in family relationships. People tend to react very subjectively, depending on their own personal history. And that is why it is so easy for the opponents of Marxism like the CP to demagogically exploit some of the most conservative and backward attitudes on the family question.

We keep these things in mind when discussing the reactionary nature of the family institution, but we do not make any theoretical concessions to the prevailing prejudices.

The family shifts from society to an individual man and/or woman the total responsibility for caring for and raising children, for taking care of the aged, for the education and inculcation of bourgeois values in children—the values they need to survive in this society—and for policing the adolescent. Intolerable economic burdens are placed on the fundamental unit which is then proclaimed sacred, and the institution destroys millions of individuals helplessly caught within its framework.

There are, of course, good husbands, good wives, good parents, and good children—as individuals. But as an institution, the family is a reactionary pillar of class society, and it is only when its individual members are freed from the economic shackles that bind them together that it will be possible for truly human relationships to blossom.

It is important for us to continue to take the lead in explaining and educating about these questions within our own movement and within the women's liberation movement. The theoretical debate underway is one that we can only be anxious to participate in.

The abolition of abortion restrictions in the United States would be a historical step forward and a tremendous boost to the burgeoning women's liberation movement. Women would see it as a direct result of their own actions, a proof of their power, and it would increase their confidence and determination to continue to fight for their liberation.

A number of the other demands that we have raised, primarily through our election campaigns, can also become focal points for mass action—free 24-hour childcare centers controlled by those who use them; equal pay for equal work; access for women to all educational opportunities; a sliding scale of hours and wages along with preferential hiring for women and oppressed national minorities; truthful teaching of women's history; free birth control information and devices on demand; and many others.

We are now seeing the dawn of a movement that will probably be one of the most important mass movements in American history. As capitalism continues to decay, to rot in its own death agony, the angers and frustrations of every oppressed sector of the population will explode with greater and greater force. We expect this, we anticipate it, we look forward to it, and we want to be right there in the middle of it helping to lead it in an anticapitalist direction. That's exactly what is beginning to happen in the women's liberation movement today, and we can greet it with nothing but extreme optimism.

NOTES

1. RYM is the acronym for Revolutionary Youth Movement.
2. YSA is the acronym for Young Socialists of America.

3

Introduction to *The Power of Women and the Subversion of the Community*

Selma James

The two articles that follow ("Women and the Subversion of Community" and "A Woman's Place") were written nineteen years and 7,000 miles apart. [Editor's Note: This is a reference to the original text. Only the first part follows in this reproduction.]

The first, "Women and the Subversion of the Community," is a product of the new women's movement in Italy. It is a major contribution to the question posed by the existence of a growing international movement of women: What is the relation of women to capital and what kind of struggle can we effectively wage to destroy it? We must hastily add that this is not the same as asking, What concessions can we wring from the enemy?—though this is related. To pose the first question is to assume we'll win; to pose the second is to calculate what we can salvage from the wreck of defeat. But in struggling to win, plenty can be gained along the way.

Up to now, the women's movement has had to define itself unaided by any serious heritage of Marxist critique of women's relation to the capitalist plan of development and underdevelopment. Quite the opposite. We inherited a distorted and reformist concept of capital itself as a series of *things* which we struggle to plan, control or manage, rather than as a *social relation* which we struggle to destroy.[1] Bypassing that heritage or lack of it, our movement explored the female experience, beginning with what we personally knew it to be. This is how we have been able for the first time on a mass scale to describe with profound insight and cutting precision the degradation of women and the shaping of our personality by forces which intended that we accept this degradation, accept to be quiet and powerless victims. On the basis of these discoveries, two distinct political tendencies have emerged, apparently opposite extremes of the political spectrum within the women's movement.

Among those who have insisted that caste and not class was fundamental, some women have asserted that what they call an "economic analysis" could not encompass, nor could a political struggle end, the physical and psychological oppression of women. They reject revolutionary political struggle. Capital is immoral, needs reforms, and should be left behind, they say (thereby implying that the reforms are a moral obligation which are themselves a negotiated and above all nonviolent transition to "socialism"), but it is not the only enemy. We must change men and/or ourselves first. So that not only political struggle is rejected; so is liberation for the mass of women who are too busy working and seeing after others to took for a personal solution.

The possible future directions of these politics vary, mainly because this point of view takes a number of forms depending on the stratum of women who hold it. An elite club of this type can remain introverted and isolated—harmless except as it discredits the movement generally. Or it can be a source of those managerial types in every field whom the class in charge is looking for to perform for it ruling functions over rebellious women and, god bless equality, over rebellious men too.[2] Integral to this participation in the marginal aspects of ruling, by the way, is an ambition and rivalry up to now primarily identified with men.

But history, past and future, is not simple. We have to note that some of the most incisive discoveries of the movement and in fact its autonomy have come from women who began by basing themselves on a repudiation of class and class struggle. The task of the movement now is to develop a political strategy on the foundations of these discoveries and on the basis of this autonomy.

Most of those who have insisted from the beginning that class and not caste was fundamental have been less able to translate our psychological insights into autonomous and revolutionary political action. Beginning with a male definition of class, the liberation of women is reduced to equal pay and a "fairer" and more efficient welfare state.[3] For these women capital is the main enemy but because it is *backward,* not because it *exists.* They don't aim to destroy the capitalist social relation but only to organize it more rationally. (The extra-parliamentary left in Italy would call this a "socialist" as distinct from a revolutionary position.) What a rationized capital—equal pay, more and better nurseries, more and better jobs, etc.—can't fix, they call "oppression," which, like Topsy, the orphaned slave child who never knew her parents, "just growed." Oppression disconnected from material relations is a problem of "consciousness"—in this case, psychology masquerading in political jargon. And so the "class analysis" has been used to limit the breadth of the movement's attack and even undermine the movement's autonomy.

The essentially similar liberal nature of these two tendencies, wanting to rationally manage "society" to eliminate "oppression," is not usually apparent until we see "political" women and these "nonpolitical" women join together on concrete demands or, more often, against revolutionary actions. Most of us in the movement belong to neither of these tendencies and have had a hard time charting a course between them. Both ask us, "Are you a feminist or are you political?"

The "political" women who talk of class are easy to identify. They are the women's liberationists whose first allegiance is not to the women's movement but to organizations of the male-dominated left. Once strategy and action originate from a source outside of women, women's struggle is measured by how it is presumed to affect men, otherwise known as "the workers," and women's consciousness by whether the forms of struggle they adopt are the forms men have traditionally used.

The "political" women see the rest of us as nonpolitical, and this has tended to drive us together in self-protection, obscuring or playing down real political differences among us. These now are beginning to make themselves felt. Groups that call themselves Psychology Groups (I'm not talking here about consciousness-raising groups) tend to express the politics of caste most coherently.[4] But whichever quarter they come from, viewing women as a caste and only a caste is a distinct political line that is increasingly finding political and organizational expression in every discussion of what to do. In the coming period of intense working-class activity, as we are forced to create our own political framework, casting away secondhand theories of male-dominated socialist movements, the pre-eminence of caste will be posed as the alternative and will have to be confronted and rejected as well. On this basis alone can the new politics inherent in autonomy find its tongue and its muscle.

This process of development is not unique to the women's movement. The Black movement in the United States (and elsewhere) also began by adopting what appeared to be only a caste position in opposition to the racism of white male-dominated groups. Intellectuals in Harlem and Malcolm X, that great revolutionary, were both nationalists, and both appeared to place color above class when the white left were still chanting variations of "Black and white unite and fight," or "Negroes and Labor must join together." The Black working class was able through this nationalism to redefine class: overwhelmingly Black and Labor were synonymous (with no other group was Labor as synonymous—except perhaps with women), the demands of Blacks and the forms of struggle created by Blacks were the most comprehensive working-class demands and the most advanced working-class struggle. This struggle was able to attract to itself the best elements among the intellectuals who saw their own persecution as Blacks, as a caste grounded in the exploitation of Black workers. Those intellectuals who got caught in the moment of nationalism after the class had moved beyond it saw race in increasingly individual terms and made up that pool from which the State Department could hook the fish of tokenism, appointing a Black as special presidential advisor on slum clearance, for example—and the personnel of a new, more integrated technocracy. In the same way women for whom caste is the fundamental issue will make the transition to revolutionary feminism based on a redefinition of class or will invite integration into the white male power structure.

But "Marxist women," as a woman from the movement in New Orleans says, "are just Marxist men in drag." The struggle as they see it is not qualitatively different from the one the organized labor movement under masculine management has always commended to women, except that now, appended to the "general struggle," is something called "women's liberation" or "women's struggle" voiced by women themselves.

This "general struggle" I take to mean the class struggle. But there is nothing in capitalism which is not capitalistic, that is, not part of the class struggle. The questions are (a) Are women except when they are wage workers auxiliary to capitalism (as has been assumed) and therefore auxiliary to a more basic, more general struggle against capitalism; and (b) Can anything ever have been "general" which has excluded so many women for so long?

Rejecting on the one hand class subordinated to feminism and on the other feminism subordinated to class, Mariarosa Dalla Costa has confronted what (to our shame) has passed for Marxism with the female experience that we have been exploring and struggling to articulate. The result has been a translation of our psychological insights into a critique of the political economy of the exploitation of women, the theoretical basis for a revolutionary and autonomous women's struggle. Based on what we know of how we are degraded, she moves into the question of why, in a depth as far as I know not reached before.

One great achievement of Marx was to show that the specific social relations between people in the production of the necessities of life, relations which spring up without their conscious planning, "behind the backs of *individuals*" (*Menschen*—previously translated as men), distinguish one society from another. That is, in class society, the form of the relation between people through which the ruling class robs the exploited of their labor is unique in each historic epoch, and all other social relations in the society, beginning with the family and including every other institution, reflect that form.

For Marx history was a process of struggle of the exploited, who continually provoke over long periods and in sudden revolutionary leaps changes in the basic social relations of production and in all the institutions which are an expression of these relations. The family, then, was the basic biological unit differing in form from one society to another, directly related to the way people produce. According to him, the family, even before class society, had the subordinated woman as its pivot; class society itself was an extension of the relations between men on the one hand and women and children on the other, an extension, that is, of the man's command over the labor of his woman and his children.

The women's movement has gone into greater detail about the capitalist family. After describing how women are conditioned to be subordinated to men, it has described the family as that institution where the young are repressed from birth to accept the discipline of capitalist relations—which in Marxist terms begins with the discipline of capitalist work. Other women have identified the family as the center of consumption, and yet others have shown that housewives make up a hidden reserve workforce: "unemployed" women work behind closed doors at home, to be called out again when capital needs them elsewhere.

The Dalla Costa article affirms all the above, but places them on another basis: the family under capitalism is a center of conditioning, of consumption and of reserve labor, but a center essentially *of social production*. When previously so-called Marxists said that the capitalist family did not produce for capitalism, was not part of social productions, it followed that they repudiated women's potential social power. Or rather, presuming that women in the home could not have social power, they could not see that women in the home produced. If your production is vital for capitalism, refusing to produce, refusing to work, is a fundamental lever of social power.

Marx's analysis of capitalist production was not a meditation on how the society "ticked." It was a tool to find the way to overthrow it, to find the social forces which, exploited by capital, were subversive to it. Yet it was because he was looking for the forces that would inevitably overthrow capital that he could describe capital's social relations, which are pregnant with working-class subversion. It is because Mariarosa Dalla Costa was looking for *women's* lever of social power among those forces that she was able to uncover that even when women do not work out of their homes, they are vital producers.

The commodity they produce, unlike all other commodities, is unique to capitalism: the living human being—the laborer himself.

Capital's special way of robbing labor is by paying the worker a wage that is enough to live on (more or less) and to reproduce other workers. But the worker must produce more in the way of commodities than what his wage is worth. The unpaid surplus labor is what the capitalist is in business to accumulate and what gives him increasing power over more and more workers: he pays for some labor to get the rest free so he can command more labor and get even more free, ad infinitum—until we stop him. He buys with wages the right to use the only "thing" the worker has to sell, his or her ability to work. The specific social relation which is capital, then, is the wage relation. And this wage relation can exist only when the ability to work becomes a saleable commodity. Marx calls this commodity *labor power.*

This is a strange commodity, for it is not a thing. The ability to labor resides only in a human being whose life is consumed in the process of producing. First it must be nine months in the womb and must be fed, clothed and trained; then when it works its bed must be made, its floors swept, its lunch box prepared, its sexuality not gratified but quietened, its dinner ready when it gets home, even if this is eight in the morning from the night shift. This is how labor power is produced and reproduced when it is daily consumed in the factory or the office. *To describe its basic production and reproduction is to describe women's work.*

The community therefore is not an area of freedom and leisure auxiliary to the factory, where by chance there happen to be women who are degraded as the personal servants of men. The community is the other half of capitalist organization, the other area of hidden capitalist exploitation, *the other, hidden, source of surplus labor.* It becomes increasingly regimented like a factory, what Dalla Costa calls a social factory, where the costs and nature of transport, housing, medical care, education, and police are all points of struggle. And this social factory has as its pivot the woman in the home producing labor power as a commodity, *and her struggle not to.*

The demands of the women's movement, then, take on a new and more subversive significance. When we say, for example, that we want control of our own bodies, we are challenging the domination of capital which has transformed our reproductive organs as much as our arms and legs into instruments of accumulation of surplus labor; transformed our relations with men, with our children and our very creation of them into *work productive to this accumulation.*

"A Woman's Place," originally published as a pamphlet, comes from the United States. It was written in 1952 at the height of the cold war, in Los Angeles, where the immigration of young working men and women had assumed Biblical dimensions (see Dalla Costa and James 1972). Though it bears my name, I was merely a vehicle for expressing what women, housewives, and factory workers felt and knew as immigrants to the Golden West from the South and East.

It was already clear even then that working outside the home did not make drudgery at home any more appealing, nor liberate us from the responsibility for housework when it was shared. It was equally clear that to think of spending our lives packing chocolates, or winding transformers, or wiring televisions was more than we could bear. We rejected both and fought against both. For example, in those days a man's friends would still laugh if they saw him wearing an apron and washing up. We changed that.

There is no doubt that the courage to fight for these changes sprang directly from that paycheck we so hated to work for. But though we hated the work, for most of us it provided the first opportunity for an independent social experience outside the isolation of the home, and it *seemed the only alternative to that isolation.* After the mass entry of women into industry during the Second World War and our brutal expulsion between 1945 and 1947, when they wanted us again in 1947 we came back and, with the Korean War (1949), in increasing numbers. For all the reasons outlined in the pamphlet, we wanted money and saw no alternative to demanding jobs.

That we were immigrants from industrial, farming, or coal-mining areas made us more dependent on that paycheck, since we had only ourselves to fall back on. But it gave us an advantage too. In the new aircraft and electronics industries of L.A., in addition to the standard jobs for women, for example in food and clothing, we—more white women than Black, who were in those days largely denied jobs with higher (subsistence) pay—managed to achieve new freedom of action. We were unrestrained by fathers and mothers who stayed "back East" or "down South." By the time trade unions, formed in the East years before by bitter struggle, were imported West, they were negotiators for a ten-cents-a-year raise, and were part of the disciplinary apparatus that confronted us on the assembly line and that we paid for in high dues taken out before we ever saw our money. Other traditional forms of "political" organization were either nonexistent or irrelevant and most of us ignored them. In short, we made a clean break with the past.

In the women's movement of the late '60s, the energy of those who refused the old forms of protection, or who never knew them, finally found massive articulation. Yet ten years before, in the baldness of our confrontation with capital (directly and via men) we were making our way through what has become increasingly an international experience. This experience taught us that the second job outside the home is another boss superimposed on the first; that a woman's first job is to reproduce other people's labor power, and her second is to reproduce *and sell* her own. So that her struggle in the family and in the factory, the joint organizers of her labor, of her husband's labor and of the future labor of her children, is one whole. The very unity in one person of the two divided aspects of capitalist production presupposes not only a new scope of struggle but an entirely new evaluation of the weight and cruciality of women in that struggle.

These are the themes of the Dalla Costa article. What was posed by the struggle of so-called "reactionary" or "backward" or at best "nonpolitical" housewives and factory wives in the United States twenty years ago is taken by a woman in Italy and used as a starting point for a restatement of Marxist theory and a reorientation of struggle. This theoretical development parallels, expresses, and is needed for an entirely new level of struggle, which women internationally are in the process of waging.

We've come a long way, baby.

NOTES

1. "... Wakefield discovered that in the Colonies, property in money, means of subsistence, machines, and other means of production, does not as yet stamp a man as a capitalist if there be wanting the correlative—the wage worker, the other man who is compelled to sell himself of his own free will. He discovered that *capital is not a thing, but a social relation between persons, established by the instrumentality of things.* Mr. Peel, he moans, took with him from England to Swan River, West Australia, means of subsistence and of production to the amount of 50,000 pounds. Mr. Peel had the foresight to bring with him, besides, 3,000 persons of the working class, men, women and children. Once arrived at his destination, 'Mr. Peel was left without a servant to make his bed or fetch him water from the river.' Unhappy Mr. Peel who provided for everything except the export of English modes of production to Swan River!" *Capital*, Vol. 1, K. Marx, p. 766, Moscow 1958 (our emphasis).

2. The *Financial Times* of March 9, 1971, suggests that many capitalists are missing the opportunity to "use" women in positions of middle management; being "grateful outsiders," women would not only lower the pay structure, "at least in the first instance," but would be a "source of renewed energy and vitality" with which to manage the rest of us.

3. If this seems an extreme statement, look at the demands we in England marched for in 1971: equal pay, free 24-hour child care, equal educational opportunity, and free birth control and abortion on demand. Incorporated into a wider struggle, some of these are vital. As they stand, they accept that we not have the children we can't afford; they demand of the state facilities to keep the children we can afford for as long as 24 hours a day; and they demand that these children have equal chance to be conditioned and trained to sell themselves competitively with each other on the labor market for equal pay. By themselves these are not just cooptable demands. They are capitalist planning. Most of us in the movement never felt these demands expressed where we wanted the movement to go, but in the absence of an independent feminist political framework we lost by default. The prime architects of these demands were women with a "class analysis."

4. Psychology itself *by its nature* is a prime weapon of manipulation, i.e., social control, of men, women, and children. It does not acquire another nature when wielded by women in a movement for liberation. Quite the reverse. To the degree that we permit, it manipulates the movement and changes the nature of that to suit its needs. And not only psychology.

> Women's Liberation needs
> —to destroy sociology as the ideology of the social services that bases itself on the proposition that this society is "the norm"; if you are a person in rebellion, you are a deviant.
> —to destroy psychology and psychiatry, which spend their time convincing us that our "problems" are personal hang-ups and that we must adjust to a lunatic world. These so-called "disciplines" and "sciences" will increasingly incorporate our demands in order more efficiently to redirect our forces into safe channels under their stewardship. Unless we deal with them, they will deal with us.
> —to discredit once and for all social workers, progressive educators, marriage guidance counselors and the whole army of experts whose function is to keep men, women and children functioning within the social framework, each by their own special brand of social frontal lobotomy ("The American Family: Decay and Rebirth," Selma James, reprinted in *From Feminism to Liberation,* collected by Edith Hoshino Altback, Schenkman, Cambridge, Mass., 1971, pp. 197–98).

4

Women and the Subversion of the Community

Mariarosa Dalla Costa and Selma James

These observations are an attempt to define and analyze the "woman question," and to locate this question in the entire "female role" as it has been created by the capitalist division of labor.

We place foremost in these pages the housewife as the central figure in this female role. We assume that all women are housewives and even those who work outside the home continue to be housewives. That is, on a world level, it is precisely what is particular to domestic work, not only measured as number of hours and nature of work, but as quality of life and quality of relationships which it generates, that determines a woman's place wherever she is and to whichever class she belongs. We concentrate here on the position of the working-class woman, but this is not to imply that only working-class women are exploited. Rather it is to confirm that the role of the working-class housewife, which we believe has been indispensable to capitalist production, is the determinant for the position of all other women. Every analysis of women as a caste, then, must proceed from the analysis of the position of working-class housewives.

In order to see the housewife as central, it was first of all necessary to analyze briefly how capitalism has created the modern family and the housewife's role in it by destroying the types of family group or community that previously existed.

This process is by no means complete. While we are speaking of the Western world and Italy in particular, we wish to make clear that to the extent that the capitalist mode of production also brings the Third World under its command, the same process of destruction must and is taking place there. Nor should we take for granted that the family as we know it today in the most technically advanced Western countries is the final form the family can assume under capitalism. But the analysis of new tendencies can only be the product of an analysis of how capitalism created this family and what woman's role is today, each as a moment in a process.

We propose to complete these observations on the female role by analyzing as well the position of the woman who works outside the home, but this is for a later date. We wish merely to indicate here the link between two apparently separate experiences: that of housewife and that of working woman.

The day-to-day struggles that women have developed since the Second World War run directly against the organization of the factory and of the home. The "unreliability" of women in the home and out of it has grown rapidly since then and runs directly against the factory as regimentation organized in time and space, and against the social factory as organization of the reproduction of labor power. This trend to more absenteeism, to less respect for timetables, to higher job mobility, is shared by young men and women workers. But where the man for crucial periods of his youth will be the sole support of a new family, women who on the whole are not restrained in this way and who must always consider the job at home are bound to be even more disengaged from work discipline, forcing disruption of the productive flow and therefore higher costs to capital. (This is one excuse for the discriminatory wages that many times over make up for capital's loss.) It is this same trend of disengagement that groups of housewives express when they leave their children with their husbands at work![1] This trend is and will increasingly be one of the decisive forms of the crisis in the systems of the factory and of the social factory.

In recent years, especially in the advanced capitalist countries, there have developed a number of women's movements of different orientations and range, from those that believe the fundamental conflict in society is between men and women to those focusing on the position of women as a specific manifestation of class exploitation.

If at first sight the position and attitudes of the former are perplexing, especially to women who have had previous experience of militant participation in political struggles, it is, we think, worth pointing out that women for whom sexual exploitation is the basic social contradiction provide an extremely important index of the degree of our own frustration, experienced by millions of women both inside and outside the movement. There are those who define their own lesbianism in these terms (we refer to views expressed by a section of the movement in the United States in particular): "Our associations with women began when, because we were together, we could acknowledge that we could no longer tolerate relationships with men, that we could not prevent these from becoming power relationships in which we were inevitably subjected. Our attentions and energies were diverted, our power was diffused and its objectives delimited." From this rejection has developed a movement of gay women which asserts the possibilities of a relationship free of a sexual power struggle, free of the biological social unit, and asserts at the same time our need to open ourselves to a wider social and therefore sexual potential.

Now in order to understand the frustrations of women expressing themselves in ever-increasing forms, we must be clear about what in the nature of the family under capitalism precipitates a crisis on this scale. The oppression of women, after all, did not begin with capitalism. What began with capitalism was the more intense exploitation of women as women and the possibility at last of their liberation.

THE ORIGINS OF THE CAPITALIST FAMILY

In precapitalist patriarchal society *the home and the family* were central to agricultural and artisan production. With the advent of capitalism the socialization of production was organized with *the factory* as its center. Those who worked in the new productive center, the factory, received a wage. Those who were excluded did not. Women, children and the aged lost the relative power that derived from the family's dependence on their labor, *which was seen to be social and necessary.* Capital, destroying the family and the community and production as one whole, on the one hand has concentrated basic social production in the factory and the office, and on the other has in essence detached the man from the family and turned him into a *wage laborer.* It has put on the man's shoulders the burden of financial responsibility for women, children, the old and the ill—in a word, all those who do not receive wages. At that moment began the expulsion from the home of all those who did not *procreate and service those who worked for wages.* The first to be excluded from the home, after men, were children; they sent children to school. The family ceased to be not only the productive, but also the educational center.[2]

To the extent that men had been the despotic heads of the patriarchal family, based on a strict division of labor, the experience of women, children, and men was a contradictory experience which we inherit. But in precapitalist society the work of each member of the community of serfs was seen to be directed to a purpose: either to the prosperity of the feudal lord or to our survival. To this extent the whole community of serfs was compelled to be cooperative in a unity of unfreedom that involved to the same degree women, children, and men, and that capitalism had to break.[3] In this sense the *unfree individual, the democracy of unfreedom,*[4] entered into a crisis. The passage from serfdom to free labor power separated the male from the female proletarian and both of them from their children. The unfree patriarch was transformed into the "free" wage earner, and upon the contradictory experience of the sexes and the generations was built a more profound estrangement and therefore a more subversive relation.

We must stress that this separation of children from adults is essential to an understanding of the full significance of the separation of women from men, to grasp fully how the organization of the struggle on the part of the women's movement, even when it takes the form of a violent rejection of any possibility of relations with men, can only aim to overcome the separation that is based on the "freedom" of wage labor.

THE CLASS STRUGGLE IN EDUCATION

The analysis of the school that has emerged during recent years—particularly with the advent of the students' movement—has clearly identified the school as a center of ideological discipline and of the shaping of the labor force and its masters. What has perhaps never emerged, or at least not in its profundity, is precisely what precedes all this; and that is the usual desperation of children on their first day of nursery school, when they see themselves dumped into a class and their parents suddenly desert them. *But it is precisely at this point that the whole story of school begins.*[5]

Seen in this way, the elementary school children are not those appendages who, merely by the demands "free lunches, free fares, free books," learned from the older ones, can in some way be united with the students of the higher schools.[6] In elementary school children, in those who are the sons and daughters of workers, there is always an awareness that school is in some way setting them against their parents *and their peers,* and consequently an instinctive resistance to studying and to being "educated." This is the resistance for which Black children are confined to educationally subnormal schools in Britain.[7] The European working-class child, like the Black working-class child, sees in the teacher somebody who is teaching him or her something against her mother and father, not as a defense of the child but as an attack on the class. Capitalism is the first productive system where the children of the exploited are disciplined and educated in institutions organized and controlled by the ruling class.[8]

The final proof that this alien indoctrination, which begins in nursery school, is based on the splitting of the family is that those working-class children who arrive (those few who do arrive) at university are so brainwashed that they are unable any longer to talk to their community.

Working-class children then are the first who instinctively rebel against schools and the education provided in schools. But their parents carry them to schools and confine them to schools because they are concerned that their children should "have an education," that is, be equipped to escape the assembly line or the kitchen to which, the parents are confined. If a working-class child shows particular aptitudes, the whole family immediately concentrates on this child, gives him the best conditions, often sacrificing the others, hoping and gambling that he will carry them all out of the working class. This in effect becomes the way capital moves through the aspirations of the parents to enlist their help in disciplining fresh labor power.

In Italy, parents less and less succeed in sending their children to school. Children's resistance to school is always increasing even when this resistance is not yet organized.

At the same time that children's resistance to being educated in schools grows, so does *their refusal to accept the definition* that capital has given of their *age.* Children want everything they see; they do not yet understand that in order to have things one must pay for them, and in order to pay for them one must have a wage, and therefore one must also be an adult. No wonder it is not easy to explain to children why they cannot have what television has told them they cannot live without.

But something is happening among the new generation of children and youth which is making it steadily more difficult to explain to them the arbitrary point at which they reach adulthood. The younger generation is demonstrating their age to us: in the '60s six-year-olds have already come up against police dogs in the South of the United States. Today we find the same phenomenon in Southern Italy and Northern Ireland, where children have been as active in the revolt as adults. When children (and women) are recognized as integral to history, no doubt other examples will come to light of very young people's (and women's) participation in revolutionary struggles. What is new is the autonomy of their participation *in spite of and because of* their exclusion from direct production. In the factories youth refuse the leadership of older workers, and in the revolts in the cities they are the diamond point. In the metropolis, generations of the nuclear family have produced youth and student movements that have initiated the process of shaking the framework of constituted power; in the Third World, the unemployed youth are often in the streets before the working class have organized in trade unions.

It is worth recording what *The Times* of London (1 June 1971) reported concerning a head teachers' meeting, called because one of them was admonished for hitting a pupil. "Disruptive and irresponsible elements lurk around every corner with the seemingly planned intention of eroding all forces of authority." This "is a plot to destroy the values on which our civilization is built and of which our schools are some of the finest bastions."

THE EXPLOITATION OF THE WAGELESS

We wanted to make these few comments on the attitude of revolt that is steadily spreading among children and youth, especially from the working class and particularly Black people, because we believe this to be intimately connected with the explosion of the women's movement and something which the women's movement itself must take into account. We are dealing here with the revolt of those who have been excluded, who have been separated by the system of production, and who express in action their need to destroy the forces that stand in the way of their social existence, but who this time are coming together as individuals.

Women and children have been excluded. The revolt of the one against exploitation through exclusion is an index of the revolt of the other.

To the extent to which capital has recruited the man and turned him into a wage laborer, it has created a fracture between him and all the other proletarians without a wage who, not participating directly in social production, were thus presumed incapable of being the subjects of social revolt.

Since Marx, it has been clear that capital rules and develops through the wage, that is, that the foundation of capitalist society was the wage laborer and his or her direct exploitation. What has been neither clear nor assumed by the organizations of the working-class movement is that precisely through the wage has the exploitation of the nonwage laborer been organized. This exploitation has been even more effective because the lack of a wage hid it. That is, the wage commanded a larger amount of labor than appeared in factory bargaining. *Where women are concerned, their labor appears to be a personal service outside of capital.* The women seemed only to be suffering from male chauvinism, being pushed around because capitalism meant general "injustice" and "bad and unreasonable behavior"; the few (men) who noticed convinced us that this was "oppression" but not exploitation. But "oppression" hid another and more pervasive aspect of capitalist society. Capital excluded children from the home and sent them to school not only because they were in the way of others' more "productive" labor or only to indoctrinate them. The rule of capital through the wage compels every able-bodied person to function, under the law of division of labor, and to function in ways that are, if not immediately, then ultimately profitable to the expansion and extension of the rule of capital. That, fundamentally, is the meaning of school. *Where children are concerned, their labor appears to be learning for their own benefit.*

Proletarian children have been forced to undergo the same education in the schools: this is capitalist leveling against the infinite possibilities of learning. Woman on the other hand has been isolated in the home, forced to carry out work that is considered unskilled, the work of giving birth to, raising, disciplining, and servicing the worker for production. Her role in the cycle of social production remained invisible because only the product of her labor, *the laborer,* was visible there. She herself was thereby trapped within precapitalist working conditions and never paid a wage.

And when we say "precapitalist working conditions" we do not refer only to women who have to use brooms to sweep. Even the best-equipped American kitchens do not reflect the present level of technological development; at most they reflect the technology of the nineteenth century. If you are not paid by the hour within certain limits, nobody cares how long it takes you to do your work.

This is not only a *quantitative* but a *qualitative* difference from other work, and it stems precisely from the kind of commodity that this work is destined to produce. Within the capitalist system generally, the productivity of labor doesn't increase unless there is a confrontation between capital and class: technological innovations and cooperation are at the same time moments of attack for the working class and moments of capitalistic response. But if this is true for the production of commodities generally, this has not been true for the production of that special kind of commodity, labor power. If technological innovation can lower the limit of necessary work, and if the working-class struggle in industry can use that innovation for gaining free hours, the same cannot be said of housework; to the extent that she must *in isolation* procreate, raise, and be responsible for children, a high mechanization of domestic chores doesn't free any time for the woman. She is always on duty, for the machine doesn't exist that makes and minds children.[9] A higher productivity of domestic work through mechanization, then, can be related only to specific services, for example, cooking, washing, cleaning. Her workday is unending not because she has no machines, but because she is isolated.[10]

CONFIRMING THE MYTH OF FEMALE INCAPACITY

With the advent of the capitalist mode of production, then, women were relegated to a condition of isolation, enclosed within the family cell, dependent in every aspect on men. The new autonomy of the free wage slave was denied her, and she remained in a precapitalist stage of personal dependence, but this time more brutalized because in contrast to the large-scale highly socialized production that now prevails. Woman's apparent incapacity to do certain things, to understand certain things, originated in her history, which is a history very similar in certain respects to that of "backward" children in ESN classes. To the extent that women were cut off from direct socialized production and isolated in the home, all possibilities of social life outside the neighborhood were denied them, and hence they were deprived of social knowledge and social education. When women are deprived of wide experiences of organizing and planning collectively industrial and other mass struggles, they are denied a basic source of education, the experience of social revolt. And this experience is primarily the experience of learning your own capacities, that is, your power and the capacities, the power of your class. Thus the isolation from which women have suffered has confirmed to society and to themselves the myth of female incapacity.

It is this myth which has hidden, first, that to the degree that the working class has been able to organize mass struggles in the community, rent strikes and struggles against inflation generally, the basis has always been the unceasing informal organization of women there; second, that in struggles in the cycle of direct production, women's support and organization, formal and informal, has been decisive. At critical moments this unceasing network of women surfaces and develops through the talents, energies, and strength of the "incapable female." But the myth does not die. Where women could together with men claim the victory—to survive (during unemployment) or to survive and win (during strikes)—the spoils of the victor belonged to the class "in general." Women rarely if ever got anything specifically for themselves; rarely if ever did the struggle have as an objective in any way altering the power structure of the home and its relation to the factory. Strike or unemployment, a woman's work is never done.

THE CAPITALIST FUNCTION OF THE UTERUS

Never as with the advent of capitalism has the destruction of woman as a person meant also the immediate diminution of her *physical integrity*. Feminine and masculine sexuality had already before capitalism undergone a series of regimes and forms of conditioning. But they had also undergone efficient methods of birth control that have unaccountably disappeared. Capital established the family as the nuclear family and subordinated within it the woman to the man, as the person who, not directly participating in social production, does not present herself independently on the labor market. As it cuts off all her possibilities of creativity and the development of her working activity, so it cuts off the expression of her sexual, psychological, and emotional autonomy.

We repeat: never had such a stunting of the physical integrity of woman taken place, affecting everything from the brain to the uterus. Participating with others in the production of a train, a car, or an airplane is not the same thing as using in isolation the same broom in the same few square feet of kitchen for centuries.

This is not a call for equality of men and women in the construction of airplanes, but it is merely to assume that difference between the two histories not only determines the differences in the actual forms of struggle but also brings to light what has been invisible for so long: the different forms women's struggles have assumed in the past. In the same way women are robbed of the possibility of developing their creative capacity, they are robbed of their sexual life, which has been transformed into a function for reproducing labor power: the same observations we made on the technological level of domestic services apply to birth control (and, by the way, to the whole field of gynecology), research into which until recently has been neglected while women have been forced to have children and forbidden the right to have abortions when, as was to be expected, the most primitive techniques of birth control failed.

From this complete diminution of woman, capital constructed the female role and made the man in the family the instrument of this reduction. The man as wage worker and head of the family was the specific instrument of this specific exploitation which is the exploitation of women.

THE HOMOSEXUALITY OF THE DIVISION OF LABOR

In this sense we can explain the extent to which degraded relationships between men and women are determined by the fracturing society has imposed between man and woman, subordinating woman as object, the "complement" to man. And in this sense we can see the validity of the explosion of tendencies within the women's movement, in which women want to conduct the struggle against men as such[11] and no longer wish to use their strength to sustain even sexual relationships with them, since each of these relationships is always frustrating. A power relation precludes any possibility of affection and intimacy. Yet between men and women power as its right *commands* sexual affection and intimacy. In this sense, the gay movement is the most massive attempt to disengage sexuality and power.

But homosexuality generally is at the same time rooted in the framework of capitalist society itself; women at home and men in factories and offices, separated one from the other for the whole day; or a typical factory of 1,000 women with 10 foremen; or a typing pool (of women, of course) that works for 50 professional men. All these situations are already a homosexual framework for living.

Capital, while it elevates heterosexuality to a religion, at the same time makes it impossible for men and women to be in touch with each other physically or emotionally—it undermines heterosexuality except as a sexual, economic, and social discipline.

We believe this is the reality from which we must begin. The explosion of the gay tendencies has been and is important for the movement precisely because it poses the urgency to claim for itself the specificity of women's struggle and above all to clarify in all their depths all facets and connections of the exploitation of women.

SURPLUS VALUE AND THE SOCIAL FACTORY

At this point then we would like to begin to clear the ground of a certain point of view which orthodox Marxism, especially in the ideology and practice of so-called Marxist parties, has always taken for granted: When women remain outside social production, that is, outside the socially organized productive cycle, they are also outside social productivity. The role of women, in other words, has always been seen as that of a psychologically subordinated person who, except where she is marginally employed outside the home, is outside production; she is essentially a supplier of a series of use-values in the home. This basically was the viewpoint of Marx, who, observing what happened to women working in the factories, concluded that it would have been better for them to be at home where a morally higher form of life resided. The true nature of the role of housewife never emerges clearly in Marx. Yet observers have noted that Lancashire women, cotton workers for over a century, are more sexually free and helped by men in domestic chores. On the other hand, in the Yorkshire coal-mining districts, where a low percentage of women worked outside the home, women are dominated more by the figure of the husband. Even those who have been able to define the exploitation of women in socialized production could not then go on to understand the exploited position of women in the home; men are too compromised in their relationship with women. For that reason only women can define themselves and move on the woman question.

We have to make clear that, within the wage, domestic work produces not only use-values, but is essential to the production of surplus value.[12] This is true of the entire female role as a personality subordinated at all levels—physical, psychological, and occupational—and which has had and continues to have a precise and vital place in the capitalist division of labor, *in the pursuit of productivity at the social level.* Let us examine more specifically the role of women as a source of social productivity, that is, of surplus value-making. First within the family.

THE PRODUCTIVITY OF WAGE SLAVERY
BASED ON UNWAGE SLAVERY

It is often asserted that, within the definition of wage labor, women in domestic labor are not productive. In fact precisely the opposite is true if one thinks of the enormous quantity of social services which capitalist organization transforms into privatized activity, putting them on the backs of housewives. Domestic labor is not essentially "feminine work"; a woman doesn't fulfill herself more or get less exhausted than a man from washing and cleaning. These are social services inasmuch as they serve the reproduction of labor power. And capital, precisely by instituting its family structure, has "liberated" the man from these functions so that he is completely "free" for *direct* exploitation, so that he is free to "earn" enough for a woman to reproduce him as labor power.[13] It has made men wage slaves, then, to the degree that it has succeeded in allocating these services to women in the family, and by the same process has controlled the flow of women into the labor market. In Italy women are still necessary in the home and capital still needs this form of the family. At the present level of development in Europe generally, and in Italy in particular, capital still prefers to import its labor power—in the form of millions of men from underdeveloped areas—while at the same time consigning women to the home.[14]

And women are of service not only because they carry out domestic labor without a wage and without going on strike, but also because they always receive back into the home all those who are periodically expelled from their jobs by economic crisis. The family, this maternal cradle always ready to help and protect in time of need, has been in fact the best guarantee that the unemployed do not immediately become a horde of disruptive outsiders.

The organized parties of the working-class movement have been careful not to raise the question of domestic work. Aside from the fact that they have always treated women as a lower form of life, even in factories, to raise this question would be to challenge the whole basis of the trade unions as organizations that deal (a) only with the factory; (b) only with a measured and "paid" work day; (c) only with that side of wages given to us and not with the side of wages taken back, that is, inflation. Women have always been forced by the working-class parties to put off their liberation to some hypothetical future, making it dependent on the gains that men, limited in the scope of their struggles by these parties, win for "themselves."

In reality, every phase of working-class struggle has fixed the subordination and exploitation of women at a higher level. The proposal of pensions for housewives[15] (and this makes us wonder why not a wage instead) serves only to show the complete willingness of these parties to further institutionalize women as housewives and men (and women) as wage slaves.

Now it is clear that not one of us believes that emancipation, liberation, can be achieved through work. Work is still work, whether inside or outside the home. The independence of the wage earner means only being a "free individual" for capital, no less for women than for men. Those who argue that the liberation of the working-class woman lies in her getting a job outside the home are part of the problem, not the solution. Slavery to an assembly line is not a liberation from slavery to a kitchen sink. To deny this is also to deny the slavery of the assembly line itself, proving again that if you don't know how women are exploited, you can never really know how men are exploited. But this question is so crucial that we deal with it separately. What we wish to make clear here is that by the nonpayment of a wage when we are producing in a world capitalistically organized, the figure of the boss is concealed behind that of the husband. He appears to be the sole recipient of domestic services, and this gives an ambiguous and slavelike character to housework. The husband and children, through their loving involvement, their loving blackmail, become the first foremen, the immediate controllers of this labor.

The husband tends to read the paper and wait for his dinner to be cooked and served, even when his wife goes out to work as he does and comes home with him. Clearly, the specific form of exploitation represented by domestic work demands a corresponding, specific form of struggle, namely the women's struggle, *within the family.*

If we fail to grasp completely that this family is the very pillar of the capitalist organization of work, if we make the mistake of regarding it only as a superstructure, dependent for change only on the stages of the struggle in the factories, then we will be moving in a limping revolution that will always perpetuate and aggravate *a basic contradiction in the class struggle, a contradiction that is functional to capitalist development.* We would, in other words, be perpetuating the error of considering ourselves as producers of use-values only, of considering housewives external to the working class. As long as housewives are considered external to the class, the class struggle at every moment and any point is impeded, frustrated, and unable to find full scope for its action. To elaborate this further is not our task here. To expose and condemn domestic work as a masked form of productive labor, however, raises a series of questions concerning both the aims and the forms of women's struggle.

SOCIALIZING THE STRUGGLE OF THE ISOLATED LABORER

In fact, the demand that would follow, namely "pay us wages for housework," would run the risk of looking, in the light of the present relationship of forces in Italy, as though we wanted further to entrench the condition of institutionalized slavery produced with the condition of housework—therefore such a demand could scarcely operate in practice as a mobilizing goal.[16]

The question is, therefore, how to develop forms of struggle that do not leave the housewife peacefully at home, at most ready to take part in occasional demonstrations through the streets, waiting for a wage that would never pay for anything; rather we must discover forms of struggle that immediately break the whole structure of domestic work, rejecting it absolutely, rejecting our role as housewives and the home as the ghetto of our existence, since the problem is not only to stop doing this work, but to smash the entire role of housewife. *The starting point is not how to do housework more efficiently, but how to find a place as protagonist in the struggle; that is, not a higher productivity of domestic labor but a higher subversiveness in the struggle.*

To immediately overthrow the relation between time-given-to-housework and time-not-given-to-housework: it is not necessary to spend time each day ironing sheets and curtains, cleaning the floor until it sparkles or dusting. And yet many women still do that. Obviously it is not because they are stupid: once again we are reminded of the parallel we made earlier with the ESN school. In reality, it is only in this work that they can realize an identity precisely because, as we said before, capital has cut them off from the process of socially organized production.

But it does not automatically follow that to be cut off from socialized production is to be cut off from socialized struggle: struggle, however, demands time away from housework, and at the same time it offers an alternative identity to the woman who before found it only at the level of the domestic ghetto. In the sociality of struggle women discover and exercise a power that effectively gives them a new identity. *The new identity is and can only be a new degree of social power. . . .*

Every place of struggle outside the home, precisely because *every sphere of capitalist organization presupposes the home,* offers a chance for attack by women; factory meetings, neighborhood meetings, student assemblies—each of these are legitimate places for women's struggle, where women can encounter and confront men, not as women versus men, if you like, but as individuals, rather than mother-father, son-daughter, with all the possibilities this offers to explode outside of the house the contradictions, the frustrations, that capital has wanted to implode within the family.

THE REFUSAL OF WORK

Hence we must refuse housework as women's work, as work imposed upon us, which we never invented, which has never been paid for, in which they have forced us to cope with absurd hours, twelve and thirteen a day, in order to force us to stay at home.

We must get out of the house; we must reject the home because we want to unite with other women, to struggle against all situations which presume that women will stay at home, to link ourselves to the struggles of all those who are in ghettos, whether that ghetto is a nursery, a school, a hospital, an old-age home, or a slum. To abandon the home is already a form of struggle, since the social services we perform there would then cease to be carried out in those conditions, and so all those who work out of the home would then demand that the burden carried by us until now be thrown squarely where it belongs—onto the shoulders of capital. This alteration in the terms of struggle will be all the more violent, the more the refusal of domestic labor on the part of women will be violent, determined, and on a mass scale.

The working-class family is the more difficult point to break because it is the support of the worker as worker, and for that reason the support of capital. On this family depends the support of the class, the survival of the class—but *at the woman's expense against the class itself.* The woman is the slave of a wage slave, and her slavery ensures the slavery of her man. Like the trade union, the family protects the worker but also ensures that he *and she* will never be anything but workers. And that is why the struggle of the woman of the working class against the family is crucial.

Meeting other women who work inside and outside their homes allows us to possess other chances of struggle. To the extent that our struggle is a struggle against work, it is inscribed in the struggle the working class wages against capitalist work. But to the extent that the exploitation of women through domestic work has had its own specific history, tied to the survival of the nuclear family, the specific course of this struggle, which must pass through the destruction of the nuclear family as established by the capitalist social order, adds a new dimension to the class struggle . . .

WOMEN AND THE STRUGGLE NOT TO WORK

Let us sum up. The role of housewife, behind whose isolation is hidden social labor, must be destroyed. But our alternatives are strictly defined. Up to now, the myth of female incapacity, rooted in this isolated woman dependent on someone else's wage and therefore shaped by someone else's consciousness, has been broken by only one action: the woman getting her own wage, breaking the back of personal economic dependence, making her own independent experience with the world outside the home, performing social labor in a socialized structure, whether the factory or the office, and initiating there her own forms of social rebellion along with the traditional forms of the class. *The advent of the women's movement is a rejection of this alternative.*

Capital itself is seizing upon the same impetus that created a movement—the rejection by millions of women of women's traditional place to recompose the workforce with increasing numbers of women. The movement can only develop in opposition to this. It poses by its very existence and must pose with increasing articulation in action the fact that women refuse the myth of liberation through work.

For we have worked enough. We have chopped billions of tons of cotton, washed billions of dishes, scrubbed billions of floors, typed billions of words, wired billions of radio sets, washed billions of nappies by hand and in machines. Every time they have let us in to some traditionally male enclave, we found a new level of exploitation. Here again we must make a parallel, different as they are, between underdevelopment in the Third World and underdevelopment in the metropolis, or, to be more precise, in the kitchens of the metropolis. Capitalist planning proposes to the Third World that it "develop"; that in addition to its present agonies, it too suffer the agony of all industrial counter-revolution. Women in the metropolis have been offered the same "aid." But those of us who have gone out of our homes to work because we had to or for extras or for economic independence have warned the rest: inflation has riveted us to this bloody typing pool or to this assembly line, and in that there is no salvation. We must refuse the development they are offering us. But the struggle of the working woman is not to return to the isolation of the home, appealing as this sometimes may be on Monday morning; any more than the housewife's struggle is to exchange being imprisoned in a house for being clinched to desks or machines, appealing as this sometimes may be compared to the loneliness of the twelfth-story flat.

Women must completely discover their own possibilities, which are neither mending socks nor becoming captains of oceangoing ships. Better still, we *may* wish to do these things, but these now cannot be located anywhere but in the history of capital.

The challenge to the women's movement is to find modes of struggle which, while they liberate women from the home, on the one hand avoid a double slavery and on the other prevent another degree of capitalistic control and regimentation. *This ultimately is the dividing line between reformism and revolutionary politics within the women's movement.*

It seems there have been few women of genius. There could not be since, cut off from the social process, we cannot see on what matters they could exercise their genius. Now there is a matter, the struggle itself.

Freud said also that every woman from birth suffers from penis envy. He forgot to add that this feeling of envy begins from the moment she perceives that in some way to have a penis means to have power. Even less did he realize that the traditional power of the penis commenced upon a whole new history at the very moment when the separation of man from woman became a capitalistic division.

And this is where our struggle begins.

NOTES

1. This happened as part of the massive demonstration of women celebrating International Women's Day in the United States, August 1970.

2. This is to assume a whole new meaning for "education," and the work now being done on the history of compulsory education—forced learning—proves this. In England teachers were conceived of as "moral police" who could (1) condition children against "crime" and curb working-class reappropriation in the community; (2) destroy "the mob," working-class organization based on a family that was still either a productive unit or at least a viable organizational unit; (3) make habitual regular attendance and good timekeeping necessary to children's later employments; and (4) stratify the class by grading and selection. As with the family itself, the transition to this new form of social control was not smooth and direct, and was the result of contradictory forces both within the class and within capital, as with every phase of the history of capitalism.

3. Wage labor is based on the subordination of all relationships to the wage relation. The worker must enter as an individual into a contract with capital stripped of the protection of kinships.

4. Karl Marx, "Critique of Hegel's Philosophy of the State," *Writings of the Young Marx on Philosophy and Society,* ed. and trans. by Loyd D. Easton and Kurt H. Guddat, New York, 1967, p. 176.

5. We are not dealing here with the narrowness of the nuclear family that prevents children from having an easy transition to forming relations with other people; nor with what follows from this, the argument of psychologists that proper conditioning would have avoided such a crisis. We are dealing with the entire organization of the society, of which family, school, and factory are each one ghettoized compartment. So every kind of passage from one to another of these compartments is a painful passage. The pain cannot be eliminated by tinkering with the relations between one ghetto and another but only by the destruction of every ghetto.

6. "Free fares, free lunches, free books" was one of the slogans of a section of the Italian students' movement, which aimed to connect the struggle of younger students with workers and university students.

7. In Britain and the United States the psychologists Eysenck and Jensen, who are convinced "scientifically" that Blacks have a lower "intelligence" than whites, and the progressive educators like Ivan Illyich seem diametrically opposed. What they aim to achieve links them. They are divided by method. In any case the psychologists are not more racist than the rest, only more direct. "Intelligence" is the ability to assume your enemy's case as wisdom and to shape your own logic on the basis of this. Where the whole society operates institutionally on the assumption of white racial superiority, these psychologists propose more conscious and thorough "conditioning" so that children who do not learn to read do not learn instead to make molotov cocktails. A sensible view with which Illyich, who is concerned with the "underachievement" of children (that is, rejection by them of "intelligence"), can agree.

8. In spite of the fact that capital manages the schools, control is never given once and for all. The working class continually and increasingly challenges the contents and refuses the costs of capitalist schooling. The response of the capitalist system is to re-establish its own control, and this control tends to be more and more regimented on factory-like lines.

9. We are not at all ignoring the attempts at this moment to make test-tube babies. But today such mechanisms belong completely to capitalist science and control. The use would be completely against us and against the class. It is not in our interest to abdicate procreation, to consign it to the hands of the enemy. It is in our interest to conquer the freedom to procreate for which we will pay neither the price of the wage nor the price of social exclusion.

10. To the extent that not technological innovation but only "human care" can raise children, the effective liberation from domestic work time, the *qualitative change of domestic work,* can derive only from a movement of women, from a struggle of women: the more the movement grows, the less men—and first of all political militants—can count on female baby-minding. And at the same time the new social ambiance that the movement constructs offers to children social space with both men and women that has nothing to do with the day-care centers organized by the

state. These are already victories of struggle. Precisely because they are the *results* of a movement that is by its nature a struggle, they do not aim to *substitute* any kind of cooperation for the struggle itself.

11. It is impossible to say for how long these tendencies will continue to drive the movement forward and when they will turn into their opposite.

12. Some first readers in English have found that this definition of women's work should be more precise. What we meant is that housework as work is *productive* in the Marxian sense, that is, produces surplus value.

    We speak immediately after about the productivity of the entire female; the productivity of the woman, both as related to her work and as related to her entire role, must wait for a later text on which we are now at work. In this the woman's place is explained in a more articulated way from the point of view of the entire capitalist circuit.

13. See introduction, p. 11. Labor power "is a strange commodity for this is not a thing. The ability to labor resides only in a human being whose life is consumed in the process of producing. . . . *To describe its basic production and reproduction is to describe women's work.*" [Editor's Note: This endnote refers to the original text.]

14. This, however, is being countered by an opposite tendency to bring women into industry in certain particular sectors. Differing needs of capital within the same geographical sector have produced differing and even opposing propaganda and policies. Where in the past family stability has been based on a relatively standardized mythology (policy and propaganda being uniform and officially uncontested), today various sectors of capital contradict each other and undermine the very definition of family as a stable, unchanging, "natural" unit. The classic example of this is the variety of views and financial policies on birth control. The British government has recently doubled its allocation of funds for this purpose. We must examine to what extent this policy is connected with a racist immigration policy, that is, manipulation of the sources of mature labor power, and with the increasing erosion of the work ethic, which results in movements of the unemployed and unsupported mothers, that is, controlling births which pollute the purity of capital with revolutionary children.

15. This is the policy, among others, of the Communist Party in Italy, who for some years proposed a bill to the Italian parliament which would have given a pension to women at home, both housewives and single women, when they reached 55 years of age. The bill was never passed.

16. Today the demand of wages for housework is put forward increasingly and with less opposition in the women's movement in Italy and elsewhere. Since this document was first drafted (June 1971), the debate has become more profound and many uncertainties due to the relative newness of the discussion have been dispelled. But above all, the weight of the needs of proletarian women has not only radicalized the demands of the movement. It has also given us greater strength and confidence to advance them. A year ago, at the beginning of the movement in Italy, there were those who still thought that the state could easily suffocate the female rebellion against housework by "paying" it with a monthly allowance of L7–L8 as they had already done, especially with those "wretched of the earth" who were dependent on pensions.

    Now these uncertainties are largely dissipated.

    And it is clear in any case that the demand for a wage for housework is only a basis, a perspective, from which to start, whose merit is essentially to link immediately female oppression, subordination, and isolation to their material foundation: female exploitation. At this moment this is perhaps the major function of the demand of wages for housework.

    This gives at once an indication for struggle, a direction in organizational terms in which oppression and exploitation, situation of caste and class, find themselves insolubly linked.

    The practical, continuous translation of this perspective is the task that the movement faces in Italy and elsewhere.

5

Not for Lesbians Only

Charlotte Bunch

The following is an expanded and revised version of a speech given at the Socialist-Feminist Conference, Antioch College, Yellow Springs, Ohio, July 5, 1975. Many of the ideas expressed here about lesbian-feminist politics were first developed several years ago in The Furies. Nevertheless, I am continually discovering that most feminists, including many lesbians, have little idea what lesbian-feminist politics is. This speech takes those basic political ideas and develops them further, particularly as they relate to socialist-feminism.

I am listed in your program as Charlotte Bunch-Weeks—a rather ominous slip-of-the-tongue (or slip in historical timing), which reflects a subject so far avoided at this conference that I, for one, want to talk about.

Five years ago, when I *was* Charlotte Bunch-Weeks, and straight, and married to a man, I was also a socialist-feminist. When I left the man and the marriage, I also left the newly developing socialist-feminist movement—because, for one reason, my politics then, as now, were inextricably joined with the way I lived my personal, my daily life. With men, with male politics, I was a socialist; with women, engaged in the articulation of women's politics, I became a lesbian-feminist—and, in the gay-straight split, a lesbian-feminist separatist. It's that gay-straight split that no one here seems to want to remember—and I bring it up now, not because I want to relive a past painful to all concerned, but because it is an essential part of our political history which, if ignored, will eventually force lesbians to withdraw again from other political women. There were important political reasons for that split, reasons explicitly related to the survival of lesbians, and those reasons and the problems causing them are still with us. It is important—especially for political groups who wish to give credence and priority to lesbian issues—to remember why separatism happened, why it is not a historical relic but still vital to the ongoing debate over lesbianism and feminism.

In my own personal experience, I and the other women of The Furies collective left the women's movement because it had been made clear to us that there was no space to develop a lesbian-feminist politics and life style without constant and nonproductive conflict with heterosexual fear, antagonism, and insensitivity. This was essentially the same experience shared by many other lesbian-feminists at about the same time around the country. What the women's movement could not accept then—and still finds it difficult to accept—is that lesbianism is political: this is the essence of lesbian-feminist politics. Sounds simple. Yet most feminists still view lesbianism as a personal decision or, at best, as a civil rights concern or a cultural phenomenon. Lesbianism is more than a question of civil rights and culture, although the daily discrimination against lesbians is real and its alleviation through civil-libertarian reforms is important. Similarly, although lesbianism is a primary force in the emergence of a dynamic women's culture, it is much more. Lesbian-feminist politics is a political critique of the institution and ideology of heterosexuality as a cornerstone of male supremacy. It is an extension of the analysis of sexual politics to an analysis of sexuality itself as an institution. It is a commitment to women as a political group, which is the basis of a political/economic strategy leading to power for women, not just an "alternative community."

There are many lesbians still who feel that there is no place in socialist-feminist organizations in particular, or the women's movement in general, for them to develop that politics or live that life. Because of this, I am still, in part, a separatist; but I don't want to be a total separatist again: few who have experienced that kind of isolation believe it is the ultimate goal of liberation. Since unity and coalition seem necessary, the question for me is unity on what terms? with whom? and around what politics? For instance, to unify the lesbian-feminist politics developed within the past four years with socialist-feminism requires more than token reference to queers. It requires an acknowledgment of lesbian-feminist analysis as central to understanding and ending woman's oppression.

The heart of lesbian-feminist politics, let me repeat, is a recognition that heterosexuality as an institution and an ideology is a cornerstone of male supremacy. Therefore, women interested in destroying male supremacy, patriarchy, and capitalism must, equally with lesbians, fight heterosexual domination—or we will never end female oppression. This is what I call "the heterosexual question"—it is *not* the lesbian question.

Although lesbians have been the quickest to see the challenge to heterosexuality as a necessity for feminists' survival, straight feminists are not precluded from examining and fighting against heterosexuality. The problem is that few have done so. This perpetuates lesbian fears that remaining tied to men prevents women from seeing the function of heterosexuality and acting to end it. It is not lesbianism (women's ties to women) but heterosexuality (women's ties to men), and thus men themselves, which divides women politically and personally. This is the "divisiveness" of the lesbian issue to the women's movement. We won't get beyond it by demanding that lesbians retreat, politics in hand, back into the closet. We will only get beyond it by struggling over the institutional and ideological analysis of lesbian-feminism. We need to discover what lesbian consciousness means for any woman, just as we struggle to understand what class or race consciousness means for women of any race or class. And we must develop strategies that will destroy the political institutions that oppress us.

It is particularly important for those at this conference to understand that heterosexuality—as an ideology and as an institution—upholds all those aspects of female oppression that have been discussed here. For example, heterosexuality is basic to our oppression in the workplace. When we look at how women are defined and exploited as secondary, marginal workers, we recognize that this definition assumes that all women are tied to men. I mention the workplace because it upset me yesterday at the economics panel that no one made that connection; and further, no one recognized that a high percentage of women workers are lesbian and therefore their relationship to and attitudes toward work are fundamentally different from those assumed by straight workers. It is obvious that heterosexuality upholds the home, housework, the family as both a personal and economic unit. It is apparently not so obvious that the whole framework of heterosexuality defines our lives, that it is fundamental to the negative self-image and self-hatred of women in this society. Lesbian-feminism is based on a rejection of male definitions of our lives and is therefore crucial to the development of a positive woman-identified identity, of redefining who we are supposed to be in every situation, including the workplace.

What is that definition? Basically, heterosexuality means men first. That's what it's all about. It assumes that every woman is heterosexual; that every woman is defined by and is the property of men. Her body, her services, her children belong to men. If you don't accept that definition, you're a queer—no matter who you sleep with; if you do not accept that definition in this society, you're queer. The original imperialist assumption of the right of men to the bodies and services of women has been translated into a whole variety of forms of domination throughout this society. And as long as people accept that initial assumption—and question everything *but* that assumption—it is impossible to challenge the other forms of domination.

What makes heterosexuality work is heterosexual privilege—and if you don't have a sense of what that privilege is, I suggest that you go home and announce to everybody that you know—a roommate, your family, the people you work with, everywhere you go—that you're a queer. Try being a queer for a week. Do not walk out on the street with men; walk only with women, especially at night. For a whole week, experience life as if you were a lesbian, and I think you will know what heterosexual privilege is very quickly. And, hopefully, you will also learn that heterosexual privilege is the method by which women are given a stake in male supremacy—and that it is therefore the method by which women are given a stake in their own oppression. Simply stated, a woman who stays in line—by staying straight or by refusing to resist straight privileges—receives some of the benefits of male privilege indirectly and is thus given a stake in continuing those privileges and maintaining their source—male supremacy.

Heterosexual women must realize—no matter what their personal connection to men—that the benefits they receive from men will always be in diluted form and will ultimately result in their own self-destruction. When a woman's individual survival is tied to men, she is at some intrinsic place separated from other women and from the survival needs of those other women. The question arises not because of rhetorical necessity—whether a woman is personally loyal to other women—but because we must examine what stake each of us has in the continuation of male supremacy. For example, if you are receiving heterosexual benefits through a man (or through his social, cultural, or political systems), are you clear about what those benefits are doing to you, both personally and in terms of other women? I have known women who are very strong in fighting against female job discrimination, but when the battle closes in on their man's job, they desert that position. In universities, specifically, when a husband's job is threatened by feminist hiring demands, I have seen feminists abandon their political positions in order to keep the privileges they receive from their man's job.

This analysis of the function of heterosexuality in women's oppression is available to any woman, lesbian or straight. Lesbian-feminism is not a political analysis "for lesbians only." It is a political perspective and fight against one of the major institutions of our oppression—a fight which heterosexual women can engage in. The problem is that few do. Since lesbians are materially oppressed by heterosexuality daily, it is not surprising that we have seen and understood its impact first—not because we are more moral, but because our reality is different, and it is a *materially* different reality. We are trying to convey this fact of our oppression to you because, whether you feel it directly or not, it also oppresses you, and because if we are going to change society and survive, we must all attack heterosexual domination.

CLASS AND LESBIANISM

There is another important aspect of lesbian-feminism which should be of interest to a socialist-feminist conference: the connection between lesbianism and class. One of the ways lesbianism has affected the movement is in changing women's individual lives. Those of us who are out of the closet have, in particular, learned that we must create our own world—we haven't any choice in the matter, because there is no institution in this society that is created for us. Once we are out, there is no place that wholeheartedly accepts us. Coming out is important, partly because it puts us in a materially different reality in terms of what we have to do. And it is the impact of reality that moves anyone to understand and change. I don't believe that idealism is the primary force that moves people; necessity moves people. And lesbians who are out are moved by necessity—not by choice—to create our own world. Frequently (and mistakenly), that task has been characterized as cultural. While the culture gives us strength, the impetus is economic: the expression of necessity is always material. For middle-class women this is especially true—lesbianism means discovering that we have to support ourselves for the rest of our lives, something that lower- and working-class women have always known. This discovery makes us begin to understand what lower- and working-class women have been trying to tell us all along: "What do you know about survival?"

I heard a lot about class analysis when I was in the Left, and some of it was helpful. But it wasn't until I came out as a lesbian and had to face my own survival on that basis—as an outlaw, as a woman alone—that I learned about class in my own life. Then I learned what the Left had never taught me—what my middle-class assumptions were and the way in which my background crippled me as a woman. I began to understand how my own middle-class background was holding me back personally and the ways in which middle-class assumptions were holding back the growth of our movement. Class affects the way we operate every day—as has been obvious in much of what has happened at this conference. And theories of class should help us understand that. The only way to understand the function of class in society, as far as I'm concerned, is to understand how it functions right here, on the spot, day to day, in our lives.

Another way in which class consciousness has occurred in the lesbian community— and I want to acknowledge it because it is frequently one of the things kept locked in the bedroom closet—is the cross-class intimacy that occurs among lesbians. This intimacy usually leads to an on-the-spot analysis of class oppression and conflict based on the experience of being hit over the head with it. Understand that I am not advising every middle-class woman to go out and get herself a lower-class lesbian to teach her about class-in-the-raw; but also understand that I am saying that there's no faster way to learn how class functions in our world.

Cross-class contact occurs all the time in the lesbian community, frequently without any self-conscious politics attached to it. For example, in lesbian bars, a political process that is often misinterpreted as a purely social process is going on in women's lives. Because there are no men in that environment, the conflicts around class and race—those issues basic to women's survival—become crystal clear, if you understand them not in rhetorical or theoretical terms but in the ways that women's lives are interacting with each other's. This is one reason why a lot of class analysis, particularly the practical kind, has come out of the lesbian-feminist movement—analysis based on our experience of class contact and conflict, our recognition of it, and our integration of its meanings in the way we live our lives. This material experience of class realities produces real commitment to struggle and to the class question, not out of idealism but as integral to our survival. Idealism can be abandoned at any time. Survival cannot.

I want to be clear about what it is that I am *not* saying. I am not saying that all lesbians are feminists; all lesbians are not politically conscious. I am saying that the particular material reality of lesbian life makes political consciousness more likely; we can build on the fact that it is not in the interests of lesbians to maintain and defend the system as it is.

I am also *not* saying that the only way to have this political analysis is to be a lesbian. But I am saying that so far most of the people with lesbian-feminist politics who have challenged heterosexuality are lesbians. But ours is not the only way, and we've got to make it not the only way. We, as lesbians, are a minority. We cannot survive alone. We will not survive alone, but if we do not survive the entire women's movement will be defeated and female oppression will be re-enacted in other forms. As we all understand survival more clearly, we see that the politics and analysis of women's oppression coming out of the lesbian's life experience have got to be integrated into the politics of socialist-feminism and the rest of the women's movement.

It is not okay to be queer under patriarchy—and the last thing we should be aiming to do is to make it okay. Nothing in capitalist-patriarchal America works to our benefit and I do not want to see us working in any way to integrate ourselves into that order. I'm not saying that we should neglect work on reforms—we must have our jobs, our housing, and so on. But in so doing we must not lose sight of our ultimate goal. Our very strength as lesbians lies in the fact that we are outside of patriarchy; our existence challenges its life. To work for "acceptance" is to work for our own disintegration and an end to the clarity and energy we bring to the women's movement.

It is not okay, and I do not want it ever to be okay, to be queer in patriarchy. The entire system of capitalism and patriarchy must be changed. And essential to that change is an end to heterosexual domination. Lesbians cannot work in movements that do not recognize that heterosexuality is central to all women's oppression: that would be to work for our own self-destruction. But we can coalesce with groups which share the lesbian-feminist analysis and are committed to the changes essential to our survival. This is the basis upon which we can begin to build greater unity and a stronger, more powerful feminist movement.

6

For a Materialist Feminism

Christine Delphy

Feminism is above all a social movement. Like all revolutionary movements, its very existence implies two fundamental presumptions. First, that the situation of women is cause for revolt. This is a platitude, but this platitude entails a corollary, a second presumption, which is much less frequently admitted. People do not revolt against what is natural, therefore inevitable; or inevitable, therefore natural. Since what is resistible is not inevitable; what is not inevitable could be otherwise—it is arbitrary, therefore social. The logical and necessary implication of women's revolt, like all revolts, is that the situation can be changed. If not, why revolt? Belief in the possibility of change implies belief in the social origins of the situation.

The renewal of feminism coincided with the use of the term "oppression." Ideology (that is, common sense, conventional wisdom) does not speak of "women's oppression" but of the "feminine condition." The latter relates to a naturalistic explanation, to a belief in the existence of a physical constraint. This puts exterior reality out of reach and beyond modification by human action. The term oppression, on the other hand, refers to something arbitrary, to a political explanation and a political situation. Oppression and social oppression are therefore synonyms; or, rather, social oppression is a pleonasm. The notion of a political (that is, a social) cause is integral to the concept of oppression.

The term "oppression" is therefore the base, the point of departure, of any feminist research, as of any feminist approach. Its use radically modifies the basic principles, not only of sociology but of all the social sciences. It nullifies any "scientific" approach which speaks of women in one way or another, at one level or another, but which does not include the concept of oppression. A feminist study is one whose objective is to explain the situation of women. When this situation is defined as a situation of oppression, theoretical premises which do not include this concept, i.e., which exclude it, can be used only at the risk of incoherence. Having a feminist approach is thus not just a matter of applying the unchanged premises of the established sciences to the study of women, with good political intent. It is useless for feminists to try to develop such studies when their premises are nullified in each particular discipline.

The premises of sociology, for example, deny the oppression of women, and in consequence the discipline (1) cannot account for it—cannot find at the end what it denied at the beginning; and (2) can only mask the oppression, and to that extent contribute to its perpetuation. There are, of course, certain approaches within sociology that are compatible with feminism, with revolt; the notion of the social origin of social phenomena for instance. But this compatibility has remained virtual, because:

1. A theory can be called sociological without so being. Most sociological theories deny not only the oppression of women, but also the social itself. Functionalism, for example, is, in the last analysis, a typical case of psychological reductionism. Structuralism is equally psychologically reductionist, although different from functionalism. Functionalism rests on Freudianism (on the universality of the emotional structures) while structuralism rests on the universality of cognitive structures. They both explain different social formations, and the phenomenon of the social itself, by human nature.

2. All these theories are expressions of idealism and thus totally incompatible with the revolt of oppressed groups. They affirm (a) that history is the product of an individual—universal—biological functioning; and, (b) areas exist which are indifferent to and independent of power between groups.

A feminist—or a proletarian—science aims at explaining oppression. In order to do this, it has to start with oppression. If it is coherent, it inevitably comes up with a theory of history in which history is seen in terms of the domination of some social groups by others. Likewise it cannot at the start consider any area of reality or knowledge as outside this fundamental dynamic. A feminist interpretation of history is therefore "materialist" in the broad sense; that is, its premises lead it to consider intellectual production as the result of social relationships, and the latter as relationships of domination.

The implications of this concern not only precise theories or areas—i.e., their content; they also directly concern the intrinsic character of these areas—the principles that constitute them (i.e., the principles according to which the real is divided into areas of knowledge). All categorization, all separation into areas actually presupposes an implicit theory of human nature, of the nature, of the social, and of history.[1]

The division of knowledge into tight areas is an effect and a tool of ideology, as is also the content of these areas or disciplines. The idea that there are separate areas of experience which are the concerns of the different disciplines, each with its own methods, and that these can afterwards be joined so as to juxtapose their findings, is typically antimaterialist. For what is this confrontation, this highly vaunted "interdisciplinarity"? It is in fact nothing but the result of the disciplinarity that it presupposes. The latter is founded on the postulate that subjectively distinct levels of experience—distinct in the subjectivity of our society—all obey their own "laws": the psychological obeys the laws of interaction, etc.

The reactionary character of this approach can be seen very concretely, for example, in studies of the family. Here the sexual relationships of husband and wife, their economic relationships, and their social relationships, etc., are studied separately, as if they each obey a distinct and heterogeneous logic. These heterogeneous "results" are then put together and we end up with an uninteresting mosaic. It is devoid of meaning; but this is precisely in the interest of "science." It thereby negates the profound unity of these "levels" and the way in which they are all locations and means of oppression.

The objective (and the result) of official science and its division into disciplines is thus the rendering unintelligible of human experience. This is true not only of sociology but of all the disciplines, which with it comprise the social sciences. Psychoanalysis, for example, claims and asserts sexuality as its domain. Yet neither psychoanalysis nor sociology takes account of the oppression of women. Not taking it into account, they necessarily interpret it in their own terms—they integrate it as a given. They thus study the domains of social life and subjective experience where and by which women are oppressed, without this oppression appearing as such. They thus have a precise ideological function: to make the oppression of women disappear from the results of their studies. Since everything is circular, this is accomplished only by having denied it at the beginning.

Can we, then, utilize the existing disciplines and their concepts at all to study the oppression of women, given that the body of knowledge they comprise presupposes it? Can we even utilize "elements" from them? The positive response to this question prevalent today suggests we can dissociate the social philosophy of certain theories from their concepts. However, even these elements are obtained from epistemological premises. Each science constructs its own object. This means that not only its theoretical content, but also its limits and the definition of its field of application, its very domain, far from pre-existing the discipline, are its creation; and the premises of all the social sciences, to the extent that they do not posit men/women relationships as relationships of oppression, posit them, by commission or omission, as something else.

These premises are thus in radical opposition to those of women's liberation and women's studies. A field of knowledge that starts from the oppression of women cannot be content with questioning this or that result of this or that discipline. We must challenge the premises themselves, and we must start with how the results were obtained; the point of view from which the "facts" were regarded; the point of view which concerns us but also the outlook which perceived the object, and the object that it constituted—right down to the most apparently "technical" and "neutral" concepts.

It is illusory to pretend to arrive at different interpretations with the same conceptual instruments. These are no more neutral, no less constructed, than the areas they delimit, nor than the theories—the content of the disciplines—they generate.

Rejecting interdisciplinarity does not, however, mean refusing to recognize that subjective experience[2] is aware of different levels. What it does mean is rejecting the current cutting up of reality into disciplinary domains—into fiefdoms; a cutting up born of, and accrediting, the idea that entire areas of experience are outside of oppression, i.e., of the political.

To the patchwork of interdisciplinarity and disciplinarity a materialist feminist approach opposes a unique dynamic which expresses itself differently at different levels. This approach has yet to be fully defined. It will challenge structuralism, for example, not because structuralism suggests that a subjectively distinct cognitive level exists, but because it imputes to this level a content independent of social relationships. This approach will challenge psychoanalysis not because psychoanalysis suggests the existence of a purely subjective level, but because it imputes to this level a content independent of social relationships.

Obviously the social which is at issue here is not "the social" of journalists. It is not the exterior as opposed to "the interior," the superficial, surface events as opposed to the inner depths. It is the political as opposed to "the private." Nor does the pre-eminence we accord this concept of the social have anything to do with the chauvinism of a specialist. It is, on the contrary, a theoretical position opposed to the prevalent concept of "specialism." It is a global view of history, hence of the social sciences; it prohibits all recourse to extra-social and extra-historical factors. Such recourse, however limited it may be, is incompatible with the concept of oppression.

It is a commonplace view that there is no neutral knowledge, but from our point of view this has a particular meaning. All knowledge is the product of a historical situation, whether it is acknowledged or not. But whether it is acknowledged or not makes a big difference. If it is not acknowledged, if knowledge pretends to be neutral, it denies the history it pretends to explain. It is ideology and not knowledge. Thus all knowledge which does not recognize social oppression, which does not take it as its premise, denies it, and as a consequence objectively serves it.

Knowledge that seeks to take the oppression of women as its point of departure constitutes an epistemological revolution, not just a new discipline with woman as its object, and/or an ad hoc explanation of a particular oppression. Such knowledge is an expression of materialism, but also a renewal of it. It applies a materialist point of view to something materialism has ignored, i.e., the oppression of women. It is a new perspective and not a new object. This perspective necessarily applies to the whole of human experience, individual and collective.

How then can materialism be "extended"? Up to now materialism has implied, denoted, a theory of history as the history of the class struggle. But women as a group were excluded from the classes involved. Their oppression was not thought of as a class exploitation. I maintain that it is the absence of women from history, from the representation of history, which has left the field open to the establishment and/or upholding of private "areas" and to the monopoly of the "disciplines," i.e., which has led to the dominance of idealist views of entire sectors of experience.

Insofar as materialism has been applied to understanding the process of the production of ideas in relation to the exploitation of the proletariat and the class struggle (as traditionally defined), so the areas of life designated as subjective—affective and sexual[3]—have escaped it. This was an obvious but inevitable contradiction. But equally it could not fail to appear insoluble. The whole intellectual history of the first, and perhaps also of the second, half of the twentieth century is marked by attempts—constantly renewed—to unify certain principles of explanation. These have predominantly taken the form of attempts at conciliation and reconciliation between Freudianism and marxism. Needless to say the fact that there have been so many is both because the contradiction is distressing and because each attempt to resolve it has ended in failure. This failure was inscribed in the very premises of the proceedings, because people have tried to reconcile the results, the findings, of the two approaches, forgetting that their epistemological premises were irreconcilable. The failure of all the attempts is due to their acceptance of the extravagant claims of psychoanalysis to be, not *a system of interpretation* of subjectivity, but subjectivity itself.

I refuse to accept that objecting to the theory of psychoanalysis is synonymous with a lack of interest in its object. Rejecting Freud's ideas does not mean one is indifferent to—or that one negates—the existence of subjectivity, though not only the adherents of psychoanalysis but also the vast majority of people claim it does. Once psychoanalysis's claim is accepted, however, attempts to resolve the contradiction of materialism's failure to come to grips with subjectivity are doomed, because to come to grips with subjectivity, it is held, one must accept the premises of psychoanalysis. And to accept them means to reintroduce idealism to the scene. Under the cover of introducing materialism into subjectivity, one in fact introduces the enemy in its place: one introduces idealism into history.

But why must attempts to reconcile marxism and Freudianism accept the premises of psychoanalysis, when the latter is only one form of "psychologism," itself a form of idealism? Especially when the areas monopolized by psychologism were *not* places of confrontation between the only groups materialist theory recognized as classes: proletarians and capitalists? For so long as only these groups were recognized as classes, and so long as the materialist theory of history was reduced to the history of *their* confrontation, the domains where this confrontation did not exist were necessarily left outside the problematic of the class struggle, and therefore of materialism. (Wilhelm Reich's attempt at reconciliation is exemplary in this respect. He believed he could reintroduce sexuality under the wing of materialism, while in reality he did nothing but betray materialism by psychologizing the class struggle.)[4]

Sexuality is, however, very much a place of class struggle. It is one of the fields of confrontation of two groups; but the groups are not the proletarians and the capitalists, but social men and social women. Only the women's struggle, and the simultaneous conceptualization of women's condition as oppression, has brought sexuality into the political arena. Feminism, by imprinting the word oppression on the domain of sexuality, has annexed it to materialism. It was the necessary condition for this annexation.

Calls for a materialist psychology are not new. How then do we explain why, despite the recognized necessity of considering "subjectivity" as one of the expressions, if not one of the mechanisms, of social organization, the reverse process has made ceaseless progress throughout the time during which these calls have been made? Why have biologism and instinctualism continued to reign over, better to constitute, the study of "the psyche"? Why has psychologism not even limited itself to the study of subjectivity, but has grabbed the study of interaction, of groups, and even of institutions? How do we explain this except by admitting that the political base for such knowledge is missing?

If the women's struggle is the necessary condition for the inclusion of new areas of experience in materialist analysis, equally materialist analysis of all the instances of women's oppression is one of the processes of this struggle—and an indispensable process.

So long as an area of experience stays outside the class struggle, it remains out of reach of materialism. To change this it was not sufficient for it to be a site of real antagonisms. It was necessary for these antagonisms to take the form of a consciously political confrontation. This was why the emergence of the WLM was significant. Conceptualization followed, because it could not but follow a real social movement. The condition of women did not give rise to a struggle because it was political. "Political" is a concept, not an element of concrete reality. The condition of women became "political" once it gave rise to a struggle, and when at the same time this condition was thought of as oppression.

Today the conditions are present for the advent of a new stage of knowledge. Women were oppressed before, and oppressed also in and by "sexuality," but that was not sufficient for sexuality to be envisaged from a materialist point of view.

In the same way, proletarian class consciousness is not the result of Marx's theory of capital. On the contrary, Marx's theory of capital was founded on the necessary premise of the oppression of proletarians. Oppression is one possible way of conceptualizing a given situation; and this particular conceptualization can originate only from one standpoint (that is, from one precise position in this situation): that of the oppressed. It is only from the point of view and life experience of women that their condition can be seen as oppression. This coming consciousness takes place neither before nor after the struggle. In other words, it is a question of two aspects of the same phenomenon, not of two different phenomena.

The women's movement is a concrete political fact, which cannot but add a new element to the political domain and which may overturn it from top to bottom. The same thing could be expressed by saying that women's consciousness of being oppressed changes the definition of oppression itself.

Materialist feminism is therefore an intellectual approach whose coming is crucial both for a social movement, the feminist movement, and for *knowledge*. This approach will not—cannot—be limited to a single population, to the oppression of women alone. It will not leave any aspect of reality, any domain of knowledge, any aspect of the world untouched. As the feminist movement aims at revolution in social reality, the feminist theoretical point of view must also aim at a revolution in knowledge. Each is indispensable to the other.

NOTES

1. For example, are "body" and "mind" divisions of something concrete, or are they entries in western dictionaries? And what is the western dictionary, if not the intellectual product of, the rationalization for, an oppressive social system?

2. I.e., in the subjectivity of this society, hence in its ideology.

3. Which is considered *a thing in and of itself* (like "the psyche") by both common sense and the "science" which reproduces these categories; and which is linked to "the psyche" by that same science which reproduces the spontaneous theory of common sense, that is, ideology.

4. What have we retained of Reich's theory? That sexual repression *caused* fascism.

7

What Is Socialist Feminism?

Barbara Ehrenreich

At some level, perhaps not too well articulated, socialist feminism has been around for a long time. You are a woman in a capitalist society. You get pissed off: about the job, about the bills, about your husband (or ex), about the kids' school, the housework, being pretty, not being pretty, being looked at, not being looked at (and either way, not listened to), etc. If you think about all these things and how they fit together and what has to be changed, and then you look around for some words to hold all these thoughts together in abbreviated form, you'd almost have to come up with "socialist feminism."

A lot of us came to socialist feminism in just that kind of way. We were searching for a word/term/phrase that would begin to express all of our concerns, all of our principles, in a way that neither "socialist" nor "feminist" seemed to. I have to admit that most socialist feminists I know are not too happy with the term "socialist feminist" either. On the one hand it is too long (I have no hopes for a hyphenated mass movement); on the other hand it is much too short for what is, after all, really socialist, internationalist, antiracist, antiheterosexist feminism.

The trouble with taking a new label of any kind is that it creates an instant aura of sectarianism. "Socialist feminism" becomes a challenge, a mystery, an issue in and of itself. We have speakers, conferences, articles on "socialist feminism"—though we know perfectly well that both "socialism" and "feminism" are too huge and too inclusive to be subjects for any sensible speech, conference, article, etc. People, including avowed socialist feminists, ask themselves anxiously, "What is socialist feminism?" There is a kind of expectation that it is (or is about to be at any moment, maybe in the next speech, conference, or article) a brilliant synthesis of world historical proportions—an evolutionary leap beyond Marx, Freud, and Wollstonecraft. Or that it will turn out to be a nothing, a fad seized on by a few disgruntled feminists and female socialists, a temporary distraction.

I want to try to cut through some of the mystery which has grown up around socialist feminism. A logical way to start is to look at socialism and feminism separately. How does a socialist, more precisely, a Marxist, look at the world? How does a feminist? To begin with, Marxism and feminism have an important thing in common: they are *critical* ways of looking at the world. Both rip away popular mythology and "common sense" wisdom and force us to look at experience in a new way. Both seek to understand the world—not in terms of static balances, symmetries, etc. (as in conventional social science)—but in terms of antagonisms. They lead to conclusions that are jarring and disturbing at the same time that they are liberating. There is no way to have a Marxist or feminist outlook and remain a spectator. To understand the reality laid bare by these analyses is to move into action to change it.

Marxism addresses itself to the class dynamics of capitalist society. Every social scientist knows that capitalist societies are characterized by more or less severe, systemic inequality. Marxism understands this inequality to arise from processes which are *intrinsic* to capitalism as an economic system. A minority of people (the capitalist class) owns all the factories/energy sources/resources, etc., which everyone else depends on in order to live. The great majority (the working class) must work out of sheer necessity, under conditions set by the capitalists, for the wages the capitalists pay. Since the capitalists make their profits by paying less in wages than the value of what the workers actually produce, the relationship between the two classes is necessarily one of irreconcilable antagonism. The capitalist class owes its very existence to the continued exploitation of the working class. What maintains this system of class rule is, in the last analysis, force. The capitalist class controls (directly or indirectly) the means of organized violence represented by the state—police, jails, etc. Only by waging a revolutionary struggle aimed at the seizure of state power can the working class free itself and, ultimately, all people.

Feminism addresses itself to another familiar inequality. All human societies are marked by some degree of inequality between the sexes. If we survey human societies at a glance, sweeping through history and across continents, we see that they have commonly been characterized by the subjugation of women to male authority, both with the family and in the community in general; the objectification of women as a form of property; a sexual division of labor in which women are confined to such activities as child raising, performing personal services for adult males, and specified (usually low prestige) forms of productive labor.

Feminists, struck by the near-universality of these things, have looked for explanations in the biological "givens" that underlie all human social existence. Men are physically stronger than women on the average, especially compared to pregnant women or women who are nursing babies. Furthermore, men have the power to make women pregnant. Thus, the forms that sexual inequality takes—however various they may be from culture to culture—rest, in the last analysis, on what is clearly a physical advantage males hold over females. That is to say, they result ultimately in violence or the threat of violence.

The ancient, biological root of male supremacy—the fact of male violence—is commonly obscured by the laws and conventions that regulate the relations between the sexes in any particular culture. But it is there, according to a feminist analysis. The possibility of male assault stands as a constant warning to "bad" (rebellious, aggressive) women and drives "good" women into complicity with male supremacy. The reward for being "good" ("pretty," submissive) is protection from random male violence and, in some cases, economic security.

Marxism rips away the myths about "democracy" and pluralism to reveal a system of class rule that rests on forcible exploitation. Feminism cuts through myths about "instinct" and romantic love to expose male rule as a rule of force. Both analyses compel us to look at a fundamental injustice. The choice is to reach for the comfort of the myths or, as Marx put it, to work for a social order that does not require myths to sustain it.

It is possible to add up Marxism and feminism and call the sum "socialist feminism." In fact, this is probably how most socialist feminists view it most of the time—as a kind of hybrid, pushing our feminism in socialist circles, our socialism in feminist circles. One trouble with leaving things like that, though, is that it keeps people wondering "Well, what is she really?" or demanding of us "What is the principal contradiction?" These kinds of questions, which sound so compelling and authoritative, often stop us in our tracks: "Make a choice!" "Be one or another!" But we know that there is a political consistency to socialist feminism. We are not hybrids or fence sitters.

To get to that political consistency we have to differentiate ourselves, as feminists, from other kinds of feminists, and, as Marxists, from other kinds of Marxists. We have to stake out a (pardon the terminology here) socialist feminist kind of feminism and a socialist feminist kind of socialism. Only then is there a possibility that things will "add up" to something more than an uneasy juxtaposition.

I think that most radical feminists and socialist feminists would agree with my capsule characterization of feminism as far as it goes. The trouble with radical feminism, from a socialist feminist point of view, is that it doesn't go any farther. It remains transfixed with the universality of male supremacy—things have never really changed; all social systems are patriarchies; imperialism, militarism, and capitalism are all simply expressions of innate male aggressiveness. And so on.

The problem with this, from a socialist feminist point of view, is not only that it leaves out men (and the possibility of reconciliation with them on a truly human and egalitarian basis) but that it leaves out an awful lot about women. For example, to discount a socialist country such as China as a patriarchy—as I have heard radical feminists do—is to ignore the real struggles and achievements of millions of women. Socialist feminists, while agreeing that there is something timeless and universal about women's oppression, have insisted that it takes different forms in different settings, and that the differences are of vital importance. There is a difference between a society in which sexism is expressed in the form of female infanticide and a society in which sexism takes the form of unequal representation on the Central Committee. And the difference is worth dying for.

One of the historical variations on the theme of sexism which ought to concern all feminists is the set of changes that came with the transition from an agrarian society to industrial capitalism. This is no academic issue. The social system which industrial capitalism replaced was in fact a patriarchal one, and I am using that term now in its original sense, to mean a system in which production is centered in the household and is presided over by the oldest male. The fact is that industrial capitalism came along and tore the rug out from under patriarchy. Production went into the factories and individuals broke off from the family to become "free" wage earners. To say that capitalism disrupted the patriarchal organization of production and family life is not, of course, to say that capitalism abolished male supremacy. But it is to say that the particular forms of sex oppression we experience today are, to a significant degree, recent developments. A huge historical discontinuity lies between us and true patriarchy. If we are to understand our experience as women today, we must move to a consideration of capitalism as a system.

There are obviously other ways I could have gotten to the same point. I could have simply said that, as feminists, we are most interested in the most oppressed women— poor and working-class women, third-world women, etc.—and for that reason we are led to a need to comprehend and confront capitalism. I could have said that we need to address ourselves to the class system simply because women are members of classes. But I am trying to bring out something else about our perspective as feminists: there is no way to understand sexism as it acts on our lives without putting it in the historical context of capitalism.

I think most socialist feminists would also agree with the capsule summary of Marxist theory as far as it goes. And the trouble again is that there are a lot of people (I'll call them "mechanical Marxists") who do not go any further. To these people, the only "real" and important things that go on in capitalist society are those things that relate to the productive process or the conventional political sphere. From such a point of view, every other part of experience and social existence—things having to do with education, sexuality, recreation, the family, art, music, housework (you name it)—is peripheral to the central dynamics of social change; it is part of the "superstructure" or "culture."

Socialist feminists are in a very different camp from what I am calling "Mechanical Marxists." We (along with many, many Marxists who are not feminists) see capitalism as a social and cultural totality. We understand that, in its search for markets, capitalism is driven to penetrate every nook and cranny of social existence. Especially in the phase of monopoly capitalism, the realm of consumption is every bit as important, just from an economic point of view, as the realm of production. So we cannot understand class struggle as something confined to issues of wages and hours, or confined only to workplace issues. Class struggle occurs in every arena where the interests of classes conflict, and that includes education, health, art, music, etc. We aim to transform not only the ownership of the means of production, but the totality of social existence.

As Marxists, we come to feminism from a completely different place than the mechanical Marxists. Because we see monopoly capitalism as a political/economic/cultural totality, we have room within our Marxist framework for feminist issues which have nothing ostensibly to do with production or "politics," issues that have to do with the family, health care, "private" life.

Furthermore, in our brand of Marxism, there is no "woman question" because we never compartmentalized women off to the "superstructure" or somewhere in the first place. Marxists of a mechanical bent continually ponder the issue of the unwaged woman (the housewife): Is she really a member of the working class? That is, does she really produce surplus value? We say, of course housewives are members of the working class—not because we have some elaborate proof that they really do produce surplus value, but because we understand a class as being composed of people and as having a social existence quite apart from the capitalist-dominated realm of production. When we think of class in this way, then we see that in fact the women who seemed most peripheral, the housewives, are at the very heart of their class—raising children, holding together families, maintaining the cultural and social networks of the community.

We are coming out of a kind of feminism and a kind of Marxism whose interests quite naturally flow together. I think we are in a position now to see why it is that socialist feminism has been so mystified: The idea of socialist feminism is a great mystery or paradox, so long as what you mean by socialism is really what I have called "mechanical Marxism" and what you mean by feminism is an ahistorical kind of radical feminism. These things just don't add up; they have nothing in common.

But if you put together another kind of socialism and another kind of feminism, as I have tried to define them, you do get some common ground, and that is one of the most important things about socialist feminism today. It is a space free from the constrictions of a truncated kind of feminism and a truncated version of Marxism—in which we can develop the kind of politics that addresses the political/economic/cultural totality of monopoly capitalist society. We could only go so far with the available kinds of feminism, the conventional kind of Marxism, and then we had to break out to something that is not so restrictive and incomplete in its view of the world. We had to take a new name, "socialist feminism," in order to assert our determination to comprehend the whole of our experience and to forge a politics that reflects the totality of that comprehension.

However, I don't want to leave socialist feminist theory as a "space" or a common ground. Things are beginning to grow in that "ground." We are closer to a synthesis in our understanding of sex and class capitalism and male domination than we were a few years ago. Here I will indicate only very sketchily one such line of thinking:

1. The Marxist/feminist understanding that class and sex domination rest ultimately on force is correct, and this remains the most devastating critique of sexist/capitalist society. But there is a lot to that "ultimately." In a day-to-day sense, most people acquiesce to sex and class domination without being held in line by the threat of violence, and often without even the threat of material deprivation.

2. It is very important, then, to figure out what it is, if not the direct application of force, that keeps things going. In the case of class, a great deal has been written already about why the United States *working class* lacks militant class consciousness. Certainly ethnic divisions, especially the black/white division, are a key part of the answer. But I would argue, in addition to being divided, the working class has been socially atomized. Working-class neighborhoods have been destroyed and are allowed to decay; life has become increasingly privatized and inward-looking; skills once possessed by the working class have been expropriated by the capitalist class; and capitalist-controlled "mass culture" has edged out almost all indigenous working-class culture and institutions. Instead of collectivity and self-reliance as a class, there is mutual isolation and collective dependency on the capitalist class.

3. The subjugation of women, in the ways which are characteristic of late capitalist society, has been key to this process of class atomization. To put it another way, the forces which have atomized working-class life and promoted cultural/material dependence on the capitalist class are the same forces which have served to perpetuate the subjugation of women. It is women who are most isolated in what has become an increasingly privatized family existence (even when they work outside the home, too). It is, in many key instances, women's skills (productive skills, healing, midwifery, etc.) which have been discredited or banned to make way for commodities. It is, above all, women who are encouraged to be utterly passive/uncritical/dependent (i.e., "feminine") in the face of the pervasive capitalist penetration of private life. Historically, late capitalist penetration of working-class life has singled out women as prime targets of pacification/"feminization"—because women are the culture-bearers of their class.

4. It follows that there is a fundamental interconnection between women's struggle and what is traditionally conceived as class struggle. Not all women's struggles have an inherently anticapitalist thrust (particularly not those which seek only to advance the power and wealth of special groups of women), but all those which build collectivity and collective confidence among women are vitally important to the building of class consciousness. Conversely, not all class struggles have an inherently antisexist thrust (especially not those that cling to preindustrial patriarchal values), but all those which seek to build the social and cultural autonomy of the working class are necessarily linked to the struggle for women's liberation.

This, in very rough outline, is one direction socialist feminist analysis is taking. No one is expecting a synthesis to emerge which will collapse socialist and feminist struggle into the same thing. The capsule summaries I gave earlier retain their "ultimate" truth: there are crucial aspects of capitalist domination (such as racial oppression) which a purely feminist perspective simply cannot account for or deal with—without bizarre distortions, that is. There are crucial aspects of sex oppression (such as male violence within the family) which socialist thought has little insight into—again, not without a lot of stretching and distortion. Hence the need to continue to be socialists and feminists. But there is enough of a synthesis, both in what we think and what we do, for us to begin to have a self-confident identity as socialist feminists.

8

The Oppression of Women
A Structuralist Marxist View

Martha Gimenez

Modern feminism has led to the emergence of an ever-growing body of literature seeking to ascertain, using social science and Marxist theories, the origin of the oppression of women, the reasons for its perpetuation throughout history, its functions in contemporary society, and the conditions that would lead to its demise. The heterogeneous class and ethnic composition of the women's movement as well as the differences in the academic training of individual writers are reflected in the political splits within the movement and in the theoretical and methodological heterogeneity of these writings. More importantly, as intellectual productions rooted in a historically specific political and ideological conjuncture, these writings have been affected by the hegemony of idealist and empiricist assumptions underlying current common-sense views of the world, social science paradigms, and dominant interpretations of Marxism. Indeed, idealist (i.e., Hegelian, phenomenological, humanistic, existentialist, psychological, voluntaristic) versions of Marxism seem to be more acceptable and respectable within feminist, Marxist, and non-Marxist academic and nonacademic circles in the United States. On the other hand, theoretical developments that claim to maintain the dialectical materialist outlook of classical Marxism and stress the nonsubjective dimension of social processes are generally ignored or criticized and dismissed on the grounds of their alleged determinism, economism, or functionalism.

An interesting case in point that highlights the nature of the parameters governing intellectual production in the United States today is the absence of Structuralist Marxism from American feminist theory. Neither non-Marxist social scientists seeking new ideas for theory construction nor feminists sympathetic to Marxism seem to have found Structuralist Marxism compelling enough to warrant some consideration.

STRUCTURALIST MARXISM:
THEORETICAL AND METHODOLOGICAL ISSUES

Structuralist Marxism is not a fully developed theory; it is a descriptive label which, although rejected by those to whom it is applied, is currently used to indicate the heterogeneous production of Marxists who have introduced structuralist terminology in their writings and have acknowledged some degree of overlap between structuralist and Marxist principles. The most important representatives are Louis Althusser and Maurice Godelier, and it is with their work that this essay will be primarily concerned.

The reason why Structuralist Marxism has had a deep impact in the development of Marxist scholarship is because it articulates fundamental methodological principles and theoretical constructs that were largely tacit in classical Marxist works. Godelier convincingly argues that the two main principles of structuralism were discovered by Marx, who can thus be considered "a forerunner of the modern structuralist movement" (Godelier 1970, 343).

The first principle is that "*a structure is part of social reality but not of visible relationships*" (Godelier 1970, 347). This principle has the following implications:

A. *There are two levels of social reality:* the level of visible social relationships and the level of invisible structures whose laws of functioning and transformation account for changes at the observable level.

B. *The aim of scientific study is to discover those hidden structures.* Marx's scientific project was precisely the discovery of the structure and laws of motion of the capitalist mode of production concealed by the visible reality created by its functioning.

C. *The systematic study of appearances cannot provide a scientific knowledge of social reality.*

D. *This failure to attain knowledge taking appearances as starting point is not a cognitive failure.* The concealment of the structure by appearance is inherent in the nature of the structure itself. Structures are made up of social relations which cannot be directly apprehended, for they vanish behind forms of physical or social objectification. For example, capital appears as machines, money, etc.

E. *To each structure corresponds a form of appearance.* And scientific study must take into account both, explaining the appearance in terms of the structure.

F. *To each structure corresponds a form of consciousness or spontaneous representations held by individuals whose activities reproduce the structure.* The systematic study of those representations, far from disclosing the underlying logic of the structure, can only reproduce, at the level of theory, the mystifications created by the very functioning of the structure.

The second principle of structuralism is that "*the study of the internal functioning of a structure must precede and will throw light on the study of its coming to being and subsequent evolution*" (Godelier 1970, 347). The historical analysis of the emergence of the constituent elements of a structure and their interrelations presupposes a prior knowledge of the structure and its processes. Thus Marx presents his brief historical discussion of the genesis of primitive accumulation *after* the basic structure, processes, and contradictions of capitalism have been identified (Godelier 1970, 348–50). After the structural level of social reality has been discovered, the next step is establishing the articulation between that structure and its observable manifestations which can now be defined according to their "real function in the system and their internal compatibility with the essential structures already studied." This process amounts to the description of "the ideal birth of the various elements of a system on the basis of its internal laws of composition" (Godelier 1970, 352). This "ideal birth" or "ideal genesis" of categories cannot be confused with their historical or real genesis. Godelier argues that Marx's stress on the priority of structural over historical analysis "is total and anticipates by more than half a century the radical rethinking in linguistics and sociology which led de Saussure and Lowie to reject the evolutionist approach of the 19th century" (Godelier 1970, 353). Marx is very specific in this respect:

> It would be impractical and wrong to arrange the economic categories in the order in which they were the determining factors in the course of history. Their order of sequence is rather determined by the relation which they bear to one another in modern bourgeois society, and which is the exact opposite of what seems to be their natural *order* or the order of their historical development. . . . We are interested in their organic connections within modern bourgeois society. (Marx 1972, 41–42)

This is an important principle which establishes the difference between Marxist historical analysis and history as chronology or as the study of arbitrary periodizations based, for example, on the dominance of specific ideas or of "great men." It indicates the methodological priority of the theoretical investigation of the mode of production as a whole over the historical investigation of the real (i.e., chronological) origin of its isolated elements.

The two main methodological principles of Structuralist Marxism have been presented. It is now necessary to examine the Structuralist Marxist contribution to the analysis of historical phenomena: the concepts of mode of production and social formation. Mode of production is a theoretical construct that denotes the historically specific combination of the elements of the production process (laborers, nonlaborers, and means of production) in the context of structurally compatible political, legal, and ideological structures. These elements are combined in two kinds of relations: relations of "*real* or material appropriation" or technical relations of production (e.g., cooperation, manufacturing, modern industry, automation); and "property connections" or social relations of production, which are the relationships between laborers and nonlaborers mediated through their property relations to the means of production. In the capitalist mode of production, these are the relations between capitalists and wage workers (Althusser and Balibar 1970, 215). The forces of production, which cannot be considered as things or techniques taken in themselves, are all the factors of production in their historically specific combination within the process of production, considered from the standpoint of their actual and potential productivity (Althusser and Balibar 1970, 233–41). Modes of production differ qualitatively from one another in the way in which unpaid surplus labor is extracted from the direct producers. The mode of surplus extraction corresponds to the level of development of the productive forces and the nature of the relations of production and constitutes the unifying principle of the mode of production as a whole (Marx 1968, 791–92).

The concept mode of production is an abstract one that captures the fundamental features that constitute the organizing principle of the economic, legal, political, and ideological structures that characterize different historical epochs. Empirically, in a given social formation, modes of production are always found in varied combinations with other modes of production. In the structuralist reading of Marx, the alternative to the abstract notion of society is the concept of social formation, a "complex structured whole where the mode of production is determinant 'in the last instance' and the superstructure (legal, political, and ideological structures) is relatively autonomous" (Althusser 1970, 111). In all social formations it is possible to identify the following: a complex economic base formed by the historically specific articulation of several modes of production, one of which is always dominant; and a complex superstructure whose elements have forms and functions the origins of which can be traced to the different modes of production that make up the economic base (Godelier 1978, 63). Scientific analysis must be aimed at establishing first the nature of the hierarchical articulation of modes of production (i.e., the specific ways in which the dominant mode of production subjects the others to its own requirements and transforms them into conditions of its own reproduction) and, second, the nature of the hierarchical articulation among the elements of the superstructure which is also constituted as a set of conditions for the reproduction of the dominant mode of production (Godelier 1978, 63). The structure of the superstructure reflects the articulation of the economic base; it overdetermines the base as it reproduces it in historically specific ways—ways peculiar to the characteristics of the social formation being considered. On the other hand, the economic base determines the superstructure "in the last instance," through a system of internal constraints which has its origins in the material conditions of production and expresses the conditions of reproduction for the dominant mode of production. The structural compatibility between the form and content of the elements of the superstructure and the system of constraints is itself a structural effect of the system of constraints which ensures the reproduction of the mode of production. It is, consequently, through the structural effects of the system of constraints, which simultaneously affect all the elements of the social formation, that the mode of production determines, in the last instance, the overall structure of the social formation as well as the form and function of its instances (Godelier 1978, 52–53). The category of determination "in the last instance" has a twofold theoretical importance: it reaffirms the materialist philosophical standpoint of Marxism (it is the base that determines the superstructure, not vice versa) and, at the same time, it stresses the dialectical nature of the Marxist concept of determination by making explicit the relative autonomy and causal efficacy of the other instances of the social formation which, in turn, "overdetermine" the base (Althusser 1976, 177; see also Althusser 1970, 89–128).

Modes of production based on the private ownership of the means of production are inherently contradictory and subject to qualitative changes brought about by the operation of those contradictions. Given that the mode of production is the locus of the two main contradictions of capitalism (the contradiction between capital and labor and the contradiction between the forces and the relations of production), the fact that the mode of production is "overdetermined by the superstructure means that those contradictions are never found 'active in the pure state but, on the contrary,' overdetermined . . . always specified by the historically concrete forms and circumstances in which it is exercised" (Althusser 1970, 106). This process of specification operates from the different elements of the social formation and includes the national and international circumstances affecting the social formation at a given time. Whatever the nature of those processes, "in the last instance" it is in the internal and contradictory properties of the mode of production that the crucial source of change is to be found.

THE STRUCTURALIST MARXIST ALTERNATIVE

From the standpoint of Structuralist Marxism, the key to developing an adequate explanation of sexual inequality is to be found not in individual biology or psychology, in the organization of parenting, in ahistorical accounts about the origins of human society, or in abstract processes of functional adaptation and structural differentiation. Instead, regardless of its ubiquitousness, sexual inequality should be investigated, in each instance, as a historically specific phenomenon with historically specific roots located in the invisible levels of social reality; namely, in structures concealed by those visible processes which are, in fact, the effects through which the existence of those structures manifests itself. This concept of structure corresponds to social relations which evolve in the process through which people produce their material and social existence and which are independent from individuals' will (Marx 1970a, 20). Production has a twofold nature: "on the one side, the production of the means of existence . . . on the other side, the production of human beings themselves" (Engels 1972, 71). The variety of visible, institutionalized ways that "men oppress women" are effects, at the levels of "society" and "market relations," of the articulation between the two aspects of the mode of production which determine relations between men and women that are independent of their will: i.e., relations determined not by what individuals think, believe, want, or need—consciously or unconsciously—or by whatever social constraints the "market" or society" imposes upon them; instead, they are relations mediated by the historically specific relation of men and women to the material conditions of production and of physical and social reproduction (Althusser 1976, 200–207). The general methodological principle is that the material basis of sexual inequality is to be sought in the articulation between class relations or relations of production and the relations of physical and social reproduction valid within a historically specific mode of production. I shall limit my analysis of the capitalist mode of production in an effort to delineate, following the second structuralist methodological principle, the capitalist basis of sexual inequality.

By mode of physical and social reproduction is meant the historically specific combination of labor and means of reproduction (the material basis for the performance of reproductive tasks: the tools, goods, utensils, raw materials, foodstuffs, etc.) with relations between men and women. Such a combination reproduces the present and future members of social groups by procreation, physical care (cleaning, food preparation, etc.), and nurturant and supportive services (sexual relations, socialization of children, cooperation, etc.). Such groups have different locations in the productive process. (For a detailed discussion of these concepts see, for example, Gimenez 1978; Secombe 1974.) The dominant visible forms taken by modes of physical and social reproduction throughout history have been family and kinship structures as well as kinship-structured groups (groups in which adults and children are not related by blood). In capitalist social formations, the nuclear family emerges as the dominant but not exclusive context in which social classes are reproduced; empirical variations documenting not only the existence of other forms (e.g., single-parent households), but also the conditions under which nuclear families remain to a greater or lesser extent embedded in broader kinship networks, must be understood in terms of underlying relations of physical and social reproduction that are determined, for each class, by the capitalist organization of production, distribution, and consumption.

Capitalist families live off profits from capital and are surrounded by extensive kinship networks which are also economic networks through which wealth is preserved, increased, and circulated. Men and women own the means of production and are free from the necessity of selling their labor to survive; they are the "bearers" or "supports" of the capitalist class (cf. Althusser 1976, 206) and reproduce it under legal and ideological conditions that ensure the preservation of property and its transmission to legitimate heirs, the future bearers of the class. Given the different biological roles of men and women in procreation, these superstructural conditions involve control over women's sexuality and reproductive capacity; the precapitalist relationship between private ownership of the means of production and class control over women as producers of the future members of the class is preserved and reproduced under capitalism through superstructural conditions (legal, ethical, religious, ideological, etc.) that universalize it for all classes, obscuring the qualitative differences between classes in the process of defining everyone as a legal, political, ethical subject (Althusser 1971, 162–86). These superstructural conditions (the legal apparatus surrounding marriage, divorce, and inheritance; bourgeois morality; ideologies about abortion, contraception, etc.) contribute to create the circumstances in which the control exerted by the capitalist class over the conditions for the reproduction of all classes, including itself, appears, at the level of visible relations, as control exerted by men over women. Class control over the means of production and over the conditions for its own reproduction as a class places capitalist men and women into social relations independent of their will. They are unequal relations in which, at the level of "society," men appear in control of capital, female sexuality, and reproductive capacity. On the other hand, within capitalist households, labor and means of reproduction are brought together through a division of labor or technical relations of reproduction that ensure women's complete freedom from the routine and menial dimensions of reproduction as well as partial freedom from social reproduction. Paid domestic workers (most of whom are likely to be women) do housework, child care, and some aspects of child socialization under the direct or indirect supervision of capitalist women, who often delegate the managing tasks to workers hired for that purpose. The existence of a primarily female strata of domestic servants is, therefore, the basic underpinning of the almost exclusive dedication of capitalist women to social reproduction on a daily and generational basis (child socialization, social activities that enhance and complement their husbands' public roles, etc.), and of the unique characteristics of domestic relations between men and women in the capitalist household; a context in which contemporary discussions about the desirability of child care by persons other than the biological parents, or about the need to change the division of labor between men and women to increase men's domestic activities in order to liberate women for greater social involvement and self-fulfillment, have no meaning.[1]

Working-class families live off the sale of the labor power of their adult members and rely on the domestic labor of women for the daily and generational reproduction of labor power. The dominant pattern is one in which men are the only or most important wage earners and wives are the primary domestic workers, whether or not they are also employed. The mutually reinforcing relationship between women's domestic responsibilities and their social and economic oppression has been discussed and documented in great lengths and need not be reexamined here. Also, I am not going to dwell on the debate about the nature of domestic labor: whether it is paid or unpaid labor and whether or not it produces surplus value (see, for example, Secombe 1974; Coulson et al. 1975; Gardiner 1975). What is relevant here is that domestic labor is a form of socially necessary labor that expands the goods and services available to the working class beyond what it would be possible to purchase with wages. Domestic labor is thus an important component of the standard of living of the working class and a source of use values which enter in the process through which labor power is produced and reproduced on a daily and generational basis. On the other hand, domestic labor benefits the capitalist class because its presence lowers the overall level of wages, thus increasing the amount of surplus that can be extorted from the direct producers. But neither the division of labor within the home and its impact on the status of women, nor the relationship between domestic labor and the level of wages, can explain the existence of sexual inequality within the working class. To find the specifically capitalist material basis of sexual inequality it is necessary to examine the material conditions leading to family formation within the working class.

Capitalism, as a historically specific mode of production, rests upon a class structure based on the private ownership of the means of production and the concomitant expropriation of the direct producers who, as free laborers owning nothing but their labor power, must sell it to the owners of capital to get access to the means of subsistence necessary for themselves and their children. Hence, there is inherent in capitalism a tendency toward the universalization of commodity production generated by the separation of the direct producers from the conditions of production and reproduction which affects not only capital goods and consumer goods but also an ever-growing variety of services. An important exception to this trend is labor power, a crucial commodity that is not produced on a capitalist basis although its daily and generational reproduction requires a constant flow of market goods and services and is, consequently, shaped by the requirements of capitalist production. Within the working class household, goods and services purchased with the means of exchange obtained through the sale of labor power are combined with domestic labor in the context of relations of reproduction that presuppose the employment, as a wage laborer, of at least one member of the household. Domestic labor produces use values for the consumption of *all* the members of the family (Benston 1969); this is "consumptive production" because persons produce their own body, and, I may add, their own physical and intellectual capacities, through the consumption of goods and services (Marx 1970, 195). The consumption of the use values produced at home is thus, simultaneously, the production and reproduction of the present and future members of the working class. The capitalist mode of producing material goods *produces* consumption, i.e., consumptive production "by providing the material of consumption. . . . by creating in the consumer a need for the objects which it first presents as products and *by determining the mode of consumption* (Marx 1970a, 197; my emphasis). Crucial for the understanding of sexual inequality in the working class is the determination exerted by the mode of production upon the mode of consumption or, which is the same, the mode of consumptive production or physical and social reproduction.

Under capitalist conditions, the production of surplus and its extraction from the direct producers is concealed by the appearances of the market and social relations; this is the sphere of Freedom, Equality, Property, and Bentham (Marx 1970b, 196). At this level, individuals meet and engage in equitable exchanges that result in the distribution of the product: rent, profits, interest, and wages are allocated to different individuals on the basis of their function in the production process. This level is an intermediate phase between production and distribution (Marx 1970a, 204). It is both a structural effect of the underlying relation of production and a crucial condition for the reproduction—over time—of the capitalist mode of production as a whole. It mystifies the nature of the production process by hiding class rule and its effects under the guise of unmanageable laws (e.g., supply and demand, the Malthusian population principle) and other "social facts."

The relations of structural compatibility between these phases or moments of the mode of production as a whole—i.e., production, exchange, and distribution—set structural limitations to the possible forms in which labor power can be reproduced. The mode of consumption or consumptive production cannot itself be isomorphic with the mode of production: the reproduction of labor power on a capitalist basis would destroy the material basis for the production of free individuals, autonomous and responsible for their own success or failure, who constitute the cornerstone of capitalist social and market relations. On the other hand, the lack of isomorphism between the mode of production and the mode of reproduction of labor power is not the product of design but the complex structural effect of the relations of production, exchange, and distribution, overdetermined by the superstructure and mediated by the biological level and by the class struggle.

At the level of production, the creation of a propertyless class, bound to capital for its survival in a context of chronic unemployment and periodic economic crises, has created an objective situation of job scarcity and fierce competition among the members of the working class. This situation is exacerbated by the tendency toward the universalization of commodity production and the concomitant transformation of all social relations into market relations.

At the level of exchange, this objectively competitive situation is ideologically understood and experienced in terms of visible and "obvious" cleavages based on sex, age, racial, or ethnic differences or differences in national origin, religion, and so forth. It is in the interest of capital to have a divided labor force, and sexual antagonism is one among the many divisions that capital uses and reinforces to its advantage. While segregated labor markets may reduce the amount of competition, they never obliterate its objective existence, which tends to reassert itself in times of economic crises, shifts in the organic composition of capital, and drastic reorganization of the labor force.

These objective conditions place men and women in antagonistic and competitive relations. At the biological level, on the other hand, men and women are placed in complementary sexual and procreative roles; this is the material basis for the fact that, at the levels of distribution, exchange, and visible social relations, they also confront each other as potential sexual partners and potential parents—i.e., as potential agents of reproduction. While other cleavages within the working class can be overcome through unionization and other forms of collective organization, the family—the major locus of the reproduction of labor power—emerges as the most important institution bringing the sexes and generations together. At this level of analysis, men and women freely meet and enter into apparently free relationships; this is the sphere not only of Freedom, Equality, Property, and Bentham but also of Love, Motherhood, ideologies about femininity and masculinity, and other forms of legitimation. These "freely" entered family relations create bonds of interdependence between men and women and between families; kinship relations become an important source of economic support for unemployed workers as well as for those unable to work because of age, illness, or other circumstances (see, for example, Humphries 1977).

But the interdependence between families and between men and women rests upon underlying relations of personal economic dependence. The relations of production, exchange, and distribution place those who earn wages in a position to gain access to the material conditions of reproduction and, consequently, in a position of power over those with little or no access to those conditions. Kinship relations legitimate the claims of the latter upon the former while the absence of such bonds place people in an objective situation of dependence leading to the emergence of forms of political control (e.g., welfare) and personal dependence. Sexual inequality is one among the many forms of inequality thus generated by the mode of production within the working class. The overall effect of the capitalist relations of production, exchange, and distribution is to recruit men and women for the positions of agents of reproduction within the mode of physical and social reproduction, in a context that places those agents of reproduction who are also wage earners in a position of power over those who are only domestic workers, and that turns the position of domestic worker into a structural alternative to that of wage worker. These conditions are outside the control of individuals, whatever their sex may be, and express the rule of the capitalist class—mediated by the anarchy of the market and the relations of dependence thereby generated at the level of distribution. Under such conditions, domestic labor becomes an unavoidable economic "option" for women that places them in a dependent position with respect to men and that is independent of their will.

It may be argued that this account does not explain why women, rather than men, are expected to become domestic workers and that an answer to this question would have to rely on arguments such as those discussed in the previous section, which seek the origins of sexual inequality outside the mode of production (on biological or psychological differences between men and women or on precapitalist "patriarchal" ideologies, division of labor, power relations, etc.). My answer to those arguments is that pre-existing structural and superstructural instances do indeed overdetermine the relations between the sexes within and outside the family. Pre-existing ideologies and practices set the parameters for the way men and women—at the level of visible relations—have perceived their options and the nature of their relationships from the very beginning of capitalism. But one must "distinguish between the material transformation of the conditions of production . . . and the legal, political, philosophical . . . ideological forms in which men become conscious of this conflict and fight it out" (Marx 1970, 21). The transformation of the conditions of production and reproduction (the mode of producing and distributing goods and its impact upon the reproduction of life) places working-class men and women in different locations which imply unequal access to the conditions of reproduction. This unequal access, which is the basis for their asymmetrical relations at the level of visible relations, stems from their relationship to the conditions of production as propertyless workers, and to the conditions of procreation and reproduction as agents involved in the daily and generational reproduction of labor power. Precapitalist sexist patterns can persist, new ones can develop, and all of them can overdetermine the relationship between the sexes because the material conditions that place men and women in an unequal relationship determine, in the last instance, the efficacy of those patterns. These material conditions are the outcome of the combined effects of the relations of production, exchange, and distribution *mediated* by the biological level of sexuality and procreation and by the class struggle and *overdetermined* by precapitalist and capitalist superstructures.

Mediation is a mode of determination according to which a given social process or a given set of material conditions shape the consequences of other processes (Wright 1976, 25). To acknowledge biology as an important mediating condition is neither "vulgar materialism" nor biological determinism; it simply means to take into account the effect of the biological level *in itself,* which cannot be reduced to its social construction or production nor to a moment in the subject-nature dialectic (Timpanaro 1975, 34). Biology shapes the consequences of capitalist relations of production, exchange, and distribution which place all individual workers in competition for scarce jobs by establishing the material conditions for the development of relations of cooperation between male and female workers based on sexuality and procreation. The class struggle, in turn, modifies the impact of the capitalist organization of production by reinforcing the working-class family as a locus of resistance. Humphries (1977) has convincingly argued that the persistence of the working-class family and its changing fortunes cannot be purely explained in terms of the sexism of male workers or the needs of capital accumulation, as an institution passively reflecting such needs while fulfilling ideological functions supporting the hegemony of the capitalist class. An adequate explanation should also take into account the state of the class struggle and its relative success in securing a family wage and other benefits.

The mode of production sets structural limitations on the possible modes of reproducing labor power that could be structurally compatible with capitalism and on the possible survival strategies that working-class people could develop to overcome their fragmentation and vulnerability to the vagaries of the labor market and to changing forms of surplus extraction. The class struggle, on the other hand, modifies and challenges those limitations in manifold ways. Through the combined mediation of the biological level and the class struggle, the working-class family emerges as the dominant survival strategy open to male and female workers. It should then be clear that it is not the power of working-class men (or women's reproductive roles) that keeps women as the primary agents of reproduction within working-class households, nor is it the power of men that creates segregated labor markets and other barriers to equality between the sexes. It is the power of capital which establishes structural limitations to the possible ways in which the propertyless class can have access to the conditions necessary for its daily and generational reproduction, and it is the relative powerlessness of working-class men and women as *individuals* struggling for survival, that forces them into these relations of reproduction, which are both relations of cooperation and unequal relations of personal economic dependence. The contradiction between capital and labor, between production and reproduction, and the protracted class struggle thereby generated are the determinants of the contradictory nature of the relations between working-class men and women. The mode of reproducing labor power can thus be accurately understood as a unity of opposites, where bonds of cooperation and solidarity are also bonds of dependency grounded in the set of structural possibilities open to male and female members of the working class under capitalist conditions.

CONCLUSION

Capitalist and working-class relations of physical and social reproduction are subject to similar structural constraints in all capitalist social formations. On the other hand, their empirically observable manifestations will reflect the unique characteristics of each social formation, such as, for example, the specific form in which capitalist and precapitalist modes of production are articulated; the characteristics of the superstructure that reflect the complexity of the base and overdetermine it; and the internal characteristics of the social formation itself as well as its location in the international structure.

The essence of my argument is that, in capitalist social formations, the observable forms of sexual inequality are determined, in the last instance, by the historically specific way in which the mode of production (conceived as a complex structured whole in which the capitalist mode of production is dominant) affects the access of the laboring and nonlaboring members of the subordinate classes (wage and salaried workers, peasants, agricultural workers, the unemployed, etc.) to the material conditions necessary for their daily and generational reproduction. While the actual effects of the mode of production upon the mode of physical and social reproduction among those classes is always modified or overdetermined by the class struggle and other mediations, the maintenance of capitalist relations of production sets structural limits to such modifications and may even reverse them on occasion, depending on the nature of the crises affecting the social formation at a given time. Moreover, in any social formation the level of social stratification reflects the complexity of the base; consequently the empirical study of sexual inequality must rest upon the previous theoretical work of developing propositions about the underlying relations of production and reproduction that determine the observable relations between men and women within classes, fractions of classes, and "contradictory class locations" (see Wright 1977 for a definition of that concept).

It should be clear, then, that from the standpoint of Structuralist Marxism, the issues of whether "class" or "sex" is primary or what forms their "mutal interdependence" may take are oversimplifications of very complex matters that cannot be resolved by a priori political commitments or by automatically reacting against the ghost of the "economism" of "orthodox Marxism" that seems to haunt the American intellectual scene. A straightforward analysis of the capitalist mode of production in all its moments (production, exchange, distribution, and consumption) clearly shows that the mode of production determines the mode of consumptive production or physical and social reproduction. The control exerted by the capitalist class over its own conditions of reproduction and over the conditions necessary for the reproduction of the laboring classes determines, in the last instance, the nature of the relations between the sexes and the relative significance of the family within social classes. The major theoretical task becomes, therefore, that of unraveling the specific parameters within which the reproduction of different classes and fractions of classes takes place under capitalism and, in so doing, mapping out the historically possible relations between the sexes that those parameters regulate. From this standpoint, all explanations of the observable forms of sexual inequality within capitalist social formations based on various analyses of the biological, psychological, or social differences between the sexes, or an analysis of

the mode of reproduction in isolation from, but "interacting" with, the mode of production, are overlooking the historically specific determinants of the phenomena they
attempt to explain. On the other hand, sociological analyses of sex differentiation and
sex stratification and feminist analyses of sexuality, reproductive oppression, psychological oppression, etc., could be *critically*—not eclectically—integrated with the
Structuralist Marxist analysis of their specifically capitalist structural and superstructural determinants. The main theoretical assumption underlying such critical
integration is the following: the capitalist relations of production and the relations of
physical and social reproduction (relations into which men and women enter independently of their will) impose historically specific structural limits to the range of
empirical variations in sexual inequality in capitalist social formations which feminist
scholarship has abundantly documented. Theoretical and empirical investigation of the
specific articulation between the visible forms of sexual inequality and their underlying
structural determinants would presuppose the investigation of the most important
mediating and overdetermining instances. This would not only heighten the scientific
understanding of sexual inequality but would also give feminists a sound basis for the
evaluation of short- and long-run political and economic objectives.

The analysis of sexual inequality developed in this essay is a preliminary contribution to the work of others similarly engaged in the task of elaborating a Marxist theory
of the oppression of women, asking Marxist questions, and developing Marxist answers
(see for example, Vogel 1979; Chinchilla 1980; Dixon 1979). Structuralist Marxism is
not indispensable for this project, but greatly facilitates it; Structuralist Marxism for-
mulates important methodological considerations and key analytical distinctions that
are not clearly and systematically stated in the works of the classics. Given the nature of
the present historical conjuncture, Structuralist Marxism is not likely to have notice-
able impact in the development of American feminist theory. But what is at stake is
more than an academic debate about the explanatory power of different theories.
Theories inform policies and political struggles, and the success of the struggle against
sexual inequality depends on the extent to which the factors that produce it and reproduce it through time are correctly identified. From the standpoint of Structuralist
Marxism, the development of theories that acknowledge the determinant role of the
mode of production are more likely to succeed in identifying those determinants and
in generating effective political strategies.

NOTE

1. The use of domestic servants is not restricted to the capitalist class; at certain levels of income,
   middle-class and upper-middle-class women do purchase domestic labor. The qualitative differences between the capitalist use of servants and the practice of hiring household "help" with
   varying degrees of regularity is a matter that cannot be fully explored at this time. It is important to point out, however, that the existence of differences in class and socioeconomic status
   that allow some women to purchase their full or partial freedom from the "drudgery of housework" contributes to the maintenance of class relations and of sexual inequality within the
   working class.

9

Feminism and Materialism

Annette Kuhn and Ann Marie Wolpe

... By the latter part of 1976, when we first discussed our general ideas for producing a collection of essays dealing with the specificity of women's position from a materialist perspective, a good deal of writing from various "feminist" points of view had been published. Since only a few years earlier there had been virtually no work in this area available at all, any published material obviously filled what was by then a very great need within the "new" women's movement, and indeed was often grasped with eagerness, sometimes regardless of its quality or coherence. Women, irrespective of nationality and class position, were seen to comprise a homogeneous group bound together by one characteristic held in common—their "oppression" in all aspects of life. Descriptions of this oppression covered mental breakdowns, discrimination in jobs and education, sexuality, dependence on men, sex-role stereotyping, and so on. The list is long, and the need evidently existed to bring to light the numerous ways in which oppression was experienced by women themselves. In the urgency to gain this recognition, little concerted effort was made to develop a systematic analysis of the situations described. When such work was begun, there was a tendency to appropriate existing theory, first by pointing to its amnesia where women were concerned, and second, by attempting to insert the "woman question" into existing work and hence to add to rather than transform it. This took place in a variety of areas—in the social sciences, psychology, history, and art history in particular.

At the same time, when feminists who were also marxists began to criticize the failure of marxist theory in coming to terms with the specificity of women's situation, attempts to construct theoretical work in this area tended, like similar projects elsewhere, to draw on existing concepts (in this case the notions of value and productive and unproductive labour) and attempted to "apply" them unproblematically in relation to their own situation. What, however, did distinguish work in these different areas at this point in time was not the nature of the work itself—progressive though it was in relation to what had, or more correctly had not, gone before—so much as the means by which it was produced: generally through group discussion and collective work, though usually with an awareness also of the needs of women working on their own. Hence, although the nature of knowledge was not yet radically challenged by the "additive" strategy, the ways in which work was produced constituted a transformation of traditional institutionalized modes of acquiring knowledge.

. . . the need for theory formulated itself precisely out of the unifying eclecticism of descriptive and empirical work undertaken under the banner of women's studies. The original aim to produce knowledge out of little or nothing meant that much work of an exploratory nature—work which would by its nature be heterogeneous—needed to be done. There was a necessary and inevitable tendency to draw on a variety of theoretical positions, often without formulating or arguing out the implications of these positions. The problematic potential of such a situation did not, however, emerge as long as the fact of work of any kind whatsoever being done was regarded as progressive. But the expansion of work meant that the very problems raised by its eclectic and largely descriptive nature had to be addressed, and the need for a more precise and explicit articulation of theoretical groundings and a greater rigor in analysis had to be faced. The risks of fragmentation and sectarianism attending such a development are evident, although the related danger of a retreat into "theoreticism"—the construction of theory for its own sake—is perhaps less so. That is why, in arguing the need for a more rigorous and analytical approach to work on the position of women—in arguing, that is, for theoretical work—we have still to question constantly the purpose of such work. The need for theory cannot be taken for granted: theory needs to be justified for each specific situation within which and for which it is produced.

At a conference in London in May 1976 organized around the concept of "patriarchy," at exactly a moment when intellectual work within the women's movement faced a crisis of unity and direction, an urgent call was made for an explanation of the need for theoretical activity. It was—in our view rightly—felt necessary to justify theoretical work of the kind articulated in the papers presented at that conference as oriented toward "the study of the forms of women's oppression both in the present and historically, the attempt to uncover the real basis for such oppression, and to explain why it takes the particular forms it does" (Himmelweit et al. 1976, p. 1). Nevertheless, some of that work did come under heavy criticism on the grounds of its inaccessibility and "elitism"; that is, it was felt that analyses were formulated in such a way as to exclude the majority of the participants from what was being said. It was also felt that any theoretically oriented enterprise by its very nature fails to take into account actions and events ordinary women experience and understand as meaningful. Criticisms such as these rest on a set of demands and positions which, because they tend to be unvoiced in the criticisms as they are formulated, need to be drawn out and examined in the light of their implications for theoretical work within a feminist problematic, however defined.

It is perhaps too easy to meet criticism of theory with counteraccusations of anti-intellectualism. If anti-intellectualism is a relevant conceptualization to employ here, it can be seen as contingently, and not necessarily, related to the subjectivism underlying—albeit often unconsciously—the position adopted by critical tendencies. The injunction to produce "analyses" that make sense of the everyday world is locatable within an epistemology articulated in the "action theory" formulated by Max Weber as embracing

all human behavior when and in so far as the acting individual attaches a subjective meaning to it. . . . Action is social in so far as, by virtue of the subjective meaning attached to it by the acting individual (or individuals), it takes account of the behavior of others and is thereby oriented in its course. (Weber 1947, 88)

In its demand for analysis—or perhaps more appropriately, description—of concrete situations, the "subjectivist" position in effect argues for a concentration on specific areas of action that have meaning for the "actors" immediately concerned: in this case, for women. The implication of the action frame of reference is that the world is reducible to and explicable in terms of subjective meanings produced and deployed by actors in concrete situations of face-to-face interaction.

From this position, criticism of theoretical work on the grounds that it does not immediately relate to "reality" may then be seen as an assertion of the impossibility of describing, let alone of analyzing, situations and instances not open to experiential observation. What must follow from the demand for making sense of the everyday world through meaningful experiences is not a rejection of all theory per se. Because such a demand is located within an epistemological base (largely unrecognized in this instance), the rejection is of specific theoretical positions, which may be described as "structural" or "holistic." We should make it clear, however, that in arguing that certain demands to justify theory may actually constitute an effective rejection of particular types of theoretical work, we certainly would not wish to suggest that no justification is required for theoretical activity.

The problematic relationship between theory and "practice" always poses itself quite acutely for the women's movement, precisely because it has been one of the projects of the movement to construct knowledge of the nature and causes of our oppression, with a view to changing that situation. The need for theoretical work arises quite simply from the very urgent and specific need for constructing an analytical and effectual understanding of women's situation. And an intervention in theory or knowledge may certainly be seen as itself constituting a change in the world. But nonetheless a distinction is to be made between theory and theoreticism. Theoreticism is not necessarily inherent in every theoretical enterprise, but tends to have its operation within a series of institutions and institutional discourses. Specifically in our society at present, the production and dissemination of knowledge is largely a specialized activity with its own institutions—a term that embodies not simply a concrete sociological conceptualization, but embraces also the very terms within which appropriate modes of inquiry, limits and boundaries of "subjects," and ways of producing and making use of knowledge are defined. This same institutional discourse incorporates also a mode of address that renders the theoretician as the authoritative source of knowledge. This is what we mean by theoreticism. But it may, even with a full awareness of this pitfall, be the case that the way in which concepts are presented and argued results in apparent inaccessibility. However, the complexity of many of the issues to be grappled with does demand an engagement on the part of the reader as much as of the author, in the sense that both reader and author are involved in the production of theory. In pointing out the dangers of theoreticism, we are calling attention also to the authoritarianism of theoreticist discourse, which constitutes the reader as a passive recipient of the privileged knowledge of another. Theorizing is not a oneway activity. The very way in which the women's movement operates—the means by which women are acquiring and using knowledge about themselves—runs counter to theoreticist tendencies: for example, women's studies is by nature interdisciplinary and hence subverts boundaries between subjects. Moreover, because of the means by which such knowledge is—or has been—produced, it may call into question the authoritarian character of traditional academic discourse. But, as we have already suggested, such a challenge is a possible and not a necessary accompaniment of the kind of work and ways of working done under the rubric of women's studies: the institutionalized character of its development can mean that work done within women's studies may become isolated from its origins and open to theorizing for its own sake . . .

In arguing for theory in feminist intellectual work, we are arguing for a theoretical contribution of a particular kind . . . materialism. We are here adopting Engels's definition of the term:

> According to the materialist conception, the determining factor in history is, in the final instance, the production and reproduction of immediate life. This, again, is of a twofold character: on the one side, the production of the means of existence, of food, clothing and shelter and the tools necessary for that production; on the other side, the production of human beings themselves, the propagation of the species. (Engels 1972, 71)

The materialist problematic is based on a conceptualization of human society as defined specifically by its productivity: primarily of the means of subsistence and of value by the transformation of nature through work. United with this is a conceptualization of history as the site of the transformation of the social relations of production and reproduction. As far as an analysis of the position of women is concerned, materialism would locate that position in terms of the relations of production and reproduction at various moments in history. In doing this, one of its central concerns would be the determinate character of the sexual division of labor and the implications of this for power relations between men and women at different conjunctures. At the same time, however, the connection between this set of relations and the social relations specific to modes of production—that is, relations between classes—must also be thought.

It is at this point that the issue at the heart of the attempt to construct a marxist feminism is raised: although we regard its production as a priority, we have to recognize that marxist feminist theoretical work is as yet in its infancy. It is for this reason that we have drawn the theoretical boundaries of our work inclusively around the terrain of materialism and have not focused attention exclusively on marxist feminist analyses; though we very much hope in doing this that some of the issues indicated in this book are of potential importance for a marxist feminist problematic and will be taken up and developed further. The starting point for a marxist—or a classic marxist—analysis, as opposed to a materialist one, would be an account of the laws of motion and transformation of modes of production, especially of the capitalist mode of production, and of the ways in which value is created and capital accumulated within this mode. The problem is that although in our view the subordination of women is to be thus analyzed historically in terms of the relation of women to modes of production and reproduction, this particular issue is scarcely addressed within traditional marxist thought. In this sense the suppression and subordination of women as such is not seen as constituting a problem requiring analysis, beyond the assertion that the prior condition of women's "emancipation" is that they be brought into the sphere of capitalist production. It is no coincidence that the attempt to construct analyses of the specificity of the subordination of women in capitalism, in terms of orthodox approaches to the labor theory of value through an examination of domestic labor, encountered such obstacles that attempts of this sort have by now been virtually abandoned. This situation suggests that Veronica Beechey is right in her assessment that "a correct analysis of the subordination of women cannot be provided by Marxists unless Marxism itself is transformed" (1971, 61)—transformed, for instance, through an attempt to come to terms properly with the sexual division of labor. It is clear . . . that much marxist analysis, in subsuming women to the general categories of that problematic—class relations, labor process, the state, and so on—fails to confront the specificity of women's oppression. There is often an automatic assumption that there is no need to do so; analysis is applicable to all groups and fractions at any moment in history, and a transformation of capitalism according to marxist precepts would entail the emancipation of all members of society, male or female. Materialist analyses of women's condition, to the extent that they constitute an attempt to transform marxism, constitute also a move toward the construction of a marxist feminism.

10

Ideology and the Cultural Production of Gender

Michèle Barrett

The concept of ideology is an intractable one for Marxist feminism, not least because it remains inadequately theorized in both Marxist and feminist theory. Although feminists have frequently posed ideology as central to women's oppression, this very centrality is presented as self-evident rather than argued for. Related to this is the inadequacy of feminist attempts to explore the ways in which material conditions have historically structured the mental aspects of oppression. Some earlier feminist writers—Simone de Beauvoir and Virginia Woolf, for example—paid more attention to this question than it has received in recent years. Approaches taken by contemporary feminism seem in comparison notably unsatisfactory. One solution has been to ground the ideology of oppression irrevocably in biology, to take procreation and its different consequences for men and women as the root cause. Another has been to present it as completely self-sustaining and in need of no further explanation; Cora Kaplan has suggested that this view of ideology—the "energy source" of patriarchal domination—underlies Kate Millett's work (Kaplan 1979). Yet another solution has been found in the application of a particular Marxist perspective that sees ideology (in this case sexist ideology) as the reflection of material conditions of male power and dominance. Hence the ideology of women's inferiority is seen as a manipulation of reality that serves men's interests, and women's own collusion in oppression is explained as a variety of false consciousness. These solutions are all unsatisfactory, and the latter is particularly so in that it simply transposes already inadequate theory of ideology on to different ground. For if a theory that sees ideology as the unproblematic reflection of class relations is inadequate, the difficulties are compounded if it is merely transferred to the question of gender.

Feminism has, however, played an important part in challenging the validity of the mechanical conception that sees ideology as the playing out of economic contradictions at the mental level. As I have already suggested, there has been a fruitful alignment of interests between those who seek to raise the question of gender and its place in Marxist theory, and those who seek to challenge economism in Marxism, insisting on the importance of ideological processes. It is clear that a conception of capitalism in which all forms of ideology are perceived as a reflection of the exploitation of labor by capital, in which gender plays no part, can be of little use to feminist analysis. It should be noted, perhaps, that the strong form of economism indicated above has never gained the hold on Western European Marxism that it has elsewhere. Indeed Perry Anderson has argued that the political context of the twentieth-century development of Western Marxism has encouraged an exploration of culture and ideology at the expense of an insistence on the primacy of economic or political considerations (Anderson 1976).

I

It is in this context that we should consider the argument that post-Althusserian developments in the theory of ideology offer an opportunity for feminist analysis that earlier versions of Marxism have denied. This claim can be identified with a particular tendency in contemporary feminist work, the appropriation of the theory developed by Barry Hindess and Paul Hirst, and is found most systematically in articles published by the journal *m/f.* It is not relevant here to enter into a sustained engagement with the ideas of Hindess and Hirst, which I will discuss only insofar as is necessary for an assessment of the claims made by feminists who have taken them over.[1]

As a basis for discussion I want to quote a passage of argument that expresses clearly the logic and assumptions of this theoretical position. My argument is that as long as feminist theories of ideology work with a theory of representation within which representation is always a representation of reality, however attenuated a relation that may be, the analysis of sexual difference cannot be advanced because reality is always already apparently structured by sexual division, by an already antagonistic relation between two social groups. And thus the complicated and contradictory ways in which sexual difference is generated in various discursive and social practices is always reduced to an effect of that always existent sexual division. In terms of sexual division, what has to be explained is how reality functions to effect the continuation of *its* already given divisions. (The different ways in which sexual differences are produced is actually denied as a political fact in this position.) In terms of sexual *differences*, on the other hand, what has to be grasped is, precisely, the *production of* differences through systems of representation; the work of representation produces differences that cannot be known in advance (Adams 1979, 52). I will come back later to the political implications of this argument. For the moment, consider the rather startling statement that sexual differences "cannot be known in advance." Let us not sink to the vulgarity of pointing out that biological differences can be known in advance, since we know that this level of reality is uncongenial to exponents of this approach. More seriously, this analysis of "social and discursive practices" appears also to deny that *gender* differences, as a set of historically constructed and systematic categories, can be predicted with any confidence within a given historical conjuncture. Underlying this argument are a series of principles that need to be examined. These can be identified (rather negatively perhaps) as (i) a rejection of theories of ideology; (ii) a denial that there is any knowable relationship between representation and that which is represented; (iii) an insistence that functionalist formulations are always and necessarily incorrect.

IDEOLOGY

It is clear that a position resting on a rejection of epistemological theories must inevitably reject any elements of determination in its approach to ideology. Paul Hirst, in a critique of Althusser, points to the "fragile" character of the thesis that ideology is "relatively autonomous" of its supposed economic determinants. He argues that the notion of relative autonomy "attempts to overcome economism without facing the theoretical consequences of doing so." On the face of it, such a criticism might point to an espousal of the view that ideology is "absolutely" autonomous. But this turns out to be a naive or willful misreading of the text.

"Autonomy from what?" asks Hirst rhetorically, insisting that even to pose questions of causality is to assume a social totality in which particular instances are governed by their place in the whole (Hirst 1979). This enlightenment induces distaste for the concept of ideology itself, and a preference for that of "discursive practices." As the editors of *m/f* emphasize: "it is indeed theories of ideology that present the categories of men and women as exclusive and exhaustive (Adams 1979, 23)." This is certainly a stylish way of dealing with the problem. But I think we have to ask whether in following it we really have shaken the mundane dust of ideology off our feet. We have, after all, been led through a series of increasingly radical breaks with the Marxism of Marx and Althusser, and the final transcendence of the epistemological problematic of "ideology" is built on the earlier advances made within this framework. In particular, the way in which the concept of discursive practice is deployed owes much to previous attempts to demonstrate the autonomy and materiality of ideology. To put this another way: they have shifted the discourse of ideology onto the terrain of the discourse of discourse and while, in their terms, this may be as real an advance as any other, to the critic of discursive imperialism it may seem a nominal rather than a conceptual gain. For this reason I want to take issue with a tenet which (although an epistemological one and therefore rejected by discourse theory) has provided for many people the stepping stone to support for the more radical position: the "materiality of ideology."

This tenet is now so much *de rigeur* in the British Marxist avant-garde that to be caught artlessly counterposing material conditions and "ideology" is an embarrassing error—"but surely ideology is material" will be the inevitable reproof. Yet this assumption will not withstand closer investigation. The insistence that ideology is *material* arises, I suspect, from an unsuccessful attempt to resolve a classic paradox in Marxism: that being may determine consciousness but revolutionary transformation of the conditions of being will depend upon raising the level of class consciousness. Virginia Woolf once said "a republic might be brought into being by a poem" and indeed it is possible, if unlikely, that a powerfully wrought poem could goad an exploited proletariat into successful seizure of the means of production. Yet however colossal the material *effects* of this poem, they would have no bearing on the question of whether the poem itself had a material existence.

To reject the view that ideology is material does not imply a retreat to the view that the economic and the ideological are related in a one-way system of determination of the latter by the former. On the contrary, it is important to stress a degree of reciprocity here. It is impossible to understand the division of labor, for instance, with its differential definitions of "skill," without taking into account the material effects of gender ideology. The belief that a (white) man has a "right" to work over and above any rights of married women or immigrants has had significant effects in the organization of the labor force. Such a belief has therefore to be taken into account when analyzing the division of labor, but its location in material practices does not render it material in the same way.

The argument turns on what might be seen as an extension of Althusser's approach to ideology. For while Althusser argues, in my view correctly, that ideology exists in (material) apparatuses and their practices, it requires a considerable leap of faith to translate this as meaning that ideology is material. Stuart Hall and Richard Johnson have made this point very clearly: Johnson suggests that a "genuine insight" here becomes reckless hyperbole and Hall argues that the "slide" from one meaning to the other enables the magical qualifier, "materialist," to serve as an undeserved emblem of legitimation (Hall 1978, 59; Johnson 1979, 116).

The notion of the materiality of ideology has been influential and has reinforced the claim that ideology should be regarded as absolutely autonomous. For why, if ideology is as material as the economic relations we used to think of as "material conditions," should it not be assigned an equal place in our analysis? The crucial questions concerning the relationship of ideological processes to historical conditions of the production and reproduction of material life are left unexamined in this attempt to colonize the world for a newly privileged concept of ideology in which everything is material. Yet in drawing the net of ideology so wide we are left with no means, no tools, for distinguishing anything. As Terry Eagleton trenchantly remarks, "There is no possible sense in which meanings and values can be said to be 'material,' other than in the most sloppily metaphorical use of the term. . . . If meanings *are* material, then the term 'materialism' naturally ceases to be intelligible. Since there is nothing the concept excludes, it ceases to have value" (Eagleton 1980).

REPRESENTATION

Parveen Adams argues that "the classical theory of representation" must be rejected. What would such a rejection entail? This classical theory, central to Marxist aesthetics, poses representation (usually seen as ideological, and often explored through the analysis of cultural products) as to some degree a reflection of specific historical conditions. Debate has raged over whether literary texts, for instance, can be understood as direct reflections, or even distortions, of reality or should be seen as mediated in complex ways. Such texts are held, however, always to bear some relation to the social relations in which they were produced. It is this relationship that is being challenged here. Paul Hirst, in the critique of Althusser already mentioned, has argued that representation must necessarily entail *means* of representation, and that once these are allowed it must follow that they "determine" that which is represented. It is but a step from this to argue that *nothing other* than the means of representation determines what is represented—that "the real" can never exist prior to its representation. This short step, however, constitutes an important break in the argument. For while it is true, as Hirst argues, that the signified does not exist (in semiotic theory) prior to its signification, this does not rule out the existence of a material referent of the sign as a whole. So Hirst's preference for the conceptual framework of signification over that of representation, and his claim that the former facilitates a break with the constraints of the classic theory of ideology, remain unjustified.

Certainly it is true that the means of representation are important. In the area of cultural production, for example, it is easy to see how forms of representation are governed by genres, conventions, the presence of established modes of communication, and so on. Yet these are not determining in the absolute sense being argued for here. They do not in themselves account for what is represented. We can approach this problem by way of an example, by looking at the imagery of gender. Suppose I am an enterprising motorcar manufacturer and it occurs to me that I can tap a market of independent salaried women for my product. I advertise my car with a seductive, scantily clad male model draped over its bonnet and an admiring, yet slightly servile, snappily dressed man politely opening the car door for my putative client. Will my efforts be crowned with success? It is unlikely—and the reason it is unlikely is, precisely, that the representation does bear a relation to something which we can know previously existed.

This point is explored in two interesting articles on the imagery, and cultural stereotyping, of gender. Griselda Pollock argues that we should not be content to view the cultural representation of gender as "images of women." She rejects this approach because it cannot explain why it should be that the inversion or reversal of accepted imagery simply does not succeed (Pollock 1977). This is so not only because the representation of women is linked to a broader chain, or system, of signification. It also occurs because representation is linked to historically constituted real relations. To put the matter simply, we can understand why female models may be more persuasive to male customers than vice versa only if we take account of a prior commoditization of women's bodies. Why this should have been so, and how, are clearly questions for historical analysis, but the fact remains that a connection has been established in which not only have women's bodies become commodities themselves (for instance, in prostitution) but the association between them and consumerism has more generally taken hold. A related case is made by T. E. Perkins in a discussion of stereotyping (Perkins 1979). Perkins argues that however irrational or erroneous a particular stereotype may be thought, we do not have the option of eradicating it by the voluntary substitution of a different one. Stereotypes are tied to historical social relations, and indeed, Perkins argues, the chances of success in challenging a stereotype will depend upon the social location of the group in question.

To argue in this way does not imply any pre-given, or ahistorical, content of representation. Parveen Adams appears to be arguing that *either* we talk of "sexual division" as "an always already antagonistic relation between two social groups who are frozen into a mutually exclusive and jointly exhaustive division (Adams 1979, 57)," *or* we talk of "sexual differences" as the apparently spontaneous production of something that we cannot know in advance. These, however, do not constitute our only options. We do not need to talk of sexual division as "always already" there; we can explore the historical construction of the categories of masculinity and femininity without being obliged to deny that, historically specific as they are, they nevertheless exist today in systematic and even predictable terms. Without denying that representation plays an important constitutive role in this process, we can still insist that at any given time we can have a knowledge of these categories prior to any particular representation in which they may be reproduced or subverted. . . .

II

I have discussed these arguments at some length, since they are proposed as a solution to the crucial question faced by Marxist feminist analysis—what is the relationship between women's oppression and the general features of a mode of production? I am unconvinced that the post-Althusserian development of discourse theory has rendered this question obsolete. These writers have, however, usefully alerted us once again to the underdeveloped nature of the theory of ideology, and in the following section I will attempt to sketch out a more useful way of deploying this concept.

I want to suggest first that for a concept of ideology to have any analytic use it must be bounded. We must retrench from a position where ideology is claimed to be as determining, as material, as the relations of production. The concept of "relative autonomy" must, whatever its apparent fragility, be further explored and defined. This need not necessarily involve intellectual acrobatics of the kind which would be required to prove that ideology is at one and the same time autonomous and not. To perceive this problem in terms of abstract logic is to misunderstand it. What it does involve is the specification, for a given social historical context, of the limits to the autonomous operation of ideology. Hence we should be able to specify what range of possibilities exist for the ideological processes of a particular social formation, without necessarily being able to predict the specific form they may take.

Second, I want to restrict the term to phenomena that are mental rather than mater-ial. Hence the concept of ideology refers to those processes that have to do with consciousness, motive, emotionality; it can best be located in the category of *meaning*. Ideology is a generic term for the processes by which meaning is produced, challenged, reproduced, transformed. Since meaning is negotiated primarily through means of communication and signification, it is possible to suggest that cultural production pro-vides an important site for the construction of ideological processes. Thus, it is not inappropriate to claim, as Eagleton and others have, that literature (for instance) can usefully be analyzed as a paradigm case of ideology in particular social formations (Eagleton 1980). Ideology is embedded historically in material practice but it does not follow *either* that ideology is theoretically indistinguishable from material practices or that it bears any direct relationship to them. We may learn much, from an analysis of novels, about the ways in which meaning was constructed in a particular historical period, but our knowledge will not add up to a general knowledge of that social forma-tion. For if literature does constitute a primary site of ideological negotiation, nonetheless it cannot provide the historian with an adequate knowledge of other, equally important aspects of a social formation. The mediation of social reality operat-ing in any fictional work will ensure that the historian will face many dangers in pillaging literature for its "social content." One reason this should be so is that literary texts operate, as Pierre Macherey has argued, through their absences as well as through what is present in them (Macherey 1978). Following Althusser's method of "symptomatic reading," in which the analyst can supposedly detect the gaps and weaknesses of the author's original problematic, Macherey suggests that we should concentrate not on what the text overtly presents to us, but on what is *not said* in it. There are clearly problems with this model . . . but Macherey points to an important danger here.

Third, lest it should be thought that this represents a return to an economistic base/superstructure model of society, I should emphasize the integral connection between ideology and the relations of production. This is particularly important and easily demonstrated, in the case of the ideology of gender. . . . This ideology has played an important part in the historical construction of the capitalist division of labor and in the reproduction of labor power. A sexual division of labor, and accompanying ideologies of the appropriate meaning of labor for men and women, have been embedded in the capitalist division of labor from its beginnings. It is impossible to overemphasize here the importance of a historical analysis. I make no claim for the inevitability of this particular ideology as a functional requisite for capitalist production—it is one of several possible options. Nevertheless there are grounds to accept a point made by Colin Sumner in his fascinating and controversial book: that once such an ideology is historically embedded it may *become* essential for the maintenance of the system (Sumner 1979).

In stressing the role of ideology in the relations of production it is perhaps necessary, to avoid misunderstanding, to stress the fact that the term "relations of production" does not refer simply to class relations. It must comprise the divisions of gender, of race, definitions of different forms of labor (mental, manual, and so on), of who should work and at what. Relations of production reflect and embody the outcome of struggles: over the division of labor, the length of the working day, the costs of reproduction, Marx's allusion to the "historical and moral element" in the value of labor-power requires further exploration and elaboration. It is, perhaps, useful here to distinguish between the "relations of production," in which the ideology of gender plays a very important part, and the means and forces of production. For while it is true that the ideology of gender plays a very significant role in the *relations* of production, it is far more difficult to argue that it plays a crucial part in the essential reproduction of raw materials, installations, and machinery; and although domestic labor is vital to the present form in which labor power is reproduced, this need not necessarily be the case. Indeed it can plausibly be argued that the wage-labor relation and the contradiction between labor and capital—the defining characteristics of the capitalist mode of production—are "sex-blind" and operate quite independently of gender.

NOTE

1. The individual and collaborative works of Barry Hindess and Paul Q. Hirst, and their collective work with Anthony Cutler and Athar Hussain, are known colloquially as "Hindess and Hirst," "post-Althusserianism" and "discourse theory." There now exist several general critical responses to their arguments, such as Andrew Collier (1979), Harris (1978), and Corrigan and Sayer (1978).

11

Socialist Feminism and the Limits of Dual Systems Theory

Iris Marion Young

Socialist feminist theory is perhaps the most vital and profound development in contemporary Marxist theory and is also central to advances in feminist social theory.[1] This growing body of theoretical and analytical literature locates itself in the tradition of Marxism, but it agrees with the radical feminist claim that traditional Marxian theory cannot adequately comprehend the bases, structure, dynamic, and detail of women's oppression. It thus seeks to supplement the Marxian theory of class society with at least elements of the radical feminist analysis of sexist society.

The predominant manner of accomplishing this synthesis of Marxism and radical feminism has been through what I call the "dual systems theory." Stated briefly, for I will define it at more length in what follows, the dual systems theory says that women's oppression arises from two distinct and relatively autonomous systems. The system of male domination, most often called "patriarchy," produces the specific gender oppression of women; the system of the mode of production and class relations produces the class oppression and work alienation of most women. Patriarchy "interacts" with the system of the mode of production—in our case, capitalism—to produce the concrete phenomena of women's oppression in society.

As one committed to the project of incorporating many radical feminist insights into a theory of women's situation within the tradition of Marxism, I used to accept the dual systems theory. Recently, however, it has begun to seem inadequate. In this paper I express some of my discomfort with the dual systems theory by raising some theoretical and practical questions about it.

My primary motive in raising these critical questions is political: I wish to see the political principles of socialist feminism furthered. By socialist feminist politics I mean the following: a socialist movement must pay attention to women's issues and support the autonomous organization of women in order to succeed, and all socialist organizing should be conducted with a feminist consciousness; and feminist struggle and organizing should be anticapitalist in its thrust and should make explicit connections between the oppression of women and other forms of oppression. The dual systems theory is a better basis for these principles than any other existing theory of women's situation under capitalism, but I have begun to think that it does not serve well enough and that it even fosters analyses and practices contrary to those principles.

THE ORIGINS OF DUAL SYSTEMS THEORY

The feminist break with the New Left and the resulting contemporary women's movement stand as perhaps the most revolutionary and lasting effect *of the movements of the 1960s.* Quickly these new-wave feminists, who called themselves radical feminists, began developing questions, categories, and analyses that broke wholly new ground and irrevocably altered the perceptions of most progressive people. For the first time we had systematic accounts of such unspeakable phenomena as rape and heterosexism. Those identifying themselves as radical feminists continue to develop their analyses with extraordinary insight.

Like the feminist politics and movement that began by distinguishing itself from the radical left, many of the early theoretical works of radical feminism, such as Firestone's *Dialectic of Sex* and Millett's *Sexual Politics,* began from a confrontation with Marxism. We do not need to summarize the details of the arguments they developed. They concluded that Marxism failed as a theory of history and a theory of oppression because it did not account for the origins, structure, and dynamic of male domination and failed to recognize sex oppression as the most fundamental oppression. Radical feminism thus rejected Marxian theory as a basis for understanding women's oppression and rejected the socialist movement as a viable means of organizing to alter the social structure.

Some feminist women, however, acknowledged the radical feminist criticisms of the socialist movement but did not wish to separate from that movement entirely. Believing that eliminating capitalist economic institutions would not itself liberate women, these emerging socialist feminists nevertheless found this a necessary condition for that liberation. The socialist feminists agreed with the radical feminist claim that traditional Marxian theory cannot articulate the origins and structure of sex oppression in a way that accounts for the presence of this oppression as a pervasive and fundamental element of most societies. But they did not wish thereby to reject entirely the Marxist theory of history or critique of capitalism.

Accepting and rejecting elements of both radical feminism and Marxist socialism, the socialist feminists found themselves with a political and a theoretical problem. The political problem was how to participate in a movement for socialism without sacrificing feminist autonomy and without forfeiting feminist criticism of socialists. Socialist feminist politics has also had to grapple with how to orient feminist organizing and self-help projects in such a way that they recognize the particular oppressions of race and poverty and promote critique of capitalist institutions.

The theoretical problem socialist feminists face is how to synthesize Marxian theory and radical feminist theory into a viable theory of social reality in general and of women's oppression in particular. The solution to this problem emerged as the dual systems theory. One of the earliest statements of the dual systems theory is Linda

Phelps's "Patriarchy and Capitalism." In discussing women's situation in contemporary society, she claims that we must talk of two distinct systems of social relations: patriarchy and capitalism.

> If sexism is a social relationship in which males have authority over females, *patriarchy* is a term which describes the whole system of interaction arising from that basic relationship, just as capitalism is a system built on the relationship between capitalist and worker. Patriarchal and capitalist social relationships are two markedly different ways human beings have interacted with each other and have built social, political and economic institutions. (Phelps 1975, 39)

According to Phelps, patriarchy and capitalism constitute distinct systems of oppression because the principles of authority differ and because they have distinct histories. Capitalism and patriarchy, moreover, contradict as well as reinforce each other as they interact in contemporary society.

More recently, Zillah Eisenstein has attempted to articulate in a more complex fashion this relation between the dual systems of capitalism and patriarchy. In her formulation, a *mode of production* (e.g., capitalism) and patriarchy are distinct systems in their structures but nevertheless support each other.

This statement of the mutual dependence of patriarchy and capitalism not only assumes the malleability of patriarchy to the needs of capital, but assumes the malleability of capital to the needs of patriarchy. When one states that capitalism needs patriarchy in order to operate efficiently, one is really noting that male supremacy, as a system of sexual hierarchy, supplies capitalism (and systems previous to it) with the necessary order and control. . . . To the extent that the concern with profit and the concern with societal control are inextricably connected (but cannot be reduced to each other), patriarchy and capitalism become an integral process; specific elements of each system are necessitated by the other (Eisenstein 1979, 27). Other dual systems theorists claim a less harmonious relationship between capitalism and patriarchy. Heidi Hartmann, for example, claims that at times during the history of modern society the interests of the system of patriarchy have struggled against the interests of the system of capitalism and that the patriarchal interests have won out.[2]

I have been referring to "the" dual systems theory not in order to designate one unified body of theory, but to refer to a general *type* of theoretical approach. Those who subscribe to a dual systems approach to understanding women's oppression differ significantly in the categories they use and in their particular formulations of the dual systems account. The two systems are not always called "patriarchy" and "capitalism." The terms "mode of production" and "mode of reproduction" frequently designate the two types of system.[3] Gayle Rubin criticizes both "patriarchy" and "reproduction" as terms to designate the system of male domination. She prefers the term "sex/gender system" as a neutral category that can stand as the analogue in the realm of sex power to the system of production in the realm of class power (Rubin 1975, 167). Among the other categories that have been proposed to designate the system underlying male domination, as distinct from the mode of production, are "sex/affective production" (Ferguson 1979) and the "relations of procreation."[4]

Development of the dual systems approach has fostered major theoretical, analytical, and practical advances over traditional Marxist treatments of "the women question" and has contributed to a revitalization of Marxist method. Socialist feminist analyses springing from the dual systems approach have examined in detail the relationship of women's specific oppression to capitalist institutions in a way that otherwise might not have occurred. The dual systems theory has directed the attention of socialists to phenomena in capitalist society that lie beyond the production process, but that nevertheless are central for understanding the contemporary economy and ideology—such as family relations, advertising and sexual objectification, consumer culture, and so on.

As the first attempt to synthesize Marxism and radical feminism, the dual systems theory has been a crucial theoretical development, and I do not wish to belittle its contribution. I suspect, however, that it may now be holding socialist feminists back from developing further theoretical insights and practical strategies. In what follows I shall argue that the dual systems theory has not succeeded in confronting and revising traditional Marxist theory enough because it allows Marxism to retain in basically unchanged form its theory of economic and social relations, onto which it merely grafts a theory of gender relations.

IDEOLOGICAL AND PSYCHOLOGICAL APPROACHES

There are numerous variations in dual systems accounts. Some develop more important insights than others. In this essay I do not wish to review the work of all the major dual systems theorists. In criticizing the dual systems approach I will be reconstructing what I see as the basic form of those accounts. Where I refer to specific works, I am using them as examples of a general approach.

All dual systems accounts begin from the premise that the system of male domination is structurally independent of the relations of production described by Marxian theory. Given this assumption, the dual systems theorists must specify the independent origins and structure of the system(s) of gender relations and articulate their relation to the system(s) of production relations. In my reading I have seen two general approaches to articulating the nature of the system of gender relations. The first understands the system of patriarchy as an ideological and psychological structure independent of specific social, economic, and historical relations. This version of the dual systems theory then attempts to give an account of the interaction of the ideological and psychological structures of patriarchy with the social and economic structures of class society. The second version of the dual systems theory considers patriarchy itself to be a particular system of social relations of production (or "reproduction") relatively independent of the relations of production that Marxists traditionally analyze. Some dual systems theorists, such as Rubin, combine both versions of the dual systems theory, but most writers tend toward one or the other.

Juliet Mitchell's approach in *Psychoanalysis and Feminism* (1974) is an example of the first ideological-psychological version, as indeed are most theories that rely on Freudian theory as the basis of a theory of male domination.[5] Mitchell clearly states the autonomy of the systems of patriarchy and capitalism, one being ideological and the other material.

> Though, of course, ideology and the given mode of production are interdependent; one cannot be reduced to the other nor can the same laws be found to govern the other. To put the matter schematically, in analyzing contemporary Western society

we are (as elsewhere) dealing with two autonomous areas: the economic mode of capitalism and the ideological mode of patriarchy. (1974, 409)

Mitchell understands patriarchy as a universal and formal structure of kinship pat-
terning and psychic development that interacts with the particular structure of a mode
of production.

> Men enter into the class-dominated structures of history while women (as women,
> whatever their work in actual production) remain defined by the kinship pattern of
> organization. Differences of class, historical epoch, specific social situation alter the
> expression of femininity; but in relation to the law of the father, women's position
> across the board is a comparable one. (1974, 409)

In this account, the patriarchal structures that Freudian theory articulates exist as a
pre- or nonhistorical ideological backdrop to transformations in social and economic
relations of the mode of production. This ideological and psychological structure lying
outside economic relations persists in the same form throughout them. Mitchell does
not wish to deny, of course, that the concrete situation of women differs in varying
social circumstances. She accounts for this variation in women's situation by the way in
which particular structures of a given mode of production intersect with the universal
structures of patriarchy.

This version of the dual systems theory inappropriately dehistoricizes and universal-
izes women's oppression. It may be true that in all male-dominated societies there are
common elements to the situation of women and the social relations in which they
stand. Relations having to do with children are not least of these. Such elements, however, by no means exhaust the distinctiveness of women's situation. It is absurd to
suggest, as Mitchell does, that women as women stand outside history. Women participate in the social relations of production, as well as most other social relations, in
gender-specific ways that vary enormously in form and content from one society or
epoch to another. Describing such differences in the specific characteristics of sexist
oppression as merely "expressions" of one and the same universal system of male domination trivializes the depth and complexity of women's oppression.

There are certain practical dangers, moreover, in representing male domination as
universal in form. On the one hand, it tends to create a false optimism regarding the
possibility of a common consciousness among women. This can lead to serious cultural, ethnic, racial, and class biases in the account of the allegedly common structures of
patriarchy.[6] On the other hand, the notion of a single system of patriarchy that persists
in basically unchanged *form* through different epochs paralyzes feminist action because
it represents the beast we are struggling against as so ancient and monolithic.

The main problem with this version of the dual systems theory, however, is that it
does not in fact succeed in giving the alleged system of patriarchy equal weight with
and independence from the system of production. It conceives of all concrete social
relations as belonging to the economic system of production. Thus it gives no material
weight to the system of patriarchy, which it defines in its basic structure as independent
of the mode and relations of production, the social relations that proceed from them,
and the processes of historical change. Thus this version of the dual systems theory
ends by ceding to the traditional theory of production relations the primary role in giving an account of women's concrete situation. The theory of patriarchy supplies the

form of women's oppression, but traditional Marxist theory supplies its content, specificity, and motors of change. Thus this version of the dual systems theory fails to challenge traditional Marxism because it cedes to that Marxism theoretical hegemony over historically material social relations.[7]

PATRIARCHY AS A SOCIAL STRUCTURE

A number of dual systems theorists have recognized these weaknesses in the first version of the dual systems theory and thus have sought to develop an account of patriarchy as a system distinct from capitalism, yet based in a set of specific social relations. Heidi Hartmann (1981), for example, maintains that patriarchy is a set of social relations with a material base that lies in men's control over women's labor and in women's *exclusion from access* to essential productive resources. She clearly subscribes to the dual systems approach: patriarchy should be understood as a system of domination distinct from capitalism, with its own "laws of motion." It is not clear, however, how one can maintain both these positions. In order to succeed in separating capitalism and patriarchy, this social-structural version of the dual systems theory requires articulating a structure by which we can isolate the social relations of production belonging to patriarchy from those belonging to capitalism. Hartmann's account does not develop such a structure of social relations, however, and she even admits that it is difficult to isolate structures specific to patriarchy (1981, 38–39).

Dual systems theorists commonly tackle this problem of isolating the material relations specific to patriarchy by positing what Rosalind Petchesky (1979) has called the "model of separate spheres." In this model women and men historically have had their primary places in separate spheres of production from which arise distinct relations of production. Almost invariably this model poses the family as the locus of the women's productive sphere and social relations outside the family as the locus of men's. The model of separate spheres seems to provide us with the distinct structures and histories that the dual systems theory requires. The history of patriarchy will be constituted in the history of relations in the "domestic" sphere, while the history of class society will be constituted in the "public" sphere, on which traditional Marxism focuses.

Ann Ferguson (1979), for example, argues that women are the exploited workers in the distinct sphere of production that she calls sex/affective production, a type of production distinct from the production of material goods. This type of production, like the production of material goods, goes through different historical states, or modes of production. In contemporary society the mode of sex/affective production is the nuclear family. Inside the family, women produce sex/affective goods that their husbands appropriate, and hence women in contemporary society constitute an exploited class in the strict Marxian sense. Those socialist feminists who regard the family under capitalism as a vestige of the feudal mode of production also hold that women's situation is structured by the interaction of two modes of production (Mitchell 1974; Rowbotham 1973), as do those who wish to distinguish a "mode of reproduction" from mode of production (Flax 1976).

The model of separate spheres appears to hypostasize a separation peculiar to capitalism—that between family and work—into a universal form. In all precapitalist societies, the family is the primary unit of production, and kinship relations are a powerful determinant of economic relations. Separation of productive activity from the household and kinship relations, and the creation of two spheres of social life, is one of the defining characteristics of capitalist society itself, as a number of writers have pointed out.[8] Projecting this separation onto the structure of all societies—or at least all male-dominated class societies—cannot but obscure crucial differences between precapitalist and capitalist societies with respect to the situation of women.

Precisely because the separation of domestic from economic life is peculiar to capitalism, use of that separation as the basis for the analysis of women's situation in contemporary society may be playing right into the hands of bourgeois ideology. Bourgeois ideology itself promoted and continues to promote the identification of women with the home, domesticity, affective relations, and "nonproductive" activity, and defines these as structurally distinct from the "public" world of "real" economic life. For this reason socialist feminists should be suspicious of this identification of women's situation with a distinct sphere of private domestic relations, and above all should be wary of utilizing such an identification as a basis of their own analytic framework.

We should also ask whether the separation itself does not obscure a more basic integration. A number of analyses have emphasized the degree to which the alleged separation of the domestic and affective sphere from the economic sphere is ultimately illusory. Weinbaum and Bridges (1979), for example, argue quite persuasively that contemporary capitalism not only has rationalized and socialized production operations in accordance with its domination and profit needs, but has rationalized and socialized the allegedly private work of consumption as well. Other theorists, such as Marcuse (1964), suggest that contemporary capitalism has actually entered into and rationalized sexual and affective relations for its own ends.

The main problem with the model of separate spheres, however, is that because it assumes the family as the primary sphere of patriarchal relations, it fails to bring into focus the character of women's specific oppression as women outside the family. For example, it is difficult to view the use of women as sexual symbols to promote consumption as a function of some separate sphere distinct from the economic requirements of monopoly capitalism. When more than half of women over sixteen are working outside as well as inside the home, the model of separate spheres, and the focus on domestic life that it encourages, may divert attention from a capitalism that increasingly exploits women in gender-specific paid work.

The character of women's oppression in the contemporary workplace has specifically sexist forms that cannot be encompassed by traditional accounts of relations of production. For example, sexual harassment is a routine way that superiors discipline women workers. More broadly, in contemporary society not only images of "sexy" women foster capitalist accumulation, but also real live women are employed for their "sexual" labor—for being sexy on their jobs, suggesting sexiness to customers, and performing many jobs whose main function is being sexy in one way or another. The dual systems theory does not seem to have the theoretical equipment to comprehend these diverse kinds of sexist oppression outside the family and personal sphere.

The only means the dual systems theory has for doing so is to view gender-structured phenomena of the capitalist economy and workplace as modeled on or as effects of relations in the family, and this in fact is the strategy for explanation adopted by many dual systems theorists. Admitting and trying to explain the pervasiveness of gender structuration in all spheres of contemporary society, however, seriously weakens the model of separate spheres on which the explanation of that gender structuration is based in the dual systems theory. It would be much more direct to construct a theory of capitalist patriarchy as a unified system entailing specific forms of gender structuring in its production relations and ideology.

Viewing gender phenomena of the contemporary capitalist workplace as modeled on or effects of family relations, moreover, still tends to play down the specific oppression of women outside family life and to give inordinate emphasis to the family. It also misses the specific character of the sexist oppression of the workplace and other realms outside the family. Patriarchal oppression outside family life in contemporary society depends on impersonal, routinized, and generalized behavior as opposed to the personal relations of oppression that characterize the patriarchal family.

My criticisms of the dual systems approach to socialist feminist theorizing ultimately issue in the claim that dual systems theory does not go far enough. The dual systems approach accepts the traditional Marxian theory of production relations, historical change, and analysis of the structure of capitalism in basically unchanged form. It rightly criticizes that theory for being essentially gender-blind, and hence seeks to supplement Marxist theory of capitalism with feminist theory of a system of male domination. Taking this route, however, tacitly endorses the traditional Marxian position that "the woman question" is auxiliary to the central questions of a Marxian theory of society.

The dual systems theory, that is, declines from confronting Marxism directly in its failure to take account of the situation and oppression of women. Our nascent historical research coupled with our feminist intuition tells us that the labor of women occupies a central place in any system of production, that gender division is a basic axis of social structuration in all hitherto existing social formations, and that gender hierarchy serves as a pivotal element in most systems of social domination. If traditional Marxism has no theoretical place for such hypotheses, it is not merely an inadequate theory of women's oppression, but also an inadequate theory of social relations, relations of production, and domination. *We need not merely a synthesis of feminism with traditional Marxism, but also a thoroughly feminist historical materialism, which regards the social relations of a particular historical social formation as one system in which gender differentiation is a core attribute.*

DUAL SYSTEMS THEORY AND POLITICS

Socialist feminists insist that no political program or political activity is truly socialist unless it attends to the unique situation and oppression of women. Likewise, socialist feminists insist that feminist analyses and political activity should always look for ways of exposing the class- and race-differentiated character of patriarchal oppression, as well as its internal connection with the dynamic of profit. For example, in the sphere of reproductive rights, socialist feminists have emphasized the racist character of sterilization abuse and recent attacks on abortion rights. They have also taken pains to expose the interests of the medical establishment and drug companies in keeping women ignorant of our bodies and dependent on expensive and often dangerous means of birth control, birthing, and "curing" menopause.

Precisely what distinguishes the politics of socialist feminism is this commitment to the practical unity of the struggle against capitalism and the struggle for women's liberation. The dual systems theory, however, can tend to sever this practical unity, which socialist feminism has been trying to achieve since its inception. Thus the politics of socialist feminism would be better served by a theory of capitalist society that explicitly incorporated gender differentiation into its structural analysis, and hence took the oppression of women as a core aspect of the system.

Some socialist feminists might fear that such a "one system" theory would undermine arguments for the necessity of an autonomous women's movement, for a cornerstone of socialist feminist politics has been its conviction that women should be organized autonomously in groups in which they alone have decision-making power. Women must have the space to develop positive relations with each other, apart from men, and we can best learn to develop our own organizing, decision-making, speaking, and writing skills in an environment free of male dominance or paternalism. Only by being separately organized can feminist women confront the sexism of socialist men. And only in an autonomous women's movement can socialist women unify with women who see the need for struggle against male domination but do not see that struggle as integrated with an anticapitalist struggle.

The dual systems theory arose at least in part from this socialist feminist recognition of the strategic necessity of a women's movement allied with but autonomous from the mixed socialist movement. If capitalism and patriarchy are each distinct systems, mutually influencing but nevertheless ultimately separate and irreducible, it follows most plausibly that the struggle against patriarchy should be organizationally distinct from the struggle against capitalism.

I am convinced of the necessity of separately organizing women around issues relating to our own situation. Without such an autonomous women's movement the socialist movement itself cannot survive and grow. One can argue for the strategic necessity of such an autonomous women's movement, however, without postulating male domination and capitalist domination as distinct social systems. One only need appeal to the indisputable practical realities that capitalist patriarchal society structures the lives of women in special ways and that these capitalist patriarchal structures give to most men relative privilege and power. From this analysis it does not follow that there are two distinct systems of social relations. The dual systems theory can have the damaging effect of justifying a segregation of feminist concerns to the women's movement. This segregation means that socialists outside the women's movement need not take feminism seriously, and those who work in that movement must justify how their political work relates to socialism.

Because it does not confront traditional Marxian theory directly enough as a theory of social relations and oppression, the dual systems theory allows many socialists not to take feminism as seriously as they should. It can tend to justify the dismissal of feminist organizing by socialists not persuaded of the centrality of women's oppression to contemporary capitalism, and it can tend to justify their not bringing issues of women's oppression to the fore in their own practice. To be sure, the failure of many socialists to take feminist concerns seriously as socialist concerns reflects a political tension that no theory will alone heal. Nevertheless, confinement of feminist concerns to the periphery of socialist organizing would be more difficult for nonfeminist socialists to justify if socialist feminists confronted them with a theory of capitalist society that showed that society to be patriarchal in its essence and internal structure.

The necessity for all socialist work to have a feminist dimension and for socialists in the mixed left to take seriously issues surrounding women's oppression becomes most pressing under contemporary conditions. The new right does not appear to separate capitalism and patriarchy into distinct systems. Those attacking women's and gay rights ally unambiguously with those attacking unions or those promoting increased armaments. The new right has a total platform, the main plank of which is defense of the sanctity of the monogamous, heterosexual, many-children family. With a theory of capitalist patriarchy that showed its relations of labor and hierarchy as one gender-structured system in which the oppression of women is a core element, socialist feminists would be in a better position to argue and enact this practical necessity.

Because the mixed left does not take feminism as seriously as it should, many socialists who choose to concentrate all their energy on women's issues feel called upon, and often enough are called upon implicitly or explicitly, to justify the socialist character of their work. On the other hand, not all socialists with strong feminist commitments wish to devote their political energies to specifically women's issues, nor should they. They then often are called upon to demonstrate the feminist meaning of their work. As a result of these tensions, many socialist feminists feel as though they ought to do twice as much work—socialist work on the one hand and feminist work on the other. As long as we define patriarchy as a system ultimately distinct from capitalism, this practical tension appears necessary.

This "double shift" syndrome, of course, cannot be overcome by theory alone. Socialist women who choose to devote all their energies to separately organizing women around women's issues, however, should have the full active support and recognition of a socialist movement that perceives such work as in itself vital political work. Within the mixed left, moreover, feminist consciousness should be so incorporated that one could justifiably understand oneself as engaging in feminist work on issues not immediately concerning women's situation. We are a long way from that situation today. A major reason for this, I claim, is lack of a theory of capitalist society that would foster analyses revealing the patriarchal meaning of nearly every aspect of society.

I have been concentrating most of my argument here on the claim that all socialist political work should be feminist in its thrust and that socialists should recognize feminist concerns as internal to their own. Likewise, socialist feminists take as a basic principle that feminist work should be anticapitalist in its thrust and should link women's situation with the phenomena of racism and imperialism. Once again, this political principle would best be served by a social theory that regards these phenomena as aspects of a single system of social relations. With such a theory we would be in a better position to argue to other feminists that they must attend to issues of class and race in their analysis and organizing.

TOWARD A UNIFIED THEORY

I am not prepared here to offer even the outlines of such a theory. In concluding I will merely offer some of the general elements I believe such a theory should contain and some of the basic issues it should address.

A feminist historical materialism must be a total social theory, not merely a theory of the situation and oppression of women. That theory will take gender differentiation as its basic starting point, in the sense that it will seek always to keep the fact of gender difference in the center of its accounts and will reject any account that obscures gender-differentiated phenomena. It will take gender statuses, gender hierarchy and domination, changes in gender relations, gender ideologies, etc., as central aspects of any social formation. These must be analyzed in any account of a social formation, and other aspects of the social formation must be linked to them.

Following the lead of the early radical feminists, a feminist historical materialism must explore the hypothesis that class domination arises from and/or is intimately tied to patriarchal domination. We cannot simply assume that sex domination causes class society, as most radical feminists have done. But we must take seriously the question of whether there is a causal relation here, to what extent there is, and precisely how the causal relations operate if and when they exist.

A feminist historical materialism must be a truly *materialist* theory. This does not mean that it must "reduce" all social phenomena to economic phenomena, narrowly understood as processes of the production and distribution of material goods. Following Delphy and Williams, among others, I understand a materialist account as one that considers phenomena of "consciousness"—e.g., intellectual production, broad social attitudes and beliefs, cultural myths, symbols, images, etc.—as rooted in real social relationships (Delphy 1980, Williams 1977). This should not imply "reducing" such phenomena of consciousness to social structures and social relationships, nor does it even mean that the phenomena of consciousness cannot be treated as having a logic of their own. Nor should it mean that phenomena like attitudes and cultural definitions cannot enter as elements into the explanation of a particular structure of social relationships, though I would claim they can never be the sole explanation. This requirement mainly calls for a methodological priority to concrete social institutions and practices, along with the material conditions in which they take place.

The concrete social relations of gender and the relations in which these stand to other types of interaction and domination must appear at the core of the theory. In another paper I have suggested that a feminist historical materialism might utilize gender division of labor as a central category. This category would refer to all structured gender differentiation of laboring activity in a particular society, where labor includes any task or activity that the society defines as necessary (Young 1980). Whether or not this is the correct approach, a feminist historical materialism should remain Marxist in the sense that it takes the structure of laboring activity and the relations arising from laboring activity, broadly defined, as a crucial determinant of social phenomena. Accepting that Marxist premise, it must also find a way of analyzing social relations arising from laboring activity in gender-differentiated terms.

Finally, a feminist historical materialism must be thoroughly historical. It must eschew any explanations that claim to apply to societies across epochs. In practice this means that a feminist historical materialism must be suspicious of any claims to universality regarding any aspect of women's situation. If there exist any circumstances common to the situation of all women, these must be discovered empirically, not presupposed. We must develop a theory that can articulate and appreciate the vast differences in the situation, structure, and experience of gender relations in different times and places. At the same time, however, we want a single theory that can be utilized to analyze vastly different social structures. This means we need a set of basic categories that can be applied to differing social circumstances in such a way that their specificity remains and yet comparison is possible. In addition to such a set of categories we need a theoretical method that will guide us in our explanation of the particular phenomena in a particular society.

The remarks in this section have been very abstract. I intend only to outline some general directions for moving toward a feminist social theory in which the basic insights of Marxism can be absorbed and developed. Whether the above criteria for a socialist-feminist theory are correct can be decided only by embarking on the theoretical task in light of our practical needs.

NOTES

1. I say feminist social theory, not all feminist theory, for I think that current works of radical feminism, like Daly's *Gyn/Ecology* (1978), make profound and in some cases unparalleled contributions to theory and analysis of cultural symbols and patriarchal mythology.

2. See Hartmann (1980); this paper, which was originally coauthored with Amy Bridges, has received wide distribution among socialist feminists over the past several years. On similar points see also Hartmann's paper, "Capitalism, Patriarchy, and Job Segregation by Sex in Eisenstein" (1979).

3. See, for example, Flax (1976, 55).

4. Alison Jaggar (1983) develops this term.

5. Compare Flax's approach in her "Do Feminists Need Marxism?" (1976).

6. See Caulfield (1977). She points to some consequences of cultural bias that result from the assumption of a universal and common sex oppression, specifically with respect to the way we regard Third World women. I have articulated in another place some contrary attributes of sexism as experienced by black women and white women in America. Eisenstein (1979) does a good job of laying out the variables that differently structure the lives of different groups of women in such a way that it is not possible to speak of a common situation.

7. Compare McDonough and Harrison's (1978) criticism of Mitchell.

8. See Zaretsky (1976), Oakley (1974), Hamilton (1978).

12

The Incompatible Ménage à Trois
Marxism, Feminism, and Racism

Gloria Joseph

THE BLACK DIFFERENTIAL

. . . The exclusion of the race question is a serious omission and the inclusion of it further complicates an already problematic affair. But such is the nature of dealing with serious and complex theoretical problems. I raise the following point on the racial issue: if one can claim that marxism is incomplete without a consideration of feminism, it is certainly true that neither is complete without a consideration of racial relations. Of course one could argue that every relationship is unique and race relations have no patent on uniqueness; that no general theories are adequate, and from this point of view, most theories are too general. However, there is ample evidence to indicate that relations between races have a long and important history which is not reducible to relations between the sexes or classes. An analysis of racism thus should be undertaken prior to, or at least in conjunction with, the discussion of marxist-feminist relations, thus facilitating a better understanding of how to integrate race into a theory of marxism-feminism.

The marxist might argue that both sexism and racism are due to an established set of classes with a proletariat engaged in producing surplus capital for the dominant classes. As the extensive brutality of women by men does not appear to be reducible to the economic factors involved, so the virulent suppression of one race by another does not appear reducible to purely economic considerations. This appears reasonable. But more than appearance of validity is required. Both empirical evidence and deeper theoretical analysis is needed. Hartmann states that sexual differences are more basic than those based on "capital," and I agree with her. But I will claim that racial differences and antagonisms are *no longer* basically due to economic exploitation.

Marxist theory did not and could not account for a role that advanced technology would play with its resulting effects on modes of production, social relations, and new social classes (e.g., nouveau riche, superstars, mafia, drug lords, etc.). Certain dimensions of marxist theory that applied to the marxist world view in the mid-1800s are no longer applicable in the 1970s. In a parallel fashion, economic considerations are no longer the basis for racial discrimination and exploitation. Racial prejudices have become so ingrained in white U.S. society that a typical racist anti-Black mentality has developed, with emotion and ignorance ruling over intellect. Education, professional jobs, and housing are three areas where empirical evidence proves that economics is no longer the prime motivator for Black exclusion and exploitation. The very fact that we had to have affirmative action plans in educational arenas speaks for itself of the depth of racial biases. School systems "prefer" to lose government funding rather than comply with desegregration laws. Professional football teams would rather go with a losing white quarterback than with a winning Black one. The fact that winning teams make money cannot compete with the powerful aversion against having a Black "director" of the team. Black school teachers and administrators are the first to be dismissed when a cutback in staffing is required. This occurs particularly in the South where the schools are predominantly Black. In many cases white teachers and administrators who remain receive higher pay than those dismissed. Realtors falsely claim that property devalues when Blacks move into a predominantly white neighborhood. Realtors systematically keep Blacks out of certain areas regardless of the Black family's income.

The claim is made, for example in banks and offices, that too many Blacks in official or administrative positions will drive away white customers and clients, and therefore for economic reasons too many Blacks cannot be hired. Where this phenomenon occurs (whites avoiding places with "too many" Blacks) the white citizens have been carefully conditioned and programmed.

Hartmann concludes her essay by saying that the struggle to establish socialism must be a struggle in which groups with different interests form an alliance; and that women should not trust men to "liberate" them "after the revolution," in part because there is no reason to think that they would know how, and in part because there is no necessity for them to do so; in fact, their immediate self-interest lies in the continued oppression of women. Black women have to be considered as one of those groups with special interests. Just as women cannot trust men to "liberate" them, Black women cannot trust white women to "liberate" them during or "after the revolution," in part because there is little reason to think that they would know how; and in part because white women's immediate self-interest lies in continued racial oppression. To date feminists have not concretely demonstrated the potential or capacity to become involved in fighting racism on an equal footing with sexism. Adrienne Rich's recent article on feminism and racism is an exemplary one on this topic.[1] She reiterates much that has been voiced by Black female writers, but the acclaim given to her article shows again that it takes whiteness to give even Blackness credibility. White feminists have to learn to deal adequately with the fact that by virtue of their whiteness they are oppressors as well as oppressed persons. "It is a mystical belief in 'womanhood' that suggests that 'woman' is the most natural and the most basic of all human groupings and can therefore transcend the race divisions of our society."[2] This is no more likely than the belief that marxist ideology can transcend sexism.

A strong viable feminist movement must give full consideration to both Black and white women. As such there is a real and obvious need for research dealing with Black feminist theory and analysis. Acknowledgement should be given to those few Black women active in these tasks. Several of these women are Barbara and Beverly Smith of the Combahee River Collective, who have made valuable contributions to Black feminist literature; Audre Lorde, whose poetry is often well grounded in a Black feminist analysis; and Carroll Oliver, whose pioneering work in the development of a revolutionary Black feminist theory is admirable . . .

Black feminists have a crucial role to play in the present movement. They must include themselves from their own organized base. "The historiography about the women's movement has been distorted to depict Black women as indifferent or hostile to the feminist movement. Rosalyn Terborg-Penn asserts that Black women were concerned about the same issues that white women campaigned against—slavery, liquor, and sex discrimination—but for the most part they were discouraged by white women from participating fully in the women's movement. Prejudice and discrimination were elements that affected the daily lives of most Blacks during the 19th and 20th centuries."[3]

In order for the current movement to avoid the mistakes of the past, it is encumbent upon Black and white feminists to discover the vulnerabilities of U.S. capitalism and imperialism, both of which embody male supremacy and white supremacy. Common strategies must be decided upon and clarified and then the two groups must utilize their various tactics in moving toward their common goals. The fight against white supremacy and male domination over women is directly linked to the worldwide struggles for national liberation. Protracted struggle must take place on an international level. As Black and white feminists combine forces in the struggle against male supremacy and white supremacy, they must be willing to communicate and follow a format consisting of dialogue (with the purpose of mutual education), practice, more dialogue, and more practice—moving slowly but inexorably toward advanced levels of understanding and respect for one another's differences. The similarities among women are easier to understand and should be used as building blocks toward understanding and respect for racial and class differences. The possibility of an alliance between Black and white women can only be realized if white women understand the nature of their oppression within the context of the oppression of Blacks. At that point we will be able to speak of "The Happy Divorce of Patriarchy, Capitalism, and Racism," and the impending marriage of Black revolutionary socialism and socialist feminism.

Author's note

Throughout my response I have referred to Black women rather than Third-World women or other specific minorities. This is due to the respect that I hold for their different historical and cultural backgrounds. I am fully cognizant of the fact that in most cases what is applicable to Black women would also be applicable to other minority women in the United States. However, I do not think that I could speak for all minority women when there are such significant differences among us.

NOTES

1. Adrienne Rich, "Disloyal to Civilization: Feminism, Racism and Gynephobia," *Chrysalis*, no. 7, 1979.
2. Pat Armstrong, "Racism and Feminism: Division among the Oppressed," unpublished paper, 1972b.
3. Sharon Harley and Rosalyn Terborg-Penn, *The Afro-American Woman: Struggles and Images* (Port Washington, New York: Kennikat Press, 1970).

13

White Woman Listen!

Black Feminism and the Boundaries of Sisterhood

Hazel V. Carby

> I'm leaving evidence. And you got to leave evidence too. And your children got to
> leave evidence. . . . They burned all the documents. . . . We got to burn out what they
> put in our minds, like you burn out a wound. Except we got to keep what we need to
> bear witness. That scar that's left to bear witness. We got to keep it as visible as our
> blood. (Jones 1975)

The black women's critique of *his*tory has not only involved us in coming to terms with
"absences"; we have also been outraged by the ways in which it has made us visible,
when it has chosen to see us. *His*tory has constructed our sexuality and our femininity
as deviating from those qualities with which white women, as the prize objects of the
Western world, have been endowed. We have also been defined in less than human
terms (Jordon 1969). Our continuing struggle with *his*tory began with its "discovery"
of us. However, this chapter will be concerned with herstory rather than *his*tory. We
wish to address questions to the feminist theories that have been developed during the
last decade; a decade in which black women have been fighting, in the streets, in the
schools, through the courts, inside and outside the wage relation. The significance of
these struggles ought to inform the writing of the herstory of women in Britain. It is
fundamental to the development of a feminist theory and practice that is meaningful
for black women. We cannot hope to reconstitute ourselves in all our absences, or to
rectify the ill-conceived presences that invade herstory from *his*tory, but we do wish to
bear witness to our own herstories. The connections between these and the herstories
of white women will be made and remade in struggle. Black women have come from
Africa, Asia, and the Caribbean, and we cannot do justice to all their herstories in a single chapter. Neither can we represent the voices of all black women in Britain; our

herstories are too numerous and too varied. What we will do is to offer ways in which the "triple" oppression of gender, race, and class can be understood, in their specificity and also as they determine the lives of black women.

Much contemporary debate has posed the question of the relation between race and gender, in terms that attempt to parallel race and gender divisions. It can be argued that as processes, racism and sexism are similar. Ideologically for example, they both construct common sense through reference to "natural" and "biological" differences. It has also been argued that the categories of race and gender are both socially constructed and that, therefore, they have little internal coherence as concepts. Furthermore, it is possible to parallel racialized and gendered divisions in the sense that the possibilities of amelioration through legislation appear to be equally ineffectual in both cases. Michèle Barrett, however, has pointed out that it is not possible to argue for parallels because as soon as historical analysis is made, it becomes obvious that the institutions which have to be analyzed are different, as are the forms of analysis needed. We would agree that the construction of such parallels is fruitless and often proves little more than a mere academic exercise; but there are other reasons for our dismissal of these kinds of debate. The experience of black women does not enter the parameters of parallelism. The fact that black women are subject to the *simultaneous* oppression of patriarchy, class, and "race" is the prime reason for not employing parallels that render their position and experience not only marginal but also invisible.

In arguing that most contemporary feminist theory does not begin to adequately account for the experience of black women, we also have to acknowledge that it is not a simple question of their absence, and consequently the task is not one of rendering their visibility. On the contrary we will have to argue that the process of accounting for their historical and contemporary position does, in itself, challenge the use of some of the central categories and assumptions of recent mainstream feminist thought. We can point to no single source for our oppression. When white feminists emphasize patriarchy alone, we want to redefine the term and make it a more complex concept. Racism ensures that black men do not have the same relations to patriarchal/capitalist hierarchies as white men. In the words of the Combahee River Collective:

> We believe that sexual politics under patriarchy is as pervasive in Black women's lives as are the politics of class and race. We also often find it difficult to separate race from class from sex oppression because in our lives they are most often experienced simultaneously. We know that there is such a thing as racial-sexual oppression which is neither solely racial nor solely sexual, e.g., the history of rape of Black women by white men as a weapon of political repression.
>
> Although we are feminists and lesbians, we feel solidarity with progressive Black men and do not advocate the fractionalisation that white women who are separatists demand. Our situation as Black people necessitates that we have solidarity around the fact of race, which white women of course do not need to have with white men, unless it is their negative solidarity as racial oppressors. We struggle together with Black men against racism, while we also struggle with Black men about sexism. (Combahee River Collective 1983, 213)

It is only in the writings by black feminists that we can find attempts to theorize the interconnection of class, gender, and race as it occurs in our lives, and it has only been in the autonomous organizations of black women that we have been able to express and act upon the experiences consequent upon these determinants. Many black women had been alienated by the nonrecognition of their lives, experiences, and herstories in the Women's Liberation Movement (WLM). Black feminists have been and are still demanding that the existence of racism must be acknowledged as a structuring feature of our relationships with white women. Both white feminist theory and practice have to recognize that white women stand in a power relation as oppressors of black women. This compromises any feminist theory and practice founded on the notion of simple equality.

Three concepts central to feminist theory become problematic in their application to black women's lives: "the family," "patriarchy," and "reproduction." When used they are placed in a context of the herstory of white (frequently middle-class) women and become contradictory when applied to the lives and experiences of black women. In a recent comprehensive survey of contemporary feminist theory, *Women's Oppression Today,* Michèle Barrett sees the contemporary family (effectively the family under capitalism) as the source of oppression of women:

> It is difficult to argue that the present structure of the family-household is anything other than oppressive for women. Feminists have consistently, and rightly, seen the family as a central site of women's oppression in contemporary society. The reasons for this lie both in the material structure of the household, by which women are by and large financially dependent on men, and in the ideology of the family, through which women are confined to a primary concern with domesticity and motherhood. This situation underwrites the disadvantages women experience at work and lies at the root of the exploitation of female sexuality endemic in our society. The concept of "dependence" is, perhaps, the link between the material Organization of the household and the ideology of femininity: an assumption of women's dependence on men structures both of these areas. (Barrett 1980, 214)

The immediate problem for black feminists is whether this framework can be applied at all to analyze our herstory of oppression and struggle. We would not wish to deny that the family can be a source of oppression for us but we also wish to examine how the black family has functioned as a prime source of resistance to oppression. We need to recognize that during slavery, periods of colonialism, and under the present authoritarian state, the black family has been a site of political and cultural resistance to racism. Furthermore, we cannot easily separate the two forms of oppression because racist theory and practice is frequently gender specific. Ideologies of black female sexuality do not stem primarily from the black family. The way the gender of black women is constructed differs from constructions of white femininity because it is also subject to racism. Black feminists have been explaining this since the last century, when Sojourner Truth pointed to the ways in which "womanhood" was denied the black woman.

> That man over there says women need to be helped into carriages, and lifted over ditches, and to have the best place everywhere. Nobody ever helps me into carriages, and lifted over ditches, or over mud-puddles, or gives me any best place! And aint I a woman? Look at me! Look at my arm! I have ploughed, and planted, and gathered into barns, and no man could head me! And aint I a woman? I could work as much and eat as much as a man—when I could get it—and bear the lash as well! And aint I a woman? I have borne thirteen children, and seen most all sold off to slavery, and when I cried with my mother's grief, none but Jesus heard me! And aint I a woman? (Loewenberg and Bogin 1978, 235)

In our earlier examination of common sense we indicated the racist nature of ideologies of black female sexuality. Black women are constantly challenging these ideologies in their day-to-day struggles. Asian girls in schools, for example, are fighting back to destroy the racist mythology of their femininity. As Pratibha Parmar has pointed out, careers officers do not offer them the same interviews and job opportunities as white girls. This is because they believe that Asian girls will be forced into marriage immediately after leaving school. The commonsense logic of this racism dictates that a career for Asian girls is thought to be a waste of time. But the struggle in schools is not just against the racism of the careers service:

> "Yes, and then there are some racist students who are always picking on us. Recently, we had a fight in our school between us and some white girls. We really showed them we were not going to stand for their rubbish."
>
> Sangeeta and Wahida's statements reflect a growing confidence and awareness amongst young Asian girls about themselves and their situations in a climate of increased racist attacks on black people generally. Many Asian girls strongly resent being stereotyped as weak, passive, quiet girls who would not dare lift a finger in their own defense. They want to challenge the idea people have of them as girls "who do not want to stand out or cause trouble but to tip-toe about hoping nobody will notice them." (Parmar and Mirza 1981)

The use of the concept of "dependency" is also a problem for black feminists. It has been argued that this concept provides the link between the "material organization of the household, and the ideology of femininity." How then can we account for situations in which black women may be heads of households, or where, because of an economic system that structures high black male unemployment, they are not financially dependent upon a black man? This condition exists in both colonial and metropolitan situations. Ideologies of black female domesticity and motherhood have been constructed through their employment (or chattel position) as domestics and surrogate mothers to white families rather than in relation to their own families. West Indian women still migrate to the United States and Canada as domestics and in Britain are seen to be suitable as office cleaners, National Health Service domestics, etc. In colonial situations Asian women have frequently been forced into prostitution to sexually service the white male invaders, whether in the form of armies of occupation or employees and guests of multinational corporations. How then, in view of all this, can it be argued that black male dominance exists in the same forms as white male dominance? Systems of slavery, colonialism, and imperialism have systematically denied positions in the white male hierarchy to black men and have used specific forms of terror to oppress them.

Black family structures have been seen as pathological by the state and are in the process of being constructed as pathological within white feminist theory. Here, ironically, the Western nuclear family structure and related ideologies of "romantic love" formed under capitalism are seen as more "progressive" than black family structures. An unquestioned commonsense racism constructs Asian girls and women as having absolutely no freedom, whereas English girls are thought to be in a more "liberated" society and culture. However, one Asian schoolgirl points out:

> Where is the freedom in going to a disco, frightened in case no boy fancies you, or no one asks you to dance, or your friends are walked home with boys and you have to walk home in the dark alone? (Parmar and Mirza 1981)

The media's "horror stories" about Asian girls and arranged marriages bear very little relation to their experience. The "feminist" version of this ideology presents Asian women as being in need of liberation, not in terms of their own herstory and needs, but *into* the "progressive" social mores and customs of the metropolitan West. The actual struggles that Asian women are involved in are ignored in favor of applying theories from the point of view of a more "advanced," more "progressive" outside observer. In fact . . . it is very easy for this ideology to be taken up and used by the state in furthering their racist and sexist practices. The way in which the issue of arranged marriages has been used by the government to legitimate increased restrictions on immigration from the subcontinent is one example of this process.

Too often concepts of historical progress are invoked by the Left and feminists alike, to create a shading scale of "civilized liberties." When barbarous sexual practices are to be described, the "Third World" is placed on display and compared to the "First World," which is seen as more "enlightened" or "progressive." The metropolitan centers of the West define the questions to be asked of other social systems and, at the same time, provide the measure against which all "foreign" practices are gauged. In a peculiar combination of Marxism and feminism, capitalism becomes the vehicle for reforms that allow for progress toward the emancipation of women. The "Third World," on the other hand, is viewed as retaining precapitalist forms expressed at the cultural level by traditions which are more oppressive to women. For example, in an article comparing socialist societies, Maxine Molyneux falls straight into this trap of "Third Worldism" as "backwardness."

> A second major problem facing Third World postrevolutionary states is the weight of conservative ideologies and practices; this is often subsumed in official literature under the categories of "traditionalism" or "feudal residues." The impact and nature of "traditionalism" is subject to considerable variation between countries but where it retains any force it may constitute an obstacle to economic and social development which has to be overcome in the formation of a new society. In some societies customary practices tend to bear especially heavily on women. Institutions such as polygyny, the brideprice, child marriages, seclusion, and forms of mutilation such as footbinding or female "circumcision" are woven into the very fabric of precapitalist societies. They often survive in Third World countries long after they have been made illegal and despite the overall changes that have occurred. (Molyneux 1982, 3)

Maxine Molyneux sees "systems of inheritance and arranged marriages" as being one of the central ways "by which forms of precapitalist property and social relations are maintained."

One immediate problem with this approach is that it is extraordinarily general. The level of generality applied to the "Third World" would be dismissed as too vague to be informative if applied to Western industrialized nations. However, Molyneux implies that since "Third World" women are outside of capitalist relations of production, entering capitalist relations is, necessarily, an emancipating move.

> There can be little doubt that on balance the position of women within imperialist, i.e., advanced capitalist societies is, for all its limitations, more advanced than in the less developed capitalist and noncapitalist societies. In this sense the changes brought by imperialism to Third World societies may, in some circumstances, have been historically progressive. (Molyneux 1981, 4)

This view of imperialism will be addressed in more detail later in the chapter. At this point we wish to indicate that the use of such theories reinforces the view that when black women enter Britain they are moving into a more liberated or enlightened or emancipated society than the one from which they have come. Nancy Foner saw the embodiment of West Indian women's increased freedom and liberation in Britain in the fact that they learned to drive cars! Different herstories, different struggles of black women against systems that oppress them are buried beneath Eurocentric conceptions of their position. Black family structures are seen as being produced by less advanced economic systems and their extended kinship networks are assumed to be more oppressive to women. The model of the white nuclear family, which rarely applies to black women's situation, is the measure by which they are pathologized and stands as a more progressive structure than the one in which they live.

It can be seen from this brief discussion of the use of the concept "the family" that the terms "patriarchy" and "reproduction" also become more complex in their application. It bears repetition that black men have not held the same patriarchal positions of power that the white males have established. Michèle Barrett argues that the term "patriarchy" has lost all analytic or explanatory power and has been reduced to a synonym for male dominance. She tries therefore to limit its use to a specific type of male dominance that could be located historically.

> I would not . . . want to argue that the concept of patriarchy should be jettisoned. I would favor retaining it for use in contexts where male domination is expressed through the power of the father over women and over younger men. . . . Hence I would argue for a more precise and specific use of the concept of patriarchy, rather than one which expands it to cover all expressions of male domination and thereby attempts to construe a descriptive term as a systematic explanatory theory. (Barrett 1980)

Barrett is not thinking of capitalist social organization. But if we try to apply this more "classic" and limited definition of patriarchy to the slave systems of the Americas and the Caribbean, we find that even this refined use of the concept cannot adequately account for the fact that both slaves and manumitted males did not have this type of patriarchal power. Alternatively, if we take patriarchy and apply it to various colonial situations it is equally unsatisfactory because it is unable to explain why black males have not enjoyed the benefits of white patriarchy. There are very obvious power structures in both colonial and slave social formations and they are predominantly patriarchal. However, the historically specific forms of racism force us to modify or alter the application of the term "patriarchy" to black men. Black women have been dominated "patriarchally" in different ways by men of different "colors."

In questioning the application of the concepts of "the family" and "patriarchy" we also need to problematize the use of the concept of "reproduction." In using this concept in relation to the domestic labor of black women we find that in spite of its apparent simplicity it must be dismantled. What does the concept of reproduction mean in a situation where black women have done domestic labor outside of their own homes in the servicing of white families? In this example they lie outside of the industrial wage relation but in a situation where they are providing for the reproduction of black labor in their own domestic sphere, simultaneously ensuring the reproduction of white labor power in the "white" household. The concept, in fact, is unable to explain exactly what the relations are that need to be revealed. What needs to be understood is, first, precisely how the black woman's role in a rural, industrial or domestic labor force affects the construction of ideologies of black female sexuality which are different from, and often constructed in opposition to, white female sexuality; and second, how this role relates to the black woman's struggle for control over her own sexuality.

If we examine the recent herstory of women in postwar Britain we can see the ways in which the inclusion of black women creates problems for hasty generalization. In pointing to the contradiction between "homemaking as a career" and the campaign to recruit women into the labor force during postwar reconstruction, Elizabeth Wilson fails to perceive migration of black women to Britain as the solution to these contradictory needs. The Economic Survey for 1947 is cited as an example of the ways in which women were seen to form "the only large reserve of labor left"; yet, as we know, there was a rather large pool of labor in the colonies that had been mobilized previously to fight in World War II. The industries that the survey listed as in dire need of labor included those that were filled by both male and female black workers, though Elizabeth Wilson does not differentiate them.

> The survey gave a list of the industries and services where labor was most urgently required. The boot and shoe industry, clothing, textiles, iron and steel, all required female workers, as did hospitals, domestic service, transport, and the women's land army. There was also a shortage of shorthand typists, and a dire shortage of nurses and midwives. (Wilson 1980, 43–44)

This tells us nothing about why black women were recruited more heavily into some of these areas than others; perhaps we are given a clue when the author goes on to point out that women were welcomed into the labor force in a "circumscribed way," as temporary workers at a period of crisis, as part-time workers, and as not disturbing the traditional division of labor in industry along sex lines. The survey reflected the view which was still dominant, that married women would not naturally wish to work (Wilson 1980, 43–44).

Not all black women were subject to this process: Afro-Caribbean women, for example, were encouraged and chose to come to Britain precisely to work. Ideologically they were seen as "naturally" suitable for the lowest paid, most menial jobs. Elizabeth Wilson goes on to explain that "work and marriage were still understood as alternatives . . . two kinds of women . . . a wife and a mother or a single career woman." Yet black women bridged this division. They were viewed simultaneously as workers and as wives and mothers. Elizabeth Wilson stresses that the postwar debate over the entry of women into the labor force occurred within the parameters of the question of possible effects on family life. She argues that "wives and mothers were granted entry into paid work only so long as this did not harm the family." Yet women from Britain's reserve army of labor in the colonies were recruited into the labor force far beyond any such considerations. Rather than a concern to protect or preserve the black family in Britain, the state reproduced commonsense notions of its inherent pathology: black women were seen to fail as mothers precisely because of their position as workers.

One important struggle, rooted in these different ideological mechanisms, which determine racially differentiated representations of gender, has been the black woman's battle to gain control over her own sexuality in the face of racist experimentation with the contraceptive Depo-Provera and enforced sterilizations (OWAAD 1979).

It is not just our herstory before we came to Britain that has been ignored by white feminists; our experiences and struggles here have also been ignored. These struggles and experiences, because they have been structured by racism, have been different from those of white women. Black feminists decry the non-recognition of the specificities of black women's sexuality and femininity, both in the ways these are constructed and also as they are addressed through practices which oppress black women in a gender-specific but nonetheless racist way. This nonrecognition is typified by a very interesting article on women in Third World manufacturing by Diane Elson and Ruth Pearson. In analyzing the employment of Third World women in world market factories they quote from an investment brochure designed to attract foreign firms:

> The manual dexterity of the oriental female is famous the world over. Her hands are small and she works fast with extreme care. Who, therefore, could be better qualified by *nature and inheritance* to contribute to the efficiency of a bench-assembly production line than the oriental girl? (Elson and Pearson 1981, 93)

The authors, however, analyze only the naturalization of gender and ignore the specificity signaled by the inclusion of the adjective "oriental," as if it didn't matter. The fact that the sexuality of the "oriental" woman is being differentiated is not commented upon and remains implicit rather than explicit as in the following remarks.

> It is in the context of the subordination of women as a gender that we must analyze the supposed docility, subservience and consequent suitability for tedious, monotonous work of young women in the Third World. (Elson and Pearson 1981, 93)

In concentrating an analysis upon gender only, Elson and Pearson do not see the relation between the situation they are examining in the periphery and the women who have migrated to the metropole. This last description is part of the commonsense racism that we have described as being applied to Asian women in Britain to channel them into "tedious, monotonous work." Elson and Pearson discuss this ascription of docility and passivity and compare it to Frantz Fanon's analysis of colonized people, without putting together the ways in which the women who are their objects of study have been oppressed not by gender subordination alone but also by colonization. The "oriental" sexuality referred to in the advertising brochure is one of many constructions of exotic sexual dexterity promised to Western male tourists to South East Asia. This ideology of "Eastern promise" links the material practice of the move from the bench—making microchips—to the bed, in which multinational corporate executives are serviced by prostitutes. This transition is described by Elson and Pearson but not understood as a process that illustrates an example of racially demarcated patriarchal power.

> If a woman loses her job in a world market factory after she has reshaped her life on the basis of a wage income, the only way she may have of surviving is by selling her body. There are reports from South Korea, for instance, that many former electronics workers have no alternative but to become prostitutes. . . . A growing market for such services is provided by the way in which the tourist industry has developed, especially in South East Asia. (Elson and Pearson 1981, 95)

The photographs accompanying the article are of anonymous black women. This anonymity and the tendency to generalize into meaninglessness the oppression of an amorphous category called "Third World women" are symptomatic of the ways in which the specificity of our experiences and oppression are subsumed under inapplicable concepts and theories. Black feminists in the United States have complained of the ignorance, in the white women's movement, of black women's lives.

> The force that allows white feminist authors to make no reference to racial identity in their books about "women" that are in actuality about white women is the same one that would compel any author writing exclusively on black women to refer explicitly to their racial identity. That force is racism. . . . It is the dominant race that can make it seem that their experience is representative. (hooks 1981, 138)

In Britain too it is as if we don't exist.

There is a growing body of black feminist criticism of white feminist theory and practice, for its incipient racism and lack of relevance to black women's lives. The dialogues that have been attempted have concentrated more upon visible, empirical differences that affect black and white women's lives than upon developing a feminist theoretical approach that would enable a feminist understanding of the basis of these differences. The accusation that racism in the women's movement acted so as to exclude the participation of black women has led to an explosion of debate in the United States.

> . . . from a black female perspective, if white women are denying the existence of black women, writing "feminist" scholarship as if black women are not a part of the collective group of American women, or discriminating against black women, then it matters less that North America was colonized by white patriarchal men who institutionalized a racially imperialist social order than that white women who purport to be feminists support and actively perpetuate anti-black racism. (hooks 1981, 123–24)

What little reaction there has been in Britain has been more akin to lighting a damp squib than an explosion. U.S. black feminist criticism has no more been listened to than indigenous black feminist criticism. Yet, bell hooks's powerful critique has considerable relevance to British feminists. White women in the British WLM are extraordinarily reluctant to see themselves in the situations of being oppressors, as they feel that this will be at the expense of concentrating upon being oppressed. Consequently the involvement of British women in imperialism and colonialism is repressed and the benefits that they—as whites—gained from the oppression of black people are ignored. Forms of imperialism are simply identified as aspects of an all-embracing patriarchy rather than as sets of social relations in which white women hold positions of power by virtue of their "race."

> Had feminists chosen to make explicit comparisons between . . . the status of black women and white women, it would have been more than obvious that the two groups do not share an identical oppression. It would have been obvious that similarities between the status of women under patriarchy and that of any slave or colonized person do not necessarily exist in a society that is both racially and sexually imperialistic. In such a society, the woman who is seen as inferior because of her sex can also be seen as superior because of her race, even in relationship to men of another race. (hooks 1981, 141)

The benefits of a white skin did not just apply to a handful of cotton, tea, or sugar plantation mistresses; all women in Britain benefited—in varying degrees—from the economic exploitation of the colonies. The proimperialist attitudes of many nineteenth- and early twentieth-century feminists and suffragists have yet to be acknowledged for their racist implications. However, apart from this herstorical work, the exploration of contemporary racism within the white feminist movement in Britain has yet to begin.

Feminist theory in Britain is almost wholly Eurocentric and when it is not ignoring the experience of black women "at home," it is trundling "Third World women" onto the stage only to perform as victims of "barbarous," "primitive" practices in "barbarous," "primitive" societies.

It should be noted that much feminist work suffers from the assumption that it is only through the development of a Western-style industrial capitalism and the resultant entry of women into waged labor that the potential for the liberation of women can increase. For example, foot-binding, clitoridectomy, female "circumcision" and other forms of mutilation of the female body have been described as "feudal residues," existing in economically "backward" or "underdeveloped" nations (i.e., not the industrialized West). Arranged marriages, polygamy, and these forms of mutilation are linked in reductionist ways to a lack of technological development.

However, theories of "feudal residues" or of "traditionalism" cannot explain the appearance of female "circumcision" and clitoridectomy in the United States at the same moment as the growth and expansion of industrial capital. Between the establishment of industrial capitalism and the transformation to monopoly capitalism, the United States, under the influence of English biological science, saw the control of medical practice shift from the hands of women into the hands of men. This is normally regarded as a "progressive" technological advance, though this newly established medical science was founded on the control and manipulation of the female body. This was the period in which links were formed between hysteria and hysterectomy in the rationalization of the "psychology of the ovary."

> In the second half of the [nineteenth] century fumbling experiments with the female interior gave way to the more decisive technique of surgery—aimed increasingly at the control of female personality disorders. . . . The last clitoridectomy we know of in the United States was performed in 1948 on a child of five, as a cure for masturbation.
>
> The most common form of surgical intervention in the female personality was ovariotomy, removal of the ovaries—or "female castration." In 1906 a leading gynecological surgeon estimated that there were 150,000 women in the United States who had lost their ovaries under the knife. Some doctors boasted that they had removed from fifteen hundred to two thousand ovaries apiece. . . . It should not be imagined that poor women were spared the gynecologist's exotic catalog of tortures simply because they couldn't pay. The pioneering work in gynecological surgery had been performed by Marion Sims on black female slaves he kept for the sole purpose of surgical experimentation. He operated on one of them thirty times in four years. (Ehrenreich and English 1979)

These operations are hardly rituals left over from a precapitalist mode of production. On the contrary, they have to be seen as part of the "technological" advance in what is now commonly regarded as the most "advanced" capitalist economy in the world. Both in the United States and in Britain, black women still have a "role"—as in the use of

Depo-Provera on them—in medical experimentation. Outside the metropoles, black women are at the mercy of the multinational drug companies, whose quest for profit is second only to the cause of "advancing" Western science and medical knowledge.

The herstory of black women is interwoven with that of white women but this does not mean they are the same story. Nor do we need white feminists to write our herstory for us; we can and are doing that for ourselves. However, when they write their herstory and call it the story of women but ignore our lives and deny their relation to us, that is the moment in which they are acting within the relations of racism and writing history.

CONSTRUCTING ALTERNATIVES

It should be an imperative for feminist herstory and theory to avoid reproducing the structural inequalities that exist between the "metropoles" and the "peripheries," and within the "metropoles" between black and white women, in the form of inappropriate polarizations between the "First" and "Third World," developed/underdeveloped, or advanced/backward. We have already argued that the generalizations made about women's lives across societies in the African and Asian continents would be thought intolerable if applied to the lives of white women in Europe or North America. These are some of the reasons why concepts which allow for specificity, while at the same time providing cross-cultural reference points—not based in assumptions of inferiority—are urgently needed in feminist work. The work of Gayle Rubin and her use of discrete "sex/gender systems" appears to provide such a potential, particularly in the possibility of applying the concept within as well as between societies. With regard to the problems with the concept of patriarchy discussed above, she has made the following assessment:

> The term "patriarchy" was introduced to distinguish the forces maintaining sexism from other social forces, such as capitalism. But the use of "patriarchy" obscures other distinctions. (Rubin 1976, 167)

In arguing for an alternative formulation Gayle Rubin stresses the importance of maintaining

> a distinction between the human capacity and necessity to create a sexual world, and the empirically oppressive ways in which sexual worlds have been organized. Patriarchy subsumes both meanings into the same term. Sex/gender system, on the other hand, is a neutral term which refers to the domain and indicates that oppression is not inevitable in that domain, but is the product of the specific social relations which organize it. (Rubin 1976, 168)

This concept of sex/gender systems offers the opportunity to be historically and culturally specific but also points to the position of relative autonomy of the sexual realm. It enables the subordination of women to be seen as a "product of the relationships by which sex and gender are organized and produced" (Rubin 1976, 177). Thus, in order to account for the development of specific forms of sex/gender systems, reference must be made not only to the mode of production but also to the complex totality of specific social formations within which each system develops. Gayle Rubin argues that kinship relations are visible, empirical forms of sex/gender systems. Kinship relations here is not limited to biological relatives but is rather a "system of categories and statuses which often contradict actual genetic relationships."

What are commonly referred to as "arranged marriages" can, then, be viewed as the way in which a particular sex/gender system organizes the "exchange of women." Similarly, transformations of sex/gender systems brought about by colonial oppression, and the changes in kinship patterns that result from migration, must be assessed on their own terms, not just in comparative relation to other sex/gender systems. In this way patterns of subordination of women can be understood historically, rather than dismissed as the inevitable product of pathological family structures.

At this point we can begin to make concrete the black feminist plea to white feminists to begin with our different herstories. Contact with white societies has not generally led to a more "progressive" change in African and Asian sex/gender systems. Colonialism attempted to destroy kinship patterns that were not modeled on nuclear family structures, disrupting, in the process, female organizations that were based upon kinship systems that allowed more power and autonomy to women than those of the colonizing nation. Events that occurred in the Calabar and Owerri provinces of Southern Nigeria in the winter months of 1929 bear witness to this disruption and to the consequent weakening of women's position. As Judith Van Allen points out, these events are known in Western social science literature as the Aba Riots, a term which not only marginalizes the struggles themselves but which makes invisible the involvement of Igbo women. "Riots" implies unsystematic and mindless violence and is a perfect example of the constructions of history. The Igbo people on the other hand remember this conflict as Ogu Umuniwanyi (the "Women's War") (Van Allen 1976, 59).

> In November of 1929, thousands of Igbo women . . . converged on the Native Administration centers. . . . The women chanted, danced, sang songs of ridicule, and demanded the caps of office (the official insignia) of the Warrant Chiefs, the Igbo chosen from each village by the British to sit as members of the Native Court. At a few locations the women broke into prisons and released prisoners. Sixteen Native Courts were attacked, and most of these were broken up or burned. The "disturbed area" covered about 6,000 square miles and contained about two million people. It is not known how many women were involved, but the figure was in tens of thousands. On two occasions, British District Officers called in police and troops, who fired on the women and left a total of more than 50 dead and 50 wounded. No one on the other side was seriously injured. (Van Allen 1976, 60)

Judith Van Allen examines in detail the women's organizations that ensured and regulated women's political, economic, and religious roles in traditional Igbo society. Although their role was not equal to that of men they did have "a series of roles—despite the patrilineal organization of Igbo society" (Van Allen 1976, 59). Two of the associations that Judith Van Allen finds relevant were the *inyemedi,* or wives of a lineage, and the *umuada*—daughters of a lineage. Meetings of the *umuada* would "settle intralineage disputes among their "brothers" as well as disputes between their natal and marital lineages." Since these gatherings were held in rotation among the villages into which members had married, "they formed an important part of the communication network of Igbo women." *Inyemedi,* on the other hand, came together in village-wide gatherings called mikri, gatherings of women who were in common residence rather than from a common place of birth (*ogbo*).

> The mikri appears to have performed the major role in the daily self-rule among women and to have articulated women's interests as opposed to those of men. *Mikri* provided women with a forum in which to develop their political talents and with a means for protecting their interests as traders, farmers, wives and mothers. (Van Allen 1976, 69)

Men recognized the legitimacy of the decisions and rules of the *mikri*, which not only settled disputes among women but also imposed rules and sanctions that directly affected men's behavior. The *mikri* could impose fines for violations of their decisions, and if these were ignored, women would "sit on" an offender or go on strike.

> To "sit on" or "make war on" a man involved gathering at his compound at a previously agreed upon time, dancing, singing scurrilous songs detailing the women's grievances against him (and often insulting him along the way by calling his manhood into question), banging on his hut with pestles for pounding yams, and in extreme cases, tearing up his hut (which usually meant pulling the roof off). (Van Allen 1976, 61)

A strike, on the other hand, "might involve refusing to cook, to take care of small children or to have sexual relations with their husbands" (Van Allen 1976, 69).

British colonizers in Nigeria dismissed all traditional forms of social organization that they found as "organized anarchy," and promptly imposed a system of administration that ignored female political structures and denied Igbo women any means of representation, leave alone any decision-making or rule-instituting power. Coming from sex/gender systems of Britain in the 1920s, these colonial males could not conceive of the type of autonomy that Igbo women claimed. When the women demanded that they should serve on the Native Courts, be appointed to positions as District Officers, and further that "all-white men should go to their own country," they were scoffed at by the British who thought they acted under the influence of savage passions. Their demands were viewed as totally irrational. The war waged by Igbo women against the British was a concerted organized mobilization of their political traditions. The fruits of colonialism were the imposition of class and gender relations that resulted in the concentration of national, economic, and political power in the hands of a small, wealthy elite. We have quoted at length this example from the herstory of Igbo women in order to illustrate the ways in which an unquestioning application of liberal doses of Eurocentricity can completely distort and transform herstory into history. Colonialism was not limited to the imposition of economic, political, and religious systems. More subtly, though just as effectively, it sedimented racist and sexist norms into traditional sex/gender systems. Far from introducing more "progressive" or liberating sex/gender social relations, the colonizing powers as

> class societies tend to socialize the work of men and domesticate that of women. This creates the material and organizational foundations for denying that women are adults and allows the ruling classes to define them as wards of men. (Sacks 1975)

Karen Sacks, in her essay "Engels Revisited," examines the ways in which these class societies have domesticated the field of activity for women to the extent that "through their labor men are social adults; women are domestic wards" (Sacks 1975, 231). Although this work agrees with much white feminist theory, which has focused on the isolation of women within the nuclear family as a prime source of oppression in Western sex/gender systems, it does not necessarily follow that women living in kinship relations organized in different sex/gender systems are not oppressed. What it does mean is that analysis has to be specific and is not to be deduced from European systems. She goes on to explain that in India,

> in untouchable tenant-farming and village-service castes or classes, where women work today for village communities . . . they "have greater sexual freedom, power of divorce, authority to speak and witness in caste assemblies, authority over children, ability to dispose of their own belongings, rights to indemnity for wrongs done to them, rights to have disputes settled outside the domestic sphere, and representation in public rituals." In short, women who perform social labor have a higher status vis-à-vis men of their own class than do women who labor only in the domestic sphere or do no labor. (Sacks 1975, 233)

Unfortunately feminist research has neglected to examine the basis of its Eurocentric (and often racist) framework. In the words of Achola O. Pala:

> Like the educational systems inherited from the colonial days, the research industry has continued to use the African environment as a testing ground for ideas and hypotheses, the locus of which is to be found in Paris, London, New York or Amsterdam. (Pala 1977)

Throughout much of this work, what is thought to be important is decided on the basis of what happens to be politically significant in the metropoles, not on what is important to the women who are under observation. Thus, from her own experience, Achola Pala relates how the major concerns of women are totally neglected by the researcher.

> I have visited villages where, at a time when the village women are asking for better health facilities and lower infant mortality rates, they are presented with questionnaires on family planning. In some instances, when the women would like to have piped water in the village, they may be at the same time faced with a researcher interested in investigating power and powerlessness in the household. In yet another situation, when women are asking for access to agricultural credit, a researcher on the scene may be conducting a study on female circumcision. (Pala 1977, 10)

The noncomprehension of the struggles and concerns of the African women Pala talks about is indicative of the ways in which much Euro-American feminism has approached the lives of black women. It has attempted to force them into patterns that do not apply and in the process has labeled many of them deviant.

Another problem emerges from the frequently unqualified use of terms such as precapitalist" and "feudal" to denote differences between the point of view of the researcher and her object of study. What is being indicated are differences in the modes of production. This distinction is subsequently used to explain observable differences in the position of women. However, the deployment of the concept sex/gender system interrupts this "logical progression" and reveals that the articulation of relations of production to sex/gender systems is much more complex. "Precapitalist" and "feudal" are often redundant and non-explanatory categories that rest on underestimations of the scope and power of capitalist economic systems. Immanuel Wallerstein, for example, has argued that the sixteenth century saw the creation of

> a world-embracing commerce and a world-embracing market . . . the emergence of capitalism as the dominant mode of social organization of the economy . . . the only mode in the sense that, once established, other "modes of production" survived in function of how they fitted into a politico-socio framework deriving from capitalism. (Wallerstein 1974, 77)

Wallerstein continues to dismiss the idea that feudal and capitalist forms of social organization could coexist by stressing that

> The world economy has one form or another. Once it is capitalist, relationships that bear certain formal relationships to feudal relationships are necessarily redefined in terms of the governing principals of a capitalist system. (Wallerstein 1974, 92)

There are ways in which this economic penetration has transformed social organization to the detriment of women in particular. Work on sexual economics by Lisa Leghorn and Katherine Parker demonstrates that the monetary system and heavy taxation that European nations imposed on their colonies directly eroded the status of women.

> In many nations the impact of the sudden need for cash was more devastating than the steep taxes themselves. Only two mechanisms for acquiring cash existed—producing the new export crops and working for wages—both of which were made available only to men. Men were forced to leave their villages and farms to work in mines, plantations or factories, at extremely low wages. Women were often left doing their own as well as the men's work, while most of the men's wages went to taxes and to support themselves at the higher standard of living in urban areas. As men who remained on the farms were taught how to cash crop, most technological aid and education went only to them, and women were left maintaining the subsistence agricultural economy that sustained themselves and their children. In Africa women still do 70 percent of the agricultural work while almost all the agricultural aid has gone to men. (Leghorn and Parker 1981, 44)

We need to counteract the tendency to reduce sex oppression to a mere "reflex of economic forces" (Rubin 1976, 203), while at the same time recognizing that

> sexual systems cannot, in the final analysis, be understood in complete isolation. A full-bodied analysis of women in a single society, or throughout history, must take everything into account: the evolution of commodity forms in women, systems of land tenure, political arrangements, subsistence technology, etc. (Rubin 1976, 209)

We can begin to see how these elements come together to affect the lives of black women under colonial oppression in ways that transform the sex/gender systems in which they live but that are also shaped by the sex/gender system of the colonizers. If we examine changes in land distribution, we can see how capitalist notions of the private ownership of land (a primarily economic division) and ideas of male dominance (from the sex/gender system) work together against the colonized.

> Another problem affecting women's agricultural work is that as land ownership shifts from the collective "land-use rights" of traditional village life, in which women shared in the distribution of land, to the European concept of private ownership, it is usually only the men who have the necessary cash to pay for it (by virtue of their cash-cropping income). In addition, some men traditionally "owned" the land, while women "owned" the crops, as in the Cameroons in West Africa. As land becomes increasingly scarce, men begin to rent and sell "their" land, leaving women with no recourse but to pay for land or stop their agricultural work. (Leghorn and Parker 1981, 45)

It is impossible to argue that colonialism left precapitalist or feudal forms of organization untouched. If we look at the West Indies we can see that patterns of migration, for both men and women, have followed the dictates of capital.

When men migrated from the islands for work in plantations or building the Panama Canal, women migrated from rural to urban areas. Both have migrated to labor in the "core" capitalist nations. Domestic, marginal, or temporary service work has sometimes been viewed as a great "opportunity" for West Indian women to transform their lives. But as Shirley-Ann Hussein has shown,

> Take the case of the domestic workers. A development institution should be involved in more than placing these women in domestic jobs as this makes no dent in the society. It merely rearranges the same order. Domestic labor will have to be done away with in any serious attempt at social and economic reorganization. (Hussein 1981, 29)

If, however, imperialism and colonialism have ensured the existence of a world market it still remains necessary to explain how it is in the interests of capitalism to maintain social relations of production that are noncapitalist—that is, forms that could not be described as feudal because that means precapitalist, but which are also not organized around the wage relation. If we return to the example of changes in ownership of land and in agricultural production, outlined above, it can be argued that

> the agricultural division of labor in the periphery—with male semi-proletarians and female agriculturalists—contributes to the maintenance of a low value of labor power for peripheral capital accumulation through the production of subsistence foodstuffs by the noncapitalist mode of production for the reproduction and maintenance of the labor force. (Deere 1979, 143)

In other words, the work that the women do is a force that helps to keep wages low. To relegate "women of color" in the periphery to the position of being the victims of feudal relations is to aid in the masking of colonial relations of oppression. These relations of imperialism should not be denied. Truly feminist herstory should be able to acknowledge that:

> Women's economic participation in the periphery of the world capitalist system, just as within center economies, has been conditioned by the requirements of capital accumulation . . . (but) the economic participation of women in the Third World differs significantly from women's economic participation within the center of the world capitalist system. (Deere 1979, 143)

Black women have been at the forefront of rebellions against land seizures and struggle over the rights of access to land in Africa, Latin America, and the Caribbean.

Adequate herstories of their roles in many of these uprisings remain to be written. The role of West Indian women in the rebellions preceding and during the disturbances in Jamaica in 1938, for example, though known to be significant, has still not been thoroughly described. White feminist herstorians are therefore mistaken when they portray black women as passive recipients of colonial oppression. As Gail Omvedt has shown in her book *We Will Smash This Prison* (Omvedt 1980), women in India have a long and complex herstory of fighting oppression both in and out of the wage relation. It is clear that many women coming from India to Britain have a shared herstory of struggle, whether in rural areas as agricultural laborers or in urban districts as municipal employees. The organized struggles of Asian women in Britain need to be viewed in the light of this herstory. Their industrial battles and struggles against immigration policy and practice articulate the triple oppression of race, gender, and class that have been present since the dawn of imperialist domination.

In concentrating solely upon the isolated position of white women in the Western nuclear family structure, feminist theory has necessarily neglected the very strong female support networks that exist in many black sex/gender systems. These have often been transformed by the march of technological "progress" intended to relieve black women from aspects of their labor.

> Throughout Africa, the digging of village wells has saved women enormous amounts of time which they formerly spent trekking long distances to obtain water. But it has often simultaneously destroyed their only chance to get together and share information and experiences. Technological advances such as household appliances do not free women from domestic drudgery in any society. (Leghorn and Parker 1981, 55)

Leghorn and Parker, in *Women's Worth,* attempt to create new categories to describe, in general terms, the diversity of male power across societies. While they warn against the rigid application of these categories—few countries fit exactly the category applied to them—the work does represent an attempt to move away from Euro-American racist assumptions of superiority, whether political, cultural, or economic. The three classifications they introduce are "minimal," "token," and "negotiating power" societies. Interestingly, from the black women's point of view, the most salient factor in the categorization of a country has

> usually been that of women's networks, because it is the existence, building or dissolution of these networks that determines women's status and potential for change in all areas of their lives. (Leghorn and Parker 1981, 60)

These categories cut through the usual divisions of First/Third World, advanced/dependent, and industrial/nonindustrial in an attempt to find a mechanism that would "free" thinking from these definitions. Space will not allow for a critical assessment of all three categories, but it can be said that their application of "negotiating power" does recognize as important the "traditional" women's organizations to be found in West Africa and described above in relation to the Igbo. Leghorn and Parker are careful to stress that "negotiating power" is limited to the possibilities of negotiating; it is not an absolute category of power that is held *over* men by women. The two examples in their book of societies where women hold this negotiating position are the Ewe, in West Africa, and the Iroquois. Both of course, are also examples where contact with the whites has been for the worse. Many of the Ewe female institutions disintegrated under colonialism while the institutions that afforded Iroquois women power were destroyed by European intrusion. In contrast to feminist work that focuses upon the lack of technology and household mechanical aids in the lives of these women, Leghorn and Parker concentrate upon the aspects of labor that bring women together. Of the Ewe they note:

> Women often work together in their own fields, or as family members preparing meals together, village women meeting at the stream to do the wash, or family, friends and neighbors walking five to fifteen miles a day to market together, sitting near each other in the market, and setting the day's prices together. They share child care, news, and looking after each other's market stalls. In addition to making the time more pleasant, this shared work enables women to share information and in fact serves as an integral and vital part of the village communications system. Consequently, they have a tremendous sense of solidarity when it comes to working in their collective interest. (Leghorn and Parker 1981, 88)

It is important not to romanticize the existence of such female support networks, but they do provide a startling contrast to the isolated position of women in the Euro-American nuclear family structure.

In Britain, strong female support networks continue in both West Indian and Asian sex/gender systems, though these are ignored by sociological studies of migrant black women. This is not to say that these systems remain unchanged with migration. New circumstances require adaptation and new survival strategies have to be found.

> Even child care in a metropolitan area is a big problem. If you live in a village in an extended family, you know that if your child's outside somewhere, someone will be looking out for her. If your child is out on the street and your neighbor down the road sees your child in some mess, that woman is going to take responsibility of dealing with that child. But in Brooklyn or in London, you're stuck in that apartment. You're there with that kid, you can't expect that child to be out on the street and be taken care of. You know the day care situation is lousy, you're not in that extended family, so you have a big problem on your hands. So when they talk about the reduction of housework, we know by now that that's a lie. (Prescod-Roberts and Steele 1980, 28)

However, the transformations that occur are not merely adaptive, and neither is the black family destroyed in the process of change. Female networks mean that black women are key figures in the development of survival strategies, both in the past through periods of slavery and colonialism, and now, facing a racist and authoritarian state.

> There is considerable evidence that women—and families—do not . . . simply accept the isolation, loss of status, and cultural devaluation involved in the migration. Networks are reformed, if need be with non-kin or on the basis of an extended definition of kinship, by strong, active, and resourceful women. . . . Cultures of resistance are not simple adaptive mechanisms; they embody important alternative ways of organizing production and reproduction and value systems critical of the oppressor. Recognition of the special position of families in these cultures and social structures can lead to new forms of struggle, new goals. (Caulfield 1974, 81, 84)

In arguing that feminism must take account of the lives, herstories, and experiences of black women we are not advocating that teams of white feminists should descend upon Brixton, Southall, Bristol, or Liverpool to take black women as objects of study in modes of resistance. We don't need that kind of intrusion on top of all the other information-gathering forces that the state has mobilized in the interest of "race relations." White women have been used against black women in this way before and feminists must learn from history. After the Igbo riots described above, two women anthropologists were sent by the British to "study the causes of the riot and to uncover the organizational base that permitted such spontaneity and solidarity among the women" (Caulfield 1974, 84). The WLM, however, does need to listen to the work of black feminists and to take account of autonomous organizations like OWAAD (Organization of Women of Asian and African Descent) who are helping to articulate the ways in which we are oppressed as black women.

In addition to this, it is very important that white women in the women's movement examine the ways in which racism excludes many black women and prevents them from unconditionally aligning themselves with white women. Instead of taking black women as the objects of their research, white feminist researchers should try to uncover the gender-specific mechanisms of racism among white women. This more than any other factor disrupts the recognition of common interests of sisterhood.

In *Finding a Voice* by Amrit Wilson, Asian women describe many instances of racial oppression at work from white women. Asian women

> are paid low salaries and everything is worse for them, they have to face the insults of supervisors. These supervisors are all English women. The trouble is that in Britain our women are expected to behave like servants and we are not used to behaving like servants and we can't. But if we behave normally . . . the supervisors start shouting and harassing us. . . . They complain about us Indians to the manager. (Wilson 1978, 122)

Black women do not want to be grafted onto "feminism" in a tokenistic manner as colorful diversions to "real" problems. Feminism has to be transformed if it is to address us. Neither do we wish our words to be misused in generalities as if what each one of us utters represents the total experience of all black women. Audre Lorde's address to Mary Daly is perhaps the best conclusion.

> I ask that you be aware of how this serves the destructive forces of racism and separation between women—the assumption that the herstory and myth of white women is the legitimate and sole herstory and myth of all women to call for power and background, and that nonwhite women and our herstories are noteworthy only as decorations, or examples of female victimization. I ask that you be aware of the effect that this dismissal has upon the community of black women, and how it devalues your own words. . . . When patriarchy dismisses us, it encourages our murders. When radical lesbian feminist theory dismisses us, it encourages its own demise. This dismissal stands as a real block to communication between us. This block makes it far easier to turn away from you completely than attempt to understand the thinking behind your choices. Should the next step be war between us, or separation? Assimilation within a sole Western-European herstory is not acceptable. (Lorde 1981, 96)

In other words, of white feminists we must ask, what exactly do you mean when you say "we"?

14

The Hoechst Chemical Company and Boredom with the Economy

Frigga Haug

I have to force myself to read the financial pages of my daily paper. The laws governing what I find there are generally familiar to me; at the same time I have absolutely no power to intervene in their workings, and they seem utterly removed from my immediate experience. The financial pages bore me. As a Marxist I know I must take an interest in the economy. So every day I force myself and read: *No increase in activity at Volkswagen. Klockner expects to be in balance. Hoechst announces an unchanged dividend for 1982.* Somehow it is simultaneously soothing and worrying. Crisis in stagnation. The laws of profit, class issues, exploitation, and, behind it all, increasing unemployment. The sheer magnitude of the phenomenon I am confronted with gives me a bad conscience for not devoting more time to studying the financial pages, and so I switch instead to the local news. *A woman leaps into the backyard from the fourth floor.* I can understand her despair. *An oil sheik has the interior of his private plane fitted out in gold; even the bathroom fittings are in twenty-four-carat gold.* This too can count on my interest. I too have a bathroom. I can assess and condemn this superfluous luxury in gold, in a plane too, and at the same time I am aware that such practices are counterproductive exceptions to the system. Production for its own sake, not for the sake of the consumption of luxury goods, is what determines the laws of capital.

I make myself return to the financial section and once again I read about capitalist normality, not its excesses. *Worldwide turnover at Hoechst rises by 15 percent to 34.4 thousand million.* That too is beyond the grasp of my imagination. I notice that I compulsively translate events in the economy into the terms of my own little household. To appropriate the laws of society as a whole means reinterpreting them in terms of the rules governing my own private life. And the other way around too. This works up to a point. Money is needed to acquire goods; use-values are created; goods are consumed; there is a division of labor. But the way in which people produce their lives, divided up into classes and for the sake of surplus-value, is not what determines the laws of the household and hence daily life. Conversely, looking after children, the form of the family and women's subordination to men are not issues that can be described in the language of exploitation, capitalist domination, and class struggle. Thus we find ourselves in the paradoxical situation that from the standpoint of everyday life the crucial questions of the laws governing society are incomprehensible and therefore boring, while the vital problems of everyday life are irrelevant from the standpoint of class struggle and therefore of radical left politics.

And yet there must be a connection between large-scale processes and the way in which the mass of the people live their ordinary lives. I laboriously force my way through the jungle of figures in the financial pages. The incomprehensible rate of growth at Hoechst, I read, is due to an above-average performance in the pharmaceutical division, which grew by 20.9 percent. The fiber division showed even stronger growth with an increase of 31.6 percent. My interest is aroused by references to particular products, which may be a matter of indifference to the manufacturers. Why did pharmaceutical production rise so dramatically? And who needs the increased quantities of fiber? How do people experience these articles? And how do they experience the system as a whole? The concepts I have derived from my study of political economy provide little guidance. *Class; class struggle; work, indifferent; forces of production; relations of production; exploitation and surplus-value*—they do not really enable me to work out how to grasp these structures. Daily life cannot simply be inferred from the laws of capital, anymore than the laws of profit can be said to have a direct impact on domestic life in the family. And what can be said of everyone's daily life, namely that it cannot be explained by the laws that govern large-scale production, is even more valid when applied to women's issues. The oppression of women is older than capitalism. The home, which tends to determine women's lives, is not directly explicable by the laws of capital. The responsibility for husband and children, the physical tasks—and these are tasks of emotional labor involved in looking after relatives—conflict with the logic of wage labor and profit-making. Love and caring are incompatible with competition and a business mentality.

This brings us to a second paradox which I should like to characterize in the following—simplified—way. Women's oppression is clearly related to the spheres of activity to which women are tied and which are by definition antagonistic to the laws of capital. That means not only that Marxism and the theory of the emancipation of the workers fail to explain this oppression, but that those aspects of a woman's life that constitute her oppression are represented by Marxism as features of liberation. Thus maternal love, the gratification of needs independently of achievement, love, care, domesticity— all these are socialist and even communist aims and yet at the same time they are the fetters in which women live today. In the labor movement, socialism was for a long time depicted as a woman. And even today women at home are given the task of redeeming men from the alien domination they encounter outside the home. (Without devoting even a fleeting thought to the oppression of women, Andre Gorz and Alain Touraine, among others, celebrate the women's movement as a liberation movement for men because it could bring domestic values into the world of men. "The task will not be to liberate women from household chores, but to achieve recognition outside the home for their non-economic rationality" (Gorz 1980, 78). "Thanks to the women's movement we men have rediscovered our right to feelings and relationships with children" (Touraine, quoted by Gorz 1980, 79).

By way of summary I would claim that boredom with the economy stems from our failure to take the trouble to study the ways in which people experience the structures described in the critique of political economy in their daily lives. And that is a question of the way in which individuals are socialized to internalize those structures and how they subjectively appropriate and transform them.

We perceive the various dimensions of life—love and work, the private and the public, the home and the economy—as separate spheres. We have our ideas and feelings about each of these spheres in isolation, in accordance with the division of labor, and yet we live out these different divisions within a coherent life. As far as women are concerned, this means that we live in almost total ignorance of the connections between capitalism and women's oppression. At most we wax indignant about unequal wages and the loss of welfare benefits, and even more indignant about the abortion laws and divorce costs. A further consequence is that we are unable to say how the entire system reproduces itself, thanks in part to the oppression of women, what action women could take to bring about their own emancipation, or even what future to predict for a labor movement that ignores women's issues.

COLLECTIVE EMPIRICISM AS MEMORY-WORK

We observe, therefore, not only that women are underrepresented in science and culture, in the government and the economy, but also that women's experience has made scarcely any inroads into theory—into the founding concepts of Marxism, for example. And difficult as it is to understand that a system based on competition, imperialism, exploitation, and war can rely on the support of its citizens, it is no easier to comprehend why women do not take up arms against a structure in which they are constantly placed in an inferior position to men, as second-class beings (see Mouffe 1982 on this point). This leads me to pose two questions. First, how are these deficiencies at the level of theory to be made good, that is to say, how can Marxism be expanded to include feminism? And second, how can women learn to intervene in their own socialization? In other words, I am asking about a practical theory that seeks to understand women's experience from the point of view of changing it.

The absence of women from all relevant social spheres of activity and the premonition that the situation in the realm of theory was not significantly different led the women's movement to resolve to go in for a politics of consciousness-raising. The personal is political—this slogan was for many women a challenge to discuss their day-to-day problems with each other in small groups. To do this would lead them out of their isolation into the sense of a collective experience. Of course, the mere exchange of personal experiences does not necessarily lead to greater understanding. Initially the recital of stories of oppression or violence does boost your self-confidence, but in the long run it saps your courage instead of making action easier. Consciousness-raising groups tend to break up after a relatively short life, or else they simply run out of steam. This is a common experience. As Brecht has said, experience does not necessarily lead to understanding, even though it is perfectly true that there is no understanding without experience (see Haug 1981).

The dilemma I have just sketched between a theory poor in experience and an experience bereft of theory leads me to propose a collective empirical project: memory-work (see the *Projekt Frauengrundstudium* [Project on the basic study of women's issues], 1980 and 1982). To discover how the lives of the majority are actually lived, we have to inspect them. One way is to write down stories—sketches of everyday life, experiences that could happen to anybody (see Haug 1980). To prevent a simple duplication of the everyday with all its prejudices and lack of theoretical insight, our task would be to *analyze these stories collectively*. In order to uncover the social construction, the mechanisms, the interconnections and significance of our actions and feelings, we must *proceed historically*. Our proposal, therefore, is to retain the strengths of the consciousness-raising groups, to make connections between the everyday and the large context, while avoiding the vices of ignoring the totality and losing ourselves in untheorized details. Our project is one of *collective memory-work,* with the emphasis on collective and memory and work. Its product would be a great and essential empirical undertaking that would be both new and enjoyable.

In this formulation the project is new, but its components have been discussed for some time. This makes it both easier and harder to implement. Precedents seem to be everywhere; at the same time, we shall be accused of crossing the borders between the various disciplines. These include the methodology of the social sciences, literature, the controversy about experience, about language and its importance, and about culture and ideology.

I shall attempt to clarify my own procedures, taking account of these controversial issues, but I do not confront them at length.

SUBJECT AND OBJECT

In the empirical social sciences, controversy has long raged about whether research into human beings does not rob them of their human specificity, the fact that they are acting subjects and not merely objects. Is it right to examine human beings as if they were insects? (See especially Adorno 1969 and Haug 1978.) Is it right to treat movements, qualities, and modes of behavior as if they were fixed things? At one end of the spectrum this has led to instructing interviewers to behave as unobtrusively as possible lest their own humanity obscure the object of investigation. At the other extreme the interview is used for educational purposes to ensure that the object under study is transformed in the process. At the heart of this disagreement about the right approach to the study of people and the right relationship between subject and object stands our view of human beings and what to do about them. Should we study their modes of behavior so that governments will be able to influence their actions better, or should we regard them as social beings who become conscious of their own actions and the obstacles that stand in their path in order to bring about change and reconstruct the world for more human goals?

My formulation reveals my own preference for upright people who stand erect and are not merely the victims of class and gender relations. This partisanship clearly affected my choice of empirical method. An approach that treats people as objects was unacceptable for us. It is obvious that the collective writing of stories as a method of finding out about life is an unambiguous invitation to conceive of research as a mode of self-activity. The researcher is identical with the object of research. This solution of the subject-object problem is almost too easy.

But making everyone a researcher is not so simple. The problems begin with the choice of theme. After all, "everyday" experience is a chaos, initially at least. Who should decide—above all in a collective what should be discussed? Questions about who has the monopoly on choosing topics for discussion raise further questions about the interests of the many. The problem is familiar to anyone who has ever taken part in a consciousness-raising group or even been forced to listen to long perorations at family reunions or on a train journey. Basically no one wants to hear what others have to say. We have heard it all before, and anyway it is not told in an interesting way. The speakers inflate their own importance and play down that of others. This universal gossip is unbearable. Even in consciousness-raising groups everyone sits waiting for her turn and would far rather talk than listen. Such justifiable complaints contain a number of practical hints about how to deal with such narratives. At issue here are the question of interest and the choice of topic.

My view of the matter is that the lack of interest in other people's stories is not just, or even principally, the result of a poor storytelling technique. It springs rather from the belief that what everyone does, experiences, or feels is basically of no importance for anyone else or, above all, for society as a whole. But since this everyday life is where society reproduces itself, an understanding of it would, or so I argue, modify each individual's attitude toward herself and to others. One would take oneself and others seriously. Questions about how social structures—such as the nature of wages, money, the growth of the textile industry, and so forth—are perceived, modified, and endured by me in my everyday life, and how others deal with the same structures, would transform us all, without our fully realizing it, into experts on our everyday life. We would cease to appear to each other as time-wasters or competitors eager to steal the show. We would become investigators with a common purpose, knowledgeable people who can supply the fragments that have been used to create the social totality and that now can be rebuilt by us. The fact that our individual experiences can come together into something shared changes our relationships with each other. The learning stance makes us impatient and eager to acquire further information and at the same time we become more tolerant toward the deficiencies of the storyteller's narrative. This holds good, I would maintain, for every topic that establishes a link between our daily experience and the larger social structures we find ourselves surrounded by. The question of which topic to single out for discussion can best be decided by the pressures individuals feel. They probably have most to say, and hence to contribute, where the pressure of suffering is greatest. And anyway, in the course of discussion the issues tend to shift, to lead on to others, open up new perspectives, and so forth.

If we decide collectively what is important to us, the group will be the guarantor from the outset that we shall not slide into sectarianism. The very consensus demonstrates that we are all concerned, that compromise is possible, that conflicting interests can be harmonized and that a process of investigation can be launched (for a detailed discussion see Haug 1983).

THE SOCIAL CONSTRUCTION OF SUBJECTIVE EXPERIENCE

It will be objected that it is an illusion to imagine that experiences can serve as the basis of knowledge. To rely on experience is to suppose, mistakenly, that individuals are in a position to make "objective" judgments about themselves. Whereas in reality they give a subjective interpretation of what has happened to them! So here the subject/object problem, which we have resolved so satisfactorily in the context of scientific research, reappears with renewed force. Objective validity must be denied to what has been experienced subjectively. The reason is that individuals twist and turn, reinterpret and falsify, repress and forget their experiences in pursuit of a construction of their personality to which the past has to be subordinated. Hence what they say about themselves and their manner of dealing with experience is of no account; it is colored subjectively.

Let us convert this criticism of "subjectivity" into the object of our research. How do people alter, falsify, and distort their everyday world, and why? The why is connected with identity. That is to say, people build the data of their lives in such a way that they can live with them in a more or less noncontradictory way. And where they cannot do so in fact, they do so in their minds or their memories. So what we can investigate is not "how it really was," but how individuals construct their identities, change themselves, reinterpret themselves and see what benefits they derive from so doing. In short, we can explore how they inscribe themselves in the existing structures.

The criticism of subjectivity gives wings to our efforts. After all, our aim had been not to identify the existing structures, but to see how they became what they are, to observe the way in which everyday life is analyzed in such a way that individuals reproduce society as a whole over and over again. The criticism has really turned into its opposite. It is actually essential to examine subjective memories if we wish to discover anything about the appropriation of objective structures. This is not to assume that these memories are wholly at the disposal of the individual, as the connotations of "subjective" might imply. On the contrary. How individuals perceive things, and whether they judge them to be well and good, beautiful or desirable, despicable and reprehensible—all that is the meat of the class struggle, as it is fought out from day to day in people's hearts and minds. Once we realize this we can look to the theory of ideology and culture for some theoretical assistance in our collective empirical enterprise. The individual's analyses of reality, which we have decoded as her or his way of appropriating the world and which we wish to track down in our everyday stories, move on the terrain of dominant cultural values and countercultural, subversive efforts to extract meaning and pleasure from life. Such analyses will end in compromises (on this point see Willis 1979 and *Projekt Ideologie-Theorie* [Project on Ideology and Theory] 1979). In order to provide a sort of theoretical framework, it is worthwhile to take account of habits, customs, rules, and norms, of what is expected and generally believed, of the moral expectations and semitheorized attitudes we entertain in our minds, and to treat them as seriously as the hopes which attach to a process of self-socialization, as opposed to molding by forces external to us. It will then turn out that our own actions, insofar as we can recall them, tend to lie to one side of social expectations and our own desires, that is to say, the problems are displaced. Investigating our own compromises also means discovering the unexplored possibilities of a different life and the areas where changes are necessary and possible.

Our collective research, then, has the ambitious goal of discovering how individuals insert themselves into existing structures. We must investigate how they construct themselves and partly modify the structures in the process; we shall see how they reproduce society, where the possibilities of change lie, where the fetters are most oppressive, and so forth.

LITERATURE OR WRITING—FIRST STEPS: LANGUAGE

Simply to write up experiences and memories changes a good deal. It is necessary to make a selection, set priorities, choose a suitable vocabulary, distance oneself appropriately, uncover similarities, posit a reader, and hence fill in necessary details and make connections between events, and so on. Above all, it is vital to make conscious what has been experienced, just as if it had already been made conscious before. That doesn't just require effort, it also calls for a quite different view of things, and, conversely, you suddenly discover in the course of writing all sorts of things that you hadn't realized you wanted to say and which now press in on you. In short, writing is a form of production, an activity that creates a new consciousness. Writing is also a source of pleasure, as can be seen when, after a long struggle, you suddenly find the right word, the one which expresses precisely what you wanted to say. Writing is a craft, a specialized skill which is part of the division of labor. Men of letters pursue it as an art.

Hence the third front on which the debate about telling stories is fought out is the front between writing and literature. When we call on women to write down their stories, are we not just following the fashion for "authentic" literature? I do not wish to intervene here in the debate about high and low art, about genius and everyday language (on this point see Manthey 1979). But I do find it necessary to draw attention to some of the undesirable side effects of such a division of labor in life and writing.

This brings us to the problems of analyzing stories. In the first place, there is the problem of inarticulateness. It appears in such stories as a verbal poverty, the inability to express oneself. Questions about what exactly happened, how someone felt, what triggered off an emotion—all come up against the same brick walls, the inability to communicate one's desires and inhibitions and hence to find a way through. I regard such inarticulateness as a real obstacle to emancipation and not just as a sign that a person is not a creative writer. If women are to emerge from the obscurity of prehistory and take their place in political life, this act requires them to be conscious about life, and that in turn means that their experiences have to be understood at the level of theory. They must therefore be conveyed in language. In this sense to delegate the power over language to the chosen few is an obstacle in the path of emancipation. One task of the collective, therefore, is to act as a "language school," but one which, unlike a real school, attempts to find words that will both describe experiences and also make action possible.

This holds good for the most common method of articulating memories: the cliche. The cliche can be described as a mode of heteronomous socialization in language. Unlike inarticulateness it is loquacious; it can reckon on a sympathetic hearing, while it effectively puts a stop to thought and understanding. "He gazed into her eyes"; "her heart gave a leap"; "the color drained from her cheeks"; "a sob rose to her throat"—it is significant that women's emotional world seems to have been colonized by cliches which, like corsets, produce the impression of the appropriate feeling and desire. The writer E. A. Rauter (1978) said of cliche that "it is like putting a plumstone in your mouth after someone else has spat it out, instead of a plum." In a sense cliches also condemn you to remain on the well-worn path of societal expectation. At all events they are an impediment to understanding. For example, during our research into the insertion of bodies into the scheme of dominant expectations, a woman wrote: "I realized that my long, curly hair was fashionable and was attracting attention." In contrast, Doris Lessing gives this description of a woman's *hair,* an issue of almost mystical importance for women:

> The hairdresser sent her out with a very dark red haircut so that it felt like a weight of heavy silk swinging against her checks as she turned her head. As she remembered very well it had once done always. (1990, 39)

My intention is not to compare the account of an ordinary woman with a successful writer, but to show the practical, political implications of the difference between the two descriptions. Lessing shows the erotic, sensual dimension of touching your own hair—something that no one would understand if it weren't so palpably obvious to everyone. In our ordinary woman's description, on the other hand, you feel that her relationship to her own hair is determined exclusively by fashion and the notice taken of it by other people. I think of it as a piece of vulgar sociology that is created by prefabricated phrases which just happen to be lying around and which are inevitably used if we fail to reflect, feel or remember. These phrases are all too quick to take the place of our own formulations and yet they can still claim to express our very own experience. In this instance they lead us away from sensuous pleasure and physicality and promise freedom only as the independence from fashion, and so on.

Quite in contrast to its reputation, our ordinary language is also fairly abstract. When feelings, thoughts, and experiences are ignored in their concrete reality and are only spoken of, as it were, from a great height, it becomes difficult to speak of women's experiences in a narrative form without a special effort. For example, a woman trade unionist wrote as follows: "In the course of his union activities he was able to make numerous contacts which will be of use to him in his application for a better position." There is no word here about what is involved in "making contacts," no word about the cost of forming such a network of relationships. Whose boots does he have to lick? Does he take care to remain in someone's good books by refraining from speaking his mind? Does he have to flatter? (Could she, a woman, make such contacts without finding herself in a highly ambiguous situation?) Why does he "need" and what is a "better position"? Such questions can be put in a collective discussion. After a time it even becomes a source of entertainment in which people compete to unmask the true meanings of events lying behind such phrases (see Morisse et al. 1982 on this point). One method of giving such conformist abstractions the slip is to concentrate on a specific situation. This makes it possible to take pleasure in describing the details involved and thereby to recognize things other than those normally allowed onto the agenda by abstraction and prejudice. In short, it makes it possible to escape the norms of behavior and to discover the sensuous dimension of experience.

CONTRADICTION, ABSENCES, AND INTEREST

Contradiction is a particular problem that arises in the process of analyzing people's stories. The collective provides a favorable context in which to criticize things that are tolerated without question in individuals. In particular, it means we can criticize the incompatible opinions, judgments, and events which normally thrive in a system of peaceful coexistence in which nonintervention is the rule. The aim in doing so is not to eliminate the real contradictions of life through one's choice of words. On the contrary, the task is to break up that peaceful coexistence which is mainly the product of non-recognition, denial, and repression. For example, we have no difficulty at all in producing endless horror stories about how our mothers prevented us from doing this or that and turned us into the stunted people we are. Equally, since most of us are now mothers in our turn, we can also write stories about the obstacles placed in our path by our daughters, or about the baneful influence of schools on an idyllic mother-daughter relationship, and so on. In my view, these perceptions, too, are based on vulgar socio-logical theories of the kind purveyed in glossy magazines, but also in "scholarly" works. These theories serve to displace structural problems into disagreements between two individuals, or, to put it another way, to make general social problems appear as the product of individual guilt or failure. Such theories have no difficulty in surviving, unless we confront them with experiences that conflict with them. This, too, is a task of the collective.

Silence is another way of coming to terms with the unacceptable. In people's memo-ries it appears as an absence or a rupture. The recognition that these silences must be investigated and that the attempt must be made to propose theories to explain them was of great importance for the women's movement (see especially Irigaray 1980). After all, we have been accustomed for so long to being absent from history that in our thoughts and speech we tend to collude in ignoring the sheer existence of women. To hear what has not been said, to see things that have not been displayed, requires a spe-cial kind of detective training (on this point see Solle 1981). But the very thought that such a thing exists and is important, that it structures the field of perception and pro-vides a guide to action, gives a significant boost to such training in detection. Collective discussion about the role of silence in our stories is particularly enjoyable because it combines a creative expansion of the stories with the discovery that different vantage points bring different ways of seeing, and that each person possesses her own vantage point which comes into conflict with the traditional way of seeing things, even if that view has been accepted hitherto.

For that matter the whole question of vantage point and interest is an education in the possibilities of action. Normally we experience and write in such a way as to suggest that something has happened to us, that our lives are organized for us by impersonal forces personified in wicked characters. Other people's actions can be explained by their qualities of character, but we are simply at the mercy of these forces. I would maintain that such a view of other people must lead to a paralysis as far as action is concerned. At best it will lead to a habit of complaint. The theoretical insight that—like myself—other people act in pursuit of various interests means that when we analyze our stories emphasis must be placed on explaining people in terms of comprehensible interests. It is this step that calls for the greatest revision in our analysis of our stories. The labor of showing other people in terms of their conditioning and their interests changes our ideas about ourselves and our own actions. Instead of seeing ourselves as the victims of people and circumstances, we must see ourselves as people who work with those people and circumstances. That this insight is important not just for writing but also for political activity in general becomes clear when women report on their defeats in political battles—for example, when they talk about the problems of creating alliances.

CONCLUSION

I shall break off my discussion of the various ways of analyzing these stories at this point and restate my practical proposal in the context of my original observations. In order to make it discussible, I shall reaffirm what it is supposed to achieve. I began with my sense of boredom with macroeconomic problems and linked this up with the failure to understand daily practices at the microlevel—female practices in particular, with their preoccupation with looking after the family, caring, the household, and so on. In order to discover how society as a whole recreates itself through the lives of the majority in their day-to-day activities, I decided to make the experience of individuals productive for the formation of theory. This is essential if women's oppression and incorporation into the reproductive processes of society as a whole are to be understood and changed.

My proposal is not intended as a substitute for politics, but as a part of cultural politics. It is aimed above all at women in the women's movement in the broader sense. It combines grassroots activities with research as it takes place in the various disciplines on the principle of the division of labor. In general it is intended to place a question mark against all divisions of labor and therefore of special claims to competence. The fact that we know so little about how people actually experience social structures seems also to be a question arising from the division of labor. There is a way of analyzing structures—this is the critique of political economy—and there are views about people. Thus the fact that women are absent from thinking about economic problems explains why they are bored by economics and regard such matters as irrelevant to themselves. There was the question of Hoechst and its growth rates, for example. There was the question of pharmaceutical products and artificial fibers. If we ask ourselves how you actually go about increasing the production of artificial fibers, we at once see the answer. We can say that one factor is that mass consumption can be increased because women fall for every change in fashion. We then lean back with a satisfied smile, exclude ourselves from this analysis, and think we have found the answer at the very point where the real questions begin. How is all this really experienced? Why do women act in this way, if indeed they do? What things matter to them? What hopes do they have? Or desires? How do they wish to live? What plans do they have? Where are they going? How can they live? How do they insert themselves into the existing structures so that "fashion," for example, can become a powerful subject that makes them the object of trade?

In conclusion I should like to present a little story which arose in the course of a project concerned with the question of how women actively turn themselves into objects, how they disappear as subjects in consequence of their own subjective activity, and how they become objects to gaze at and touch—the objects of male desire. What triggered off our investigation was an encounter with a woman at the university who wore a transparent dress and, underneath it, tiny purple bikini panties. Dressed thus and wearing very high-heeled shoes, she moved through the landscape waggling her bottom and issuing a generalized invitation. We wondered what she really intended to achieve and could not imagine that her unambiguous appearance really represented an unambiguous intention, although we had no idea what else it could mean. We realized that without going as far as her, we, too, were constantly monitoring our own appearance and somehow displaying ourselves and as it were judging ourselves with the eyes of others according to unknown criteria. In short, like her we failed to live in a straight-forward manner, in tune with ourselves, and instead made more or less successful efforts to influence the impression we made. Our aim then was to research our public selves, the images we had made of ourselves, the sense in which we were living as objects (see Haug 1983). This is the story:

The Knickers

At long last spring came round again and it became warmer. Soon she began to pester her mother to allow her to wear knee-socks once again. One morning, when the thermometer climbed to 13° the much longed for knee-socks were laid out with her other clothes. It was still absolute madness to wear them and her mother warned her that she would not fail to come down with the flu. So she would also have to wear pale-blue woollen knickers over her pants. She found this dreadful, because the wool was scratchy and the knickers were so babyish. But for the moment she acquiesced, because it meant that her heavy tights would come that much closer to being stored away in the attic. How wonderful to feel the air around her legs again at long last, she thought on her way to school. Most of the other girls were not yet wearing knee-socks and she was the object of envy, since it showed what fantastic parents she had and that she was able to get her own way with them. During break they played french skipping for the first time that year and they all tried to outdo each other with high jumps and complicated maneuvers. From about knee-high she began to hold her skirt down at the back so that no one, and the cheeky boys least of all, should be able to catch a glimpse of the blue knickers. That was difficult; it spared her their teasing but made her make mistakes, which annoyed her. In the afternoon she went into town with her grandmother. In the underwear department she complained that the knickers were stupid and that she would take them off on the stairs before going into school and that she would not put them on again until just before she was back home again. Her grandmother asked the salesgirl about woollen knickers for her. In addition to the familiar blue ones, only in a slightly stronger blue, they had the very latest thing, just in: white knickers made of very soft material and with three rows of ruching at the back. They were made of an easy-care fabric—much more convenient than wool as well. She thought they were brilliant. The same material as her mother's underwear. She begged and begged until her grandmother gave in and agreed she could have them for Sundays. Sure thing, she thought and the very next morning she stuffed the woollen knickers back into the wardrobe and put the frilly knickers on in barely contained excitement. She could hardly wait until break, or rather until the jumping at french skipping had reached knee-high. Using her arms to help her she jumped as high as she could go. The girls all asked her where she had bought them. That's what they would like too. The boys all shouted, "Bum-wiggler, bum-wiggler!" Let them shout, that's what grown-ups wear. Boys just don't understand.

I can scarcely offer a detailed interpretation of this story, or even describe the process of interpretation which was followed by further versions of the story. But I should like to point to a number of features of the story which in my view have a general significance.

The story is written from experience, with empathy. None of us would find it difficult to recall similar incidents and feelings. We can all identify with it and at the same time we can observe some peculiarities.

In the first place there is a contradiction. In the beginning it was the boys who were to be prevented at all costs from seeing the pale-blue knickers; at the end, their views are insignificant, because they are stupid. We find both points of view comprehensible—in other words, the importance of people's opinions changes according to the context. The fear of being ridiculed by the boys pales into significance before the prospect of being grown up. Moreover, there is the complex situation that the girl is doing something for other people, but accepts the fact that they have misinterpreted it and despite this she is able to construct her identity in terms of the way she appears to others.

No less clear, in my view, is the compromise she makes. Linguistically, the writer incorporates other points of view by an act of legerdemain in which alien phrases are imported into her own speech. For example, "It was absolute madness"—here you can hear her mother's voice. Or again, "They had the very latest thing, an easy-care fabric"—that is the salesgirl talking. These standards will be taken over later on; their origins will be forgotten.

The story is silent about certain relationships, relationships which seem to have fossilized: the knickers *are* babyish. The story of this effort to become grown up still has to be decoded. Why is it important to show that we can get our own way with our parents? Since we like to represent ourselves in later years as victims, we should look for the break in continuity and examine the true strength of those situations in which we appeared as the victors.

But we also learn something about the triumphal progress of the Hoechst Chemical Company. Its products encounter a manifold complex, for the most part unconscious, of feelings, bodily sensations, smells, tastes, personal relationships, memories of victories and defeats, of friendships and voices, hopes and plans. A white frill in a shop window releases a violent feeling of freedom and excitement, triumph and energy, sun and friendship. The connection is then broken off. It is with such things that the advertising industry works as it prepares the way for high sales. We too must work at it in our efforts to increase our consciousness of life.

15

From the Woman Question to Women's Liberation

Lise Vogel

How can Marxist theory address the problem of women's oppression? For most of the 1970s I wrestled with this conundrum. Beyond a critique, I wanted to come up with an alternative. First in "Questions on the Woman Question" and then more fully in *Marxism and the Oppression of Women: Toward a Unitary Theory* (1983), I offered the beginnings of a materialist analysis that put childbearing and the oppression of women at the heart of every class mode of production.

Central to my approach was a confrontation with the Marxist tradition on the woman question. Texts long regarded by socialists as canonical in fact offered, I thought, only an unstable hodgepodge of fragments pertaining to women. I therefore undertook a lengthy critical reading of such concepts as the reproduction of labor power, individual consumption, and the industrial reserve army as they appeared in the writings of Marx, Engels, Bebel, Lenin, Zetkin, and others. Once disentangled, reworked and supplemented, these concepts became the starting point for the construction of a more adequate theoretical framework.

This chapter provides an overview of what that framework might took like. Responding to a 1983 critique by Johanna Brenner and Nancy Holmstrom, I challenge conventional socialist-feminist analysis of women's oppression in capitalist societies on two counts (Brenner and Holmstrom 1983; Vogel 1984, 1995). Where socialist feminists commonly locate women outside the processes of capitalist accumulation, I position them at their center. And where socialist feminists often assume female subordination to be rooted solely in women's relation to the economy, I argue that it is established by their dual situation, differentiated by class, with respect to domestic labor and equal rights. That is, capitalism stamps the subordination of women with a twofold character, political as well as economic.

My advocacy of Marxist-feminist theory did not come at an auspicious moment. In the early 1980s neither of my intended audiences was likely to pay much attention. The U.S. Left, never that strong and always hostile to feminism's supposedly inherent bourgeois tendencies, was losing ground in an increasingly conservative political climate. American feminism, by contrast, had at last achieved a more mainstream, if always vulnerable, acceptance, together with new kinds of concerns. Several years after the unhappy marriage of Marxism and feminism seemed to have ended in divorce, socialist feminism was a minor trend within the rapidly growing women's movement.

Meanwhile, postmodernist theorists had launched a quite persuasive attack on the Enlightenment notion of a universal human subject—autonomous, coherent, unencumbered, and without gender, race, or class. In many ways a theorization of understandings developed by the social movements of the 1960s, this analysis also entailed rejection of the modernist quest for an all-embracing single theory. Postmodernists targeted Marxism as an emancipatory grand narrative that had to be abandoned. To argue in 1983 for a unitary Marxist-feminist theory was thus to be, at the very least, seriously out of step.

Readers will notice that I take issue with the claim that empirical accounts of the history of women constitute the appropriate basis for feminist theory. This is because I resist the temptation to collapse theory into history or, more generally, to theorize directly "from experience." Theory, it seems to me, is necessarily abstract and quite limited in its role. I find it helpful to use a metaphor. Theory is something like a skeleton—different from but necessary to the flesh and blood data of history it supports. A skeleton must be structurally coherent, of course, but the Marxist theoretical tradition fails to meet this condition. In my work I therefore put a great deal of effort into the rigorous reconstruction of a set of concepts pertinent to women's position within social reproduction. When, for example, I define domestic labor or generational replacement and consider their articulation within the social reproduction of class-stratified societies, I only identify possible mechanisms and tendencies. These can then be of use in the study of a specific historical situation, but the scope of what they can explain is severely restricted. Even less can they directly suggest strategy or an evaluation of the prospects for political action. These are matters for concrete analysis and historical investigation. The bare bones of theory only spring to life, in other words, when they encounter the rich data of history.[1]

In "Questions on the Woman Question" (1979) I addressed the problem of the relationship between women's liberation and the struggle for socialism in three ways. First, I criticized the ambiguities of theoretical work in the socialist tradition on the so-called woman question. Second, I sketched what I believe to be a more rigorous theoretical approach. Third, I offered a brief consideration of strategic orientations. Packing so much into the article format, I was unavoidably too brief and some of what I wrote is open to misinterpretation. I am therefore happy to have this opportunity to respond to Johanna Brenner and Nancy Holmstrom's comments and to clarify my analysis of women's oppression.

The bulk of "Questions on the Woman Question" consisted of a critique of the socialist tradition. I organized my discussion in terms of an opposition between two approaches, then called the "family argument" and the "social production argument." I now conceptualize these as the "dual-systems perspective" and the "social reproduction perspective," and I continue to believe that only the latter can adequately situate women's oppression within the framework of Marx's analysis of social development. This position has little in common, however, with the view attributed to me by Brenner and Holmstrom, namely that "women's oppression stems from their marginalization from social production." I seek to understand women's oppression in terms of the differential location of women and men within, not at the edge of, the social reproduction processes of class society, most especially those involving the reproduction of labor power.

To theorize women's oppression, I do not take the notions of reproduction of labor power and domestic labor for granted, as is common in the socialist feminist literature. For example, I restrict the meaning of reproduction of labor power to the processes that maintain and replace exploitable labor power. That is, the concept is pertinent only to subordinate classes. (Propertied-class women also experience gender oppression, but it is associated with their role in the maintenance and reproduction of the property-owning class, not of labor power.) I also detach the concept of reproduction of labor power from customary assumptions of biological procreation in family contexts. Although the reproduction of labor power usually involves child-rearing within kin-based settings called families, it can be organized in other ways. From a theoretical point of view, it does not necessarily entail heterosexuality, family forms, or even generational replacement. That these institutional arrangements are so common reflects their advantages over the alternatives.

In capitalist societies, labor power takes the form of a commodity and the reproduction of labor power has specific features, shaped in the workings of capitalist social reproduction. At its heart is working-class women's historically evolved, disproportionate responsibility for domestic labor. By domestic labor I do not mean housework but, rather, a particular set of activities involving the maintenance and replacement of the bearers of labor power and of the working class as a whole. Capitalism stamps this domestic labor with its own character: as in no other mode of production, maintenance and replacement tasks become spatially, temporarily, and institutionally isolated from the sphere of production, with serious consequences for relations between working-class women and men and for the nature of women's oppression.

Domestic labor constitutes, I also suggest, an important but heretofore invisible component of what Marx termed necessary labor. As such it is both indispensable to capital and an obstacle to accumulation. If capitalist production is to take place, it must have labor power—the essential force that propels its advance. And if labor power is to be available, domestic labor must be performed. At the same time, domestic labor to some extent stands in the way of capitalism's drive for profit, for it limits the availability of labor power that might otherwise be exploited in the value-producing process. The capitalist class is thus caught between the conflicting pressures of its long-term need for a labor force, its short-term requirements for different categories of workers, and its desire to maintain hegemony over a divided working class. In response it adopts a variety of strategies, some of which involve manipulating domestic labor in ways that create absolute or relative surplus value.

Over the long term, the capitalist class seeks to stabilize the reproduction of labor power at a low cost and with a minimum of domestic labor. At the same time, the working class strives to win the best conditions for its own renewal, which may include a particular level and type of domestic labor. Because both capital and labor are ordinarily fragmented into distinct sectors, the results are not uniform across the working class. A contradictory tendential dynamic thus threads through historical struggles over the conditions for the reproduction of labor power. Particular outcomes include the family wage for certain groups, protective legislation covering female and child industrial workers, sex- and race-segregation in the labor market, migrant labor housed in barracks, and so forth.

While only certain women perform domestic labor in capitalist society, all women suffer from lack of equality. Women's lack of equality constitutes a specific feature of women's oppression in capitalist societies. As Marx and Lenin argued, equality of persons is not an abstract principle or false ideology but a complex tendency with roots in the articulation of the spheres of production and circulation. "Capitalism," observed Lenin, following Marx, "combines formal equality with economic and, consequentially, social inequality" (Lenin 1966, 80).

Given the contradictory character of equality in capitalist society, struggles to expand its scope threaten the dominance of capitalist social relations on two fronts. First, they tend to reduce divisions within and among oppressed classes, as well as between these classes and other sectors, by moving all persons toward a more equal footing. Second, they reveal the foundation of bourgeois society to be class exploitation, not individual equality, for the further democratic rights are extended the more capitalism's oppressive economic and social character stands revealed. Far from a useless exercise in reformism, the battle for equality can point beyond capitalism.

Lack of equality as a group constitutes the basis for movements that bring women from different classes and sectors together—movements that Holmstrom, Brenner, and I agree are critical to socialist transformation. These movements may hold varying interpretations, explicit or implicit, of the meaning of the equality they seek. Some, for example, may regard equality of women and men within capitalist society as a sufficient goal. The contradictions of modern capitalism make it likely, however, that twentieth-century women's movements will have at least some insight into the deficiencies of a liberal conception of equality. This can form a basis for the development of a women's movement oriented toward socialism, as recent historical research documents.[2] Since the 1960s, women's movements in the advanced capitalist countries as well as in some Third World countries have also shown such potential. Unfortunately, the left has rarely been capable of intervening constructively. Its weakness has its origin, in part, in the lack of an adequate theory of women's oppression and of the role of the demand for equality and democratic rights in social change.

To sum up my theoretical position: the logic of capitalist accumulation and the articulation between the spheres of production and circulation doubly constitute women's subordination. On the one hand, women and men are differentially located with respect to important material aspects of social reproduction. On the other, women, like other groups, lack full democratic rights. The dynamics of female oppression in capitalist society respond to this dual situation, varying along dimensions of social class, race, ethnicity, etc.

Women in capitalist societies, in short, have a distinctive political as well as economic location. Their disadvantaged position in the political sphere is a phenomenon that is analytically separable from, yet rooted in, their subordinate place within capitalist relations of production. Marxists who ignore this political aspect of women's status in capitalist societies open themselves up to the age-old canard that takes Marxism to be a theory of economic determinism.

In their critique, Brenner and Holmstrom misread my theorization of social reproduction and ignore my discussion of equal rights, thereby generally distorting the theoretical approach I propose. Along with much socialist and socialist-feminist analysis, they argue that "women's oppression is a function of both their role in the family and their role in wage labor." That is, they locate female oppression in women's dual position as domestic workers and wage laborers. The problem with this kind of analysis is that it focuses solely on economic phenomena, fails to account for the oppression of non-working-class women, and cannot explain the basis for movements of women that cross class, race, and other divisions. Despite professed commitments to the liberation of all women, to organizational autonomy, and to the importance of subjective experience, activists who hold this view paradoxically embrace an analysis of women's oppression with weaknesses quite similar to those of the socialist tradition. By contrast, I consider women's oppression in terms of their dual position with respect to domestic labor and equal rights. In this way I offer a framework for both analyzing working-class women's position and understanding how a broad-based women's liberation movement may represent an essential component in the struggle for socialism.

In making their comments, Brenner and Holmstrom claim to offer "a theory of women's oppression based on the actual conditions of material production." In their view, theory is built out of full-blown historical accounts of the evolution of social relations. In contrast, I distinguish between history and theory, and my presentation is necessarily abstract. My critics' disappointment in the theoretical adequacy of my arguments thus reflects a misplaced demand for detailed empirical descriptions of the history of women's oppression. Historical accounts alone, no matter how detailed and accurate, cannot provide a theoretical foundation.

Where my emphasis in "Questions on the Woman Question" was on theory, Brenner and Holmstrom focus on the practical questions facing socialist feminists and socialists committed to women's liberation. As a basis for their strategic outlook, they examine the evolution of women's oppression in the course of capitalist development. From this history they derive a strategic corollary: women must organize "separate from and independent of men." Such self-organization must include both a women's movement and women's caucuses in all mass organizations as well as socialist organizations. In contrast, I suggested that such questions were strictly a matter of concrete analysis, and some readers have concluded that I do not support the independent organization of women. Let me restate my views more positively. Because of the history of women's oppression and the revolutionary edge inherent in the issue of democratic rights, it seems highly likely to me that the independent organization of women will be and must be a feature of struggles for socialism—both before and after the attainment of state power. I see this, however, as a strategic orientation flowing from concrete analysis rather than an abstract principle of socialist organization. Despite their disclaimer, Brenner and Holmstrom come dangerously close, I think, to the position that "organizational structure provides an ironclad guarantee" of commitment to women's interests.

In conclusion, I want to observe that my critics and I agree on many points. Above all, we share what Gail Omvedt has delineated as a socialist-feminist outlook—"a feeling of a need for revolutionary change and a genuine commitment to the left, coupled with a distrust not only of the bourgeois establishment but also of the traditional left bureaucracy and its economistic neglect of women's oppression" (Omvedt 1980). And we share as well the view that, as Crystal Eastman put it, "we will not wait for the Social

Revolution to bring us the freedom we should have won in the nineteenth century" (Eastman 1978, 51).

NOTES

1. My understanding of theory as skeletal in nature to some extent converges with Iris Young's discussion of a "pragmatic theorizing [that] is not concerned to give an account of a whole" (1994, 718). In terms of Young's concept of gender as seriality, my project here has been to identify aspects of the way women are serialized by the processes of capitalist social reproduction.

2. For example, Meredith Tax (1980), Kumari Jayawardena (1986); and Sonia Kruks, Rayna Rapp, and Marilyn B. Young, eds. (1989).

16

Theories of the Family

Lindsey German

Feminist theory has become established in society over the past twenty years. Feminism in university courses is now an accepted area of study. This is demonstrated both by the substantial number of women's studies courses which now exist and by feminist approaches to history, sociology, economics, and media studies which are now widespread. It is argued that due to women's oppression, the women's dimension in academic study has been ignored. The common response is for feminism to be integrated into academic study.

There are, of course, many different theories of women's oppression. But increasingly one theory has become hegemonic, not just among radical feminists but among socialists and Marxist feminists too. That is the theory of patriarchy. It is now almost universally accepted by feminists and among the left that patriarchy, the patriarchal family, or even patriarchal capitalism is responsible for the oppression of women. Sometimes it is even said that patriarchy is women's oppression.

There is obviously a conceptual problem: What does the term mean? "Patriarchy" literally means "rule of the father." Marx used it in this sense to describe the domestic household system of production. He applied it to a historically specific form of the family, not as a general phrase meaning women's oppression and certainly not in any transhistorical sense.

Clearly most feminist theorists do not use the term in this manner; their application is much less rigorous. What most of their theories have in common, however, is an insistence that male domination exists over and above the particular economic mode of production in which it features—and that it therefore cannot be explained either in class terms or by reference to Marx's economic theory. According to many feminist theorists, although the forces of production advance, and although revolutionary social change takes place, male domination still remains something constant and given for all time. Women's oppression has always existed, we are told, and will continue to exist even after a socialist revolution.

Such ideas are often put forward by those who consider themselves Marxists. But Marx and Engels approached the question quite differently and came to different conclusions. They started from the assumption that women's oppression arose alongside the division of society into classes and the development of private property. Alongside this went, in Engels's phrase, "the world-historic defeat of the female sex" (Engels 1942)—the defeat of mother right and the establishment of the family.

As society developed, oppression took on different aspects. The development of the forces of production gave rise to different forms of society; and as society changed so the family form changed. All forms of consciousness are rooted in social being. So both the ideas and material reality of women's oppression changed along with the change from one mode of production to another.

A famous passage from Marx's writing makes the point that it is the way in which workers are exploited which determines their oppression:

> Morality, religion, metaphysics, all the rest of ideology and their corresponding forms of consciousness, thus no longer retain the semblance of independence. They have no history, no development: but men, developing their material reduction and their material intercourse, alter, along with their real existence, their thinking and the products of their thinking. Life is not determined by consciousness, but consciousness by life. (Marx and Engels 1976)

Ideas, then, are rooted in material reality. However, when we talk of women's oppression and capitalism, there are other features to consider. In particular, Marx saw capitalism as a totality: an economic system which encroached into every area of life, throughout every part of the world; which changed all previous production; which altered all the social relations of production. It involved constant processes of change, and this in itself set the capitalist mode of production apart from all previous modes. Whereas in all previous modes of production the ruling classes attempted to conserve the old ways of producing, the capitalist ruling class—the bourgeoisie—behaves in exactly the opposite way:

> Constant revolutionizing of production, uninterrupted disturbance of all social conditions, everlasting uncertainty and agitation distinguish the bourgeois epoch from all earlier ones. All fixed, fast-frozen relations, with their train of ancient and venerable prejudices and opinions, are swept away, all new-formed ones become antiquated before they can ossify. (Marx and Engels 1988)

Every area of life—including the family and women's oppression—is rooted in social production. The implication in Marx's theory is that socialist revolution will dissolve the old family, end the legal restraints on women's equality and lay the basis for genuine women's liberation. Such a view cuts across the views of the patriarchy theorists.

From the Marxist point of view there are two major flaws with patriarchy theory. It is idealist—there is no conception of ideas being rooted in material reality; and it does not consider the capitalist system as a whole.

The early patriarchy theorists are clear examples of both propositions. Their assumption is that patriarchy exists, is embracing and ahistorical, and they are overtly opposed to any class analysis. Kate Millett argues in her book *Sexual Politics* that no major differences of class exist between women (Millett 1971), while Shulamith

Firestone subverts most categories to argue that sexual struggles, not class struggles, have been the real dynamic of history—so she argues for a separate revolution (Firestone 1970). Women's oppression is explained either by biological difference (which cannot be overcome until women wrest control of their reproductive functions) or simply in terms of male chauvinist ideas.

Such arguments have provided the basis of radical or separatist feminism throughout the existence of the women's movement. They have recently been more widely adopted by socialist feminists of all descriptions. In the process they have been much embellished. But crucially they have retained the idea of separateness: of ideology as autonomous from economic struggle; of patriarchy as separate from capitalism. Class antagonisms are therefore overlaid, it is argued, by the antagonisms between men and women.

The theoretical basis for the theory of patriarchy is that there are two areas of production, or modes of production, not one. Hence there are two separate struggles—economic struggle and ideological struggle. Juliet Mitchell puts it succinctly: "we are dealing with two autonomous areas, the economic mode of capitalism and the ideological mode of patriarchy" (Mitchell 1974). Others find this formulation too idealist and try to develop a Marxist interpretation. Descriptions of patriarchy as an "ideological mode" tend to abandon any idea of a materialist analysis.

Attempts to couple the two theories are common: they too express themselves in the formulation of two modes—the capitalist mode of production and the family mode of reproduction. This is widespread among separatist feminists. So the French feminist Christine Delphy argues:

> There are two modes of production in our society. Most goods are produced in the industrial mode. Domestic services, childrearing and certain other goods are produced in the family mode. The first mode of production gives rise to capitalist exploitation. The second gives rise to familial, or more precisely, patriarchal exploitation. (1984, 69)

Delphy considers both spheres to be completely separate—what goes on at work is totally divorced from what takes place in the family. Whereas the male worker has to depend on the employer for his sustenance, the wife has to depend on the man. Her relationship to him is *totally* subordinate; she is dependent on him for her well-being in every sense. "Her standard of living does not depend on her class relationship to the proletariat; but, on her serf relations of production with her husband" (1984, 71). Again, for Delphy, class is not key: she argues that wives of the bourgeoisie are not themselves bourgeois, and that women who see themselves in class terms suffer from false consciousness and an identification with "enemy patriarchal classes" (1984, 76).

From a Marxist point of view there are fundamental problems with this analysis. It totally abandons any analysis of class differences. It also misunderstands the nature of capitalism by arguing that feudal relations of production can exist within the capitalist family. That a radical feminist like Delphy takes such a view is no surprise. But many socialist feminists who would agree with few of her conclusions have accepted similar arguments.

Even Sheila Rowbotham in one of her earlier books, *Woman's Consciousness, Man's World*, argued that women's subordinate role within the family could only be explained with reference to precapitalist modes of production. While not explicitly developing a patriarchy theory (and indeed later attacking the whole concept), she put forward similar arguments:

> In the relation of husband and wife there is an exchange of services which resembles the bond between *man and man* in feudalism. (1973, 62)

Sheila Rowbotham draws back from arguing that the relationship is *actually* feudal. However, she then refers to women's labor as maintaining a subordinate mode of production within capitalism which "retains elements of earlier forms of production" (1973, 62).

Such formulations are used to justify the separation of struggles—against capitalism and against men. Endorsement of this position is taken from Engels's famous passage on the production and reproduction of human life, part of which was quoted above, where he talks of the production of everyday life on the one hand, and of the family on the other:

> According to the materialistic conception, the determining factor in history is, in the final instance, the production and reproduction of immediate life. This, again, is of a twofold character. On the one side, the production of the means of subsistence, of food, clothing and shelter and the tools necessary for that production; on the other side, the production of human beings themselves, the propagation of the species. The social institutions under which people of a particular historical epoch and a particular country live are conditioned by both kinds of production; by the stage of development of labor on the one hand and of the family on the other. (Engels 1942)

Any feminist theorist who wants to retain some commitment to socialist theory (and some who don't) will use this passage in an attempt to argue that even Engels acknowledged a separation and therefore at least some degree of autonomy between the two modes. But their argument is flawed and stems from a misunderstanding or wrong interpretation of what Engels actually wrote. For he goes on to argue that as human beings developed production, so the family became relatively less important:

> the less the development of labor and the more limited the amount of its products . . .
> the more the social order is found to be dominated by ties of lineage. (1942, 4)

The development of the forces of production bring about changes in how people live. In particular, the rise of the state and the establishment of groups based on geographical connection rather than lineage leads to a society in which the family structure is completely dominated by the property structure (1942, 5).

On this construction, the more developed a society, the more the family form is subordinated to production. However there is always of necessity a connection between the two; the family and the form it takes arises from the particular mode of production. It is not autonomous, separate or distinct from that mode of production. Reproduction is tied up with production.

Most feminist theorists would disagree. Annette Kuhn argues for example that:

> Patriarchal structures have their operation within history, but not within modes of production: they are overdetermined in particular modes of production by more immediate characteristics of the social formation. (1978, 65)

Many argue from this that Marxism can only be used to explain the *economic* development of society; the *ideas* which arise in any particular society cannot be explained in these terms. Accordingly Marxism is supposedly inadequate to explain the ideological or the unconscious. This approach involves abandoning some basic ideas of Marxism: that social being determines consciousness, and that there is a distinction between base and superstructure. The "relations of production" do not arise from any separate mode of *reproduction*. They are a product of the particular mode of production in which they exist.

This is clear if we start from an understanding of how societies change and develop. Marx's description went like this:

> At a certain stage of their development the material forces of production in society come in conflict with the existing relations of production or—what is but a legal expression of the same thing—with the property relations within which they had been at work before. From forms of development of the forces of production these relations turn into their fetters. Then comes the period of social revolution. With the change of the economic foundation the entire immense superstructure is more or less rapidly transformed. (1971, preface)

Marx's analysis differs from feminist ones in that it talks about change and contradiction. For Marx there is nothing static or eternal about society, and the change from one mode of production to another brings about a transformation in every area of life. The description exactly fits the changes that took place in the transition from feudalism to capitalism. The old forms of family became obstacles to new methods of production. For the new methods to succeed, among other things the old family has to be smashed and this obstacle removed.

Production then moves from the family to the factory—the separation of work from home—and is transformed completely in the course of the ensuing social upheaval. The family becomes, for Marx, part of the immense superstructure of society which is changed as society itself changes.

The distinction between base and superstructure attempts to show the relationship between economic production and ideas: that the forces of production themselves give rise to particular ideas, cultural and social formations. Many feminists try to ditch any such connection, talking instead of the "relative autonomy" of patriarchy from the capitalist mode of production, so it can be seen as "a relatively autonomous structure whose operation is overdetermined conjuncturally by precisely such structures as class" (Kuhn and Wolpe 1978, 53).

This leads to the kind of distinction made by Roisin McDonough and Rachel Harrison:

> Although as Marxists it is essential for us to give analytic primacy to the sphere of production, as feminists it is equally essential to hold on to a concept such as the relation of human reproduction in order to understand the specific nature of women's oppression. (1978, 28)

In doing so, they are unable to explain either the development of society or the connection of ideas to economic change. Concepts such as patriarchy become free floating, transcending modes of production. Any relationship between the two—as when class "overdetermines" patriarchy—is seen as purely accidental. So these feminists abandon any Marxist theory of change and resort to a combination of economic determinism and complete idealism.

The theories are only sustained by maintaining them at the highest level of abstraction. Any connnection with changes in the family or with the real lives of women today would point to too many inconsistencies.

The basic flaw in the argument is a failure to see the link between production and reproduction. This link exists for all class societies, both in the narrow biological sense of the reproduction of the species and in the wider sense of the reproduction of the labor force. Capitalist production gives rise to the capitalist form of family. This last point is clearly accepted by Joan Smith in her article "Women and the Family" (1977). However she makes the opposite error from the patriarchy theorists by arguing that the capitalist family is not superstructural at all, but is part of the economic base of capitalism.

Like many patriarchy theorists, Joan Smith misinterprets Engels's formulation and adopts the two-modes theory, claiming that the family constitutes the mode of reproduction; capitalism could not abolish the family without abolishing the very basis of capitalism itself. For her, the family is as central to the capitalist system as wage labor or accumulation.

But her thesis is not tenable. Even within capitalism there have been *major* changes in the way labor power is reproduced. Capitalism does not depend for its existence on privatized domestic labor. In theory the family could be abolished without that spelling the end of capitalist society. The interests of the capitalist class are not *necessarily* served by maintaining women as unpaid laborers in the home, rather than as wage laborers in social production directly producing value for the capitalist class. What evidence there is seems to suggest the reverse is true. It is at least arguable that massive investment in the socialization of aspects of the family, thus releasing more women workers to produce surplus value for the capitalist class, would be of greater economic benefit to the capitalist system than the existing method of reproduction of labor power (Bruegel 1978).

It is important to stress this, because to view the family as central to the capitalist system as the process of exploitation itself leads to serious political problems: in particular, equating the fight against oppression with that against exploitation. But while the privatized family is not essential to the survival of capitalism, its abolition is not at all likely while capitalism exists. There are a number of reasons for this. Centrally, the level of investment in the socialization of the family which each capitalist state would have to undertake would be massive. Any individual state undertaking this task would be massive. Any individual state undertaking this task would be at a disadvantage, at least in the short term, with regard to its main rivals internationally. In periods of prosperity and expansion socialization might be considered, but the crisis-ridden nature of the system is such that it becomes far too daunting for any single capitalist class. It is worth remembering that even in the record postwar boom, the level of spending on public child-care provision by the advanced capitalist countries remained appallingly low.

Despite all the inefficiencies and inconsistencies of the privatized family in terms of the reproduction of labor power, any alternatives to it in a crisis-ridden, profit-oriented system are highly unlikely. The present combination of increased state intervention, a growing level of public child care (though often through private capitalist investment), and women's jobs "fitting in" with the care of young children is therefore likely to continue.

Joan Smith's analysis fails to take into account the contradictions present in the family, and so it slips into an almost mystical faith in the family's centrality to capitalism. By sticking rigidly to the two-modes theory, she ends up moving back toward patriarchy analysis, with its transhistorical features, rather than breaking from it.

One of the problems in developing a theory of the family has been the abandonment by so much of the academic left of any notion of base and superstructure. This abandonment developed at least in part from a rejection of rigid Stalinist notions of a deterministic relationship between the two. Today, however, it is widely but erroneously accepted that there is *no* real connection between the economic base of a particular society and the ideas that develop within it.

Some of the confusion over the base and superstructure distinction arises from the belief that by allocating the family to the superstructure, its economic role is thereby diminished, as is its importance as a unit of women's oppression. This is not the case. As Chris Harman has put it:

> The distinction between base and superstructure is a distinction between social relations which are subject to immediate changes with changes in the productive forces, and those which are relatively static and resistant to change. The capitalist family belongs to the latter rather than the former category, even in its "economic" function of reproducing the labor force. (Harman 1986, 32)

The family has a very important economic role. This is equally true of other superstructural formations such as the capitalist state. But it does not form its own dynamic, nor is it part of the dynamic of capitalist production. Indeed as we have seen, it can act as a conservative force, a defense mechanism for the protection of its members against the ravages of class society. And its economic role is subordinate to the process of accumulation. This was the point made by Engels, and Marx gave a similar description of the family. The development of social production brought with it a corresponding decline of the family form of production:

> The family, which to begin with is the only social relationship, becomes later, when increased needs create new social relations and the increased population new needs, a subordinate one. (1976, 49)

THE DOMESTIC LABOR DEBATE

Recognition of the centrality of the family to capitalism was one feature of attempts by Marxists in the late 1960s and early 1970s to theorize women's oppression. The domestic labor debate was about the economic contribution of women's labor in the home to the capitalist system of production. It was characterized by academicism and a level of abstraction. While it was a serious attempt to locate women's oppression in capitalist society and to use Marxist terminology to explain oppression, it was also a concession to feminist ideas. It was a response to the criticism that Marxism only concerned itself with production and that Marxists always regarded housework as a totally separate sphere.

So while some of the writing on domestic labor produced some valuable insights, there were a number of major flaws in the arguments.

The early domestic labor theorists tended to emphasize the two modes of production and reproduction and accepted that housework formed a separate mode of production. Many fell into the functionalist trap of believing that capitalism could not under any circumstances manage to survive without the privatized family. Others argued that the labor of women in the home was productive of surplus value through the commodity of labor power. So women constituted a separate class which had an interest in fighting for wages for housework (Dalla Costa and James 1975).

The problem with these theories was that both, in their different ways, separated housework from social production. They first put domestic labor on a par with wage labor performed for the employer, equating it with socialized commodity production. Secondly, they implicitly assumed the continued existence of privatized domestic labor by claiming that it constituted a separate mode of production.

Several critics of these various positions pointed out that housework could not be equated with wage labor in this way:

> To compare domestic labor with wage labor in a quantitative way is not comparing like with like. However unevenly it operates, the process of value creation within commodity production enables one to talk about quantities of abstract labor in the case of wage labor in a way that is not valid for domestic labor. It is therefore not possible to add together domestic labor—time and wage labor—time in order to calculate the wife's surplus labor because the two are not commensurate. (Women's Collective 1977, 10)

The housewife has no rigid distinction between work and leisure; she is not directly controlled or supervised; and she is not producing for a market. She is atomized rather than part of a collective. Because market forces do not directly govern her work, the tasks connected with the reproduction of labor power are performed whether that labor power is in immediate demand or not (due to old age, unemployment, and so on).

Nor is the housewife directly productive of surplus value. It is often argued that what the housewife produces are simply use-values:

> Domestic labor is the production of use-values, the physical inputs for the production being commodities bought with part of the husband's wage. The housewife produces directly consumable use-values with them. . . . Child-care is the most time-consuming part of the work of full-time housewives . . . it is the most essential task performed by the housewife for the continuance of capitalism. (Women's Collective 1977, 9)

To say simply that the housewife is concerned with the production of use-values implies that she is merely a servant to her husband and children. However, domestic labor has a social role. The reason child care is the most essential task performed for capitalism within the home is that there is a connection between this work and the production of surplus value. Put succinctly, "the relation of domestic labor to the production of surplus value is simply that the former makes the latter possible" (Women's Collective 1977, 13).

Domestic labor can be seen as *indirectly productive* of surplus value, through being directly productive of labor power. This feature is important in order to retain what is central to the domestic labor debate and to draw the correct conclusions from it. The two dominant strands of the debate in fact lead to wrong conclusions: either to the wages-for-housework campaign espoused by Selma James, or to the idea that the use-values produced by the housewife have little to do with commodity production or indeed capitalism. This analysis leads to the view that the reproduction of labor power takes place outside the capitalist mode of production. Either theory leads yet again to complete separatism in terms of struggle and embracing patriarchy theory.

The connection of domestic labor with capitalism lies not in the production of values but in the reproduction of labor power. The housewife produces only use-values; but these in turn affect the value of labor power.

Separatist conclusions may not have been the intention of many of the domestic labor theorists. They saw their work as a serious attempt to theorize Marxism and women's oppression. But their attempt to put unpaid work in the home on a par with the categories of Marx's *Capital* led to a major weakness: the lack of an understanding of the connection between family and work.

This may appear to be a contradiction, for after all one of the central aspects of the reproduction of labor power under capitalism is the separation of home and work. But the two complement and reflect one another as well. Domestic labor exists in the form it does precisely because of wage labor and commodity production.

The domestic labor theorists instead saw the family as a separate sphere. They therefore set out to prove that women's domestic labor was central not just to the family but to the capitalist system as well. This led away from attempts to synthesize the two. It similarly failed to take sufficiently into account the fact that women's labor was increasingly social outside the home, in the workplace. Consequently, the theory was only able to give a partial view of women's oppression.

MALE BENEFITS

By the late 1970s, the domestic labor theory was being usurped by more overtly patriarchal theory: in particular the view that men gained some material benefit from women's oppression in the home. Woman's oppression was seen as maintained through men's control of every aspect of her life, including work. So it has been argued that

> at marriage, the wife gives into the control of her husband both her labor power and her capacity to procreate in exchange for subsistence for a definite period, for life. (McDonough and Harrison 1978, 34)

Heidi Hartmann, who describes Marxism as sex-blind, has attempted a similar materialist, rather than purely idealist, analysis of patriarchy by arguing that "the material base upon which patriarchy rests lies most fundamentally in men's control over women's labor power" (1979, 11).

For Hartmann, control does not merely lie within the family but throughout the structures of capitalist society. She too bases her ideas on the two-modes-of-production analysis and states quite categorically that fledgling capital and men of all classes went into alliance in order to maintain this control over women. Working-class men achieved this through ensuring protective legislation and a family wage. This kept women in the home and gave men a "higher standard of living than women in terms of luxury consumption, leisure time and personalized services" (1979, 6).

Similar arguments are put by Zillah Eisenstein, who explicitly refers to "capitalist patriarchy" in her attempt to define women's oppression (1978, 5–40). The substance of this argument has been dealt with already, but it is worth pointing to a couple of its weaknesses. First it stems from a total misunderstanding of women workers' relationship to the labor market. The woman worker sells her labor power on the market in exactly the same way a male worker does. No mediating structure exists between female wage laborers and the capitalist class, preventing her from being able to sell her labor power. She is employed directly, without reference to her husband.

To pretend that women are somehow in a servile or bond relationship to their husbands with relation to the labor market is simply denying the facts. More important, it leaves patriarchy theorists with no understanding or explanation of the continued preference of the capitalist class for employing cheap female labor.

Protective legislation and the family wage were, as we have seen, the result of class interests and part of a class response to the worst ravages of the system, when there seemed little alternative to the awful conditions the working class lived under. Nor were male workers in a powerful position over female ones: only a minority were even in unions and protective legislation was nowhere near as devastating to women's work as some feminists imply. For example, hardly any such legislation existed in the United States until well into the twentieth century, yet the structure of the working-class family in the United States was similar to that in Britain.

Johanna Brenner and Maria Ramas make this point in their article "Rethinking Women's Oppression":

> It is very difficult to make a convincing case that so precarious a socio-political edifice could have played a major role in conditioning the sexual division of labor or the family household system, either in England or the United States. (1978, 40)

In Britain, reductions in hours for women and children were often seen as beneficial for the whole working class, since they tended to shorten the working day. Where the unions did act to exclude women from work, they often did so for the most *class-conscious* reasons: to prevent the undercutting of wages and conditions.

> it is entirely unnecessary to resort to ideology to explain why trade unions were particularly adamant in their opposition to female entry into their trades. It is quite clear that when unions were unable to exclude women, a rapid depression of wages and general degradation of work resulted. (Brenner and Ramas 1978, 45)

Although it may be relatively easy to point to the inconsistencies of Hartmann's historical analysis, it is much harder to defeat the *thrust* of her argument, which does not depend on historical accuracy for its appeal. The idea that men do gain substantial benefits from women's labor in the family is widespread. Most feminists argue that men receive these real benefits—more leisure, more food, more power—and it is this which leads them to support the status quo.

These ideas are powerful precisely because they reflect the appearance of the society in which we live. After all, the common sense of society points to the fact that men get their meals cooked, that they have control over family finances, that they retain control over their wives and children. This is certainly how things would appear and, most feminists would argue, how they actually are.

Yet again, the argument centers on the role of the family under capitalism. Is it for the reproduction of labor power or is it additionally for the benefit of individual men? If the latter proposition is true, then does this mean that working-class men have a *material* interest in defending the capitalist system?

To argue that men do have such an interest leads away from a class analysis of women's oppression. It is in the overwhelming interest of the working class to fight for the overthrow of the society that exploits them and therefore to fight for—among other things—the liberation of women. It is in the interests of the capitalist class, on the other hand, for labor power to be reproduced privately as it is at present: for women to labor inside and outside the home, being paid low wages for work outside and nothing for domestic labor; and for the man to see his responsibility in society as providing, however inadequately, for his wife and family.

This situation leads to unequal relationships between the sexes and within the family. But it does not lead to a situation where the man benefits. On the contrary, all members of the family would benefit from being able to live in a society where relationships were not straitjacketed as they are at present.

Often the question of male benefits is reduced simply to one of power. The argument, put at its most basic, is that whereas the male worker is exploited, alienated, and downtrodden through his relationship to the capitalist at work, at least in the home he is boss. He can bully and sometimes physically assault his offspring and wife. Even where he does not do so, he controls the home, both financially and ideologically.

But the working class as a whole is characterized not by its power but its *powerlessness*. The worker is denied access to the product of his or her labor, and through this is denied access to property or to any real standing inside capitalist society. The only worth of the worker to capitalism is his or her ability to sell labor power. Once this ability no longer exists—through age, sickness, or a surplus of labor power—then workers are denied even the few crumbs granted to them while in work.

Some feminists talk about patriarchy as a hierarchical pyramid, with old, white men at the pinnacle. The picture could not be more misleading, for inside capitalist society it is only rich old white men who have any real power. Once workers are too old to sell their labor power, they are hardly valued at all by capitalist society, since they no longer possess the ability to earn and therefore to spend money. This contrasts strongly with feudal society, where old men (heads of the patriarchal family) often have the monopoly of power within the family. But a crucial feature of capitalism is the lack of power of the working class.

Images of the man as an all-powerful and dominant figure inside the family are in reality a capitulation to the stereotypical "Andy Capp" view of what the working class looks like. They degrade the role of working-class women within the family and suggest that women and children are totally passive and submissive. There are, of course, families which fit the mythical stereotype; many more do not. In some families the women have control of finance within the family. In some men and women coexist happily; in others the family becomes an arena of struggle between different family members.

The idea that the family is a patriarchal plot can be rapidly dispelled when considering the often quite backward role of the woman in socialization within the family. It is simply not true that sex roles and gender definition are always forced on women. Often women are some of the strictest enforcers of oppressive sex roles, as for example when mothers force their daughters to conform to these roles.

The argument about male benefits clearly reinforces patriarchy theory and predicates two separate and autonomous spheres of struggle. It also leads to another argument quite dominant among the left: that the unequal situation in the home can be solved by either reversing the roles of men and women or by evening up the amount of housework done by both sexes. The argument is put, for example, by Beatrix Campbell and Anna Coote in *Sweet Freedom:*

> If women are to share domestic labor equally with men, then men will have to increase their time spent on unpaid work. (1982, 247)

Few could argue with the sentiments of equal work-sharing in the home. But the political argument often takes the form of utopianism. Although the strategy can improve the lot of individual women, it does not raise the question of why anyone should have to engage in boring repetitive drudgery around the home. In addition, because work-sharing does not challenge the fundamental structure of society, it is likely to remain a utopian dream. Given that society is structured so that men tend to work longer hours for more money, altering women's role in the household will require more far-reaching changes than work-sharing.

The division of labor in the home today is reinforced by the patterns of work in the workplace—the fact that men work far more overtime than women (especially when they have young children, because women are least able to work at this time) and that they tend to travel further to work. That is why it is much easier for middle-class men—who are more likely to earn a reasonable income without overtime—to share child care.

Failure to understand this leads to the sort of narrow reformism expressed by Michele Barrett and Mary McIntosh in *The Anti-Social Family.* They argue that feminists should avoid oppressive relationships and live pure feminist lives, avoiding coquettish behavior and marriage—even avoiding going to other people's weddings. Their real concerns are revealed in one of the most telling statements of modern feminism:

> for those who can afford it, paying someone to clean the house or cook meals is preferable to making it the duty of one household member. Many socialists have qualms about this, without being very clear why. . . . It should be more like engaging a plumber and less like having a skivvy. (1982, 144–45)

Most women, of course, are likely to be the ones doing the paid cleaning rather than employing the cleaner; even if such an option were desirable, which it is not, it is simply not available for most women workers. Role reversals do not begin to challenge the privatized family and its role in the reproduction of labor power.

Yet the reason many feminists put forward such arguments is not simply to do with their feminism. Their politics rests on the reform of the existing system, rather than its revolutionary overthrow. Patriarchy theory fits exactly with such an outlook.

Ideas of patriarchy allow the continuation of the existing privatized family regardless of the social conditions under which it exists. Patriarchy theory can coexist with the gradual reforms of the Labor Party. It is a welcome alibi for Communist Party feminists such as Beatrix Campbell. She and others influenced by Stalinist ideas played a major role in popularizing these theories throughout much of the 1970s. They provided a justification for continuing support for the oppressive and exploitative regimes in Eastern

Europe by giving a feminist veneer to explanations for the various inequalities there. How else, after all, could one explain the oppression of women in the "socialist countries" or the discrimination against gays in Cuba or East Germany? One can either conclude that these countries have nothing to do with socialism, or that socialism cannot bring women's liberation—and a separate fight against patriarchy is needed.

The extent to which patriarchy theory has been adopted shows the dominance of reformist ideas within the socialist and women's movements. Most feminists are happy to concur with Heidi Hartmann when she argues:

> I do not agree with those who argue that the USSR, China, and Cuba are not socialist—they may not have the socialism we would like, but they regard themselves as socialist and so do most other folks. (1981, 364)

This may not be the most scientific analysis, but it has the virtue of encapsulating the dominant view in the women's movement.

It is also typical of an anti-intellectual approach common among many patriarchy theorists. This leads them to attack any serious or rigorous attempt to theorize women's oppression. So Jane Humphries is described as "nonfeminist" (Campbell and Charlton 1978), while the domestic labor debate is derided as "functionalist" (Barrett 1980, 172–75).

Perhaps the greatest weakness of patriarchy theory, however, is that it parallels the separation of home from work, which is a feature of capitalist society. Feminists as a whole were slow to recognize or acknowledge that women were no longer simply housewives but played a crucial role in the workforce; many have still not come to terms with this fact. The separation is convenient for those who pretend that economic struggle goes on at work, whereas political or ideological struggle takes place elsewhere. Some of these people even try to deny that women workers really are part of the working class—relegating only manual workers to the proletariat. So men are seen stereotypically as manual workers, while women are seen equally stereotypically as oppressed housewives.

This is a major error in considering the working class today. Women are a major and permanent part of the working class. As we shall see, there are major divisions inside the working class, that between the sexes being one of the most fundamental. But that women are part of the working class is indisputable. To see them as separate means developing only a partial understanding of women's oppression.

To develop a total picture we need to look at the working class as a totality. We must also see the family as part of class society—a product of the capitalist mode of production. Viewed like this, the fate of the family is seen to be tied up with the fate of capitalism itself. The ending of women's oppression is inextricably linked to the self-emancipation of the working class.

ARCHIVE II

THINKING DIFFERENCE GLOBALLY

Race, Class, Sexuality

17

Women Working Worldwide

Swasti Mitter

NO FAREWELL TO THE WORKING CLASS

A significant yet grossly underemphasized aspect of the current global restructuring is, as we have seen, the emergence of an acutely polarized labor market. In such a market, increasingly, a small number of core workers is going to coexist with a vast array of peripheral workers. There are many names for these peripheral workers: flexible workers, casual workers, or, as in the context of Free Trade Zones, temporary or part-time proletariat. All these terms have the same or similar connotations and conjure up invariably the image of a worker who is a woman, and whose status as a wage-earner does not necessarily carry with it an automatic prospect of career progression. Nor does the image imply job security or other employment-related benefits such as a core worker enjoys.

Who are these peripheral or casual workers? They work for small subcontracting firms or are young recruits in the Free Trade Zone areas, where hiring and firing are easy. In larger companies, they provide services on a contract basis to meet sudden or seasonal upturns in demand. These predominantly female workers are called casual not because of a lack of commitment or experience on their part, but simply because their conditions of work have been deliberately casualized. They provide the base of a growing "shoe-shine" economy even in the affluent West.

Equally striking is the creation of a small but highly privileged and multi-skilled elite of workers in corporate organizations. With a well-defined career path in a secure job, such workers are likely to identify themselves more with company ethics and corporate management than with casual workers. Significantly, the majority of core workers are men, and the trade unions still maintain commitment to their cause.

The division of labor along these lines is influenced by the Japanese system of management; in fact, the system is an extension of the principle used by Japanese companies for a successful method of stock control. It is known as the "kan ban" system and implies having materials "just in time" rather than "just in case." The principle is applied equally effectively by management to the problem of recruiting labor at the lowest possible cost.

This approach to manpower planning, novel in the West, has begun to change the composition of the working class. This change is becoming more pronounced with the growth of home-based work. Increasingly, the self-employed and the hidden workers of the "sweatshop economy" complement the flexible workers of the "shoe-shine economy." Unfortunately, in spite of their growing numbers, they remain, like the flexi-workers on the factory floor, at the margins of the mainstream labor movement.

These changes imply that the working class no longer consists mainly of white male workers; instead, the concept "working class" increasingly covers blacks, women, and in many sectors black women workers. This new working class is largely ignored not only by the mainstream labor movement but by most writers on economic and political issues. Whereas literally thousands of articles have been written on the labor-replacing aspect of new technology, only a handful have been written on the casualization of work, and these mostly by committed women scholars. Titles such as *Collapse of Work* or *World Without Work* are commonplace on library shelves. Videos also take up the theme: *Chips Are Down, Mighty Micro, Chips with Everything*. All these remind us of a future in which the inputs of human labor will be totally unnecessary for the production of goods and services. Concerned philosophers attempt to alter our world view in order to help us come to terms with the changed material conditions of production. In his thought-provoking book *Farewell to the Working Class,* André Gorz, for example, looks forward longingly to the abolition of most kinds of work, which will usher in the "non-class of non-workers" who are not conditioned to believe in the sacredness of work. His nonclass, unlike the outmoded Marxist concept of the working class, is not a "social subject":

> It has no transcendent unity or mission . . . it has no prophetic aura. Instead, it reminds individuals of the need to save themselves and define a social order compatible with their goals and autonomous existence. (Gorz 1982, 10–11)

Striving toward this new social order would involve, according to Gorz, a coherent "policy of time" which would involve reduction of working hours and sharing of jobs. But most of all it would entail learning to appreciate the pleasures of unpaid jobs and being prepared to relinquish the right to paid jobs (Gorz 1982).

This scenario does not appear plausible at present, when the major impact of new technology seems to be in the intensification of the work process through massive subcontracting and casualization of employment. Moreover, to strive for a future of this kind may not seem so attractive either, especially to millions of women workers. In fact, the "labor of love" or "unpaid work" is not a new experience to women. Society's expectation that women will provide such labor at home does not disappear even when they are in paid jobs. As a result, in market-oriented as well as in socialist countries, increased wage employment for women in the postwar years has almost invariably meant burdening women with two jobs. In spite of the burden of a double day, however, most women would welcome the opportunity of going out to work, as only this gives credibility to their status as workers. The limited achievement of such credibility that women have gained in the last two decades has in fact been entirely due to the expansion of paid work outside the home, however exploitative. Not surprisingly, therefore, in a trade-off between the oppression of family life and the drudgery of ill-paid work, most women prefer the latter.

Ironically, it is the access to paid outside work that has given many women a chance to reclaim dignity for themselves in the domain of their own family lives. Unwaged hours of work, by general consensus, are seen as an extra-economic activity, however essential they may be for the productive sphere of a society. The hidden labor of women becomes unrecognized labor, and there is always a pressure not to subject this labor to the cool calculations of economic accounting. As André Gorz writes: "Raising children, looking after and decorating a house, repairing or making things, cooking good meals . . . none of these activities is carried out for economic ends or for consumption" (Gorz 1982, 82).

Much to the chagrin of romantic visionaries, however, women's movements have adopted the strategy of demanding wages for housework. Alternatively, they demand greater social provision of care facilities for children and the old. This is because only by bringing some of these occupations out of the private sphere into the social domain have women in the West achieved some power in the political system. It is power of this kind that could be used effectively for an equitable distribution of work and leisure in tomorrow's society.

Indeed one looks with some trepidation at the glorification of the family, not only by the Moral Majority in America and the Thatcherites in the U.K., but also by an iconoclast of the radical world such as Ivan Illych. He sees the sexual division of labor in and outside the home as based on "vernacular gender," that is, of a natural complementarity which he claims is clearly visible in preindustrial societies. To question it leads him to "the conclusion that the struggle to create economic equality between genderless humans of two different sexes resembles the efforts made to square the circle with ruler and straight edge" (Illych 1983, 66).

In Father Illych's natural order, it is the women who are to contribute most of the unpaid work, "shadow work" as he calls it. For this type of work, women ought not to ask for remuneration, because "the best they can hope for is not a shadow price but a consolation prize" (Illych 1983, 57). In his bitter critique of the women's movement Illych concludes that the demand to end sex discrimination is an idle luxury of elite women who have benefited somehow from economic growth:

> The Mexican woman with the two-car garage leaves the house in charge of a domestic when she escapes to a feminist gathering. . . . Her experience is totally beyond that of her distant cousin, who lives with the tooth puller in the village. . . . The tooth puller's concubine still knows by magic and gossip how to keep men in their place. The bourgeois Latina has traded both for the servant plus car, and the right to flirt with feminist rhetoric. (Illych 1983, 60)

A priest's vision of a womanly woman in her natural habitat is a far cry from the vernacular women I know of who frantically search for paid employment to escape poverty, the oppression of family life, and bride-burning. In a world where one in three families is headed by a woman, and where the number of such families is increasing at an alarming rate, the idealized image of a woman immersed contentedly in her "shadow work" while her vernacular hunter man brings the bacon home ought to be confined only to a romantic's dream. It is the woman's urgency and desire to work outside the home that have created a new working class.

WOMEN ORGANIZING INTERNATIONALLY

The power of the stereotype dies hard. The myth of a male breadwinner perpetuates a convention where it is considered just for women to receive lower wages even when they perform similar jobs. So, too, it is considered natural for women to accept jobs which are part-time, temporary, or performed in home-based units. In the ideology of a patriarchal family unit, a woman's primary role is considered to be in the area of domestic work and in the care of children and older relatives. Hence her commitment to paid work outside her home is seen by society and by her family as less than perfect. However exacting her profession may be, however many hours she may put into her work, a woman worker is always seen as a "permanent casual."

Indeed, because of the accepted notion of a "natural" sexual division of labor at home, the male members of a society tend to view a woman's commitment to paid work as an aberration that should be resisted. Such politics of gender within the family unit extend themselves to the conflict between male and female workers on the factory floor, thereby unwittingly giving transnational corporations an added power to counteract the challenge of the organized labor movement.

The common experience of male attitudes has brought about, especially in the 1980s, a sense of solidarity among female workers, a new awareness of a bond that transcends racial and geographical boundaries. The new technology has been instrumental in fragmenting the production process to the advantage of the transnational corporations (TNCS), but it has also, by facilitating improved communication and transport, helped women workers exchange their experiences. Feminist conferences on the labor movement in recent years bear testimony to this contribution of new technology (NT).

Here I shall document only a few such conferences, of which I have had personal experience, to illustrate the objectives and mechanism of establishing such worldwide networks. In October 1982, twenty-six women from the North and the South met at the Transnational Institute in Amsterdam to consider together the communality as well as the divergences in their experiences as workers in the global clothing and textiles industry. In a colloquium that lasted over three days, the contributors included trade unionists and activists as well as committed researchers in this area. Not only were they all women, most of them were mothers of young children. Their concern with the political and economic issues was understandably interspersed with concern for the children or babies they left at home. One brought her young son with her, and women felt and showed deep sympathy for the delegate from the Philippines whose husband was in prison for his political activism against President Marcos. The participants were by no means the usual crowd one finds at an international conference. For some, this was the first visit away from their home and country. Women came from England, Scotland, Eire, Holland, Canada, the United States, Germany, India, the Philippines, the Mexican-American border, Hong Kong, Brazil, and Australia. Of course, the experiences of these women were diverse, rooted as they were in their cultural and social specificities. But what emerged from the discussion was the striking common element in their experiences as workers, especially in the treatment they received from the TNCs and from their male colleagues (Chapkis and Enloe 1983). A woman from Hong Kong—Choi Wan Cheung—gave an account of the disillusionment of female workers during the Control Data hostilities in South Korea in 1981–82. During the strike staged by women operatives, male workers connived with the management and assumed a disciplinary role to keep women workers in their place. Exactly the same tactic was used by the Levi's company in Tennessee, said Corky Jennings, a union organizer of women workers in that state. Levi's used husbands, older brothers, and fathers to oversee the women workers.

The feminist conference of women workers in the electronics, clothing, and textiles industries on 24 April 1983 also represents a landmark in international solidarity of workers for transnational corporations. The conference was organized at County Hall in London by War on Want and the Archway Development Education Center. It gave a forum to 170 women from the labor, trade union, and women's movements from countries as far apart as Sri Lanka, Malaysia, the Philippines, Holland, and Scotland. The analysis and discussion of the conditions of work in global companies at the conference clarified the role of TNCs in creating an unstable and vulnerable pattern of employment, be it in Malaysia or in Scotland. The exchange of information also confirmed the determination of workers to resist the divisive strategies of multinationals that set black women against white and Third World women against First. The conference affirmed the need for establishing a continuous and powerful international network for disseminating information regarding conditions of work and resistance to the conditions imposed by TNCs. As a result of the conference, the now well-known network "Women Working Worldwide" was set up (War on Want 1983).

Apart from sharing the conviction that knowledge is power, women are increasingly becoming aware that togetherness is power. This new sense of solidarity brings female white-collar workers closer to their manual counterparts. The logic behind this solidarity is obvious: the twin effects of NT—automation and fragmentation—affect office and service work in the same way as they do manufacturing work. Flexi-workers in office jobs share the same vulnerability as casual workers on the factory floor, and the "runaway" office jobs increasingly follow the well-trodden path of "runaway" factory jobs. Awareness of this bond between manual and office workers brought together sixty women from rich and poor countries in Geneva on 19 June 1983, under the auspices of ISIS, a resource center in the international women's liberation movement. The contributions of participants confirmed the need for increased solidarity to resist low wages and health hazards that are often associated with NT in office work as well as in factory work. The discussions in fact successfully challenged the notion of NT as the liberator: the experiences of women workers confirmed that advances in technology had given a potent toot to management to intensify the work process. Hence it was agreed that there was a need to reorient the labor movement to protect the interests of the growing number of low-paid workers and flexi-workers. Again an effective network was begun (ISIS 1983).

The nascent parallel labor movement based on the exchange of information among women workers cannot afford to be blind to the racial dimension in the division of labor. Indeed, it would be unrealistic, in the name of womanly solidarity, to ignore the evidence of history. The distrust black women feel is voiced poignantly by Buchi Emecheta:

> Do you then blame us for being careful in following the white woman's footsteps? The blood of the black woman (for example) has helped so much in building the America of today; but look at her, living in poor areas of Palo Alto in California, look at her shacks in Sacramento, to say nothing of the east . . . (Emecheta 1985, 19)

The labor movement is also tarnished by its record of racism. The treatment of black workers by trade unions in the 1983 strike at the Peugeot-Talbot factories in

France makes black women workers understandably cautious. Here the Communist-led Confédération Général du Travail (CGT) readily agreed to a redundancy plan that laid off mainly the black workers. This is particularly ironic as it is the struggle of Arab and North African workers in the Citroen-Aulney plant in 1982 that gave the CGT the strength it needed to gain organizational control from the "yellow" union (International Labor Reports 1984).

The Imperial Typewriters strike, organized mainly by Asian men and women, in Leicester in 1974 also typifies the difficulty black workers face in identifying themselves with the white-dominated mainstream labor movement. The strike, which started as a protest against economic and racial exploitation, developed into "an all-out battle against the management, the agencies of the state which attempted to mediate, and the Transport and General Workers' Union (TGWU), which denied support to the strikers and attempted to assist the management in defeating them" (Parmar 1982, 264).

In those cases where trade unions did come out in support of black women workers, the issue of race, if not of sex, became subsumed under the cause of defending the trade union movement. The Grunwick strike in 1977, one of the major and most publicized strikes of the 1970s, drew the support of white workers, who attended the mass pickets organized by the strike committee. Indeed, the Grunwick struggle soon became symbolic of the fundamental right of a worker to belong to a union. The fact that most of the strikers were Asian women was seen as incidental. As Pratibha Parmar documents, this negation of the race and gender of the strikers was exemplified by one miner saying, "We are right behind the lads here, they have our full support" (1982, 267).

The need to be aware of the importance of racial issues, both in understanding the emerging structure of employment and in establishing bonds based on realistic awareness, was the guiding principle behind launching the third National Homeworking Conference. The conference was organized by the National Steering Group, an umbrella organization for U.K.-based homeworking campaign groups. It took place on 2 June 1984, at County Hall in London, and was attended by 150 participants from places ranging from Dundee to Amsterdam. The speakers highlighted the racist and sexist practices prevailing in society that give the TNCs easy access to the cheapest and most hidden type of labor in the form of homeworking. The participants, with justifiable humility, remembered the thousands of homeworkers who could not come to the conference. A woman from Lambeth said:

> We must not forget the number of women who are not in the conference today. They could not come because of racist and sexist practices, because they have no childcare, could not get on the trains (for lack of money) and could not come up to the microphone to speak (from fear of the authorities or lack of English). (Greater London Council 1986)

It was recognized particularly at this conference that institutional racism places black women at a special disadvantage. Faced with additional obstacles, black women at times feel that racism is more of an evil in their lives than sexism. An Asian woman from the Greenwich Homeworking Project voiced the dilemma:

> For many Asian and black women, there are greater problems than [the loneliness, health hazards, and financial insecurity] associated with homeworking: there are racist attacks, being a single parent in an alien culture, and fear of immigration authorities. (GLC 1986)

To challenge the racist element in the spread of homeworking, therefore, became a major objective in the Charter of Homeworking formulated by the Steering Group.

One of the important contributions of the feminist labor movement is that it seriously challenges the male-dominated, class-biased, and Eurocentric vision of growth and development. The postwar flourishing academic discipline of "development economics" was based on the unquestioned superiority of European societies (Mitter 1986). The socioeconomic maturity of a non-European nation was measured against a norm prevailing and accepted in white society. The ethos of international agencies reflected the nineteenth-century social Darwinism that viewed all non-European cultures simply as poorer versions of European civilization. Black societies were regarded as belonging to the childhood of mankind, whose maturity had been reached only in white societies. The desirability and the necessity of evolving one's own path of development, oriented toward a country's history, tradition, and specific needs, were not seen as important. The concept of "appropriate technology" was regarded as eccentric. In this intellectual milieu, TNCs were seen as welcome and universal revelers, as harbingers of modern and superior societies.

Similarly, in white societies the improvement of the working class was planned for them by the elite. The people were treated as a "dull compendious mass," to borrow Thomas Carlyle's phrase, in the restructuring of the postwar economy. Bea Campbell describes the disastrous consequences of such attitudes in the context of housing policy:

> The municipal merchants of mass housing for the people planned homes for the people, not with them; they forced high-rise blocks, for example, on reluctant inhabitants. They knew people did not like them, but they built them nonetheless. (Campbell 1984, 232)

The zeal of doing things for people rather than with people permeated left-wing political thinking as well. Bea Campbell recounts:

> A contemporary of mine once said, self-critically, "I used to think that what I was fighting for was for the people to have access to a good education, good housing, good books, to be fearless, to be like me, actually." (Campbell 1984, 232)

Such condescension in planning, as well as the class-biased, neocolonial policies of national and international agencies, are now being rejected by the grassroots feminist movements in favor of a more caring, sharing, and cooperative economic structure. In the search for this, women in the West are looking for models to emulate in non-Western societies—models such as GABRIELA in the Philippines or the Self-Employed Women's Association (SEWA) in India. GABRIELA, as we have seen, is a movement of women workers who aim to restructure their society in order to use the nation's resources for the betterment of all its people. As a precondition of this goal, they wage a struggle to free the Philippines from the military and economic domination of foreign powers, especially the United States. In addition, the movement provides the strength and inspiration behind a new type of unionism where both the leadership and the membership consist entirely of women workers.

The Kilusan Ng Manggagwang Kababaihan (KMK) is the Philippine Women Workers' Movement; a union since 1984, it is linked to Kilusan Mayo Uno (KMU), the May 1 Movement of militant workers. KMU, organized clandestinely under martial law in 1980, is distinct from "yellow unions" and includes both men and women. Women workers can be members of KMU as well as of KMK. KMK concentrates on the gender-specific issues, such as child care, low pay, maternity leave, flexible working time—the kinds of issues that tend to get lost or diffused in a male-dominated trade union movement. This dual structure heralds an organizational innovation in trade unionism reflecting the commonality as well as the divergences in the interests of men and women workers.

SEWA is also a trade union movement of a novel kind. Its membership consists of scattered, self-employed, and home-based women workers who constitute a major part of the female workforce in the famous textiles city of Ahmedabad, in the western province of India. Its 25,000-odd members are recruited from a variety of professions. The women in SEWA may be petty roadside vendors, rollers of "Bidi" (indigenous cigarettes), basket-makers, or vegetable sellers. They represent the poorest and the most exploited sections of the community, and a great many of them are Harijans (untouchables). In some trades, nearly half of the women are the sole supporters of their family, as their men have either deserted or migrated in search of better jobs. Although potentially vulnerable, the lives and working conditions of these women have been transformed by this immensely successful union of self-employed women. SEWA—the acronym resembles the word that means "service" in most Indian languages—was founded in 1972 and became an autonomous movement when it broke away from its parent organization, the Textiles Labor Association, in 1981. The split came about as a result of SEWA's taking up the cause of Harijans in the outbreak of violence over the issue of positive discrimination in favor of this lowest of castes. All along, under the inspiring guidance of Ela Bhatt, SEWA has provided a constructive, rather than merely reactive, approach to the labor movement. In her words:

> The purpose of trade unionism is not only for agitation. It is about solidarity and development: 89 percent of women workers in Ahmedabad are self-employed. If they are excluded from the labor movement, you are cutting off the vast majority of workers, and those who most need protection. (Seabrook 1985, 14)

This broad vision of the labor movement can sustain itself only through the economic strength of its members. Hence SEWA arranges not only for upgrading the skills of its members in production, retailing, and marketing, but also for giving them adequate access to finance. The most impressive achievement of SEWA to date has been to set up its own bank for its members, who are poor and mostly illiterate, and who cannot provide any collateral to an ordinary finance house. Based on the strength of the small savings of its members, SEWA can now boast a rate of default that is much lower than that in commercial banks (SEWA 1983).

As the casualization of employment becomes all-pervasive in the West, the achievement of SEWA provides a model for organizing women workers in the advanced economies of Europe. Echoing the messages of Ela Bhatt, the women's movement in the West now also questions the present trend in the trade union movement that marginalizes the ever-growing number of casual and home-based workers.

ALTERNATIVE ECONOMIC STRATEGIES

Reversing this trend will imply recognizing a fresh definition of the working class. It will also necessitate, in the spirit of GABRIELA, a revaluation of the instruments as well as the goals of economic planning.

This new approach is as important for the mature West as it is for the newly emerging non-European countries. An awareness of this has led to formulations of a number of alternative strategies in Western Europe. The experiments with "municipal socialism" under the labor-controlled Greater London Council (GLC) between 1981 and 1986 have been among the most comprehensive. In 1981 the GLC, under the leadership of Ken Livingstone, pledged its commitment to a new version of socialism. Over the brief period of five years, it tried to build a participatory socialism, bringing together women, ethnic minorities, and other new social forces. There was a fresh vision of economic renewal: the plan was to work toward the restructuring of labor, to borrow Robin Muffay's phrase, rather than the restructuring of capital (Murray 1983, 103).

In this brand of socialism, there was no reason to make the state the center of power. Of course, a certain amount of state support was necessary, but only insofar as it increased the competitive power of labor. To what extent the experiment with municipal socialism was successful is for the historians to evaluate, but it definitely mobilized support from the general public on a scale that challenged the philosophy of the central monetarist government, committed to its belief in free market mechanisms and the invigoration of international capital. The experiment had to be stopped. The abolition of the GLC by the central government in March 1986 was itself a tribute to the success of the GLC's policies.

In case the experiment should simply disappear into the folk history of London, the GLC in 1985 produced a document entitled *The London Industrial Strategy 1985 (LIS)* to enable its strategy to obtain the serious consideration it deserved (GLC 1985, 17–18). In it, the socialist GLC provided a coherent and detailed blueprint for an alternative economic strategy in the context of Greater London, based on some in-depth research on the main industrial sectors that generate employment for Londoners.

The radical new departure in LIS is that it acknowledges the crucial roles of domestic work and child care in restructuring the local economy. By extending the social provision of caring, it promises to reverse the central government policy that "is shifting work back into the household" (GLC 1985, 22). This promise is particularly significant as the document explicitly relates the discrimination women face in paid jobs to the role of women at home. It is for this reason perhaps that LIS, uniquely among socialist blueprints, incorporates a chapter on the growth of homeworking. The GLC recognizes that this represents the logical outcome of the current restructuring of capital, which thrives on increased subcontracting and on the racial and sexual divisiveness among workers.

Increasing the competitiveness of workers in relation to monopoly capital is the aim of the GLC's strategy. In this connection, the production of goods and services plays a central role. The council's approach contrasts sharply with mainstream economic philosophy embedded in monetarism and Keynesianism, both of which place undue emphasis on financial indicators relating to foreign exchange, the stock market, or the money supply. The establishment economists, obsessed with the money veil of the economy, have shown too little concern for the vital issues of people and production. As the LIS states:

> Thus, ignored by economists, production has been left as the province of the engineer, the production manager and the industrial relations consultant [who give] . . . overriding priority to private market production and to the military sector, and the technological replacement of awkward labor. We can call this *militarized market production*. It represents the economics of capital.

The alternative, therefore, is to work toward the economics of labor, where the planners aim to provide work for all those who wish it in jobs geared to meeting social needs. The role of technology, in such a scheme, is to reskill labor and thereby improve its competitiveness, rather than to deskill workers for the benefit of management.

The Greater London Enterprise Board (GLEB) was set up in 1983 precisely to augment this aim. It still exists, but with much-reduced resources now that the GLC is gone. As a vital institution of the GLC, it provided assistance to create or save jobs in firms that offered better wages and greater control by workers, and manufactured socially useful goods. The principal aim of the Board was to evolve what Mike Cooley, the Director of GLEB, called a "human-centered technology." His commitment to promote this was based on the current feminist critique of science and technology. In his words:

> The prevailing technology reflects the economic base and power relations of the society which has given rise to it, and displays predominantly the value system of the white male capitalist warrior hero. (*Computing* 1980, 16)

To change this value system meant, therefore, altering the power base itself and thereby the accepted social relations of production.

The GLC and GLEB fall somewhat short of offering the steps for achieving such an alteration. The promises of crèche facilities, of an expansion of social provisions, and of urging or forcing firms to be equal opportunity employers are important but by no means sufficient steps for achieving gender equality at work. The LIS, for example, does not take up the issue of hours of work—a question that many feminist economists see as crucial to progress in achieving equality between genders (Phillips 1984). Without a provision for shorter working hours and a more flexible pattern of employment, which would make it possible for the tasks involved in bringing up children to be shared, gender equality will be hard to achieve. By not stressing the importance of such a demand, therefore, even the LIS would seem to be building its socialist base on the accepted image of a woman who is or should be solely responsible for the caring jobs. As long as this assumption remains, it becomes difficult to make a dent in the myth of the male breadwinner—hitherto the crucial concept in constructing a role for women in the job market.

Again the LIS, representing an island of socialism in a market-oriented society, can pose only a limited challenge to the large corporations. The hope of counteracting the power of the global corporations is seen primarily in obtaining a deep knowledge of the interconnection between different sectors: "The French refer to it as the *filière,* the thread of industrial organization" (LIS 1985, 40). In the absence of such knowledge, however, the LIS states, "public intervention itself may become in the end a mere support for those who control the commanding economic heights and who have themselves decentralized to subcontractors" (Cochrane 1986).

The knowledge itself can hardly alter the existing social relations of production unless we demand accountability regarding the corporations' sources of supply. The multinational retailers are precisely the ones that the LIS fears as commanding "economic heights." By accepting their power in the market, the LIS at times appears like a report written by "radical management consultants" helping the small and ailing firms in the inner city to win the custom of the big retailers.

Municipal socialism can be fully successful only with the support of central government. The political mobilization at the grassroots level can then be used to bring about the desired changes in the structure of the market as well as in the accepted social relations of production. In this future scenario, it may be possible to demand accountability from the flexible international companies, but only with the help of firsthand knowledge of the hierarchy of subcontracting that links homeworkers and other vulnerable workers to the worldwide strategies of the multinationals.

The grassroots organizations of women workers, such as homeworking campaign groups in the U.K., can offer precisely this vital knowledge regarding industrial organization that the restructuring of labor requires. In London since 1981, such organizations have been funded by the GLC, which has also provided the facilities for them to meet comparable groups from other countries. Thus, the strong links that are being forged among such organizations across national boundaries can provide the force for taking up the challenge of the multinationals internationally.

The growing awareness of the limited ability of nation-states to counteract the supranational powers of global corporations has already led to a visibly transnational approach in the socialist planning of West European countries. In the well-publicized manifesto, *Out of Crisis—A Project for European Recovery,* the need for a concerted European plan for a socialist expansionary policy of reflation, redistribution, and restructuring has been stressed. The manifesto, known as the "Alternative Economic Strategy" (AES), demands, in Stuart Holland's phrase, an end to "beggar my neighbor" deflation and the adoption of coordinated "better my neighbor" expansionary policies (Holland 1983). Such a mechanism of European macromanagement to replace national management seems particularly urgent when, to quote Ken Livingstone, "Europe . . . is overcast by the shadow of the American economy just as it is overcast militarily by the shadow of the American arsenal." To change course is not going to be easy. It would involve, as Ken Coates argues, "a new set of relationships with the Third World and with developing China. This would be a coalition for peace, as well as development and recovery" (Coates 1985). In particular this new internationalism, as Frances Morrell reminds us,

> is anti-Atlanticist. If it is to be carried through, then conflict with the current Presidency of the United States is inevitable. Equally inevitable is some conflict with major American and Japanese multinationals trading in Europe, with international financial institutions like IMF, and with the EEC over some of the clauses of the Treaty of Rome. (Morrell 1985, 9)

Implementing a transnational socialist program of recovery would involve the linking of the labor movement across Europe in a plan to enlist the explicit cooperation of the workers of the countries concerned. John Palmer envisages establishing such links through agitations or campaigns for jobs and welfare rights by trade unions, following the model set by the European Nuclear Disarmament movement (Palmer 1983).

In such a vision, however, the labor movement is being assigned only a reactive role (Teague 1985). At the same time, it implies a too facile identification of the labor movement with the mainstream trade union–based workers' movement. At the current stage of global industrial restructuring, when the growth area of employment is only in casualized jobs and home-based work, the strategy for participatory socialism is certain to founder unless it reckons with the cooperation: of the grassroots organizations representing women and black workers.

It is on the basis of reasoned analysis, therefore, that the "Alternative Economic Strategy" of the left is viewed by women and blacks as a manifesto written by white male activists, reflecting the traditions of the male-dominated labor movement. The agenda puts more emphasis on the manufacturing sector, which is viewed as the engine for growth, and less on the services that are the basis for distributive justice. Neither does the AES consider the arbitrariness in the definition of skills and the notion of a family wage—two factors that have been instrumental in subjecting women to the status of low-pay workers (Campbell 1982).

If women feel marginalized in the European plan for socialist expansionary policy, so too do blacks. In a society where black families live in constant fear of violence and where black youth face overt discrimination in jobs and training, socialism becomes an empty promise without a positive assurance of distributive justice.

Nor should such a strategy overlook the basic tenets of feminist socialism, rooted in a belief in the equality of gender as well as class. It is imperative therefore that, in an alternative economic strategy, the household should be seen as a focal point and domestic work seen to play a vital role. As we have observed, the division between core male workers and peripheralized women workers in the international political economy is based precisely on the generally accepted role of women in the domestic sphere. Hence it will be futile to counteract the challenges of the global corporations until and unless there are extended social provisions for the care of the young and the elderly, and men are willing to share domestic work.

Finally, an alternative strategy needs to build its base on the ongoing socialist experiments at the community level. It is indeed only a community-based network that can effectively assess and harmonize economic, emotional, and environmental needs. Through their campaigns for organizing homeworkers, flexi-workers, and workers in the unregulated economy, feminist labor movements are offering different variants of such community networks. In spirit, their vision is akin to what Rudolf Bahro would have called a "noncapitalist path of production" (Bahro 1978). In the Lega delle Cooperative in Rome, Italian feminists have, for example, submitted such a blueprint of grassroots socialism. I cannot do better than quote them:

> Would it not be possible, for instance, to introduce a modernized version of the old practice whereby a housing cooperative would be regarded as being not only the group of people living in the same building, but also as the place where the services needed by these people are organized? And would it not be possible to encourage members of the producers' cooperatives to create ways of channeling company profits to benefit the community (in cultural, touristic, welfare and other activities)? Could consumers' cooperatives not come to an agreement with social services cooperatives to allow their members to have privileged rates for specific services? This would stimulate new experiments in the areas of social services, which then would be assured of a stable market within the cooperative circuit. And women would benefit from this, since they would once again find an effective channel for voicing their collective needs: they would have a new—though at the same time a very old—weapon in their battle for emancipation and freedom. (Nicolini 1982)

When such grassroots experiments gather momentum, one hopes that the mainstream labor movement will reach out to join the new yet already dynamic women workers' movement. A British trade union banner of the early twentieth century proclaimed:

> The world is my country,
> Mankind are my brethren,
> To do good one to another is my religion. (*New Internationalist* 1982, 7)

The time has now come to make explicit room for womankind in these phrases if we are to build solidarity for employment and justice.

18

Colonization and Housewifization

Maria Mies

WOMEN UNDER COLONIALISM

As Rhoda Reddock (1984) has shown, the colonizers' attitude to slavery and slave women in the Caribbean was based clearly on capitalist cost-benefit calculations. This was particularly true with regard to the question of whether slave women should be allowed to "breed" more slaves or not. Throughout the centuries of the modern slave trade and slave economy (1655 to 1838), this question was answered not according to the principles of Christian ethics—supposedly applicable in the "Motherlands"—but according to the accumulation considerations of the capitalist planters. Thus, during the first period, from 1655 to the beginnings of the eighteenth century, when most estates were small holdings with few slaves, these planters still depended, following the peasant model of reproduction, on the natural reproduction of the slave population. The second period is characterized by the so-called sugar revolution, the introduction of large-scale sugar production in big plantations. In this period, beginning around 1760 and lasting until about 1800, slave women were actively discouraged from bearing children or forming families. The planters, as good capitalists, held the view that it "was cheaper to purchase than to breed." This was the case in all sugar colonies whether they were under Catholic (French) or Protestant (British, Dutch) dominion. In fact, slave women who were found pregnant were cursed and ill-treated. Moreover, the backbreaking work in the sugar plantations did not allow the slave women to nurse small babies. The reasons behind this antinatalist policy of the planters are expressed in the statement of one Mr. G. M. Hall on Cuban planters:

> During and after pregnancy the slave is useless for several months, and her nourishment should be more abundant and better chosen. This loss of work and added expense comes out of the master's pocket. It is he who has to pay for the often lengthy care of the newborn. This expense is so considerable that the negro born on the plantation costs more when he is in condition to work than another of the same age bought at the public market would have cost. (G. M. Hall, quoted in Reddock 1984, 16)

In the French colony of St. Dominique the planters calculated that a slave woman's work over a period of eighteen months was worth 600 livres. The eighteen months were the time calculated for pregnancy and breast feeding. During such a time the slave woman would be able to do only half her usual work. Thus, her master would lose 300 livres. "A fifteen-month-old slave was not worth this sum" (Hall, quoted by Reddock 1984, 16). The effect of this policy was, as many observers have found, that the "fertility" of slave women was extremely low during this period and far into the nineteenth century (Reddock 1984).

Toward the end of the eighteenth century, it became evident that western Africa could no longer be counted upon as fertile hunting ground for slaves. Moreover, the British colonizers saw it as more profitable to incorporate Africa itself into their empire as a source of raw material and minerals. Therefore, the more "progressive" sections of the British bourgeoisie advocated the abolition of the slave trade—which happened in 1807—and the encouragement of "local breeding." The colonial government foresaw a number of incentives in the slave codes of the late eighteenth and nineteenth centuries to encourage local breeding of slaves by slave women on the plantations. This sudden change of policy, however, seems to have had little effect on the slave women. As Rhoda Reddock points out, in the long years of slavery the slave women had internalized an antimotherhood attitude as a form of resistance to the slave system; they continued a kind of birth strike until the middle of the nineteenth century. When they became pregnant, they used bitter herbs to produce abortions or, when the children were born, "many were allowed to die out of the women's natural dislike for bearing them to see them become slaves, destined to toil all their lives for their master's enrichment" (Moreno-Fraginals 1976, quoted in Reddock 1984, 17). Rhoda Reddock sees in this antimotherhood attitude of the slave women an example of "the way in which the ideology of the ruling classes could, for different though connected material reasons, become the accepted ideology of the oppressed" (Reddock 1984, 17).

The colonial masters now reaped the fruits—or rather the failures—of treating African women as mere conditions of production for capital accumulation. The problem of labor shortage on the plantations in the Caribbean became so acute, due to the slave women's birth strike, that in Cuba virtual "stud farms" were established and slave breeding became a regular business (Moreno-Fraginals quoted in Reddock 1984, 18). Rhoda Reddock summarizes the changing policy of the colonizers regarding slave women's procreative capacities in the following manner:

> As long as Africa was incorporated in the capitalist world economy only as a producer of human labor, there was no need to produce labor locally. Through the use of cost-benefit analysis the planters had taken the most profitable line of action. When this was no longer profitable for them, they were surprised by the resistance shown by the slave women who . . . recognized clearly their position as the property of the plantation owners. The fact is that for more than 100 years, the majority of slave women in the Caribbean were neither wives nor mothers and by exercising control over their reproductive capabilities were able to deeply affect the plantation economy. (Reddock 1984, 18)

These more than a hundred years that "slave women in the Caribbean were neither wives nor mothers" were exactly the same period that women of the European bourgeoisie were domesticated and ideologically manipulated into wifehood and motherhood as their "natural" vocation (Badinter 1980). While one set of women was treated as pure labor force, a source of energy, the other set of women was treated as "nonproductive" breeders only.

It is, indeed, an irony of history that later in the nineteenth century the colonizers tried desperately to introduce the nuclear family and the monogamous marriage norm into the ex-slave population of the Caribbean. But both women and men saw no bene-fit for themselves in adopting these norms and rejected marriage. Now their own double-faced policy boomeranged on the colonizers. In order to be able freely to exploit the slaves, they had for centuries defined them outside humanity and Christianity. In this they were supported by the ethnologists who said that the negroes did not belong to the same "species" as the Europeans. Hence, slaves could not become Christians because, according to the Church of England, no Christian could be a slave.

When, around 1780, the new slave codes began to encourage marriage among the slaves as a means to encourage local breeding of slaves, the slaves only ridiculed this "high caste" thing and continued with their "common law" unions. This meant that each woman could live with a man as long as she pleased; the same also applied to the man. Slave women saw the marriage tie as something that would subject them to the control of one man who could even beat them. The men wanted more than one wife and therefore rejected marriage. The missionaries and planters who tried to introduce the European middle-class model of the man-woman relationship were exasperated. A church histori-an, Caldecott, eventually found an explanation for this resistance to the benefits of civilization in the fact that negroes were not able to "control their fancy" (their sexual desires), and therefore shrank from constancy: "With them it is the women as much as the men who are thus constituted; there is in the Negro race a nearer approach to equality between the sexes than is found in the European races . . ." (Caldecott, quoted in Reddock 1984, 47). "Equality between the sexes," however, was seen as a sign of a primitive, back-ward race, a notion common among nineteenth-century colonizers and ethnologists.

That equality of men and women is a sign of backwardness and part of the "civiliz-ing mission" of the British colonialialists to destroy the independence of colonized women, and to teach the colonized men the "virtues" of sexism and militarism, are also clearly spelled out by one Mr. Fielding Hall in his book, *A People at School*.[1] Mr. Hall was political officer in the British colonial administration in Burma between 1887 and 1891. He gives a vivid account of the independence of Burmese women, of the equality between the sexes, and of the peace-loving nature of the Burmese people, which he ascribes to Buddhism. But instead of trying to preserve such a happy society, Mr. Hall comes to the conclusion that Burma has to be brought by force on the road of progress: "But today the laws are ours, the power, the authority. We govern for our own subjects and we govern in our own way. Our whole presence here is against their desires." He suggests the following measures to civilize the Burmese people:

1. The men must be taught to kill and to fight for the British colonialists: "I can imagine nothing that could do the Burmese so much good as to have a regiment of their own to distinguish itself in our wars. It would open their eyes to new views of life." (Hall 1915, 264)

2. The women must surrender their liberty in the interests of man.

Considering equality of the sexes a sign of backwardness, this colonial administrator warned, "It must never be forgotten that their civilization is relatively a thousand years behind ours." To overcome this backwardness, the Burmese men should learn to kill, to make war, and to oppress their women. In the words of Mr. Hall: "What the surgeon's knife is to the diseased body that is the soldier's sword to the diseased nations." And again:

> the gospel of progress, of knowledge, of happiness . . . is taught not by book and sermon but by spear and sword . . . To declare, as Buddhism does, that bravery is of no account; to say to them, as the women did, you are no better and no more than we are, and should have the same code of life; could anything be worse?

He also seeks the help of ethnologists to defend this ideology of Man the Hunter: "Men and women are not sufficiently differentiated yet in Burma. It is the mark of a young race. Ethnologists tell us that. In the earliest peoples the difference was very slight. As a race grows older the difference increases." Then Mr. Hall describes how Burmese women are eventually "brought down" to the status of the civilized, dependent housewife. Local home industries, formerly in the hands of women, are destroyed by the import of commodities from England. Women are also pushed out of trade: "In Rangoon the large English stores are undermining the Bazaars where the women used to earn an independent livelihood."

After their loss of economic independence, Mr. Hall considers it of utmost importance that the laws of marriage and inheritance be changed so that Burma, too, may become a "progressive" land where men rule. Woman has to understand that her independence stands in the way of progress:

> With her power of independence will disappear her free will and her influence. When she is dependent on her husband she can no longer dictate to him. When he feeds her, she is no longer able to make her voice as loud as his is. It is inevitable that she should retire. . . . The nations who succeed are not feminine nations but the masculine. Woman's influence is good provided it does not go too far. Yet it has done so here. It has been bad for the man, bad too for the woman. It has never been good for women to be too independent; it has robbed them of many virtues. It improves a man to have to work for his wife and family; it makes a man of him. It is demoralizing for both if the woman can keep herself and, if necessary, her husband too. (Hall in Anonymous 1915, 266)

That the African women brought to the Caribbean as slaves were not made slaves because they were "backward" or less "civilized" than the colonizers, but on the contrary were made "savages" by slavery itself and those colonizers is now brought to light by historical research on women in West Africa. George Brooks, for example, shows in his work on the *signares*—the women traders of eighteenth-century Senegal—that these women, particularly of the Wolof tribe, held a high position in the precolonial West African societies. Moreover, the first Portuguese and French merchants who came to Senegal in search of merchandise were totally dependent on the cooperation and goodwill of these powerful women, who entered into sexual and trade alliances with these European men. They not only were in possession of great wealth, accumulated through trade with the inferior parts of their regions, but had also developed such a cultured way of life, such a sense for beauty and gracefulness, that the European adventurers who first came into contact with them felt flabbergasted. Brooks quotes one Rev. John Lindsay, chaplain aboard a British ship, as having written:

> As to their women, and in particular the ladies (for so I must call many of those in Senegal), they are in a surprising degree handsome, have very fine features, are wonderfully tractable, remarkably polite both in conversation and manners; and in the point of keeping themselves neat and clean (of which we have generally strange ideas, formed to us by the beastly laziness of the slaves) they far surpass the Europeans in every respect. They bathe twice a day . . . and in this particular have a hearty contempt for all white people, who they imagine must be disagreeable, to our women especially. Nor can even their men from this very notion, be brought to look upon the prettiest of our women, but with the coldest indifference, some of whom there are here, officers' ladies, who dress very showy, and who, even in England would be thought handsome. (Brooks 1976, 24)

The European men—the Portuguese and French who came to West Africa first as merchants or soldiers—came usually alone, without wives or families. Their alliances with the "ladies" or *signares* (from the Portuguese word *senhoras*) were so attractive to them that they married these women according to the Wolof style, and often simply adopted the African way of life. Their children, the Euroafricans, often rose to high positions in the colonial society, and the daughters usually became *signares* again. Obviously, the Portuguese and the French colonizers did not yet have strong racist prejudices against sexual and marriage relationships with West African women, but found these alliances not only profitable but also humanly satisfying.

With the advent of the British in West Africa, however, this easy-going, Catholic attitude toward African women changed. The British soldiers, merchants, and administrators no longer entered into marriage alliances with the *signares,* but turned African women into prostitutes. This, then, seems to be the point in history when racism proper enters the picture: the African woman is degraded and made a prostitute for the English colonizers, then theories of the racial superiority of the white male and the "beastliness"of the African women are propagated. Obviously, British colonial history is as discreet about these aspects as the Dutch. Yet Brooks says that the institution of "signareship" did not take root in Gambia because it was

> stifled by the influx of new arrivals from Britain, few of whom, whether traders, government officials, or military officers—deviated from "proper" British behavior to live openly with Euroafrican or African women, whatever they might do clandestinely. British authors are discreet about such matters, but it can be discerned that in contrast to the family lives of traders and their *signares,* there developed . . . a rootless bachelor community of a type found elsewhere in British areas of West Africa. Open and unrepentant racism was one characteristic of this community; two others were reckless gambling and alcoholism. (Brooks 1976, 43)

These accounts corroborate not only Walter Rodney's general thesis that Europe underdeveloped Africa, but also our main argument that the colonial process, as it advanced, brought the women of the colonized people progressively down from a former high position of relative power and independence to that of "beastly" and degraded "nature." This "naturalization" of colonized women is the counterpart of the "civilizing" of the European women.

HOUSEWIFIZATION

First Stage: Luxuries for the "Ladies"

The "other side of the story" of both the violent subordination of European women during the witch persecution, and of African, Asian, and Latin American women during the colonizing process is the creation of the women first of the accumulating classes in Europe, later also in the United States, as consumers and demonstrators of luxury and wealth, and at a later stage as housewives. Let us not forget that practically all the items stolen, looted, or traded from the colonies were not items necessary for the daily subsistence of the masses, but luxury items. Initially these items were only consumed by the privileged few who had the money to buy them: spices from the Molluccan islands; precious textiles, silk, precious stones, and muslin from India; sugar, cacao, and spices from the Caribbean; precious metals from Hispano America. Werner Sombart, in his study *Luxury and Capitalism* (1922), has advanced the thesis that the market for most of these rare colonial luxury goods had been created by a class of women who had risen as mistresses of the absolutist princes and kings of France and England in the seventeenth and eighteenth centuries. According to Sombart, the great cocottes and mistresses were the ones who created new fashions in women's dress, cosmetics, eating habits, and particularly in furnishing the homes of the gentlemen. Neither the war-mongering men of the aristocracy nor the men of the merchant class would have had, if left to themselves, the imagination, the sophistication, and the culture to invent such luxuries, almost all centered around women as luxury creatures. It was this class of women, according to Sombart, who created the new luxury "needs" that gave the decisive impetus to capitalism because, with their access to the money accumulated by the absolutist state, they created the market for early capitalism.

Sombart gives us a detailed account of the development of luxury consumption at the Italian, French, and English courts of the sixteenth and seventeenth centuries. He clearly identifies a trend in luxury spending, particularly during the reign of Louis XIV. Whereas the luxury expenses of the king of France were 2,995,000 livres in 1542, these had steadily risen and were 28,813,955 in 1680. Sombart attributes this enormous display of luxury and splendor to the love of these feudal lords for their courtesans and mistresses. Thus, the king's fancy for La Vallière prompted Louis XIV to build Versailles. Sombart is also of the opinion that Mme. de Pompadour, the representative of the culture of the *ancien régime,* had a bigger budget than any of the European queens had ever had. In nineteen years of her reign she spent 36,327,268 livres. Similarly Comtesse Dubarry, who reigned between 1769 and 1774, spent 12,481,803 livres on luxury items (Sombart 1922, 98–99).

Feminists will not agree with Sombart, who attributes this development of luxury—first centering around the European courts and later imitated by *the nouveaux riches* among the European bourgeoisie—to the great courtesans with their great vanity, their addiction for luxurious clothes, houses, furniture, food, and cosmetics. Even if the men of these classes preferred to demonstrate their wealth by spending on their women and turning them into showpieces of their accumulated wealth, it would again mean making the women the villains of the piece. Would it not amount to saying that it was not the men—who wielded economic and political power—who were the historical "subjects" (in the Marxist sense), but the women who were the real power behind the scenes, who pulled the strings and set the tune according to which the mighty men danced? But, apart from this, Sombart's thesis that capitalism was born out of luxury consumption and not in order to satisfy growing subsistence needs of the masses has great relevance for our discussion of the relationship between colonization and housewifization. He shows clearly that early merchant capitalism was based almost entirely on trade with luxury items from the colonies which were consumed by the European elites. The items which appear in a trading list of the Levant trade include *oriental medicines* (e.g., aloes, balm, ginger, camphor, cardamon, myrobalam, saffron, etc.); *spices* (pepper, cloves, sugar, cinnamon, nutmeg); *perfumes* (benzoin, musk, sandalwood, incense, amber); *dyes for textiles* (e.g., indigo, lac, purple, henna); *raw materials for textiles* (silk, Egyptian flax); *precious metals and jewelry and stones* (corals, pearls, ivory, porcelain, glass, gold, and silver); *textiles* (silk, brocade, velvet, fine material of linen, muslin, or wool).

In the eighteenth and nineteenth centuries many more items were added to this list, particularly items systematically produced in the new colonial plantations like sugar, coffee, cacao, and tea. Sombart gives an account of the rising tea consumption in England. The average tea consumption of an English family was 6.5 pounds in 1906. This level of consumption could be afforded in

1668 by	3 families
1710 by	2,000 families
1730 by	12,000 families
1760 by	40,000 families
1780 by	140,000 families (Source: Sombart 1922, 146)

What did this tremendous deployment of luxury among the European rich, based on the exploitation of the peoples of Africa, Asia, and America, mean for the European women? Sombart identifies certain trends in the luxury production, which he, as we have seen, attributes to the passions of a certain class of women. They are the following:

1. *a tendency toward domesticity:* Whereas medieval luxury was public, now it became private. The display of luxury does not take place in the marketplace or during public festivals, but inside the secluded palaces and houses of the rich.

2. *a tendency toward objectification:* In the Middle Ages wealth was expressed in the number of vassals or men a prince could count upon. Now wealth is expressed in goods and material items, commodities bought by money. Adam Smith would say one moves from "unproductive" to "productive" luxury, because the former personal luxury puts "unproductive" hands to work, whereas the objectified luxury puts "productive" hands to work (in a capitalist sense, that is, wage workers in a capitalist enterprise) (Sombart 1922, 119). Sombart is of the opinion that leisure-class women had an interest in the development of objectified luxury (more items and commodities), because they had no use for more soldiers and vassals.

Similar trends can be observed with regard to sugar and coffee. For most people in Europe in the eighteenth century, sugar had not yet replaced honey. Sugar remained a typical luxury item for the European rich until far into the nineteenth century (Sombart 1922, 147).

Foreign trade between Europe, America, Africa, and the Orient was, until well into the nineteenth century, mainly trade in the above-mentioned luxury goods. Imports from East India to France in 1776 were to the value of 36,241,000 francs, distributed as follows:

coffee	3,248,000 fr.
pepper and cinnamon	2,449,000 fr.
muslin	12,000,000 fr.
Indian linen	10,000,000 fr.
porcelain	200,000 fr.
silk	1,382,000 fr.
tea	3,399,000 fr.
saltpetre	3,380,000 fr.
Total	36,241,000 fr.

(Source: Sombart 1922, 148)

Sombart also includes the profits made by the slave trade in the figures for luxury production and consumptions. The slave trade was totally organized along capitalist lines.

The development of wholesale and retail markets in England followed the same logic from the seventeenth to the nineteenth centuries. The first big urban shops which came up to replace the local markets were shops dealing with luxury goods.

3. *a tendency toward contraction of time:* Whereas formerly luxury consumption was restricted to certain seasons because the indigenous production of a surplus needed a long time, now luxuries could be consumed at any time during the year and also within the span of an individual life.

Sombart again attributes this tendency—in my opinion, wrongly—to the individualism and the impatience of leisure-class women who demanded immediate satisfaction of their desires as a sign of the affection of their lovers.

Of the above tendencies, the tendency toward domestication and privatization certainly had a great impact on the construction of the new image of the "good woman" in the centers of capitalism in the nineteenth and twentieth centuries, namely, woman as mother and housewife and the family as her arena, the privatized arena of consumption and "love," excluded and sheltered from the arena of production and accumulation, where men reign. In the following, I shall trace how the ideal of the domesticated privatized woman, concerned with "love" and consumption and dependent on a male "breadwinner," was generalized, first in the bourgeois class proper, then among the so-called petty bourgeoisie and finally in the working class or the proletariat.

Second Stage: Housewife and Nuclear Family–
The "Colony" of the Little White Men

While the Big White Men—the "Dominant Men" (Mamozai)—appropriated land, natural resources, and people in Africa, Asia, and Central and South America in order to be able to extract raw materials, products, and labor power which they themselves had not produced, and while they disrupted all social relations created by the local people, they began to build up in their fatherlands the patriarchal nuclear family, that is, the monogamous nuclear family as we know it today. This family, which was put under the specific protection of the state, consists of the forced combination of the principles of kinship and cohabitation and the definition of the man as "head" of this household and "breadwinner" for the nonearning legal wife and their children. While in the eighteenth and early nineteenth centuries this marriage and family form were possible only among the propertied classes of the bourgeoisie—among peasants, artisans, and workers women had always to share all work—this form was made the norm for all by a number of legal reforms pushed through by the state from the second half of the nineteenth century onward. In Germany—as in other European countries—there existed a number of marriage restrictions for people without property. These were only abolished in the second half of the nineteenth century, when the state intervened to promote a pronatalist policy for the propertyless working class (Heinsohn and Knieper 1976).

Recent family history has revealed that even the concept "family" became popular only toward the end of the eighteenth century in Europe, particularly in France and England, and it was not before the middle of the nineteenth century that this concept was also adopted for the households of the workers and peasants because, contrary to general opinion, "family" had a distinct class connotation. Only classes with property could afford to have a "family." Propertyless people—like farm servants or urban poor—were not supposed to have a "family" (Flandrin 1980; Heinsohn and Knieper 1976). But "family" in the sense in which we understand it today—that is, as a combination of coresidence and blood relationship based on the patriarchal principle—was not even found among the aristocracy. The aristocratic "family" did not imply coresidence of all family members. Coresidence, particularly of husband and wife and their offspring, became the crucial criterion of the family of the bourgeoisie. Hence our present concept of family is a bourgeois one (Flandrin 1980; Luz Tangangco 1982).

It was the bourgeoisie which established the social and sexual division of labor characteristic of capitalism. The bourgeoisie declared "family" a private territory in contrast to the "public" sphere of economic and political activity. The bourgeoisie first withdrew "their" women from this public sphere and shut them into their cozy "homes," where they could not interfere in the war-mongering, moneymaking, and the politicking of the men. Even the French Revolution, though fought by thousands of women, ended by excluding women from politics. The bourgeoisie, particularly the puritan English bourgeoisie, created the ideology of romantic love as a compensation for and sublimation of the sexual and economic independence women had had before the rise of this class. Malthus, one of the important theoreticians of the rising bourgeoisie, saw clearly that capitalism needed a different type of woman. The poor should curb their sexual "instincts," because otherwise they would breed too many poor for the scarce food supply. On the other hand, they should not use contraceptives, a method recommended by Condorcet in France, because that would make them lazy because he saw a close connection between sexual abstinence and readiness to work. Then Malthus paints a rosy picture of a decent bourgeois home in which "love" does not express itself in sexual activity, but in which the domesticated wife sublimates the sexual "instinct" in order to create a cozy home for the hard-working breadwinner who has to struggle for money in a competitive and hostile world "outside" (Malthus, quoted in Heinsohn, Knieper, and Steiger 1979). As Heinsohn, Knieper, and Steiger point out, capitalism did not, as Engels and Marx believed, destroy the family; on the contrary, with the help of the state and its police, it *created* the family first among the propertied classes and later in the working class, and with it the housewife as a social category. Also, from the accounts of the composition and condition of the early industrial proletariat, it appears that the family, as we understand it today, was much less the norm than is usually believed.

As we all know, women and children constituted the bulk of the early industrial proletariat. They were the cheapest and most manipulable labor force and could be exploited like no other worker. The capitalists understood well that a woman with children had to accept any wage if she wanted to survive. On the other hand, women were less of a problem for the capitalists than men. Their labor was also cheap because they were no longer organized, unlike the skilled men who had their associations as journeymen and a tradition of organizing from the guilds. Women had been thrown out of these organizations long ago, they had no new organizations and hence no bargaining power. For the capitalists it was, therefore, more profitable and less risky to employ women. With the rise of industrial capitalism and the decline of merchant capitalism (around 1830), the extreme exploitation of women's and child labor became a problem. Women whose health had been destroyed by overwork and appalling work conditions could not produce healthy children who could become strong workers and soldiers—as was realized after several wars later in the century.

Many of these women did not live in proper "families," but were either unmarried or had been deserted and lived, worked, and moved around with children and young people in gangs (cf. Marx, *Capital,* vol. 1). These women had no particular material interest in producing the next generation of miserable workers for the factories. But they constituted a threat to bourgeois morality with its ideal of the domesticated woman. Therefore, it was also necessary to domesticate the proletarian woman. She had to be *made* to breed more workers.

Contrary to what Marx thought, the production of children could not be left to the "instincts" of the proletariat, because, as Heinsohn and Knieper point out, the propertyless proletariat had no material interest in the production of children, as children were no insurance in old age, unlike the sons of the bourgeoisie. Therefore, the state had to interfere in the production of people and—through legislation, police measures, and the ideological campaign of the churches—the sexual energies of the proletariat had to be channeled into the straitjacket of the bourgeois family. The proletarian woman had to be housewifized too, in spite of the fact that she could not afford to sit at home and wait for the husband to feed her and her children. Heinsohn and Knieper (1976) analyze this process for nineteenth-century Germany. Their main thesis is that the "family" had to be forced upon the proletariat by police measures, because otherwise the propertyless proletarians would not have produced enough children for the next generation of workers. One of the most important measures—after the criminalization of infanticide, which had already taken place—was, therefore, the law that abolished the marriage prohibition for propertyless people. This law was passed by the North German League in 1868. Now proletarians were allowed to marry and have a "family," like the bourgeois. But this was not enough. Sexuality had to be curbed in such a way that it took place within the confines of this family. Therefore, sexual intercourse before marriage and outside it was criminalized. The owners of the means of production were given the necessary police power to watch over the morality of their workers. After the Franco-Prussian War in 1870–71, a law that made abortion a crime was passed—a law against which the new women's movement fought with only small success. The churches, in their cooperation with the state, worked on the souls of the people. What the secular state called a crime, the churches called a sin. The churches had a wider influence than the state because they reached more people, particularly in the countryside (Heinsohn and Knieper 1976).

In this way the housewifization of women was also forced into the working class. According to Heinsohn and Knieper (1976) and others, the family had never existed among the propertyless farm servants or proletarians; it had to be created by force. This strategy worked because, by that time, women had lost most of their knowledge of contraception and because the state and church had drastically curbed women's autonomy over their bodies.

The housewifization of women, however, had not only the objective of ensuring that there were enough workers and soldiers for capital and the state. The creation of housework and the housewife as an agent of consumption became a very important strategy in the late nineteenth and early twentieth centuries. By that time not only had the household been discovered as an important market for a whole range of new gadgets and items, but also scientific home management had become a new ideology for the further domestication of women. Not only was the housewife called on to reduce the labor power costs, she was also mobilized to use her energies to create new needs. A virtual war for cleanliness and hygiene—a war against dirt, germs, bacteria, and so on—was started in order to create a market for the new products of the chemical industry. Scientific homemaking was also advocated as a means of lowering the men's wage, because the wage would last longer if the housewife used it economically (Ehrenreich and English 1975).

The process of housewifization of women, however, was not only pushed forward by the bourgeoisie and the state. The working-class movement in the nineteenth and twentieth centuries also made its contribution to this process. The organized working class welcomed the abolition of forced celibacy and marriage restrictions for propertyless workers. One of the demands of the German delegation to the 1863 Congress of the International Workingmen's Association was the "freedom for workers to form a family." Heinsohn and Knieper (1976) point out that the German working-class organizations, at that time headed by Lassalle, fought for the right to have a family rather than against the forced celibacy of propertyless people. Thus, the liberation from forced celibacy was historically achieved only by subsuming the whole propertyless class under bourgeois marriage and family laws. As bourgeois marriage and family were considered "progressive," the accession of the working class to these standards was considered by most leaders of the working class as a progressive move. The struggles of the workers' movement for higher wages were often justified, particularly by the skilled workers who constituted the "most advanced sections" of the working class, by the argument that the man's wage should be sufficient to maintain a family so that his wife could stay at home and look after children and household.

NOTE

1. I found the astounding extracts from Mr. Hall's book in a text entitled *Militarism versus Feminism,* published anonymously in London in 1915 by George Allen and Unwin, Ltd. The authors, most probably British feminists, had written this most remarkable analysis of the historical antagonism between militarism and feminism as a contribution to the women's movement, particularly the international women's peace movement which tried, together with the International Suffrage Alliance, to bring European and American women together in an antiwar effort. Due to the war situation, the authors published their investigation anonymously. They do not give complete references of the books they quote. Thus Mr. Fielding Hall's book, *A Nation at School,* is referred to only by its title and page numbers. The whole text, *Militarism versus Feminism,* is available at the Library of Congress in Washington, D.C.

19

The Construction of Woman in Three* Popular Texts of Empire
Toward a Critique of Materialist Feminism

Rosemary Hennessy and Rajeswari Mohan

In the late 1970s, materialist feminism emerged in the West from a feminist critique within Marxism. Annette Kuhn and Anne Marie Wolpe in Britain and Christine Delphy in France were among the promoters of materialist feminism, favoring that term over Marxist feminism on the basis of an argument that Marxism cannot adequately address women's exploitation and oppression unless the Marxist problematic itself is transformed so as to be able to account for the sexual division of labor (Kuhn and Wolpe 1978, 1–10; Delphy 1984). With its class bias, its emphasis on economic determinism, and its focus on a history exclusively formulated in terms of the laws of motion and transformation of capitalist production, classic Marxism had barely begun to analyze and critique patriarchal systems of exploitation. At the same time there was a marked tendency in feminist theory to conceptualize woman in essentialist and idealist terms. In this context, materialist feminism provided a historically urgent ground from which to launch a critical counterknowledge to mainstream feminism and classic Marxism.

While it has continued to be a source of powerful critiques of liberal and essentialist feminisms, materialist feminism's radical edge has blunted over time in the arenas of oppositional political struggles. As multinational capitalism systematically expands its network of exploitative relations of production and consumption, patriarchal and capitalist relations become even more securely imbricated—witness the growing disciplinary violence against Third-World women by multinational corporate research, the increasing sexualization of women by an all-pervasive commodity aesthetics, and the intensified contestation over woman's body as the site of reproduction in the first world

*Only two texts are covered in this excerpt.

and of production in the third world. How we make sense of these disparate instances of women's oppression in our historical present will affect their perpetuation or elimination. It has therefore become urgent to adopt theoretical frames that can account for the complex interconnections between the various axes along which exploitation and oppression take place. A philosophy of praxis capable of directing a globally articulated revolutionary struggle gains a certain urgency as the confinement of oppositional struggles to regional and isolated sites becomes a widely deployed strategy of crisis management. In this respect, what was once materialist feminism's greatest strength is now being pressured by increasing calls to recognize difference within the category "woman." From the beginning, materialist feminism gave priority to the social construction of gender while simultaneously avowing commitment to the analysis of gender in its intersection with class. It is only recently that race and sexuality have become part of materialist feminist concerns, but the articulation of class, race, gender, and sexuality has for the most part merely been used as the legitimizing cliché of a leftist discourse.

Early second-wave feminist critiques within Marxism produced at best a dual systems theory acknowledging women's positioning within patriarchal and capitalist systems, but often relegating patriarchy exclusively to ideological practice or explaining it only in terms of a specific social formation. One consequence of this theoretical impasse was the inability to draw out the complex interrelations of support and opposition between capitalism and patriarchy (Sargent 1981). More recent developments in an increasingly loosely defined materialist feminist project indicate a continued propensity toward regional analysis enhanced by an uncritical appropriation of postmodern discourses. . . .

Because materialist feminism's emphasis on gender has involved the backgrounding of other modalities of exploitation, the project is fraught with an ideologically charged discrepancy between its political desires and its effectivity. . . .

As we live out the postmodern moment under the crisis conditions of multinational capitalism, materialist feminism does not have the same historical urgency it had at its inception. However, in arguing that the materialist feminist project has lost its radical edge we are in no way making the postfeminist argument that feminist struggles are irrelevant. Our critique is a critique for feminism. Only it is directed as much against new imperialism, white supremacy, homophobia, and class exploitation as it is against patriarchy. In doing so we argue for a globalizing reading strategy. Such a strategy attends to the interconnection between various modalities of oppression and exploitation at any one instance of the social while situating that instance in the global deployment of capitalist power relations.

Calling for such a strategy requires a particular understanding of feminism and a way of distinguishing between the point of entry of critique and its aims. Feminism is a discourse that critiques hegemonic constructions of woman as a social subject, advances an understanding of the historical factors that necessitate these constructions and the interests they serve, and in doing so seeks to end the self-perpetuating circuit of relations that alienate women from their labor, their sexuality, their comrades in struggle. So long as patriarchal and capitalist arrangements maintain a system of hegemonic relations wherein constructions of the feminine enable and support global exploitation and domination, feminism's point of entry to critique of those relations is urgent. In trying to destabilize mutually imbricated systems of exploitation and domination, however, feminism is just one oppositional discourse. It has to develop strategies to follow through all the lines of force that radiate from the category "woman" to other categories and vice versa. In doing so feminism works toward change wrought through overdetermination, change which is the effect of a collective, not just a feminist, subject.

Implicit in a global reading strategy is a theory of history contrary to the understanding of history as distinct from theory that runs like a fault line through much materialist feminist criticism. . . . Th[e] separation of the way of knowing from the object of knowledge is itself ideologically produced and serves to resecure an idealist understanding of theory as metadiscourse and an empiricist notion of history as data. Even new historicist notions of theory as mediating the relationship between historical object and investigating subject often implicitly posit history or the body as existing outside of ways of knowing.

. . . In renarrating [two] texts of the nineteenth century—"The Adventure of the Speckled Band" (1892) by Arthur Conan Doyle [and] "Mussumat Kirpo's Doll" (1894) by Flora Annie Steel, our essay intervenes in current understandings of alterity, sexuality, and patriarchal controls.[1] As responses to and interventions in the transition into monopoly capitalism that was building up slowly and unevenly across the social formation through the latter part of the nineteenth century, the texts we study are part of the general work of crisis containment performed by ideology. Competition from Germany, Russia, and Japan, and nationalist struggles in the colonies, undermined the global reach of British imperial might, while domestic social order was threatened by a burgeoning feminist movement, working-class insurgency, and the growing power of socialist movements. While all these crises were affected and made possible by the global reach of capitalism, part of the work of crisis containment has been directed toward reading them as isolated phenomena, thereby mystifying their systemic implication in capitalist and patriarchal relations. In Britain, the transition into monopoly capitalism took place under the pressures generated by the Great Depression (1873–96) and the adventures of New Imperialism (1870–1902). The enormity and obviousness of the economic benefits accompanying the Great Depression and Britain's New Imperialism in the last two decades of the nineteenth century have often resulted in an exclusive emphasis on the economic sphere in theories of imperialism. This tendency has been further sanctioned by a long tradition of economism in Marxist theory—where the economic level of a social formation is seen to determine or express its political and ideological practices. Because economic determinism understands the social formation as a homogeneous and monolithic expression of economic forces, it cannot explain the unevenness of a social formation nor account for the strong cross-currents impelling social change. Furthermore, locating the economic sphere as the prime mover of social change ignores the crucial work performed by ideology in reproducing existing modes of production through its work of interpellating or constituting subjects.

From a post-Althusserian understanding of the social, popular culture can be seen as not just a reflection of economic and political forces, but as a site where ideological work is continuously produced out of diverse political and economic interests to disrupt or resecure existing social arrangements. In this sense, popular culture is a terrain of contestation. The ideological struggles waged in popular texts of the late nineteenth century were crucial in constituting the modalities of the relations between the dominant and subordinate sectors of the social formation. It is important to locate these struggles in the global logic of capitalism in order to understand the containment of subaltern interests on which the western "democratic way of life" is secured.

In nineteenth-century Britain, popular culture was an influential site for the circulation of discourses of alterity and served as a powerful medium through which a rearticulated array of subject positions necessary for all emerging social order could be established. Narratives celebrating imperial and patriarchal authority were immensely popular in music halls, popular fiction, sensationalist "new" journalism, and advertising. As reading became a leisure-time activity to be slipped into the daily routine of travel and work, the long triple-decker novel lapsed from its privileged position into the cultural margin. Its place was taken by such popular productions as the "railway novel" and variety magazine. Developments in printing and paper technology which made books cheaper than ever, greater access to education, increased literacy levels after the Education Act of 1870, and the emergence of the advertisement-supported magazine all greatly enhanced the influence of popular narratives. In the colonies—particularly in India, after Macaulay's infamous minutes of 1835—teaching English, studying English literature, and reading popular British texts were integral elements in the maintenance of imperial control. . . .

The periodically recurring crises that marked the second half of the nineteenth century signaled the rearticulation of alterity as previously prevalent ideologies of otherness disintegrated against the force of the contradictions accompanying the global shift to monopoly capitalism. This shift required a redefinition of alterity around the issue of discipline to help produce the good subject necessary under the emergent conditions of production, exchange, and consumption, and to serve as the ideological foundation for new laws marking increased state control over the family, sexuality, and labor in both the colonies and the metropole. The rearticulation of alterity and its systemic recruitment to justify new forms of control and exploitation was aided by emergent knowledges of the nineteenth century. While the same discourses of social Darwinism, eugenics, civic health, medicine, and secular morality were drawn upon in the articulation of race, class, and gender difference, the location of the subject across several positions often resulted in contradictions that required the important but local and contingent work of crisis containment carried out by popular narratives such as the stories of Conan Doyle and Steel.

"The Adventure of the Speckled Band" is one of several stories Conan Doyle published in *The Strand Magazine* in the 1890s that negotiates these contradictions through a variety of narrative strategies: the construction of Holmes as rational protector, the resolution of the narrative's enigma, and the positioning of the reader. The problem presented in the case involves a father's control over his unmarried daughter's property. Thirty-year-old Helen Stoner turns to Holmes for help in solving the riddle of her twin sister Julia's death a fortnight before her marriage. Helen's anxiety is based on vague suspicions sparked by the recurrence before her own impending marriage of a series of events similar to those surrounding Julia's death. The Stoner sisters live in a decaying ancestral manor with their stepfather, Dr. Grimsby Roylott, the last son of a pauperized aristocratic family. In India where he practiced medicine, Roylott married the Stoners's widowed mother who bequeathed a considerable sum of money ("not less than £1,000 a year") entirely to Roylott so long as the twins lived with him, with a provision that a certain annual sum should be allowed to each daughter in the event of her marriage (196). Holmes's detection discloses Roylott as his daughter's murderer, motivated by greed for the money he would lose when she married. In staging the murder as symbolic rape (Roylott kills Julia by means of a poisonous snake sent through a vent connecting his bedroom to hers) the narrative dramatizes the sexual economy of patriarchy: the equation of woman and property. At the same time, it presents Holmes as woman's protector, rescuing her from the villainous patriarch's domination and defending her right to control over her own property and person.

In the construction of Holmes as hero, the narrative draws upon the codes of otherness such as irrationality, lack of control, and dissipation, set by the discourses of alterity, and in so doing redefines subjectivities in ways historically necessitated by the regional and global rearrangements taking place in the late nineteenth century. Holmes's heroic status is constructed relationally in the narrative through a semic code that links various subject positions. Examining these links makes visible a network of gaps and contradictions that are suppressed in the interests of the narrative's coherent resolution. These gaps, associated with both Roylott and Helen, are details which exceed the solution to the crime—details the solution does not and cannot explain—specifically, Roylott's association with the gypsies, his possession of an excessive number of Indian animals, and Helen's silencing. As we will show, Holmes's status as hero depends on the downplayed existence of these details.

Holmes's opposition to and complicity with the villainous patriarch, Roylott, indicates the articulation of a "new" masculine subject. Roylott is coded as a failed aristocrat whose decline is owing to a weakness of both moral fiber and blood, a hereditary mania that translates into lack of self-control and results ultimately in his criminal fall from respectability. His friendship with the gypsies upon his return from India is related to this fall and is presented as simultaneously self-explanatory and suspicions. Helen's suggestion that the "band" of gypsies are linked to her sister's death draws on a commonly held suspicion of gypsies, but it does not explain the association between them and the lapsed aristocrat, Roylott. Nonetheless, this unexplained contradictory class coding of Roylott helps valorize Holmes's status by positioning him in opposition to the negative upper- and lower-class alternatives associated with the villain. Holmes's amateur detective work (bearing the marks of an emergent professionalism: wage work as skilled yet artful dedication) takes on its value in opposition to Roylott's association with both aristocratic squandering and lower-class shiftlessness.

In conjunction with his contradictory class location, Roylott's links to the Orient encode him with multiple semes for otherness in overdetermined opposition to the western, rational, middle-class Holmes. Semically marked for aristocratic dissipation, lower-class unrespectability, and eastern irrationality, Roylott presents a profile of the criminal as all that Holmes, the middle-class restrained gentleman, is not. The semic association of Roylott with the wild Orient is also in excess of the requirements of the solution—Holmes's disclosure of the phallic murder weapon. Roylott has lived in Calcutta, has access to knowledge of poisons available only to "a clever and ruthless man with ill Eastern training" (209), keeps a baboon and a cheetah as well as the deadly swamp adder, and in his death scene is wearing Turkish slippers. Like the gypsies, the Indian animals are decoys in the untangling of the enigma, possible suspects that establish a false lead but ultimately are not required by the logic of the solution. However, Roylott's association with the East blurs with his ties to the gypsies—long figures of alterity in the West—and qualifies as explanation for his violence. The hereditary mania blamed for his outbursts "had been intensified by residence in the tropics" (196), and it is his robbery by a native in Calcutta that incites Roylott to beat his butler to death, an act that lands him in prison. While Roylott's violence is associated causally with the East, its enactment in relation to three significant figures—the colonial servant, the white daughter, and the village blacksmith he assaults—constructs him in opposition to a series of others arranged along race, gender, and class lines. However, Holmes's privileged position in the narrative as subject of knowledge with which the reader identifies serves to dissociate him from these scenes of violence and to downplay any possible connections among imperial domination, patriarchal control, and class privilege.

Still, as opposed as Roylott and Holmes are made to appear, the narrative resolution that valorizes Holmes as hero depends on his links to Roylott in a system of patriarchal gender relations that set both of them apart from woman as other. It is the threatened disruption of this system that occasions the murder constituting the narrative's enigma. In his daughter's murder and symbolic rape Roylott enacts the ultimate patriarchal privilege: control over women as property that simultaneously denies them access to property and to sexual consent. The narrative makes use of the twin sisters to negotiate woman's contradictory positioning as subject and object within capitalist patriarchal arrangements, simultaneously canceling and affirming woman's claim to property as she shifts positions from daughter to wife. It is the management of the "moment" of transition between these two highly controlled positions that comprises the ideological work of the story as it eliminates the threatening position of the independent, propertied female subject by means of the band of paternal protectors.

Questions about woman's status as subject in relation to property and sexual consent that are raised and quickly resolved in the narrative are symptomatic of the contest over woman's ambiguous social position, a struggle waged in the long campaign for reform of married women's property rights. The Married Women's Property Act (1882) overturned the common law of coverture, according to which a wife forfeited all property upon marriage to her husband because husband and wife were one person and that person was the husband. While the formal arrangement of the family remained the same, legalized in the heterosexual monogamous Christian marriage, profound changes in property during industrialization—from land to money—created entirely new forms of wealth. By the late nineteenth century a transformation of entrepreneurial activity, brought about by the development of finance capital exemplified in the creation of the Stock Exchange and the legal recognition of limited liability companies, encouraged the investment of risk capital. These changes in economic practice meant that landed property inherited through a family line was no longer the sole source of wealth, a shift that paved the way for legal reforms relating to the family. These legal reforms were also part of a process in the late nineteenth century by which the state, mediated by voluntary organizations, gradually intervened further in the private sphere in response to demands for civil equality from trade unions and women. These demands provided the state with opportunities to control and direct the emergence of an expanded and reconstructed middle-class workforce whose social position was grounded on education and business skills rather than inheritance. As a result, the division between public and private domains which undergirded the development of industrialization was rearticulated as the private family was gradually permeated by the disciplinary apparatuses of state intervention. In the process patriarchal gender relations were reshaped.

The Married Women's Property Act exemplifies the dynamics of this rearrangement. The contest over property rights simultaneously constituted and managed a crisis in woman's social position brought on by changes across the social formation, making visible woman's contradictory social status and spanning positions as property and property owner. Legal reforms addressed this crisis by giving women control over their property; but by doing so in terms of male protection, the law kept in place woman's position as nonrational other.

Because feminist histories of the Married Women's Property Act have been based on a liberal humanist understanding of social relations, they leave unquestioned the notions of equity, property, and the marketplace western women struggled to gain access to.[2] In opposition, our reading suggests a radical rethinking of these unquestioned categories in terms of the global exploitative relations they help to sustain. From this position, property reforms can be seen to readjust the patriarchal family alliance in Britain by perpetuating women's exclusion from full social participation. But this exclusion was only a regional aspect of the global social relations these reforms both depended on and affected. Reform of women's property rights also contributed to a shift in productive relations that would allow middle-class women in Britain to be recruited into a newly structured marketplace. In turn, the emergence of the tertiary sector in Britain depended on the shift to the colonies of production and exploitable labor no longer viable in the metropole.

As the campaign for property reform made clear, the subject position most endangering the patriarchy—both sexually and economically—was the femme sole, a position made available by the shift in productive relations and threatening to elude the discourses of male protection that secured the feminine as other. Like all men, the single woman had legal control over her property. But because the skills thought to be needed for the administration of her property were locked in the male professions, the single woman's ability to exercise that control was curtailed. Women's increasing demands in the late nineteenth century for access to the professions threatened the Victorian ideology of separate spheres by transgressing the paternalistic management of the division between the subject of property and the subject as property that constituted the feminine as other. The unusual terms of Mrs Stoner's will in "The Speckled Band"—foreclosing the possibility that either daughter will occupy the position of femme sole—functions to suppress the availability of this dangerous feminine subject position, one that by the 1890s—when large numbers of single middle-class women were recruited into a newly formed clerical workforce—was becoming increasingly available.

The same discourse of protection used in the law to justify women's limited liability and mystify the operation of patriarchal control underlies Holmes's defense of Helen's property right in "The Speckled Band," and to a similar end. Holmes's opposition to Roylott's control over his daughter's sexual and economic power might seem at first glance to define a position that opposes traditional patriarchal domination. However, Holmes's inclusion in a circuit of exchange that enables Helen's passage from father to husband makes his role as protector problematic. As the go-between from the father who symbolically strangles his daughter with his poisoned phallic band to the fiance whose power is encoded in his silencing of the daughter-wife's secret rape, the position of Holmes is in collusion with a "band" of patriarchs implicated in suppressing that which poses an economic and sexual threat to patriarchal gender relations. Holmes's position as opponent to the traditional patriarch defines him as a "new" man, but, as we will show, this "newness" is more a rearticulation than a transformation of the sexual economy of patriarchy.

The construction of Helen as "silent" provides the premise for Watson's narrative and allows Holmes the last word on it: Helen has pledged Watson to secrecy and he can only tell her story now because she is dead. Like Roylott's association with the gypsies and Oriental beasts, this detail—that Helen's story must be suppressed until after her death—is not explained. In this sense it lies outside the logic of the solution to the case. Moreover, Helen's version of events is suppressed as soon as Holmes takes over the case, and it never features in the official report. In the absence of her narratives after Roylott's death, Holmes's "protection" of Helen elides easily with both the patriarch's phallic poisoning of his daughter until she "choked her words" (198) and could not name her murderer, and the "protection" of her husband-to-be, who censors Helen's narrative as "the fancies of a nervous woman" (195). Silencing the rescued daughter effectively protects patriarchy's privileged "play": the inquest simply "came to the conclusion that the Doctor met his fate while indiscreetly playing with a dangerous pet" (208). Firmly situated within a protective circle of male kin, Helen's position as consenting subject is so overwritten by paternal authority that it is virtually effaced. Thus, she serves the function of the feminine "other" in the economy of patriarchy: the conduit through which the phallus can be passed from father to son. The sexualization of the female body that serves as the symbolic ground for the narrative's enigma manages woman's contradictory position as property and property owner, a contradiction simultaneously being managed in the legal sphere by property reform and reform in the age of consent. Passed on the heels of the Married Woman's Property Act, the Criminal Law Amendment Act (1885) legislated a complementary shift in patriarchal arrangements affecting the status of woman outside the home. In raising the age of consent for girls from thirteen to sixteen, the act and its supporters purported to defend and protect the interests of girls from sexual offenders. However, as with property reform, the discourse of protection, which threads its way through the reform campaign and the law, conceals the class and gender interests served by the amendment.

The passage of the Criminal Law Amendment Act was punctuated by one of the first and most effectively waged campaigns of sensationalist journalism and inaugurated a broad-based social purity movement that would extend through the next few decades. The "Maiden Tribute of Modern Babylon," a series of stories written and published in *The Pall Mall Gazette* by its editor, W. T. Stead, provided the catalyst for passage of the Criminal Law Amendment Act by purportedly exposing extensive white slave trade between Britain and the continent as well as pervasive child prostitution in London. The exposé demonstrates the class lines along which the age of consent battle was fought and indicates the historical conditions of possibility for the overdetermined network of sexual and class codes in "The Speckled Band." In targeting the foreign aristocrat as procurer and the "daughters of the poor" as his victims, the campaign for raising the age of consent used one of the most familiar themes of popular melodrama—the seduction of the poor girl by the wealthy lecher—to sexualize threats to capitalist production: foreign competition, collective unrest fueled by feminist and socialist reform movements, and the destablization of gender arrangements by the recruitment of "redundant" single middle-class women into the workforce. The patriarchal gender ideology that commodified bourgeois woman as ornament of the home was thereby rearticulated in age of consent legislation and the social purity campaigns that this reform movement spawned. By constructing woman outside the home as sexual commodity in need of state protection, the law addressed the increasing numbers of single middle-class women working outside the home and helped contain the threat they posed. In the name of protecting girls against sexual abuse, the law went a long way in resecuring the destablized patriarchal family, severely undermining the position of female "consenting" subject outside the private sphere by constituting it as a position in which woman was still encircled by patriarchal controls, subject to the "reasonable beliefs" of both her legal representative and her violator.

Like the Married Women's Property Act, the age of consent law focused on issues central to patriarchal control—"protection" and "possession"—extending the protective arm of the state to girls and women outside the possessive claims of father or husband. But while the Married Women's Property Act emphasized woman as *subject of* property, age of consent legislation foregrounded woman *as* property. Both reforms managed complementary adjustments in the contradictory position of woman as the relationship between public and private spheres and middle-class women's place in both was gradually shifting. Most historical studies have treated one or the other of these reforms, but not both in conjunction.[3] Seeing them in adjacency rather than in isolation makes visible the mutual determination of woman's position as married property owner and as sexualized subject outside the home. Taken together, they comprise two sides of the same coin of patriarchal control under capitalism.

The symbolic appearance of the incest motif in "The Speckled Band" is symptomatic of the contradictions that produced this desecuring of the patriarchal gender system from one set of social arrangements and its resecuring in another. As it is encoded in the story, the daughter's seduction demonstrates the class interests this sexualization of the family alliance served by disarticulating the masculine subject from aristocratic aspirations and rearticulating it as the rational professional. Furthermore, the daughter's seduction enacts cultural anxiety about incest, which helped reinforce the mutually supporting feminine subject of property—bound as nonperson to patriarchal protection/possession within a father-daughter or a husband-wife relationship—and the nonsubject of consent subjected to the state's (read Holmes's) protection in lieu of adequate protection from the father-husband.

The sexualization of woman through the narrative of the daughter's seduction took place in multiple sites of culture from sensationalist newspaper accounts of spoiled maidens to the theoretical discourses of Freudian psychoanalysis. Crucial to the elaboration of this narrative in the discourses of psychology and psychoanalysis is the construction of the bourgeois family romance as a universal arrangement. . . .

The sexualized subject of the late nineteenth century, inscribed by the disciplinary interventions of the state, did not supplant the subject of familial alliance. Rather, as Foucault has argued, the family provided an anchor of sorts whereby alliance and sexuality could be interchanged (Foucault 1980). Universalizing the incest taboo made the law of the patriarch secure even in the new mechanics of power (Foucault 1980, 109). At the same time, the proliferation of incest motifs in the discourses of the social sciences—in particular, through the hystericization of the middle-class daughter—signaled a reformation of patriarchal gender arrangements that loosened the bonds of family alliance in order to construct an individualized, sexualized feminine subject. The symbolic encoding of the daughter's seduction in "The Speckled Band," including Holmes's complicity with Roylott, is an instance of the ideological function of incest motifs: managing the threat to family alliance posed by the individualized, single, middle-class daughter by reinstalling her within patriarchal control through a narrative of the family romance.

The narrative handling of the daughter's seduction in "The Speckled Band" demonstrates the alliance between the rearticulation of woman as other and the discourses of scientific rationalism. The daughter's seduction, along with the race, class, and gender hierarchies it supports, is silenced by the narrative's coherent solution, a coherence that depends on the reader taking up the position of the subject of knowledge offered by Holmes. Holmes's ability to "explain it all" by pointing to the perfectly obvious "elementary" details that have passed before the reader's unwitting eyes (as well as the reader's stand-in, Watson's) explains the enigma and gives Holmes his status as genius of detection. Holmes's authority as rational, scientific investigator works with the narrative movement toward resolution to seal over contradictions and gaps undermining both the coherence of the explanation and the obviousness of Holmes's authority as subject of knowledge.

If read from the subject position the story invites the reader to take up, these contradictory links and the fissures they open in Holmes's air-tight explanation are invisible. This invisibility is in itself a clue to the ideological force of both this position and the deductive logic it offers as an obviously enlightened way of seeing. Reason is presented simultaneously as a universal human attribute and a gratuitous gift of birth available only to a fortunate few. While the qualifications for those "few" are not overtly explained—in this sense they are navigable—they are nonetheless encoded in Holmes, the consummate rational subject. The reader is invited to "identify" with this subject through Watson, the classic participant-observer in awe of Holmes's superior reasoning power and yet similarly qualified in terms of class, race, and gender positions. Holmes's empiricist emphasis on the visible as self-explanatory mystifies the ways the narrative's endorsement of deductive logic naturalizes the visible marks of difference in order to sustain a social hierarchy. Thus, Roylott's associations with the Orient and the gypsies serve as obvious clues—visible signals to the reader—of his unreasonableness, just as mud splashes on a sleeve are visible evidence that Helen has ridden in a dog cart.

The ratiocination that employs an empiricist mode of knowing as a weapon for criminal justice explicitly sets the rational subject of knowledge apart not only from the criminal (who, as Roylott's overdetermined encoding indicates, is often a collective outlaw) but also from the pedestrian masses: "Crime is common, logic is rare," Holmes tells Watson. "What do the public, the great unobservant public, who could hardly tell a weaver by his tooth or a compositor by his left thumb, care about the finer shades of analysis and deduction?" (Doyle 1986, 253). This subject position endowed with heroic stature recruits the discourse of scientific rationalism increasingly taken up for state intervention into various domains of the social, to present as obvious and natural a hierarchy that protects the interests of the middle-class, western, white male. By privileging this subject position through Watson's narration, the narrative offers the reader a way of making sense by which the contradictory links between the science of deduction and the interests of patriarchy and imperialism are glossed over.

A similar strategy is adopted in Flora Annie Steel's "Mussumat Kirpo's Doll," whereby a privileged and approved subject position is marked out through the oppositions generated by the discourse of colonialism. However, while the subject of knowledge in "The Speckled Band" is the exemplary rational subject, the subject of knowledge here is the cosmopolitan ironic subject who occupies the same class and race positions as Holmes. While Steel's work does not enjoy the continuing popularity that Conan Doyle's does, her stories hold a privileged position in Raj mythology. As we will show, the tropes of alterity functioning in Steel's story are exemplary of the discursive strategies used to justify colonial control, not just in the imperialist high noon but also in our current era of neo-imperialism and multinational capitalism.

"Mussumat Kirpo's Doll," set in India, is the story of a fourteen-year-old child bride, Mussumat Kirpo, who is given a doll by the local missionary teacher, Miss Julia Smith, as part of an incentive program to encourage the people of the city to send their children to the British school for secular and Christian education. However, Kirpo has to fight hard to keep her doll. In the struggle for possession of the doll we see the various contesting forces seeking to control Kirpo. The school's policies dictate that married girls should be given cloth rather than dolls as prizes, and Miss Smith attempts to set aright her mistake by retrieving the doll from Kirpo. In the meantime, Mai Gungo threatens to sell Kirpo's doll, since as mother-in-law she has absolute control over the girl and her possessions. Mai Gungo also forces Kirpo to spend long hours making combs for sale, and thus prevents her from going to school. Miss Smith, fearing that Mai Gungo's ire will arouse the disapproval of other Indians and thus limit her chances of saving heathen souls, refrains from pleading Kirpo's case or alleviating her misery. Torn between the dictates of imperial policy and Christian kindness, Miss Smith seeks to solve the problem altogether by taking back Kirpo's doll. However, in a moment of compassion she allows Kirpo to keep the doll for a short while and play with it in secrecy.

In a year, Miss Smith learns that Kirpo has delivered a baby boy. Now that Kirpo has her own child, Miss Smith feels less remorse over complying with the school's policies and takes the doll back. A few days later, she learns that Kirpo is dying in childbed and goes to visit her. She finds Kirpo restless and believes that she longs to hold her baby, which Mai Gungo has taken away from her, just as she threatened to do with the doll. Miss Smith persuades Mai Gungo to let Kirpo hold the baby, only to have Kirpo refuse him. What she wants is her doll. Kirpo dies before Miss Smith can bring the doll to her.

The story begins with a horticultural metaphor describing the young students in the Mission House compound, set out in "companies on the bare ground like seedlings in a bed—a perfect garden of girls" (53). The narrative then proceeds to build upon the metaphor at some length, generating a series of implicit and explicit oppositions—gardens/bare ground, seedlings/tree of knowledge, nurturance/exploitation, etc., through which a symbolic field is set up. The codes of horticultural symbolism bring together the discourses of imperialism and patriarchy in a way that is symptomatic of the contradictions within and between imperial and patriarchal practices. For in the description of the kindly attempts of some of the English ladies to encourage "some young offshoot of the Tree of Knowledge—uncertain either of its own roots or of the soil it grew in—by directing its attention to the tables set out with toys" (52), the ideological fabric of the narrative momentarily parts to reveal the contradictions of colonial education and its (ir)relevance for the young students situated within the mutually implicated systems of patriarchy—indigenous and western—and imperialism. Significantly enough, the young girls are not compared to Eve as consumers of the fruit of the Tree of Knowledge; they are the very offshoots of the tree, the potential sites and causes of disruption. As the colonial rulers were to discover soon, the "hotbeds of learning" (53) were also potential hotbeds of sedition. Their very existence in the narrative signals temptation and bodes ill for the inhabitants of this latter-day Eden—particularly the English, whose expulsion is threatened above all else by the existence of these offshoots of the Tree of Knowledge. The threat of a Fall, then, undermines from the start the pastoral construction of the civilizing mission of the British. Further intensifying this hint of crisis is the reference to "many a critical mother, determined that her particular plant shall receive its fair share of watering" (53–54). The narrative makes it very clear that this solicitude is reserved only for the prizes and not for the knowledge the school imparts, thus reinforcing the indigenous patriarchal arrangements coding the good woman as ignorant. Underlying the logic of the narrative is a deep ambivalence around the issue of colonial and women's education which implicitly raises these questions: For women positioned within the strictly private space of the home, what could be the uses and consequences of education? What is the double threat of knowledge placed in the hands of natives and women—of native women? Like the silence in Conan Doyle's story, these unanswered questions circle around the issue of political and economic control over women.

However, the uncertainty and disruptiveness produced by these details are quickly glided over by the self-conscious and ironic gesturing toward the paltry but valued material compensation the students get for attending the British school. The dolls and cloth the young girls receive annually as prizes for their attendance are enough, the narrative suggests, to quell their doubts about what they are taught. The narrative's irony is grounded on the construction of the native as avaricious, a construction that simultaneously defends the bribery and glosses over the missionaries' anxieties. Through the gift item—dolls and cloth—the ideological and political weight of imperialism exerts a subtle but insistent pressure on the narrative. The Japanese doll—brought into circulation in India through the emergent global economic and commercial network dominated by Britain—is emblematic of the passage from childhood to womanhood, a passage that in this context is also one from indigenous family arrangements into those modeled on the Victorian bourgeois family. The contestation over the doll in the narrative is symptomatic of the contestation of various political and ideological interests over the modalities of this dual passage. Cloth partakes similarly in the economic and ideological arrangements of imperialism. In the hands of Victorian missionaries, the cult of "Christianity and Calico" forged an alliance between the forces of civilization and commerce. Wearing English cloth served as a token of acceptance of Christian faith and became in the colonies a sign of the spiritual grace that distinguished the converted from the "naked savages." As a symbol of civilization, English cloth conferred status upon its wearers by associating them with the imperial rulers.

The gesture toward the prizes, however, is not really a containment but a deferral that cannot be sustained for long. The repressed crisis returns, this time in the form of dissatisfaction over the adequacy of the compensation, as one of Miss Smith's underlings complains that the prize is not enough of an incentive:

> If Miss-sahib thought she was going to slave as she has done for the past year for a paltry eight yards of cotton trousering, which would not be enough to cut into the "fassen"—why, the Miss-sahib was mistaken. And then with the well-known footfall on the stairs came smiles and flattery. (55)

The narrative's dis-ease about the civilizing mission of the British is now displaced onto the Indians and rearticulated as native discontent, which in the figure of Mai Gungo is overlaid by Orientalist tropes of avarice. Once again, we see the evasiveness of the narrative as the arrival of Miss Smith signals the setting aside of the problem of dissatisfaction in favor of "smiles and flattery." From this point on, the narrative focuses exclusively on the tragedy of Mussumat Kirpo, but doubts about the imperial mission persist even as the logic of the narrative consistently evades the troubling questions raised in the text.

Implicit in the horticultural symbolism is the logic of labor and value that serve as the pole between which Mussumat Kirpo is situated in relation to both her mother-in-law,

Mai Gungo, and the evangelist Julia Smith. The young girls under Miss Smith's tutelage are not just seedlings to be nurtured to maturity and set out in the world; they are also "part of the harvest necessary for a good report" (54). In other words, Miss Smith has an investment in the success, well-being, and receptivity of her students. The labor expended on them is not the disinterested labor of philanthropy, but the prudent work of cultivation that augments the symbolic capital of Miss Smith in particular and the British in general. The trope of harvest, furthermore, firmly links the symbolic capital of good will and spiritual gain with the mercantile capital of dividends and profits from exploitative labor relations and commodity exchanges. Mussumat Kirpo is particularly important because as the daughter-in-law of Kuniya, the head of the comb-makers, she can open many doors to Miss Smith, whose "gentle, proseletysing eyes cast glances of longing on every house where she has not yet found entrance" (55). Therefore, Julia Smith tolerates Kirpo's slowness and stupidity because, more than anyone else, Kirpo serves as the strategic investment likely to produce rich dividends—professional as well as spiritual. At this point, a crucial equivocation is introduced in a sentence that attempts to summarize Miss Smith's feelings toward Kirpo:

> Hence her reluctance to quarrel definitely with her pupil's belongings, since poor Kirpo did not count for much in that bustling household. (56)

While the first part of the sentence seems to follow the previous discussion of Kirpo's position of influence, the second part—while seeming to offer another supporting argument—explicitly contradicts all that has preceded it. More interesting is the insertion of the discourse of Christian kindness and compassion central to evangelism, in the reference to "poor Kirpo," whose oppression is explained by implicitly invoking Orientalist understandings of the inherent despotism of Hindu religious practices and family arrangements. However, the rift in the sentence is symptomatic of deeper contradictions. First, between the secular interests and spiritual claims of Miss Smith's evangelism; second, and more important, the contradictory positioning of Mussumat Kirpo not only in relation to Miss Smith but also within the economic arrangements of the family.

If Kirpo is seen by Miss Smith as an investment, she is more explicitly coded as property in her relation to Mai Gungo. This narrative development draws upon the patriarchal-capitalist logic which, by inscribing the female body as property, renders female labor invisible. The invisibility of woman's domestic labor as mother and housewife and the devaluation of her income-generating labor as "casual" or "supplementary" work serve the ideological function of lowering women's wages and creating a casual labor force that greatly increments capital's profits. But the narrative directs the horror of this process of dehumanization exclusively toward the figure of Mai Gungo. The burden of responsibility of Mussumat Kirpo's oppression is, by this narrative strategy, displaced onto the community of women, with the bulk of the blame falling upon Mai Gungo, the exemplary figure of alterity constructed as pathetic, disgusting, and inhumane. For Mai Gungo blatantly treats Kirpo as labor—that commodity whose consumption generates surplus value. As a comb-maker, Kirpo labors to add to the family income; as irregular student, she brings in the annual bonus of free books and cloth which Mai Gungo can sell; most of all, her very existence in the family depends on her capacity to labor forth the male child who will continue the family line. That she is remiss in the last of her duties almost costs her a place in the family, and it is in fulfilling her obligation in this respect that her life is consumed. The narrative's silence about the market for which Kirpo labors—the urban anglicized centers of the colonies or the metropole—is symptomatic of its implication in the oppressive practices it seems to bemoan. The combs and the infant son that Kirpo produces serve as the conduit linking the positioning of Kirpo as invisible producer of luxury, cosmetic commodities, and, more importantly, of exploitable colonial population with the concomitant production of woman as the sexualized object taking place in the metropole. This, then, is the argument for our adjacent readings of Kirpo's exploitation and Helen Stoner's assault. Kirpo's labor is crucial for the reproduction of the circuit of production: she keeps the craft alive through her labor, a significantly feminine component of most forms of cottage industry; and she produces the labor force necessary for the continuation of the value inscribed in commodity and phallus. But paradoxically, she is constructed as a cipher within the economy of this circulation.

Both Kirpo and Mai Gungo are constructed such that alterity serves to justify control. This, then, is one of the ideological functions of the narrative. In both instances, alterity is invoked to explain and contain feminine resistance—Kirpo's to her construction as mother and Mai Gungo's to her position as colonial subject. Kirpo's inability to assume the position of good mother, an inability overdetermined by physical deformity and mental dullness, is transformed by the end of the narrative to willful and cunning resistance to motherhood. She is considered by the community to be a "bad bargain" (54), the victim of ill luck but also the potential source of "evil influences" (59). The narrative constructs her as excess, beyond the limits of proper femininity, but at the same time overlays her figure with an implicit comment on the superstitious, backward, and uncivilized ways of the natives. By constructing Kirpo as excess while at the same time attributing this construction to the Indians, the narrative is able to distance itself from the exploitative arrangements it implicitly critiques. Furthermore, by locating Mai Gungo as a figure of rapacious matriarchal authority, the narrative mystifies not only the patriarchal arrangements within which Mai Gungo derives her power, but also the exacerbation of Kirpo's oppression within the indigenous patriarchal family system by the dislocation of traditional support systems brought about by the penetration of capitalist values into Indian social arrangements through colonialism.

If the text constructs Kirpo as refusing to take up the position of good mother in rejecting her infant son, it nevertheless firmly positions her as potential good mother in her intense desire for the doll. This, then, is the logic underlying Kirpo's construction as "childlike, yet unchild-like" (56). Her desire for the doll is merely the deferral of desire for motherhood; moreover, the deferral is also an occasion for rearticulating the meaning of motherhood so that the traditional expectations and attitudes voiced by Mai Gungo are replaced by a more Eurocentric notion of motherhood. Signaling this shift is Kirpo's preference for the "Japanese baby-doll with a large bald head" over her infant son. What the narrative enacts is the dislocation of indigenous social arrangements to make way for the colonial subject as producer and consumer in a modernized capitalist arrangement that is nonetheless implicated in patriarchal power relations.

It is at this point that the narratives of patriarchal and imperial control produced by Conan Doyle and Steel can be seen to be mutually enabling and implicated in the same global shift in patriarchal and capitalist productive relations. The contestation between Mai Gungo and Miss Smith over differing ideals of womanhood complements the struggle between Roylott and Holmes over changing ideals of manhood, for, as Maria Mies has argued, the "rise and generalization of the 'decent' bourgeois marriage and family as protected institutions are causally linked to the disruption of clan and family relations of the 'natives'" (98). The economic advantages accompanying the erosion of indigenous kinship networks and cultural practices in the colonies together with the universalizing ideology of Victorian domesticity helped install bourgeois notions of marriage and womanhood in the colonies as well as across the class divisions in European social formations, thereby homogenizing domestic society and containing upheavals such as labor unrest at home and anticolonial insurgencies abroad. In other words, the Married Women's Property Act and age of consent legislation in Britain—the context of Conan Doyle's stories—were enabled by the disruptions in India that Steel's story mediates.

The nexus of desire and rejection operating around the baby-doll is ideologically significant in light of the important and highly charged debate over age of consent and child marriage that had taken place immediately prior to 1894, when Steel's story was published. In fact, the narrative explicitly refers to the debate in the course of the embarrassed explanation offered for Miss Smith's mistaken decision to award Kirpo a doll:

> Of course, as a rule, we always draw the line about dolls when a girl is married. Sometimes it seems a little hard, for they are so small, you know; still, it is best to have a rule; all these tiny trifles help emphasize our views on the child-marriage question. (54)

However, the allusion to the child-marriage question is ambiguous. The exact terms of "our views on the child-marriage question" are not elaborated. Withholding the doll from a married girl, however young, can serve as a penalty, reminding her family of what is lost to the girl through early marriage. It can also serve to underwrite the transition from childhood to adulthood implicit in marriage and reinforce demands placed on the young girl to graduate from dolls to babies. Furthermore, Kirpo is legally not a child. The narrative, however, offers no help in resolving this ambiguity. Its silence on the issue is ideologically necessitated by the terms and consequences of the child-marriage debate in the late nineteenth century.

From the start, the debate on child marriage and age of consent that took place in Britain and India in the late nineteenth century was caught up in the complexities of imperial control and nationalist resistance. Initiated largely by reform-minded British and westernized Indians, the attempt to raise the minimum age of marriage and consent was part of a larger social movement to change traditional social and religious customs in the name of modernization. However, the reform was not without opposition from revivalist religious and conservative upper-class segments of Indian society. For the British who were anxious to prevent large-scale opposition to the idea of imperial rule from gathering around the child-marriage issue, it was nonetheless important to make the scope of imperial power clear to the Indian bourgeoisie. The British viceroy, Lord Landsdowne, therefore refused to concede to the opposition and passed the Age of Consent law in 1891, but issued a circular soon after the act was passed, making it virtually impossible to enforce it in protection of child brides. Thus, whatever might have been the initial commitments of the age of consent debate to lessen the plight of women, it soon became the occasion for various political agendas to secure their influence. While legislation on age of consent sought to alleviate Indian women's oppression within traditional social arrangements, paradoxically, it installed the female body as the site of contest between larger political interests (Sinha 1986). In so doing, both British and Indian sides of the argument invoked patriarchal responsibility: while the British argued that the legislation was necessary to protect Indian women from Indian men, the counterargument was that young Indian women had to be protected from their own sexuality. The issue for both sides was the control of female sexuality—and by implication, female labor—by situating women as mother and housewife. One significant consequence was the reinscription of the Indian woman as subject of consent, thereby continuing a trend initiated in the Sati legislation of 1829. The disarticulation of woman as subject of religion and indigenous culture and her re-articulation as subject of law, together with the awarding of consent to women, must be seen as necessary aspects of the imposition in India of western social models based on the division of the civil society from the state. Viewed this way, the protectionist rhetoric accompanying the legislation can be seen as an attempt to validate the contradiction of state intervention in civil society.

It is therefore not surprising that Steel's story equivocates on this crucial issue. For the official British position on the issue was scrupulously non-committal. However, while British administrators did their best to avoid taking a position on the question of reform, it was in their interests to acknowledge and indeed play up the oppressiveness of local practices. It was only by continuously emphasizing the depravity of the natives that Britain could argue for its presence in India as a civilizing force. But Britain's long-term imperial plans also meant that it had to maintain the state of dependence, hence its resistance to modernizing reform and its alliance with conservative elements on the child-marriage issue. In the meantime, the prevalent ideological project was to get as much mileage as possible from the child-marriage question, and this is what Steel's story achieves most effectively. Situating Mussumat Kirpo's plight in relation to the child-marriage act, the narrative avoids taking a position on the issue, while at the same time taking advantage of the emotional appeal gathered around the issue to advance an implicit argument for imperial presence.

The success of this argument in the story depends on the construction of the subject of knowledge, the position from which the narrative becomes intelligible and compelling as an account of British India. The ironic self-consciousness of the early sections of the narrative presumes a subject who is distanced as much from the proselytizing Miss Smith and the condescending British as from the Indian characters. By treating the British characters with a certain degree of amused sarcasm, the narrative puts under pressure the traditional paradigms of imperialism—philanthropy and evangelism. However, while the irony dissolves previously held positions, it offers nothing in return. The point of intelligibility marked in the narrative is congruent with the imperious, paternal gaze typical of Orientalist discourse. This is the uncommitted position from which all the observations are made and from which alone the narrative makes sense. While the ironic mode relentlessly pushes contradictions to the foreground, it is not bound to resolve them. The subject of irony, then, holds in unresolved balance the conflicts and contradictions implicit in imperialist and patriarchal authority. And the realization of this position of balance without commitment is the emerging modernist, cosmopolitan, liberal subject. This subject position is also the ideal reformist subject of transition which acknowledges the inadequacy of the old paradigm without conceding to any uncomfortable and disruptive demands for a radical change. In delineating the tragedy of Mussumat Kirpo, the narrative draws upon the liberal colonial tradition of outrage in the face of indigenous practices, and grafts on to the ironic subject of knowledge an implicit acknowledgement that the Miss Smiths of British India do indeed have an urgent and important mission. . . .

As we have seen, historical pressures on hegemonic constructions of alterity require its rearticulation along race, class, and gender lines. In the nineteenth century, the principal medium for this rearticulation was the ensemble of discourses on sexuality. As one of the most emotionally charged conflicts within Britain and the colonies, control of female sexuality served as a politically and ideologically crucial battleground, on which the constellation of relations that constituted the new hegemonic subject including the category "woman" as other could be reconstructed. Reading changes in the construction of the feminine subject in terms of the global relations of empire, as they functioned in Britain and India in the 1880s and 1890s, explains the sexualization of woman in Britain and the colonies as mutually dependent. A global reading of the representation of the sexualized feminine subject recasts the narrative of history and the construction of woman in the West, making visible the mechanisms by which the self-contained western version of the sexualized woman is produced by both patriarchal and imperialist arrangements and depends on the sexualization of the colonized feminine other.

The sexualized subject is not exclusively feminine (the precocious child as well as the homosexual male were also products of the deployment of sexuality). However, the sexualization of woman is an integral part of the general deployment of sexuality to produce subjects more adequate to the shifting relations of production. This deployment of sexuality had a direct bearing on the reconstruction of the feminine subject as the subject of state. Through legislation like the Criminal Law Amendment Act in Britain and the Age of Consent Act in India, control of female sexuality was gradually moved out of the private space of the patriarchal family and into the domain of state regulation. In the process, woman as subject of the law was constituted as a sexualized body to be protected by the state when the respectable father or husband was absent or, as in the case of the colonies, when the uncontrolled sexuality of tile colonial male rendered him unfit to protect the colonial woman. The issue of control over female sexuality in Britain and India took the form of a response to specific but interdependent crises in each social formation, reproduced and managed in the stories of Steel and Conan Doyle. In both social formations, "protection" of women by men served as the signifier of the respectable or good society, marking a moment when that society emerged out of domestic crisis (Spivak 1988). In both England and India, "protection" of women served as a premise for redefining the relation between the private and the public as the state moved into the previously inviolable space of the family. The struggle over woman's body in the stories of Steel and Conan Doyle is delineated by drawing upon interdependent versions of this discourse of protection deployed through state apparatuses: the philanthropic paternalism of the missionary school and the rational paternalism of the amateur detective, mediating between law enforcers and the private citizen.

The entangled encoding of the feminine and the Oriental as sexualized other in the Holmes story is an instance of the ways the sexualization of woman and Oriental male resecured patriarchal and imperial interests across a range of class positions. Both Helen and the Orientalized Roylott are traversed by semes for unreason, figured as a wild, animal-like lack of self-possession. When Helen is first "unveiled" she presents to Holmes a face "all drawn and grey, with restless, frightened eyes, like those of some hunted animal" (194), fitting complement to Roylott, that "fierce old bird of prey" (201). As with Roylott's unreasonable passions, Helen's feeble rational powers set her apart from Holmes. The darkness that envelops Helen's mind makes her only able to entertain "vague fears and suspicions" in contrast to Holmes's enlightened rapid deductions, "as swift as intuitions and yet always founded on a logical basis" (194). This seme of animal irrationality sexualizes both patriarchal-predator and daughter-victim, entangling the feminine and the Oriental as other in opposition to Holmes's rational, reserved, western, middle-class norm.

The sexualization of western woman in the late nineteenth century was the outcome of a complex of economic and political pressures exerted on the sexual division of labor across the classes: working-class women were gradually pushed back into the home as a result of the decline in the predominantly female textile industry and the growth of male-dominated heavy industry; unions won higher wages for men; and a rigorous social purity campaign for working-class respectability stressed woman's natural place in the home as health-conscious and efficient mother (Davin 1978). While the gradual movement of working-class women back into the home helped rigidify the sexual division of labor, the increasing recruitment of middle-class women into the developing tertiary sector in Britain bred a certain cultural anxiety over the residual flexibility of that division. The construction of woman in the public space as object of desire in need of protection helped tame the threat independent women posed to the family (by implicitly calling into question the equation between domesticity and respectability) and to the male workers they at least potentially competed against in the market. At the same time, the sexualization of woman in the private sphere as reproductive body served to relegitimate her invisible labor in the home not just as civilizing moral agent—the mid-Victorian angel in the house—but as mother of the race and domestic consumer; the concomitant rearticulation of her labor as a civic responsibility was aided by the increased permeability between the private and public spheres. The overall effect was to mystify woman's role in both spheres as social producer.

In colonial India sexuality became the ground on which alterity was invoked to legitimate British presence. The sexualization of the colonial subject drew upon the contradictory Victorian construction of the feminine as both uncontrolled and passionless. In the economy of the distribution of gender roles by the British, these two faces of the feminine were split between the colonial male constructed as sexually uncontrolled and the colonial female constructed as passionless. Anglo-Indian objections to Hindu child marriage focused on the rapacious sexuality of Bengali men who were accused of essentially raping their child brides. This perceived lack of sexual restraint signified for the Anglo-Indian reformer the otherness of the Oriental male and confirmed his naturally lower position on the evolutionary scale, less civilized and controlled and therefore more effeminate than his manly British counterpart. In equating marriage with the ritual of consummation, traditionally tied to the onset of puberty, the British enacted a political misreading of the Hindu child-marriage custom (D. Engels 1983). Both British and Hindu ideologies, however, proposed distinctly patriarchal versions of female sexuality: the Victorian ideology of female passionlessness allowed the imposition of all arbitrary age of consent since women (at least good ones) were never sexual subjects, although they could be victimized as sexual objects. In contrast, the Hindu ideology of feminine sexuality as active and in need of male control called for the consummation of marriage at the onset of puberty. In "protecting" Indian daughters from their sexually uncontrolled and therefore unmanly "protectors," the British state "emasculated" Indian men, stripping them of their status as controllers of "their" women's sexuality." For the colonial woman the effect was doubly devastating: her status as social subject in the law was completely circumvented by competing protectors.

Historical studies of the conflicts around the age of consent legislation have for the most part been descriptive rather than analytical. For instance, while both Engels and

Forbes present with great detail British and Indian attempts to use the legislation to stake out positions on colonial rule and emphasize the redefinition of sexuality accompanying social reform, their account stops short of explaining why social reform became a necessary aspect of imperial administration in India in the late nineteenth century (Forbes 1979). Furthermore, in discussing the consequences of the legislation, both Engels and Forbes restrict themselves to the Indian social formation and ignore the crucial connection between the redefinition of sexuality in India and the rearticulation of femininity in the metropole. The absence of a conceptual framework that situates sexuality as a important discursive category in a globally operative economic and political system makes it impossible for them to see the age of consent debates in England in relation to those in India. Thus Engels is left with the simplistic observation that "social control in Britain emerged as colonial domination abroad. Domestic class attitudes translated smoothly into racist attitudes in Africa or India" (124). As the specificities of the deployment of patriarchal ideologies in England and India elide in this narrative of displacement, the economic and political implications for monopoly capitalism of the age of consent legislation in India are overlooked. In this sense, even overtly feminist historical accounts of colonization are implicated in the mystification of the globality of patriarchal relations under capitalism. The simultaneous construction of woman as subject of consent and of property and as object of desire and of knowledge in both the metropole and the colonies kept in place the gap between subject and object status which constituted woman's ambiguous position in a patriarchal gender system, a status that served the interests of an emerging consumer culture. As reproductive mother of the race, the sexualized feminine subject in Britain helped to quell threats to empire along the axis of racial superiority, and in this way she complemented the Orientalist discourse of native inferiority. As reproductive subject she was not very unlike the eroticized, hysterical woman whose body was taken up by medicine and psychology and read as sexual excess and cured if subjected to patriarchal control.

The sexualization of woman in the West was only possible because of the shift in production, which recruited women in the colonies into the workforce. Development of colonial markets and production during the transition to new imperialism laid the groundwork for the gradual convergence of the international and sexual divisions of labor—a division between producers (mainly in the colonies and in the countryside) and consumers (mainly in the metropole and the cities) and a division between men and women (men as free wage laborers and women as nonfree housewives). Maria Mies has called this process the "housewifization" of women in the global relations of production (Mies 1986). Across the international sexual division of labor, articulated differently according to class and social formation, women were recruited as invisible labor, providing the subsistence basis for male wage labor. The sheltered nest of respectable western housewives provided a breeding ground for the production of new needs and a large market for new gadgets as scientific home management became the basis for a new ideology of domestication which stressed woman's function as mother rather than wife (Davin 1978; Lewis 1984, 92ff). The "good" first-world woman was thus constructed ideologically as breeder and as consumer, while her position as producer of labor power was obscured (Mies 1986, 125). This "internal" colony of patriarchal relations in the respectable home (as well as in the developing gendered service sector) in the metropole depended on the exploitation of the external colony (Mies 1986, 110).

On the other side of the globe the colonial woman, secreted within her isolated household routine, labored under a double yoke: she no longer produced just for the use of the patriarchal household but now also for the rise of urban consumers, with the surplus value she produced being appropriated by the capitalist. It is precisely these links between Mussumat Kirpo, who produces combs for the feminine middle-class urban market within a household handcraft industry owned by her father-in-law, and the sexualized feminine middle-class consumer of the product of Kirpo's labor, that the narrative strategies of Steel's story and the western hegemonic ideology of the sexualized self work to conceal. While they share a position as exploited workers, the colonial housewife as producer and the metropolitan housewife as consumer-breeder occupy positions in the circuit of production and consumption that are sharply differentiated by the political and ideological lines along which their exploitation is determined. In the western hegemonic ideology the respectable (white) mother and consumer qualifies as the "good" woman, while the lower-class or colonial mother and consumer is constructed as "bad" woman. As breeder of nonwhite children, the colonial mother threatens imperial racial dominance and as consumer she constitutes only an expendable drain on the capitalist economy she services.

The incipient threat to imperial hegemony which woman poses at both ends of the globe is visible in violence against women in its various manifestations—ideological, political, economic. Violence against women is one element in the ongoing primitive accumulation of capital which, by perpetuating the equation of woman with property, sustains a set of social arrangements wherein woman's labor is a potential source of surplus value (Mies 1986, 171). Both Conan Doyle's and Steel's stories are symptomatic of this perpetuation in that both construct distinct versions of woman as victim of violence, either through aggression or neglect. The figure of Mussumat Kirpo clutching her Japanese doll and dying after childbirth traces a trajectory along which economic and political violence against the colonized woman is reproduced ideologically in the western construction of the "bad" colonial woman as breeder and consumer. Julia Stoner's murder-rape enacts a complementary trajectory of violence against the "bad" western feminine subject who claims social agency in the form of control over property. What neither narrative can speak (except obliquely through the contradictory semic coding of Grimsby Roylott) are the objective links that bind the ideological construction of the violated individualized western woman of property to her complement in a global economy and imperialist gender ideology, the inconsequential brown-skinned mother. The struggle over control of female sexuality in Britain and colonial India constructed the category "woman" in ways that confirmed the ambiguous position of women in patriarchal arrangements. For the colonial woman this ambiguity was doubly compounded by her invisibility to the West. The profound irony that in both Britain and India women's status as subject of consent was constructed in laws regulating their often violent passage from one man to another—through marriage, rape, abduction, or prostitution—goes to the heart of this ambiguous status. Like the feminine subject of property in the nineteenth century who is a nonperson, the feminine subject of consent is in fact the object of possession. Between subject constitution and object formation lies the breach that engulfs western woman's threatening agency; shuttled between patriarchy and imperialism, caught in the overdetermined gap between subject and object status, the colonial woman disappears, her invisibility the substantive collective shadow on which the increasingly individualized western woman depends.

The continued circulation of the Holmes and Kirpo figures in various sites of culture today helps to manage the crises of multinational capitalism where western hegemony, political influence, and economic power are threatened by internal competition, cold war politics, and third-world resistance. Holmes's hold on the dominant ideology of western culture as a figure of rational paternalism is reinforced by his valorization on the fringes of the literary establishment: Holmes stories appear in Norton anthologies for college fiction classes and are still celebrated in the *New York Times Book Review*. These institutions legitimate the ideological function of Holmes through the discourse of permanence that informs the study of literature. At the same time, the obviousness and universality of Holmes's virtues are further reinforced by the circulation of this trope of rationalism within the multinational commodity culture of advertising and media entertainment: in ads for the New York Stock Exchange, in popularized rewrites of these "classic" tales in book and video form and in box-office hits like *The Young Sherlock Holmes* or *The Seven Percent Solution*. The circulation of the Holmes figure in various domains of culture underscores the naturalization of the semes for rationalism and paternalism that construct Holmes and in so doing mystifies their legitimating function for late capitalist technocracy, patriarchy, and imperialism.

Although Flora Annie Steel's stories have long been forgotten by the western literary establishment, the cultural figure of Mussumat Kirpo—the neglected brown-skinned third-world child—has a similar continuing hold on the western imagination and as an ideological trope performs a complementary function. The most visible instance is the appropriation of this figure by the discourse of paternalism in ads for first-world aid agencies. Faces of girls much like Kirpo stare out with hungry eyes and child-like yet unchild-like face[s] from placards in buses and subways and from advertisements in the pages of popular magazines—more often than not women's magazines. Under the signature of Save the Children or any one of a number of international agencies, the figure of Kirpo is recirculated in the discourses of late capitalist philanthropic reform helping to cultivate the continued mission of first-world developers in countries like India.

These contemporary constructions of the detective and third-world child as timeless human figures are possible in part because they are read as disconnected from each other and from the political and economic relations that produce them and in which they intervene. Our reading of their circulation in late nineteenth-century texts is an ideological intervention in the contemporary historical moment to the extent that it critiques and offers an alternative to prevailing regional reading practices, which gloss over the ways third-world populations, racial "minorities," and women continue to be the unacknowledged crucial links in the global circuit of capitalist production.

NOTES

1. All quotations from Conan Doyle will be taken from Doyle (1986); all quotations from Steel are from Cowasjee (1982, 53–60).

2. Feminist histories of this legislation have either applauded the reform as a landmark victory in feminist struggles for equality or in a more critical mode pointed to the ways equality under the new law was undermined by other legal and economic structures. For an example of the former see Holcombe (1973); the latter position is exemplified in Stetson (1982); Sachs and Wilson (1978) point out that although the act gave women the right to their separate earnings and property, it did not grant them legal status as persons.

3. See for example Holcombe (1983); Poovey (1988); Sachs and Wilson (1978) on property. On reform of consent law see Bristow (1977) and Gorham (1978).

20

Socialist Feminism
Our Bridge to Freedom

Nellie Wong

We work for enough to live each day,
    Without a day off, like the labor laws say.
The price of noodles, 12 hours' work don't pay,
    So, change our working conditions. Hey!
(Refrain)
Fellow workers, get it together,
    For prosperity in our land
Fellow workers, rise up together,
    To right things by our hand.
When we get our monthly paychecks,
    Our monthly worries merely grow,
Most of it goes for some rice and the rent—
    Our private debts we still owe.
Lifeless, as if they were poisoned,
    Are those fine young men,
Who once promised to work hard for us—
    Oh, revive your lost bravery again.
      —Song of factory women, February 1973
       ("Change Our Working Conditions" 1982, 13)

This song illustrates only one of many working-class struggles being waged by women throughout the world. It shows that Korean women workers recognize their multi-issue oppression; their low wages won't pay for the price of noodles, their monthly paychecks do not alleviate their ongoing private debts, and they must take action into their own hands, independent from the men in their lives who act as if they were "poisoned" by their government's antilabor stance. South Korea's leading exports are textiles, shoes, and electronic goods—industries with a mostly female work force ("Change" 1982, 13). A primarily female work force has helped maintain Korea's economic growth. However, women workers are the lowest paid and work under the bleakest conditions. Sister workers in the Philippines, Singapore, Japan, Hong Kong, and Taiwan also suffer long hours, unpaid overtime, and sexual harassment. The conditions of Korea's women workers are typical of the majority of Asia's industrial workers.

Women continue to be a part of the ongoing liberation movements throughout the world. In 1982, during International Women's Day, I spoke at a public forum sponsored by the Anti-Family Protection Act Coalition in Los Angeles, California, where I paid tribute to international working women:

> Women workers started the Russian Revolution.
> Women workers sparked the shipyard strikes in Poland.
> Women workers and housewives marched by the thousands to protest the inhumane,
>   antiwoman repression in Iran.
> Women workers protested the sexist antiworker conditions in textile factories in Korea.
> Women militants fought the Kisaeng tourism/prostitution in Korea.
> Women workers formed a 100-year marriage resistance in Kwangtung, China.
> Women fighters, young and old, fought in liberation struggles in Vietnam,
>   Nicaragua, Cuba, El Salvador, South Africa, Lebanon.
> Women workers are fighting to end nuclear testing in the Marshall Islands.

And in the United States, women continue to participate on all political fronts, from reproductive rights to union organizing, for social, economic, political, racial, and sexual equality.

Dine and Hopi women, mostly grandmothers and mothers, in 1986 were leading the resistance to the U.S. government's forced "relocation" from Big Mountain, Arizona, of people from ancestral homelands in an area jointly held by the Navajo and Hopi nations. Giant energy corporations such as Peabody Coal, Kerr McGee, and Exxon want unhampered access to the estimated 44 billion tons of high-grade coal and deposits of oil, natural gas, and uranium found on and around Big Mountain (O'Gara and Hodderson 1986).

The resistance of women is nothing new; however, it must be seen in the context of political, social, and economic conditions in which the total emancipation of women, as a sex, is hampered. The liberation of women cannot be relegated to simply overthrowing the patriarchy because male chauvinism is not eternal, any more than racism, anti-Semitism, or anti-gay bigotry is eternal. They are all products of the historical development of private property, where a few had everything, and most had virtually nothing (Hill 1984, 19). Resistance to the patriarchal institutions of private property has always existed. Opposition to the current epoch's patriarchal institution—capitalism—is, by definition, socialist. Without overthrowing the economic system of capitalism, as socialists and communists organize to do, we cannot liberate women and everybody else who is also oppressed.

Socialist feminism is our bridge to freedom. By feminism, I mean the political analysis and practice to free all women. No woman, because of her race, class, sexuality, age, or disability, is left out. Feminism, the struggle for women's equal rights, is inseparable from socialism—but is not identical to socialism. Socialism is an economic system which reorganizes production, redistributes wealth, and redefines state power so that the exploiters are expropriated and workers gain hegemony. Feminism, like all struggles for liberation from a specific type of bondage, is a reason for socialism, a catalyst to organize for socialism, and a benefit of socialism. At the same time, feminism is decisive to socialism. Where male supremacy functions, socialism cannot, because true socialism, by definition, connotes a higher form of human relations that can't possibly exist under capitalism. Revolutionary Trotskyist feminism sees the most oppressed sections of the working class as decisive to revolution—working women and particularly working women of color. This is the theory which integrates socialism and feminism.

Socialist feminism is a radical, disciplined, and all-encompassing solution to the problems of race, sex, sexuality, and class struggle. Socialist feminism lives in the battles of all people of color, in the lesbian and gay movement, and in the class struggle. Revolutionary feminism also happens to be an integral part, a cornerstone, of every movement. It objectively answers the ideological search of black women and men. It is the political foundation of the new revolutionary vanguard: socialist feminist people of color (Hill 1984, 19).

As a Chinese American working woman, I had been searching for many years to arrive at the heart and soul of my own liberation struggle. As a long-time office worker, I was laid off after eighteen and one-half years' service with Bethlehem Steel Corporation, the second-largest steel maker in the United States. As a Chinese American, one of seven children of Cantonese immigrants, I questioned over and over why our lives were shaped by racism and sexism and our oppression as workers in this country. Historically, our lives as Chinese Americans are linked to those of other Asians, all people of color—of blacks who have been enslaved, and who are still fighting for their civil rights; of Japanese Americans who were incarcerated during World War II; and of other groups of workers who were brought in to build America.

I did not have the opportunity to attend college immediately after I graduated from high school. Economics, and the Confucianist and feudal ideology pervasive in the Chinese American community, dictated my taking a secretarial job at the age of seventeen. As a young office worker, I learned that my secretarial career was supposed to be temporary—that if I met the "right" man, got married, and had children, I would become a "real" woman fulfilling what society ordained; and that in itself, life as a woman worker had no value, particularly when that woman worker took shorthand, typed, and filed for a living.

My feminist consciousness began to take hold when I got married and when I began college in my mid-thirties while still working full-time. Silenced most of my life, I began to articulate my experiences through creative writing courses. My seemingly personal and private deprivation and angst as a Chinese American working woman began to express itself in a social milieu—with other women, other Asian Americans, other people of color, other feminists, and other workers. What I had thought was personal and private was truly political, social, and public. What a jolt it was to realize what I had learned from a capitalist bourgeois society—through the public school system and the workplace—that as a woman-of-color worker, I was simply an individual left to my own capacities and wiles! What a revelation, as long in coming as it was, to learn that workers everywhere were connected to one another—that it was our labor that provided wealth for a few, and that a class analysis of our lives was essential to find the root causes of our multifaceted oppression.

My development to integrate all parts of me—my gender, my ethnicity, my class, and my worker status—grew by leaps and bounds when I joined Radical Women and the Freedom Socialist party, two socialist feminist organizations which integrated the study of class, race, sex, and sexuality as interlocking roots of the capitalist system. Not only did we study, but we were consistently active in the democratic movements for radical social change.

To speak seriously as one who is committed to building a socialist feminist society at home and abroad takes real change; it takes examining one's attitudes which have been shaped by a powerful capitalist system through the institutions of the state, the schools, the media, the church, and monogamous marriage. I had absorbed "my place." I had kept silent because I was Asian and a woman, and I had been determined not to appear too smart because I wouldn't be able to attract and hold a man.

Attending college at night as an adult, being married, working full-time, and organizing and socializing with feminists and radicals brought me to socialist feminism: the belief that unless every woman, every lesbian and gay man, every worker, and every child is free, none of us is free. Such is the beauty and triumph of radical, social knowledge. Such is the basis upon which I have committed myself to working for a socialist feminist society. Such is the foundation upon which the leadership of all the oppressed is being built.

Socialist feminism is the viable alternative to capitalism and world imperialism, which use sexism, racism, colonialism, heterosexism, homophobia, and class oppression to keep us down. Although revolutions waged in Soviet Russia, Cuba, Vietnam, Nicaragua, and China have brought about changes, oppression against women, sexual minorities, and workers still exists. While we can learn from the gains made by women in countries where revolutions have taken place, many inequalities still exist, and nowhere have women achieved total liberation. Gay oppression and racism still exist in these countries, and there are far too few democratic freedoms. For example, abortion rights are denied in Nicaragua, as the influence of the Catholic church dominates in Latin America. In China, feminism—at least officially—is deemed to be a product of decadent, bourgeois capitalist society.

While true socialism is to be strived for in each context, socialism cannot exist within a single country but must be a worldwide system, supplanting world capitalism. The nations of the world are wholly interdependent, and without an international system of socialism, countries can share only their poverty, rather than the world's wealth. Worldwide socialism will break the stranglehold of worldwide imperialism. It will end the exploitation of one country for the profit of another country's capitalist class. And that is why the U.S., as the most powerful capitalist country in the world, dominates the global market, and why there is a need for a socialist feminist revolution in the U.S. Socialism alone is not the answer. Feminism alone is not the answer. There won't be a socialist revolution in this country without socialist feminists in the lead, and there won't be true emancipation of women without a socialist overthrow of capitalism. Socialism without feminism is a contradiction in terms (Hill 1984, 21).

Our oppression as workers is rooted in the capitalist system. As women workers of color, we get the message, loud and clear, that if we only pull ourselves up by our own bootstraps, we will "succeed" as members of a capitalist society, and miraculously, our multi-issue oppressions as women and people of color will disappear. Within the women's movement, bourgeois feminist ideology teaches us that if we take the path of *partial* resistance, we might just make it to the executive boardroom. And if we do, we can become one of the bosses to stifle worker militance and to uphold the profit-seeking status quo. Or radical feminist ideology teaches us that if we just overthrow the patriarchy, women will truly be free. Radical feminism does not take into account the oppression of gay men and men of color.

Multi-issue feminism is necessary to fight back and win against all forms of oppression. As my Asian American comrade Emily Woo Yamasaki says, "I cannot be an Asian American on Monday, a woman on Tuesday, a lesbian on Wednesday, a worker/student on Thursday, and a political radical on Friday. I am all these things every day." We are discriminated against as *workers* on the economic plane, as racial *minorities* on the economic and social planes, and as women on all three planes—economic, social, and domestic/family. We must cope with the world and with men as a unique category of people—women-of-color workers. We have been subjected to humiliations and brutalities unknown to most whites or even to men of color.

Feminism, in general, and socialist feminism, in particular, do have a vibrant history of militant struggle in this country. Today, increasing numbers of women of color and their allies are calling for an end to racism, sexism, and homophobia. Black women, Chicanas and Latinas, Native American women, and Asian/Pacific women have already demonstrated to the world their capacity for taking upon their shoulders the responsibility for social leadership. This talent and drive stem directly from the triple oppression unique to our position.

Women leaders have emerged from the radical movements of the 1950s, 1960s, and 1970s. In 1959, a black woman, Rosa Parks, refused to move to the back of the bus, inspiring the Montgomery Bus Boycott. In 1974, a Jewish woman, Clara Fraser, walked out on strike at Seattle City Light to protest unfair working conditions. Clara won a seven-year fight against the public utility based on a historic suit of political ideology and sex discrimination. Her fight and victory inspired a class-action suit against the utility by many more women workers who were fed up with sexism and racism on the job!

In 1982, a Chinese-Korean American lesbian, Merle Woo, was fired from her job as a lecturer in Asian American Studies at the University of California, Berkeley, for openly criticizing the right-wing moves of the Ethnic Studies Department. Merle was fired unfairly, though she received outstanding student evaluations and had been promised Security of Employment when she was first hired. Her firing, based on the pretext of an arbitrary rule limiting lecturers' employment to four years, was imposed upon two thousand lecturers throughout the university system. Although the Public Employment Relations Board (PERB) had ruled that Merle and other affected lecturers were to be rehired with back pay, the university appealed the decision. Merle then filed a federal complaint charging discrimination based on race, sex, sexuality, and political ideology and abridgment of her First Amendment free-speech rights, which were the real reasons she was fired. In 1984, she was reinstated at the university. Merle fought back by organizing with the Merle Woo Defense Committee, composed of people of various communities who believed in the necessity of unifying around all of the issues.

Henry Noble, a Jewish socialist feminist man, also fought an employment-rights case in Seattle. After several years with the Hutchinson Cancer Research Center, Henry's hours were reduced to 75 percent time. Why? Because he actively and successfully organized a union with his primarily female coworkers.

The workplace, where workers—people of color and white—often work side by side, offers a social arena in which the struggle against multi-issue oppressions can take place. Clearly, class analysis and action strike at the heart of capitalist exploitation of workers, whose rights are denied as workers, as women, and as people of color. The economy of capitalism could not have survived as long as it has if it did not depend on sexism and racism to split workers apart, and on the immense profits from paying people of color and women low, low wages. After all, combined, we represent the majority of workers, and that adds up to a lot of profits (Hill 1984, 19)!

Our politics and strategies must be forged through political action independent of the twin parties of capitalism, the Republicans and the Democrats. It was two Democratic presidents—Roosevelt and Truman—who signed Executive Order 9066 and dropped the first atomic bombs on the Japanese cities of Hiroshima and Nagasaki during World War II. Militarism engenders profits. Defense contracts and the manufacture of guns, airplanes, and bombs perpetuate the warmongering drive of the capitalists, both Republicans and Democrats. A labor party could further our multi-issue political struggle, and that labor party must be led by women of color, lesbians, and feminist men. Its program would express the interests and needs of workers and their allies. It would provide an effective alternative and challenge to the boss-party politics dominating the electoral arena. It would be democratic. Anyone could join who agreed with the program, and it would be ruled by the will of the majority, not the labor bureaucrats.

But whether the road taken is via a labor party or some other organization or a combination of strategies for struggle, solidarity and victory will be realized only through the understanding that in unity there is strength. There must be solidarity and mutual aid between all the oppressed for the genuine liberation of any one group. But that unity can come about only if it is based solidly on the demands of the most oppressed strata. We need the unity of blacks, Native Americans, Jews, Chicanos, Latinos, Asian Americans, Puerto Ricans, the working class, the elderly, youth, women, sexual minorities, the disabled—all of the oppressed groups—to win our liberation.

And it is women, especially women of color, who are equipped by our bottommost socioeconomic position to serve as the vanguard on the way to solidarity. We must because nobody needs revolutionary social change as much as we—working women of all races and orientations—need it to survive. We can honor and support the revolutionary and working-class struggles throughout the world by building a socialist feminist revolution here on the soil of the United States. The American revolution will be decisive to international socialism because when U.S. capitalism is dismantled, world capitalism will be dismantled, along with its tyrannical and oppressive forms of institutionalized racism, sexism, and homophobia, and its global greed for profits. While we fight for a socialist feminist society, however, we must, at the same time, fight for reforms under capitalism. Reforms alone, though, are not enough, for they provide only a band-aid solution to the tremendous political, social, and economic problems that we face.

Radical labor history and women's history have taught us that women workers/leaders of all races will lead the way for our total emancipation, as shown in this poem titled "A Woman":

> I am a woman
> and if I live
> I fight and
> if I fight

I contribute to
the liberation
of all Women
and so victory
is born even in the darkest hours. ("Good News" 1980, 19)

A new song of factory women, under a vibrant socialist feminist society, might go like this:

We work for enough to live each day.
    With three days off, like the labor laws say.
The price of noodles, 15 minutes' work will pay.
    So, our working conditions are better. Hey!
(Refrain)
Fellow workers, get it together,
    For prosperity in our land
Fellow workers, rise up together,
    We've made things right with our hand.
When we get our monthly paychecks,
    Our monthly worries do not grow,
Some it goes for some rice and the rent—
    Our private debts are part of the old.
Spirited as they smile and work with us
    Are those fine young men,
Who promise to work and keep fighting back
    Oh, our bravery is revived again.
Sisters, brothers, we now have time
    To write and paint and dance together
Our backs no longer ache from working all day
    We love our children, with them we learn and play.

21

Marxism, Feminism, and the Struggle for Democracy in Latin America

Norma Chinchilla

One of the liveliest debates in Western European and North American feminism during the 1970s was over the past, present, and future relationship of Marxism to feminism. In a paper first circulated among U.S. feminists in 1975, Heidi Hartmann and Ann B. Bridges argued that "the 'marriage' of Marxism and feminism has been like the marriage of husband and wife depicted in English common law: Marxism and feminism are one and that one is Marxism. . . . [e]ither we need a healthier marriage or we need a divorce" (Hartmann 1981, 21).

Marxist-feminists such as Mary Bailey acknowledged that, all too often, women who identified with the hyphenated theoretical perspective and political strategy had been seen as "Marxists to our feminist sisters and feminists to our Marxists brothers" and urged that work be intensified to dissolve the hyphen rather than accepting it "comfortably as self-explanation, a cipher, instead of a project" (cited in Petchesky 1979, 375).

During the 1980s, however, work on dissolving the hyphen and transforming Marxist-feminism into a political project languished on the back burner in the United States and Eastern Europe as a result of a call to "join ranks" against the right-wing attack on feminism and women's rights. Toward the end of the decade, efforts to revive a Marxist-feminist dialogue were further hampered by confusion over the content of socialism and the meaning of Marxism in light of developments in the Soviet Union and Eastern Europe and the lure of a postmodern critique of the notions of "truth" and "progress." Ironically, however, it has been in the effort to build a common-denominator defense of women's rights and the corresponding critique of racism in the women's movement by women of color that the need to understand differences among women, and interrelationships between gender, class, and race/ethnicity and between feminist and class politics is finally beginning to be understood.

In contrast, by the end of the 1980s, the synthesis of ideas from contemporary Marxist and feminist traditions and their transformation into a concrete political strategy for social change had become a high priority for a growing number of Marxists and feminists in Latin America, especially in Mexico, Nicaragua, Peru, Brazil, Chile, and the Dominican Republic.[1] While the views of activists and groups who enthusiastically embrace Marxism *and* feminism still represent a minority perspective within the organized Marxist and non-Marxist Latin American left, they are growing in popularity as a result of their potential to link opposition movements together. This difference in emphasis in the Latin American and North American feminist movements is directly related to the different political and economic contexts within which social movements in the two areas have developed over the last decade. Conservative governments in the United States and Britain have reduced or dismantled social programs that benefit the poor and increased investment and tax incentives for the rich while maintaining the illusion that capitalism will continue to provide for all who are deserving. Events in the Soviet Union and Eastern Europe are generally interpreted by the press in those countries as definitive proof that socialism is terminally ill while capitalism is eternally young.

Meanwhile, the basically capitalist Latin American economics are undergoing one of their worst crises in history, with devastating effects on the living standards of the majority of people. Widespread opposition to the human rights abuses of authoritarian military governments in some countries has resulted in chronically unstable elected civilian governments unable to retain legitimacy because of their inability to overcome a massive foreign debt, stagnant or negative economic growth, and antipopulist economic policies imposed by the International Monetary Fund. In other countries, such as Mexico, ostensibly civilian democratic governments have become increasingly identified with human rights abuses at the same time that their traditionally populist internal economic policies are increasingly dismantled by austerity programs demanded by foreign banks.

In response to these crises, a myriad of social and political groups have mobilized with new demands, tactics, utopian visions, and definitions of what it means to "be political" or "do politics" (*hacer politica*) or, in the case of Central America, "make revolution" (*hacer revolución*) (see Kirkwood 1987; Nun 1989). The range of issues represented in such groups and organizations is great—daily survival, independent labor organizing, human rights, democracy, antiracism, autonomy for indigenous peoples, feminism, and the environment. Their degree of autonomy from the state, political parties, or armed revolutionary organizations in the cases of Nicaragua, El Salvador, and Guatemala varies—but all are experimenting with new ways of facilitating direct political participation by the diversity of groups that arise from capitalism's multiple and complex contradictions. In the process, the unilateral "either/or" choices that dominated Latin American Marxist discussions in the 1970s (reform *or* revolution, class *or* ethnicity, rural *or* urban, armed *or* electoral struggle, etc.) are giving way to a more complex view of how individuals and social groups influence the course of history.[2] The issues raised by these contemporary social movements in their search for a more democratic and egalitarian society have profoundly affected the thinking of key feminist activist-theorists and adherents to what might be called, for lack of a better term, *the New Marxism* in Latin America.[3] The ideas that have emerged from these experiences are important for anyone interested in forging a class- (and racial/ethnic-) conscious feminism and feminist Marxism and for those interested in assessing the significance of such efforts.

This article presents a discussion of the relationship of feminism and Marxism to ideas about democracy and socialism and about the relationship of Marxist and feminist perspectives to each other in the context of contemporary social movements in Latin America. The basic argument is that there is a growing convergence of thinking on issues that once divided or were the sources of serious tension: the importance of pluralism and democracy and its relationship to the idea of plural (potentially revolutionary) social subjects or actors (such as women) and the relationship of democracy to the principle of autonomy for popular organizations (such as those composed of women) in their relationship to the state and to political parties (including vanguard or cadre organizations). Related to each of these debates are new conceptions of the relationship of class to gender and of daily life to the struggle for democracy and socialism. Before discussing the content of these converging ideas, the evolution of contemporary feminist and New Marxist movements in Latin America will be reviewed to provide a context for discussion.

LATIN AMERICAN FEMINISM'S "SECOND WAVE"

The appearance of a second wave of Latin America feminism is often attributed to an external international event: the United Nations Conference on Women held in Mexico City in 1975. The conference was undeniably an important catalyst in many Latin American countries for discussions about women's situation. Preparations for and follow-up from the conference stimulated the formation of many official and unofficial groups and conferences, conferring on them a degree of legitimacy, protection from political persecution, and, in some cases, access to external funding. Although government-sanctioned activities were often short-lived and heavily biased toward the involvement of elite professional women, official party female office holders, and spouses of high government officials, individuals and groups with other agendas (particularly journalists, students, academics, trade union activists, and opposition party activists) were able to take advantage of the political and intellectual opening created by this international event to hold their own discussions of women's condition and proposals for improving it (see Alvarez's [1991] description of this process in Brazil).[4]

But to link Latin American second-wave feminism so intimately to the conference is to underestimate the importance of feminist activities prior to the conference, in countries such as Mexico, Brazil, and Argentina, and the hostile environment that kept the ranks of feminism small and relatively isolated from other social and political sectors until the end of the decade (see accounts by Alvarez 1991; Chester 1986; Kirkwood 1986, 1987; Lau Jaivan 1987; Lozano and Gonzales 1986).

During official and unofficial proceedings of the conference and in a wide variety of public arenas afterward, religious and political groups representing a range of political inclinations argued that feminism was alien to or inappropriate for the Latin American context or both. The Catholic church argued that women were destined, by nature and divine plan, to be self-sacrificing and self-abnegating vessels of virtue and guardians of family and public morality. Feminism, they argued, pointed women in the direction of materialism, individualism, and egotism and, thus, was inherently opposed to church doctrine.

Liberal and nationalism politicians, on the other hand, declared that males and females were already "different but equal" in Latin American culture and argued that feminism demotes women from their elevated special status. Left groups, influenced by Stalinism's hostility to feminism and its mechanical, economistic stagist conceptions of social change ("first the socialization of the means of production and the incorporation of women into wage labor, then automatic equality for women in the family and society" [see Molyneux 1982]), warned women that feminism was a bourgeois deviation from the primary focus of the class struggle. This sequencing of demands was justified by some Marxists on the grounds that sexism could not be eliminated *without* the overthrow of capitalism. Other Marxists argued, however, that capitalism was gender neutral and could theoretically *concede* gender equality as a result of its pursuit of cheap labor and profits while still leaving exploitation on the basis of class intact.[5]

Reinforcing traditional religious and left thinking, the Latin American mass media stigmatized feminism as a "radical and crazy" movement of relatively privileged, but unhappy, women from economically developed countries (Chinchilla 1977, 1985–86, 1990; Cordero 1986; Molina 1986; Murguialday 1989; Portugal 1986). The low level of class, ethnic, and international political consciousness among U.S. women constituted a serious obstacle to fruitful exchange of ideas and experiences with Latin American women during the international conferences held during this early period.[6] Latin American women who had attempted to organize feminist groups after having lived or traveled abroad tended to be viewed as having lost their cultural and national perspective.

The birth of second-wave feminism in Latin America was made more difficult by the loss of a collective memory of the earlier period of Latin American feminism, particularly the ideas and organizing experiences of radical, socialist, and anarchist women. Historical accounts of earlier feminist efforts available during the later 1970s emphasized reformist tendencies in nineteenth- and twentieth-century Latin American feminism and the upper- and middle-class origins of radical as well as reformist feminist leaders.[7] It took a while to rediscover and disseminate examples of socialist and working-class women's efforts to make women's equality a priority in early twentieth-century social movements, such as the socialist women in the autonomous Movement for the Liberation of Chilean Women (MEMCH) in the 1930s and the more than 50,000 Mexican women representing some 800 organizations and a variety of social sectors and classes organized in the autonomous coalition Frente Unico Pro Derecho de la Mujer (Molina 1986, 19; Rascon 1975, 60–61). It is not surprising that the growing influence of feminism in many Latin American countries (most notably Mexico and Chile) coincides with the recovery of a progressive women's history that had been hidden for many years.

Despite the ideological containment of previous decades, by the mid-1980s, conditions for and attitudes toward women's involvement in politics had begun to change in dramatic ways throughout the hemisphere. First, women were involved in politics to a degree and in a variety of forms without precedent in Latin American history (Alvarez 1989, 1991; de Barbieri and de Oliveira 1986; Jacquette 1989; Jelin 1990). Second, women's organizations were beginning to carve out a space for themselves in local and national political life and feminism was slowly making inroads into political and academic institutions as reflected in a growing number of consciousness-raising and political action groups, service and popular education centers, research institutes, and university-based women's studies programs (Deutsch 1988). Finally, a conscious Marxist-feminist tendency had begun to appear, in theory and in practice, in Latin American Marxism; and the diffusion of a feminist perspective and agenda within popular movements had been adopted as a priority by a number of feminist groups (Flora 1984; Gonzalez, Loria, and Lozano 1988; Lozano and Gonzales 1986).[8]

The most dramatic early examples of women's contributions to a redefinition of what constitutes political activity or "doing politics" in Latin America come from the protests of Argentine and Chilean women against miliary dictatorships in their countries, even when other groups were still reluctant to confront the regimes openly and directly. Women in Argentina used their "moral force" as mothers, grandmothers, and sisters of the disappeared to demand an accounting of relatives who had been victims of political repression, while in Chile women converted homes and neighborhoods into centers of collective resistance and survival after the emergence of the Pinochet dictatorship (Agosin 1987; Feijo 1989). In both cases, these struggles by women contributed significantly to the demise of the respective military regimes. In the last two years before the Somoza dictatorship in Nicaragua was overthrown in 1979 (and throughout the hemisphere during the decade of the 1980s), women acquired unprecedented importance in opposition movements, often through new organizational forms and with new tactics that they themselves helped to invent. In rural areas, women became active in peasant organizations and in ethnic/racial movements in urban areas; they formed the backbone of neighborhood-based grassroots protest movements. In both rural and urban areas, they formed the foundation of the Christian-based community and human rights movements (Alvarez 1988; Chinchilla 1990; Jacquette 1989; Jelin 1990; Randall 1981).

Women's growing participation in these protest and social change movements during the 1980s were often derived from an attempt to fulfill, rather than subvert, the traditional gender division of labor (mothers entering the public sphere to save the lives of their children, housewives turning to collective action to provide for the survival of their families, etc.). But the experiences women gained in the process often created fertile ground for links between a gender-specific consciousness (what Molyneux [1986] calls "women's strategic interests") and social consciousness (consciousness of class, social sector, nation, etc.).

Parallel to women's growing visibility in nontraditional forms of civilian politics was the unprecedented incorporation of women in cadre revolutionary organizations and political parties in countries with broad-based revolutionary movements, such as Nicaragua, El Salvador, and Guatemala (Chinchilla 1990; Gargallo 1987; Murguialday 1990). The ties of these women with women in neighborhood and other organizations nurtured their appreciation of women's potential for courageous and creative protest and encouraged them to analyze the concrete conditions of women's lives in greater depth (Randall 1981; author's interviews with Guatemalan women participants in politico-military organizations). Women's visibility in human rights organizations and groups for the defense of basic survival, in turn, encouraged women in traditionally male-dominated class organizations (such as trade unions) to form women's caucuses and commissions and create mechanisms for greater representation of women in leadership—for example, the Nicaraguan Agricultural Workers Union (Chinchilla 1990;

Criquillon and Espinoza 1987; Murguialday 1990). Increased contact with feminist ideas within and without the movement, at international conferences and as a result of international solidarity efforts, and the ability to test ideas in practice served as incubators for a new-born revolutionary Marxist-feminist current within socialism and the feminist movement.

LATIN AMERICAN MARXISM'S INTERNAL CRITIQUE

As early as the 1950s, decades before the changes in Eastern Europe and the dramatic increase of women's involvement in Latin American politics, Latin American Marxists critical of traditional communist parties' intellectual and strategic dependence on the Soviet Union embarked on a search for an indigenous version of Marxism capable of guiding movements for social change. The search led to experiments with various revolutionary strategies and theoretical perspectives and the eventual rediscoveries of works of earlier Latin American Socialist and nationalist revolutionary thinkers, such as Jose Carlos Mariategui (Peruvian), Agusto Cesar Sandino (Nicaraguan), and Carlos Fonseca Amateur (Nicaraguan). During the 1970s and 1980s, these discussions drew in the writings of Italian Marxist Antonio Gramsci and "liberal socialist" Norberto Bobbio (1989), the experiences and ideas of 1960s social movements from around the world, and theoretical debates among Western European and U.S. Marxists (see Barros 1986; Burbach and Nuñez 1987; Cueva 1987; Hodges 1974; Moulian 1982; Munck 1990; Portantiero 1982; Vasconi 1990; Winn 1989).

Democracy and feminism were not, however, topics of serious discussion in the search for an indigenous Latin American Marxism until the 1980s. During the 1960s the Latin American (noncommunist party) New Left revolutionary groups' assessment of the alternatives for the region "left very little room for seriously integrating democracy" into their theory and practice (Barros 1986, 53). Reformist democratic governments were seen as incapable of breaking the cycle of economic stagnation; economic development was seen as the key missing element for Latin America, with little attention paid to political institutions. No form of development was seen as possible unless it challenged the dominance of (capitalist) imperialism; socialism or fascism were seen as the only alternatives, and the only road to socialism was a revolution (like that of Cuba). Democracy was seen as a facade used by anticommunist reformist governments posing as alternatives to the Left. The New Left and the Old Left (the Soviet-aligned communist parties) disagreed on the need for development of the productive forces in stages and the potentially progressive character of a "national bourgeoisie." Both shared, however, "the objectivistic Marxism of the Third International":

> The communist parties, ideologically subordinate to the international line of Moscow, despite their electoral activities, never produced any democratic theory. In the term "bourgeois-democratic" the weight has always been on the side of the "bourgeois" with the "democratic" side of the conjunction left dangling. For the revolutionary Left, on the other hand, democracy could have no value as a mode of will formation; ends were known; the real problem was one of the proper combination of tactics and strategy. (Barros 1986, 53–54)

The underlying view of politics was instrumental, even for groups that emerged in countries with formal democratic political structures (periodic elections, etc.). "At best," Barros concludes, "democracy presented the possibility of 'an additional form of struggle.' But just as often, it was rhetorically cast off as a bourgeois trap" (1986, 54).

By the mid-1970s the economic expansion of the 1960s had been replaced by significant economic stagnation and a decline in living standards of the majority of people. Right-wing military dictatorships had replaced civilian governments in a majority of countries in the hemisphere (e.g., Brazil, Argentina, Uruguay, Chile, Peru, Guatemala, El Salvador); officially sanctioned repression and torture became commonplace. These trends, together with changes in the demand for women's labor (as the result of the internal capitalist expansion and increased penetration of foreign multinational corporations), heightened women's importance as economic producers, sustainers of household units, and spokespersons for human rights, social justice, and peace (Chinchilla 1990; Murguailday 1989). They also created a broad spectrum of individuals and organized groups that stood to benefit from an end to dictatorship.

In response to the systematic violence and intolerance of differences imposed by authoritarian governments, Marxists joined others in the denunciation of authoritarianism in the name of human rights. The defense of life replaced the defense of a political agenda. All statist perspectives (including socialist ones) were reconsidered with a critical eye; formal and "real" democracy came to be seen as compatible by some and necessarily interconnected by others. Brazilian Marxist Michel Lowy's argument that democracy is the essence of socialism reflects the latter view:

> Democracy is not a problem of "political form" or institutional "superstructure": it is the *very content* of socialism as a social formation in which workers and peasants, young people, women, that is, the people, effectively exercise power and democratically determine the purpose of production, the distribution of the means of production, and the allocation of the product. (1986, 264)

Just as important, because of its link to contemporary feminism, was the discovery by some male leftists of the importance of the invisible activities that make up daily life (*lo cotidiano*). This discovery, made because survival itself was threatened by the harsh conditions of military dictatorship, was interjected by some into theoretical discussions of the relationship between democracy and socialism. Norbert Lechner, for example, linked successful democratization to changes in daily life and political culture:

> [Democracy's] possibilities and tendencies are conditioned by the standards of normalcy and naturalness that common people develop in their daily life. It is the concrete experiences of violence and fear, misery and solidarity, that give democracy and socialism their meaning. (1990, 4)

Critics have argued that Marxist advocates of a greater emphasis on democracy have not clearly articulated its relationship to socialism, particularly under the precarious material conditions of Third World societies, and that some position statements seem to imply that democracy can automatically evolve into socialism. Nevertheless, the attempt to elaborate a Marxist understanding of democracy and daily life is an important step forward and, in my opinion, an essential precondition for a convergence with contemporary feminism and with contemporary social movements in general. The discussions of feminist and Marxist views on the notion of a plurality of potential revolutionary actors (as opposed to simply the industrial working class) and the application of the principle of autonomy to popular and vanguard or cadre organizations, to which we now turn, are meant to underscore this point.

DEMOCRACY AND THE PLURALISM OF SOCIAL SUBJECTS

The tendency of orthodox Marxists to rank social sectors and classes according to their revolutionary potential, with industrial wage workers at the top, has always been a problem for feminists who, as housewives and nonindustrial workers, have frequently been seen only as auxiliaries to the "central actors" in the class struggle. Feminist arguments about the interrelatedness of production and reproduction have helped to clarify the centrality of women to the struggles of the classes and social sectors to which they belong.

But, in addition to the new awareness of women's roles in reproduction, another important conceptual revolution within Latin American Marxism has begun to take place, influenced by the social movements of the 1960s and 1970s, the writings of Italian Marxist Antonio Gramsci, and the experience of the Nicaraguan revolution: the acceptance of the view that the contradictions of contemporary capitalism may create a plurality of potential social subjects (i.e., people who act politically on their own behalf) that any broad social or revolutionary movement must learn to articulate (i.e., coordinate or interrelate) for long-term revolutionary change. While this is true for contemporary capitalism generally, it is particularly true where capitalism has developed extremely unevenly as a result of conquest, colonialism, intervention, the appropriation of precapitalism structures, and a continuing pattern of external economic and political dependence. Class struggles, in and of themselves, are necessarily complex and multidimensional. Within the working class alone in Latin America, there are often large differences in age (an age structure highly skewed toward those under 25 years), ethnicity, employed and unemployed status, concentration in services versus manufacturing, formal and informal sectors, rural versus urban areas, and so on (Chinchilla and Dietz 982; Petras 1981; Portes 1985, 16, 22–23; Vilas 1986). Beyond that, class struggles can combine with cross-class aspects of gender, ethnic, generational, and other struggles in important and potentially powerful ways.

The extent to which these various social groups, fractions of classes, or classes gel as a coherent political force depends not only on the political character of the opposed regime (e.g., the internal divisions in its base of support or factors such as the indiscriminate character of its repression), but also on the capacity and political will of the vanguard organization, if such an organization exists. The character and coherence of the opposition force is also determined by the past history of resistance and protest and the way in which real alliances have been forged in struggle (Vilas 1986, 21).

Roger Burbach, a U.S. Marxist theorist/activist, and Orlando Nuñez, a Nicaraguan Sandinista theorist/activist, refer to this pivotal group who can spark revolutionary movements and help lead them as a "third force" that, unlike propertyless wage laborers, is "not a new class or even a single consolidated class" but a category made up of "diverse social groups and social moments that are more defined by their social and political attributes than by their relationships to the work-place" (1987, 64). The radical potential of this force comes from the "discrimination and oppression they experience in the general social structure . . . in the evolution of capitalist society as a whole, i.e., in the totality of social and class structure" (1987, 64). Although the composition of the third force will "vary from country to country, and particularly between the developed and underdeveloped countries" (1987, 65), examples of social groups in Central America that make up this category, some of which have a multiclass composition themselves, include women, ethnic minorities, and young people.

Burbach and Nuñez do not point out any particular contribution that women's organizing or feminism can make toward the class struggle and the building of socialism. Latin American Marxist-feminists do, however, explicitly discuss these contributions and interconnections in their writings and documents. Activists in mixed groups such as shantytown and trade union organizations in Chile, for example, turn the traditional argument that feminism is divisive on its head and argue instead that men and women will remain divided unless they engage in a common political project that acknowledges women's subordination and directly confronts machismo. A feminist perspective thus can make the class struggle "more efficient."

> It is not part of the [feminist] project to deny the reality and validity of the analysis of class domination. On the contrary, a feminist analysis, which exposes the economistic bias of class analysis enriches it. . . . In fact, feminism truly constitutes a social movement for liberation in Chile because it successfully links the struggle against class and sex oppression simultaneously. (1987, 8–9)

While this formulation leaves questions about the interrelationship between class and gender unanswered, it is not a dismissal or underestimation of the importance of class. On the contrary, second-wave Latin American feminism has generally been distinguished by a high level of class consciousness since its emergence, and this class consciousness is central to its theoretical and practical discussions.

There is a growing recognition, for example, that women of different classes and sectors are likely to come to feminism in different ways: some struggle around practical gender interests (which tend to be highly differentiated by class and ethnicity), and some through an analysis of gender subordination (strategic gender interests). These diverse starting points inevitably imply diverse forms of action through which women may contribute to the construction of an individual and collective gender identity (Murguailday 1990).

The central knot of feminist practice, particularly for those who aspire to create a feminist current within popular movements, is how to link practical (women's) interests derived from the existing gender division of labor and strategic (feminist) gender interests derived from a critique of the existing gender hierarchy. Chilean feminists have attempted to do so when they link authoritarianism in the family to authoritarianism (dictatorship) in society and Nicaraguan feminists do when they link women's demands to the overall success of the revolution.

Neither aspect of women's interests, Peruvian feminist Virginia Vargas points out, is complete without the other: "The challenge is to achieve the articulation of both. This means politicizing practical gender interests in such a way that they advance towards a modification in the situation of the subordination of women" (1989, 82–83).

DEMOCRACY, AUTONOMY, AND VANGUARD ORGANIZATIONS

Closely related to the notion of a plurality of social subjects is the argument that popular organizations have the right to autonomy in relation to the state and political parties, that is, the right to carve out a political space within which they can choose their own leaders, criteria for membership, and political agenda. In the case of women's organizations, Gonzalez, Loria, and Lozano suggest that it also means "the creation of a correlation of forces favorable to the raising of women's demands, one which does not imply their subordination" (1988, 22). At the same time, it means the existence of safe spaces where women can discover their identities, give mutual support, build trust, explore previously forbidden topics (such as women's bodies and sexuality), and invent new forms of political struggle or definitions of what it means to do politics. In Latin America these safe spaces are usually linked to political activity in such a way that autonomy, for the majority of groups, is not simply a defensive concept and does not signify isolation or ghettoization in a "world of women" (Vargas 1989, 97). Murguailday points out that, in fact, the spaces that women have created in different Latin American countries over the last decade have facilitated coordination with other struggles and social groups such as Christian-based communities, urban social movements, human rights groups, ethnic movements, and youth groups. Meetings conducted in these spaces have been the catalyst for theoretical and ideological discussion about the ways in which different contradictions intersect and different demands and struggles interconnect (e.g., domestic violence and political violence, male dominance over women and children in the domestic sphere, capitalist dominance in society, the interaction of inequalities based on class, gender, and ethnicity, etc.) (1989, 9). This emphasis on understanding interconnections represents an important break from the past when debates centered around the ranking of different oppressions. Autonomy thus defined "entails a recognition of the diversity of social interests, the refusal of class reductionism, and, above all, of economism" (Munck 1990, 117–18).

An important aspect of the autonomy of popular organizations involves their relationship to a vanguard or cadre political organization (where it exists). Some Latin American feminists have argued that the concept of a revolutionary "vanguard" is inherently inconsistent with the kind of democratic, popular movement of which the women's movement is, or aspires to be, a part (see, for example, Costa Rican feminist Ana Sojo 1985, 90). Vargas, a founding member of the feminist movement in Peru, is critical of cadre organizations' tendencies toward "homogenizing opinions, of liberating subjects from their responsibility for vital decisions, of repressing their freedom and creativity" (1989, 37). She believes that she and other activists were guilty, in the early stages of the Peruvian women's movement, of reproducing some of the negative characteristics they had learned in cadre organizations.

> We conceived of ourselves as a group of people who were holders of the truth. We considered that only those were faced with double exploitation, of class and gender, were justified in demanding their rights. . . . We accepted the principle of the vanguard as the superior bearer of knowledge, which was characterized by messianism and "machismo." In this view, people—in our case women—were regarded as virgin lands where the seeds of wisdom could be sown. (1988, 137)

Others argue, however, that the concept of a vanguard is not inherently problematic, but certain definitions and practices that have characterized it in the past are (for example, a sense of elitism, a "top-down" internal and external leadership style, intolerance of minority views, suppression of gender, and racial/ethnic conflict within the vanguard organization). Burbach and Nuñez, for example, believe that "there is a need for direction and guidance in any revolutionary process but this direction should help nurture and organize the democratic tendencies rather than repress them" (1987, 49), and some feminists use the term to describe the role feminists should play within the broader (nonfeminist or prefeminist) women's movement (i.e., as teacher and student, repository organizer, and interpreter of past and present experiences and as a link between the different parts of a global cause or struggle; EMAS et al., 1987, 293, 332–33; Gonzalez, Loria, and Lozano 1988, 22). This latter view seems to be consistent with other attempts to redefine the role of vanguard groups or parties in Latin American political struggles (see Brown 1990; Lowy 1986, 272).

While Latin American feminists, including Marxists feminists, vary in the degree to which they believe a vanguard political organization is necessary for revolution, there is a considerable consensus about the reasons why organizational autonomy for popular organizations is essential for democracy and the building of socialism. The strong arguments of independent feminists (many of whom are ex-party militants) in favor or autonomy frequently put them in conflict over mass organizations. This also creates tensions between independent feminists and female political party militants when they work together in the same coalitions and attend the same conferences; it adds to the pressure on those who try to be activists in both types of groups at once, the condition Latin American feminists refer to as "double militancy." Female militants of political parties frequently feel that independent feminists regard them as impure in their feminism and inherently subordinate to men in their political party activities. Feminists, on the other hand, often feel that their credentials as revolutionaries and commitment to class as a fundamental axis for understanding Latin American society are constantly being challenged (Bonder 1989; Chuchryk 1989; Kirkwood 1986).

In the best of circumstances, however, the interaction between women militants of political parties and independent feminists in a multiplicity of forms (in consciousness-raising groups, battered women's shelters, and soup kitchens as well as multiorganizational bodies coordinating political protest) has a positive effect on both groups of women, reinforcing the goal of a class-conscious current among feminists and making left political parties more open to feminism (Molina 1986).

CONCLUSION

It is common for Marxists critical of feminism and feminists critical of Marxism to see their own intellectual tradition and the social movements based on it as dynamic, evolving, and self-correcting while regarding the other as unable to transcend earlier weakness. Thus, Marxism is often seen by feminist critics as inherently economistic, reductionist, and gender blind, whereas Marxist critics of feminism often regard it as inherently white, middle class, "First World," and reformist.

The reality is, of course, that both Marxist and feminist thinking have changed in important ways over the last two decades. For Latin American Marxists, for example, the hope of overthrowing corrupt, unpopular, and elite-based authoritarian regimes as a result of the efforts of a small but dedicated clandestine guerrilla band has been exchanged for the growing consensus that the power of entrenched privileged elites and their external allies can only be overcome by the broadest, most democratic grassroots movement possible. Feminism is seen by a growing number of Latin American Marxists as not only compatible with this effort but essential to it. The very existence of new social movements in Latin American societies (i.e., the multiplicity of class, sectoral, and other opposition groups that challenge some aspects of authoritarian relationships, exploitation, or alienation) challenges left political parties to develop more tolerant, democratic, and pluralistic political practices in spite of a weak democratic tradition.

The mainstream of Latin American feminism takes Marxist contributions to the understanding of class and the mode of production seriously, while contributing to an understanding of the interconnectedness of production and reproduction, practical and strategic gender interests, and an evolving understanding of the relationship between class and other forms of oppression. In addition, feminist demands for equality in the social relations of daily life, control over reproduction, and greater freedom in sexual expression draw attention to the need for a holistic view of change and offer a vision of the future in a context decidedly lacking in alternative utopias (Arizpe 1990; Lozano and Gonzales 1986; Vargas 1988).

Thus, while many feminists in developed capitalist countries choose to ignore or consciously reject Marxism as outmoded, irrelevant, or worse yet, an obstacle to the emancipation of women, feminist activists in Latin America are adding to and converging with new Marxist thinking in important ways. Their debates and discussions are not simple reflections of changes in intellectual trends in the developed countries (although they are inevitably influenced by them) but are also reflections of changed social, economic, and political structures within such societies as well as conclusions drawn by activists from their own and others' successful and unsuccessful organizing experiences. The evolving understanding of the interrelationship between women's movements, the class struggle, and the struggle for socialism is not only grounded in the particular realities of Latin American societies (the complexity of the class structure, for example, and the extent to which it has been conditioned by external forces, i.e., imperialism) but in a new appreciation of the role of culture, ideology, democratic practice, and daily life in the struggle against capitalism and the construction of socialism. These are insights that have potentially universal importance for anyone who seeks to understand the link between class, race/ethnicity/nationality, and gender and between Marxism and feminism.

NOTES

1. See, for example, *Debate feminista* (Lamas 1990); *FEM* magazine; the publications of ISIS International; reports (*memorias*) from hemisphere-wide conferences, such as the Fourth and Fifth Feminist Encuentros. Ironically absent from the list of countries is Argentina, which had one of the hemisphere's strongest first-wave feminist movements (see Carlson 1988). Since the 1970s, a variety of feminist groups and research centers has existed in Argentina, with a resurgence of feminist activity in the 1980s, but they appear to be smaller in size and influence than in the other countries listed and reflect a separation between activists and professionals (Chester 1986). Recently, however, some 5,000 women attended the national feminist conference in

preparation for Argentina's hosting the Fifth Latin American and Caribbean Feminist Encounter in November 1990, and the encounter itself was more than twice as large as the previous one in Taxco, Mexico.

2. This is not to imply that economically and politically conservative "New Right" and "neo-liberal" (free market) ideas do not have a growing number of followers among intellectuals and politicians in Latin America as elsewhere in the world, but it is to argue that these intellectual and political trends offer little hope for improvement in the situation of the vast majority of Latin Americans who are poor, peasant, and working class and are thus likely to continue to encounter relatively strong organized opposition. Postmodernism has also begun to be discussed among Latin American intellectuals, but it would be logical to anticipate that it will undergo significant adaptation to the Latin American reality before gaining many adherents.

3. The term New Marxism is problematic in that it is not necessarily used by the adherents themselves; nor is it particularly accurate, since some of the ideas it encompasses have roots in early twentieth-century Marxist writings and social movements. Nevertheless, I have chosen to use the term because a more satisfactory term does not appear to be available.

4. For more detailed descriptions of the origins of recent feminist movements in Latin America, see articles in EMAS et al. (1987), Jacquette (1989), *FEM* (numerous issues), and works by Alvarez (1991), Chuchryk (1984), Murguialday (1989, 1990), Vargas (1989), and Chinchilla (1990).

5. For a succinct composite of other objections to feminism advanced by Chilean Marxists as recounted by past and present women militants, see Chuchryk (1984).

6. See, for example, Bolivian Indian Domitila's account of her encounter with U.S. feminist Betty Friedan (Barrios de Chungara 1978).

7. The educated middle-class origins of earlier feminists were seized on by male-dominated left groups in the 1970s as evidence that feminism in Latin America had been an inherently middle-class concept. In fact, the social origins of core Latin American feminist activists, past and present, had not been that different from that of the leadership of many male-dominated left groups, especially in their early stages of formation. While bourgeois historians are partly to blame for overlooking this earlier history, the close ties between Latin American Marxism and the international line of the Soviet Union are also at fault. The Soviet-inspired antifascist popular front policy of the late 1930s and early 1940s led to the dissolution of the Mexican women's front (in favor of undifferentiated support for Cardenas) and a lack of support for the principle or organizational autonomy for popular organizations, thus contributing to the prolonged period of feminist silence.

8. In the Fourth Latin American Feminist Encounter held in Taxco, Mexico, in October 1987, this "popular feminist" perspective appeared to have the sympathy of the majority of the 1,500 women in attendance, many of whom were grassroots activists in unions, neighborhood, housewife, and peasant organizations, and religious groups, who publicly declared their receptivity to feminism for the first time (Monroy Limon 1987; *Off Our Backs* 1989; Zimmerman 1987).

22

Transgender Liberation
A Movement Whose Time Has Come

Leslie Feinberg

BREAKING THE SILENCE

This pamphlet is an attempt to trace the historic rise of an oppression that, as yet, has no commonly agreed-upon name. We are talking here about people who defy the "man"-made boundaries of gender.

Gender: self-expression, not anatomy.

All our lives we've been taught that sex and gender are synonymous—men are "masculine" and women are "feminine." Pink for girls and blue for boys. It's just "natural," we've been told. But at the turn of the century in this country, blue was considered a girl's color and pink was a boy's. Simplistic and rigid gender codes are neither eternal nor natural. They are changing social concepts.

Nevertheless, there's nothing wrong with men who are considered "masculine" and women whose self-expression falls into the range of what is considered "feminine." The problem is that the many people who don't fit these narrow social constraints run a gamut of harassment and violence.

This raises the question: Who decided what the "norm" should be? Why are some people punished for their self-expression?

Many people today would be surprised to learn that ancient communal societies held transgendered people in high esteem. It took a bloody campaign by the emerging ruling classes to declare what had been considered natural to be its opposite. That prejudice, foisted on society by its ruling elite, endures today. . . .

Many of the terms used to describe us are words that cut and sear.

When I first worked in the factories of Buffalo as a teenager, women like me were called "he-shes." Although "he-shes" in the plants were most frequently lesbians, we were recognized not by our sexual preference but by the way we expressed our gender.

There are other words used to express the wide range of "gender outlaws": transvestites, transsexuals, drag queens and drag kings, cross-dressers, bulldaggers, stone butches, androgynes, diesel dykes, or berdache—a European colonialist term.

We didn't choose these words. They don't fit all of us. It's hard to fight an oppression without a name connoting pride, a language that honors us.

In recent years a community has begun to emerge that is sometimes referred to as the gender or transgender community. Within our community is a diverse group of people who define ourselves in many different ways. Transgendered people are demanding the right to choose our own self-definitions. The language used in this pamphlet may quickly become outdated as the gender community coalesces and organizes—a wonderful problem.

We've chosen words in this pamphlet we hope are understandable to the vast majority of working and oppressed people in this country, as a tool to battle bigotry and brutality. We are trying to find words, however inadequate, that can connect us, that can capture what is similar about the oppression we endure. We have also given careful thought to our use of pronouns, striving for both clarity and sensitivity in a language that only allows for two sexes.

Great social movements forge a common language—tools to reach out and win broader understanding. But we've been largely shut out of the progressive movement.

It was gay transvestites who led the 1969 battle at the Stonewall Inn in New York City that gave birth to the modern lesbian and gay movement.

But just as the lesbian and gay movement had to win over the progressive movement to the understanding that struggling shoulder to shoulder together would create a more powerful force for change, the transgendered community is struggling to win the same understanding from the lesbian and gay movement.

Many people think that all "masculine" women are lesbians and all "feminine" men are gay. That is a misunderstanding. Not all lesbians and gay men are "cross"-gendered. Not all transgendered women and men are lesbian or gay. Transgendered people are mistakenly viewed as the cusp of the lesbian and gay community. In reality the two huge communities are like circles that only partially overlap.

While the oppressions within these two powerful communities are not the same, we face a common enemy. Gender-phobia—like racism, sexism and bigotry against lesbians and gay men—is meant to keep us divided. Unity can only increase our strength.

Solidarity is built on understanding how and why oppression exists and who profits from it. It is our view that revolutionary changes in human society can do away with inequality, bigotry, and intolerance.

In the spirit of building that fighting movement, we offer this view of the sweeping patterns in history, the commonality of women and men who have walked the path of the berdache, of the transgendered—walked that road whether we were held in high esteem or reviled.

Look at us. We are battling for survival. Listen. We are struggling to be heard.

TRANSGENDER PREDATES OPPRESSION

Jazz musician Billy Tipton died in 1989 at the age of 74. He will be remembered most not for his music, but for the revelation that Tipton was born a woman. Tipton died of an untreated bleeding ulcer rather than visit a doctor and risk exposure.

After his death this debate began: did Tipton live as a man simply in order to work as a musician in a male-dominated industry or because of lesbian oppression?

It is true that women's oppression, especially under capitalism, has created profound social and economic pressures that force women to pass as men for survival. But this argument leaves out transgendered women—women who are considered so "masculine" in class society that they can endure extreme harassment and danger. Many of these women are forced to "pass" in order to live. Of course transgendered women also experience the crushing weight of economic inequity and, in many cases, anti-lesbian oppression. These factors also play a role in forcing "masculine" women as well as non-transgendered women to pass.

If "masculine" women are acknowledged at all, it is implied that they're merely a product of decadent patriarchal capitalism and that when genuine equality is won, they will disappear.

IT'S "PASSING" THAT'S NEW

Transgendered women and men have always been here. They are oppressed. But they are not merely products of oppression. It is *passing* that's historically new. Passing means hiding. Passing means invisibility. Transgendered people should be able to live and express their gender without criticism or threats of violence. But that is not the case today.

There are legions of women and men whose self-expression, as judged by the Hollywood stereotypes, is "at odds" with their sex. Some are forced underground or "pass" because of the repression and ostracism they endure.

Today all gender education teaches that women are "feminine," men are "masculine," and an unfordable river rages between these banks. The reality is there is a whole range of ways for women and men to express themselves.

Transgender is a very ancient form of human expression that pre-dates oppression. It was once regarded with honor. A glance at human history proves that when societies were not ruled by exploiting classes that rely on divide-and-conquer tactics, "cross-gendered" youths, women, and men on all continents were respected members of their communities.

"SHE IS A MAN"

"Strange country, this," a white man wrote of the Crow nation on this continent in 1850, "where males assume the dress and perform the duties of females, while women turn men and mate with their own sex."

Randy Burns, a founder of the modern group Gay American Indians, wrote that GAI's History Project documented these alternative roles for women and men in over 135 North American Native nations.

The high incidence of transgendered men and women in Native societies on this continent was documented by the colonialists, who referred to them as *berdache*.

Perhaps the most notable of all berdache Native women was Barcheeampe, the Crow "Woman Chief," the most famous war leader in the history of the upper Missouri nations. She married several wives and her bravery as a hunter and warrior was honored in songs. When the Crow nation council was held, she took her place among the chiefs, ranking third in a band of 160 lodges.

Today transgender is considered "anti-social" behavior. But among the Klamath nations transgendered women were given special initiation ceremonies by their societies.

Among the Cocopa, Edward Gifford wrote, "Female transvestites were called war'hameh, wore their hair and pierced their nose, in the male fashion, married women and fought in battle alongside men."

Wewha, a famous Zuni berdache who was born a man, lived from 1849 to 1986. She was among the tallest and strongest of all the Zuni. When asked, her people would explain, "She is a man." Wewha was sent by the Zuni to Washington, D.C., for six months where she met with President Grover Cleveland and other politicians who never realized she was berdache.

Osh-Tische (Finds Them and Kills Them), a Crow berdache or bade who was also born a man, fought in the Battle of the Rosebud. When a colonial agent tried to force Osh-Tisch to wear men's clothing, the other Native people argued with him that it was against her nature and they kicked the agent off their land. They said it was a tragedy, trying to change the nature of the bade.

A Jesuit priest observed in the 1670s of the berdache, "They are summoned to the Councils, and nothing can be decided without their advice."

But the missionaries and colonialist military reacted to the Native berdache in this hemisphere with murderous hostility. Many berdache were tortured and burnt to death by their Christian conquerors. Other colonial armies sicked wild dogs on the berdache.

WHY SUCH HOSTILITY?

Why were the European colonialists so hostile to transgendered women and men? The answer can be found back on the European continent in the struggles that raged between the developing classes of haves and have-nots.

Ancient societies on the European continent were communal. Thousands of artifacts have been unearthed dating back to 25,000 B.C. that prove these societies worshiped goddesses, not gods. Some of the deities were transgendered, as were many of their shamans or religious representatives.

We have been taught that the way things are now is roughly the way they have always been—the "Flintstones" school of anthropology. The strong message is: don't bother trying to change people. But a glance at history proves that human society has undergone continuous development and change.

A great debate has raged for more than 150 years about the role of women in ancient societies. To hear Jesse Helms and his ilk rant, you'd think that the patriarchal nuclear family has always existed. That's not true.

Twentieth-century anthropologists recognize that matrilineal communal societies existed all over the world at an early stage in social development. Women were the heads of gens or clans that bore little resemblance to today's "family."

But many argue that matrilineage could co-exist with the subjugation of women, and that there is no confirmed documentation of any culture in history in which women consistently held leadership positions. This ignores the relationship between male domination and private property, and implies that women's oppression is merely a result of "human nature."

This ideological argument is as much a weapon of class warfare as prisons are.

Rosalind Coward offers an invaluable overview of this debate in her work *Patriarchal Precedents*. Coward shows that most 19th-century European scholars held the patriarchal nuclear family and male inheritance to be universal. But by the latter part of the century, European colonialists studying the peoples of Southern India and Southwest Asia disputed that view.

In 1861, Johann Bachofen published his famous book *Das Mutterrecht* (Mother Right)—a scientific study of the family as an evolving social institution. His work was regarded as a fundamental contribution to modern anthropology.

Lewis Henry Morgan, the great ethnologist and one of the founders of anthropology, wrote his significant work *Ancient Society* in 1877—an exhaustive study of communal societies with kinship systems based on women. He studied the Haudenosaunee (Iroquois Confederacy) on this continent, and numerous indigenous peoples in India and Australia. His research on social evolution confirmed that the patriarchal form of the family was not the oldest form of human society.

The research of Bachofen and especially Morgan was the basis for Frederick Engels's great 1884 classic, *The Origin of the Family, Private Property and the State*. Engels argued that early societies were based on collective labor and communal property. Cooperation was necessary for group survival.

Engels, Karl Marx's leading collaborator in developing the doctrine of scientific socialism, found that these ancient societies showed no evidence of a state apparatus of repression, large-scale warfare, slavery, or the nuclear family. Engels and Marx saw Morgan's studies as further proof that the modern-day oppression of women was rooted in the cleavage of society into classes based on private ownership of property. The fact that oppression was not a feature of early communal societies lent greater weight to their prognosis that overturning private ownership in favor of socialized property would lay the basis for revolutionizing human relations.

THE NATURAL BECOMES UNNATURAL

Ancient religion, before the division of society into classes, combined collectively held beliefs with material observations about nature. Christianity as a mass religion really began in the cities of the Roman empire among the poor and incorporated elements of collectivism and hatred of the rich ruling class. But over several hundred years, Christianity was transformed from a revolutionary movement of the urban poor into a powerful state religion that served the wealthy elite.

Transgender in all its forms became a target. In reality it was the rise of private property, the male-dominated family, and class divisions that led to narrowing what was considered acceptable self-expression. What had been natural was declared its opposite.

As the Roman slave-based system of production disintegrated it was gradually replaced by feudalism. Laborers who once worked in chains were now chained to the land.

Christianity was an urban religion. But the ruling classes were not yet able to foist their new economic system, or the religion that sought to defend it, on the peasantry. The word "pagan" derives from the Latin "paganus," which meant rural dweller or peasant. It would soon become a code word in a violent class war.

Even after the rise of feudalism, remnants of the old pagan religion remained. It was joyously pro-sexual—lesbian, gay, bisexual and straight. Many women were among its practitioners. Many shamans were still transvestites. And transvestism was still a part of virtually all rural festivals and rituals. In the medieval Feast of Fools, laymen and clergy alike dressed as women. The Faculty of Theology at the University of Paris reported priests "who danced in the choir dressed as women."

But in order for the land-owning Catholic church to rule, it had to stamp out the old beliefs that persisted from pre-class communal societies because they challenged private ownership of the land.

Ancient respect for transgendered people still had roots in the peasantry. Transvestism played an important role in ritual cultural life. Many pagan religious leaders were transgendered. So it was not surprising that the Catholic church hunted down male and female transvestites, labeling them as heretics, and tried to ban and suppress transvestism from all peasant rituals and celebrations.

By the 11th century, the Catholic church—by then the largest landlord in Western Europe—gained the organizational and military strength to wage war against the followers of old beliefs. The campaign was carried out under a religious banner—but it was a class war against the vestiges of the older communal societies.

TRANSGENDER ENDURES

As the old land-based feudal order was replaced by capitalism, the very existence of transvestite and other transgendered women and men had been largely driven underground. Many were forced to pass as the opposite sex in order to survive. Transvestite women passed as men and became soldiers, pirates, and highway robbers. Yet transvestism continued to emerge culturally throughout Europe in holiday celebrations, rituals, carnival days, masquerade parties, theater, and opera.

These transgender traditions persist today in the Mummer's Festival, Mardi Gras, and Halloween. In contemporary imperialist Japan cross-gendered roles are still at the heart of ancient Noh drama and Kabuki theater. But these are not merely vestiges of tradition. Transgendered women and men still exist, no matter how difficult their struggle for survival has become.

TRANSGENDER AROUND THE WORLD

Our focus has been on European history and consciously so. The blame for anti-transgender laws and attitudes rests squarely on the shoulders of the ruling classes on that continent. The seizures of lands and assets of the "accused" during the witch trials and Inquisition helped the ruling classes acquire the capital to expand their domination over Asia, Africa, and the Americas. The European elite then tried to force their ideology on the peoples they colonized around the world.

But despite the colonialists' racist attempts at cultural genocide, transvestism and other transgenderd expression can still be observed in the rituals and beliefs of oppressed peoples. It is clear that they held respected public roles in vast numbers of diverse societies in cultures continents apart.

Since the sixteenth century, "transvestite shamans have . . . been reported among the Araucanians, a large tribe living in southern Chile and parts of Argentina. . . . Male transvestite shamans have also been reported for the Guajira, a cattle-herding people of northwest Venezuela and north Colombia, and the Tehuelche, hunter-gatherers of Argentina" (Greenberg 1988).

Transvestism also used to be practiced by shamans in the Vietnamese countryside, Burma, in India among the Pardhi, a hunting people, and in the southeast, by the Lhoosais, as well as in Korea (Greenberg 1988).

Transgender in religious ceremony is still reported in areas of West Africa. . . . Cross-dressing is a feature in Brazilian and Haitian ceremonies derived from West African religions.

The Chukchee, Kamchadal, Koryak, and Inuit—all Native peoples of the Arctic Basin—had male shamans who dressed as women.

"In India the Vallabha sect, devotees of Krishna, dressed as women. Reports of the 1870s and 1930s describe the priests (bissu) of the Celebes who live and dress as women" (Ackroyd 1979).

PASSING FOR SURVIVAL

By the time the Industrial Revolution in Europe had forged plowshares into weapons and machinery, prejudice against transgendered women and men was woven deep into the tapestry of exploitation.

But mercantile trade and early industrial capitalism created opportunities for anonymity that seldom existed under feudalism, where the large serf families and their children and their neighbors lived and worked on the land.

Capitalism unchained the peasants from the land—but chained them to machinery as wage slaves, or sent them off in armies and armadas to conquer new land, labor, and resources.

Not only transgendered women but men now had the opportunity to pass. The oppression of women under capitalism forced many thousands of women who weren't transgendered to pass as men in order to escape the economic and social inequities of their oppression.

The consequences for passing were harsh. At the close of the seventeenth century the penalty in England was to be placed in the stocks and dragged through the streets in an open cart. In France as late as 1760 transvestites were burned to death.

Despite the criminal penalties, women passed as men throughout Europe—most notably in the Netherlands, England, and Germany. Passing was so widespread during the seventeenth and eighteenth centuries that it was the theme of novels. . . .

While it is biologically easier for a woman to pass as a young man than for a man to pass as a woman, many transgendered men have lived sucessfully without discovery.

Mrs. Nash, for example, married a soldier at Forte Meade in the Dakota Territory. After her husband's transfer, Mrs. Nash married another soldier. After she died, it was discovered she was a man (Garber 1992).

CAPITALISM WIELDS OLD PREJUDICE

In capitalism's early competitive stage, when the new bourgeoisie were fighting feudalism and all its ideological baggage, they prided themselves on their enlightened and scientific view of the world and society.

But once in power, the capitalists made use of many of the old prejudices, particularly those that suited their divide-and-conquer policies.

"Liberty, fraternity, and equality" soon became a dead letter as hellish sweatshops expanded into the factory system. Colonized peoples were seen as subjects to be used up in the production of wealth. As the new ruling class established itself, it demanded conformity to the system of wage slavery, and shed its radicalism.

But despite long being termed "illegal" and "unnatural" and still carrying with it an "unofficial" death penalty, transvestism is still a part of human expression.

Transvestites and other transgendered people were leaders of the first wave of gay liberation that began in 1880s in Germany. That movement enjoyed the support of many in the mass Socialist parties.

Magnus Hirschfield, a Jewish gay leader of first-wave gay liberation in Germany in the 1880s was also reported to be transvestite. He wrote a groundbreaking work on the subject. Most of the valuable documentation this movement uncovered about transgender throughout history, along with research about lesbians and gay men, was burned in a pyre by the Nazis.

LIVES RENDERED INVISIBLE

While, as we have seen, transgendered expression has always existed in the western hemisphere, the need to "pass" washed upon these shores with the arrival of capitalism. Many women and men have been forced to pass. Some of their voices have been recorded.

Deborah Sampson passed as a male soldier in the American War of Independence. She once pulled a bullet out of her own thigh to avoid discovery. She later published her memoirs, titled *The Female Review,* and went on a public speaking tour in 1802.

Jack Bee Garland (Elvira Mugarrieta), born the daughter of San Francisco's first Mexican consul, was detained by police in Stockton, California, in 1897, charged with "masquerading in men's clothes." A month later the gregarious and outspoken Garland was made an honorary member of Stockton's Bachelor's Club.

Lucy Ann Lobdell, born in New York State in 1829, was a renowned hunter and trapper. She explained her painful decision to leave her young daughter with her parents and venture into "a man's world" as Rev. Joseph Lobdell:

> "I made up my mind to dress in men's attire to seek labor, as I was used to men's work. And as I might work harder at housework, and get only a dollar a week, and I was capable of doing men's work and getting men's wages. I feel that I cannot submit to see all the bondage with which women is oppressed, and listen to the voice of fashion, and repose upon the bosom of death. I am a mother; I love my offspring even better than words can tell. I cannot bear to die and leave that little one to struggle in every way to live as I have to do." Lobdell died in an asylum. . . .

Cora Anderson lived as Ralph Kerwinieo for thirteen years before being brought up on charges of "disorderly conduct" in 1914 in Milwaukee after her sex was disclosed. After being ordered by the court to don "women's" apparel, Anderson, a South American Indian, explained, "In the future centuries it is probable that woman will be the owner of her own body and the custodian of her own soul. But until that time you can expect that the statutes [concerning] women will be all wrong. The well-cared for woman is a parasite, and the woman who must work is a slave. The women's minimum wage will help, but it will not—cannot—effect a complete cure. Some people may think I am very bitter against the men. I am only bitter against conditions—conditions that have grown up in this man-made world" (Katz 1976).

FROM JOAN OF ARC TO STONEWALL

In the last decades, the development of technology rendered many of the occupational divisions between men and women obsolete. Women were joining the work force in large numbers, becoming part of the working class in the most active and immediate sense. This shaped a whole new consciousness.

The contraceptive pill, first produced in 1952, virtually revolutionized social relations for many women, and allowed women to participate in all phases of life with the same freedom from unwanted pregnancy as men.

Rigidly enforced gender boundaries should also have been scrapped. But the motor force of capitalism still drives prejudice and inequity as a vehicle for division. It took monumental struggles—and still greater ones remain on the horizon—to right these wrongs. . . .

From peasant uprisings against feudalism in the Middle Ages to the Stonewall Rebellion in the twentieth century, transvestites and other transgendered people have figured in many militant struggles, both in defense of the right of personal expression and as a form of political rebellion.

But from the violence on the streets to the brutality of the police, from job discrimination to denial of health care and housing—survival is still a battle for the transgendered population.

Transgendered people are the brunt of cruel jokes on television and in films. Movies like *Psycho, Dressed to Kill,* and *Silence of the Lambs* create images of transgendered people as dangerous psychopaths.

This point was driven home by activists who disrupted the National Film Society awards in the spring 1992. They passed out fliers highlighting the real-life murder of transsexual Venus Xtravaganza, who appeared in the documentary *Paris Is Burning.* Xtravaganza was murdered before the film on Harlem's balls was finished.

Silence of the Lambs swept the Academy Awards. *Paris Is Burning* wasn't even nominated.

FIGHTING FOR A BETTER WORLD

The institutionalized bigotry and hatred we face today have not always existed. They arose with the division of society into exploiter and exploited. Divide-and-conquer tactics have allowed the slave owners, feudal landlords, and corporate ruling classes to keep for themselves the lion's share of the wealth created by the laboring class.

Like racism and all forms of prejudice, bigotry toward transgendered people is a deadly carcinogen. We are pitted against each other in order to keep us from seeing each other as allies.

Genuine bonds of solidarity can be forged between people who respect each other's differences and are willing to fight their enemy together. We are the class that does the work of the world, and can revolutionize it. We can win true liberation.

The struggle against intolerable conditions is on the rise around the world. And the militant role of transgendered women, men, and youths in today's fight-back movement is already helping to shape the future.

23

Theorizing Race, Class, and Gender

The New Scholarship of Black Feminist Intellectuals and Black Women's Labor

Rose M. Brewer

At the center of the theorizing about race, class, and gender in the USA is a group of Black feminist intellectuals. These are academics, independent scholars, and activists who are writing and rethinking the African-American experience from a feminist perspective. In this chapter, I am most concerned with the ideas of those women involved in knowledge production who are situated in the academy: colleges and universities throughout the United States. Their insights are essential to the rethinking which must occur in conceptualizing the African-American experience. Although they are few in number, their recent placement in Women's Studies, Ethnic Studies, and traditional disciplines such as sociology, political science, history, English, anthropology, comparative literature, and so on, is strategic to the current upsurge in Black feminist scholarship.

What is most important conceptually and analytically in this work is the articulation of multiple oppressions. This polyvocality of multiple social locations is historically missing from analyses of oppression and exploitation in traditional feminism, Black Studies, and mainstream academic disciplines. Black feminist thinking is essential to possible paradigm shifts in these fields; for example, in Black Studies to begin explaining the African-American experience through the multiple articulations of race, class, and gender changes the whole terrain of academic discourse in that area. Black feminist social scientists deconstruct existing frameworks in sociology, history, and a range of other disciplines.

In the ensuing discussion I look more carefully at how Black feminist theorizing is central to our rethinking the African-American experience. I examine Black women's labor and African-American class formation to illustrate how race, class, and gender in intersection contribute to our understanding of African-American life. I organize the chapter around the following three themes: (1) an examination of the context of recent Black feminist theorizing in the social sciences; (2) a closer analysis of a major proposition of Black feminist thought, "the simultaneity of oppression," given race, class, and gender as categories of analyses in the social sciences; and (3) sketching out a reconstructed analysis of Black women's labor and African-American class formation through the lenses of race and gender.

THE SOCIAL CONTEXT OF RECENT BLACK FEMINIST THEORIZING

The theory and practice of Black feminism predates the current period. Even during the first wave of feminism, according to Terborg-Penn (1990), prominent Black feminists combined the fight against sexism with the fight against racism by continuously calling the public's attention to these issues. Turn-of-the-century Black activist Anna Julia Cooper conceived the African-American woman's position thus: She is confronted by a woman question and a race problem, and is as yet an unknown or unacknowledged factor in both (Cooper 1892).

Although early twentieth-century Black suffragettes saw women's rights as essential to relieving social ills, they repeatedly called attention to issues of race. Nonetheless, within the vise of race, African-American women forged a feminist consciousness in the USA. Such women might be called the original Black feminists. Again, the life and work of Anna Julia Cooper is a case in point. Guy-Sheftall and Bell-Scott (1989, 206) point out that Cooper's work, *A Voice from the South by a Black Woman of the South* (1892), "has the distinction of being the first scholarly publication in the area of Black women's studies, though the concept had certainly not emerged during the period."

Yet the gateway to the new Black feminist scholarship of the past twenty years is the civil rights movement and the mainstream feminist movement of the late 1960s and early 1970s. E. Frances White, an activist in the civil rights movement, captures the recent historical context in which contemporary Black feminists are located. She says: "I remember refusing to leave the discussion at a regional black student society meeting to go help out in the kitchen. The process of alienation from those militant and articulate men had begun for me" (1984, 9). White goes on to point out that

> many of today's most articulate spokeswomen, too, participated in the black student, civil rights, and black nationalist movements. Like their white counterparts, these women felt frustrated by restraints imposed on them by the men with whom they shared the political arena (1984, 9).

For Cynthia Washington, an activist in the Student Nonviolent Coordinating Committee (SNCC), this incipient Black feminism is given a different slant. She points out that although Black women's abilities and skills were recognized in the movement, the men categorized the women as something other than female (Echols 1989). Both these positions reflect the historic path of Black feminist development in the second wave of U.S. feminism. White and Washington's interpretations of the movement point to the multiple consciousness which informs Black feminist thinking and struggles. Black feminism is defined as a multiple level engagement (King 1988).

This is strikingly exemplified by the Combahee River Collective. The organization was formed by a group of Black lesbian feminists in the mid-1970s. In the context of murder in Boston, Barbara Smith and a group of other Black women founded the collective. Smith was insistent that the murder of Black women was not only a racial issue. The fact that thirteen Black women were killed cruelly exhibited how sexism and racism intersected in the lives of African-American women. Given this, the collective argued:

> The most general statement of our politics at the present time would be that we are actively committed to struggling against racial, sexual, heterosexual, and class oppression, and see as our particular task the development of an integrated analysis and practice based upon the fact that major systems of oppression create the conditions of our lives. As Black women we see Black feminism as the logical political movement to combat the manifold and simultaneous oppressions that all women of color face. (Smith 1983, 272)

Importantly, Black feminist theorizing places African-American women at the center of the analyses (Hull et al. 1982; Collins 1986, 1990; King 1988; Dill 1979). By theorizing from the cultural experiences of African-American women, social scientists such as Collins argue epistemologically that experience is crucial to Black women's ways of knowing and being in the world. Thus capturing that cultural experience is essential to a grounded analysis of African-American women's lives. This means analysis predicated on the everyday lives of African-American women. More difficult has been linking the everyday to the structural constraints of institutions and political economy (Brewer 1983, 1989). Indeed, a challenge to Black feminist theory is explicating the interplay between agency and social structure. However, nearly all the recent writing has been about everyday, lived experiences. Less successful and visible is the explication of the interrelationship between lives and social structure. Finally, running through Black feminist analyses is the principle of "the simultaneity of oppression" (Hull et al. 1982). This is the conceptual underpinning of much of recent Black feminist reconceptualization of African-American life. In the following discussion, "the simultaneity of oppression" is examined more carefully and is central to our understanding of Black women's labor and African-American class formation. Furthermore, rethinking the social structure of inequality in the context of race, class, and gender intersections are crucial to this discussion, using Black women's textile industry work in North Carolina as a case in point.

RACE, CLASS, AND GENDER: "THE SIMULTANEITY OF OPPRESSION"

The conceptual anchor of recent Black feminist theorizing is the understanding of race, class and gender as simultaneous forces. The major propositions of such a stance include:

1. critiquing dichotomous oppositional thinking by employing both/and rather than either/or categorizations

2. allowing for the simultaneity of oppression and struggle, thus eschewing additive analyses: race + class + gender which leads to an understanding of the embeddedness and relationality of race, class and gender and the multiplicative nature of these relationships: race x class x gender

3. reconstructing the lived experiences, historical positioning, cultural perceptions, and social construction of Black women who are enmeshed in and whose ideas emerge out of that experience, and

4. developing a feminism rooted in class, culture, gender, and race in interaction as its organizing principle.

Importantly, the theorizing about race, class, and gender is historicized and contextualized.

RACE, CLASS, AND GENDER AS CATEGORIES OF ANALYSIS

Race has been defined in a number of ways, yet a few powerful conceptualizations are useful to our discussion of Black feminist theory. Recently, feminist historian Higginbotham noted: "Like gender and class, then, race must be seen as a social construction predicated upon the recognition of difference and signifying the simultaneous distinguishing and positioning of groups vis-à-vis one another. More than this, race is a highly contested representation of relations of power between social categories by which individuals are identified and identify themselves" (1992, 253). The embeddedness of gender within the context of race is further captured by Higginbotham. She notes that

> in societies where racial demarcation is endemic to their sociocultural fabric and heritage—to their laws and economy, to their institutionalized structures and discourses, and to their epistemologies and everyday customs—gender identity is inextricably linked to and even determined by racial identity. We are talking about the racialization of gender and class. (1992, 254)

Omi and Winant point out:

> The effort must be made to understand race as an unstable and decentered complex of social meanings constantly being transformed by political struggle. (1987, 68)

And finally, Barbara Fields conceptualizes race ideologically:

> If race lives on today, it does not live on because we have inherited it from our forebears of the seventeenth century or the eighteenth or nineteenth, but because we continue to create it today. (1970, 117)

Relatedly, gender as a category of analysis cannot be understood decontextualized from race and class in Black feminist theorizing. Social constructions of Black womanhood and manhood are inextricably linked to racial hierarchy, meaning systems, and institutionalization. Indeed, gender takes on meaning and is embedded institutionally in the context of the racial and class order: productive and social reproductive relations of the economy. Accordingly, class as an economic relationship expressing productive and reproductive relations is a major category of analysis in the notion of the simultaneity of oppression. Yet recent Black feminist writers (hooks 1984; Collins 1990; King 1988) point out the tendency of theorists writing in the class traditions to reduce race and gender to class. Similarly Black feminist economist Rhonda Williams (1985) places changes in the labor market squarely in a race, gender, and class framework that cannot be explained through traditional labor/capital analyses.

Yet we can fall into the trap of overdetermination, especially in the case of race as a category of analysis. In fact, Higginbotham (1992) draws our attention to the metalanguage of race in which internal issues of gender and class are subsumed to a unitarian position of African-Americans. Here, class is hidden or misspecified and gender is rendered invisible in this conceptualization of African-American inequality. Indeed, race in the context of the globalization of capitalism makes gender the center of the new working class. Thus the following discussion draws upon recent Black feminist theorizing to place Black women at the center of an analysis of labor and African-American class formation emphasizing the relational and interactive nature of these social forces.

BLACK WOMEN'S LABOR AND AFRICAN-AMERICAN CLASS FORMATION THROUGH THE PRISM OF RACE, GENDER, AND CLASS

The contestation among scholars on race and class reflects conceptual, political interests and careerist concerns. Yet, the debate on the relative importance of race and class has been fought largely on a nongendered terrain. The writings of Black feminist intellectuals give us some new insight into how the race and class might be viewed in the context of gender. Indeed, as theorists explicate the intersection of race, gender, and class, our conceptualizations of racial inequality will change. The complexity of race, gender, and class interactions suggests that scholarly work must accomplish a number of difficult theoretical tasks especially around interrelationships. Thus, in the context of explaining Black women's labor and class formation, at least one question is key: How does explicating African-American's women poorly paid productive or unwaged social reproductive labor recenter our understanding of African-American inequality and class formation? I can begin to answer this question by examining more closely the changes in Black women's labor, drawing upon the insights of Black feminist theorizing.

Striking is the research on race and labor. Baron (1971), in a classic essay titled "The Demand for Black Labor," essentially discusses Black men's labor. This tendency is pervasive in a good deal of the work on the Black experience (Collins 1986, 1990). Consequently, the inequality of African-American life is conflated with Black men's inequality. Indeed, much of the discussion of inequality in the USA has been centered on the dynamics of either race or gender, which translates into discussions of white women or Black men. Dismissing intersections of race and gender in such autonomous analyses conceptually erases African-American women. Recent Black feminist thinking strongly emphasizes the error in this kind of analysis. Accordingly, a critical defining element of the current time is the regionalization and internationalization of women's work. Indeed, a crucial determinant of Black life today is not simply Black men's marginalization from work but the social transformation of Black women's labor. Furthermore, the transformation of Black women's labor is tied to structural changes in the state and economy as well as to shifts in the racial/gender division of labor. Three major labor transformations in Black women's waged labor are key: (1) movement from domestic to industrial and clerical work, a process still incomplete and particularized by region and class (Simms and Malveaux 1986); (2) integration into the international division of labor in low-paid service work, which is largely incapable of providing a family wage (Brewer 1983); and (3) the increasing impoverishment and fragmentation of Black women, children, and families (Sidel 1986). An analysis of the

North Carolina textile industry is a good case in point of the above processes. These changes are matched by the pervasive peripherization of Black men from manufacturing work and the labor force (Beverly and Stanback 1986). Theorizing race, class, and gender in the context of these broad-based structural changes in Black women's labor exemplifies a division of waged labor built on racial norms and values, as well as material arrangements embedded in a gendered division of labor. More recently, uneven economic growth and internationalization have involved Black women in the complex circuitry of labor exchange of women nationally and globally. In short, capitalist firms do not have to depend upon Black labor, either male or female. Low-wage, low-cost labor can be found all over the world. The world labor force is a cheap substitution for Black labor in the USA. Yet this is further complicated by the feminization of much of labor (low-paid women within the USA and outside). Furthermore, women's work in the USA is gender/race divided. Disproportionate numbers of Black women are at the bottom of this division of labor, rooted in social meanings systems which get remade in the material context of social practices as well as the calculus of profit. Structurally, such processes anchor a disproportionate number of African-American women at the bottom of the service sector with some regional variation and some convergence of women's status across race in gender-segregated jobs. Thus African-American women represent a significant component of the new working classes. What more can be said about the social forces integral to African-American labor changes and class formations? To answer this, I will look carefully at the structural shifts of the last thirty years. The concrete manifestation of regional political economy is uneven capitalist development (Clavell et al. 1980). Today, U.S. workers compete in an international market for labor power. There is a worldwide latent reserve labor force which competes with unskilled and semiskilled labor in both the USA and Europe. White women, men and women of color, and increasingly white male workers in the USA either directly compete with or are bypassed in favor of cheaper labor in Malaysia, Mexico, Singapore, the Philippines, and the Dominican Republic, among others (Williams 1985).

Thus, a regional and international approach to political economy is central to this analysis. However, this must be matched by a concern with racial/cultural formation, gender inequality, and concrete political struggles. White workers have historically been in competition with Black workers (Bonancich 1976). They have been able historically to close ranks against Black labor for the best jobs. Black women and men have often been left with the least desirable work, but some work. Today, this is not so for many African-Americans. During the era of advanced capitalism, competition moves beyond the confines of single industries and nations and becomes internationalized (Williams 1985).

Economic changes are not abstractions from the activities of agents. Choices are made: who will be used, who will not. These choices are not wholly separated from cultural/racial/gender practices which get remade under conditions of internationalization of the economy. This means that much of the explanation of African-American marginalization from the economy is explained as cultural deficit. The economic locking-out of the Black poor and working poor is defined as a reflection of a culture of poverty rather than the remaking of racism, sexism, and economic oppression under conditions of advanced capitalism. The white power elite makes decisions based on profit as well as the ideology of race and gender.

Given this, uneven economic development encompasses more than a labor/capital struggle. It is shaped by cultural processes reflecting longstanding definitions, perceptions of what is natural and given around hierarchies of race and gender. It is the issue of who loses. And, increasingly, the answer is young Black women and men of American inner cities. Moreover, the concern with the changing division of labor through economic restructuring is matched in this discussion by a concern with racial and gender divisions of labor. Pivotal here is the intersection of race/gender hierarchies and the way contemporary economic restructuring is shaped by existing arrangements of race and gender divisions. Furthermore, class fractioning within the racial/ gender divisions of labor intersects with racial constraints within the gender/class division of labor. These processes take on an urban, regional and international form. Consequently, although at issue is the transformation of Black women's labor, it should be viewed as a transformation in three moments: race, gender, and class simultaneously. Finally, historically and currently, politics and the state appear to mediate the process of class, race and gender struggle. Hence, uneven economic development and economic restructuring are a political process, too. The state and its political relations are part of the calculus of change and restructuring engaged in by capital. For example, Perry and Watkins (1977) explain the political and economic nature of sunbelt growth and development: a state/business coalition created desirable conditions in the sunbelt. So, moving defense money to sunbelt-based industries, providing tax breaks and R & D subsidies, was essential to early sunbelt growth. It was as much a political as an economic process.

Thus, economic restructuring, uneven economic growth and internalization of the labor force embody cultural, gender, political, and economic moments. The consequence of this now in the USA is that about two-thirds of all working persons are engaged in services (Williams 1985). A good number of these are African-American women performing public reproductive work in the form of nurses' aides and old-age assistants, and in fast food outlets and cafeterias. Indeed, nearly all new job growth during the 1970s and 1980s was in the service category. Externally and internally, women are filling these new service jobs. They are the new working class. Under conditions of economic restructuring, highly skilled labor is largely technical labor and unskilled labor is largely manual and clerical labor. Thus, Black women's work today in the USA reflects the high demand for clerical labor emerging out of restructuring. Moreover, Black women's clerical work reflects the partial collapsing of a racial/gender division of labor. Both Black and white women do the same work in most places in the USA. Even so, Black women are more likely to be supervised and white women are more likely to supervise (Simms and Malveaux 1986). Nonetheless, structural changes in the American economy and globally are changing cities and regions. This restructuring is changing Black women's work and all women's relation to work.

The second transformation in Black women's labor reflects a changing relationship to the new international division of labor. There is a diasporic connection with African women in the Americas, the USA, the Caribbean, and South America. In sub-Saharan Africa, in the wake of colonialism and imperialism, there has been a profound reconstitution of African women's productive and reproductive labor (Amadiume 1988). What is not well understood in this process is what further changes African women globally will undergo. Within the USA, shifts will be costly in human terms under conditions of uneven economic development, restructuring, regional and international labor change. Job loss is occurring for many Black women or they are in part-time rather than full-time jobs (Woody and Malson 1984). Their unemployment rate is among the highest in the USA (Simms and Malveaux 1986). And paradoxically, just as some Black women are being more firmly tied to white-collar/clerical work, others are being excluded from the economy altogether. This job loss is linked to the replacement of the most vulnerable women of color with women workers outside the country and new immigrant women within the society.

This labor exchange process is increasingly being studied by scholars in research on labor transformation and Third World women globally (Nash and Safa 1976, Fernandez-Kelley 1983, Leacock and Safa 1986). These writers discuss the impact of the new international division of labor on women of color globally. It is arguable that Third World women internationally are an essential part of the search for cheap labor (Safa 1983). Fuentes and Ehrenreich concur (1983). Women generally, and Third World women specifically, have become essential to cheap labor in the global capitalist economy.

Hence, given the international division of labor, some Black women within the USA are losing work just as they are making a niche for themselves in regional industries such as textiles. The racial/gender division of labor historically in the USA has opened from the bottom for Black women. This continues to be the case. For example, as southern white women in textiles moved to more desirable industrial jobs in the past two and half decades, Black women in North Carolina, South Carolina, and across the textile South have filled the unskilled and semiskilled jobs. Black women now hold over 50 percent of the operative positions in many southern plants (Woody and Malson 1984). Yet, with plant closedown and internationalization, many of these women are being fired. Textile workers peaked at over 1 million in the 1950s; in 1978 there were 754,296 (Sawars and Tabb 1984). As usual Black women were again the last hired, the first fired.

Given the regional evolution of Black women's work within the USA, North Carolina serves as a good case study of the racial/sexual division of labor for African-American women. Some work has already been done on this process in the state through the 1930s (Janiewski 1985). Clearly, Black women's work has been carefully crafted by economic and cultural forces. Well into the 1960s, economically and politically the state of North Carolina was completely dominated by whites. Jim Crow was only officially coming to an end, and the vestiges of the civil rights struggle lingered. White males dominated the state politically and socially. Nonetheless, all whites shared in a cultural heritage of white supremacy, dating back to the days of slavery, accepting the notion of their specialness vis-à-vis Black women, whether they themselves were economically privileged or not. This meant that poor white women were committed to the premises of white supremacy as well as wealthier women.

Despite a shared heritage around white supremacy, a racial order built on the belief and ideology of white supremacy alone would have toppled. It was solidified and maintained through the domination of political institutions and the economic control by white male elites. Economics, politics, and culture meshed to form a special kind of racial order in North Carolina, but the linchpin of the system was white male domination and control of key political and economic institutions. Certainly by the time of the incorporation of Black women into the textile mills of the region, usually in the dirtiest and most distasteful jobs, the racial and gender distinctions were strong enough to generate four separate groups of labor: white men, white women, Black men, Black women. The gender distinctions generated a different kind of labor hierarchy: white men, Black men, white women, Black women.

Black women in North Carolina have been overwhelmingly concentrated in the secondary sector of the state. Secondary jobs are dirtier, harder, and lower waged than primary sector jobs. Job turnover is greater and job benefits are fewer in the secondary sector. Indeed jobs are different in the secondary and primary sectors. U.S. census data for 1980 show that Black and white women held different types of jobs in North Carolina. A typical job for a white woman was white collar. A large number of white women were clerical workers, and others were involved in teaching, health-allied professions, and retail sales work. Black women in the state were in blue-collar occupations. These include nondurable goods, operatives, private household workers, service workers. And unlike the nearly complete shift of Black women out of domestic work nationally, a somewhat greater percentage of the Black women in the state were involved in domestic work. Overall, there had not been major penetration into white-collar clerical work for these women. They were nearly all in the lower reaches of the occupational structure.

Thus, when Black women moved into industrial work in North Carolina textile mills, they did so without parity with white women. The gender division of labor was overlaid with the particularities of race. Only in the 1980s did Black and white women begin to share a common occupational trajectory. Currently, there is some convergence similar to the national convergence of all racial ethnic women. Some Black women in the state are moving into clerical work. Moreover, there is a racially mixed workplace for women in North Carolina textile mills today. Even still, Black women occupy a disproportionate percentage of low-income work in this industry in the South (Woody and Malson 1984). They bear the brunt of lay-offs, and the industry has been devastated by plant mobility and closedowns.

More broadly, as noted earlier, uneven economic growth and internationalization have involved these women in a complex circuitry of female labor exchange nationally and globally. Racial segmentation of labor persists, rooted in cultural assumptions and social practices as well as the calculus of profit. Consequently, although occupational segregation separates all women from men in the labor process, there is noise around race. Race in the context of gender and class means African-Americans are quite vulnerable. For example, Black women are still more likely than white women to be paid less, to be unemployed, to be supervised rather than to supervise (Simms and Malveaux 1986). Given these differences (Wallace 1980), their relationship to capital is different from that of white women. Even still, a small group of Black women are moving into the white-collar occupations. Their numbers are indicative of the growing significance of class relative to race in national labor markets.

Nonetheless, it is the service sector in which a disproportionate number of African-American women work. This job slot for Black women cannot provide a family wage for high-school educated and/or less-skilled urban Blacks. This is highly problematic in the midst of extremely high Black male unemployment rates. In the case of African-American adolescents, the nearly complete erasure of their labor force participation has occurred. Phyllis Wallace (1974) is one of the few early scholars who place this reality in context. She points out that:

> Black teenage females constitute one of the most disadvantaged groups in the labor markets of large metropolitan areas. (1974, 8)

Woody and Malson elaborate this point:

> Current employment patterns indicate substantial under representation in hiring black women in all income levels in key U.S. industry and a strong possibility of discrimination based on race. (1984, 3)

Indeed, the working poor as a significant segment of the working class must be understood in a gendered context. Black male joblessness alone does not account for the tremendous disadvantage of the Black pool. Race/gender segmentation and low wages as reflected in the positioning of African-American women are conceptually central to African-American class inequality today.

SOCIAL REPRODUCTION: GENDER INEQUALITY AT HOME AND WORK IN THE CONTEXT OF BLACK WOMEN'S LABOR TRANSFORMATION

Labor is not simply about waged work at the site of production. Within households, Black women perform a significant portion of the social reproductive labor. The socialization of children and the cleaning, cooking, and nurturing functions are all disproportionately Black women's work. Indeed, poor Black women are often expected to do everything. Their work within the home is devalued, even though housework is accomplished under trying circumstances: substandard housing, no household washers and dryers, or few appliances. Yet these women are increasingly expected to work in low-paid jobs to qualify for Aid to Families with Dependent Children (AFDC). Indeed "workfare" is the key to recent public "welfare reform" legislation. Here again, race and gender intersect to anchor African-American women in a different stratum from white women or Black men.

Furthermore, the public service work referred to earlier is increasingly public social reproductive work—care for the aged, sick, and children. It falls disproportionately on Black women and other women of color. Yet, wages are very low and the average service salary is less than $12,000 per year (Williams 1985). There simply is not enough money to support a family. Given this, some form of state support should make up a portion of the social wage for young Black people. Realistically, with severe cutbacks in the social wage, increasing immiseration for poor African-Americans is likely. Thus, Black male marginalization from work, and a particular type of work and welfare for the poorest African-American women, point to extremely difficult times ahead for the Black population in the USA. The increasing impoverishment of the Black family must be viewed in this context: Black women's placement in poorly paid jobs, Black men's increasing marginalization from work altogether, and little state social support for men, women, or children. Out of these processes emerges the lowest sector of the Black class structure.

For this reason, although there has been an assault on the Black working class, there is still a working class. It is conflated with the working poor. It is highly exploited and has experienced heavy assaults on its wage. It is a class which is often poor and female. Sidel (1986) points out that many poor families are headed by women who work all year long. For those households, the problem is not lack of work, it is low wages. The problem is also, as noted in the North Carolina example, sex segregation demarked by a racial/gender division of labor. The labor force participation of Black men has dropped precipitously and now about 55 percent of them are in the labor force. Such realities have profound implications for African-American life. Understanding Black men's placement in the economy provides only a partial analysis of what is happening. Explicating Black women's labor transformation in the context of race, class, and gender gives us a fuller understanding of the African-American experience in the 1990s.

SUMMARY

My purpose in this chapter has been to explicate some of the recent theorizing on race, class, and gender by Black feminist thinkers in the academy. This theorizing is further explored in an analysis of Black women's labor and African-American class formation. The labor transformation of Black women has been explicated in terms of economic restructuring and capital mobility, racial formation and gender inequality. It is a process linking Black women in the Northeast and Midwest to the South and Southwest, Asia, Africa, and the Caribbean. It is not the tie of poverty to prosperity, but the tie of subordinate status to subordinate status crosscut by internal class differences in all these regions. Because of class, which intersects with race and gender, a sector of Black women is in the upwardly mobile, integrated sector of a servicized economy. These are women who are moving out of the fast-growing female service sector made up of clericals into the somewhat slower-growing high technology fields which are male dominated. Even still, the rate of change into high-paying fields has been slow for Black women. In 1970, 1 percent of African-American women were engineers and by 1980 only 7 percent were (Amott and Matthaei 1991). More often Black women professionals are ghettoized in the lowest-paying professional fields. They are poorly represented in engineering, computer science, and other highly skilled fields with high pay. Currie and Skolnick (1984) aptly note that "short of an unprecedented shift in the sex composition of these occupations, their growth (highly paid professionals) seems unlikely to have a very strong effect on the overall distribution of (Black) women in the job hierarchy." Finally, a discernible number of Black women are subemployed (desire full-time rather than the part-time work they have) or have been marginalized from work altogether (Woody and Malson 1984). This occurs across regions; it is especially evident in northern and southern inner cities and rural areas. About half of all poor female-headed Black families are in the South. Additionally, the bifurcation of Black women's labor plays out a certain logic. Somewhat higher levels of clerical and white-collar service work are being performed by skilled Black women in the Northeast, Midwest, and West while capital mobility has devastated the Black male semiskilled and unskilled working class in older industrial areas. What is left is a service sector of racial minority women working for low wages. Simultaneously, there is a marginalization of some Black women from work altogether. They depend upon transfer payments, the informal economy of bartering, hustling, exchange, and kinship support.

Even now, the largest category of Black women workers in the USA is clerical and service workers (Simms and Malveaux 1986). The latter is a category encompassing household workers, cleaners, janitors, and public service workers, jobs which are extensions of the private household service role. Internationally, there is a broad base of women doing semiskilled labor in the electronics, computer, and other "sunrise" industries which have gone abroad. This is the work, primarily, of the white and Asian working-class female in the international women's economy.

Finally, the intersection of race, class, and gender, in interplay with economic restructuring, accounts for the internal fractioning and separation of women from one another. Yet, this is not the entire story. Cultural practice, beliefs, and ideology also structure female labor. The ideology of what is appropriately Black women's work is played out in the arena of the public social reproduction of labor. Kitchen and cafeteria workers, nurses' aides—these are defined as appropriate jobs for Black women, very much as the domestic labor of a generation ago was defined as "Black women's work." It is only when all these processes are better understood that perspectives on African-American inequality will be more accurate.

Crucially, the Black class structure is made in the context of economic, state restructuring and political struggle, and the recreation of race, and a gender/racial division of labor. These are not unrelated phenomena. The result is a highly complicated positioning of the Black population, with some sectors clearly worse off than in the past and other sectors more securely tied to mainstream institutions. African-American women are at the center of this reconstitution of Black labor and class formation. Most importantly, only in theorizing the complexity of the intersections of race, class, and gender can we adequately prepare to struggle for social change in the African-American community.

CONCLUSIONS

In theorizing the construction of race, class, and gender in intersection, three key themes are apparent. First, gender alone cannot explain the African-American woman's or man's experience. Feminism must reflect in its theory and practice the race and class terrain upon which hierarchy and inequality are built globally and within the USA. Secondly, the simultaneity of these social forces is key. In turn, practice and struggle must be anti-sexist, anti-classist, anti-racist and anti-homophobic.

Finally, the "gender, race, class" dynamic is the major theoretical frame through which gender is incorporated into discussions of the position of Black women. Alone, they are rather sterile categories, infused with meaning developed out of many decades of social thought on class and race. In interplay with the concept gender, the paradigm becomes fairly rich (Brewer 1989). It is the simultaneity of these forces which has been identified and theorized by Black feminist thinkers. Preliminary thinking in this direction suggests that any such analyses must be historically based and holistic.

Given the writings of Black feminist thinkers in the social sciences, social scientific analyses embodying race, class, and gender are growing. Simms and Malveaux (1986), Dill (1979), Collins (1986), King (1988), and Higginbotham (1992) are among a growing number of Black feminist social scientists. These writers critique parallelist tendencies and oppositional dualistic thinking. The old additive models miss an essential reality: the qualitative difference in the lives of African-American women through the simultaneity of oppression and resistance. Thus we must rethink many of the extant analyses on African-Americans through the lenses of gender, race, and class. This is just the beginning phase of the kind of work which must be done for a robust and holistic understanding of African-American life.

24

Where's the Revolution?

Barbara Smith

When I came out in Boston in the mid-1970s, I had no way of knowing that the lesbian and gay movement I was discovering was in many ways unique. As a new lesbian I had nothing to compare it with, and there was also nothing to compare it with in history. Stonewall had happened only six years before and the militance, irreverence, and joy of those early days were still very much apparent. As a black woman who became politically active in the civil rights movement during high school and then in black student organizing and the anti-Vietnam War movement as the sixties continued, it seemed only natural that being oppressed as a lesbian would elicit the same militant collective response to the status quo that my other oppressions did. Boston's lesbian and gay movement came of age in the context of student activism, a visible counterculture, a relatively organized left and a vibrant women's movement. The city had always had its own particularly violent brand of racism and had become even more polarized because of the crisis over school busing. All of these overlapping influences strengthened the gay and lesbian movement, as well as the political understandings of lesbian and gay activists.

Objectively, being out and politically active in the seventies was about as far from the mainstream as one could get. The system did not embrace us, nor did we want it to. We also got precious little support from people who were supposed to be progressive. The white sectarian left defined homosexuality as a "bourgeois aberration" that would disappear when capitalism did. Less doctrinaire leftists were also homophobic even if they offered a different set of excuses. Black power activists and black nationalists generally viewed lesbians and gay men as anathema—white-minded traitors to the race. Although the women's movement was the one place where out lesbians were permitted to do political work, its conservative elements still tried to dissociate themselves from the "lavender menace."

Because I came out in the context of black liberation, women's liberation, and—most significantly—the newly emerging black feminist movement that I was helping to build, I worked from the assumption that all of the "isms" were connected. It was simply not possible for any oppressed people, including lesbians and gay men, to achieve freedom under this system. Police dogs, cattle prods, fire hoses, poverty, urban insurrections, the Vietnam War, the assassinations, Kent State, unchecked violence against women, the self-immolation of the closet, and the emotional and often physical violence experienced by those of us who dared leave it made the contradictions crystal clear. Nobody sane would want any part of the established order. It was the system—white supremacist, misogynistic, capitalist, and homophobic—that had made our lives so hard to begin with. We wanted something entirely new. Our movement was called lesbian and gay *liberation* and more than a few of us, especially women and people of color, were working for a *revolution.*

Revolution seems like a largely irrelevant concept to the gay movement of the nineties. The liberation politics of the earlier era, which relied upon radical grassroots strategies to eradicate oppression, have been largely replaced by an assimilationist "civil rights" agenda. The most visible elements of the movement have put their faith almost exclusively in electoral and legislative initiatives, bolstered by mainstream media coverage, to alleviate *discrimination.* When the word "radical" is used at all, it means confrontational, "in your face" tactics, not strategic organizing aimed at the roots of oppression.

Unlike the early lesbian and gay movement, which had both ideological and practical links to the left, black activism, and feminism, today's "queer" politicos seem to operate in a historical and ideological vacuum. "Queer" activists focus on "queer" issues, and racism, sexual oppression, and economic exploitation do not qualify, despite the fact that the majority of "queers" are people of color, female, or working class. When other oppressions or movements are cited, it's to build a parallel case for the validity of lesbian and gay rights or to expedite alliances with mainstream political organizations. Building unified, ongoing coalitions that challenge the system and ultimately prepare a way for revolutionary change simply isn't what "queer" activists have in mind.

When lesbians and gay men of color urge the gay leadership to make connections between heterosexism and issues like police brutality, racial violence, homelessness, reproductive freedom, and violence against women and children, the standard dismissive response is, "Those are not our issues." At a time when the gay movement is under unprecedented public scrutiny, lesbians and gay men of color and others committed to antiracist organizing are asking: Does the gay and lesbian movement want to create a just society for everyone? Or does it only want to eradicate the last little glitch that makes life difficult for privileged (white male) queers?

The April 25 March on Washington, despite its historical importance, offers some unsettling answers. Two comments that I've heard repeatedly since the march is that it seemed more like a parade than a political demonstration and that the overall image of the hundreds of thousands of participants was overwhelmingly Middle American, that is, white and conventional. The identifiably queer—the drag queens, leather people, radical faeries, dykes on bikes, etc.—were definitely in the minority, as were people of color, who will never be Middle American—no matter what kind of drag we put on or take off.

A friend from Boston commented that the weekend in Washington felt like being in a "blizzard." I knew what she meant. Despite the fact that large numbers of lesbians and gay men of color were present (perhaps even more than at the 1987 march), our impact upon the proceedings did not feel nearly as strong as it did six years ago. The bureaucratic nineties concept of "diversity," with its superficial goal of assuring that all the colors in the crayon box are visible, was very much the strategy of the day. Filling slots with people of color or women does not necessarily affect the politics of a movement if our participation does not change the agenda, that is, if we are not actually permitted to lead.

I had my own doubts about attending the April march. Although I went to the first march in 1979 and was one of the eight major speakers at the 1987 march, I didn't make up my mind to go to this one until a few weeks before it happened. It felt painful to be so alienated from the gay movement that I wasn't even sure I wanted *Outlook* to be there; my feelings of being an outsider had been growing for some time.

I remember receiving a piece of fundraising direct mail from the magazine *Outlook* in 1988 with the phrase "tacky but we'd take it" written next to the lowest potential contribution of $25. Since $25 is a lot more than I can give at any one time to the groups I support, I decided I might as well send my $5 somewhere else. In 1990 I read Queer Nation's manifesto, "I Hate Straights," in *Outweek* and wrote a letter to the editor suggesting that if queers of color followed its political lead, we would soon be issuing a statement titled "I Hate Whiteys," including white queers of European origin. Since that time I've heard very little public criticism of the narrowness of lesbian and gay nationalism. No one would guess from recent stories about wealthy and "powerful" white lesbians on TV and in slick magazines that women earn 69 cents on the dollar compared with men and that black women earn even less.

These examples are directly connected to assumptions about race and class privilege. In fact, it's gay white men's racial, gender, and class privileges, as well as the vast numbers of them who identify with the system rather than distrust it, that have made the politics of the current gay movement so different from those of other identity-based movements for social and political change. In the seventies, progressive movements—especially feminism—positively influenced and inspired lesbians' and gays' visions of struggle. Since the eighties, as AIDS has helped to raise consciousness about gay issues in some quarters of the establishment, and as some battles against homophobia have been won, the movement has positioned itself more and more within the mainstream political arena. Clinton's courting of the gay vote (at the same time as he did everything possible to distance himself from the African-American community) has also been a crucial factor in convincing the national gay and lesbian leadership that a place at the ruling class's table is just what they've been waiting for. Of course, the people left out of this new gay political equation of mainstream acceptance, power, and wealth are lesbians and gay men of color.

Our outsider status in the new queer movement is made even more untenable because supposedly progressive heterosexuals of all races do so little to support lesbian and gay freedom. Although homophobia may be mentioned when heterosexual leftists make lists of oppressions, they do virtually no risk-taking work to connect with our movement or to challenge attacks against lesbians and gays who live in their midst. Many straight activists whose politics are otherwise righteous simply refuse to acknowledge how dangerous heterosexism is and that they have any responsibility to end it. Lesbians and gays working in straight political contexts are often expected to remain closeted so as not to diminish their own "credibility" or that of their groups. With so many heterosexuals studiously avoiding opportunities to become enlightened about lesbian and gay culture and struggle, it's not surprising that nearly twenty-five years after Stonewall so few heterosexuals get it. Given how well organized the Christian right is, and that one of its favorite tactics is pitting various oppressed groups against one another, it is past time for straight and gay activists to link issues and work together with respect.

The issue of access to the military embodies the current gay movement's inability to frame an issue in such a way that it brings various groups together instead of alienating them, as has happened with segments of the black community. It also reveals a gay political agenda that is not merely moderate but conservative. As long as a military exists, it should be open to everyone regardless of sexual orientation, especially since it represents job and training opportunities for poor and working-class youth who are disproportionately people of color. But given the U.S. military's role as the world's police force, which implements imperialist foreign policies and murders—those who stand in its way (e.g., the estimated quarter of a million people, mostly civilians, who died in Iraq as a result of the Gulf War), a progressive lesbian and gay movement would at least consider the political implications of frantically organizing to get into the mercenary wing of the military industrial complex. A radical lesbian and gay movement would of course be working to dismantle the military completely.

Many people of color (Colin Powell notwithstanding) understand all too well the paradox of our being sent to Third World countries to put down rebellions that are usually the efforts of indigenous populations to rule their lives. The paradox is even more wrenching when U.S. troops are sent to quell unrest in internal colonies like South Central Los Angeles. Thankfully, there were some pockets of dissent at the April march, expressed in slogans like: "Lift the Ban—Ban the Military" and "Homosexual, Not Homophobic—Fuck the Military." Yet it seemingly has not occurred to movement leaders that there are lesbians and gays who have actively opposed the Gulf War, the Vietnam War, military intervention in Central America, and apartheid in South Africa. We need a nuanced and principled politics that fights discrimination and at the same time criticizes U.S. militarism and its negative effect on social justice and world peace.

The movement that I discovered when I came out was far from perfect. It was at times infuriatingly racist, sexist, and cutist, but also not nearly so monolithic. There was at least ideological room to point out failings, and a variety of allies willing to listen who wanted to build something better.

I think that homosexuality embodies an innately radical critique of the traditional nuclear family, whose political function has been to constrict the sexual expression and gender roles of all of its members, especially women, lesbians, and gays. Being in structural opposition to the status quo because of one's identity, however, is quite different from being consciously and actively opposed to the status quo because one is a radical and understands how the system works.

It was talking to radical lesbians and gay men that finally made me decide to go to the April 25 march. Earlier in the month, I attended an extraordinary conference on the lesbian and gay left in Delray Beach, Florida. The planners had made a genuine commitment to racial and gender parity; 70 percent of the participants were people of color and 70 percent were women. They were also committed to supporting the leadership of people of color and lesbians—especially lesbians of color—which is almost never done outside of our own autonomous groupings. The conference felt like a homecoming. I got to spend time with people I'd worked with twenty years before in Boston as well as with younger activists from across the country.

What made the weekend so successful, aside from the humor, gossip, caring, and hot discussions about sex and politics, was the huge relief I felt at not being expected to cut off parts of myself that are as integral to who I am as my sexual orientation as the price for participating in lesbian and gay organizing. Whatever concerns were raised, discussions were never silenced by the remark, "But that's not our issue!' Women and men, people of color and whites, all agreed that there desperately needs to be a visible alternative to the cut-and-dried, business-as-usual agenda of the gay political mainstream. Their energy and vision, as well as the astuteness and tenacity of radical lesbians and gays I encountered all over the country, convince me that a different way is possible.

If the gay movement ultimately wants to make a real difference, as opposed to settling for handouts, it must consider creating a multi-issue revolutionary agenda. This is not about political correctness, it's about winning. As black lesbian poet and warrior Audre Lorde insisted, "The master's tools will never dismantle the master's house." Gay rights are not enough for me, and I doubt that they're enough for most of us. Frankly, I want the same thing now that I did thirty years ago when I joined the civil rights movement and twenty years ago when I joined the women's movement, came out, and felt more alive than I ever dreamed possible: freedom.

25

Touring Thailand's Sex Industry

Lillian S. Robinson

The stories you've heard about the sex shows are all true. . . . It is not a place for the squeamish or for those with feminist leanings.
— Steve Van Beck, *Insight Guide to Thailand*

"You have to do it," Ryan tells me. "You have to go there the way you have to visit Dachau." It's my first evening in Thailand and I met my dinner partner, an American resident in Bangkok, just half an hour ago. After some general conversation involving our whole party, he addresses me privately for the first time, saying "I want to take you to the sex shows."

"You what?" That's when he adds the remark about Dachau—a line circulated to provoke—and declares that, as a feminist, I must not leave without exploring international sex tourism as practiced in the nightspots of Bangkok. When I accept the invitation, I become, in essence, a sex tourist's tourist.

Bangkok, the sexual Disneyland of the world, a place where everything is offered to anyone at all times—at little or no cost.
— Linda Ellerbee, "'And So It Goes': Adventures in Television"

Sex isn't sold everywhere in Bangkok, but it's available in enough places and enough kinds of places at a low enough price to confirm the First World view that the whole city it an erotic theme park. In addition to traditional brothels—many of them labeled "teahouses"—there are massage parlors, floor shows, and bars, some of each type featuring boys rather than girls. A freelance tourist with a taste for variety might, in theory, sample all these venues. In practice, customers—always men—seem to make their choices for cultural reasons, seeking the familiar even when "exotic" and "erotic" are sold as synonymous. The Japanese and the Arabs go to the brothels, and there are also clubs catering to Japanese tourists. But the bars seem to be the primary way of American sex.

The three blocks of Patpong and the single one of Soi Cowboy are lined with these establishments. Each bar on these streets has several small stages decorated with fire-house-style poles, a long bar, tiny tables crowded together, flashing colored lights, and loud rock music. The sound is so intense, in fact, that I felt that John Fogerty and the rest of Creedence Clearwater Revival were leading me through the scene, running me personally through the jungle.

On stage, the women dance. (I say women out of respect. The ones I see are teenagers, and in the gay bars they're boys.) Each dancer stands beside a pole that she caresses as she makes some rudimentary dance movements. They are dressed in beach-wear, the youngest in one-piece numbers, while the most seasoned wear bikinis. When actually at the beach, Thai women are almost pathologically modest, undressing furtively for a swim and covering up as soon as they come out of the water. For a teenager fresh from a country village in the Northeast and now awkwardly on stage in a bathing suit, fiddling with the crotch to make it cover more than it does or can, this public exposure is the first shame—after which, perhaps, all the others seem inevitable.

The girls are not skilled dancers, and through a long night they put minimal energy into it. Their gestures are suggestive but not sensuous, understood as sexy only if the observer, too, has learned the erotic code as language foreign to the body. Like the girls in the massage parlors, who are displayed in glass cages for the customers to choose, the dancers have numbers pinned to their costumes. Waitresses move among the tables and along the bar, ready to take drink orders and girl orders. When her number is selected, the girl stops dancing and joins the customer, donning a bright silk robe like a prizefighter's except that its hem stops at the top of the thigh. If she can get the man to buy her a drink, the fact is noted. At the very least, this contributes to job security and may even earn her a percentage of the sale.

At the tables, there is not much talk, what with the volume of the music and the lack of a common language, and a lot of casual horseplay. This mostly takes the form of teasing and shoving, the occasional arm around a shoulder or waist, sometimes a girl sitting briefly on a customer's lap. The giggles and pushes take me back to the tentative interactions of junior high. And why not? That's the age of a lot of these girls; the customers, meanwhile, are old enough to be their uncles, fathers, grandfathers. In the brothels serving local men, where there's a premium on extreme youth and virginity, a girl who has not yet menstruated brings a price that is more than sixty times the usual. Deflowering a virgin is said to increase virility, and fresh prepubescent crops are brought into the city for good luck at the Chinese New Year. Very young girls, even if no longer virgins, are also believed likelier to be free of disease. However, one study estimates that 50 percent of the child prostitutes in Thailand are HIV positive.

A 1992 survey by the Thai Public Health Ministry indicated that 76,863 prostitutes were working nationwide at 5,622 establishments (20,366 at 688 places in Bangkok). The numbers suggest precision, but the figures are generally considered absurdly low. Pasuk Phongpaichit's study for the International Labor Organization (I.L.O.), pub-lished ten years earlier, states that "conventional estimates of the number of masseuses and prostitutes in Bangkok start at around 10,000. Most estimates cluster around 200,000." Pasuk, a Thai sociologist, also speculates that 6.2 to 8.7 percent of the female population between the ages of 15 and 34 is or has been employed in the sex industry. Resistance efforts are on a considerably smaller scale. Empower, an organization serving prostitutes, enrolls more than 100 women in English classes so that they might avoid being cheated by foreign customers or eventually qualify for other employment. And the bar girls' *Patpong Newsletter,* sponsored by Empower, has not yet had much impact.

> *"A whorehouse is always a good investment."*
> —Jack Flowers in Peter Bogdonovich's film, *Saint Jack*

In 1967, Thailand contracted with the U.S. government to provide "rest and recreation" services to the troops during the Vietnam War. Today's bar customers are white American, but also European and Australian—all *fahrang* to the Thais. In addition to tourists, they include permanent residents—what *New Statesman* writer Jeremy Seabrook calls "sexpatriates"—and workers rotated in and from isolated, all-male environments like oil rigs, corporate entertainment contracts having effectively replaced the military ones. The men look pink and flabby, and in the tropical heat (90 degrees every day in the "cool" season), I've become very sensitive to the strong *fahrang* body odor, wondering whether I smell like that, too.

After playing around for a drink or two, a pair may come to an agreement to go off together for the night. It's the overnight one-partner arrangement that makes this a comparatively privileged form of sex work. The customer pays the bar management a "fine" for taking away a dancer. There are so many dancers that it is impossible to imagine what rush of clientele beyond the current full house would create a dearth of entertainers. The fleet is always in, and the sexual message is always about abundance. The sex worker may also receive a tip, but the basic transaction is between the bar owner and the customer.

The current official crackdown on child prostitution (there's always a crackdown on something, Thai friends explain) has focused the glare of publicity on the money earned, which is at once very high and very low. In her 1982 study, Pasuk estimates the income of sex workers at twenty-five times that attainable in other occupations. Entire families in the countryside are supported on the earnings of one daughter in Bangkok, and entire rural villages are made up of such families. Indeed, the *Bangkok Post*'s two-page feature on the subject earlier this year was headed "Ex-Child Prostitutes Facing Many Hardships After the Crackdown." It centered on one peasant family "hoping for a miracle" for their collective survival now that their daughter has been summarily returned home. Yet the same article places the girl's monthly salary as a dancer in the resort town of Phuket at 1,000 baht—about $40. The estimates I heard in Bangkok ran four times as high, bringing monthly wages in the big city to an amount roughly equal to the cost of two nights at an international-class hotel but, by the same token, considerably higher than the earnings of seamstresses or domestic workers. The hideous fire at a doll factory outside Bangkok in May dramatized the conditions of employment available to young Thai women working outside the sex industry.

Vietnam-born feminist writer Thanh-Dam Troung insists that the relationship between tourism and prostitution should not be understood "only as an issue of employment alternatives available to women" but also in relation "to the international structure of the tourist industry and to vested interests of a financial nature." But it's impossible not to see these as organically linked. It was in 1971, while the war in Southeast Asia raged, that the World Bank recommended the development of mass tourism in Thailand. (The bank at that time was headed by Robert McNamara, who had been U.S. Secretary of Defense when the R&R contract with Thailand was signed).

The economic initiatives consequent on the bank's report led to what is routinely described today as a $4 billion a year business involving fraternal relationships among airlines, tour operators, and the masters of the sex industry. In this sense, sex tourism is like any other multinational industry, extracting enormous profits from grotesquely underpaid local labor and situating the immediate experiences of the individual work-er—what happens to the body of a fifteen year old from a village in Northeast Thailand—in the context of global economic policy. From the perspective of First World customers, the international inequities translate into a great bargain, while their personal experiences of cut-rate ecstasy combine to make up these totals in the billions.

Traditional discussions of imperialism turn on the exploitation of labor and natural resources in the colonized territory. The neocolonialist leisure industry tends to identi-fy the two. In a public speech in 1980, Thailand's vice premier asked all provincial governors "to consider the natural scenery in your provinces, together with . . . forms of entertainment that some of you might consider disgusting and shameful, because we have to consider the jobs that will be created." Landscape, sexual entertainment and labor thus converge in a single economic image of Thailand.

> "The first thing you learn after fallatio is how to listen."
> —Jane Wagner, The Search for Signs of Intelligent Life in the Universe

In the West, too, travel to Thailand is promoted through a double association of the available female body with usable nature and with the benevolent creation of employ-ment. A Swiss tour operator describes Thai women as "slim, sunburnt and sweet . . . masters of the art of making love by nature." Meanwhile, a Dutch agency's brochures explain that in the depressed rural regions of Thailand and the slums of Bangkok, "it has become a habit that one of the nice-looking daughters goes into the business in order to earn money for the poor family . . . you . . . get the feeling that taking a girl here is as easy as buying a package of cigarettes." Customers are lured by an appealing conflation of natural, social, and cultural forces, while they themselves are represented as inherently desirable. Thai girls "love the white man in an erotic and devoted way", which is why sexual services cost no more effort, and only a bit more money, than that pack of cigarettes.

In the imperial rhetoric of the Dutch agency, the sex workers are described as "little slaves who give real Thai warmth," thus naturalizing servitude. In fact, economically speaking, most of the women are not slaves, although the most recent I.L.O. findings include disquieting evidence of Thai "child catchers," who buy or steal children for sale to "private households, restaurants, factories and brothels."

Pasuk prefers the word "indenture" to describe the economic relationship that the tourist literature characterizes in cultural terms. Sex workers are typically recruited from rural families, the sum given to the parents representing several months' advance salary, with the rest to be remitted after a ten-month or one-year term. The lump-sum payments provide subsistence for a family with few other resources and many even finance a new house, cultivation of the family land, or schooling for younger siblings. This kind of contract binds the sex worker to her job, the sense of family obligations overwhelming negative feelings about the work itself.

First World feminists are frequently criticized for culture-bound insensitivity to dif-ferences in values, needs, and desires of women in other parts of the world. Warnings against cultural blindness—not to say arrogance—are never misplaced. But it is worth noting how neatly the enlightened relativist position dovetails with the language of the sex tourism industry, which also hypes cultural difference. Thanh-Dam Truong argues that the past two decades have witnessed a change in rural attitudes toward the value of female children. As the result of new opportunities to sell a daughter into prostitution, female sexual capacity is perceived as having market value taking "predominance over male labor . . . Families actually celebrate the birth of a daughter, because she now has potentially more access to social mobility." So, in this case, "Thai values" amount not only to what I might unsympathetically call traditional sexism but also to something considerably more familiar, the commodification of sexuality.

Even given our vast differences of experience, in the latitude allowed to sexual subjectivity there is something in the bar girls' experience that is recognizable to a heterosexual First World woman like me. We are linked by men's ability to turn their own desire and its object into things, as well as by an international system of labor and consumption in which all of us are actors. And we are linked in another way too. The sickness of the head and heart I see in these transactions in Bangkok is not the only disease they foster. Nor is that sickness entirely eclipsed by the concrete bodily realities of AIDS. Each is the deadly mirror of the other.

The Public Health Ministry, which has instituted an extensive testing program, estimates that between 200,000 and 400,000 Thais are infected with the AIDS virus. Australian professor John Dwyer, president of the AIDS Society for Asia and the Pacific, calls Thailand and Burma the nexus of the Asian sex and drug traffic, the "epicenter of the epidemic" on the continent. Thailand's projected population growth has already been affected by the epidemic, and Dr. Werasit Sittitrai of the Thai Red Cross estimates that by the year 2000, one-third of all deaths in the country may be caused by AIDS. Meanwhile, the *Bangkok Post*'s egregious night-life columnist, Trink, assures visitors, who get free copies of the daily distributed to their hotel rooms, that there is no AIDS or HIV among the bar girls of Soi Cowboy and Patpong.

One of the most explicit official acknowledgements of the connection between the AIDS crisis and international economic relations, Dr. Michael Merson, director of the Global Program on AIDS of the World Health Organization, stated recently, "It's extremely important that the developed nations understand that the focus of this epidemic is going to end up being Asia and the Pacific. We are all dependent for survival on having this region of the world become prosperous."

> *As a rule, literary treatment of the orgasm in Thai literature is implicit and genteel. It is considered a kind of miracle.*
> —Prapart Brudhiprabha, "A Sociolinguistic Analysis of the 'Marvel Act' of Love in Thai Literature: The Case of Phra Abhaimani"

"We have Japanese men here but we have never had a Japanese woman before!" exclaimed the madam of a Bangkok teahouse to journalist Yayori Matsui. Matsui was researching the chapter on the sex industry for her 1989 book *Women's Asia*, but even once they let her in, she could not experience the brothel as a brothel. Similarly covering bars where my countrymen buy women, I could see only the form of transactions, not their content. It's as if the whole scene takes place inside a translucent bubble and I'm on the outside looking in. I'm told the sex itself is strictly missionary position vanilla.

What the customer is buying, in addition to the unimaginative but unproblematic experience, is the woman's undivided attention. His overnight companion will also bargain with the cabdriver, work the unfamiliar payphone, and order food. I have no idea how this social submission translates into an erotic vocabulary. But nights that start with sexual exhibitions, where women demonstrate remarkable control of their vaginal sphincter—"smoking" cigarettes and catching ping pong balls with their genitals or extracting a string of razor blades from them—must be conducted in a different dialect.

What's missing from all this talk of sex bars, sex tours, sex workers, is, of course, sex—at least, sex as women imagine and experience it. Classic Thai poetry, with orgasm as a gift of divine grace, articulates a male fantasy. Elsewhere on the erotic register, established Thai institutions like concubinage and prostitution put arguably less delicate male fantasies into action. On the *fahrang* side, the European travel agencies hawk their wares in a commercial poetry that also evokes and stimulates fantasy. This fantasy isn't about the male orgasm as a breathtaking miracle but as the material goal of scores of pleasure-seekers avid for exotic techniques. Bangkok's sexual entertainment is the concrete expression of this fantasy. Desire and fulfillment seem to have no female voice in either the traditional or the contemporary culture of Thailand. For women, eros took a holiday and it wasn't a trip to Bangkok.

26

Identity and the Lifestyle Market

Nicola Field

In February 1993 the lesbian and gay rights group Outrage! organized a Queer Valentine's Carnival in London's West End "to celebrate the growing number of shops, restaurants and bars in and around Soho which cater exclusively for lesbians and gay men" (5 February 1993). Since then, Soho Pink Weekends have been regular occasions. The events have grown into full-scale carnivals, with gay businesses using the events to promote themselves. Corporate advertising banners, born by company employees, are carried along the streets in a grotesque parody of a political demonstration. Extolling the potential power of the pink pound to buy influence and legal reform, organizers pull thousands of gay and lesbian people into the shopping area. These defiant tourists crowd the streets, downing cappuccinos, cream cakes, and designer beers, maneuvering packed shopping bags, and cheering on a program of raunchy entertainment. The message is clear: "We're here, we're queer, get used to it, get out of our faces, we're not going away, we've got talent and a bloody big community. Most of all we've got money. So there." Events like this, whether they take place in the gay villages of Manchester, London, San Francisco, or New York, express the logical outcome of identity politics. If sexual orientation is the primary factor uniting people who want gay rights, then lesbians and gays can be seen as a discrete social group and potential market sector. Never mind differences in class, wealth, and social position. Rich gay business people who own magazines and nightclubs are put in the same category as gay men who work in the printshops or the bars. Property-owning entrepreneurs are classified in the same social grouping as single lesbian mothers on benefits.

Political organization by lesbians and gay men as a discrete or separate group in society is based in the 1990s on a sense of collective consumer power. This consumer power is perceived as the basis of citizenship: "We pay our taxes, we should get our rights." Meanwhile, the establishment of gay markets is applauded as a means of achieving collective, cross-class gay confidence, of proving the significance of the pink economy, of providing a focus for lesbians and gays to recognize common references. These references have to be consumable and are popularly located in fashion, interior design, publishing, restaurants, and bars. Through these reference points is constructed a loose consensus on what constitutes a gay lifestyle and, consequently, what contributes to gay identity. Gay lifestyle is visible as a specialized form of middle-class lifestyle and therefore is second nature to some, completely unattainable and meaningless to many.

This chapter argues against the notion that "buying gay" or attempting to wield power through bolstering the pink economy as a progressive political activity. It shows how the politics of identity are based on misleading and divisive ideas which weaken the fight against gay oppression. Identity, politicized and commodified, is not a basis for unified action; instead it is an insidious and complex framework of competing positions. It creates a false premise upon which to make hopeless and unfounded alliances across class. These alliances do not ensure that the powers of the few ensure the betterment of the many. On the contrary: the gay bourgeoisie (entrepreneurs, intellectuals, and media celebrities), which dominates the movement today, sets a political agenda that suits its interests alone. This does nothing to increase the power of working-class lesbians and gays to kick back at the bosses and bigots where it really hurts: in the bosses' pockets. Instead it reduces the exciting prospect of sexual liberation for all to a dreary set of proposed legal reforms and isolated single-issue campaigns. It is obviously important to support any move aimed at alleviating oppression. However, there are many reasons why lifestyle and identity politics can never bring about real freedom for all lesbian, gay, and bisexual people.

IDENTITY TAGS

The politics of identity are about bypassing the roots of oppression and concentrating on the symptoms. Obviously identities exist; they are products of our place within capitalist society. Identities define our place within the global conditions that oppress us: our nationality, sexuality, the social meaning of our gender, our physical dis/abilities, our experience of family relationships. In capitalist society where people's needs are subordinated to the tyranny of profit, identities provide a focal point for making some sense of who we are, what has happened to us, and what we would like to do about that. They are a survival mechanism, accommodated within capitalism as a sweetener for individuals who are denied any other control over their lives. They appear to lend a sense of individuality in a world where most people are treated as factory-, office- or gun-fodder. But forming a political agenda on the basis of identity is to mistake identity as an end in itself. Identity politics celebrate and sanctify our oppression—rooting our individuality in a system of exploitation and compulsion rather than a context where we are free to fulfill our individual potentials. They divide up what we know to be a multiplicity of identities (gay, black, woman, African) into single, monolithic concepts that compete with one another for ascendancy. They say that if you are not specifically oppressed on the basis of identity then you must surely be oppressing. Identity politics separate oppression from exploitation, thus divorcing cause from effect. They assert that only those who personally experience a type of oppression (homophobia, sexism, racism) can lead or even be involved in the fight against discrimination and prejudice. Identity politics revere lifestyle, saying that it is how you live that constitutes political action. They concede the commodification of identity and encourage the fetishization of identities in the marketplace. They compete for visibility and influence. They concentrate on one symptom of oppression—abusive language, say—and promote a futile system of language reform as a way of changing society. The leaders of identity politics fail to recognize class society as the root cause of stigma and blame and enter "working class" as an optional item halfway down the shopping list, or hierarchy, of oppressions. In identity politics it is what and how you consume that defines you, not what and how you produce. This ideological distortion . . . is the basis on which the family is retained as a social norm. Conservatives always try to see people as individuals defined by the methods in which they consume rather than by their role in the creation of wealth.

THE MARGIN FETISH

Gay journalist Colin Richardson describes the cultural marginalization of homosexuality as an opportunity for radical consumption. He celebrates the building of a corporate "gay sensibility" as a way of looking at, being in and consuming mainstream culture:

> We are used to seeing things differently. We grew up in a heterosexual culture which banishes positive images of homosexuality. So we read between the lines, take our own meanings from books and films we are allowed to access and call it camp. Our first images of sex are heterosexual images, but we can still enjoy them. I remember when I first saw simulated sex on TV, putting myself in the place of the woman, the man on top of me. Lesbian and gay porn frees our imagination from such trickery. When I watch a gay video I can imagine myself as any or all of the participants, or just sit back and enjoy being a voyeur. (Richardson 1991)

Identity politics, fetishizing this position of marginalized consumer, essentially seek to accommodate gay people within an unjust class society. They do not offer any solution for revolutionary action or change—suggesting that it is within individual lifestyle and personal decisions that political action is wrought. Cause and effect are thus interchanged with the result that the politics of identity are shot through with themes of guilt, binary oppositions, endless self-examination. Being gay or lesbian means sharing a common victimhood, collectively suffering the oppressive behavior of virtually all heterosexuals. According to the politics of identity, all women and men in heterosexual relationships are universally privileged as heterosexuality is promoted as the norm. Homosexual relationships are universally oppressed. The idea that it is heterosexuality itself which mainly causes gay oppression, rather than the system that calls it normal, is a misapprehension shared by protagonists across the gay identity politics spectrum.

Sheila Jeffreys is a radical lesbian feminist writer who believes, against evidence to the contrary, that all women, whatever their class or position within society, share a common interest in overthrowing what she calls "male supremacy." However exploited men are, however poor or abused, Jeffreys believes that they maintain power over women and will always, given the chance, oppress women and treat them as sex objects. She claims that not even lesbians and gay men have any interests in common and defines *all men* as a ruling class. Fantastically, she calls on all women to give up the power imbalances of heterosexuality and embrace homosexuality, or, as she puts it, the eroticization of "equality and mutuality":

> It is not to be expected that men, gay or straight, will voluntarily choose to relinquish the pleasure and privilege they derive from the eroticized subordination of women. Though some are capable of political integrity and of working against their own interests as a class, we cannot expect this to take place on any mass scale.
>
> As women and as lesbians our only hope lies in other women. (Jeffreys 1990, 313)

Jeffreys's scenario is profoundly depressing on many levels. Firstly, she denies that there could be any common interest between women and men in improving relationships between them. Secondly, it appears men are, on the whole, so aggressive and abusive they are incapable of any real change. She also ignores the oppressive and exploitative roles played by ruling class and rich women. Finally, she places all hopes for change on women having some kind of inner transformation of their feelings—a metaphysical counterweight to the thought crime of hetero-sex:

> The "thought" of women's sexual subordination delivers powerful reinforcement to men's feelings of dominance and superiority. The liberation of women is unimaginable in this situation . . . if we cannot imagine our liberation then we cannot achieve it. Male sexuality must be reconstructed . . . (Jeffreys 1990, 313)

It is inconceivable that any kind of oppression can be got rid of simply by wishing or "imagining" it away, or by putting forward some kind of model for "equal" (good, homosexual) sex as opposed to "oppressive" (bad, heterosexual) sex. Jeffreys's arguments are dangerously close to those of the moralists on the right of the Conservative Party who, quite unrealistically, demand that everyone should aspire to "normal" family values. Her point is that everyone should aspire to the "good" sex to which only lesbians (because of their supposed common, cross-class experience of oppression) can point the way. This proscriptive message is thankfully held in disdain by those who position themselves on the left wing of identity politics.

Many sections of the black, women's, and other identity-based movements reply to prejudice and bigotry by creating defensive myths that aim to counteract stereotypes. These responses, however, often end up by reworking the stereotypes and creating new ones. Parts of the women's movement, for instance, have often responded to sexism and misogyny by resorting to right-wing biological determinism. They declare that women are naturally more caring and less aggressive than men. Quite apart from the fact that this can be disproved by any number of the women who do not fit this romanticized model, such a tactic leads nowhere because it suggests that women and men will always be unequal. Similarly, suggesting that gay people are leading a messianic sexual revolution through simply being gay does nothing to address the real reasons for gay oppression. Neither does it explain how gay people who are not even out, let alone participating in the heady, sex-positive, cruisy, commercial scene, benefit from this stereotypical lifestyle.

AUTONOMY VERSUS UNITY

Peter Tatchell, self-styled "queer emancipation" leader in the UK, is a forceful proponent of lesbian and gay identity politics as the only way forward to equality:

> What unites lesbians and gay men are our common sexual experiences and our suf-
> fering discrimination as a result of prejudice against our sexuality. A wealthy white
> gay man is in much the same boat if he loses his job because he is gay as a poor, black
> lesbian who loses her job for the same reasons. (*Gay Times,* August 1993)

Tatchell tries to arrive at a state of unity by denying the divisions of class. He ignores
the fact that wealthy gay people do not experience oppression in the same way as the
rest of us. They can afford to cushion themselves against the sharp ends of oppression.
They travel by taxi and avoid being out late at night in the streets, vulnerable to attack.
They do not feel the squeeze of insecurity and poverty because they have property and
insurance schemes. They do not endure constant fear of ill-health because they can buy
private care. They do not feel the grind of daily toil and long working hours because
they pay childminders, cleaners, and secretaries. Tatchell implicitly defies working-class
lesbians and gay men who have no choice but to fight on the basis of class. While setting the ground for inevitable fragmentation, he appears to support a united front and
leaves the way open to accuse others of divisiveness. His thinking claims to rescue a
strategy for "advancement" from revolutionary black leader Malcolm X. Tatchell advocates the creation of lesbian and gay institutions and a "community" power-base from
which to push for changes in the law and in society. Like other reformists, he writes as
though gay liberation can come about without fundamental political and economic
upheavals. He also defines mainstream society as "heterosexual" rather than bourgeois
and implies that we can change society simply by enlightenment or persuading the ruling class to change its mind.

> By developing the lesbian and gay community as a focus of counter-culture and
> counter-power, we are helping to subvert and undermine the ideas and institutions
> that sustain heterosexual supremacism. In effect, we are withdrawing our allegiance
> from the dominant culture and denying it moral legitimacy. (Tatchell 1993)

By doing this he stamps "heterosexual" on the institutions and power structures
whose primary function is to control workers. He implies that heterosexual people as a
whole have no interest in the eradication of homophobia and that oppressions can be
fought on separate fronts with optional coordination on special occasions.

> Self-reliance does not mean that we retreat into our own separatist ghetto, give up the
> campaign for equal rights, or reject working with others suffering discrimination. On
> the contrary. It simply means that we make lesbian and gay self-help and community
> empowerment our priority. From a position of strength, we will be better able to
> make effective alliances with others fighting discrimination and to bargain with
> straight society for meaningful legislative changes. (Tatchell 1993)

"Prioritizing" lesbian and gay rights has turned the lesbian and gay movement in on
itself, over and over again. There are continual retreats back into single issues and
woolly separatism. This has led to a complete divorce from the revolutionary ideas of
lesbian and gay liberation. It has distracted activists from the root causes of gay oppression. It has thrown all the energies of lesbian and gay anger into the marketplace.
Tatchell's proposal to "bargain" for civil rights is a clear outcome of the disaster of
seeking "self-reliance and autonomy." Factions and figureheads cannot look to a mass

movement to demand equality and justice. They really are, as Tatchell knows, not self-reliant at all but heavily dependent upon the maneuverings and negotiations between the rich and powerful. By separating, even for a moment, the fight against homophobia from the fights against sexism and racism, activists weaken the struggle. Our most important task is to show how oppressions affect everyone because they divide us. Racism, sexism, and homophobia all come from the same system. Women and black people want and need a movement that links all our concerns. Statistically speaking, the majority of homosexuals in the world are female, nonwhite, and working class or poor. We have to fight collectively against the common enemy.

The fear that there will be no gay movement left if lesbians and gays don't concentrate on the single issues that affect them does indeed echo Malcolm X's early ideas. Malcolm claimed at the beginning of his political life that all whites are racist. He later changed his mind, though, and asserted that black and white workers had a mutual interest in working together to fight oppression and overcome prejudices. He recognized that the roots of oppression were embedded in the common experience of exploitation, across racial differences. His later writings and speeches, when he was breaking with the separatist Nation of Islam, resonate with his growing conviction that the racism of the white working class is a divisive set of ideas that can be challenged and changed—rather than an inherent characteristic born of self-interest:

> We are living in an era of revolution, and the revolt of the American Negro is part of the rebellion against the oppression and colonialism which has characterized this era. . . . It is incorrect to classify the revolt of the Negro as simply a racial conflict of black against white, or as purely an American problem. Rather, we are today seeing a global struggle of the oppressed against the oppressor, the exploited against the exploiters. (Breitman 1990, 217)

It was not an imaginary "white society" that was the source of racism, but a society controlled by a privileged minority consolidating its power by the systematic exploitation of workers: black and white. In the same way there is really no such thing as an oppressive "straight society" benefiting from gay oppression. The only people who materially benefit from gay oppression are the bosses, property owners, and the business classes. For them, racist, homophobic, and sexist ideas which confuse, distract, and divide workers are useful, ensuring that there is no united opposition to their systems of exploitation. Control of the media is an essential component of a strategy of oppression whereby divisive ideas are continually paraded through our consciousness. It is in this sense that ideology reinforces economic structures, honing, shifting, and manipulating their effectiveness.

Many activists and supporters on the left of the gay movement today not only acknowledge but insist that unity with other oppressed groups is essential if any progress is to be made in bringing about equality for gay people. Leaders within the movement pay lip-service to the principle of unity while all the time dragging people back to the futile ideas of autonomy. Peter Tatchell believes that heterosexuals, while benefiting from gay oppression, also often suffer as a result of homophobia. However, he does not begin to explain that homophobia short-changes straights because it stops them from uniting with gay workers against a common oppressor. His idea is that homophobia prevents heterosexuals from experiencing the liberating erotic and emotional potentials of homosexuality:

No-one should have to suffer guilt, ostracism or discrimination because of who they love. Most heterosexuals seem incapable of understanding what it is like to be told that your feelings are immoral, sinful, abnormal and unnatural . . . Homophobia also forces many heterosexuals to police their own image and mannerisms, out of a fear of being labeled homosexual. . . . The result is that heterosexual women are pushed into a feminine passivity which limits their independence and freedom. . . . Ultra machismo in heterosexual men is not unrelated to social problems such as rape and domestic violence as well as football hooliganism, racist attacks, vandalism and queer-bashing. (Tatchell 1994)

Tatchell rightly points to the complex consequences of homophobia and their fatal implication in other forms of oppression like sexism. Homophobia is a powerful weapon preventing people of all sexualities from realizing their potentials, socially as well as sexually. But he fails to make the essential connection between the personal responses of ordinary people trying to form satisfying and rewarding relationships and a society beset with prejudices, fantasies, and divisions. Demonization of sexual relationships on the ground of morality, religion, biology, psychiatry, and the law is experienced by many sections of society and not just lesbians and gay men. Multiracial, intergenerational, and interdenominational relationships are all stigmatized to differing degrees. People with disabilities, prisoners, the mentally ill, women of all sections of society, children, and many others are constantly told that their feelings and desires are illegitimate.

Lesbians and gay men occupy a pivotal and explosive position within the whole system of sexual regulation, but their experiences are the tip of the iceberg. Homophobia is part of a huge economic, political, social, and ideological system of mass oppression. Even if it could be eradicated without changing this system, many other forms of sexual oppression would remain. Tatchell avoids this by ignoring the fact that lesbians and gay men, even those who are out and active, are often limited and constrained by ideals of femininity and masculinity. Lesbians are no less likely than heterosexual women to take passive roles at home and work and have difficulty in asserting their views and wishes. Gay men are by no means immune to the pressures of machismo that enforce codes of behavior supposedly signifying mental strength, sexual prowess, physical supremacy. Yes, homophobia does indeed affect everyone, but not on the simplistic level implied by idealist radical reformers.

Peter Tatchell's "solution" is to create an alternative society, a dimension of citizens who share common lifestyles, aspirations and interests based on their sexual identities:

. . . the quality of life for most lesbians and gay men has dramatically improved over the last two decades. This has been largely the result of our own self-help initiatives. We have created a safe and supportive lesbian and gay community; with switchboards and social behavior, bars and discos, employment and legal advice organizations, publishers and book shops, housing and immigration rights groups, counseling and befriending services, newspapers and magazines. . . . Effective use has never been made of the economic power of the pink pound or the electoral power of the pink vote. . . . We've therefore got to start changing ourselves and our community, as well as changing society. (Tatchell 1994)

This "self-helping community" would exist to nurture homosexual identity. It would be founded on and strengthened by the power of its own capitalists and bourgeoisie.

Tatchell's vision is underpinned by the mistaken belief that only by separate self-organization will gay people overthrow their oppression. Like Jeffreys's, his is also a counsel of despair because it is founded on the belief that only lesbian and gay people can wage a fight against gay oppression. This can only lead to fragmentation and weakness.

Separatism, whether seen as a political principle of purity or simply a means to an end, is destructive because it alienates and overlooks the mass of potential allies and supporters who have a material and immediate interest in fighting all the forms of oppression which proceed from exploitation and divisiveness. Divisiveness, fragmentation, separation—all these are weaknesses which prevent any force for liberation from gaining strength in numbers. Sharon Smith, in her powerful analysis of identity politics, "Mistaken Identity," points to the most imperative example of why unity in action is of the utmost importance and why autonomy and all other forms of separatism are deeply dangerous:

> For people newly active on the left, this way of organizing may seem like common sense: it should go without saying that those who are oppressed should fight against their own oppression. . . . For this same reason it follows that each oppressed group should have its own distinct and separate movement. Such movements therefore tend to be organized on the basis of "autonomy" or independence—from each other and from the socialist movement. They tend also to be organized independent of any class basis. But this logic is flawed. It would be disastrous for example if the fight against fascism in Europe today were limited to members of those racial groups who are immediately targeted by fascists. The advance of the fascist movement is not only a threat to "foreign born" workers but to all workers. To most effectively counter the recent rise of fascism in Europe, all those who oppose the far right, whatever race they happen to be, should be encouraged to join the anti-fascist movement. *Any fight against oppression, if it is to succeed, must be based upon building the strongest possible movement.*" [my emphasis] (Smith 1994, 4)

Smith also refers to Lenin's criticism of Jewish separatist organization in 1903. His warning represents a important lesson for lesbians and gays in the 1990s. Some Jewish workers called for a separate revolutionary organization, saying that gentile workers were too anti-semitic to unite. Lenin pointed out that autonomous organization compartmentalizes and fragments. He described the Jewish Bund as having "stepped onto the inclined plane of nationalism" which must inevitably lead to isolation of different groups and weakness in the overall struggle:

> one who has adopted the standpoint of nationalism naturally arrives at the desire to erect a Chinese Wall around his nationality, his national working class movement; he is unembarrassed by the fact that it would mean building separate walls in each city, in each little town and village, unembarrassed even by the fact that by his tactics of division and dismemberment he is reducing to nil the great call for the rallying and unity of the proletarians of all nations, all races and all languages. (quoted in Smith 1994, 44)

We can add to that rallying cry: "and all sexualities." This call for unity was not one of a movement which ignored oppression. Bolshevik revolutionaries were committed to eradicating the many divisions of nationality and racism which existed at that time in Russia, as they do across the world today. Time and history proved that Lenin had been right to argue against autonomous organization:

> In 1917 the same Russian workers who the Bund had argued in 1903 were too backward to champion the rights of Jewish workers elected Trotsky, a Jew, as chairman of the Petrograd soviet, Kamenev, a Jew, as chairman of the Moscow soviet, and Sverdlov, a Jew, as chairman of the Soviet Republic. (quoted in Smith 1994, 44)

THE POSTURINGS OF POST-MARXISM: WHERE IDENTITY POLITICS COMES FROM

How have we arrived at this stage where we, as a movement, have become so confused and divided over the route to gay liberation? An important factor in the fragmentation of the left into identity politics and groupings around personal characteristics has been the growing influence of the theories of post-modernism and post-Marxism across political, social and cultural fields.

. . . both of these inter-linked schools of thought are based on the ideas that the old certainties of class and a society divided by wealth and class interests are over. The idea that the world is largely divided into exploiters and exploited is simplistic and outdated. Workers experience modern capitalism as individuals, not collectively. They therefore identify not with a large working class, but severally, across alternative groupings, according to their particular individual identifications (national, racial, gender, sexual, etc.). Hence the collapse of class struggle into various "movements" (environmental, gay, women's, disabled, etc.).

Furthermore, because ordinary people are so divided and so fragmented by the present system, they will never again organize on the basis of class to improve their conditions or to take control of the means of production. The academics and intellectuals who articulate these new conditions are therefore crucial to any form of resistance because it is their ideas (of identity, of groupings) which make sense of the apparent lack of cohesion. Any revolution, revolt, or reform will therefore be led by intellectuals rather than workers.

Post-Marxist academics and intellectuals fill a lot of published space with theoretical writing intended to be read by other academics. Their writings tend to be highly obscure and full of impenetrable jargon. Their treatment of sex, whilst often providing indepth explorations of the highly complex ideological function of "sexuality" in capitalist culture, does little to offer any kind of tangible theoretical basis for ordinary people working in the world to tackle sexual oppression at the roots. For instance, cultural theorist Dugald Williamson is willing to approach the much neglected subject of bisexuality and its position within contemporary ideas about individuality and gender. This issue could be of interest to all women and men wishing to create a society where everyone has the right and the opportunity to explore their full sexual and creative potentials. Williamson, though, submerges the implications of talking and writing about bisexuality in a morass of abstraction with no connection to the material world:

> In some current writing, a notion of bisexuality has been invested with a new (or greatly altered) potential, where it can give sexual content to a residually Romantic

notion that true subjectivity is to be found in the incompletion of the self, the active tension between thought and feeling, mental consciousness and pulsational experience, and indeed, between the masculine closure of representation and the feminine possibility of excess. In this case, it becomes possible to speak in the same breath of a plethora of unrealized differences for the subject positioned in the signifying process, and an oscillation between sexual polarities, not bisexuality in any fixated form, but a continual androgynous deferral of identity, the intermediate space of desire: these two terms coming together to create a sense of the radical possibilities of the subject's realization in history. (1987)

Academic theories are generated to provoke further theoretical response, not to inspire revolutionary action among ordinary people. However, we need to be clear that ideas are not the property of an intelligentsia or academic elite. Issues of sexuality, representation, and liberation belong to everyone and they relate to all of us on a theoretical level as well as a practical and everyday basis.

Post-Marxists deny that the root of oppression lies in class society. Oppression itself, instead of being objectively identifiable through systematic discrimination, media misrepresentation, and popular prejudice, is seen as something only definable by the people who experience it. They see the state itself as essentially neutral and not inextricably bound up with the interests and methods of capital. They deny, for instance, that the welfare benefits system is a means of class control. The state, according to post-Marxism, is up for grabs to anyone who can get the power to influence it. This concurs with the current Tory philosophy of free market choice. Under this system public services are privatized. This involves "contracting out" health care, education, and advice provision to independent "providers" who are forced to monitor their clientele as "units" or sources of income which collectively attract the providers' cash. Thus, for example, services for people with sickle cell anemia are put in competition for funds with services for people with HIV. Refugee students needing English language support are put in competition with women students needing creche provision under the "special needs" budgets. In reality, the free-for-all is a free-for-no-one. The choice on offer is obliterated by a total absence of opportunity. In the same way, by offering all things to all people, post-Marxism ends up by articulating almost nothing that relates to the everyday experiences of ordinary people. In this sense it would be more accurately described as "anti-Marxism."

Post-Marxists explain that more fragmented, individualized identities are really the basis upon which people are galvanized into radical or reformist action, because they do not see class divisions as universal and applicable to everyone. Thus movements based on identity politics can compete with one another and with institutions to influence the "neutral" state. Sharon Smith points out yet another feature of post-Marxism which helps to explain the divisions and squabbles within the gay identity politics movement:

... according to Laclau and Mouffe [post-Marxist theorists], oppression is not only completely subjective, but it can also result from any relationship in which one group of people are subject to the authority of another or others. This method borrows heavily from the blind anti-authoritarianism of anarchism—which opposes any form of authority, regardless of who is wielding it and for what purposes. But there is a difference between the authority of those who are democratically elected and of those whose authority is imposed from above. Similarly, the authority of a picket captain in a strike is of an entirely different nature from the authority of a police officer, based upon each one's objective interests—based upon class position. But taken out of the context of class society, all forms of authority are equal and should be equally opposed. . . . The forms of struggle which flow from post-Marxist theory consist of separate, autonomous struggles against specific relations of "subordination." (1994, 30)

By this logic we can begin to see how identity politics so frequently collapse into bitter schisms and antagonisms. If oppression can also result from any relationship, then political differences and various tactics can be ascribed to oppressive behavior. Women declare they can't fight alongside "oppressive men"; black people won't unite with "oppressive whites"; lesbians and gays (if they get as far as working together) won't align with supportive heterosexuals, seeing them instead as "oppressive straights."

SIGNPOSTS TO UTOPIA:
RADICAL PLURALISM AND MULTICULTURAL DEMOCRACY

The proponents of post-Marxist identity politics describe their ideas as a radical step forward, leaving behind the old-fashioned Marxist ideas of class analysis and class struggle. Their rhetoric, however, reveals a deeply reactionary despair that socialism is no longer possible or even desirable. Cloaked in language which suggests optimism based on fresh, diverse, and vibrant new energies, their vision suggests an illusory "pluralistic" society where all kinds of different groups compete on a friendly basis for ascendancy within the neutral state:

> . . . the central questions confronting the left aren't located within the left itself but in the broader, deeper currents of social protest and struggle among non-socialist, democratic constituencies—in the activities of trade unionists, gays and lesbians, feminists, environmentalists, people of color, and the poor. . . . This means advancing a politics of radical, multicultural democracy, not socialism. (Aronowitz, quoted in Smith)

So, not only are identity politics entirely compatible with the forces of market capitalism, we now see that they are entirely incompatible with socialism. Unsurprisingly, these ideas of pluralism find support in intellectual coteries that once supported the now defunct Soviet Stalinist regime, believing it to be a progressive socialist society, and who now find themselves floundering without a substantial political program. Rosalind Brunt gives a good account of the appeal of identity politics to those who want to stay on the left but who don't want the embarrassment of admitting that they might have been wrong. She cheerfully paints a horrifying picture of a political program with no basic philosophy or analysis. Brunt also denies the disastrous splits, accusations, and fragmentations resulting from the worst excesses of 1980s identity politics and buys wholesale into the idea that politics should be expressions of people's personal feelings:

> A politics of identity . . . is indeed a very welcoming kind of politics because everyone can have a go at defining it in their own terms . . . [It] has been current for some time

as a contextual shorthand for movements organizing around sexuality, gender and ethnicity and working to translate "the personal is the political" into everyday practice. Learning the lessons of these movements, we can begin applying notions of identity, and identities, to a political agenda for all. A politics whose starting point is about recognizing the degree to which political activity and effort involves a continuous process of making and remaking ourselves—and ourselves in relation to others—must rightfully be available for anyone to make up as they go along. (1989, 15)

Celebrating fragmentation to this extent goes hand in hand with the consumer lifestyle politics of the gay bourgeoisie. Identity politics are claimed as the potential liberator of everyone, as though everyone in society has the same interests. Quite clearly this is not the case. Class interests are, by their very nature, oppositional and cannot be reconciled through an attractive-sounding program for breaking down sexual boundaries. The post-Marxist proponents of identity politics see a multiplicity of identities being marketed to consumers through the sounds and images of advertising. They claim that "old certainties" are "gone" and that people have become caught up in the plethora of options and identities on offer through consumerism. They cannot be "made classconscious"—the argument goes—their imaginations and their aspirations are too fragmented. The left intelligentsia, then, must respond to this psychic splintering with a program of political ideas that will appeal to these fragmented consciousnesses. There's no point, they say, in reiterating "the old certainties" because people will just not understand them. They ignore the fact that society is galvanized by a continual struggle between those who produce the wealth and those who own the wealth.

UNITE! DON'T FOLLOW THESE LEADERS!

Proponents and supporters of identity politics were very active in the 1980s in city-based movements to reform public and social services. Their aims were to pressurize local governments and city councils—from the inside or from the fringes—to accommodate diverse lifestyles in their policies and practices. While the demands for equality had clearly emerged from the sense of confidence which had been built by the class struggles of the 1970s, the pattern of "interest groups" and "movements," all trying to push for their particular projects of advancement, owed its origins to the diverse radical struggles of the 1960s. During this period modern ideas of feminism, black liberation, and gay liberation were formed and they went on to become the basis of identity politics in the 1980s, through a process of pluralistic accountability based on the politics of identity. The "top down" consultative democracy that grew up in this brief era of reform holds many attractions for lesbian and gay "opinion formers" today. But for many others, this outcome heralded the virtual collapse of any kind of popular belief in working from inside to change the system. Many socialists are still wondering nearly ten years later where gay liberation will come from.

The danger is that the lesbian and gay leaderships in Europe and the U.S. will step even deeper into the pitfalls and minefields of identity politics, embracing wholesale the cynical business solutions of buying our way out to freedom. Most lesbians and gays know that a new brand of sexual politics is desperately needed, one that will make sense of the failures and splits of reformist organizations, one that will be able to explain why lesbians and gays cannot unite across chasmic class differences, one that will offer a way forward for black and white gays to unite and fight a common enemy. But while a comprehensive class analysis of gay oppression remains sidelined, this development is inhibited. It is not in the interests of the bourgeoisie and their supporters (business people, managers, media cliques) to admit the truth about where sexual liberation for all will come from. It is only the working class which has a material and unifying interest in bringing about a society where sexual oppression is no longer needed. Identity politics offer none of the crucial theoretical and practical links between gay oppression and the exploitation which workers experience every day of their working lives. They foster the illusory hope that the state is indeed neutral and that by increasing pressure we can gain more influence over it. They encourage those of us who are not in influential positions to hand over the task of gay liberation to a select few who set themselves up as our representatives. Yes, we have to recognize and confront the awesome developments in the modern world which have alienated millions of people from any sense of control over their own lives. But at the same time we have to be aware that the old divisions, the ones which divide people through society and create basic antagonisms, are still very much alive and still the primary influence upon our lives.

The proliferation of identities in modern capitalism is about the commercialization of "alternative lifestyles." It is not about sanctioning diversity or undermining the structures and systems which create oppression. While the institution of the family may appear to decline, its ideological function as a regulating ideal remains intact. At best, identity politics offers a route for oppressed individuals to understand the symptoms of their oppression—on the way to understanding its causes. At worst, the politics of identity provides a vehicle for the middle classes to make money and nurse their own careers, enabling the capitalist state to continue repression while appearing to bow to organized pressure. Identity politics only offers solutions to certain individuals through selective "empowerment." It has nothing to offer the mass of people for whom sexual liberation will be attainable only when the battle against class oppression has been fought. This battle can only be won by a movement which unites all workers across boundaries of race, gender, and sexuality.

ARCHIVE III

ONGOING WORK

27

The Heterosexual Imaginary
Feminist Sociology and Theories of Gender

Chrys Ingraham

Feminist sociology, once at the vanguard of academic feminism, is showing signs of losing its conceptual and political edge. Feminists once sought to effect transformative social change by making visible the investment of sociology in practices contributing to the reproduction of gender inequality and relations of ruling.[1] But in the 20 years since feminists announced the need for sociology to attend to gender as an organizing social category, gender studies have been gradually canonized; more than that, the founding concept, gender, has come to be taken as obvious. From textbooks to research studies to theory, there is little or no debate over what is meant by gender. In this essay I make the argument that feminist sociological understandings of gender need to be reexamined for the ways in which they participate in the reproduction of what I call "the heterosexual imaginary." The "imaginary" is a Lacanian term borrowed by Louis Althusser for his theory of ideology. Defining ideology as "the imaginary relationship of individuals to their real conditions of existence" (1971, 52), Althusser argues that the imaginary is that image or representation of reality which masks the historical and material conditions of life. The heterosexual imaginary is that way of thinking which conceals the operation of heterosexuality in structuring gender and closes off any critical analysis of heterosexuality as an organizing institution. The effect of this depiction of reality is that heterosexuality circulates as taken for granted, naturally occurring, and unquestioned, while gender is understood as socially constructed and central to the organization of everyday life. Feminist studies of marriage, family, and sexual violence (which might seem to cover this ground) invariably depend upon the heterosexual imaginary deployed in a variety of heteronormative assumptions. Heteronormativity—the view that institutionalized heterosexuality constitutes the standard for legitimate and prescriptive sociosexual arrangements—represents one of the main premises not only of feminist sociology but of the discipline in general. As such, it underlies and defines the direction taken by feminist sociology and by gender studies in particular.

If this is to change, feminist sociology must develop a critique of institutionalized heterosexuality which does not participate in the heterosexual imaginary. To interrupt the ways in which the heterosexual imaginary naturalizes heterosexuality and conceals its constructedness in the illusion of universality requires a systemic analysis of the ways in which it is historically imbricated in the distribution of economic resources, cultural power, and social control.

It will be the work of this essay to call for a reconsideration of gender as the key organizing concept of feminist sociology. The main argument of this article is that the material conditions of capitalist patriarchal societies are more centrally linked to institutionalized heterosexuality than to gender and, moreover, that gender (under the patriarchal arrangements prevailing now) is inextricably bound up with heterosexuality. By re-articulating some of the critical strategies of early feminist sociology within a materialist feminist framework, it is possible to both redress and disrupt the heterosexual imaginary circulating in contemporary gender theory.

Gender, or what I would call "heterogenders," is the asymmetrical stratification of the sexes in relation to the historically varying institutions of patriarchal heterosexuality. Reframing gender as heterogender foregrounds the relation between heterosexuality and gender. Heterogender confronts the equation of heterosexuality with *the natural* and of gender with the cultural, and suggests that both are socially constructed, open to other configurations (not only opposites and binary) and open to change. As a materialist feminist concept, heterogender de-naturalizes the "sexual" as the starting point for understanding heterosexuality, and connects institutionalized heterosexuality with the gender division of labor and the patriarchal relations of production.

MATERIALIST FEMINIST CRITIQUE

Materialist feminism developed in response to a series of global social changes and associated critical currents in intellectual and political work. Western materialist or marxist feminists attempted to expose and disrupt the interface of patriarchal social structures with multinational (particularly U.S.) corporate capitalism's expanding sphere of accumulation and exploitation (Barrett 1980; Hennessy and Mohan 1989; Kuhn and Wolpe 1978; Landry and MacLean 1993; Mies 1986). Complaints about the global effects of patriarchy and capitalism provoked protests from non-western or U.S. Third World feminists about western feminism's own racist, classist, and colonialist assumptions in attempting to "speak for" all women (Minh-ha 1989; Mohanty 1988; Sandoval 1991; and Spivak 1985, 1988). These criticisms were buttressed by escalating claims in the west that feminism privileged the interests of white, middle-class, heterosexual women at the expense of an emancipatory project which could intervene in white supremacist, classist, and heterosexist social arrangements (E. Brown 1989; R. Brown 1976; Bunch 1976; Carby 1982; Collins 1991; Combahee River Collective 1983; Davis 1981; Giddings 1984; hooks 1984; Lugones 1989; Moraga 1986; Rich 1980; Spelman 1989). This call for an internal re-evaluation of western feminism intersected with the circulation of newly forming critical knowledges such as Afrocentrism, postcolonial criticism, poststructuralism, neo-marxism, and postmodernism, and brought about a rethinking of feminist concepts and politics.

Throughout the struggles and debates within feminism over the past 20 years, materialist feminists have continually worked to develop an analytic capable of disrupting the taken-for-granted in local and global social arrangements and of exposing the economic, political, and ideological conditions upon which exploitation and oppression depend. Materialist feminism, however, is not to be confused with vulgar Marxism, with what is frequently referred to as base-superstructure Marxism or economic determinism. Rather, *materialism* here means a mode of inquiry that examines the division of labor and the distribution of wealth in the context of historically prevailing national and state interests and ideological struggles over meaning and value. Employing both marxist and feminist critiques of ideology, materialist feminism breaks away from the growing trend toward discursive politics—postmodern and poststructuralist feminism—and takes as its object the "social transformation of dominant institutions that, as a totality, distribute economic resources and cultural power asymmetrically according to gender" (Ebert 1993, 5). Committed to systemic analysis, materialist feminism is

> an inquiry intended to disclose how activities are organized and how they are articulated to the social relations of the larger social and economic process . . . how our own situations are organized and determined by social processes that extend outside the scope of the everyday world and are not discoverable within it. (D. Smith 1987,152)

This form of analysis asserts the systematic operation of historically specific social totalities that link the local to the macrolevel of analysis. It is not, however, a "totalizing" theory in that it does not generalize its findings to apply to absolutely all phenomena, nor does it argue from an abstract or objectivist stance.

As a form of "critical postmodernism" (Agger 1992), materialist feminism argues that the nexus of social arrangements and institutions which form social totalities—patriarchy, capitalism, and racism—regulates our everyday lives. They are not monolithic, but consist of unstable patterns of interrelations and reciprocal determinations which, when viewed together, provide a useful way of theorizing power and domination. To theorize in terms of social totalities is to have a way of making sense of events in relation to pervasive social patterns. Rape and domestic violence, for example, can be seen as the effect of social structures that situate men in a hierarchical relation to women and to each other according to historical forms of social differentiation such as heterosexuality, with its historically specific heterogendered and racial components. According to Dorothy Smith, "relations of ruling" such as patriarchy

> bring into view the intersection of the institutions organizing and regulating society . . . a specific interrelation between the dynamic advance of the distinctive forms of organizing and ruling contemporary capitalist society and the patriarchal forms of our contemporary experience . . . a complex of organized practices, including government, law, business and financial management, professional organization, and educational institutions as well as the discourses in texts that interpenetrate the multiple sites of power. (1987, 3)

Significant in Smith's theory of ruling is her reference to forms, complexes, and "multiple sites of power." It is evident that for Smith, capitalism and patriarchy are organizing structures which are varied and multiple, institutionally as well as textually. Before returning to the role of ideology in materialist feminist work in this essay, let us first address the struggles over concepts such as capitalism and patriarchy.

Theories which focus on capitalism and patriarchy as social totalities are becoming less and less acceptable. In recent years an important debate about the explanatory reach of such frameworks has challenged feminists to defend or rethink many of their assumptions. In particular, many postmodernist and poststructuralist theorists have criticized the use of "master narratives" such as marxism as "totalizing," and have disputed any theory which conceptualizes in terms of social totalities, such as capitalism or patriarchy. For example, Jean Francois Lyotard argues against master narratives, but his argument confuses ever-changing and historically specific social totalities with totalitarianism and (for some) positivism. These ideological debates are crucial and consequential. When critiques of western culture's master narratives privilege the local and the particular at the expense of making connections, these arguments endanger any effort to conceive a "social change movement designed to remake the world" (Agger 1992, 113). Furthermore, they fail to acknowledge the significant rewriting that social totalities and marxism have undergone in recent years (Hennessy 1993a, Walby 1989).

It is my position that we should continue to critique capitalism and patriarchy as regimes of exploitation which organize divisions of labor and wealth, national and state interests, and those ideologies which legitimize the ordering and justification of these totalities and the production of social hierarchies and difference. In particular, we need to examine their varying historical, regional, and global conditions of existence. For instance, capitalism in Japan is not the same as capitalism in the U.S., even though they are interrelated and reciprocal and produce similar effects. They emerge from different historical and material relations of production and therefore defy reductive generalization.

Patriarchy is also historically variable, producing a hierarchy of heterogender divisions which privileges men as a group and exploits women as a group. It structures social practices which it represents as natural and universal and which are reinforced by its organizing institutions and rituals (e.g., marriage). As a totality, patriarchy organizes difference by positioning men in hierarchical opposition to women and differentially in relation to other structures, such as race or class. Its continued success depends on the maintenance of regimes of difference as well as on a range of material forces. It is a totality that not only varies cross-nationally, but also manifests differently across ethnic, racial, and class boundaries within nations. For instance, patriarchy in African American culture differs significantly from patriarchy in other groups in U.S. society. Even though each group shares certain understandings of hierarchical relations between men and women, the historical relation of African American men to African American women is dramatically different from that among Anglo-European Americans. Among African Americans, a group which has suffered extensively from white supremacist policies and practices, solidarity as a "racial" group has frequently superseded asymmetrical divisions based on gender. This is not to say that patriarchal relations do not exist among African Americans, but that they have manifested differently among racial-ethnic groups as a result of historical necessity. Interestingly, racism has sometimes emerged in relation to criticisms of African American men for not being patriarchal enough by Euro-American standards. As a totality, patriarchy produces structural effects that situate men differently in relation to women and to each other according to history.

To critique the way gender is theorized in feminist sociology, a materialist feminist mode of inquiry begins by investigating foundational assumptions. This investigation is followed by an examination of what is concealed or excluded in relation to what is presented. A materialist feminist critique attempts to determine the ideological foundations of a particular set of knowledges and the interests served by the meanings organizing a particular theory. For example, theories which foreground gender and bracket off its link with heteronormativity—the ideological production of heterosexuality as individual, natural, universal, and monolithic—contribute to the construction of (patriarchal) heterosexuality as natural and unchangeable.

To examine the ways in which feminist sociology reproduces the heterosexual imaginary requires a theoretical framework capable of investigating the interests and assumptions embedded within any social text or practice. This mode of inquiry would make visible the frames of intelligibility or the "permitted" meanings in constructions of gender and heterosexuality. More than this, it would connect heterosexuality and interests to a problematic. As Althusser has argued, "A word or concept cannot be considered in isolation; it only exists in the theoretical or ideological framework in which it is used: its problematic" (1982, 253). To determine a text's problematic is to reveal another logic circulating beneath the surface. It appears as the answer to questions left unasked. It is not that which is left unsaid or unaccounted for, but that which the text assumes and does not speak. What is required, then, is a process of analysis capable of inquiring into the power relations organizing the allowed as well as the disallowed meanings in an effort to expose the artificiality of the theories and ideologies organizing the use of particular concepts.

The practice of ideology critique used by Marx (1985, 1986) and rewritten as symptomatic reading by Althusser (1968) has had a significant influence on sociology, most recently in the work of Dorothy Smith (1987, 1990). Ideology critique seeks to demystify the ways in which dominant or ruling-class ideologies are authorized and inscribed in subjectivities, institutional arrangements, texts of ruling, various cultural narratives, and, in this case, feminist sociological theories of gender. Like those taken-for-granted beliefs, values, and assumptions encoded as power relations within social texts and practices, ideology is central to the reproduction of a social order. Because it produces what is allowed to count as reality, ideology constitutes a material force and at the same time is shaped by other economic and political forces. As Althusser theorized it, ideology is the "'lived' relation between [persons] and their world, or a reflected form of this unconscious relation" (1986, 314), or imaginary.

This theory of ideology addresses the meaning-making processes embedded within any social practice, including the production of (social) science. Inherently contradictory, capitalist and patriarchal social arrangements are in a continual state of crisis management. The work of dominant ideologies is to conceal these contradictions in order to maintain the social order. At the same time, however, these breaks in the seamless logic of capitalism and patriarchy allow oppositional social practices and counterideologies to emerge.

Central to a materialist feminist analytic is its critical focus on ideology (see Althusser 1971; D. Smith 1987). Critique is a mode of inquiry which makes use of what is and what is not said in any social text, and theorizes the disjuncture between the two. Of particular importance is the examination of what is missing from the text. What is unsaid can be read symptomatically[2] to reveal the organizing problematic, or how the text raises certain questions while suppressing others. The unsaid of a text also reveals the interests served by what is left out. This understanding of absence speaks to the boundaries established by any conceptual or theoretical framework, which distinguish that which is addressed and that which is constructed as outside the limits of the theory at hand. What is unsaid is as constitutive of the problematic as what is said. Critique is a "decoding" practice which exposes these textual boundaries and the ideologies which manage them, revealing the taken-for-granted order they perpetuate and opening up possibilities for changing it. Materialist feminism then situates these ideologies historically and materially in relation to the division of labor and the relations of production. Finally, critique inquires into the political consequences of theorizing from this site of opposition. This approach attempts to put into crisis those organizing ideologies which naturalize or universalize particular sets of power relations implicated in the production of exploitation and oppression.

Feminist sociology has long made use of critique in order to pressure the discipline for its participation in relations of ruling. Many critical works served as significant interventions in the business-as-usual of sociology, and stand as landmarks from which to extend the reach of feminist theory. Although the following sections of this essay examine feminist sociology for its participation in the heterosexual imaginary, I think it only fair to say that some of the challenges to disciplinary authority by feminists were made at great risk and that much can be learned from these early critiques of sociology. The strategies used by feminist sociologists created the opening for further critical social inquiry and should be considered in their historical and material contexts.

FEMINIST SOCIOLOGY AND THE HETEROSEXUAL IMAGINARY

Feminist sociology has been a powerful force for change since its emergence in the 1960s and 1970s. In addition to its significant contribution to gender studies, feminist sociology has provided a critical evaluation of mainstream sociology. Contesting the foundations upon which the production of sociological knowledges depends, feminist sociologists have provided a profound critique and rewriting of both the theoretical and the methodological assumptions of mainstream sociology (Acker 1973; Bart 1971; Bernard 1973; Deegan 1981; Hacker 1969; Hughes 1975; Long Laws 1979; Millman and Moss Kanter 1975; Oakley 1974; Reinharz 1983, 1984; Schwendinger and Schwendinger 1971; D. Smith 1974, 1975, 1987, 1990; Spender 1985; Stanley and Wise 1983). In a recent essay, Patricia Lengermann and Jill Niebrugge-Brantley (Ritzer 1990) discuss the defining characteristic of feminist sociological theory:

> Feminist sociological theory attempts a systematic and critical reevaluation of sociology's core assumptions in the light of discoveries being made within another community of discourse—the community of those creating feminist theory. (1990, 316)

Central to this description is a reading of feminist sociological theory as responsive to "discoveries" and critical insights emanating from feminist theory and research. Feminist sociological theory has continually pressured the discipline to account for its political investments. In this regard, a key feature of feminist theory in sociology has been its exposure of sociological inquiry as value-laden and implicated in ruling practices. If it is to continue as a vital critical force in the discipline, feminist sociology must attend to contemporary theoretical and political debates, even those which question the problematics of feminist sociology. Recent trends in social thought, especially in what is becoming known as queer theory or lesbian/gay/bisexual/transgendered studies, are challenging the very foundations of feminist sociology and indeed of sociology in general.

Critiques which reveal the implicit perpetuation of a normative heterosexuality require new ways of thinking for feminist sociology. Significant insights for this kind of analysis can also be found, however, in the works of those whose critical sociology questions the assumptions of the discipline. Of particular importance are the contributions of feminist sociologists whose analyses provide the possibility for examining the circulation of the heterosexual imaginary in sociology, even as their work also bears the marks of participating in it.

Two feminist theorists who have been highly influential in this regard are Shulamit Reinharz and Dorothy Smith. Reinharz argues that sociology is a field of study which demonstrates its conservative politics by "reinforc[ing] the current order and its values" (1983, 165) rather than taking into account "specific historical, cultural, ideological" contexts (162). Arguing from a sociology of knowledge perspective, Reinharz asserts the importance of explaining "the relationship between the knowledge produced or accepted in a particular society at any time, and the other dimensions of that society" (163). She is referring to mainstream sociological knowledge, but her critique can be applied as well to feminist sociology. For instance, feminist theories of gender which posit males and females, masculine and feminine, heterosexual and homosexual, as opposites participate in dominant ways of thinking which organize all areas of difference as hierarchical and oppositional binaries. To produce theories of gender which bracket off heterosexuality as a social organizing structure is to "reinforce the current order and its values" by participating in the production of "acceptable" knowledges or ideologies. This closes off the possibility of theorizing the complex ways in which gender is tied to heterosexuality as institutionalized and hegemonic, as organizing the division of labor, and as instrumental to capitalism and patriarchy. If heterosexuality is assumed to be the natural attraction of opposites, somehow outside of social production, it does not require explanation. Feminist theories of gender, as well as common sense and acceptable knowledges, reflect these assumptions. By not considering the "historical, cultural, and ideological" contexts in which gender circulates—the heterosexual imaginary—feminist theories of gender not only are contradictory but also leave heterosexuality as the unsaid on which gender depends.

Gender cannot be simultaneously an achieved status and an organizing concept for a "naturally occurring" heterosexuality. If both gender and heterosexuality are socially produced, then feminist sociology should be engaging with both of them at that level. Heterogender and its corresponding heterosexual imaginary are among those "other dimensions" which can affect the organization of knowledge and the reach of feminist sociology.

Dorothy Smith (1974, 1987, 1990) also takes the discipline to task, in this case for participating in the production of "objectified modes of knowing characteristic of the relations of ruling" (1990, 13) and for using ideas exclusive to a "male social universe" (13).

> The profession of sociology has been predicated on a universe grounded in men's experience and relationships and still largely appropriated by men as their "territory." Sociology is part of the practice by which we are all governed; that practice establishes its relevances. (13)

Smith critiques the disjuncture between women's experience and the prevailing "male" sociological frameworks, raising feminist sociology to a new height by making visible the significance of knowledges pertaining to women which sociology has typically ignored. She theorizes the silences in sociological theory as implicating sociology in male domination and rewrites sociological practice to attend to women's everyday lives.

The neglect of women's everyday lives by sociology is of central concern to Smith, who argues for a sociology from the standpoint of women. This means not only analyzing women's daily lives and practices but also placing women within the larger social context of capitalist and patriarchal relations. Smith aims to explicate the "actual social processes and practices organizing people's everyday experience from a standpoint in the everyday world" (1987, 151). Her argument differs from Reinharz's in that she links the organization of women's lives to political economic dynamics. Of particular importance here is Smith's contribution to a theory of the everyday. In rewriting Marx for a feminist sociology, she opens up the study of the everyday as organized by relations of ruling.

In her contribution to the study of women's invisible labor and everyday experience, however, Smith makes repeated reference to the work of mothering and housework as largely overlooked by social scientists.

> Expanding the concept of work for our purposes requires its remaking in more ample and generous form . . . to include all the work done by women to sustain and service their and men's functioning in the wage relation. (1987, 165)

In her references to mothering and women's domestic labor as enabling the work of men, heterosexuality once again appears as the assumed and unacknowledged structure organizing women's lives as well as the division of labor. Heterosexuality is a natural or universal condition that Smith's theory of gender assumes. Although Smith makes great strides in shifting the starting point of feminist sociology to incorporate a version of ideological critique, her own work reveals a political investment in a heteronormative social order, which by definition maintains the very relations of ruling that she tries to put into crisis.

Feminist sociologists have challenged sociology to account for its "politics"—its investment in practices and knowledges organized hierarchically along lines of power. As can be seen in the work of Reinharz and Smith, these analytical strategies indeed create important conceptual and political openings, but by participating in the heterosexual imaginary they also reproduce some of the very social conditions they seek to interrupt.

In addition to Reinharz and Smith, other feminists have challenged the discipline (Abbott 1992; Lengerman and Niebrugge-Brantley 1990; Maynard 1990; Stacy and Thorne 1985). Their groundbreaking efforts have also paved the way for a critique of feminist sociology. Yet, at the same time they, too, participate in the reproduction of the heterosexual imaginary. In their overview of the contributions of feminist sociology, Lengermann and Niebrugge-Brantley (1990) outline the ways feminists have challenged sociology, beginning with questioning the absence of women and of knowledges related to women in all areas of sociology. This heuristic is particularly important for questioning the circulation of the heterosexual imaginary in feminist sociology.

A particularly important pattern that these authors identify in feminist sociology is the contestation of the andronormative starting point of sociological inquiry, which relegates all other knowledges to the margins and thereby reinforces patriarchal authority and value. For example, studies of mothering, teaching, child care, caregiving, and other aspects of the "domestic sphere" have been either ignored or devalued by mainstream sociology. Patriarchy, however, is not only andronormative; it is also heteronormative. Those aspects of the division of labor which are trivialized and neglected in sociological research and theory are also those practices which count as "women's work" in heterogendered social arrangements. By shifting the focus from gender to heterogender as the primary unit of analysis, institutionalized heterosexuality becomes visible as central to the organization of the division of labor. This shift also reveals the ways in which the heterosexual imaginary depends on an abject "other," which is regulated as deviant. This "other" consists of any sexual practice which does not participate in dominant heterogender arrangements and therefore does not count as legitimate or normal.

When I say that the critical insights of feminist sociologists can be employed to interrogate the heterocentrism of feminist sociology, I am not talking only about the marginalization of lesbian/gay/bisexual knowledges from sociological inquiry, but also about the way in which heteronormative assumptions organize many conceptual and professional practices. For instance, many social science surveys ask respondents to check off their marital status as either married, divorced, separated, widowed, single, or (in some cases) never married. Not only are these categories presented as significant indexes of social identity; they are offered as the only options, implying that their organization of identity in relation to marriage is universal and not in need of explanation. Questions concerning marital status appear on most surveys regardless of relevance, in some cases as "warm-up" questions. The heteronormative assumption of this practice is rarely, if ever, called into question; when it is questioned, the response is generally dismissive. Heteronormativity works in this instance to naturalize the institution of heterosexuality.

For those who view questions concerning marital status as benign, one need only consider the social and economic consequences for those respondents who do not participate in these arrangements, or the cross-cultural variations which are at odds with some of the Anglocentric or Eurocentric assumptions regarding marriage. All respondents are invited to situate themselves as social actors according to their participation in marriage or in heterosexuality as a "natural" and monolithic institution. This invitation includes those who, *regardless of sexual (or asexual) affiliation,* do not consider themselves "single" or defined in relation to heterosexuality and do not participate in these arrangements. Above all, the heterosexual imaginary working here naturalizes the regulation of sexuality through the institution of marriage and state domestic-relations laws. These laws, among others, set the terms for benefits such as tax, health, and housing on the basis of marital status. Rarely challenged except by nineteenth-century marriage reformers and early second-wave feminists (Bunch 1974, 1976; Harman 1901; Heywood 1876; MacDonald 1972; Sears 1977; Stoehr 1979; Wittig 1992), these laws and public policies use marriage as the primary requirement for social and economic benefits rather than distributing resources on some other basis, such as citizenship.

Heteronormative sociology, then, plays its part in what Dorothy Smith has conceptualized as textually mediated social practice.

> Such textual surfaces presuppose an organization of power as the concerting of people's activities and the uses of organization to enforce processes producing a version of the world that is peculiarly one-sided, that is known only from within the modes of ruling, and that defines the objects of its power. (Smith 1990, 84)

To not answer such seemingly innocent or descriptive questions is to become deviant according to sociology's enactment of modes of ruling, which signal to respondents in a variety of ways—from theory to surveys—what counts as normal. Under these conditions, sociology is a political field of study, invested in the reproduction of a heteronormative social order and closed off to struggles over the construction of sexuality and to the exploration of social relations in *all* their layered and complex configurations.

Dorothy Smith's theory of the everyday world as problematic can be particularly useful for investigating the circulation and production of heteronormativity in sociological practice. As a mode of inquiry which begins with people's everyday lives, it illustrates and explains how individual lives are organized by extralocal social arrangements. For instance, to study how institutionalized heterosexuality organizes everyday professional activities in sociology, consider the case of the two nontenured faculty members competing for the same job in a department which was allotted funds for only one. One candidate was a heterosexual man; the other, a lesbian. Two weeks before the final decision is made concerning hiring, the heterosexual man announces his engagement to a local woman and sends out wedding invitations to all members of the department. Well situated within the heterosexual imaginary, members of the department do not view this event in relation to the decision concerning the job but rather respond to it as a celebratory occasion and a chance to have a good time. The effect of this event on the material life of the candidates is never considered.

Weddings, like many other rituals of heterosexual celebration such as anniversaries, showers, and Valentine's Day, provide images of reality which conceal the operation of heterosexuality both historically and materially. In this sense they help constitute the heterosexual imaginary's discursive materiality. When used in professional settings, for example, weddings work as a form of ideological control to signal membership in relations of ruling as well as to signify that the bride and groom are normal, moral, productive, family-centered, good citizens, and, most important, appropriately gendered. (Or I should say "heterogendered"?) Although these patterns pervade the culture at large in everything from Tums commercials to the "Style" section of the *New York Times*—not to mention their prolific use in soap operas and prime-time television—little work has been done to critically examine their reasons for being and their effects.

Other examples abound regarding the heteronormativity or heterocentrism of sociology (e.g., privileging married couples in hiring practices, sanctions against research on lesbian/gay/bisexual/transgendered people, use of heteronormative concepts to describe nonheterosexual relationships, invisibility of nonheteronormative parenting practices), but to critique them is beyond the scope of this essay. Certain questions can be raised here, however, as a way to convey the extent to which heterosexuality remains an unexamined issue in the discipline. Of particular interest from a materialist feminist perspective are the complex ways in which institutionalized heterosexuality helps guarantee that some people will have more class, power, and privilege than others. Sociologists need to ask not only how heterosexuality is imbricated in knowledges, but how these knowledges are related to capitalist and patriarchal social arrangements. How does heterosexuality carry out the project of capitalism and patriarchy ideologically and institutionally? How do so many institutions rely on the heterosexual imaginary? Considering the rising levels of violence and prejudice in U.S. society, how are we to understand the social and ideological controls regulating sexuality? What would a critical analysis of institutionalized heterosexuality reveal about its relationship to divisions of labor and wealth, national and state interests, and the production of social and economic hierarchies of difference? And, finally, how will sociology change if we shift away from a heteronormative or heterocentric sociology through a critique of heterosexuality?

Lengermann and Niebrugge-Brantley point to the contribution of feminist sociology in critiquing the discipline for its lack of social activism. Sociological studies rarely examine how women's lives are organized by dominant ideology and practice, or what role sociological inquiry plays in the maintenance and production of social inequality. Feminist sociologists insist that the discipline be reflexive, accountable for its politics, and actively engaged in reducing any oppressive consequences of its practices.

Reclaiming the critical legacy of feminist sociology not only promises to advance the theoretical reach of sociological inquiry, but also restores the activist orientation of feminist sociology. By questioning the starting point of gender studies while denaturalizing the institution of heterosexuality, feminist sociology once again can become politically reflexive and active in ideological struggle. The following section is a step toward initiating this process through an exploratory examination of contemporary gender texts.

CRITIQUING HETERONORMATIVE GENDER THEORY

Over the past quarter-century, feminist sociologists have made an enormous contribution to the study of gender across all social institutions and categories of analysis, theorizing everything from gender-based power arrangements to sex difference development. Moreover, they have pressured the discipline to account for the ways in which it is implicated in the reproduction of gender oppression and exploitation. As a formidable force for change, feminist sociology, with its counterpart, the Section on Sex and Gender of the ASA, has established itself as one of the largest and most successful areas of inquiry in the discipline.

Feminist sociology, however, is losing its impetus for intervention or for ideological debate. Recent works within areas of inquiry covered by the sociology of sex and gender[3] generally assume a level of agreement on what gender is, how to study it, and why it is important. Gender, family, and introductory sociology textbooks, journal articles, and conference presentations in recent years show little variation in definitions of sex and gender.

A sampling of gender texts within sociology reveals the presence of a dominant framework in gender theory. Sex is typically defined as "the biological identity of the person and is meant to signify the fact that one is either male or female." Gender is described as "the socially learned behaviors and expectations that are associated with the two sexes" (Andersen 1993, 31). The idea of sex as biological and gender as socio-cultural was originally theorized by Oakley (1972) and then again by Gould and Kern-Daniels (1977), and has become the standard for most of sociology. In addition to Margaret Andersen's widely used text, *Thinking About Women,* Laurel Richardson's *The Dynamics of Sex and Gender* describes sex as "the biological aspect of a person" and gender as the "psychological, social, and cultural components . . . an achieved status" (1981, 5). Laura Kramer's *The Sociology of Gender* employs a similar version, arguing that "physically defined categories are the sexes" and that the "system of meaning, linked to the sexes through social arrangment constititues gender" (1991, 1). Likewise, in Clare Renzetti and Daniel Curran's *Women, Men, and Society,* sex is a "biological given . . . used as the basis for constructing a social category that we call gender" (1989, 2). In each case, sex is distinguishable as biology, implying that it is natural, while gender is viewed as learned or achieved. Even in essays offering an overview of the field of gender studies within sociology, gender is perceived as an established concept in a discipline which needs only to take it more seriously as a central category of analysis (Abbott 1992; Maynard 1990; West and Zimmerman 1987).

These patterns suggest that the biological-cultural differentiation of sex and gender has become "normalized" in sociology generally and among feminist sociologists in particular. Although inclusion of gender studies in "legitimate" sociology may be cause for celebration for some, the lack of debate over such a crucial concept as gender—not to mention its companion concept, sex—should be grounds for concern among feminists. Acquiescence to an unexamined gender concept goes against the grain of two of feminist sociology's founding principles—to keep a critical eye on the disciplining of knowledge and on forms of gender bias.

Consider some of the contradictions present in the acceptance of these theories of sex and gender. As Maria Mies (1986) points out, separating sex from gender reinforces the nature/culture binary, opening the study of sex to the domain of science and closing off consideration of how biology is linked to culture. Sex, as a biological category, escapes the realm of construction or achieved status, even though it is "defined" or "constructed." Because we are always engaged in giving meaning to the natural world, how we do that and to what end are questions of major significance. Sex as a category of analysis can never exist outside prevailing frames of intelligibility. It is a concept that is related to ways of making sense of the body, often by those—sociologists and biologists—who have a great deal of authority in the creation of knowledges. As a socially constructed category, sex must be scrutinized in relation to the interests that its definition furthers. That is, as sociologists we need to ask what ends are served by constructing sex as "the division of humanity into biological categories of female and male" (Macionis 1993, 350).

The institution of science and its authority in relation to the production of biological knowledges have far-reaching effects. It is one thing to assert that two X chromosomes produce a female and that an X plus a Y chromosome produces a male. But what happens when introductory sociology texts claim that it is a "hormone imbalance" which produces "a human being with some combination of female and male internal and external genitalia" (Macionis 1993, 351)? What investment or perspective is present in connoting this hormonal and genital configuration as an imbalance? Or, reading the unsaid here, what constitutes balance according to these knowledges?

Clearly, a society of scientifically defined and authorized males and females is considered the "natural" order of things. How, then, do we make sense of cross-cultural difference in the "treatment" of sex variation? For example, the Dine (Navajo) view persons born with a combination of male and female genitalia as the exemplification of complete humanness, not as evidence of some dis-order (Geertz 1973).

Contemporary sex-gender ideology provides limited options for how we organize sexuality, but expanding these options is not simply a matter of attending to marginalized sexualities. Instead, it seems to me that we need to question our assumptions about sex and gender as to how they organize difference, regulate investigation, and preserve particular power relations, especially those linked to institutionalized heterosexuality.

All of the institutions involved in the production of sex as a biological category defined as male or female, where each is distinct and opposite from the other, are participating in reproducing lines of power. Claims that XX is female and XY is male are just that: scientific *claims* about the natural world, authorized by the ruling order and processed through organizing structures which assign meanings based on frames of intelligibility already circulating in the culture at large. What counts as normal and natural or as "fact" comes out of ways of making sense already ideologically invested in the existing social order. Often it closes off our ability to imagine otherwise. Any manifestation which does not fit the facts is rendered abnormal, deviant, or (worse) irrelevant. Consider, for instance, that the same institutions which organize these knowledges also historically neglected the study of women, scientifically justified the inferiority of non-white people, and claimed that social Darwinism was fact. These "findings" were coherent with dominant ways of thinking about sex, race, and class, and worked in their historical moment to legitimize prevailing practices and policies (Gould 1981; Takaki 1990).

Currently, with the rise of the lesbian/gay/bisexual rights movements, many "factual" knowledges concerning gender, sexuality, desire, morality, sex differences, labor, and nationality have been put into crisis. The more these critiques challenge the taken-for-granted concerning sex and gender, the clearer it is that current ways of thinking in sociology do not adequately account for sex variation. This investment in the dominant construction of sex begs the question of what interests are served by the disciplining of knowledge in sociology and what social arrangements that disciplining makes possible. The uncritical participation of feminist sociologists in these knowledges implies the possibility that there exists an investment in "naturalized" social arrangements at the risk of rendering invisible the interests that organize these ideas and benefit from their production. At the present, the dominant notion of sex in feminist sociology depends upon a heterosexual assumption that the only possible configuration of sex is male or female as "opposite sexes," which, like other aspects of the physical world (e.g., magnetic fields), are naturally attracted to each other. Masking the historical relation of sex to history and to heterosexuality is guaranteed by what I have defined as the heterosexual imaginary.

Gender, as the cultural side of the sex-gender binary, is frequently defined by sociologists as either achieved or constructed through a process of "socialization," whereby males and females become men and women attaining opposite and distinct traits based on sex. In addition to appearing in prominent texts and articles on gender, this understanding of gender circulates in introductory sociology texts. For instance, Hess,

Markson, and Stein's *Sociology* asserts that gender is made up of "femininity and masculinity as *achieved* characteristics" but that maleness and femaleness are "*ascribed* traits" (1989, 193). Although this particular text makes reference to gender as variable cross-culturally and historically, its reliance on an unsaid heterosexual dualism implies a static or normative understanding of gender. In addition, this definition of gender illustrates the need for the concept of heterogender as a more appropriate description of the relation between sex and gender. Finally, this explanation does not account for the "necessity" of gender. This theory of gender as an "achieved" status does not address to what ends gender is acquired. Nor does it account for the interests served by ascribing or assigning characteristics based on sex. In other words, this text, as well as many others, does not examine what historical and material arrangements organize or are organized by gender. By foregrounding gender as dependent on the male-female binary, the heterosexual assumption remains unaddressed and unquestioned.

A similiar approach is evident in John Macionis's introductory textbook, where he defines gender as

> society's division of humanity, based on sex, into *two* distinctive categories. Gender guides how females and males think about themselves, how they interact with others, and what positions they occupy in society as a whole. (1993, 352; my emphasis)

Likewise, consider Craig Calhoun, Donald Light, and Suzanne Keller's text, which claims that sociologists conceptualize gender as "nonbiological, culturally and socially produced distinctions between men and women and masculinity and femininity" (1994, 269). Again we see the dependence of theories of gender on the existence of two distinct categories, male and female. This so-called biological configuration is actually the foundation of established definitions of gender. Accordingly, gender is not treated as variable; rather, it is made up of two distinct entities, unquestioned, ahistorical, static, and consequently normative. These understandings serve as the standard in mainstream sociology and legitimize the organization of all other manifestations as deviant, alternative, or nontraditional.

Evident in most conceptualizations of gender is an assumption of heteronormativity. In other words, to become gendered is to learn the proper way to be a woman in relation to a man, or feminine in relation to the masculine. For instance, consider Mary Maynard's argument that "a significant factor in understanding the organisation of society is women's socially constructed difference from men" (1990, 281). Patricia Lengermann and Ruth Wallace state that "exploring the gender institution means looking at the identity of females in relation to males and vice versa . . . in the context of a two-gender social reality" (1985, 3). As Margaret Andersen explains, "Gender refers to the complex social, political, economic, and psychological relations between women and men in society" (1993, 34). These are just a few examples among many that identify gender as a cultural binary organizing relations *between* the sexes. Ask students how they learned to be heterosexual, and they will consistently respond with stories about how they learned to be boys or girls, women or men, through the various social institutions in their lives. Heterosexuality serves as the unexamined organizing institution and ideology (the heterosexual imaginary) for gender.

Most important in these theories is the absence of any concept of heterosexuality as an institutional organizing structure or social totality. The cultural production of behaviors and expectations as "socially learned" involves all social institutions from family, church, and education to the Department of Defense. Without institutionalized heterosexuality—that is, the ideological and organizational regulation of relations between men and women—would gender even exist? If we make sense of gender and sex as historically and institutionally bound to heterosexuality, then we shift gender studies from localized examinations of individual behaviors and group practices to critical analyses of heterosexuality as an organizing institution. By doing so, we denaturalize heterosexuality as a taken-for-granted biological entity; we begin the work of unmasking its operations and meaning-making processes and its links to larger historical and material conditions. Although feminist sociologists have made important contributions to the analysis of the intersection of gender and social institutions, they have not examined the relation of gender to the institution of heterosexuality. By altering the starting point of feminist sociology from gender to heterosexuality, or heterogender, as I have defined it, we focus on one of the primary roots of exploitation and oppression rather than on one of the symptoms.

CONCLUSION

The position I am taking in this essay is not new. It has a long and controversial history in feminist thought. Early second-wave feminists such as the Furies Collective, Purple September Staff, Redstockings (1975), Rita Mae Brown (1976), and Charlotte Bunch (1976) challenged dominant notions of heterosexuality as naturally occurring and argued that instead it is a highly organized social institution rife with multiple forms of domination and ideological control. Adrienne Rich's (1980) article "On Compulsory Heterosexuality and Lesbian Existence" and Monique Wittig's (1992) "The Straight Mind" confronted the institution of heterosexuality head on, asserting that it is neither natural nor inevitable but instead is a contrived, constructed, and taken-for-granted institution or, as Wittig argues, a political regime. Now classics in feminist theory, these works have left a legacy that can be found in knowledges circulating primarily in the humanities.

In relation to other disciplines, sociology is losing ground on these issues as the contest over sexuality and gender escalates in other areas of the social sciences and in the humanities. For example, debates within gay/lesbian theory, cultural studies, and feminist theory in the humanities indicate that a major rethinking of gender and heterosexuality is underway (Butler 1989; de Lauretis 1987; Fuss 1991; Hennessy, 1994–95; Hennessy and Ingraham 1992; Parker et. al. 1992; Plummer 1992; Sedgwick 1990; Seidman 1991, 1992, 1993; Warner 1993; Wittig 1992). Queer theory, as it is now called, has emerged as one of the prominent new areas of academic scholarship. A virtual explosion of books, articles, and special issues has issued from major academic publishers and high-level journals. Yet these new knowledges have been produced primarily within the humanities. Queer theory has been dominated by postmodern cultural theorists such as Butler (1989), de Lauretis (1987), and Sedgwick (1990), who posit heteronormativity and gender as performative aspects of postmodern culture. More recent materialist approaches to rethinking gender and sexuality include the works of Delphy (1980), Evans (1993), Hennessy (forthcoming), George Smith (1988, 1990, 1991), and Wittig (1992), to name a few.

I am arguing in this essay for a return to feminist sociology's political high ground. By "political" I mean all those social, material practices in which the distribution of power is at stake. Attending to these practices requires an internal critique of sociological gender theory for its participation in the very conditions feminism seeks to pressure and for its reproduction of the heterosexual imaginary. In the interests of materialist feminism and the lesbian/gay/bisexual rights movements, I am arguing for an examination of the ways in which feminist sociology's theories of gender contribute to the production and institutionalization of hegemonic heterosexuality. Finally, I am calling for something really queer: a critique of institutionalized heterosexuality as a formal area of inquiry within feminist sociology.

NOTES

1. The phrase *relations of ruling* can be attributed to Dorothy Smith. According to Smith, "'Relations of ruling' is a concept that grasps power, organization, direction, and regulation as more pervasively structured than can be expressed in traditional concepts provided by the discourses of power. I have come to see a specific interrelation between the dynamic advance of the distinctive forms of organizing and ruling contemporary capitalist society and the patriarchal forms of our contemporary experience" (1987, 3).

2. This refers to Louis Althusser's theory of symptomatic reading, which he ultimately attributes to Marx: "A word or concept cannot be considered in isolation; it only exists in the theoretical or ideological framework in which it is used: its problematic. . . . [it] is not a world-view. It is not the essence of the thought of an individual or epoch which can be deduced from a body of texts by an empirical, generalizing reading; it is centred on the *absence* of problems and concepts within the problematic as much as their presence; it can therefore only be reached by a symptomatic reading" (1968, 316).

3. These areas include marriage and family, human sexuality, homosexuality, and any other category which makes use of sex or gender for its secondary level of analysis.

28

A Materialist Feminist Reading of Jeanne Duval

Prostitution and Sexual Imperialism from the Mid-Nineteenth Century to the Present Day

Victoria P. Tillotson

Prostitution has had a long-term and entirely unsatisfactory relationship to capitalism. This seemingly simple claim can be read along any number of axes, interpreted as drawing attention to the status of prostitution as a criminalized, rather than commercial, activity to vaunting prostitution's existence as a result of the ever-changing social desires and demands for affective services mediated by the capitalist entrepreneurial system. While both of these interpretations of my initial claim give a partial story about the complexity of this dysfunction—for the prostitute, anyway—relationship, neither entirely hit the mark. The aporia is in the socially sanctioned refusal to view prostitution as a form of alienated labor, and, more specifically, women's alienated labor. Capitalism benefits greatly on a systemic level from labor such as prostitution, and while claims can be made that prostitutes individually benefit from capitalism in their earning of wages, women on a global level pay dearly for capitalism's minoritizing, stigmatizing, and exploitation of women's affective labor such as prostitution.

Prostitution needs to be removed from the realm of ethical consideration as the subject of potential social and religious reform and recast as an economic issue—reflecting the status of women's sexuality under capitalism. The stigmatizing of prostitution is not merely an issue of superstructural representation, but a result of the interworkings of the capitalist system of global accumulation in conjunction with patriarchy and imperialism. This "threesome" works on a global level to extract surplus value from paid and unpaid women's labor—such as prostitution and housework—while simultaneously yoking various ideologies to mask this exploitation in this process and misrepresent women's labor as a moral issue.

Prostitution is the subject of much academic writing in the humanities, most notably in the arena of literary criticism and theory, which is devoted to the task of debunking cultural myths about "the oldest profession," and most effectively elides the issue of labor in its "reading" of the "text" of prostitution. I cite two recent examples of this elision, which come from two ends of the spectrum of literary criticism: deconstruction and cultural materialism. While seemingly worlds apart in ideology and methodology, these two texts both participate in an aestheticizing of prostitution, which disregards it as an issue of women's sexual labor. My own essay is an attempt to restore the issue of women's labor to the heart of prostitution. This work follows the work of Rosa Luxemburg and, more recently, Gayle Rubin, Maria Mies, Leopoldina Fortunati, and other material feminists in the exploration of the political connection of imperialism, capitalism, and women's labor. My argument is that nineteenth-century European literary representations of prostitution, informed by the dual ideologies of territorial and religious expansionism combined with the intensified industrial capitalism, worked to reinforce and maintain an ideology doubly damaging to women. This ideology, which I term sexual imperialism,[1] supports the extraction of greater and greater surplus value from the labor acquired through women's unpaid affective labor, such as housework and prostitution, alongside the extraction of value from the appropriation and maintenance of colonial economies. While nineteenth- and twentieth-century capitalism upholds the affective value created through women's sexual and domestic labor, it disavows it as labor as such. In other words, prostitution continues to provide the commodity of sexual pleasure that has been established as a social need at the same time that it is denied validity as commodity-producing labor. Furthermore, the ideologies that oversaw representations of prostitution in the nineteenth century create the space for the production of a romanticized, "exotic" service which was utilized by the dominant Judeo-Christian moral ideology, which underscored and secured prostitution's illegitimacy and moral decrepitude.

I look at a series of writings on Jeanne Duval, Créole prostitute and longtime companion to Charles Baudelaire. Duval was indubitably the inspiration for a number of poems in Baudelaire's opus The Flowers of Evil, but she has received little positive attention. Rather, Baudelaire's biographers and critics have sought to demonize and malign Duval as a negative influence on the poet. Contemporary British author Angela Carter re-imagines Baudelaire's relationship with Duval in her 1986 short story "Black Venus" (1985, 111–26). Carter attempts to rewrite the relationship from Duval's point of view, restoring a voice to the historically silenced Duval and critiquing Baudelaire and his biographers for their prejudicial representations of her. I read these texts for their truth value and critique both the "original" representations of Duval and Carter's late capitalist one for failing to foreground the historical conditions that massively overdetermined both Baudelaire's relationship with Duval and Duval's subsequent denigration. These historical conditions are the relations of capitalism and hyperbolic imperialist conquest and domination, at their apex in the mid- to late nineteenth century. These economic and political conditions ushered in the era of exoticism and primitivism that would enjoy a hegemony in the realms of literature and the fine arts well into the twentieth century.

In chapter three of his recent work, Given Time (1992), Jacques Derrida uses the figure of an indiscriminate prostitute to illustrate the relationship between counterfeit money and the "poetics" of gift giving. This chapter, "Counterfeit Money 1: Poetics of

Tobacco," opens with Derrida's brief consideration of Honoré de Balzac's treatise on prostitution, "Splendeurs et misères des courtisanes"—a typically moralistic, nine-teenth-century treatise on the atavism and ethical rectitude of the prostitute—and ends up with a lengthy consideration of another commodity prone as well to the imdemni-fying fetishistic and moralizing rhetorical treatment: tobacco. However, in the shift in this chapter from prostitution to tobacco, women "go up in smoke." The prostitute in the section of Balzac's récit quoted by Derrida functions only as a marker for women's sexual indiscrimination and greed—traits that Derrida obliquely links with tobacco consumption as it is represented in the writings of Charles Baudelaire. Derrida barely considers the prostitute herself and rather hurries along to a more controllable subject of inquiry: the circulation of tobacco within nineteenth-century European literature. To be fair, prostitutes, or women in general, are not the foremost concern of this chap-ter. However, in his elision of women, Derrida unwittingly makes a point which is of great interest to material feminists: despite his best intentions, perhaps, Derrida has brought to the foreground the explicit linking of women, sexuality, imperialism, and capitalism in nineteenth-century fiction. Because Derrida chose to concentrate only on the discursive connection—that is, a connection existing solely on the linguistic and narratological level of the texts in question—between prostitution, luxury goods, and money, he left the material realities of woman living under this ideological construct marooned in the footnotes of his text, replicating the textual and material exiling of women by his literary and theoretical forefathers. He did not see the more critical, and to my mind, more compelling, question of the persistent nineteenth-century ideologi-cal linkage of prostitution and exoticism to women's sexual labor and the politics of imperialism. This persistent linkage of prostitution with the exotic, with the Other, is discursively registered at the level of numerous nineteenth-century fictional writings, medical reports, visual representations, and inflammatory pamphlets—to name just a few cultural representations—and cannot be written off as accidental, happenstance. Rather, it occurs as a result of a particular matrix of economic and political and ideo-logical relationships, which determine and govern the linkage. These material circumstances must be identified, explored, and critiqued because the ideology that oversaw the representation of prostitutes in nineteenth-century Europe continues to influence representations of prostitutes and other sex industry workers today. While prostitution may no longer be romanticized in the same agonistic fashion in which Baudelaire, for example, indulged, prostitutes and other sex workers continue to be subject to both personalized and state violence, denied access to fair legislation, and represented as the source of many of today's urban woes. Furthermore, in perpetuating the spirit of nineteenth-century moral rhetoric, the figure of the prostitute is still ideo-logically utilized by state and Judeo-Christian ideology alike as the ur-complement to the "good" married woman and, critically, is repudiated and denounced as a worker. Her labor is not recognized as such, but rather written off as one more instance of socially necessary affective work which should be done out of "love" and therefore not subject to fair and legitimate wage relations.

Recent attempts by scholars have sought to critique the current representation of prostitution and the gender hierarchy it helps support. One such attempt is a special edition of *Social Text,* edited by Anne McClintock (1993). This volume, written by scholars and activists in conjunction with sex industry workers' own accounts, claims to "collectively explore the difficult frescoes of power, profit, and pleasure that crisscross the commercial sexual body" (1993, 1). While *Social Text* acknowledges that the crucial issue regarding sex work is "a labor issue" (4), no sustained materialist analysis is effected. That is, in no part of this volume is sex work analyzed from the position of the status of women's sexuality and its relationship to capital. Rather, most of the articles focus on the "stigma" of prostitution that "short-circuit[s]" the women's movements and offer personalized accounts of sex worker/client relations that deal only on an individual level with the politics of capitalism. Finally, and crucially, there is no consideration of the relationship between capitalism and patriarchy, which sanctions the continuing colonization of women's bodies and the many values they produce. Instead, *Social Text* "tarts up" the issue of sex work with sexy photos of dominas and cross-dressers, replicating, in a slightly more self-conscious and progressive way, the nineteenth-century exoticization which simultaneously fetishizes the "dark continent" of sex work while performing lip service, so to speak, to a liberatory and demystifying agenda.

This essay hopes to offer a remedy to the present and not-so-distant past aporias that continue to permeate the theorizing of prostitution as a feminist issue. These aporias exist on both ends of the theoretical spectrum concerning prostitution, as I hope to have illustrated with the examples of Derrida and *Social Text:* a reinvigorated form of new criticism and a politically anemic brand of cultural materialism. I hope to ameliorate both positions by combining feminist historical materialist analysis with close textual and rhetorical analyses of past and recent representations of prostitution. In other words, my analysis insists that ideological representations such as Balzac's *Splendeurs,* Derrida's text, and *Social Text* do not operate within a vacuum, but rather are shaped by a number of social forces, the most important of which is the economic, or the base. The conjoining of economic determinants with the political or ideological sector provides the structure which governs the emergence of certain discourses at certain and specific historical moments.

This is certainly clear in the case of the proliferation of travel writings and exotica that achieved prevalence as literary genres during the mid- to late nineteenth century in Europe as a direct response to the ideology and practice of imperial conquest. France, especially, ushered in, with the dual influences of hyperbolic imperial practices and the growing industrial revolution, a taste for the exotic and the strange. The category of the exotic became a novel way to organize and articulate a new relationship between the familiar and the Other, the domestic and the foreign, the desired and the dreaded. Exoticism is particularly evident in the literature of this period, from the travel writings of George Sand and the poetry of Theophile Gautier to Jules Verne's *Les enfants du capitaine Grant,* which literalized the psychic space of exoticism and "brought it home," so to speak, to be commoditized, purchased, and set into circulation as a category of value.

The notion of the exotic is almost inconceivable when disassociated from its perpetual bearer: the image of woman. Long before Freud's pronouncement, woman emerged as the predictable "dark continent" in travel and exploration narrative, simultaneously in need of corrective civilizing procedures and offering the promise of unexplored and potentially dangerous territory, replete with the promise of sexual abundance and fulfillment. The former representation of the exotic woman confirms and positivizes modernity, while the latter inculpates it as a destructive force to "nature." Nonetheless, as Chris Bongie (1991) points out, both representations are bound to the notion that the "dark continent" exists in a pure state of nature, untouched as yet by the redemptive or damaging forces of capitalist modernity. While writers such as Verne partook of the former representation, adopting a paternalistic and condescending attitude toward the subject of their observations, Charles Baudelaire adopted the second and consistently represented woman in his most famous work, *The Flowers of Evil*—as "wild," in need of domestication, and unabashedly exotically arousing. Baudelaire enacted what could be termed a self-conscious textual paternalism toward the image of the exotic woman—the woman who guides his anguished erotic exploration in *The Flowers of Evil*.

While Baudelaire's so-called exoticism is the subject of many critical texts, it is obsessively treated as an aesthetic, rather than political, issue. Even Joseph E. Nnadi (1980), who claims that his work on Baudelaire's exoticism considers it strictly outside the parameters of the poet's relationship with the "Madone noire" Jeanne Duval, manages to reinscribe Baudelaire's exoticism and primitivism within strictly aesthetic and psychologistic terms. Thus Nnadi states:

> In a study on Baudelaire's tropical exoticism one acquires little new knowledge about the real tropical world. Rather, the reader has the impression of penetrating further and further into the soul, the sensibility and the thought of Baudelaire. This poet-critic is the perfect example of the artist who, as with his subject, "never goes out of himself." (1980, 141)

Although Nnadi claims to restore a fuller sense of the term "exoticism" to the work done on Baudelaire, he, too, fails to consider it as anything but an emotional or literary issue.

On a material level, Baudelaire was the economic and emotional partner of Jeanne Duval for twenty-five years. Duval became Baudelaire's mistress in 1842, when Baudelaire was twenty-one, and subsequently became the inspiration of the "Black Venus Cycle" of *The Flowers of Evil*. The poems attributed to Duval include "Sed Non Satiata," "The Jewels," "Of Her Hair," "The Dancing Serpent," "Exotic Perfume," "The Cat," and "I Worship You . . ." In François Porché's biography of Baudelaire (1928), Duval is introduced initially as Baudelaire's "Black Venus," a mulatto with an "undeveloped mind," an "obtuse intellect," who had only "instinctive knowledge" at her disposal to ingratiate herself to the young man with a checkbook. Furthermore, Porché represents Duval in characteristically racist terms, describing her motions as "the movements of a monkey," her character as "bestial," and herself as a "vulgar half-caste" (73). Porché repeatedly claims that Duval had a negative effect on Baudelaire:

> [c]onfronted with Mlle. Duval, endlessly retailing [sic] her silly tittle-tattle, Baudelaire began to suffer cruelly from a degrading companionship: before this dark body, naked save for its jewels, which in the firelight threw an immense shadow on the wall, like that of the Genius of Evil stretched over the world, the poet bowed his head and worshipped. (79)

Porché's narrative bears all the markers of exoticism, from the transvaluation of skin color onto Duval's consciousness to Baudelaire's worshipful posture in deference to the Great Unknown. He outwardly blames Baudelaire's relationship with Duval for Baudelaire's later insanity and claims that Duval was ruthlessly money-hungry, would spitefully burn Baudelaire's manuscripts, and was too indolent and animalistic to understand the poems Baudelaire wrote for her (133). Finally, in another work he consistently characterizes Baudelaire's relationship with Duval as merely sexual and perverse in order to better deny Baudelaire's evident long-term fascination with and affection for his "Black Venus":

> In Jeanne's flesh he found what he dreamed of—but this word "flesh" only coarsely and badly expresses the powerful and subtle bundle of his instincts—he found all that his being then called his vows: to know the opposite of the "Beautiful and Good," the opposite of Decency, the opposite of healthiness, the opposite of the norm. (1930, 75)

Duval fit the image of exoticism and primitivism but did not conform to nineteenth-century physical and symbolic norms or ethical codes of behavior. Physically, as a "quarteroon"—French racial nomenclature for a person of mixed ethnic background—Duval did not fit the norm of white continental bourgeois subjectivity. On the level of occupation, Duval's labor as a small-time vaudeville actress and prostitute rendered her susceptible to a matrix of degenerate assumptions about her sexual voracity, atavism, and health. Duval did have syphilis, but unlike her syphilitic counterpart Baudelaire, the disease served as a marker of her prostitution, considered a form of societal pollution and perversity, rather than as an unfortunate individualized affliction. The color of Duval's skin, "a dark complexion, yellow rather than black," according to Porché, sealed her image as an exotic dangerous object in need of moral and psychological redemption. Another biographer, Pierre Flôttes, succinctly summarizes Baudelaire's critics and biographers' attitude toward Duval when he refers to her as "a deformed [or twisted] woman of color" (1992, 109).

Other writers have been more generous to Duval, but most relegate her to the realm of the unimportant, claiming, for example, that what Baudelaire cherished in Duval was her ability to reconnect him with a past constructed during his voyage to Mauritania in 1841, shortly before he met her. This past is spatialized into the image of the tropics and is represented by the infiltration of exotic images which permeate his work thereon. Thus Duval has been recast in the role of a convenient vessel into which Baudelaire poured and contained his erotic and cultural obsessions. Recently, others have attempted to redefine Baudelaire's relationship to Duval. Marc-A. Christophe (1990, 428–39) has gone far to "rescue" the figure of Duval from the prejudicial rhetoric of Baudelaire's many biographers and critics. Investigating Baudelaire's correspondence to elucidate his relationship with Duval, Christophe found that Baudelaire exploitatively used Duval for the purpose of extorting money from his mother (1990, 431). This discovery points out that at least one of the assumptions about Duval was in fact the work of the bankrupt and money-hungry Baudelaire. Regarding the relationship itself, however, Christophe is inclined to impose an Oedipal hermeneutic in which Duval is linked to Baudelaire as a substitute for his largely absent mother. Christophe thus characterizes the triad of mother, son, and lover as a "love/hate relationship [in which] these women crystallized the two components of Baudelaire's personality, the 'satanic' and the 'angelic'" (1990, 430). Within this overdetermined Judeo-Christian symbolic structure, Duval emerges as the "dark angel" Baudelaire employed in his money-making "schemes." Christophe replicates, with an economic twist, the self-same prejudicial rhetoric from which he claims to have saved Duval. In other words, he fails to provide a new understanding of Baudelaire's relationship with Duval. For one, Christophe insists on psychologically polarizing Baudelaire's life. Furthermore, while he relieves Duval of responsibility for her own representation as atavistic, he does little to explain her influence on Baudelaire and instead relegates their relationship to the saccharine realm of "together[ness] in the same love of beauty" (1990, 438). Despite, perhaps, his best intentions, Christophe aestheticizes this relationship and so partakes in the literalization to which Baudelaire's biographers resort. This inattention to material and ideological circumstances glosses the imperial practices and exoticist ideology that inform and complicate Baudelaire's relationship with Duval. Lastly, Christophe all but denies Duval's economic status as a "kept woman" and denies that there is nothing in this relationship but a normative heterosexual contract based on mutuality of feelings.

In keeping with the dominant tropes of these writings on Duval—the structuring dyads of disease and passion, dread and desire, Other and same—Angela Carter's recent rewriting depicts Baudelaire literally and figuratively treating Duval as an exoticized fetish despite her frequent protestations. In Carter's representation, Duval is a far cry from Porché's villainous, greedy whore who burned Baudelaire's manuscripts, but rather a simple woman who "ached, raged and chafed under [Baudelaire's verse] because his eloquence denied her language" (Carter 1985, 120). Not cruel, but a dispossessed "Empress . . . in exile," Carter re-imagines Duval as a disinherited colonial subject. Carter brings Duval's genealogy to the foreground of her story and mocks its relevance to Baudelaire as the link with a utopian past. Baudelaire emerges in Carter's rewriting as a prototypical nineteenth-century, imperial exoticist who "pretend[s] [Duval] has a fabulous home in the bosom of a blue ocean" and who will "force a home on her whether she's got one or not" (1985, 113). Duval may not really be all that different from Baudelaire, Carter implies, but Baudelaire will fabricate the myth of cultural difference to match his exoticist interests.

For example, Carter portrays Baudelaire as an indefatigable collector of exotic goods. His Paris apartment is full of what he believes to be "authentic" Oriental treasures. In reality, Carter tells us, these goods are fakes sold to him by dishonest dealers. The prize of his collection is, of course, the spectacle of Duval dancing, "sulking sardonically through Daddy's sexy dance" (1985, 114). The narrator of "Black Venus" tells the reader that Duval is Baudelaire's most precious *objet d'art*, but that he does not realize or rather categorically denies that Duval's origins are not authentically exotic. They are *colonial,* themselves created by Europe's "indefatigable" quest to conquer and collect territories, and as such are in fact not "authentically" distinguishable from Baudelaire's own: "[t]he colony—white, imperious—had fathered her" (1985, 119). In Carter's rewriting, it is not Duval who scams and impoverishes Baudelaire, but the art dealers who sell him "fakes." Baudelaire's poverty, she suggests, is the product of his "indefatigable" quest for exotic goods and services. Thus, Baudelaire "buys" Duval's identity as a "fake" authentic West Indies subject, whom he believes is "made of a different flesh than his." His longing for the authentic transforms the culturally orphaned Duval into a "real" spectacle of the islands. The model for Baudelaire's metaphysical desire for authenticity in Duval is the material process of European colonization, which robs peoples and cultures of their land, customs, and possibility of a self-determined future. Colonization renders these peoples "fakes"—peoples who have "authentic" claims to certain cultural—via genealogical—associations and material history are denied the geography and psychical space that would substantiate and validate those cultural claims. In other words, the demand for authenticity at the heart of colonial exoticism in nineteenth-century Europe governs the production and dissemination of "fakes."

The displacement Carter foregrounds in Baudelaire's activities—from collector of things to collector of the image of a woman, or voyeurism—is attested to in many nineteenth-century texts, from Laure Adier's *La vie quotidienne dans les maisons closes, 1830–1930* and J. K. Huysmans *A rebours,* to the writings of the Goncourt brothers and Zola. This voyeurism is expressed by an intensified interest in "les maisons closes" or brothels, and more specifically in the figure of the prostitute herself. For Emily Apter, "these slippages sharpen our understanding of how woman, and most specifically, the *fille de noce* came to be fetishized as an erotic commodity within the fin-de-siècle Imaginary" (Apter 1991, 43). From commodities to women, exotica to prostitutes, Apter claims that these displacements signal a crisis in bourgeois male subjectivity, and that the prostitute provides the bourgeois male with the opportunity for the exercise of total power and control (59). However, the obsession with prostitutes is much more than an issue of male control over the trafficking of things.[2] Rather, the fetishization of prostitutes' erotic commodities is a product of the metropole's adoption of the logic of imperial acquisition and colonization of the peripheries. The model of accumulation adapted for colonial economies directly informed the "collectomania" and erotomania of the nineteenth-century narrative. The relegation of the series of narrative displacements to individualized and psychologized motives ("male control") eradicates the role of capitalist and imperial division and conquest which overdetermined the metropolitan relationship to the exotic.

Baudelaire's radical disavowal of mutual origins is one of the most distinguishing features of Carter's construction of his character. Carter's Baudelaire stubbornly imagines Duval as "the perfect stranger"—utterly alien and therefore not bound to him and his country by imperialistic land acquisition and colonial intermarriage. Carter suggests that Baudelaire is just as culturally dispossessed as Duval, that in fact "neither has a native land" (1991, 113), but Baudelaire enslaves Duval in an imaginary home on a "lovely, lazy island where the jewelled parrot rocks on the enamel tree" and where they will "live together in a thatched house with a veranda overgrown with flowering vine" and "sway in our hammock" (112). Furthermore, Duval's actual genealogy matters little to Baudelaire, Carter tells us: "[h]er *pays d'origine* [is] of less importance than it would have been had she been a wine" (118). Baudelaire's willful ignorance of Duval's history creates the possibility of imagining Duval's "home" as anything but a French colony.

In "Black Venus" Duval, however, has a force that exists outside the narrative frame suggested by the historical representation of her relationship with Baudelaire. Unlike the "stupid," "bestial," and "twisted" Duval of Baudelaire's biographers and critics, Carter's Duval is imbued with an interior consciousness that talks back to Baudelaire's incessant romanticization and fetishization of her body, sexuality, and origins. In response to Baudelaire's romantic imaging of her "home," Duval thinks:

> Go, where? Not *there!!* The glaring yellow shore and harsh blue sky daubed in crude, unblended colors squeezed directly from the tube, where perspectives are as abrupt as a child's painting, your eyes hurt to look. Fly-blown towns. All there is to eat is green bananas and a brochette of rubber goat to chew. (Carter 1991, 112)

In contrast to Baudelaire's "fine" portrait of the imaginary island, Duval impatiently offers a "child's drawing" which hurts the eyes in more than one way. Carter sharply contrasts Duval's empirical realism with Baudelaire's imaginative primitivism and offers a "true" portrait of a colony. Furthermore, Carter's Duval refuses to participate in Baudelaire's fantastic journey and matter-of-factly calls his bluff: "No! . . . Not the bloody parrot forest! Don't take me on the slavers' route back to the West Indies, for godsake! And let the cat out before it craps on your precious Bokhara!" (1991, 113). While Baudelaire is "off in the clouds," Duval is "down to earth," crankily demanding attention to material things, such as the potential ruin of an expensive carpet. Duval introduces and forces the grotesque body that defecates as an antidote to the self-contained bodies which sway in the hammock of Baudelaire's portrait. The intrusion of the material serves to abruptly displace the exotic space with the domestic, and underlines the fact that the ideology which governs the desire for individual collection and coincides shockingly with that which potentiates and governs global accumulation.

Little work has been done on Carter's fiction to date, and only one scholarly article has been written specifically on "Black Venus." In "Blond, Black and Hottentot Venus," Jill Matus explores "Black Venus" as a subversive example of the Venus mythology (1991, 467–76). Matus draws attention to the iconoclastic features of Carter's text and maps out the ideological opposition between Baudelaire's mythical construction of Duval and Carter's representation of her as a simple "good for nothing black woman." While Matus makes mention of the imperial emphasis in Carter's narrative, she does not foreground it or discuss "Black Venus" as an imperial critique. Rather, for Matus the historical fact of imperialism is no more than a convenient topos into which Carter inscribes and subverts Duval's putative history. Furthermore, Matus makes no mention of the different economic models described in Carter's text as embodied by Duval and Baudelaire, which inform what I see as the basis for the text's unexplored potential of creating extended imperialist critique. In other words, I am not suggesting that an imperial critique should be replaced or superseded by a materialist economic analysis, but rather that the imperialist ideological critique cannot be understood without a more nuanced and foregrounded economic consideration. As it stands both Carter's and Matus's texts are missing crucial economic parameters, although Carter herself draws attention to competing economies within Baudelaire and Duval's relationship, economies that circulate around differing notions of what constitutes sexual and affective labor.

Carter's narrative itself must be critiqued for its role in perpetuating the circumscription of Baudelaire's relationship with Duval within a colonial or exoticist fantasy. Carter lays a claim to represent the "authentic" voice of Duval. This plea for authenticity is problematic on a number of levels, and the question must be raised about what historical circumstances have occurred in the last hundred years to account for the possibility of Carter's "authentic" rewriting of Duval's history. On an axiomatic level this can be articulated by the following question: What claims can a white, middle-class British author writing in the heyday of Thatcherism have on the life of a culturally and economically dispossessed woman of color? Carter ameliorates Baudelaire's fetishization of Duval by offering an alternative reading of their relationship, but ultimately constructs another, albeit late capitalist, fantasy in which Duval figures as the exoticized "native" intellectual with a clear understanding of what it means to be exploited. The material figure of Duval should in no way be written into an imperial scene to begin with, and that imperial romance with which Baudelaire imbued his writing on Duval provides precisely the formula into which Baudelaire and his biographers first inscribed the figure of Duval, and which Matus and Carter herself have mistakenly repeated and replicated by adopting the terms of textual imperial analysis. In other words, the textual imperial critique adopted by Matus and Carter in their efforts to rectify and revivify the figure of Duval is nothing more than the flip side of Baudelaire's adoption of the ideology, which supports the fantasy of an exoticist romance that originally informed his relationship with Duval.

However, Carter's representation differs from Baudelaire's and his biographers insofar as she introduces a level of economic analysis which is absent from their texts. For Porché and Flôttes, for example, Duval's prostitution is strictly an ethical, rather than an economic, issue. The recourse to ethics legitimates the vituperative moralizing that characterizes their writing on Duval. Regarding Duval's initial meeting of Baudelaire, Porché remarks, "This by no means austere young woman must without a doubt have cut short the addresses the poet was paying her: for she was eager to come to a conclusion—that is, to find out if this individual who moved only in a maze of incomprehensible politeness was a serious customer" (1928, 72). Carter, on the other hand, heuristically suggests that one of the problems with Duval's historical treatment is that she operates in a different economy than Baudelaire. Carter engages Duval's labor in prostitution to illustrate this difference: "Jeanne never had this temperament of the tradesperson" (1985, 122), "[w]hen she slept with anyone else but Daddy, she never let them pay" (114). Carter suggests that Duval did not recognize in herself the figure of the exotic, so that she "squandered her capital" and offered sexual services without demanding compensation. Rather, Duval is "kept," according to Carter, but not in the usual understanding of the term: she is kept "off the streets," exploited within the space of domesticity rather than the public sphere. Duval is not expressly paid for her sexual services, although Carter claims that Baudelaire "allocat[es] her the occasional lump of hashish" (113). She is alienated from her own labor while surplus value in the form of an affective commodity is extracted through the trafficking in affective values such as sexual pleasure—which patriarchy demands of women in its support of capitalist accumulation.

Thus in Carter's rewriting, Duval functions not as a prostitute but as a sexual slave to Baudelaire; not an inept whore but an exploited woman who "did not feel she was her own property" (1985, 123). Carter tells us that Duval's misrecognition of herself as a prostitute, "seller and commodity in one," is the result of her colonial upbringing, during which she experienced firsthand simple economic transactions based upon the exchange of commodities for commodities: barter. Carter's Duval has a purchase on the history in which women's labor and commodity production has no monetary value. She understands commodities, rather, in terms only of their relational value.

Furthermore, Carter states that Duval exchanges her labor and herself from a pre-capitalist, "peripheral" economic model within the metropole, an economy which is based on the logic of simple gift exchange. Duval's economy can be termed, *tout court*, a "Maussian" economy, and as such threatens to disrupt traditional notions of value and exchange by disregarding the capitalist insistence on the third term of exchange: money (Mauss 1967). Duval's alternative economy is also complicated by her own labor within capitalism, sexual labor which is not recognized as producing surplus value for accumulation. Duval's inability to be compensated for her sexual labor can be attributed not to a mishandling of resources, as Carter insists, but rather as tantamount to the continuing exploitation of women's bodies as they exist as natural resources within patriarchal capitalism. The problem with Carter's analysis of Duval's "primitive" economy is that it unspecifies women's labor as a commodity from others, and focuses on the cultural system of circulation which influences, but does not supersede, capitalist accumulation as the dominant economic paradigm of nineteenth-century Europe. Carter's Duval operates in a principally gift- or commodity-based economy that *theoretically,* or idealistically, may threaten capital's hegemony but is ultimately subsumed under the force of capitalism in the same way that value produced in the colonies is introjected into the metropole.

In a gift-based economy, potlatch—extravagant gift-giving—is an "agonistic type of total prestation" by which hierarchies of nobles are established in certain Indian tribes (Mauss 1967, 5). Its logic is one of total expenditure, in which one must give back more than one receives. Mauss claims this "total prestation" is the oldest economic system, from which contemporary gift exchange arose (68). It is a less "prosaic" economy, in which something other than utility (exchange value) is circulated, and thus, Mauss claims, is directly opposed to a capitalist mode of production. He states "[i]t is only our Western societies which quite recently turned man [sic] into an economic animal" (74), and says that employers are responding to the loss of many forms of "irrational expenditure" by

> making men [sic] work . . . by reassuring them of being paid loyally all their lives for labour which they give loyally not only for their own sakes but for that of others. The producer-exchanger feels now as he always has—but this time he feels it more acutely—that he is giving something of himself, his time and his life. Thus he wants recompense, however modest, for this gift. And to refuse him is to incite him to laziness and lower production. (75)

Western capitalist societies capitalize on the logic of gift-giving to ensure loyalty from workers. But rather than being subversive of capitalism, this logic fits into its mechanism. Mauss's critique is naive insofar as it excises the place of capitalist accumulation in the history of territorial and sexual imperialism. Primitive or colonial economies have been brought into the service of capitalist accumulation through the practice of imperial conquest and colonization. Furthermore, Maria Mies has shown that the metropole's attitudes toward the colonies reflect careful capitalist cost-benefit analysis and calculations in its assimilation of surplus value, extracted from primitive and colonial economies (Mies 1986).

Arjun Appadurai has recently expanded on the work of Mauss. In his introduction to *The Social Life of Things,* Appadurai outlines a theory of economics based on the dynamics of commodity exchange and value (Appadurai 1986). The traditional Marxian conception of a commodity is simply an external object that satisfies some form of human desire. Engels amended this definition of commodity by drawing attention to a commodity as a historical product of labor produced for others and transformed through "value-form" into a commodity (67). Based on these formulations, Appadurai pithily states that a commodity is "*anything intended for exchange*" (9). Rather than widening the gap in economic theories between commodity-based theories of exchange and gift-based theories of exchange, Appadurai treats both as convergent under the rubric of commodity circulation. And rather than foreground a Marxist insistence on the primacy of production of products for exchange, Appadurai states that a commodity-based economics means looking at the commodity potential of all things rather than searching fruitlessly for the magic distinction between commodities and other sorts of things. It also means breaking significantly with the production-dominated Marxian view of the commodity and focusing on its total trajectory from production, through exchange/distribution, to consumption (13).

Appadurai heuristically proposes that commodity exchange is not significantly different from other kinds of exchange. This reading is consistent with Carter's construction of Duval, who de-differentiates between economic systems of commodity exchange. Commodity exchange for Appadurai constitutes a "politics," that is, a system that "links value and exchange in the social life of commodities" (1986, 57). This relation of commodities is political insofar as it "signifies and constitutes relations of privilege and social control . . . and the tensions between these two tendencies" (57). Implicit in this construction is the creation and discrimination of certain forms of desire and demand for commodities, which Appadurai defines as neither a mechanical response to the structure and level of production nor a bottomless natural appetite.

> It [demand] is a complex social mechanism that mediates between short- and long-term patterns of commodity circulation. Short-term strategies of diversion [a sign of creativity or economic or aesthetic crisis] . . . might entail small shifts in demand that can gradually transform commodity flows in the long run . . . long-established patterns of demand act as constraints on any given set of commodity paths. (41)

For Appadurai, demand is not structurally managed by capital production; thus it does not enjoy a direct and necessary relationship to the circulation of products. Nor is it "natural," unmediated by social relations. Nor does Appadurai link the "politics" of commodity exchange to demand, because in certain instances demand subverts the direct and necessary relationship between value and exchange, so that value and price (exchange value) become "unyoked." Appadurai relegates demand to the realm of "complex social mechanism[s]" which his account of commodity circulation can only tangentially explain. Demand has to do with the *context* of commodity exchange; that is, "the variety of *social* arenas, within or between cultural units" (15). It is not infrastructural, but exists in relation to external events. There exists a clear relation of necessity between "cultural units" and demand for certain commodities.

The problem, as noted before, with commodity-based theorizing exemplified by Mauss, Appadurai, and, more distantly, Carter, is that it separates the commodity from its relationship to capitalist value and, more importantly, the alienated labor of the worker who produced it. In other words, the production and process of capitalist accumulation is lost within this model of exchange, and with it, capitalism's relationship to the systems of patriarchy and imperialism. Certainly, "cultural units" such as desire and demand oversee the emergence of certain types of commodities at certain historical moments—the exotic in mid-nineteenth-century Europe, for example—but these "social arenas" are not the only determinants. Cultural units are linked to capitalist accumulation by relations of necessity, which include the historical mode of production and imperialist conquest and expansion. Furthermore, the "diversion" of commodities cannot be written off as the pathologized "function of irregular desires and demands," but rather operate at a systemic level within the dual modalities of capitalism and imperialism. For a material feminist critique of the labor theory of value, commodity-based theorizing excludes women's labor and the processes of production integral to capitalist accumulation. Furthermore, it ignores the role of demand insofar as it mediates the historical valuation of certain commodities. Not all commodities have an equal purchase, so to speak, on value at equal points in history.

In a footnote to *The Gift* (1967, 93), Mauss proffered the suggestion that the definition of money as it is used his discussion of primitive economies be widened. It should include material stuff, "precious objects," "condensed wealth," even *"lifegivers,"* he notes.[3] Thus money is recast into an alternative mode and is subsumed by the commodity itself. The last definition explicitly links money—the expanded form of the commodity—as a category of value to women's labor and the products of their bodies. The story about simple commodity exchange becomes much more complicated when the commodities being exchanged are women. As Rubin (1975) notes in "The Traffic in Women," exchange becomes a matter of continuing kinship relations, a process that typically excludes women. The historical trafficking of women inaugurated the bifurcated gender hierarchy that elevates men to the level of sexual subjects in control of the objects of their exchange: women. Under capitalism, this trafficking takes on more complicated forms, the most evident evident of which is the continued delegitimation of women's labor and the products of its labor. Leopoldina Fortunati (1995) has shown that capitalist ideology operates hand in hand with patriarchy to make women's labor appear valued, while the brute material reality is that it is not. As Thanh-dam Truong notes, "[t]he effect of such ideological constructs [biology, heterosexual love] is the concealment of the value of specific types of sexual labor which, in turn, facilitates the process of accumulation from such labor" (1990, 91). Instead, Fortunati argues that women's labor, such as prostitution, which does not produce an obvious surplus value, works in conjunction with unpaid housework to compensate for a sexual deficit in the domestic realm. More crucially, because the female housewife's (and prostitute's) relationship to capital is mediated by the male worker, the labor produced by both in what she calls the "reproductive" sector creates a value which has to appear as a nonvalue in order to be subsumed to the "higher" sector of recognized commodity production (Fortunati 1995, 20). Thus, this reproductive labor is not recognized as part of capitalist production and is therefore not subject to fair wages or legitimacy. For "who are prostitutes but housewives who go out for an evening job?" (Truong 1990, 51). Furthermore, reproductive labor falls on the side of the private sector, which ideologically operates in contradistinction to the public, "social" sector of wage labor. Reproductive labor is constructed to appear natural," "personal," and motivated by "love," and therefore is not considered wage labor.

Capital's ideological recourse to affect and the notion of "personal services" works to mask socially sanctioned exploitation of this type of women's labor. Patriarchy works to secure this misrepresentation in its dual servicing of capitalism through the realm of women's unpaid women's work within the family as mothers and wives, and in reinforcing women's position as low-wage workers within the labor market itself through sexual stereotyping. Because personal services such as housework and sexual service are considered to possess only immediate use value and not *value* proper they immediately reenter circulation and exchange via their consumption by the waged male worker. Thus, Fortunati argues, they are considered to provide part of the subsistence of the waged male laborer and not to contribute to the greater production of wealth (1995, 54).

However, although Fortunati extends and adds consistency to Marx's notorious inattention to sexual labor, she eventually falls into the same trap as Marx insofar as she repudiates the production of a surplus value in sexual labor. While Fortunati critiques Marx for his "redemptive" attitude toward prostitution and his refusal to include it in his class analysis, she ultimately excludes it as well. Prostitution, Fortunati argues, following Marx, does not contribute to the production or retention of wealth because it consumes a portion of the waged laborer's stored wealth. However, the services are bought with the goal of producing a commodity, she admits, which ostensively would ameliorate its initially consumptive effect. This commodity—sexual pleasure—adds to the subsistence of the worker. And the goal aimed for in the purchasing of a commodity *immediately* is sexual pleasure, as noted, and more distantly the continuation of the laborer's capacity to labor, his labor power. Fortunati unfortunately also takes a "redemptive" stance toward prostitution—though interestingly, not housework, which she seems to unconditionally valorize—and replicates Marx's definition of productive labor as labor which *directly* is transformed into capital. However, she levels a critique against Marx for not adequately accounting for the legitimacy of "reproductive"—domestic and sexual—labor in its capacity to produce capital, by drawing attention to the fact that the value produced by this labor is regarded only as a use value to be exchanged for another, and not a value proper (1995, 54). Thus this type of women's labor continues to be unrecognized by capital as labor, but recognized and legitimized only as a nonproductive affective "activity" (53).

Moreover, this type of "activity" is ideologically represented as "natural," and its status as "natural" identifies it within the taxonomy of natural resources. The housewife and the prostitute produce not only immediate use values, but enable the reproduction of labor power that can then be sold in the labor market. However, because women's labor is continuously represented as personal and natural it appears as a resource to be exploited. The logic which governs imperialism can be seen as an accumulation theory of natural resources (Mies 1986, 17), and the status of women under capitalism bears the same relationship that colonies bear to the continent (25). Thus, Mies writes, it is not that women have a colonial status, but that the colonies have a woman's status under capitalism (25). Rosa Luxemburg's analysis of capitalist accumulation accounts for the necessary relationship between capitalism and imperialism (Luxemburg 1972). Imperialist expansion is crucial to the expansion of capitalism in its creation of a "third market." Luxemburg writes, "[I]mperialism is the political expression of the accumulation of capital in its competitive struggle for what remains still open of the non-capitalist environment" (425). While Luxemburg can rightly be faulted for the voluntaristic bent in her accumulation theory, her model is an important corrective to Marx's assumption that capitalism is a closed system because, as Mies notes, it opens up the possibility for an expanded economic analysis that includes previously discounted nonwaged labor by women and in the colonies (Mies 1986, 34). This inclusion provides the groundwork for understanding the relations of necessity that exist between patriarchy and capitalism. For each system works through the logic of imperialism: to appropriate, exploit, and exclude women's labor and simultaneously rob women of the possibility of managing their own representations.

Women's sexual labor continues to be unfairly represented by the essentializing and individuating categories of love and duty. The figure of Jeanne Duval is a trenchant reminder of the pervasiveness of these ideologies and the seeming permanence of the patriarchal capitalist economy, which legitimates its exploitative accumulation through the renunciation of women's affective labor as labor. Emphasizing the material production of the discourses that organize and control the continuing representation of prostitution and other unrecognized forms of women's labor is crucial to revealing the inauthenticity of these representations. The future of all women workers under capitalism depends on the continued collective efforts by feminists and prostitutes to intervene in current prejudicial discourses and practices, such as legislation and the criminal system, which oversee the continued obfuscation of the labor in prostitution and other affective work. Until prostitution is recognized as legitimate wage labor and the stigma lifted, the taxonomy of misrepresentations galvanized by nineteenth-century capitalism and imperialism will continue to influence the many ways in which prostitution is represented. Until liberation is achieved, women as a class will continue to pay dearly for the current and future forms of sexual imperialism.

NOTES

1. According to Thanh-dam Truong (1990, 56), this term was coined by the Japanese Women's Christian Temperance Union in 1973, during the time of massive protests in Japan and South Korea against Japanese sex tourism. My adoption of the term reflects the belief that prostitution does not exist in a vacuum, but is shaped by market relations which continue to maximize the difference between prostitutes and "other women" and simultaneously ignore the fact that sexual services operate under the aegis of exchange relations.

2. This reference is to Gayle Rubin's seminal article, "The Traffic in Women" (1975).

3. It is necessary to point out that Mauss's redefinition itself is determined by a complex set of ideological and historical facts and not just ludic linguistic reform. *The Gift* was written shortly after World War I and the massive expansion and reorganization of empires that accompanied it. The age of imperialism refigured and redynamized space as historically and economically significant, and this re-evaluation had a significant impact upon the boundaries, valuation, and expansion of lanuage as well. Discursively speaking, imperialism offers the image of transgression of boundaries, or de-territorialization. In the spirit of the avant-garde aesthetic of transgression of linguistic and discursive boundaries, Mauss refigures the definition of money to include all forms of exchange, all stuff of value.

29

Motherhood in Crisis

Women, Medicine, and State in Canada, 1900–1940

Cynthia R. Comacchio

Motherhood has historically constituted the beating heart of women's identities. Images, ideals, discourses, and definitions have varied with time and place. At no time during the past century, however, have women been delimited in "nature," ability, or socioeconomic position without reference to the primacy of the maternal: the twentieth century dawned as "the Century of the Child." Maternalism became the central strategy of a politics of regeneration, emerging from pervasive discourses of anxiety grounded in the rapid, intensive, disruptive socioeconomic changes perceived to be corroding the very framework of the industrial-capitalist order.[1]

The objective reality of motherhood is relationship: the biological, emotional, social, economic bonds that exist between women, men, and children. Even on the level of ideas and the ideal, motherhood is configured always in relation to fears, aspirations, and projections specific to time and context, and subject to the intersections of class, race, age, and regional culture. The so-called "new woman" of modernity was conceived of and constructed primarily as a "new mother."[2] And what was new about her was the specific locus of her reconfiguration. For the new woman/new mother was the ergonomic design of emergent "scientific experts," largely in medicine, psychology, and social work, almost exclusively men, and now given explicit support by the state.

This essay considers maternalism, related issues of individual and collective health and welfare, and the evolution of social policy within a historical framework of materialist feminism that stresses their intrinsic connection. It was the permeability of boundaries between capitalism and patriarchy, between private and public, that permitted the coalescence of ideas, ideals, and policies in the construction of the maternal and its politics.

Although the specific location of this maternalist campaign is early twentieth-century Canada, it unfolded within an international crusade of broad-ranging social reform. The Canadian campaign shared with its counterparts in other industrial democracies the material context of socioeconomic change, the ideological context of "modernity," and notably, parallel reformist discourses that were adamantly maternalist and pronatalist. The explicit connections between motherhood and a widely defined national "health" were drawn from a particular material setting. Compelling reformist discourses repeated, enhanced, and reinforced these connections through an apocalyptic imagery of disorder and degeneration. The circulation and politicization of such discourses helped shape modern understandings of gender, family, health in its every connotation, citizenship, and state.[3] More than anything, the story reveals the many ambiguities and ambivalences that characterize the historical reformulation of relationships.

What follows is an outline of the principal ideas motivating a campaign of social regeneration premised on an ideology of "scientific motherhood." The constant and consistent, expounding, admonishing, and bleak prophecy in the pages of professional journals, mass-circulation newspapers and magazines, institutional and government reports, medical literature, and diverse social commentaries meant that the message was bound to be heard, repeated, circulated, and politicized. An ideal of what should constitute "the family," as opposed to what did, or had, constituted real families, was constructed in critical commentaries and reformist proposals meant to impress upon the inattentive and unseeing both the current seriousness of these interrelated crises and their social portents. Battle metaphors and military imagery resounded through these discourses long after the end of the Great War. Their very language testifies to the war's tremendous impact on collective memory, but also suggests reformist perceptions of the scope and magnitude of contemporary social disorder, giving rise to the central image of "the family besieged." The patriotic and imperialistic tones of these discourses also point to their intended effect as a "call to arms," and the expected response of worthy citizens: self-sacrifice for the greater good. Their creators, largely drawn from the white, Anglo-Saxon, urban, Protestant middle class, established themselves as the natural commanders of any regenerative campaign; the target group was preponderantly working class, immigrant, and deemed racially "inferior"; and within that target group, women were both the particular cause of the problem and the particular instrument of salvation.

Given the clashing aims and conflicting images that suffused these discourses of anxiety, it is not surprising that the solution proposed should be paradoxical. The only possible agent for the family's salvation and modernization—concepts so intertwined as to be synonymous—was its traditional heart and center: the mother. The response, therefore, was a maternalism depicted as regenerative while operating in a fundamentally regulatory manner. And the chief ideologues of maternalism, sanctioned as appropriate commentators on morality, arbiters of social custom, and guardians of the nation's health, were medical doctors. Their position ensured them not only a receptive audience, but an influential role in the translation of ideology into state policy. Medicine and the state would see that mothers were "educated": modernized, upgraded, and re-formed, in effect, so that "the family" could meet the needs of modern industrial society while preserving its traditional form, function, gender roles, and relations of inequality.[4]

CONTEXT: MODERNIZATION AND THE CRISIS IN PATRIARCHY

The historical relations of motherhood are constituted from the multiplicity of biological and ideological threads woven into the material basis of society and culture. These threads are never separated out to any degree that does not oversimplify. An exclusive gender focus, for example, will tell an inflexible story of women's subordination that leaves little room for consideration of class, age, race, family, and other such relations comprising social identity, and even less for agency and contestation. A close reading of the discourses, by downplaying the contexts of modern industrial capitalism embedded in the symbols and metaphors that permeate them, inadvertently weakens arguments about their instrumentality. Emphasis on the rise of the interventionist state risks its depiction as an autonomous regulatory entity, stretching out its newly spun bureaucratic web over an insensate citizenry—over its female citizens in particular. Historians need to consider the relationship of maternalist ideologies, sociocultural change, and welfare policy in a dialectical manner that allows for ambiguity, unresolved paradox, and internal contradiction; for the necessary acknowledgment of overlapping categories, of the persistence of old and new, "traditional" and "modern," and emergent and residual, in the shaping of modern motherhood.

To make sense of these historical complexities without unraveling them entirely requires an interpretive framework that will uncover the issue of social reproduction at their base. Marx never developed a comprehensive theory of social reproduction, all the while conceding its importance to capitalism: "the maintenance and reproduction of the working class is, and must ever be, a necessary condition to the reproduction of capital." Any production is at once reproduction: "a society can no more cease to produce than it can cease to consume. When viewed, therefore, as a connected whole, and as flowing on with incessant renewal, every social process of production is, at the same time, a process of reproduction."[5] The day-to-day restoration of human beings, enabling them to continue these social processes, takes place largely although not exclusively within the family, the usual site for procreation, nurture, and replenishment.[6]

Understanding social reproduction as a relational concept that is culturally and historically specific exposes the swirl of motion, back and forth, among and between the ideal, the material, and the political. At times the lines we have imposed between gender, class, and race blur in ways that are uncomfortable to historians accustomed to highlighting each in turn. Yet scrutinizing these "motherhood issues" in this manner will permit us to glimpse the ever-transforming dance of power that is the adaptive mechanism sustaining patriarchy and capitalism in their historic mutuality.

At the turn of the century, structural economic changes spurred concomitant changes in the material conditions of life, changes that were accelerated and intensified by the military exigencies of world war. The accompanying social stresses ignited multiple discourses of anxiety, but their focus was singular. The family, immutable icon of tradition, symbol of social health and stability, appeared to be floundering. The reasons for this crisis in the family were precisely those invoked to explain the wider social crisis, a litany of contributory ills at once specific and amorphous—most having to do with the negative repercussions of the very modernization also celebrated as "progress." Internal logic and consistency were secondary to dramatic impact. Canadians were warned that social disorder had opened a vacuum of authority in the nation's homes, fueling further social disorder and threatening the imminent collapse of the system itself.

The perceived crisis in the family naturally pointed to fathers' weakened ability to carry out their traditional paternal duties of protection, sustenance, and discipline, just as it pointed to a failure in motherhood. The turn-of-the century popularization of eugenic theory intensified anxieties about declining manhood, at least that of the white, Anglo-Saxon, Protestant "better stock." The decreasing birth rate represented not only the selfishness of modern women, but also manly failure to perform the requisite manly duty. The sorry state of army recruits for the First World War and the hideous toll of casualties of "young men in their prime" and "future fathers of the race" sparked all manner of concerns about race suicide and social degeneration.[7] Was there a related crisis in masculinity that caused some men [doctors, psychologists, scientific experts] to believe that they were better equipped than the vast majority of men [ordinary fathers] to rule over families? The crisis in the family, in short, was a crisis in patriarchy with systemic repercussions. And women would be affixed both the majority of the blame and the burden of setting things right.

All these fears about reproduction derived from perceived, more than actual, dangers. But to anxious Canadian middle-class observers and [male] social critics, this was a modernizing nation peopled by new and "strange" immigrant "strains" who imported worrisome "foreign" customs and values. The strongest, bravest, most worthy of "Canadian" fathers were helpless to protect their families from the growing menace to health and life that this changing society seemed to pose. The state was required to step in as protector and guarantor of the family's safety. The shift from familial patriarchy to social patriarchy, as Jane Ursel has pointed out, was meant to buttress the sinking father. It was not meant to sink him further, any more than it was intended to restructure the existing system.[8] But fathers could not be approached directly by the new experts in science and state, as this was too obvious a slight to the very patriarchal authority they wanted to uphold. And so mothers were targeted as both problem and solution. Among the new relationships of the modern order would be an ever-closer one between medicine and the state, the nexus of which was the regulation of reproduction.

These early twentieth-century reformist discourses influenced, and were addressed by, a maternalist ideology focused on potential. Science, technology, and a sanctified womanhood would together generate a shiny new world. The contours of this gleaming future were at once innovative and familiar. Modern citizens borne by modern mothers would be healthy, fit, productive, and content with their places within a refurbished hierarchical order that looked remarkably like that which was currently threatened. A utopian vision inspired by faith in modern science was sustained by faith in the traditional family, and by unwavering commitment to existing social inequalities.[9]

MEDICINE AND STATE, REPRODUCTION AND REGULATION

In capitalist societies, health, too, is a commodity. Economic exploitation of large portions of the population has adverse effects for health and well-being, in proportion to the position of those exploited, as this is defined by their own productive/reproductive roles within the system. Those at a relative economic advantage naturally fare better than the marginal; men have commonly fared better than women because they have not been subject to the risks surrounding maternity; the very old and the very young are vulnerable not only because of health difficulties pertinent to age, but because of their dependent status as nonworking members of society.[10]

Health care delivery is shaped by direct profit and efficiency objectives, and by the particular health needs of the economy. Care is bought and sold in the marketplace at whatever price the market will sustain, with minimal consideration to the concept of health as a universal need and fundamental right. Elizabeth Fee has observed that health care systems invariably mirror the priorities and organization of the larger socioeconomic system, thereby replicating its relations of inequality. Power is situated and affirmed in class and gender stratification and is perpetuated in the gendered division of labor. The system's accountability to those it purports to serve is minimal, ultimate responsibility resting, paradoxically, in the hands of the ruled and not the rulers.[11] The socioeconomic system and the health care system jointly support the symbiosis of economic production and social reproduction. The gendered division of labor, despite historical evidence of women's productive work both within and outside the home, explicitly designates women to the work of social reproduction. As women's work, it must serve the productive work that properly belongs to men and must consequently be regulated by the state as the source of healthy, reliable, efficient, and productive bodies.[12]

The distribution of health care also reflects the status of the medical profession as a vital sector of the dominant class. That medicine has historically been a near-exclusive masculine profession underscores the status doctors have enjoyed in modern society. Class, gender, and modernist ideas linking progress, science, and technology have granted doctors an impressive social and political power that has gone remarkably unchallenged during the course of the twentieth century. The medicalization of twentieth-century life is concomitant to its rationalization, encouraging and sustaining, in Foucault's terminology, a "biopolitics" of regulation and supervision as a joint project of medicine and the state. Modern medicine has contributed, in ways both overt and insidious, to the production and reproduction of the "healthy" national body.

Prevailing constructions of what signifies "health" in a given historical moment owe much to the complicated relationship between economy and culture: the very definitions of health and illness are overdetermined. Differences in individual and class behavior and in cultural patterns are obviously significant. The explanation for ill health remains fundamentally materialist, however, in that these individual choices and broader patterns are themselves derived from existing inequalities.[13] A period's predominant health difficulties are delimited by the conditions of work and life that are the common experience of the majority of the population. Late nineteenth-century social critics who recognized these links between socioeconomic status and health advocated "social medicine," which they envisaged as radical state intervention on behalf of public health.[14] But the rise of "scientific" medicine at this time dismissed the relevance of the social contexts of health. The medical focus was fixed on the body as object of scientific examination and physician intervention, negating any concept of the patient as an embodied subjectivity.[15] The "social" and the "scientific" were reconciled, to some degree, in campaigns of public education, supported by minimalist legislation, which used interventionary agencies to encourage, regulate, and monitor individual responsibility for collective welfare.

The body, of course, lives within, responds to, and is affected by the material circumstances of its owner. It is surrounded nonetheless by subjective ideas that are formulated in accordance with sociocultural values and aspirations.[16] By the end of the nineteenth century, western medicine favored a mechanistic conception of the body that emphasized the objective, organic basis of illness. The body was represented as a machine, absorbing industrial symbolism in its conceptualization as the "human motor" and the "human factory." Representations of the body, and consequently bodily health, were responses to the requirements of particular modes of production and the way in which these influenced the organization of social relations. We can understand the disciplinary requirements of capitalism in terms of the particular practices employed to "manage" and regulate the body, from diet, to exercise, leisure, sleep, and sexuality, to name only a few. In turn, constructs about the body are significant referents for state policy concerning labor, family, health, and social welfare. What was happening, to varying degrees, in western industrial nations at the turn of the century prompted an adaptive shift in the socioeconomic delineation of human bodies, and consequently in scientific understandings of how they worked and how they could be put to work. Emphasis necessarily devolved upon the productive body. Women and men both own productive bodies, but the nature of that production was defined in gender-specific ways that replicated the gendered division of labor and life in the material world.[17]

The turn-of-the-century transition to monopoly capitalism from its earlier competitive form, and the onslaught of a "second industrial revolution" fueled by technological innovation, changed the labor process. Production now required an intensification of labor that made worker efficiency—bodily efficiency—paramount. Emerging interest in the "psychophysics" of industrial labor in Europe also turned the attention of scientists and social scientists to the physiological and mental impact of the altered nature of work. The "science of work" investigated and redefined the relationship between machine and human being to allow for the "calibration" of workers—the "mechanical" finetuning of their bodies—to fit them to machinery.[18] The corresponding definition of health also shifted from emphasis on physical endurance, which could be secured by simple replacement of "outworn" workers, to optimum labor efficiency, which had to be actively promoted and instilled in all workers and potential workers.

The medical profession also espoused a cultural/behavioral explanation of class differences, locating predisposing factors to ill health in individual life-style choices that amounted to personal failings. Prescribed changes in individual behavior were considered the most efficacious approach to illness.[19] From a historical perspective, however, cultural and behavioral patterns cannot be excised from the structural and environmental whole, essentially what contemporary doctors were attempting to do. The connections among health, medicine, and the nature of production in different societies at specific moments are crucial: health, like wealth and power, is an unequally distributed social resource. It is affected as much by the social identities and roles inscribed in categories of class, race, gender, and age as it is by individual choice or genetic makeup.[20] Doctors, while conceding that low wages contributed to ill health and economic dependency, argued that "inefficiency of labor" was itself responsible for low wages. This circular reasoning made labor inefficiency both the source and the outcome of mass physical deterioration. Ill health was due to poor choices, ignorance, incorrect behavior—in short, to personal deficiency now classified as "inefficiency."[21] The body had to be harnessed to the needs of industrial capitalism. The object was the productive, disciplined body, as a widening regimen of "body regulation" took root in public institutions such as factories, schools, and prisons, as well as in the realm histor-ically deemed private—the family.[22]

Production, consumption, and reproduction are obviously integral to capitalism, yet they are all threatened by the very exploitation the system demands, none more so than the reproduction essential to this dynamic. The system's innate potential for self-destruction revealed itself already in the early stages of industrialization, when its damaging impact on living standards and public health became all too apparent. Women and children were the earliest victims of the new industrial order. It was their situation that sparked the concern of those advocating state protection and regulation of families.[23]

In Canada, much as was the case in reformist circles throughout the western world, concerned citizens operating largely under the aegis of the Social Gospel were moved to organize in support of child and maternal welfare.[24] The campaign's immediate pur-pose was to lower the horrific infant and maternal mortality rates. Though scant and frequently impressionistic, statistics confirmed that this was a class mortality, afflicting primarily the ill-fed, ill-housed, often recently arrived families of workers. Added to this bourgeois guilt/responsibility was the effect of current eugenic theory, which warned against the imminent degeneration—even devolution—of humanity because of reckless and ill-thought intermingling of the "races"; because of ill-advised marriages and unconsidered reproduction; and because of ill-informed child care and childrear-ing practices. Illness and deviance appeared to be endemic. Management and efficiency, order and discipline, individual and collective responsibility, citizenship in the sense of duty to nation and state—these were profoundly lacking in the nation's homes, profoundly affecting the national body. Recognizing the enormity of the prob-lem and the threat of its long-term effects for the social order and their privileged place within it, reformers looked to the state to intervene in social reproduction.[25]

Social critics of the time understood that reproduction encompasses more than the biological. It comprises the socialization, physical maintenance, and emotional nurture of family members, and it constitutes the basis of the dialectical interchange between family and society. What happens in the home affects the capacity of human beings to work, to function socially, to continue to exist. Women have historically carried the primary responsibility for the domestic labor that ensures the maintenance and renew-al of the nonworking as well as the active labor force.[26]

Both patriarchy and capitalism hinge upon the survival of the family, with its gen-dered structures and unequal power relations. Childrearing and all forms of unpaid domestic work are central to these mutually supportive systems. The feminine respon-sibilities of household production and reproduction meant that women's bodies had to be conceptualized as potentialities: for their own potential to give birth and for the future potential of the children that they bore.[27] The metaphors of mass production were borrowed by the medical profession to describe sex and reproduction, tending to the transformation of reproductive relations, biological and social, into what Juliet Mitchell describes as a "sad mimicry of production."[28]

While it is clearly in the general interest that families be healthy, when the require-ments of production conflict with those of reproduction, the family cannot protect the health and welfare of its members on its own. Because employers preferred to avoid the costs of doing so, the state was obliged to play a more active role in regulating and pro-viding services for the workforce to ensure its reproduction.[29] The corollary to this state regulation is the legitimation and valorization of certain classes and interest groups, to whom are relegated the definition of the normative [derived from ideal more than "objective" knowledge], and consequently the deviant; and second, the nature and distribution of health and welfare services in accordance with their definitions. The expansion of the bureaucratic state in early twentieth-century western democracies placed the medical profession in an ideal mediatory position between the social and the scientific. Doctors played an integral role in delineating both the targets of social and moral reform and the means to approach these. They reinforced patriarchal values through their "scientific" constructions of normal womanhood. Professional groups thus play an invaluable part in the system's functioning, contributing directly to the management and surveillance of the working class, of women, of children, and of those "marked" by race and ethnicity, by regulating on behalf of capital under the auspices of the state.[30]

Because they discounted environmental and subjective components of health, factors that all too often hinged on family economics, the explanation for the crisis in reproduction epitomized by high infant mortality could only be found on the other side of the equation. It must lie with parents, especially mothers. The poor, particularly those classified as "inferior" by virtue of ethnicity and race, were providing the victim's sanction by refusing to take responsibility for their own health and that of their children. Mothers were feckless and ignorant. Because children are the most subordinate of all social groups and because it is clearly impossible to make dependent infants and children responsible for their own health and upbringing, mothers had to be made responsible according to medical dictates and by means of medical regulation. In striving toward these ends, doctors became the foremost proponents of the modern family.[31] The impact of medical leadership in this area was a measure of their ability to make women recognize their fundamental inadequacy in raising children without modern scientific instruction—without being led to knowledge by the men of the medical profession. The disruption of traditional support networks by immigration, urbanization, and mass culture made women particularly vulnerable to the exhortations of emergent scientific experts. Given the stakes that were depicted by those intent on such regulation, society and state were obliged to support it.[32]

The regulation of reproduction, doctors argued, required nothing less than a state-funded, professionally directed, actively interventionist, and "scientific" program. Such a program would ensure the health of prospective "mothers of the land" and produce healthy infants, its first objective. But it would also, as all nature of maternalist reformers believed, encourage the "proper" nurture, maintenance, and socialization of those infants in the interests of the future health and well-being—in terms of social progress and economic productivity—of the nation as a whole. The one true hope of race, nation, and system subsided in the child, whose modernity was self-evident, whose existence embodied potential. As science and technology continued to restructure the world around children, childhood had to be reformulated to reflect evolving social needs and aspirations and to eradicate the difficulties, individual and collective, that doctors attributed to improper, inferior, and outmoded childrearing practices.[33] For its part, the state attempted to meet the changing, at times conflicting, requirements of both capitalism and patriarchy by institutionalizing class relations and upholding gender and racial distinctions, often using the authority of scientific experts to substantiate its policies, or, conversely, to dismiss any need for policy.[34] Throughout this century, the state has become increasingly important in the regulation of human bodies and human relationships through medical legislation, including mandatory blood tests and physical examinations for immigration and marriage, compulsory immunization, sanctions against abortion and birth control, enforced quarantine, and myriad public health laws. Contemporary understandings of the relationship between citizen and state politicized the body in a manner that placed specific value on the bodies of women, with their maternal potential.[35] But at no time during the course of this physician-led crusade to save infants and mothers did either medicine or the state argue in favor of universal, state-supported health care or any redistribution of wealth that might attack the material foundations of illness and mortality. With their combined focus on personal [maternal] responsibility, the solution idealized was medically directed, state-supported education for motherhood.

Although child and maternal welfare were fundamentally health issues, the "problem" was defined from the viewpoint of the material realities and ideological imperatives of industrial capitalism. If infants could be saved and their physical, mental, and moral health regulated, the benefits in socioeconomic terms would more than offset any state investment. The result would be a modern nation worthy of the most favorable implications of modernity: progress, efficiency, productivity, and the triumph of reason that were signified by advances in science, industry, and technology. Child nurture and family health were appropriated as state interests, as child and maternal welfare shifted out of the voluntarist reform sphere to become the object of a male-dominated professional body and a state-sponsored campaign. No argument was made by medicine or the state against the view that these subjects should remain the primary concern of women. But women had to be shown that the way to health, to familial contentment—to the future in all its glorious promise—was a carefully regulated maternity. The inherent paradox was that these newly constructed modern mothers were, through the ideological mists, "traditional" women in all their subordinate reality.

Patriarchal ideas and class dynamics, colored by notions of racial superiority, thus shaped maternalist discourses. The solutions proposed sought to reinforce family and state as mutually supportive entities. For all the rhetoric of separate spheres that sustained patriarchy, it was recognition of the fluid boundaries between private and public that led to attempts by medicine and the state to intervene in intimate human relationships. They did not encourage adaptation of the family to the modern industrial order in any true sense; their stance was defensive and protective. The traditional mother-centered family was vital to the welfare of Canadian society and essential to the quality of its future. The maternal potential had to be channeled to that end.

FIRST LINE OF DEFENSE: THE "NEW AND IMPROVED" MOTHER

In Canada, the much-heralded "return to normalcy" in the immediate aftermath of the Great War prepared a receptive audience for contemporary medical constructions of maternity. The carnage and futility of war, the stresses induced by socioeconomic modernization, the decline in the birth rate, the emergence of the "flapper" who seemed more interested in pleasure and career than in marriage and family—their conjuncture inspired a backlash against further change made the more curious because the "traditional" was held in such contempt in this newly modern world.

Physicians lent their voices to the public debate on the modern woman's place and role with the same force and conviction that underlay their nineteenth-century pronouncements on the "woman question."[36] If modernization had introduced a host of new possibilities to answer that question, their own response was formed within the ideological framework of the system that worked best for them as leading male members of the dominant class. The modern argument, therefore, was contiguous with that which had long preceded it. Both "traditional" and "modern" conceptualizations of family were premised on the mutuality of the ideal civilization and the ideal home. Naturally, gender roles were idealized to fit.[37] The mother-centered family carried out the essential task of social reproduction, both in the sense of reproducing the labor force and the equally important sense of reproducing sociocultural norms.[38] Against this background, motherhood had to be defined as a matter of national importance.

What is striking about these maternalist discourses is their grounding in economic principles of cost and investment. It was reasoned that saving children from death and debility and supervising their upbringing by educating mothers would more than justify public expenditure in redoubling the prospects of turning out a productive citizenry. Parents who were unwilling or unable to acknowledge children as "national assets" and to carry out their duties accordingly became "liabilities" to state and society.

Equally striking is the ambivalence and ambiguity surrounding the issue of modernity itself. On one hand, the modern was depicted in positive reference to the traditional, which had taken on connotations of the decadence and sordid aggression that had led to world war. In this sense, the modern connoted "better than before" and was regenerative. On the other hand, the modern, with its machine focus, was also held to be "unnatural" in the sense of anti-human; in this sense it was a major cause of physical and spiritual degeneration. Modern industry meant "progress" in terms of material wealth. But modern industry was also undermining the health of the current generation of workers, and consequently damaging the potential of future workers, hence national potential. The "unfit" were reproducing themselves and perpetuating their "unfitness" at an escalating socioeconomic cost. Modern industry attacked the patriarchal basis of society: "the innumerable machines of industry . . . have brought women from the home and field into factories, and limited their maternal powers and instincts."[39] While workers protested the importation of "foreign" bodies to replace the damaged bodies of their own class, racist/imperialist attitudes construed immigration as another means of increasing the numbers of the unfit and aggravating the menace they represented.[40] Whatever meaning was ascribed to the modern, neither its critics nor its proponents intended a return to a mythic golden age, a preindustrial Eden. Nothing that had existed and nothing currently in existence represented "the modern" in its true glory, merely projecting a particular social vision of what ailed society and its favored cure. And as is invariably true of ideologies-in-the-making, this futuristic wishful thinking created important positions in that new world for its makers.

In the end, modern industry itself was decidedly not the problem. The problem was the unnatural gender roles it had inspired, the unnatural mingling of races, the unnatural class antagonisms, all spurring the dissolution of "natural" social relations that was culminating in crisis. While few maternalists were strict eugenicists who advocated institutionalization and sterilization of the "unfit," the notion of selective breeding gave a much-coveted scientific gloss to their ideas. They contended above all that prevention was more effective and less costly than any attempts to deal with the problem of degeneration after the fact.[41] More interventionary than curative medicine, the preventive ideal necessitated effective state machinery for the required medical regulation of the public. In the language of battle, the modern public health department would be "the first line of defense of the people," while the mother was evoked as "the first line of defense" for the helpless "infant soldier" whose preservation depended entirely on her "training, education and preparation."[42]

The Great War impressed upon physicians "as never before" that they had "a patriotic duty as well as a professional one" to save infants and keep them healthy. War naturally drew attention to the population as a biological resource. The class that produced the majority of workers and soldiers alike was also the most vulnerable in terms of health. The exigencies of war brought production and reproduction to the point of crisis "as never before." That "inferior" immigrants might fill the places of the fallen and of those damaged physically and emotionally by war now appeared an ever more pressing threat. The war magnified corresponding middle-class fears about "race suicide," which had been developing since the turn of the century. Recent statistics confirmed that the birth rate was indeed dropping within the "better stock," adding quantifiable force to maternalist and pronatalist arguments.[43] Middle-class women's organizations adopted these arguments, contending that the victory won on the actual battlefield had to be followed by "a realization of the power of consecrated motherhood." Similarly, trade unions and women's labor associations urged that women, "as mothers of the race," use their "mighty power for the uplift of womanhood, the family and the home." As non-medical supporters of these notions picked up the medical discourse and repeated and embellished it, motherhood was transformed into a "science" and a "profession of the highest order," in deliberate contrast to the "natural" and "instinctive" relation it had traditionally been.[44]

Maternalist reformers were intent on saving children, but they were equally intent on adjusting the attitudes and behavior of women to fit their particular analysis of the social ailments of their time. By the end of the Great War in 1918, doctors were establishing moral sanctions on the grounds of health and national interest and denigrating traditional childrearing methods. Ever more forcefully, they began to dispense advice to women in ways that were not purely medical, arguing that this was an integral part of their community function because they possessed "the types of knowledge not likely to be had by lay groups."[45] Around this axis of knowledge and its interpretation revolved the new expert/mother relationship. They had to impress upon women that only they held the interpretive skills to mediate that knowledge through the mother/child relationship. While women could become more informed about child care, they still had to make doctors and other such experts an integral part of their mothering experience. Between knowledge and its application existed a social space wherein both medical dominance and the power relations subordinating women found reinforcement.[46]

The medicalization of social problems created newly activist roles for doctors and the state in private lives and private relations. The wartime intensification of concerns about social reproduction, the maternalist platforms of various reform organizations and voluntary agencies, and the establishment of a federal health department and various provincial divisions with stated commitments to maternal education and child welfare facilitated both state and popular acceptance of attempts to fortify maternal responsibility and modernize motherhood. "To glorify, dignify, and purify motherhood, by every means in our power" became the call to arms of a massive campaign of medical regulation of motherhood on behalf of the state.[47]

ADVICE LITERATURE: SCIENTIFIC MANAGEMENT/MOTHERHOOD

The heady maternalist rhetoric that underscored these intentions to "elevate" motherhood implies that it had somehow been debased and demeaned. Such is the principal irony of maternalist discourses: modern women, with their ambitions for education, career, and life experience, and with their obvious lack of respect for the traditional, were themselves to blame for the devaluation of the maternal. Yet, in this newly modern world the traditional was not supposed to be worthy of respect. Women had to be re-formed, in short, in order to be modern mothers—but significantly not modern women in the sense of fitting themselves in new ways to a new order. It was of the first importance, therefore, that the training of young women should always be directed "wisely, tacitly, with no fuss or protestation" toward the "one great fact" of maternity—about which, despite its primacy, they were profoundly ignorant.[48] Charges of maternal ignorance respected no barriers of class or race, providing for the experts a potentially unlimited audience of women who needed their instruction simply because they were women.

Through the medium of advice literature, predominantly medical in authorship or at least in inspiration, the key themes of the varied maternalist discourses were compressed into directives for women who aspired to "perfect parenting."[49] This mass-production advice to mothers articulated emergent theories of scientific motherhood in a determined effort to change maternal behavior. During the interwar years, advice literature was produced apace by medical professionals and new health and welfare agencies at all levels of government, and in conjunction with private insurance companies and voluntarist health and social service organizations. It was further popularized in the ubiquitous advice columns and "women's pages" of mass-circulation magazines and newspapers, through radio shows [often sponsored by medical associations, health promotion agencies, and women's organizations], through government films shown in the newsreels that introduced feature films in this period, and by public health nurses who held "demonstrations" at baby clinics and in home visits. Its immediate purpose was to promote improved health and hygenic standards. Far from being purely informative, however, it was also intentionally "formative." The advice strove to establish doctors as maternal mentors and child saviors, to associate maternalism with national interest, and to reformulate motherhood and consequently childhood.

In the modern scheme of things, raising a family was an "exceedingly complex job," while the sort of training needed for the task was itself becoming complicated. Children were being born into a world changing so rapidly that "each day is as new to the adult as to the child." The traditional precepts that had served as guideposts for child nurture had been swept away.[50] Medical professionalization and specialization meant that information about the body and the feminine activity of child nurture were gradually removed from the stock of folk knowledge. Here was justification for medical management of all aspects of motherhood and childhood, and hence all familial relations. Modernization had opened a leadership vacuum that was manifesting itself in the homes of the nation, where the old values had become outmoded and meaningless. Mothers were confronted with the crumbling of traditional childrearing culture and urged to embrace scientific methods within a context of pervasive social optimism about the capacity of science and technology to improve the earth and its inhabitants. Under those circumstances, they could reasonably be expected to look to the new authorities for guidance.[51]

The production of childrearing information was not in itself new to the 1920s and 1930s. What was "modern" about this advice was the fact that it was predominantly medical in authorship and that the state took active part in its production and distribution. To reach the broadest sector of society, the advisory texts directed specifically at the middle class through childrearing manuals, child study courses, and popular publications had to be supplemented by mass distribution of free advisory publications. In no other area did the reformist call for intervention receive such enthusiastic state support for the public management and socialization of future citizens. To those ends, new public health and social welfare bureaucracies printed and disseminated their advisory literature, established supervisory clinics and community centers, and sent out their field workers to pay "home visits" and make "demonstrations." State forays into this arena, while focused narrowly on the educational, were nevertheless historically unprecedented. But neither maternalist ideologues nor state policymakers wanted more than to "fix" what in their shared view was undermining existing social relations.

The child care instructions tendered by the medical advisers and their state and media popularizers were uniformly prescriptive. Analysis of the literature reveals much about the sort of familial relationships they idealized, and equally about the ideal role for medicine in family and society. Doctors would be overseers, training, regulating, and supervising mothers so that they, in turn, could "manage" their pregnancies effectively and efficiently. The production line culminated in the desired product: the healthy modern child. The child was further "managed" all along its healthy way to attaining its adult potential as the model citizen. There was universal agreement that maternal ignorance was endemic, that traditional patterns of child nurture were outdated and harmful, and that doctors alone could effectively cure family and nation. Science and state lent the weight of their combined authority to social constructions depicting the ideal mother, the ideal child, and ideal family relationships.[52]

While disparaging modern women, the advice literature nonetheless invoked the creation of a new, improved, scientific mother, a thoroughly modern mother befitting the new industrial order. The new order was itself quite literally man-made, and so was the modern mother. The model proposed for the home, world of women, was the masculine model of the workplace, the man's world that attempted to shut out women. "Management," an almost uniquely masculine endeavor, was the core concept informing the experts' childrearing prescriptions. There was much borrowing of ideas and principles from the productive setting for attempted transferral to the home. Frederick Winslow Taylor's *Principles of Scientific Management* was translated into the language of every industrial nation by 1913. Against the background of industrial consolidation and technological innovation, the early twentieth century witnessed increasing professionalization of management and an all-out campaign for the systematization of the industrial setting. But the application of science to industry had ideological implications far surpassing the original intentions of its advocates. The term "efficiency" was not to be confined to the "mere speeding up of production." "By efficiency," proclaimed one expert, "we mean an understanding working knowledge of human nature and how to put it to the best use."[53]

Just as "efficiency" and "productivity" became keywords of modern industry, the metaphors of scientific management imbued the professional ethos and made their way into public discourses. The application of scientific management to the reproductive setting of the woman-centered household, it was argued, would be just as beneficial as it was in the productive setting of the man-centered workplace. The two would serve as mutual reinforcement, first upgrading the health, welfare, and productivity of the family, and ultimately improving the productivity and efficiency of the nation as a whole.[54] Modern motherhood was infused with the spirit of industrialism, with its unrelenting demands for regularity, repetition, scheduling, systematization, discipline, and productivity. The "kitchen timepiece" was proclaimed to be the most important tool of modern childrearing, analogous in function and effect to the stopwatch and punch clock that regulated production.[55] In keeping with the rigidly behaviorist psychological theories increasingly influential during the 1920s, every child would be "conditioned" to respond properly and efficiently to maternal directives.[56] Effective maternal management of children would quickly transform them into "little machines." The period's triumphalism about technology ensured that the machine represented the most evolved human type. This mechanistic approach to motherhood made women responsible more for "engineering" a specific child-type than for mothering as commonly signified in the biological and emotional bond between mother and child.[57] But the constant and unwavering objective was national regeneration through the training of model citizens, and the success of this "scientific programme" depended on the efficacy of maternal regulation.

In tone, nature, and intent, the advice literature infantilized women, resonating constantly with reminders of their intellectual, emotional, and physical inferiority. Women were symbolic children, addressed by speakers of greater wisdom and stature as they would speak to an unschooled, unformed, and not very astute child. The experts spoke with the unquestionable and unquestioned authority conferred by their status as professional men of science. In effect, the maternal tutors who directed, counseled, managed, and "made" modern motherhood represented the patriarchal archetype, the traditional father figure, to be revered and obeyed. Their exalted image of the modern mother scarcely masked its own antithesis: the real woman of the day, in her position of real subordination—a position her promoters themselves underscored in their rhetoric. Reconfiguring the willful child-woman of old as the modern mother did not signify enhanced social, economic, and political status for her. The cult of motherhood made her a sanctified subject of the state and the object of tutors who were invariably male and her "superiors" on many counts.

What was new about this family with its new mother at the helm was clearly more rhetorical than real. But the language of newness, as Rosemary Hennessy has argued, is a seller's language: it captured the popular imagination in a time when the "modern" was a particular selling point, the "traditional," associated with those left "behind the times."[58] In fact, the sellers were themselves promoting new ideas about motherhood. The media were very effective in disseminating maternalist discourses. Through radio, magazines, and newspapers, ideas about scientific motherhood entered countless homes in ways that doctors and nurses and state agents could not. Uneasy about its ability to resolve the "problems" drummed into its consciousness, the public is usually willing to grasp a solution that appears reasonable, especially when the solution is also relentlessly pushed through the sort of current imagery whose infiltration of popular culture guarantees its familiarization, if not its acceptance. In this manner, ideology becomes popular opinion.[59]

With their practiced eye for trends, advertisers were quick to sense the interwar generation's hunger for the modern. The new child-centeredness of modern life was sold through advertisements depicting the importance of a particular product or service in any truly modern childrearing system. In the "photonovella" style popular at the time—a series of photograph frames depicting a morality tale—advertisements for Castoria, "the special children's laxative," repeatedly pitted the modern mother against the forces of outmoded tradition and misinformation in the guise of the protoypical bogeys: the interfering mother-in-law, the nosy neighbor, the old-fashioned aunt, the unprogressive father. The modern mother inevitably emerged victorious because she had the modern doctor and the special scientific child-care product on her side.[60]

The modern child glowing with health and self-confidence was also a popular sales image for products not specifically linked to child health and welfare. In such advertisements, involving all manner of new consumer goods, the connection was made clear. Parents who put their child's well-being first recognized the value of this investment. So confident were advertisers about the popular understanding of the new relationship between family and medicine, they sometimes seemed to "sell" medical supervision over any specific product. One of the largest international pharmaceutical companies, which produced a line of baby care goods, did not name or illustrate these goods in any of its full-page advertisements in various popular magazines during the 1930s. With photographs capturing charming scenes of family activity, parents were urged to take advantage of modern medical expertise because "the two pairs of hands of even the most conscientious parents are not enough to guide a child safely past the hazards that confront her. A third parent should be added to the family circle . . . the doctor."[61] Mothers, the real "parent" in the traditional family, would have to surrender some of their own authority and autonomy, but this was assuredly a small price to pay for the benefits of medical guidance. This sort of advertising not only reflected the period's sociocultural currents, but contributed in no small way to their assimilation by the public at a time when consumerism was hitting new strides in mass culture.

The advice literature aimed at mothers during the interwar period was attempting to inculcate certain standards and values, deemed modern, that its authors believed were woefully lacking in Canadian homes. Doubtless the medical profession attained social dominance and political influence because state and society, in some measure, accepted and upheld its claims to knowledge, power, and authority. But do we accept, on the basis of discursive analysis, that the insistent maternalist ideals of early twentieth-century reformers were embraced and embodied in maternal practices? Obviously this is too facile a conclusion for what was, just as obviously, the complex and confused nature of cultural change. An additional complication rises directly from the avowed purpose of the advisory sources. They represent an ideology in the making rather than an established value system. Mother-roles as depicted in the prescriptive literature can neither be assumed to have reflected the "average" parenting experience nor to have been implemented by the majority of even the most engaged would-be modern mothers.

Analysis of the discourse on these issues suggests that doctors and other supporters of maternal education fretted, declaimed, and expounded as much as they did because they knew that no amount of propaganda, regulation, and surveillance, however unprecedented, was sufficient to eliminate *every* possibility of maternal agency. Judging by the views of the mothers themselves, it is likely that they incorporated into their practices those ideas that best suited them in terms of practicality, personality, and economics. More than this cannot be said with any certainty. However fixed the images of the ideal modern mother, there were in reality, in practice, many permutations of this relationship; shifting and changing with moment and context, replacing older images or harkening back to them nostalgically, even coexisting in unacknowledged contradiction. Representation, in short, is not reality.

Maternalist discourses affected the way society regarded motherhood and the way governments inscribed those constructions of the maternal into social policy. But they did not necessarily make women the passive and submissive "patients" doctors wanted them to be. Far from simply taking in the entire modern motherhood package as presented by the new experts, women themselves recognized the limits of maternalist ideologies. Ultimately, the way most women in this period raised their children had more to do with the material conditions of their lives and the way these circumscribed their choices, than with any amount of advice or medical supervision delivered through baby clinics and nurse visits. Most did not resist their delimitation as mothers, and many responded gratefully to medical instruction and supervision—but they also wanted tangible help in the form of affordable health care for themselves and their families. And they believed that such assistance was owed them by the state as a right of citizenship.[62] This is where maternalist politics failed to deliver on promises to have medicine and the state serve as joint guardians of the beleaguered modern family.

The campaigners' dismissal of poverty as a health issue was echoed in provincial and national legislatures by all but a few lonely voices. The education of poor mothers in modern principles of health and child care, consequently, was often futile. Despite expressions of discontent from some physicians, politicians, labor and women's groups, and the clients themselves, no alternative was promoted or attempted by organized medicine or the state. No legislation was enacted in the first forty years of this century, in Canada, to provide adequate health service, much less supplementary income, better housing, or nutrition, to needy pregnant women or mothers and their children.[63] While purporting to be scientific, the medical approach to the problem was clearly selective in its analysis. Its proponents consistently failed to deal with the material basis of infant and maternal mortality. If the medical program was bound by the limits of contemporary science, as indeed it was, it was proscribed as much by ideological confines and material realities. Because doctors failed to take the complicating factor of social inequality into account in their profoundly individualist theories of health, they were able to make maternal ignorance the foremost cause of high infant and maternal mortality, and scientific motherhood the principal remedy.

The campaign contributed significantly to the ongoing trend toward increased professional authority and state intervention. The medical profession's determination to make the state recognize its authority in all matters of public health, and its success in doing so, meant significant medical influence on state health and welfare policy. This influence, however, was often in the interests of medicine rather than the interests of health. Moreover, as doctors increasingly persuaded mothers to look to them in child-rearing matters, their power to influence social customs expanded. The overall effect for women was to enhance the focus on maternity as their reason for being, and especially on feminine ineptitude in carrying out a social role that was supposed to be biologically determined. By the Second World War, the care of expectant and parturient women and their children was firmly in the hands of the medical profession, a monopoly over health services only challenged within the past few years.

CONCLUSION: MATERNALIST POLITICS AND MODERN MOTHERHOOD

In framing their concerns about social anomie around the issue of reproduction, Canadian doctors echoed the interpretations of their colleagues in the United States and Western Europe. More than a medical position, this was a view grounded in the capitalist and patriarchal systems of these nations. Internationally, maternalist campaigns adhered remarkably to the regulatory, educational, mother-focused paradigm. Notwithstanding differences in timing, content, and delivery of maternalist ideologies, what is striking about motherhood in the industrial-capitalist democracies of North America, Western Europe, Australia, and New Zealand is the twentieth-century move toward its deliberate modernization. The making of modern mothers in all these nations required, first, public recognition of the mother-centeredness of national welfare; second, maternal education and supervision by an emerging caste of childrearing professionals, especially doctors, public health nurses, child psychologists, and social workers; and ultimately, to sustain and promote the first two requirements, the subtle but unrelenting process of state regulation. The language of science, modernity, and futurism that permeated reformist discourses in all these nations belied the conservatism, nostalgia, and anxiety about the future motivating their creators, themselves caught in an uncomfortable space between the traditional and the modern in a rapidly changing world.

Despite the vast historical differences between early and late twentieth-century western capitalist societies, the similarities and continuities ensure that this story remains starkly relevant to our own time. These understandings of gender, motherhood, and family—and their reciprocal relations—persist in spite of their all too evident inadequacies in the face of material, behavioral, and even widespread cultural changes. While twentieth-century advances in the rights of women and children, most attained in the aftermath of the Second World War, are real, they were designed as reinforcements for patriarchal and capitalist social relations. Moreover, they are not universal; not democratic in the sense of rights equally enjoyed by all citizens on the basis of citizenship alone; and not permanently inscribed in the social contract, as current attempts to dismantle them clearly indicate. Nowhere is this more apparent than in health and welfare, where the historical subordination wrought by gender and age is perpetuated and intensified by class and race, where those materially most vulnerable have ever been, and continue to be, women and children.

NOTES

1. Recent examples of the historiography on maternalism include T. Skocpol, *Protecting Soldiers and Mothers: The Political Origins of Social Policy in the United States* (Cambridge, Mass.: Belknap Press, 1992); G. Bock, P. Thane, eds., *Maternity and Gender Policies: Women and the Rise of European Welfare States* (London: Routledge, 1991); S. Koven and M. Michel, eds., *Mothers of the New World: Maternalist Politics and the Origins of Welfare States* (New York: Routledge, 1993); H. Marsland, L. Marks, V. Fildes, eds., *Women and Children First: Maternal and Infant Welfare in International Perspective* (London: Routledge, 1992); S. Pedersen, *Family,*

Dependency, and the Origins of the Welfare State (Cambridge: Cambridge University Press, 1994); M. Ladd Taylor, *Mother-Work: Women, Child Welfare and the State* (Chicago: University of Illinois Press, 1994); C. R. Comacchio, *Nations Are Built of Babies: Saving Ontario's Mothers and Children* (Montreal/Kingston: McGill-Queen's University Press, 1993).

2. On the new woman/new mother within the context of a "crisis in subjectivity" respecting bourgeois femininity, see R. Hennessy, *Materialist Feminism and the Politics of Discourse* (New York: Routledge, 1993), pp. 104–6.

3. I am using discourse/ideology in the relational sense outlined in D. Landry and G. McLean, *Materialist Feminisms* (Cambridge, Mass.: Blackwell, 1993), especially "Introduction," p. 6; also Hennessy, *Materialist Feminism and the Politics of Discourse,* especially ch. 4, pp. 100–38.

4. On the social influence of doctors in Canadian history, see W. Mitchinson, *The Nature of Their Bodies* (Toronto: University of Toronto Press, 1991); A. McLaren, *Our Own Master Race* (Toronto: McClelland and Stewart, 1990), p. 9, pp. 28–29; M. Valverde, *The Age of Light, Soap and Water* (Toronto: McClelland and Stewart, 1991), p. 47. Foucault sees doctors replacing priests as custodians of social values, as the ecclesiastical institutions of surveillance are replaced by those of scientific medicine: M. Foucault, *Madness and Civilization* (New York: Pantheon, 1965), *The Birth of the Clinic* (New York: Pantheon, 1973), *The History of Sexuality* (New York: Pantheon, 1979). For the impact of medical regulation on the family, see C. Lasch, *Haven in a Heartless World* (New York: Basic Books, 1977); J. Donzelot, *The Policing of Families* (New York: Harper, 1979).

5. Marx, *Capital,* 1 (New York: Vintage Books, 1977), pp. 168, 531, 537. Recent studies on the social reproduction process have focused on the social construction of factors of material production, in particular that of labor power as a commodity, and the reproduction of capitalist social relations. See J. Dickinson and B. Russell, "Introduction: The Structure of Reproduction in Capitalist Society," in Dickinson and Russell, eds., *Family, Economy and State: The Social Reproduction Process under Capitalism* (Toronto: Garamond, 1986), pp. 1–4; J. Ursel, *Private Lives, Public Policy: 100 Years of State Intervention in the Family* (Toronto: Women's Press, 1992), pp. 17–58; and J. Conley, "More Theory, Less Fact? Social Reproduction and Class Conflict in a Sociological Approach to Working-Class History," in G. S. Kealey, ed., *Class, Gender and Region: Essays in Canadian Historical Sociology* (St. John's, Newf.: Memorial University Press, 1988). See also L. Vogel, *Marxism and the Oppression of Women* (New Brunswick, N.J.: Rutgers University Press, 1983), pp. 64, 129, 151.

6. Feminist research has brought to light the often-obscured connections between household structures, family relations, and the social position of women. See, for example, M. Abramovitz, *Regulating the Lives of Women* (New York: South End, 1977), pp. 27–28; the collection of essays in B. Fox, ed., *Hidden in the Household: Domestic Labor under Capitalism* (Toronto: Women's Press, 1980); M. Luxton, *More Than a Labor of Love* (Toronto: Women's Press, 1980), pp. 14–19.

7. Dr. P. H. Bryce, "The Scope of a Federal Department of Health," *Canadian Medical Association Journal* 10, no. 1 (1920): 3; Dr. H. MacMurchy, "The Baby's Father," *Canadian Public Health Journal* 9, no. 7 (1918): 318; Editorial, "The War," *CMAJ* 4, no. 10 (1914): 803; Editorial, "The Canadian Mother," *Social Welfare* 5, no. 8 (1923): 158. The problem of army rejects was also cause for fears about social degeneration in the U.S. and Britain; see D. Dwork, *War Is Good for Babies and Other Young Children* (London: Routledge, 1987), pp. 208–20. On associated fears, see McLaren, *Our Own Master Race,* pp. 13–27; G. R. Searle, *Eugenics and Politics in Britain* (Leyden: Noordhoff, 1976); D. Kevles, *In the Name of Eugenics: Genetics and the Uses of Human Heredity* (Berkeley, Calif.: University of California Press, 1985).

8. J. Ursel, "The State and the Maintenance of Patriarchy," in Dickinson and Russell, eds., *Family, Economy and State,* p. 151; further developed in Ursel, *Private Lives, Public Policy.*

9. For Britain, see J. Lewis, *The Politics of Motherhood* (London: Croom Helm, 1980); Dwork, *War Is Good for Babies;* on Britain and France, S. Pedersen, *Family, Dependency, and the Origins of the Welfare State;* for the U.S., Skocpol, *Protecting Soldiers and Mothers;* for a comparison of similar occurrences in the U.S. and Europe, see S. Koven and S. Michel, "Womanly Duties: Maternalist Policies and the Origins of Welfare States in France, Germany, Great Britain and the United States," *American Historical Review* 95, no. 4 (1990). For Australia, see P. M. Smith, "That Welfare Warfare: Sectarianism in Infant Welfare in Australia," in Fildes, Marks, Marland, eds., *Women and Children First.*

10. Medical sociologists have theorized the relationship between health, health care, and capitalism. See, for example, V. Navarro, *Medicine under Capitalism* (New York: Prodist, 1976), *Class Struggle, the State and Medicine: An Historical and Contemporary Analysis of the Medical Sector in Great Britain* (London: Martin Robertson, 1978); V. Navarro and D. M. Berman, eds., *Health and Work under Capitalism* (Farmingdale, N.Y.: Baywood, 1977); B. Turner, *Medical Power and Social Knowledge* (London: Sage, 1987), especially pp. 193–97; S. Kelman, "The Social Nature of the Definition of Health," in V. Navarro, ed., *Health and Medical Care in the United States* (New York: Tavistock, 1977), pp. 8–13; M. Renaud, "On the Structural Constraints to State Intervention in Health," in Navarro, ed., *Health and Medical Care,* p. 136; V. Navarro, "The Political Economy of Medical Care," in Navarro, ed., *Health and Medical Care,* p. 86–89.

11. E. Fee, "Women and Health Care," in Navarro, ed., *Health and Medical Care,* p. 128.

12. On the production/reproduction relationship see C. Brown, "Mothers, Fathers and Children: From Public to Private Patriarchy," in L. Sargent, ed., *The Unhappy Marriage of Marxism and Feminism* (London: Pluto Press, 1986), p. 243. Brown's ideas are further developed and applied historically to Canada in Ursel, *Private Lives, Public Policy.* See also B. Turner, *Regulating Bodies* (London: Routledge, 1992), pp. 18–21.

13. Turner, *Medical Power and Social Knowledge,* p. 195.

14. D. Porter and R. Porter, "What Was Social Medicine?" *Journal of Historical Sociology* 1 (1988): 102; also Turner, *Regulating Bodies,* pp. 130–34.

15. Turner, *Regulating Bodies,* p. 24.

16. Turner, *Regulating Bodies,* pp. 55 and 89, discusses the materiality/subjectivity arguments about the body, which lean toward a discursive understanding of materiality regarding both the body and "the social." For example, Bourdieu's conceptualization of the body as "cultural capital" emphasizes the impact of social constructions on the raw material of the body; see P. Bourdieu, *Distinction: A Social Critique of the Judgement of Taste* (London: Routledge, 1984). Judith Butler, *Bodies That Matter* (New York: Routledge, 1994), p. 17, considers discourses about the body to demonstrate how power relations work in the very formation of "sex" and its "materiality."

17. B. Turner, *The Body and Society* (London: Sage, 1980), p. 6; Foucault, *History of Sexuality* 1: 139. On medical constructions of women's bodies, see Mitchinson, *The Nature of Their Bodies.* See also Brown, "Mothers, Fathers and Children," pp. 243–45; Hennessy, *Materialist Feminism and the Politics of Discourse,* pp. 103–6.

18. R. Brain, "The Extramural Laboratory Limited: German *Arbeitswissenschaft* versus Max Weber," unpublished paper, presented to the British-North American Joint Meeting, Canadian Society for the History and Philosophy of Science/History of Science Society/British Society for the History of Science, University of Toronto, 26 July 1992.

19. Turner, *Medical Power and Social Knowledge,* pp. 195–96.

20. Fee, "Women and Health Care," p. 128; Turner, *Medical Power and Social Knowledge,* p. 217.

21. "Everyman's Child," undated manuscript, Dr. E. Smith-Shortt Collection, University of Waterloo Archives, Box 46, File 1813.

22. Turner, *Regulating Bodies,* pp. 6, 192–93.

23. D. Chunn, *From Punishment to Doing Good* (Toronto: University of Toronto, 1992), pp. 45–47; W. Mitchinson, "Early Women's Organizations and Social Reform," in A. Moscovitch and J. Albert, eds., *The Benevolent State* (Toronto: Garamond, 1987), pp. 77–92; Skocpol, *Protecting Soldiers and Mothers,* especially ch. 4, pp. 373–423.

24. On social reform in Canada, see R. Allen, *The Social Passion* (Toronto: University of Toronto Press, 1971); N. Sutherland, *Children in English Canadian Society* (Toronto: University of Toronto Press, 1976); and the essays on women and reform in L. Kealey, ed., *A Not Unreasonable Claim* (Toronto: Women's Press, 1976). For the United States and Western Europe, see Koven and Michel, "Womanly Duties"; and Pedersen, *Family, Dependency, and the Origins of the Welfare State.*

25. Dr. P. H. Bryce, "The Scope of a Federal Department of Health," 3; Dr. A. Meyer, "The Right to Marry: What Can a Democratic Civilization Do about Heredity and Child Welfare?" *Canadian Journal of Mental Hygiene* 1, no. 2 (1919): 145; Dr. H. MacMurchy, "The Parent's Plea," *CJMH* 1, no. 3 (1919): 211; see also MacMurchy's reports for the Ontario government, "The Feeble-Minded in Ontario," in Legislature of Ontario, *Sessional Papers,* 1907–15, annually; and

MacMurchy, *Sterilization? Birth Control?* (Toronto: King's Printer, 1934). All of these use blatant class and race arguments in explaining perceived social degeneration.

26. On women's productive/reproductive work, see L. Tilly and J. Scott, *Women, Work and Family* (New York: Routledge, 1989), pp. 14–45; S. Rose, "Proto-industry, Women's Work and the Household Economy in the Transition to Industrial Capitalism," *Journal of Family History* 13, no. 2 (1991): 183; Luxton, *More Than a Labor of Love,* p. 17. See also the essays in Fox, ed., *Hidden in the Household,* especially E. Blumenfeld and S. Mann, "Domestic Labor and the Reproduction of Labor Power," pp. 271–301, and W. Seccombe, "The Expanded Reproduction Cycle of Labor Power," p. 225. The longstanding debates about the theoretical significance of domestic labor and its nature and relationship to production are complicated, unrelenting, and largely unresolved. For an overview of these debates, which commenced in the mid-1960s, see Vogel, *Marxism and the Oppression of Women;* P. Armstrong and H. Armstrong, *Theorizing Women's Work* (Toronto: Garamond, 1990), pp. 67–97.

27. Turner discusses "the body as potentiality" in *The Body and Society,* and *Regulating Bodies;* also, Martin, *The Woman in the Body,* ch. 4, pp. 54–67.

28. Martin, *The Woman in the Body,* pp. 66–67; J. Mitchell, *Woman's Estate* (New York: Vintage, 1971), p. 108.

29. D. Wayne, "The Function of Social Welfare in a Capitalist Economy," in Dickinson and Russell, eds., *Family, Economy and State,* p. 55; Brown, "Mothers, Fathers and Children," in Sargent, ed., *The Unhappy Marriage of Marxism and Feminism,* p. 244.

30. V. Navarro, "The Political Economy of Medical Care," in Navarro, ed., *Health and Medical Care,* pp. 104–6; D. Naylor, *Private Practice, Public Payment* (Kingston/Montreal: McGill-Queen's University Press, 1986), p. 15.

31. Charges of maternal ignorance and negligence run rampant through the medical and social service journals of the early twentieth century. Some examples include Editorial, "Save the Children," *Canada Lancet* 40, no. 10 (1907): 934; Editorial,"The Health of the Child," *CMAJ* 2, no. 7 (1912): 704; Dr. B. F. Royer, "Child Welfare," *CPHJ* 12, no. 8 (1921): 293; Dr. H. MacMurchy, "A Safety League for Mothers," *Social Welfare* 13, no. 9 (1931): 184. Dr. Helen MacMurchy, who became the first chief of the federal Division of Child and Maternal Welfare in Canada in 1920, was instrumental in motivating public interest in child and maternal welfare with the publication of her three special reports on infant mortality, commissioned by the Ontario government, in 1910, 1911, and 1913. These themes are further developed in Comacchio, *Nations Are Built of Babies.*

32. Dr. C. Hodgetts, "Infantile Mortality in Canada," *CMAJ* 1, no. 8 (1911): 720; MacMurchy, *Infant Mortality: Third Special Report* (Toronto: King's Printer, 1912), p. 30.

33. S. M. Carr-Harris, "Reasons for Parental Education," *Canadian Nurse* 22, no. 6 (1926): 312–14; A. Mackay, "Caring for the Children," *Maclean's* (15 August 1928): 25; Dr. E. K. Clarke, "Community Responsibility for Habit Training in Children," *Social Welfare* 13, no. 11 (1931): 228; K.W. Gorrie, "Parent Education and Social Work," *Canadian Child and Family Welfare* 11, no. 5 (1936): 33–34.

34. Ursel, "The State and the Maintenance of Patriarchy," pp. 155–57; M. Abramovitz, *Regulating the Lives of Women,* pp. 30–31; Wayne, "The Function of Social Welfare in a Capitalist Economy," p. 81.

35. Editorial, "Free Mothers of a Free Race," *CPHJ* 4, no. 1 (1913): 40–41; Dr. W. B. Hendry, "Maternal Mortality," *CMAJ* 13, no. 4 (1923): 253–54; Dr. B. Atlee, "The Menace of Maternity," *Canadian Home Journal* (May 1932): 8. See also Turner, *Regulating Bodies,* p. 46; A. Davin, "Imperialism and Motherhood," *History Workshop Journal* 2, no. 5 (1978); A. Oakley, *The Captured Womb* (Oxford: Oxford University Press, 1984).

36. B. Ehrenreich and B. English, *For Her Own Good: 150 Years of the Experts' Advice to Women* (Garden City, N.Y.: Anchor, 1978), pp. 26–29; also W. Mitchinson, "The Medical Treatment of Women in Canada," in S. Burt, L. Code, and L. Dorney, eds., *Changing Patterns: Women in Canada* (Toronto: McClelland and Stewart, 1988).

37. The "cult of motherhood" was international: see Ellen Key, *The Century of the Child* (New York: Putnam, 1909); Key, *The Renaissance of Motherhood* (New York: Putnam, 1914). Contemporary Canadian examples include Editorial, "Free Mothers of a Free Race," *Canadian Public Health Journal* 4, no. 1 (1913): 40–41; "Mother and Baby," *Family Herald* (26 July 1919); Editorial,

"The Value of Motherhood," *Industrial Banner* (26 March 1920); Dr. W. B. Hendry, "Maternal Welfare," *Social Welfare* 13, no. 9 (1931): 180. On the postwar celebration of maternalism see V. Strong-Boag, *The New Day Recalled* (Markham: Penguin, 1988), especially ch. 5; B. Ehrenreich and D. English, *For Her Own Good;* R. Bridenthal, "Something Old, Something New: Women Between the Two World Wars," in R. Bridenthal and C. Koonz, eds., *Becoming Visible: Women in European History* (Boston: Houghton Mifflin, 1977).

38. A. W. Coone, "The Child as an Asset," *Social Welfare* 1, no. 2 (1918): 38; Dr. A. Brown, "Child Health," *CPHJ* 11, no. 2 (1920): 49; Dr. P. Bryce, "Recent Constructive Developments in Child Welfare," *Social Welfare* 2, no. 10 (1920): 19; H. E. Spence, "For a Healthy Canada," *Chatelaine* (August 1930): 29.

39. Dr. P. H. Bryce, "The Scope of a Federal Department of Health," 3–4; also G. I. H. Lloyd, "The Relation of Preventable Sickness to Poverty," *CPHJ* 6, no. 5 (1915): 244.

40. For anti-immigration labor views, see Editorial, *Industrial Banner* (20 April 1920); for racist medical views, see Dr. J. Halpenny, "One Phase of the Foreign Invasion of Canada," *Canadian Journal of Mental Hygiene* 1, no. 3 (1919): 224–26; J. Crosbie, RN, "The Foreign Problem as Related to Public Health," *Canadian Nurse* 26, no. 3 (1920): 136–37. See also McLaren, *Our Own Master Race,* pp. 46–67.

41. Editorial, "Child Welfare," *CPHJ* 4, no. 4 (1913): 162; E. M. Chapman, "Paying the Doctor to Keep You Well," *Maclean's* (1 January 1921); J. Miller, "Preventive Pathology," *Queen's Quarterly* (October 1922); Dr. A. Brown, "The General Practitioner and Preventive Paediatrics," *CPHJ* 21, no. 6 (1930): 268; Dr. A. G. Fleming, "Education of the Public in Health Matters," *CMAJ* 20, no. 10 (1930): 562.

42. H. M. Cassidy, "The Economic Value of Public Health," *CPHJ* 23, no. 2 (1932): 52; also Editorial, "Public Health and Social Welfare," *CPHJ* 23, no. 10 (1932): 493; Dr. W. W. Chipman, "The Infant Soldier," *Social Welfare* 4, no. 3 (1921): 48–49.

43. Dr. A. G. Fleming, "Study of Infant Deaths in Toronto," *CPHJ* 13, no. 5 (1922): 199; Dr. J. J. Heagerty, "Birth Control," *Social Welfare* 6, no. 3 (1924): 57; Editorial, "Birth Control," *Social Welfare* 5, no. 12 (1923): 243–44; on birth control and abortion, see A. McLaren and A. T. McLaren, *The Bedroom and the State* (Toronto: McClelland and Stewart, 1986).

44. R. Torrington, Presidential Address, National Council of Women of Canada *Yearbook* (1917): 16; also *Women's War Conference* [pamphlet] (Ottawa: Dominion Government, 1918), p. 33; Editorial, "Infant Mortality," *CPHJ* 6, no. 10 (1915): 510; Editorial, "These Little Ones," *Social Welfare* 1, no. 3 (1918): 53. For labor views, see Editorial, "A Splendid Move," *Industrial Banner* (7 May 1920); also Editorial, "The Value of Motherhood," *Industrial Banner* (26 March 1920).

45. Editorial, "Child Welfare," *CPHJ* 6, no. 3 (1915): 162; Editorial, "A Children's Bureau for Canada," *Social Welfare* 1, no. 4 (1919): 84.

46. Turner, *Medical Power and Social Knowledge,* pp. 10–12, discusses the knowledge/power relationship as developed by Foucault; see also Foucault, *Discipline and Punish* (New York: Pantheon, 1977), pp. 27–28.

47. Dr. H. MacMurchy, "The Baby's Father," 315. MacMurchy is actually citing Dr. John Burns, who presided over Britain's First National Council on Infantile Mortality in 1906; see Dwork, *War Is Good for Babies,* p. 114.

48. Dr. E. Guest, "Problems of Girlhood and Motherhood," *CPHJ* 18, no. 5 (1927): 195–98; Dr. W. W. Chipman, "Preparing Women for the Greatest of Professions," *Maclean's* (15 October 1921); Dr. Woods Hutchinson, "The Modern Mother," *Maclean's* (15 July 1920); Editorial, "The Health of Women," *CMAJ* 26, no. 11 (1936): 572.

49. S. Pines, RN, "We Want Perfect Parents," *Chatelaine* (September 1928): 29. On advice literature, see Comacchio, *Nations Are Built of Babies,* ch. 5–6; K. Arnup, *Education for Motherhood* (Toronto: University of Toronto Press, 1994); see Ehrenreich and English, *For Her Own Good;* D. Beekman, *The Mechanical Baby* (London: Dobson, 1979); C. Hardyment, *Dream Babies* (New York: Harper and Row, 1983); M. Ladd-Taylor, *Mother-Work.*

50. Dr. E. K. Clarke, "Community Responsibility for Habit Training," p. 228; Gorrie, "Parent Education," p. 33.

51. J. Mechling, "Advice to Historians on Advice to Mothers," *Journal of Social History* 9, no. 1 (1973): 65; V. Strong-Boag, "Intruders in the Nursery," in J. Parr, ed. *Childhood and Family in Canadian History* (Toronto: McClelland and Stewart, 1982), pp. 169–73.

52. To name just a few examples of the advice literature: the federal government's Division of Child and Maternal Welfare produced *The Canadian Mother and Child;* the Ontario government produced *The Baby;* the Canadian Welfare Council published a series of newsletters for mothers entitled *Prenatal Letters, Postnatal Letters,* and *Preschool Letters.* These circulated, with various updates, throughout the 1920s and 1930s; *The Canadian Mother and Child* remains in publication today. Advice manuals included Dr. Alan Brown, *The Normal Child, Its Care and Feeding* (Toronto: Macmillan, 1923); Dr. F. F. Tisdall, *The Home Care of the Infant and Child* (New York: Harper, 1931). Brown and Tisdall, Canada's foremost pediatricians during this period, worked out of Toronto's Hospital for Sick Children; with Dr. T. H. Drake, they were the creators of Pablum.

53. Dr. W. A. Evans, "Human Efficiency," *CPHJ* 4, no. 3 (1913): 138; K. Derry, "Morale, National and Industrial," *Canadian Congress Journal* 12, no. 3 (1933): 23; N. S. Rankin, "100 Percent Efficient," *CCJ* 3, no. 12 (1924): 78. On Taylorism, see B. D. Palmer, *Working Class Experience,* 2d ed. (Toronto: McGraw-Hill, 1992), pp. 160–62.

54. C. E. Hamilton, "The Scientific Management of Household Work and Wages," *CPHJ* 4, no. 1 (1913): 30–31; see also V. Strong-Boag, *The Parliament of Women* (Ottawa: Museum of Man, 1976), p. 187, on the National Council of Women of Canada's support of scientific management in the household; also R. Apple, *Mothers and Medicine* (Madison, Wisc.: University of Wisconsin Press, 1987), pp. 97–113; Ehrenreich and English, *For Her Own Good,* pp. 196–210.

55. W. Blatz and H. Bott, *Parents and the Preschool Child* (Toronto: Macmillan, 1928), p. vii. All the advisers were strict on the subject of a four-hour feeding schedule.

56. J. B. Watson, *Behaviourism* (New York: Norton, 1925), p. 4; Hardyment, *Dream Babies,* and Beekman, *The Mechanical Baby,* provide a good overview of Behaviourism's main tenets.

57. Brown, *The Normal Child;* Tisdall, *The Home Care of the Infant and Child;* and Ontario, Department of Health, *The Baby* all employ this "little machine" metaphor. The concept was prevalent in international child welfare circles; see Beekman, *The Mechanical Baby;* and Ehrenreich and English, *For Her Own Good.*

58. Hennessy, *Materialist Feminism and the Politics of Discourse,* pp. 103–4.

59. S. Fox, *The Mirror Makers* (New York: William Morrow, 1984) argues that the 1920s were the high point of advertising in America and the peak of its ability to influence consumer purchasing patterns.

60. For example, "Let's duck . . . here comes that nosey pest again," Castoria advertisement, *Maclean's* (15 September 1939).

61. "Are two pairs of hands enough?" Parke-Davis company advertisement, *Maclean's* (15 September 1937).

62. Letters from dissatisfied mothers to the federal government's Division of Child and Maternal Welfare and the Canadian Welfare Council expressed both gratitude for information and public health nurse visits and the great need for provision of real medical care; see Comacchio, "Nations Are Built of Babies," pp. 209–11. Similar testimony is found in M. Ladd-Taylor, ed., *Raising a Baby the Government Way: Mothers' Letters to the Children's Bureau* (New Brunswick, N.J.: Rutgers University), and M. Llewelyn Davies, ed., *Maternity: Letters from Working Women* (1915), reprint (London: Virago, 1978).

63. In Great Britain, the Maternity and Child Welfare Act of 1918 established prenatal supervision, medical consultations for preschoolers, milk and meals for toddlers and pregnant and nursing women, and dental care for mothers and children, regardless of socioeconomic status; see Dwork, *War Is Good for Babies,* pp. 208–14. In the U.S., the Sheppard-Towner Act of 1921 made available to the states grants of federal money for maternal and child welfare purposes, if matched by equal sums by the states themselves; see M. Ladd-Taylor, *Mother-Work,* pp. 168–69, 177–79. In Australia, the vital introduction of maternity allowances in 1912, limited implementation of a child endowment, and a royal commission on health in the 1920s also testified to more activist state efforts than in Canada; see K. M. Reiger, *The Disenchantment of the Home* (Melbourne: University of Melbourne, 1985), especially ch. 6, pp. 128–52.

30

A Value-Theoretic Approach to Childbirth and Reproductive Engineering

Kathryn Russell

In advanced capitalist societies today, reproduction is undergoing revolutionary change. Heated social debates echo new relations among people as we engage in practices that bring childbirth more and more under human control. Industry, hospitals, lawyers, insurance companies, social services, and a burgeoning cadre of professionals are increasingly involved in the central relation between a birth mother and her child.

Scientific advance is irretrievably changing human possibilities. Though artificial insemination, drugs for treating infertility, and abortion are perhaps the most recognized forms of interfering in the biological process, other more interventionist techniques are now a reality or are being researched. Sperm banks are available, some enticing customers with products produced by men with "special" intellectual and physical properties. A variety of techniques are being tried for sex preselection, including antibody injection against female- or male-determining sperm (Hull 1990, 242). In vitro fertilization and embryo transfer have helped some infertile people have children, while freezing embryos makes it possible to store them for future thawing and implantation.

New developments in genetics have further enlarged our capability actively to direct the outcome of human reproduction. Genetic defects can be discovered through amniocentesis or chorionic villus sampling, so fetuses can be identified for potential abortion; screening embryos after in vitro fertilization can prevent having to make an abortion decision by allowing for selective implantation. Research from the human genome project may someday make it possible to correct abnormalities through gene splicing. The first fetal tissue transplant to treat a patient for Parkinson's disease occurred in Colorado in 1988. Some 150 other types of genetic disorders may be so treated, raising the controversial possibility of producing a fetus for the sole purpose of its being aborted for medical use (Begley 1993). Research in genetics is not without detractors, however. Demonstrators have marched outside laboratories, opposing the specter of eugenic manipulation of embryos.

People interested in having children these days can look to friends, relatives, and agencies to provide sperm, egg, and uterus if necessary. Professionals are working on quality control! The class nature of the new services is evident, as many are extremely expensive and often not covered by insurance policies. Thus they are available only to those who can afford them. Women are now hired as gestational surrogates, although the fetus they carry and give birth to is not the result of their own ovulation and copulation. The first birth through gestational surrogacy, where an embryo was transferred into a woman who had no genetic relation to the egg used during fertilization, occurred in April 1986 (American Fertility Society 1986, 58S). A postmenopausal South African grandmother gave birth to her own granddaughter in 1992, serving as her daughter's surrogate. Lawmakers are considering making it illegal for post-menopausal women to bear children in France. In the United States, controversy rages over paying surrogates, and legal guidelines promise to be in a state of flux for the foreseeable future. In 1986, the Kentucky Supreme Court ruled that such payments did not violate state laws against baby selling (American Fertility Society 1986, 13S); in 1992, New York State became the eighteenth state to ban payment for surrogacy. The confused nature of the controversy is symbolized by the fact that both the National Organization for Women and the New York State Catholic Conference endorsed the ban. There are no clear political sides in this battle, revealing just how necessary careful analyses of the problems are.

In many ways reproductive relations are becoming more impersonal, even intrusive. The behavior of pregnant women is increasingly being controlled. Women are sometimes treated as human incubators with little capacity for self-direction. Katha Pollitt reports that a pregnant woman was confronted in a restaurant for supposedly endangering her fetus by drinking a glass of wine. Women who abuse drugs and alcohol are jailed in the name of fetal protection. Doctors performed a Cesarean section on Angela Carder, a Long Island woman who was dying of cancer, to "save her baby" before her family could stop them through the courts (Pollitt 1990, 409). *The New England Journal of Medicine* reveals that almost 50 percent of the physicians directing programs in maternal-fetal medicine think that court action should be sought to save the life of a fetus in case the pregnant woman refuses to give her consent (Hull 1990).

The involvement of reproductive technologists and agencies in childbirth as well as the increasing social scrutiny of pregnant women suggest that childbirth is becoming less private. It is important to analyze what economic developments these new social relations herald. Sensing the possibility of profit maximization, capital has pushed itself into what was once thought to be one of the most intimate—even sacred—of human activities: conception, gestation, and birth. This is a continuation of the process whereby a male-dominated medical profession has struggled to take childbearing and birth control over from women.

In this paper, I draw an analogy between childbearing and social labor. My work is exploratory and intended to show that a value-theoretic approach to childbirth can be illuminating. It can provide an interesting example of how private labor becomes social and extends the Marxist research program into a new area. My argument is not without problems, as I will make clear; but, in my view, the labor theory of value can provide necessary conceptual foundations for understanding childbirth and its social functions under capitalism. I will contend that childbearing is being socialized and commodified, brought into a material relationship with other forms of labor. It thus functions in ways similar to abstract labor. Moreover, contemporary social and technical developments enhance the valorization of childbirth, deepening its value-theoretic aspects and making it more crucial to turn to Marxist theory to account for this.

It is important to realize that the valorization of childbirth stands in contradiction to the fundamental need of capital for an independent working-class household sector, where labor power is reliably produced without direct capitalist support. Women's contributions are crucial in the domestic sphere, because they maintain the daily subsistence of the labor force and give birth to and socialize future workers. Thus, with respect to children, women's role in childrearing as well as childbearing is important. I will focus here on the latter and discuss childbirth as providing for the generational replacement of labor power necessary for capitalism to succeed.

Before I explain how childbearing is being drawn into the market, I want to lay out a framework for my argument by making some general comments in Section I about the way birth is often centered in feminist and Marxist theories. In my view, women can be oppressed because of their biological capacities, but these are not the root causes of our problems. The connection between childbearing and women's disadvantaged status changes throughout history. My work on the valorization of childbirth is an attempt to avoid biological determinism by situating birth in a social context.

Section II presents a value-theoretic analysis of childbirth, followed by Section III on the social reproduction of labor power. Section IV addresses implications of the new scientific technologies, since these developments have an impact on the quality of women's lives and the degree of oppression they experience. Women of color and women in nations dominated by imperialism are particularly affected. I will not attempt to develop a general theory of women's oppression; nor will I discuss the ethical and legal issues involved in reproductive and genetic engineering. My focus is political economy, and my remarks are tentative. The reproductive changes I will discuss have both liberatory and exploitative potential. The valorization process provides a context that can reveal how women will fare under these changes, because the higher the value extracted from childbirth and the greater control over bearing children achieved by capital, the greater the oppression of women in this arena. Social relations are crucial, however, not technology and not biology. Productive or reproductive forces themselves do not determine the quality of women's lives. Women should have the new technologies at their disposal, but in ways that we control. Understanding the valorization process can help to make this more likely.

I. CHILDBEARING IN FEMINIST AND MARXIST LITERATURE

Anthropologists and historians have sought the origins of patriarchy by concentrating on several problems: the development of production for exchange; specialization of work; colonization; centralization of political authority; the use of warfare to plunder other groups for slaves and riches; and the dissolution of communal kinship networks (Engels 1972; Leacock 1981a; Sayers, Evans, and Redclift 1987). Despite the richness of these scholarly traditions, both feminists and Marxists have had a tendency to focus on childbearing capacity as the source of women's differential status. An undue emphasis has been placed on childbearing capacity as culturally and psychologically significant and on its presence as a source of the division of labor between women and men.

My approach to childbearing does not center on it. Centering a theory on a particular phenomenon assigns that feature special and unique status; it assumes that everything else revolves around that factor, is tied to it, is given meaning by it, or is conditioned by it. I want to contextualize childbirth, situating it within the development of historical contradictions to show how the current social relations of bearing children are benefiting capital. Thus, neither biological capacity nor reproductive engineering can be studied by itself to understand women's oppression. We need to understand the context—in this case, valorization—that creates the significance of reproductive difference.

Feminists have often treated women's capacity to bear children as crucial to the cultural construction of gender. Monique Wittig and Jeffner Allen, for example, explain that childbearing defines what a woman is and that patriarchy depends on women's functioning as breeders for the benefit of men (Allen 1983, 315–16). Other feminists suggest that the fact that women give birth and men do not is so primordial that it structures human consciousness. Breast or womb envy has been portrayed as a central psychological mechanism determining personality development and structuring meaning in social ideology (Kittay 1983; Al-Hibri 1983). The phenomenology of childbirth has been said to define woman as the Other. Mary O'Brien (1982) uses a version of Hegelianism to argue that men dominate women to compensate for the "alienation of the male seed in the copulative act," but that women's birthing labor cancels their alienation from their product, causing them to be uniquely connected to the historical process. Simone de Beauvoir (1953) has been influential in arguing that bearing children limits women's capacity to achieve transcendence and thus accomplish genuine human projects. Thus, for many, feminist childbearing capacity sets the stage for a psychosexual drama that draws men and women into a struggle for power.

Childbirth can also be centered theoretically by assuming that this reproductive difference between men and women gives rise to a division of labor between the sexes, not only in child care but also in other activities of a broader scope. On this view, specialization of task develops because women give birth and men do not, and responsibilities vary in such a fashion that benefits accrue to men but not to women. This is, of course, a more materialist approach than those previously mentioned. For example, Maria Mies (1986) argues that women were the first to develop practical ways to gather food and nonviolent tools like baskets and digging sticks because of the necessity of feeding themselves and their offspring. According to her, patriarchal divisions of labor developed during the pastoralist phase when the breeding of animals led to men's understanding of their own role in reproduction and eventually to their appropriation and control of female birthing capacity. There is a long tradition within Marxist scholarship that sees the sexual division of labor as natural, as based on biological difference (Vogel 1983). Theorists influenced by Engels often explain that men's status improved and women's declined when the sphere of activities men were engaged in changed due to the use of new forces of production, such as the domestication of animals, and surplus goods were produced that could be exchanged (Engels 1972; Leacock 1981a). Engels's explanation for the "world historical defeat of women" shows how developments within the sphere of production caused the subordination of women in the sphere of reproduction.

I would argue that women are bit disadvantaged because they are different from men, but that biological difference is used as a stigma or mark to identify them, and that this stigmatization is used to justify keeping women subordinate after their oppression has already developed. In trying to understand gender and male dominance, we should emphasize the contextual social and historical processes that create relations of power, rather than biological difference. These relations require legitimization and maintenance; significant difference is created, not discovered.

Furthermore, although thinking about childbearing is a meaningful way to understand how the reproductive roles women play articulate with the production process, it is an inadequate approach to conceptualizing gender. In *Marxism and the Oppression of Women,* Lise Vogel argues that at the level of abstraction reached when one considers the reproduction of labor power in any society, workers are genderless. This is because she is considering the renewal of workers as a set of abstract labor units, no matter their sex or national origin. Gender becomes relevant for her only when we realize that generational replacement rests on the capacity of women to bear children.

> From a theoretical perspective, it does not yet matter whether they are women or men, so long as they are somehow available to make up the labor force. What raises the question of gender is, of course, the phenomenon of generational replacement of bearers of labor power—that is, replacement of existing workers by new workers from the next generation. (Vogel 1983, 141)

Vogel does place birth in a context, because, as an aspect of total social reproduction, she does not see it as valuable in and of itself. But Vogel contextualizes birth too late. The contextualization is made *after* women's childbearing capacity is abstracted from the social whole and identified as an absolute biological fact. For Vogel, "biological differences constitute the material precondition for the social construction of gender differences." From my point of view, biological differences are an *aspect* of gender differences, but not the root, or base, or precondition for the emergence of gender. According to Vogel, the biological difference between men's and women's bodies with respect to childbearing is the basic reason for the constitution of gender relations (1983, 141):

> [Generational replacement] requires, in an *absolute* sense, that there be a sexual division of labor of at least a minimal kind. If children are to be born it is women who will carry and deliver them. . . . While they may also be direct producers, it is their differential role in the reproduction of labor power that lies at the *root* of their oppression in class society. (1983, 145; emphasis added)

In my view, focusing on childbearing as the "root" of women's oppression is a problematic way of thinking about biological difference. It is true that women's and men's bodies are qualitatively different, but is this difference the *source,* the *root,* of women's oppression? How do we tell when a difference *makes* a difference historically?[1]

An examination of various periods in history shows that the birth rate and other demographic and political considerations seem to be more critical to the generational replacement of labor power than the brute biological "fact" of women's birthing. This "fact" exists within a myriad of considerations influencing the availability of new people and the significance of their existence. If we consider the need for a new generation of workers to replace those spent in the labor process, the need for new humans is not simply satisfied by saying that we will get babies from the women.

For example, bringing women to the British colony in North America did not ensure the reproduction of labor power. Factors like the timing of marriages, the mortality rates of either men or women, the ratio of women to men, and people's standards of living were as important as the availability of women. Both servant and slave women born in the colonies had higher fertility rates than women brought from Europe or Africa, so the index of generational replacement also depended on the percentage of women available who were born in North America. The likelihood of people reaching adulthood and also beginning to reproduce was influenced by marriage and household formation, which among whites involved the availability of land. The relations of production affected the latter, because an increase in the use of slave labor made less land available for settlement by new white families. Slave household formation was tied to the degree of their exploitation and depended on the demands of their white masters, the health of the economy, and the amount of ethnic division in the slave community (Kulikoff 1986).

Therefore, as a form of concrete material activity, childbearing is a capacity that is internally related to its conditions of existence. Its effectiveness in enabling the generational replacement of the work force is dependent on other considerations. Since it does not transcend these factors, it cannot be the key to understanding how the need to replace workers affects the oppression of women. Stress, diet, prenatal care, environmental factors like natural disasters and the carrying capacity of the land, and the existence of oppression due to race, class, or nationality are all vital influences on childbearing. We should look at the relationship between childbearing and other factors that cause disadvantages for women, not at childbirth itself. Discussing how procreative labor is being valorized is an example of how to explicate the concrete relations within which childbearing exists, the context that should be specified to avoid biological determinism.

II. A VALUE-THEORETIC APPROACH TO CHILDBIRTH UNDER CAPITALISM

In this section I examine the two-fold nature of childbearing labor that is emerging under late twentieth-century capitalism. As concretely useful labor, it is an activity that ties biological parents to a particular child. Now that the social and abstract character of childbirth is developing, however, these organic links are being ruptured. Simultaneously, new social relations are forming. I will first explain why childbearing can be viewed as a form of labor. Then I will show how it is being drawn into capitalist exchange relations. I will also argue that what commentators have said about abstract labor can be applied to childbearing, as material economic processes and new social relations create an abstract equivalence between ways of creating children and other forms of social labor. Finally, I will address some problems with my application of value theory to childbirth.

Instead of viewing childbirth solely as a biological, natural function, we can see it as genuine human productive activity. Human labor is the appropriation of the natural environment through conscious, purposive activity. Marx defines it as "productive activity of a definite kind, carried on with a definite aim . . . it is an eternal natural necessity which mediates the metabolism between man [sic] and nature, and therefore human life itself" (1977a, 133). Childbearing is unique in several respects, but it involves a unity of conception and execution sufficient to call it a human labor process, which expends physiological energy and has "material-technical properties" (Rubin 1972, 141). It involves an interchange with nature, is planned, and utilizes instruments of (re)production. It is not merely directed by animal instinct.

Women have had children "unconsciously" only after a male-dominated medical profession began to view childbirth as a dangerous disease-like state against which the woman had to be protected by a man and from which she had to be insulated by being "put to sleep." Throughout history, women have regulated their births, have planned how to have births, and have thought about and reacted to the changes their bodies were undergoing during pregnancy. This understanding of childbirth moves away from common assumptions about early human history, but is consistent with research into birth control. Women used devices like pessaries, sponges, and cervical caps to prevent pregnancy, and potions made from plants and herbs as abortifacents; they timed the spacing of their births by extending lactation; some practiced infanticide (Mies 1986, 54; Gordon 1976, 26–46). We need to be aware that we are using a linear conception of history in presupposing that today's birth control practices are better than those used by women long before us. It is possible they had more control over their fertility than do many women in twentieth-century industrialized countries who are alienated from their bodies under conditions where birth control and birth itself are commodified. Also, we need to view women as active historical agents, not passive animals at the mercy of their biology. Surely instincts are involved and uterine contractions are to some extent automatic, but women intervene in these processes and condition them according to their historically constituted needs. Social relations mediate what would otherwise be a purely physiological act.

Thus, procreative labor can be viewed as concrete, useful labor because it is a definite form of activity carried out to achieve a definite aim. It can be undertaken to produce use values, ones needed by others. Increasingly, childbearing is being drawn into the market, and the actual labor involved is being transformed into different concrete forms. These events are interesting examples of what I. I. Rubin considers to be central problems in Marxist political economy: understanding how private labor becomes social and explaining how production taking place dispersed throughout society in distinct, private firms becomes part of a unified economic system exhibiting characteristics that are regular and describable by laws (1972, 129). As he explains, under capitalist commodity production, ". . . *private* labor acquires a supplementary characteristic in the form of *social* labor, *concrete* labor in the form of *abstract* labor, *complex* labor is reduced to *simple* labor, and *individual* to *socially necessary* labor" (1972, 128). Let us apply Rubin's ideas to childbearing.

Private labor becomes social when it becomes part of the mass of productive labor in society. Consider how childbearing becomes interconnected with other labor processes. Today, developments in reproductive engineering such as in vitro fertilization, embryo transfer, fetal tissue transplants, and the freezing of sperm and embryos have transformed the options available for generational reproduction. These changes are now part of the new material relations of social labor because they involve more people than birth parents in the creation of children. Those who also participate do so as part of their work. We notice even more social labor that is drawn into these relations if we consider the construction of necessary facilities, the products produced for use in the laboratories, the schooling of workers, and the capital investment necessary to support such undertakings. A growing service sector is developing to satisfy the needs of those unable or unwilling to reproduce the "standard" way. The movement of capital into these new fields should be studied. We can also appraise, as I do below, the mobility of labor into what may someday be considered the "birth industry."

The idea of simple labor, which ignores the different qualitative properties of individual laborers, can also be applied to childbearing. Simple childbearing labor power is possessed by every average, biologically capable woman. Thus, what Marx says of productive labor applies also to her parturitive labor. It is part of her "bodily organism . . . without being developed in any special way" (Marx 1977a, 135). One woman can function as the surrogate for another, providing ova or uterus. More importantly, social relations are separating women from the means and forces of reproduction.

In a sense, a process similar to deskilling is taking place in reproduction. These biological processes are being isolated and assigned to different people: the provision of gametes, fertilization and the acquisition of an embryo, implantation, and gestation and birth. All these can be separated from social parentage. With hormones, a woman's ovaries can be stimulated to produce eggs which can then be harvested through laparoscopy. Sperm can be acquired from a donor or bank. Fertilization can occur in a petri dish, and the resulting embryo frozen or placed in the uterus of a woman. Individual women are to a great extent interchangeable; within certain medical parameters, one uterus or egg is as useful as another. News reports reveal that through continued research, female cadavers and particularly fetuses may provide good sources of eggs. Thus, the childbearing labor of women is being made materially equivalent through a historical process. Through reproductive engineering, however, this equalization of labor involves several people, male or female, since the labor components involved in bearing a child can be distributed among different people. If we use the language of political economy, we see that reproductive engineers are engaging in productive consumptions, expending their labor power in uniting the raw material (eggs and sperm) with a functioning uterus (means of production) to create a product.

It is interesting to consider how childbearing might be compared to socially necessary labor, wherein the labor time required to produce a product could be compared across a particular sphere of production. Reproductive and genetic engineering will continue to develop. Perhaps someday it will be possible to quantify the various forms of simple childbearing labor power required to produce new people. The labor used in individual laboratories and service agencies involved in the new technologies may be equalized through competition among them for funding and customers. But problems exist with this analogy, as I will show below.

In what sense is procreation being commodified? The social nature of childbearing unfolds as its material relationship with other labors is enhanced through exchange. Under commodity production, private labors expended in different firms are connected only indirectly as the products created circulate in a money economy. Marx says, "Since the producers do not come into social contact with each other until they exchange their products, the specific social characteristics of their private labors appear only within this exchange" (1977a, 165). The same point seems applicable to reproduction, for during in vitro fertilization or surrogacy the relationship among the different people involved is not direct. Parents, biological and social, are brought into contact by the activity of technicians, agency workers, and often lawyers. These services must be paid for. The social character of the activity of joining egg, sperm, uterus, surrogate mother, or future parents comes about through the introduction of money. In *The Human Body Shop* (1993), Andrew Kimbrell states that at least six companies supply fetal tissue to customers, with sales of several million dollars per year. Sperm can be stored, embryos frozen, and the future children "used" by any potential household. The value form of childbearing develops when the use value of its various biological components can be consumed outside the private production site. Arguments are being advanced to require that "extracorporeal" body parts and bodily organs be considered private property that can be sold or rented (Andrews 1986; American Fertility Society 1986; Hull 1990). Childbearing labor is thus becoming indirectly social, a form appropriate to capitalism. The social nature of producing eggs for the market or renting one's uterus expresses itself indirectly in the exchange relation.

Is childbearing labor becoming abstract? The use value of the baby, uterus, sperm, or eggs is the form through which a particular way of acquiring the universal equivalent, money, is expressed. The equalization of this form and money shows that the labor of childbearing is being brought into relation with other social labor as an abstraction. Chris Arthur explains: "The abstraction inherent in value-equivalence can occur only through a social process of unconscious character, which equates transitively all the labors carried on in the different branches or production as if each in itself were nothing more than a fraction of a homogeneous substance" (1979, 99). The social substance here is abstract value. Arthur's analysis is directed at productive labor, but a similar point is relevant for my purposes. The choice involved in deciding to make money through surrogacy, selling eggs or fetal tissue, or by having a job is represented through the possibility of the valorization of birthing. Childbearing labor is being made similar to the universal character of labor under capitalism, and this suggests its practical equivalence with other kinds of human labor.

In discussing controversies surrounding reproductive technology, some commentators draw an analogy between social and childbearing labor which presupposes the material equivalence I have pointed out. Lori Andrews, who was part of the working group "Reproductive Laws for the 1990s" at Rutgers University in 1987, argues that people who give up their sperm, eggs, and other body parts should be paid.

> In any paid labor, we are giving our body. . . . How much risk should a paid donor be allowed to run? One way of deciding would be to compare the level of risk people face when they donate organs with the risk of selling another product of their body, their labor. (1986, 32)

Here, a direct comparison is being made between the exchange of productive labor power for wages and the selling of reproductive labor. In defending surrogacy contracts, John Robertson makes a similar point.

> Even though blood and sperm are sold, and miners, professional athletes, and petrochemical workers sell some of their health and vitality, some persons think it wrong for women to bear children for money, in much the same way that paying money for sex or body organs is considered wrong. . . . Since blocking this exchange stops infer-

tile couples from reproducing and rearing the husband's child, a harm greater than moral distaste is necessary to justify it. (Hull, 1990, 162)

Once again childbearing labor is said to be similar to other forms of social labor.

The ideas of these theorists reflect the material developments that are taking place today, perhaps without our notice. Through the inclusion of childbearing labor in a money economy, a transitive equivalence is being created between childbirth and productive labor. The formerly private and intimate nature of childbearing is diminishing as it becomes part of the social economy. This addresses the central problem Rubin is interested in: "The comprehensive equilization (through money) of all concrete forms of labor and their transformation into abstract labor simultaneously creates among them a social connection, transforming private into social labor" (1972, 130).

This abstract equivalence among different kinds of labor, including reproductive labor, is being created as a particular social and historical form of childbearing in advanced capitalism. Discussing social labor, Marx points out the following in the "Introduction" to the Grundrisse:

> . . . this abstraction of labour as such is not merely the mental product of a concrete totality of labours. Indifference towards specific labours corresponds to a form of society in which individuals can with ease transfer from one labour to another. . . . Not only the category, labour, but labour in reality has here become the means of creating wealth in general, and has ceased to be organically linked with particular individuals in any specific form. . . . The simplest abstraction, then . . . achieves practical truth as an abstraction only as a category of the most modern society. (1973, 104–5)

If we apply this analysis to childbearing, comparing the new forms of conception to other labors is not simply a mental act of theory construction. Homogeneous human labors, including the creation of children, are being made equivalent materially as part of the abstract universal labor which is the social expression of value. Thus, the organic link between a child and a particular woman is being ruptured, and there is a separation of genetic, gestational, and social parentage. These disruptions are to be expected when concrete labor becomes abstract: "Abstract labor stands separated from, and opposed to, the richness of the concrete. It transcends, but does not preserve, the concrete labors' specificity" (Arthur 1979, 100).

We can also draw an analogy to the mobility of social labor. Consider the movement of service workers, clerical workers, educational, industrial, and construction workers, as well as professional technicians into the economic spheres connected to reproductive and genetic engineering. As these spheres continue to expand, more labor power of various types will be drawn in, and their rate of development will increase as more profit is able to be extracted by capital. We can also consider the mobility of women's reproductive labor. Today, women hire themselves out as surrogates and poor women and women in countries exploited by imperialism put their children up for adoption by people in core capitalist countries in a fashion suggestive of simple commodity production. The money received for their "product" can be used to buy necessities for their family or other commodities and services they desire (C-M-C). One could earn $10,000 having a surrogate child, or earn a similar amount working for wages.

Surrogacy is distinguished from "baby selling" because the former is regulated by a contract set up before a pregnancy occurs. The American Fertility Society insists that women are being paid for their labor, not their product, "for their help in creating a child," not for a child they have in their possession (1986, 66S). This distinction is spurious. My analysis of the valorization of childbearing shows that the new reproductive activities cannot be defended by separating a women's labor from her product, the infant. A labor process and its product are intimately related, and they are torn asunder only under conditions of alienation. It is the extraction of value from their labor that causes problems for women, not the activities themselves.

A Michigan psychiatrist, Phillip Parker, investigated over 275 surrogate applicants. Though several factors seem to motivate women to become surrogates, Robertson reports Parker's research showing that "they choose the surrogate role primarily because the fee provides a better economic opportunity than alternative occupation . . ." (Hull 1990, 158). In the future, women may be able to make money not only by gestating a fetus to term, but also by producing ova for embryo transfers, or a fetus for a tissue transplant or scientific research. The character of their product will have to be taken into account. Race will be relevant, for just as in adoption, white infants will probably continue to be in great demand. Gender and class-linked properties ideologically associated with intelligence and physical form will also be sought after. Family medical history will count in determining the likelihood of transmission of genetic disease.

If childbearing labor were not being socialized and becoming more abstract, those who find it necessary to make money in these ways would not be conditioned by race, class, and nationality. The set of women participating in the new forms of reproduction would be simply biologically determined. As the valorization of childbirth develops, a division of labor is developing among women. Those who acquire babies are benefiting from the labor of surrogates, egg donors, technicians, and service workers. I am not insinuating that adoptive women are callous or that working-class women are opportunists. Women's involvement in such transactions indicates their lack of suitable alternatives and loss of control over their own bodies.

Of course, the childbearing power of women is not yet being bought in order to sell its product for a profit on a large scale. At this point, I will consider some conceptual problems that arise for my analogy between childbirth and productive labor and my use of Marx's labor theory of value.

Let us look more closely at commodity production and the nature of full-blown capitalist exchange. "Marx distinguishes between the case in which particular useful objects are produced for direct use and only accidentally or occasionally find their way into the sphere of exchange, and the case in which goods are produced in order to be exchanged" (Shaikh 1990, 43). When goods or services are normally created to be used in the immediate household or self-sufficient small community, their exchange or barter is not expected, and the activities involved in creating them occur in a fashion that is not regulated by exchange. As Shaikh says, the labor involved is only valorized in the act of exchange, which "creates a temporary equivalence" (43). The social nature of the labor is transitory. In cases of the second variety, however, the goods or services are created for the express purpose of selling them and the abstract character of the labor expended is a necessary part of the process. There is an important difference, then, between producing something rarely sold and producing something only to sell it, under conditions in which exchange relations are determined by labor values. "It is only the latter instance, in which capitalism has effectively generalized commodity production, that the reproduction of society is regulated by the law of value" (Shaikh 1990, 44).

As childbearing is being integrated into the market, it takes on the characteristics of petty commodity production. Surrogate mothers are not merely providing a personal service. That they are producing for exchange can be seen by noting that they take the sum they will receive into account and produce a child to turn their "product" into money. But since childbearing has not yet become part of full-blown commodity production, its valorization must be regarded as incomplete. The situation lies somewhere between the two extremes mentioned above. Perhaps it never will be completely integrated. There are several inherent economic problems with the commodification of childbirth that may prevent the full capitalization of reproduction. How can the exchange value of infants or embryos be measured? Women's gestation and delivery times vary in ways that might preclude their measurement as well. How would we specify the total labor time needed to produce a baby? How would this time be compared with that of other labor processes occurring in the capitalist economy? These problems make it difficult to see how the market prices of reproductive products could be regulated by the productivity of the people involved in producing them.

III. THE SOCIAL REPRODUCTION OF LABOR POWER

As I indicated earlier, capitalism has a fundamental need for an independent household sector providing for the reproduction of labor power with little direct support from the capitalist. An interesting theoretical issue is whether the valorization of childbirth fundamentally conflicts with this capitalist form of procuring labor power and therefore with the stable reproduction of capitalist production relations in general. I will show, however, that the new social forms of childbearing are consistent with other developments that have taken place in the twentieth century. The reproduction of capitalist relations has led to the socialization of the reproduction of labor power in many ways.

Traditional Marxist analyses have treated reproduction and the family, as well as the state, as social spheres that are external to the accumulation process though structured by it (Smith 1978). In the transition to capitalism from feudalism, production is socialized, individual ownership of the means of production persists, and the household-based reproduction of labor power stays private. Marx says: "The maintenance and reproduction of the working class remains a necessary condition for the reproduction of capital. But the capitalist may safely leave this to the worker's drives for self-preservation and propagation" (1977a, 718). Childbirth provides for the generational replacement of labor power, and Marx stipulates that it takes place privately. This autonomy is required for the successful valorization of labor power. However, the relation between socialized production and privatized reproduction under capitalism is contradictory. Furthermore, in many Marxist theories of the oppression of women, it is the privatization of work in the household that lies at the core of their subordination. Thus, socialist suggestions of liberating women often recommend the socialization of domestic labor (Leacock 1981b; Davis 1981). It is essential to analyze then how the contradiction between reproduction and production is unfolding. What has been separate from production is becoming integral to it as the process of valorization creeps into every possible nook and cranny of capitalist society and sucks new value-creating activities into itself.[2]

This contradiction between reproduction and production is developing in ways that tie the former into the latter. Their material interpenetration can be theoretically discussed by recognizing the internal relation between the two spheres. Indeed, for Marx, reproduction becomes production when it is ". . . productive to the capitalist and to the state, since it is the production of a force which produces wealth for other people" (Marx 1977a, 719; Russell 1984). Moreover, "when viewed . . . as a connected whole, and in the constant flux of its incessant renewal, every social process of production is at the same time a process of reproduction" (Marx 1977a, 711). The reproduction of capital involves institutions and struggles growing out of the continuation and expansion of capitalism; the provision and reprovision of exploitable labor power is relationally identical to the continued accumulation of capital.

Marx asks us to look at how a mode of production reproduces itself to continue as an identifiable way of life. Under capitalism, it is expanded, not simple, social reproduction that is most interesting, since the former is required for increasing the scale of the economy and fostering the growth of capital. Marx identifies productive and individual consumption as aspects of social reproduction. Productive consumption brings together the expenditure of human labor power, the means of production, and raw materials to create a product which can be sold to realize value greater than the variable and constant capital originally invested. The actions of the worker during the labor process renew capitalist relations by providing for the metamorphosis of labor into capital. Through productive consumption, the worker creates a commodity existing independently of her or himself. Individual consumption reproduces the workers themselves, however, because it entails the "reconversion of means of subsistence given by capital in return for labor power into fresh labor power" (Marx 1977a, 718); it keeps workers alive from day to day and able to participate in production. Women's domestic labor is integral to this process. Not only childrearing, but also childbearing is important because it creates new generations of workers. Most individual consumption takes place in households of one form or another, though this location is not necessary since workers might be fed and cared for in hostels, as in South Africa, or even in prisons (Russell 1984).

Today's governmental services are part of the social, not private, reproduction of labor power, and they are necessary for maintaining labor in a suitable form for capitalist production. The expansion of governmental entitlement programs in areas like food stamps, Medicaid, and welfare reflects the move away from privatized reproduction. As Dickinson and Russell point out, "this growth reflects the increasing contradiction between the imperatives of social production on the one hand and the limitations of privatized reproduction on the other" (1986, 11). Neither the reserve army of labor nor much of the working class can sustain itself privately. Historically, working-class women have been entangled most within this contradiction and have been particularly vocal in demanding that the state assume more and more responsibility for the reproduction of labor power, calling for child care, public health facilities, welfare, and housing (Leacock 1981b, 485). These demands ask for the socialization of childrearing. A similar form of struggle is developing around childbearing. Many argue that reproductive technologies should be available to all, as a state-sponsored entitlement (Hull 1990; Arditti 1984). This is especially important in preventing a situation where only the rich have access to the new services. A demand for government assistance is based on an argument of the positive right to reproduce and the government's obligation to provide health care for all its citizens.[3]

Thus, capital is proving itself to be resilient and resourceful. The valorization of childbirth and other forms of socializing the reproduction of labor power do not seem to interfere with the successful reproduction of capitalist relations of production, despite the move away from privatization. The interpenetration of reproduction and production has drawn capital into the relations of childrearing and childbirth. These developments are one way to resolve tensions inherent in the contradiction between privatized reproduction and socialized production. Here we see socialized forms of reproduction developing in the worm of capitalism. We might remember, however, that Marx never thought the transition to socialism inevitable. Capitalism might degenerate into a form of "barbarism." Since the commodification of embryos, infants, and women that protects the interest of capital is not liberating, the full development of capitalist relations of reproduction may represent a turn to barbarism.

IV. SOCIAL IMPLICATIONS OF THE NEW REPRODUCTIVE TECHNOLOGIES

Just as in the transition from feudalism to capitalism, relations among people are changing to be consistent with the unfettered development of the new reproductive forces. Struggle is heightening and playing an important role in defining these new relationships. The commodification of childbearing is blocked by the immediate organic unity of household relations and laws that codify the nuclear family as the reproductive norm. Maria Mies points out that during a 1985 congress in Bonn, members of the group "Women against Reproductive and Genetic Engineering" complained that though the new sciences were being promoted as a way to help people overcome infertility, in reality the goal was solving problems posed by stagnating industrial capitalism: "The female body with its generative power has been discovered as a new 'area of investment'" (1988, 225). Lawyers, the medical establishment, insurance companies, the pharmaceutical industry, and scientific laboratories are eagerly pursuing options for proficient new forms of procreation.

The American Fertility Society and the reproductive industry need to make sure the activities of surrogates and donors are undertaken in ways consistent with a more generalized form of commodity production, to ensure that the labor is performed *only* for exchange. This is why they want a contract set up *before* pregnancy occurs and why they want to formalize the endeavors and set-up procedures to sell or rent body parts and capacities. Non-marketplace behavior on the part of surrogates must be stopped. As Mies points out:

> . . . the surrogacy industry faces problems similar to those old home-based industries had to contend with in the beginning. It is to make sure that the producers deliver the products and do not keep them for themselves. This means that they have to be forced into accepting that what they produce is a commodity, not something of their own, and that they are doing alienated labour. (1988, 229)

This analogy between reproductive engineering and home-based cottage industry is particularly appropriate when the egg and/or embryo, the "raw materials," are supplied to the surrogate mother. The infants cannot simply be made available accidentally or occasionally. They need to be produced only for the market, not immediate use. Restrictive family and state practices that interfere with the valorization of childbirth must be replaced.

Tremendous controversies have ensued over the use of reproductive technologies and the changes in relations among people they are stimulating. Many people are struggling to prevent monetary transactions from being allowed. Humanist objections to setting a price for people's bodily organs and products, and above all for infants, are raised often. But some see the free market and liberal contract law as the solution to the tensions that have arisen. For example, the Ethics Committee of the American Fertility Society argues that the right to reproduce should be considered a negative one[4] based on the constitutional right to privacy, and that non-coital reproduction should be regulated through contracts enforced by the government: "Refusal to enforce a reproductive contract or to ban payment would amount to an interference with procreative liberty because it would prevent couples from acquiring the donor or surrogate assistance needed to acquire a child genetically" (American Fertility Society 1986, 5S). Surrogate mothers should not refuse to give up their gestational product, and state or federal laws should not prohibit arrangements which pay providers of biological components for their services. According to Andrews, "A market in body parts and products would require consent to all categories of research and ensure that patients are protected from coercion and given the chance to be paid fairly for their contribution" (Andrews 1986, 28). This argument, however, demonstrates the extreme degree of alienation potentially involved in surrogacy. The socialization of childbearing labor is taking place within market relations that divorce the owners of the labor power from the products of their labor.

The commodification of childbearing represents a further loss of women's control over birth as well as over other aspects of their lives. *The Handmaid's Tale* by Margaret Atwood (1985) is a powerful warning that historical forces are creating a class of women who can be exploited as baby makers. This arrangement is not entirely new. Gertrude Himmelfarb's comments on the etymology of "proletarian" reveal the use value of women's procreative labor long ago: "Derived from *proles,* offspring ['proletarian'] originally referred to the lowest class of Roman citizen who served the state only by producing children" (1983, 283). Contrary to the American Fertility Society and its allies, selling body parts and procreative labor power will not free women, just as liberal contract law will not protect people from exploitation. The subsumption of childbearing labor into capitalist market relations represents an extreme example of dehumanization and alienation, and it may be laying the foundation for new forms of exploitation. A positive right to reproductive freedom will not be found in the marketplace.

Since childbearing is being valorized, it is not surprising that the new social relations create a form of alienation. Women are estranged from the product of their reproductive labor—ova, fetal tissue, or infant—if it is taken over by others who decide who will use it and how and when it will be used. They are alienated from the process of reproductive labor when they have no control over the course of their own pregnancy. If a woman is unable to care for her own medical needs and those of her fetus, some form of oppression or drug or alcohol addiction is preventing her from doing so. The root causes of infant morbidity are not addressed by incarcerating her or by trying to contractually guarantee that she will behave cautiously. Moreover, women are alienated from themselves when their childbearing potential cannot be expressed in ways that allow them to personally and creatively define themselves. They are alienated from others when they cannot establish relationships that enable them to create satisfying communities.

Genetic and reproductive engineering should be available to women as an aspect of reproductive freedom, broadly defined. Many features of life would have to change if women and men were genuinely free to control their own procreation. Safe and inexpensive birth control and abortion services would be obtainable. People would receive adequate counseling and sex education, and sexually transmitted disease would not be targeted at women of color and poor women. If people were free to have children when and how they wanted, living conditions would have to improve so that decent childcare and education, housing, and medical care were available. Wages would have to be sufficient to support a household, and men and women would have to participate equally in family life. People would not be oppressed because of their sexual orientation, and many forms of nontraditional lifestyles would be accepted. Genetic and reproductive engineering would fit well into such a context. For women and men, these services would simply be another option for procreative self-determination and expression.

It is conceivable that the socialization of reproductive labor under capitalism is a necessary precondition for its liberation, just as Marx theorized that the commodification of labor power creates the possibility for a society free from drudgery and domination. In a socialist society that is anti-racist and anti-sexist, childbearing might still be socialized. Reproductive technology and scientific advancement would benefit children and adults rather than ministering to the needs of capital. New forms of conception would be a source of fulfillment, not merely a means to acquire money.

As explained above, under commodity production, childbearing is indirectly social because the marketplace establishes relations among people and value is extracted from their labor. In a socialist society, however, labor is directly social. Marx hints at the kinds of relationships that might be involved, though his subject matter is not reproduction:

> I would have been for you the mediator between you and the species and thus been acknowledged and felt by you as a completion of your own essence and a necessary part of yourself and have thus realized that I am confirmed both in your thought and in your love. In my expressions of my life I would have fashioned your expression of your life, and thus in my own activity have realized my own essence, my human, my communal essence. (1977b, 121–22)

Dividing gamete production, fertilization, implantations, gestation and birth, and social parentage among different people might enhance our ability to live cooperatively. They might be creative expressions of the kind of community people themselves desired. It will be important for Marxists to examine the current process of the socialization of childbearing to understand how its commodification will develop and to determine whether potential liberatory forces are contained therein. Reproductive technology cannot itself liberate women, however, though some radical feminists like Shulamith Firestone (1970) have supposed that it would since they thought of reproductive difference as the source of women's oppression.

CONCLUSION

In this paper, I have argued that a value-theoretic approach to childbirth can be helpful in understanding how reproduction is being socialized in late twentieth-century capitalism. I have also discussed how new social relations are separating genetic, gestational, and social parentage and how capital is benefiting from reproductive engineering. I have explained that the valorization of childbearing is consistent with other ways of making reproduction less private, as the contradiction between socialized production and privatized reproduction develops. Though the analogy I have drawn between childbearing and social labor is exploratory, I feel that the theory of value provides an essential way to conceptualize how childbirth is being drawn into relationship with other labor under capitalism. Without an understanding of valorization, it may seem that the new sciences themselves are a source of difficulty for women. Furthermore, given the tendency to focus on biological differences as the root of women's oppression, it may seem that reproductive engineering deepens an already basic and primary contradiction between women and men. I offer instead an approach grounded in political economy. We can then begin to understand how childbearing can become a form of alienated labor. Thus, the new developments in reproductive relations are neither inherently liberating nor automatically dehumanizing. It is the context of commodification of childbirth that must be analyzed to chart the way forward.

NOTES

1. In a very interesting new book, Vogel has developed a more sensitive, finely grained account of sexual difference. *Mothers on the Job: Maternity Policy in the U.S. Workplace* (1993) strikes a balance between gender-neutral policies that emphasize men's and women's fundamental sameness and sexually specific strategies that stress reproductive difference. Using a notion she calls "differential consideration," she recommends the approach taken in family and medical leave legislation, which, she argues, recognizes women's special needs within the context of struggle for equality.

2. Marx uses organic metaphors to discuss the process of the self-expansion of value. For example, capital is "value that sucks up the worker's value-creating power" (1977a, 716).

3. Positive rights are appealed to by progressives and leftists. They are sometimes called "welfare rights" and require government intervention to insure people have the material means to actually carry out their individual choices.

4. Negative rights are those that represent the right of people to be free from the interference of other people or the government. They are basic to the formulation of classical liberalism.

31

Standing on Solid Ground
A Materialist Ecological Feminism

Gwyn Kirk

- A billion people in the world lack safe drinking water, and some 80 percent of all disease in poor countries is caused by contaminated water (Seager and Olson 1986). An estimated 40,000–50,000 children die each day worldwide, mainly in Africa and Asia, from malnutrition and a lack of clean water.

- Millions of industrial and agricultural workers are employed in hazardous conditions. Oil companies, chemical companies, and textile and electronics producers are responsible for severe environmental devastation through their regular manufacturing processes as well as industrial "accidents," but operate without meaningful environmental constraints (Chavez 1993; Noble 1993).

- In India, Africa, and Latin America, vast acres once used for subsistence crops have been diverted into cash crop production to earn hard currency to pay the interest on overseas loans. In some places new dams make water available for large-scale irrigation of cash crops, but many poor women have to carry water and firewood increasing distances for home use (Shiva 1988).

- A significant number of babies without brains have been born to women on both sides of the Rio Grande, polluted by U.S.-controlled *maquiladora* industries on the Mexican side of the river, and to Pacific Island women who were exposed to radiation during atomic tests or subsequently through irradiated land and water (de Ishtar 1994; Dibblin 1989; Women Working for a Nuclear Free and Independent Pacific 1987).

- In the U.S., children's health is compromised by environmental factors such as lead in paints and gasoline, air pollution, traffic hazards, and violence that often involves the use of handguns, with significant differences between those living in inner cities and suburban neighborhoods (Hamilton 1993; Phoenix 1993).

- Under pressure of poverty, some Native American reservations in the U.S., as well as African and Pacific Island nations, import toxic wastes from industrialized countries and regions as one of the few ways they can earn income, particularly foreign exchange, by providing landfill sites (Center for Investigative Reporting 1990; Center for Third World Organizing 1991; Third World Network 1988).

- In the U.S., breast cancer, which is increasingly linked to environmental causes, affects one woman in nine—many more in some areas—and has killed more women than the AIDS epidemic (Arditti and Schreiber 1992). Native American women whose land and water are heavily polluted have initiated research into the likelihood that their breast milk is toxic (Cook 1985, 1993).

- In the past few years several patents have been taken out on genetically engineered parts of plants and animals, including the cell lines of a U.S. man and an indigenous man from Papua New Guinea, and many more patents are pending (Juma 1989).

The purpose of this chapter is to show how gender, race, class, imperialism, and the global capitalist economy are connected to ecological destruction, and how effective analysis and activism need to be informed by a broad, integrative materialist framework. Given the vast scope and critically serious nature of environmental devastation, I am dismayed that relatively few feminists in the U.S. appear to be concerned with this issue. I see the theoretical frameworks that dominate U.S. feminist discourse and activism—liberalism, radical feminism, and postmodernism—as the least useful approaches for understanding ecological issues, and the pre-eminence of these perspectives is a serious limitation to feminist work in this area.

Women are the backbone of grassroots organizing around ecological issues worldwide. Well-known examples come from the Chipko (tree-hugging) movement in India (Anand 1983; Shiva 1988), the Kenyan women's green belt movement (Maathai 1988), Micronesian women working in communities devastated by atomic testing (de Ishtar 1994; Women Working for a Nuclear Free and Independent Pacific 1987), U.S. women organizing against toxic dumps and incinerators (Zeff 1989), Native American women's research on toxicity in breast milk (Cook 1985, 1993), and many projects in Asia, Africa, and Latin America that promote sustainable agriculture (Durning 1989b). Much environmental activism in the U.S. is currently undertaken by women of color and poor white women, arising from their daily experiences of poverty and degraded physical environments and often drawing on analyses of race and class rather than gender. While women's engagement with environmental issues comes out of a variety of situations and experiences, I argue that an understanding of their close material connection to the nonhuman environment puts such women on the cutting edge of resistance to ecological destruction, and that such analysis should also be a crucial part of any feminist oppositional project.

Ecological feminists and women environmental activists need to understand and challenge the source of environmental devastation: the unsustainable priorities, values, and living standards of industrialized countries based on highly militarized, capitalist economies. A materialist framework identifies economic and political institutions as the perpetrators of ecologically unsound investment; it offers a basis for understanding how the seemingly random instances listed above are connected and suggests appropriate public action—locally, nationally, and internationally. It allows one to see global connections across lines of race, class, and nation, and to build alliances across these lines of difference. While emphasizing women's activism here, I do not consider women to be solely responsible for planetary caretaking.

FEMINISM AND ECOLOGY: SEEING THE WOOD FOR THE TREES

There are several ways to make theoretical links between feminism and ecology, with varied roots in feminist theories (Daly 1979; Griffin 1978; Warren 1991), feminist spirituality (Sjöö and Mor 1987; Spretnak 1982; Starhawk 1987), social ecology (Bookchin 1990; King 1990), and socialism (Mellor 1992). While some ecofeminists embrace this eclecticism (Spretnak 1990), many proponents and detractors find it confusing and incoherent. Some reject ecofeminism as essentialist; others see it as synonymous with goddess worship and earth-centered spiritualities (Biehl 1991) or animal rights (Adams 1990; Gaard 1993). Women of color critics argue that, as with much western feminism, ecofeminism privileges gender over race and class (Agarwal 1992). English-language ecofeminist anthologies have been dominated by a concern with ethics, personal transformation, and earth-centered spirituality drawn from prehistoric Europe-idealist rather than materialist concerns (Adams 1993; Caldecott 1983; Diamond and Orenstein 1990; Plant 1989), and the contributions and perspectives of women of color are marginal in these collections, which tend to assume a unitary theoretical framework. Joni Seager uses the term "ecological feminism" in an attempt to sidestep the confusion surrounding ecofeminism (Seager 1991). I consider this theoretical quagmire briefly in order to define a solid place to stand.

AN ESSENTIAL, CARING WOMEN'S NATURE?

The fact that women are disproportionately involved in campaigning around environmental issues and against militarism at a grassroots level worldwide is a phenomenon for explanation. Some ecofeminist writers assume an essential, caring woman's nature (Gray 1979); many critique this as a facile essentialism that necessarily limits women's activities and perspectives within the constraints of traditional roles as wives, mothers, domestic workers, and caretakers (paid and unpaid). For the past decade academic discussions of ecofeminism in the U.S. have been bogged down by arguments about essentialism and the related claim that women are closer to nature—a complex concept—than men. This claim implies a separation between people and the nonhuman world that is highly problematic. Nature is not something "out there" somewhere. Rather, people are intimately connected to the nonhuman world in the most profound yet mundane way, through the air we breathe, the food we eat, the water we drink, and so on. But this long drawn out argument about essentialism is also unnecessary and can be avoided by focusing on women's socialization as caretakers across many cultures, with overwhelming responsibility for caring for children, the sick, the elderly, and the well-being of their communities, as family members, friends, and neighbors, or professionally as nurses, teachers, and social workers. I see women's caring work—and this includes environmental knowledge and activism, especially in rural areas where women are farmers and herbalists who understand the visceral interconnections between people and the nonhuman world—as part of this gendered division of labor. Women and men are socialized very differently in many cultures. While it may be fascinating to hypothesize about why this gendered socialization and division of labor first arose, one does not need to speculate about "essentials" to see a clear experiential connection between these aspects of women's lives and their environmental activism.

CONNECTING SPIRITUALITY AND POLITICS

As many scholars have noted, the European "Enlightenment" tradition—from which such liberatory political philosophies as liberalism, Marxism, and socialism have been developed—is fundamentally dualistic and constructs hierarchical relationships between polarized concepts such as mind and body, matter and spirit, and reason and spirituality, which are also basic oppositional categories of contemporary western thought (Merchant 1981; Plumwood 1993). This routine construction of hierarchy and the justification of difference in terms of inequality has had profound consequences. Pre-Enlightenment philosophies such as European paganism and the worldviews of indigenous peoples in the Americas, India, Australia, New Zealand, and the Pacific do not make these separations (Booth 1990; LaDuke 1993; Sanchez 1993; Shiva 1988; Starhawk 1987). On these views, spirituality and politics, for example, are not dissociated categories but interrelated approaches to life. A spiritual belief in the interconnectedness of all life forms is then the springboard for environmental activism against governments and corporations that repudiate such connections by destroying or contaminating the earth, air, and water as well as a multitude of life forms.

This question of a legitimate connection between politics and spirituality—also a complex term—seriously divides U.S. environmentalists, ecosocialists, and ecofeminists. For some, ecofeminism is held to be synonymous with goddess worship and embraced or rejected on that basis. Distinctions should be made here between goddess religions, earth-centered spiritualities in their many cultural forms and contexts, rituals and the cultural underpinnings of specific rituals, organized male-dominated religions, and the origins of people's passionate but seemingly secular beliefs which lead them into political action. This issue needs exploring in more depth, but I note that many Native American, African American, and Chicano environmentalists in the U.S. do not polarize spirituality and politics as some U.S. Greens and ecofeminists do, though even the most secular activists derive their passion for social and economic justice from a fundamental belief, for example in people's equality or intrinsic value. Indeed, the perspective I put forward here may also run into this problem. In an attempt to avoid charges of essentialism and goddess-worship I emphasize the material basis for women's environmental activism, because western thought has no conception of a blended spiritual politics. This is very different from individualist spiritualities that focus on personal growth, betterment, and salvation without also incorporating an oppositional political practice. Particularly egregious in this respect are those "New Age" spiritualities that appropriate Native American rituals and concepts, often turning them into commodities for sale without taking on a wider concern for and resistance to the continuing oppression of Native Americans. Scientists who have proposed that the earth is a self-regulating system, personified as Gaia, the ancient Greek goddess of the earth (Lovelock 1988; Margulis and Lovelock 1974), have attracted "New Age" environmentalists as well as hardcore polluters to the idea that Gaia can look after herself. But to throw out all spiritual beliefs as superstitious mumbo-jumbo, as Bookchin and Beihl do, is to continue to uphold a disconnected view of life, which ecological feminism should seek to transcend (King 1990).

INTEGRATIVE FRAMEWORKS: CLASS, RACE, GENDER, AND NATION

A key insight of ecofeminism put forward in the germinal works of Susan Griffin and Carolyn Merchant, for example, is the connection between the domination of women and the domination of nature, often feminized and sexualized as in "virgin forest," "rape of the earth," "penetrating the wilderness," and so on. Sources—whether forests, seeds, or women's bodies—are turned into resources to be objectified, controlled, used, and only valued when placed in a system that produces profits (Mies and Shiva 1993; Shiva 1988). But this is not just a matter of women and nature. In the service of capital accumulation, white-dominated, capitalist patriarchy also creates "otherness" and oppresses people of color and poor people worldwide. This continual process of objectification is the central mechanism underlying systems of oppression based on class, race, gender, and nation (Plumwood 1993). Thus the oppression of women, racism, and ecological destruction are directly linked to economic exploitation.

In practice there is an enormous gap between much U.S. ecofeminist writing and the perspectives of grassroots activists involved in the environmental justice movement—predominantly women, many of whom see their activism not only in terms of gender, but also and often more importantly in terms of race and/or class arising from their daily experiences and understandings of the world as women of color or white working-class women. As I outline briefly below, the global capitalist economy is intrinsically antiecological. If ecological feminism is to inform a vital ecological politics in the U.S. we need to emphasize the interconnections among oppressions, activists, and movements; to frame issues broadly to mobilize wide-ranging involvement and support, rather than emphasizing points of disagreement; and to show how the process of capital accumulation is reinforced by the ideological articulation of difference based on gender, ethnicity, and culture. While I agree with those who argue that much U.S. ecofeminism is overly concerned with sexism at the expense of class and race, what is often missing from environmental justice activism is an explicit recognition of sexism as a crucial mechanism of oppression. This is very different from acknowledging that most grassroots environmental activists are women, and it means embracing theoretical perspectives that see women's liberation as fundamental to ecological soundness and a sustainable world.

In summary, I argue for an ecological feminism that focuses on the social and material reasons for women's environmental concerns, has an integrated view of spiritual politics, and can integrate class, race, and gender in theory and practice. Fundamental to this approach is an understanding of the profoundly antiecological nature of the global capitalist economy.

THE ANTIECOLOGICAL GLOBAL ECONOMY

The widespread nature of environmental destruction is an integral part of capitalist as well as state-planned economies (O'Connor 1994). This discussion focuses on capitalist economics now dominant worldwide, which, while not identical, share a logic of capital accumulation. Key principles of capitalist economies include the following:

- They are based on production for profit, not needs—admittedly a tricky concept that varies from context to context—and inevitably result in considerable inequalities of wealth, material comfort, safety, social standing, and opportunities for work, education, and self-expression among people in the same nation and between nations.

- They are inherently expansionist, always seeking new markets, new commodities, and generating new "needs."

- They are intrinsically wasteful, routinely producing trash, derelict land and buildings, and polluted environments as businesses establish themselves, operate until they have exhausted the opportunities for profit-making, and either close down or move on.

- Growth = Progress. There is an inbuilt assumption that economic growth is the same as progress—a more complex concept with economic, intellectual, social, and moral dimensions. Wealth is seen only in terms of material wealth.

- Capital must be able to move at will and without loyalty or commitment to the people of a particular area, so that businesses can always maximize their operating costs, pitting workers in one region or country against those in another.

- Immediate costs and short-run considerations dominate corporate and government decision-making. The role of governments is to maintain political and economic conditions favorable to profit-making through laws, regulations, tax breaks, and other incentives.

Current inequalities between countries are often based on older inequalities resulting from colonization. While the details differed from place to place and from one colonial power to another, colonialism invariably involved the distortion of local economies with dependence on a few agricultural products or "raw materials"—people, timber, minerals, and cash crops. Throughout the second half of the twentieth century, virtually all former colonies have gained political independence but have remained linked to their colonizers politically through organizations like the British Commonwealth and economically through the activities of established firms and transnational corporations and loans from governments and banks based in northern countries. There are also ties of culture and language, as many members of the new political and business elites were educated at prestigious universities in colonial capitals. Whether the hand-over of political power was relatively smooth or accompanied by extreme turmoil and bloodshed, newly independent governments have been under pressure to improve living conditions for their populations and have borrowed capital to finance economic development. This combination of circumstances has led many commentators to characterize the continuing economic inequalities between rich and poor countries as "neocolonialism" (George 1988; Payer 1991).

EXTERNAL DEBT AND STRUCTURAL ADJUSTMENT

This is the contemporary context for international trade. Currently many countries pay more for imports than they earn in exports, leading to external debt or a balance of payments deficit. In 1991, for example, the U.S. budget deficit dropped to $66.2 billion, the first time it had fallen below $100 billion since 1983. Over $1.3 trillion is jointly owed by governments of Latin America, Asia, Africa, and the Caribbean to northern governments and commercial banks. The sixteen major borrowers in Latin America owe a total of $420 billion; between 1982 and 1990, $160 billion was transferred from Latin America to the developed world in debt repayments (O'Reilly 1991). Partly because countries of western Europe and North America have such serious balance of payments problems themselves—increasingly a focus of political debate and domestic policy-making—they have put a great deal of pressure on other debtor countries to repay loans. Indeed, since the mid-1980s, African governments have transferred $2 billion more to the International Monetary Fund in interest payments than they have received in new loans (Beresford 1994). Loans have to be repaid in "hard" currency— U.S. dollars, Japanese yen, British pounds, French francs, Swiss francs, and German marks—which can be exchanged on world currency markets. Thus debtor nations have to sell goods and services that richer countries want to buy, or that can earn hard currency from poorer countries, with clear implications for the physical environment. Such products include raw materials (hardwoods, oil, copper, gold, diamonds); cash crops (sugar, tobacco, coffee, tea, tropical fruits and flowers); drug-producing crops (coca, marijuana, opium poppies), processed illicit drugs, and weapons. Debtor countries may also export labor (construction workers, maids, and mail-order brides); lease land for military bases or trash dumps; or develop their tourist assets—sunny beaches, beautiful landscapes, and "exotic" young women and children involved in sex tourism.

As well as selling goods and services to offset their external debt, the World Bank and the International Monetary Fund have pressured all debtor nations to make stringent changes in their economies to qualify for new loans, with the aim of increasing the profitablity of the economy and making it more export-focused (Barnet and Cavanagh 1994; Danaher 1994; Reed 1992; Sparr 1994; Vickers 1990). Measures relevant to environmental concerns include

—cuts in government subsidies and the abolition of price controls, particularly on food, fuel, and public transportation;
—selling nationalized industries or at least a majority shareholding to private corporations often from outside the country;
—improving profitability for corporations through wage controls, tax breaks, loans, and credit, or provision of infrastructure such as better roads or rail transport; and
—increasing the output of cash crops by increasing yields and/or increasing the amount of land in cash crop production.

In parts of Latin America, governments have been willing to allow international environmental organizations and foreign banks exclusive control of specific parcels of land to be left undeveloped—"debt-for-nature swaps"—as a way of dealing with a small proportion of their debt (Madrid 1990; O'Cleireacain 1990). Many activist groups in southern countries oppose the repayment of external debts and challenge the structural/social adjustment policies that are making many people's lives much harder. They argue that many foreign loans were used by their countries' elites for inappropriate, prestige development in urban centers that have not benefited the majority of the population, or that the country has already lost enormous wealth to northern countries due to centuries of colonization.

THE POLITICS OF SURVIVAL

This global economic context—characterized by complex inequalities based on class, race, gender, and nation—frames ecological issues and politics. I now look at several examples which illustrate how such inequalities impact ecological concerns and grassroots environmental projects, particularly focusing on development and health. These examples come from the U.S. and southern countries, from very different contexts and life situations; not all of them concern women exclusively. Thus my discussion has an inevitable unevenness and requires the reader to shift between varied contexts while at the same time keeping in mind the overarching framework, so that these are not seen as random cases.

AGRICULTURAL DEVELOPMENT: FEEDING THE WORLD

Women's role as primary agricultural producers in many parts of Africa, Latin America, and Asia gives them direct experience and detailed knowledge of ecological issues. Women make up 80 percent of the subsistence farmers in sub-Saharan Africa, for example. They are the main users of water in agriculture and forestry, as well as domestic life, and they carry it each day, sometimes several miles. Women are also responsible for finding fuel—wood, crop residues, and manure—another time-consuming and arduous daily task. While some women are involved in cash crop production, a gendered division of labor and the gender bias of many economic development projects means that men produce most cash crops and receive the income from them. Increasingly, cash crops compete with subsistence agriculture for available land, labor, and water. To provide food for their families, women farm more marginal land and walk further for water and fuel (Agarwal 1992; Dankelman and Davidson 1988). They may well understand ecologically sound agricultural practices but are pressured into farming steep hillsides or cutting trees for fuelwood, for example, thus worsening soil erosion and flooding during heavy rains. Such women work sixteen-hour days, seven days a week, juggling farming with cooking, cleaning, laundry, and child care—though according to national income accounting none of this counts as productive work because it is not done for wages (Waring 1988).

The world of agricultural development agencies, transnational corporations, and government policy-makers is dominated by capitalist and neo-colonial notions of economic development and material progress, where large-scale, chemically dependent, capital-intensive mechanized agriculture, usually producing cash crops for export, is the model promoted and funded by international financial institutions. An extensive literature on women and development offers trenchant critiques of such maldevelopment for its emphasis on cash crops at the expense of viable subsistence agriculture; its exclusion of women from much development policy-making; and its promotion of ecologically unsound agricultural practices (Braidotti and others 1994; Dankelman and Davidson 1988; ISIS Women's International Information and Communications Service 1984; Rodda 1990; Sen and Grown 1987; Shiva 1988). The so-called Green Revolution with hybrid "high-yield" seeds that require massive inputs of chemical fertilizers, pesticides, and regular irrigation, has not improved food security for poor people in the "two-thirds world,"[1] but has been an ecological disaster that has turned plants and farmers into consumers of chemicals (Shiva 1991). New hybrid varieties are more susceptible to drought, disease, and pests, and—the biggest contradiction of all—are not fertile, so farmers cannot recycle their own seed for the next year's planting but must buy more each season from chemical companies—an example of a new commodity creating new "needs" as part of the expansionist process of capital accumulation.

SCIENCE REDESIGNS NATURE: BIOTECHNOLOGY AND GENETIC ENGINEERING

Going beyond this plant-breeding technology is genetic engineering, a remarkable new form of biotechnology capable of changing the very nature of life itself (Juma 1989; Spallone 1992). It involves the manipulation of genetic material—DNA—so that it is possible to implant human genes in animals, for example, and animal genes in people, creating combinations that could never be achieved through selective breeding as traditionally practiced. Other examples include research on human embryos intended to identify genes responsible for various genetic "defects" that can be corrected in the womb, making genetically engineered designer babies a real possibility. A cancerous mouse, created and patented by Harvard University and DuPont, is already available for sale to cancer researchers. The use of genetically engineered bovine growth hormone, introduced in the U.S. in 1994, will increase milk production. Genetically engineered bio-pesticides and seeds will have far-reaching effects on agriculture and are considered the most lucrative products of this technology—seeds being the crucial first link in the food chain (Mather 1995; Raeburn 1995). Enormous profits are to be made, as is clear from even a casual glance at the business pages.

Genetic engineering is being vigorously promoted as the answer to many problems: curing disease, eliminating mental illness and physical disabilities, reducing crime, curing infertility, as well as increasing genetic diversity and ridding the world of hunger, claims which need to be looked at very critically. While researchers, promoters, and investors argue that everyone stands to benefit from this new technology, it is important to note that it is controlled by a small number of transnational corporations and research facilities in northern countries, in contrast to traditional plant and animal breeding practices developed in specific settings, known to many farmers and passed on from generation to generation. Clearly this will reinforce the power of elites and further marginalize the poor. World hunger, for example, is not caused by deficiencies in crop varieties but by the consumption habits of rich countries and the unequal distribution of wealth and political power in the world (Moore Lappé and Collins 1986). Pineapples from the Philippines, strawberries from Mexico, and carnations from Colombia are all imported into the U.S. and are grown on land that could otherwise produce food for local needs, as is also the case with sugar cane, tea, and coffee. As well as increasing milk production, bovine growth hormone makes cows more vulnerable to disease, for which they are given powerful antibiotics and other drugs on a regular basis, which in turn affects the quality of their milk. The percentage of human diseases whose cause can be traced to genetic defects is very small. Most disabilities are caused by accidents and environmental or occupational exposure. By focusing on a tiny proportion of diseases, genetic engineering gives them enormous attention, while the study of most illnesses is ignored and poorly funded. Social causes are also ignored. Rather than genetic factors, poor prenatal care, directly traceable to socioeconomic class, is the primary cause of birth defects, with environmental or drug-related effects close behind.

Besides engineering genetic material, people's thinking is also being engineered to accept it (Shiva 1993). Genetic engineering suggests fantastic or terrifying possibilities and assumes that there are technical solutions to problems with economic and social causes. Thus, discussions that should be taking place in the political arena have been transferred to biological experts who present their work to their funders and professional colleagues in obscure, scientific language. Research and activist groups like the Research Foundation for Science, Technology and Natural Resource Policy in India,[2] the Pure Food Campaign in the U.S.,[3] and the Feminist Network of Resistance to Reproductive and Genetic Engineering[4] (with groups in sixteen countries) are piecing together available information and challenging the underlying assumptions and practices of genetic engineering as it affects agriculture and human reproduction, though there is little public debate in the U.S. on this issue, which has such far-reaching effects—many of which, like the release of genetically engineered organisms into the environment, are simply not known. Beyond the political and economic details, what is at stake here are opposing systems of knowledge and value.

WHO OWNS LIFE? ETHNOSCIENTIFIC KNOWLEDGE, INTELLECTUAL PROPERTY

Despite the incursions of profit-driven agriculture in Africa, Asia, Latin America, and the Caribbean, there are thousands of small-scale, ecologically sound development projects, many of them organized by women, described by Alan Durning as the "best hope for global prosperity and ecology" (Durning 1989a). Many rural farmers struggle to continue to use ecological practices and appropriate technology, and to draw on long-standing ethnoscientific knowledge—for instance, the National Council of Women of Kenya's Green Belt Movement, which has spread to many other African countries. Started in 1977 by biologist Wangari Maathai, this program was initiated and promoted by women as a solution to diminishing supplies of fuelwood and desertification in rural Kenya. By the mid-1980s Kenyan women had planted more than 2 million trees (Maathai 1988; Maathai 1991). Other projects rely on the introduction of appropriate technology to reduce the long hours women spend working for subsistence (Charlton 1984; Dankelman and Davidson 1988; Leonard 1989).

Ecologically sound development projects also have their counterparts in the U.S., including women's economic projects in rural and urban areas and on Native American reservations; organic farms; seed banks that safeguard genetic diversity and promote the use of old, established seed varieties that can withstand drought and pests; and community gardening in inner cities (Bagby 1990). The 4-H Urban Gardening project in Detroit,[5] for example, coordinates well over 100 small gardens citywide and relies on the expertise of local people, mostly elderly African American women, who raise vegetables for individual use and to supplement food prepared at senior centers, as well as producing crops for sale: loofah sponges, fresh herbs, honey, and worm boxes for fishing. Many of these women were brought up in rural areas in the southern United States, where they learned about gardening before coming to Detroit for work in the 1930s and '40s. By drawing on local people's knowledge and interests, providing fresh produce at little financial cost, and using the land in an ecologically sound and productive way, these gardening projects combine aspects of economic, ecological, and cultural survival. Besides growing vegetables and flowers, they contribute to the revitalization of inner-city communities and a sense of empowerment that comes from self-reliance. When people are outdoors working they also make neighborhoods safer by their presence, watchfulness, and care. An additional goal is to teach young people about gardening, strengthening connections between the generations and helping young people become more self-supporting. A rural example from the U.S. is Ganados del Valle/Tierra Wools in northern New Mexico, a worker cooperative of twenty people—most of them women—which owns some 3,000 head of Churro sheep and produces high-quality, handwoven rugs and clothing and organic lamb.[6] Its objectives include economic development, environmental protection, cultural revival and conservation, workplace democracy, and social justice (Jackson 1991; Pulido 1993).

Sociologist and activist Devón Peña notes that, as ethnobotanists, Chicanas in northern New Mexico know the backcountry in great detail because they go there at different seasons to gather herbs for medicinal purposes (Peña 1992). This detailed knowledge has been passed on by older people, as is also the case with some Native Americans and others who live in rural areas. Though many who have been raised in cities have not had the opportunity to learn such things, feminists involved in women's health in the past twenty years have encouraged women to become more knowledgeable and self-reliant with regard to health, and have published herbal guides as part of this work (Gladstar 1993; Potts 1988). On other continents, indigenous people—often women—also have a detailed knowledge of local plants—their medicinal properties and usefulness for many domestic tasks—learned from their mothers and grandmothers and gradually developed over many generations. Increasingly, the pharmaceutical industry is interested in developing medicines from plant material from tropical regions, which are the richest and most diverse sources of plant life. Seventy-five percent of plants that "provide active ingredients for prescription drugs originally came to the attention of researchers because of their uses in traditional medicine" (Kloppenburg 1991). Western agribusiness insists that plant and animal resources from the two-thirds world are public property, part of a common human heritage, but when they are developed by pharmaceutical companies they become private property for sale, graphically described by Vandana Shiva as "biopiracy." As well as medicines, many staple food crops now produced in northern countries, such as corn and potatoes, have been adapted from tropical crops. According to Jack Kloppenburg, "Indigenous people have in effect been engaged in a massive program of foreign aid to the urban populations of the industrialized north" (Kloppenburg 1991). This commodification of knowledge in a capitalist context raises complex questions about who owns knowledge of life forms and whether indigenous peoples should have intellectual property rights and be compensated for their knowledge, a debate that feminists in industrial countries should participate in. Genetic engineers who seek protection for modified life forms by taking out patents on their "inventions" pose a similar challenge.

WORKING FOR WELLNESS: ENVIRONMENTAL HEALTH

Capitalist production processes—whether in the agricultural, industrial, service, or information sectors—are a crucial aspect of health for workers and those who live and work near toxic workplaces. The explosion of the Union Carbide chemical plant near

Bhopal, India, in 1984, which killed and maimed thousands of people, is a graphic example of lax safety standards routinely adopted as a way to cut production costs (Kurzman 1987; Shrivastava 1987). While many labor organizers oppose unsafe working conditions, companies often frame the issue in either/or terms and pit jobs against a better working environment. Firing particular individuals or threatening to relocate the plant elsewhere are common management strategies in this struggle for improved working conditions (Moses 1993; Noble 1993).

In the U.S., hazardous working conditions and toxic wastes disproportionately affect lower-income neighborhoods, particularly those housing people of color, in a correspondence so striking it merits the term "environmental racism" (Bullard 1990; Bullard 1993; Hofrichter 1993; Lee 1987; Schwab 1994; Szasz 1994). Many women are involved in campaigning against toxic pollution in the workplace and the community in an environmental justice movement significant for its racial diversity (Kraus 1993; Zeff et al. 1989). Typically they get involved because they become ill themselves or through caring for a sick relative, often a child. Activists piece together information to find the source of the illness, publicize their findings, and take on agricultural or industrial corporations and city agencies responsible for contamination. The Citizens' Clearinghouse for Hazardous Wastes,[7] founded by Lois Gibbs in the early 1980s, provides resource materials to local groups and publishes news of local campaigns (Gibbs 1995). Other organizations actively pursuing these issues at regional and national levels include the National Women's Health Network[8] (Nelson et al. 1990), the Southwest Organizing Project,[9] the Center for Third World Organizing,[10] and the United Farm Workers of America (U.F.W.),[11] which opposes the extensive use of pesticides in commercial fruit and vegetable production. For some years the U.F.W. has called for a boycott of California table grapes to protest the fact that farm workers and their families, particularly women and children, suffer severe health effects due to pesticide exposure, and as leverage in negotiating better conditions in work contracts. Such produce is not good for consumers either. Middle-class parents were very effective in getting the pesticide Alar banned in the late 1980s because it damaged children's health (Mott and Snyder 1987; Witte Garland 1989), with no apparent awareness or concern for farm workers exposed to it in the course of their work. In many parts of the U.S. mainly white, middle-class consumers avoid contaminated produce by buying organic, which does nothing to improve conditions for most farm workers or to reduce the effects of chemical pesticides and fertilizers on land and water. Much more needs to be done to build alliances between farm workers—many of whom are Mexican Americans and Central Americans—and consumer groups. This will include increased education and public awareness of the dangers of pesticides and the low nutritional value of much mass-produced food, as well as support for farmer's markets, producer/consumer cooperatives, and other alternative agricultural projects.

WOMEN'S HEALTH, FETAL HEALTH

For U.S. women, cancer is the second leading cause of death, and breast cancer currently affects one in nine women, though the figures are much higher in some areas. Rita Arditti and Tatiana Schrieber argue that cancers have environmental causes, evidenced by dramatic differences in cancer rates between geographical locations and the identification of specific substances including asbestos, chemicals, and ionizing radiation, which are linked to cancer (Arditti and Schreiber 1992). They conclude that cancer is not only largely environmental in origin but also largely preventable, a view that underlies the work of groups like the Women's Community Cancer Project.[12]

Women and children are "ecological markers" with regard to toxics and often show signs of disease earlier than men do, either due to low body weight in the case of children, or because their bodies are said by health professionals to be "unhealthy environments" for their babies (Chavkin 1984; Nelson 1990). In some cases women in the U.S. have been barred from jobs involving routine exposure to toxic chemicals so that they cannot sue their employers should they give birth to a disabled child—a form of fetal protection where women are seen in terms of their reproductive potential rather than as people in their own right. A Supreme Court decision in April 1991, for example, barred Johnson Controls, an auto battery manufacturer in Milwaukee, from keeping fertile women out of high-paying jobs involving exposure to lead (Daniels 1993). While some feminists hailed this as a victory for equal rights, others saw it as the right to be treated equally badly. The decision does not address the more fundamental issue of hazardous workplaces, regardless of gender. Men's reproductive systems are also affected by toxics—as has at last been officially accepted in some extreme cases, such as exposure to the defoliant Agent Orange during the Vietnam War, and exposure to radioactivity in nuclear plants and through nuclear weapons tests (Gibbs 1995). A Native American women's initiative concerning connections between the health of a mother and the health of her baby is the Akwasasne Mother's Milk project, started in the early 1980s by midwife Kasti Cook (Cook 1985, 1993). Akwasasne, "the land where the partridge drums," home of the Mohawk Nation (near Rooseveltown, NY), is affected by severe chemical pollution flowing through the Great Lakes system as well as from nearby industries. Akwasasne women became concerned that by eating local vegetables, fish, and other wildlife they might be exposing their babies to toxic pollution through their breast milk and questioned whether they should continue breast feeding. Despite the economic costs and against their tradition of supporting themselves from the land, they decided to stop eating locally produced food—garden produce, fish, and small game animals—and to monitor their situation carefully. More recent analysis of breast milk samples is not as bad as originally feared but still gives no cause for complacency. Another egregious example involves women from Micronesia in the western Pacific who have been campaigning for years about the catastrophic effects of atmospheric atomic tests conducted by the British, French, and U.S. governments in the 1950s and early 1960s (de Ishtar 1994; Women Working for a Nuclear Free and Independent Pacific 1987). Whole islands have been irradiated and soil and drinking water contaminated. Some women have given birth to "jelly fish babies" without skeletons who live only a few hours. Other children survive despite severe illnesses and disabilities caused by radiation.

The general relationship between environmental hazards and health needs much more detailed research and public debate (Gibbs 1995; Nelson 1990), including research on environmental causes of illnesses like cancer, chemical sensitivities to pollution, and allergies, and support for holistic medical practices that do not rely on drugs and surgery.

POPULATION: TOO MANY PEOPLE FOR WHAT?

The issue of population is another key one for ecological feminism. The discourse about fertility and population is also a discourse about race. With white populations falling in comparison to people of color in the U.S., it is white women who are offered so-called fertility treatments and whose right to safe, accessible abortion is being eroded. The question of why so many young people in this country are apparently infertile, for example, is salient here. In the U.S. infertility is looked upon as a personal failing to be remedied by treatment, another example of a new product meeting a new "need," even though infertility treatments have a spectacularly low success rate so far and are very expensive. They are aimed at middle-class women as a way of widening individual choice, but the relationship between infertility and environmental hazards is rarely examined, and feminist critiques of reproductive technologies have tended to focus on their invasiveness and the lack of power and knowledge consumers have compared to medical experts (Arditti et al. 1984; Corea 1985, 1987; Stamworth 1988). Sterilization without women's full knowledge or under duress has been a common practice in the U.S. among poor women, especially Latinas, African Americans, and Native Americans. In the 1950s and '60s Puerto Rican women were used in trials of contraceptive pills later made available in the U.S. in much lower dosages. Currently poor African American women and Latinas are much more likely than white women to be encouraged to use the long-acting contraceptive Norplant, implanted under the skin, on the assumption that their pregnancies are not desirable and that these women would be unreliable if they used other contraceptive methods.

There is also a similar, distinctly racist dimension to the environmental debate about population globally. Simply looking at numbers of people and rates of population growth, prominent environmentalists in northern countries argue that many nations, particularly in Africa and Asia, must cut their high rates of population increase. They talk in terms of the limited carrying capacity of the planet to support human life and pose the "problem of overpopulation" as a central (sometimes *the* central) environmental concern. Anne and Paul Ehrlich, for example, emphasize the inevitable, destructive potential of this "population bomb," implying that two-thirds world women, more than anyone else, threaten the survival of the planet (Ehrlich and Ehrlich 1990). Deep ecologists have gone much further, calling for drastic reductions in population. An *Earth First!* contributor who wrote under the pseudonym Miss Ann Thropy made the outrageous claim that if AIDS did not exist it would have had to be invented, or that starving people in Africa should be left to die so that the human population can be brought back into balance with the carrying capacity of the land (Miss Ann Thropy 1991). Framing the issue this way is ideologically loaded and racist and obscures several central questions: the varied cultural and economic reasons poor people have children; the inverse relationship between women's status and family size; why men are not required to take responsibility for their sexuality and fertility; the political reasons for starvation and hunger; the skewed distribution of wealth on an international level, where industrialized countries consume most of the world's resources and generate most of the waste, especially the chemicals and gases that deplete the ozone layer. The U.S., for example, which has 6 percent of the world's population, uses some 40 percent of the world's resources. "A family of eight in Rwanda or Nicaragua neither depletes nor pollutes the Earth anywhere near the amount that does a family of four in Great Britain or the United States" (Hynes 1991). Feminist researchers like Betsy Hartmann, director of the Population and Development Program,[13] emphasize this relationship between population and consumption, positing a "problem of overconsumption" on the part of the North (Bandarage 1994; Hartmann 1991; Hartmann 1995; Moore Lappé and Schurman 1988). Many southern countries are working to reduce their population growth and recognize only too well the difficulties they face in terms of food security. It is important to see this in the context of external debt outlined above. One reason it is difficult to feed fast-growing populations in southern countries is that an increasing acreage once used for subsistence crops now produces cash crops for export as a way of earning hard currency and making repayments on foreign loans.

MILITARY SACRIFICE AREAS: OUTPOSTS OF EMPIRE

A final example to illustrate my general argument concerns military activities, which cause the most severe, long-term environmental destruction worldwide (Seager 1993). This includes weapons production, storage, and testing, as well as outright war. In many wars farmland, deserts, and forests are routinely mined, making them extremely dangerous and unusable for years to come. In the Vietnam War, chemical defoliants were used to destroy the forests. During the Gulf War, U.S. bombers did untold environmental damage, including an unprecedented attack on oil wells that continued to burn for many months after the war was officially over, giving off a thick, noxious smoke that completely blotted out the light. The production of nuclear weapons is another case in point. The mining of uranium, the development of weapons-grade plutonium, and the assembly and testing of warheads have contaminated indigenous peoples' lands in North America, southern Africa, Australia, and the Pacific, and have affected the health of countless people through contaminated air and water (Birks and Ehrlich 1989; Christensen 1988). The half-life of weapons-grade plutonium is 24,000 years, so this is a long-term problem of overwhelming dimensions, currently with no solution. Many community organizations in the U.S. have been campaigning for years against nuclear processing plants and dump sites, which leak radioactive particles into the air and ground water, ironically in the name of national security.[14] Not only do these processes treat the land as disposable, they treat people the same way. Many Native Americans see uranium mining on reservations as racist and genocidal, though it often provides the only well-paid work available. People from the Pacific view the decision to test atomic weapons in their islands, which France continued in French Polynesia until January 1996, as imperialist and racist in the extreme. During agreements to end the UN Trusteeship of Micronesia in 1969, then U.S. Secretary of State Henry Kissinger said, "There's only 90,000 people out there, who gives a damn?" (Women Working for a Nuclear Free and Independent Pacific 1987). He did not say people of color, but the implication is clear.

As the world economy becomes more integrated and more reliant on automation, there are fewer chances of employment for many people. At the same time military budgets have risen in virtually every country to a staggering total, with arms sales a major export for many industrialized countries (Collinson 1989; Leger-Sivard 1991).

Poorer countries also trade arms, a key source of hard currency. For many young men, whether in U.S. inner cities or war-torn countries like Afghanistan and Sri Lanka, guns are far easier to get than jobs, while many women worldwide campaign against militarism and military values. Women in Sri Lanka have come together across lines of ethnicity and culture to try to stop civil war. Jewish and Palestinian women are working together to oppose the military violence of the Israeli state. Women in the Pacific Island of Belau have been crucial in the campaign to retain their country's nuclear-free constitution—incidentally the only one in the world—against great political and economic pressure from the U.S. to use Belau as a navy base. Women's antimilitarist campaigning in northern countries, especially in the 1980s, included many demonstrations, vigils, and peace encampments outside military bases, factories making weapons components, bomb assembly plants, and military tracking stations. The Women's Pentagon Action (1983) protested military priorities and the vast resources allocated to them, and the widespread, everyday culture of violence manifested in war toys, films, and video games, an important factor in the construction of militarized masculinity (Enloe 1990). Greenham Common Women's Peace Camp in England, which started in 1981 as a protest against the siting of U.S. nuclear cruise missiles, linked violence against women and children, military violence, and ecological destruction. Greenham inspired dozens of other peace camps in North America, western Europe, Australia, and New Zealand, and many thousands of women there participated in campaigns of nonviolent direct action—protests that were imaginative, colorful, and assertive, with powerful artistic and ritual elements (Cook and Kirk 1983; Harford and Hopkins 1984). Greenham women also campaigned for the demilitarization of what used to be common land, making connections with others whose land has been annexed in the interests of military domination, including indigenous people of North America, Australia, Aoteroa (New Zealand), and the Pacific Islands. This antimilitarist activism was the source of much ecofeminist theorizing and practice, though it was criticized by women of color for being overly concerned with gender at the expense of race and class (Amos and Parmer 1984; Omolade 1989). This tendency, together with the inevitable ebb and flow of any voluntary campaign, made for a limited theoretical understanding, and this feminist peace movement has not sustained itself into the 1990s.

PRINCIPLES OF A MATERIALIST ECOLOGICAL FEMINISM

With these examples I have outlined a broad basis for a materialist ecological feminism, which will have many cultural variants depending on specific circumstances. Based on this discussion I suggest the following general principles for a materialist ecological feminist theory and practice. It should

- include the experiences and perspectives of women dealing with ecological issues as a matter of survival;
- recognize the linear expansionism of capitalist economies as fundamental to ecological devastation;
- link the domination of women by men, people of color by white people, nonhuman nature by human beings—understanding that the connection between ecological sustainability and social justice is structural and not just a campaigning strategy based on coalitions of different groups;

- challenge existing industrial and agricultural production processes that involve the routine use of toxics, excessive packaging and waste, the pollution of the workplace and surrounding environment, and the oil-intensive transport of goods over great distances;

- challenge the overconsumption and materialism of rich countries and elites in poor countries, opposing prevalent ideas about modernization, growth, and progress;

- call for a reduction in production such that the goals of the economy are reoriented to the production and reproduction of life;

- frame issues in ways that include women and men of different backgrounds and experience, to enable diverse groups to work together across race, class, and national lines;

- move from a framework of oppression to a framework of resistance;

- oppose personal and military violence;

- promote sustainable, life-affirming projects that link economic and cultural survival.

AGENDAS FOR ACTION

These principles give rise to extensive agendas for action. I see two fundamental questions for feminists in industrialized countries who are concerned about ecological issues. What is involved in creating sustainable economies worldwide? How can we work toward this change?

Ecological feminism needs to be involved with sustainable agriculture, restoration ecology, and health in the broad sense of well-being. It must oppose the structural/social economic adjustment policies of northern governments, as well as militarism and the culture of violence it generates and requires. This means opening up a public debate that challenges and opposes the values and practices of this economic system—its hazardous production processes as well as its consumerist ideology—rather, framing progress in terms of sustainability, connectiveness, and true security. It involves promoting vibrant local economic projects so that people are not dependent on the whims of corporate investors and developers, building up communities where young people are needed, where they can develop skills and gain respect for themselves and each other through meaningful work and participation in community projects and decision-making (Boggs 1994; Kirk 1996). It involves expanding and strengthening many existing, small-scale projects including community gardens; farmers' markets; cooperative organic farming; backyard gardening and composting; the design and building of eco-housing; repairing, reusing, and recycling discarded materials, vacant land, and derelict buildings, especially in blighted postindustrial cities; promoting technologies that rely on renewable resources. There need to be many more such projects, though the next challenge is to scale them up without destroying them.

This agenda also means questioning what constitutes valid knowledge and who can claim authority and expertise. It assumes that people may need to be made aware of these issues—a task for formal schooling and informal community-based education—and that they should be active participants in decision-making with control over their means of livelihood. It means challenging the assumptions and practice of genetic engineering as it applies to the production of seeds, plants, and animals, as well as human reproduction; challenging institutionalized science as a major contributor to ecological destruction—indeed, as Carolyn Merchant puts it, the death of nature—but promoting what Lin Nelson calls the "kitchen table science" of women piecing together information about polluters, and the ethnoscience of women farmers in the Himalaya or Native American and Chicana herbalists. It requires research which is of interest and value to activists and policy-makers, rather than an abstract academic feminism increasingly coopted by patriarchal notions of scholarship. It needs organizations and contexts where working relationships between activists, researchers, and policy-makers can develop, and where students can learn this approach in practice. It will require extensive democratization of political processes and institutions locally, nationally, and internationally.

Clearly, what I am outlining here is both a long-term agenda and something already happening in small ways through many projects. Such a broad perspective may seem utterly daunting given the basic contradiction between exploitative economic systems and a world without environmental destruction or violence, but many women and men are grappling with these issues and making changes. Local, regional, national, and international networks of feminists and environmental justice activists, admittedly small and rather fragile, currently link organizers, researchers, and policy-makers around many of the issues I raise here. Examples include Development Alternatives for Women in a New Era (DAWN) active in Asia, Africa, Latin America, and the Caribbean; Women Working for a Nuclear Free and Independent Pacific, with groups in Britain, Australia, and the Pacific; and Women's Environment and Development Organization in New York. Fifteen hundred women from all continents gathered in Miami in November 1991 to develop a women's agenda to take to the UN Conference on Environment and Development in Brazil in June 1992. This World Women's Congress for a Healthy Planet[15] included women who work for UN agencies, elected politicians, teachers, scholars, journalists, students, and activists—women who are working inside formal governmental structures, in lobbying and educational work, and through grassroots organizing. It was the first major international women's gathering to discuss ecological issues and showed the growing strength of women's analysis and organizing.

Environmental issues have enormous potential for bringing people together across lines of gender, race, class, and nation in projects and movements that radically challenge white-dominated, patriarchal capitalism and include transformative agendas and strategies for sustainable living. At root this is about taking on the whole economic system and the systems of power—personal and institutional—that sustain it, working to transform relationships of exploitation and oppression. This means that northern countries must consume far fewer of the world's resources. Feminists and environmentalists need to challenge the fundamentals of materialism and consumerism, creating a definition of wealth that includes health, physical energy and strength, safety and security, time, skills, talents, wisdom, creativity, love, community support, a connection to one's history and cultural heritage, and a sense of belonging. This is not a philosophy of denial nor a romanticization of poverty, though it does involve a fundamental paradigm shift in a country—indeed a world—so dominated by the process of capital accumulation and the allure of material wealth. There is a need for greater dialogue between those from rich and poor countries, and between middle-class and poorer people in rich countries like the U.S., but this needs to move from a politics of solidarity—implying support for others in struggle—to a politics of engagement, where we are in struggle together.

This is a pivotal time in human history. The point is not to pursue the liberal ideal of equal opportunity for material development in a world that is heading toward even greater ecological destruction; to intellectually deconstruct the complexities of reality without apparent interest in practical reconstruction; or to buy "Green" products—where the emphasis is still on consumption (Hynes 1991; Mies 1993), but to transform relationships among people and between people and the nonhuman world so there is the possibility that our children's children will inherit a healthier planet and will be able to live in more truly human ways.

NOTES

1. I follow Charlotte Bunch in using this term to emphasize the fact that the majority of the world's people live in the so-called Third World, while recognizing that such shorthand terms are all problematic: "First World/Third World" assumes the superiority of North America and Western Europe. Economic development terms, which rank countries as "developed," "undeveloped," "underdeveloped," or "developing" assumes a unitary view of development and progress following the industrial capitalism of western Europe and North America. Hemispheres of political influence—West and East—is also a simplification; as is the distinction between countries of the North and South. Comparing countries also masks serious inequalities within them.

2. Research Foundation for Science, Technology and Natural Resource Policy, A60 Hauz Khas, New Delhi, 110 016, India. Journal: *Bija—the Seed: A Quarterly Monitor on Biodiversity, Biotechnology and Intellectual Property Rights.*

3. The Pure Food Campaign, 1130 17th Street NW, #300, Washington, DC 20036.

4. Feminist Network of Resistance to Reproductive and Genetic Engineering (FINRRAGE). The U.S. contact is Janice Raymond, Women's Studies Department, University of Massachusetts, Amherst, MA 01003.

5. 4-H Urban Gardens is a project of Michigan State University, Department of Agriculture, Wayne County Cooperative Extension Service, 640 Temple Street, sixth floor, Detroit, MI 48201.

6. Tierra Wools, P.O. Box 118, Los Ojos, NM 87551.

7. Citizens' Clearinghouse for Hazardous Wastes, P.O. Box 6806, Falls Church, VA 22040. Newsletter: *Everyone's Backyard.*

8. National Women's Health Network, 1325 G Street N.W., Washington, DC 20005.

9. Southwest Organizing Project, 211 Tenth Street S.W., Albuquerque, NM 87102.

10. Center for Third World Organizing, 1218 East 21 Street, Oakland, CA 94606. Bimonthly journal: *Third Force.*

11. United Farm Workers of America, P.O. Box 62–La Paz, Keene, CA 93531. Film; *The Wrath of Grapes.*

12. Women's Community Cancer Project, c/o The Women's Center, 46 Pleasant Street, Cambridge, MA 02139.

13. Population and Development Program, Hampshire College, Amherst, MA 01002.

14. Radioactive Waste Campaign, 625 Lafayette Street, New York, NY 10003; the Military Toxics Project, Tides Foundation, P.O. Box 845, Sabattus, ME 04280.

15. Women's World Congress for a Healthy Planet, 845 Third Avenue, 15th floor, New York, NY 10022.

32

"History Is What Hurts"[1]

A Materialist Feminist Perspective on the Green Revolution and Its Ecofeminist Critics

Meera Nanda

In the end, the glorification of the splendid underdogs is nothing other than the glorification of the splendid system that makes them so.

—Adorno, *Minima Moralia*

Emancipation depends upon the transformation of structures, rather than just the amelioration of the state of affairs.

—Roy Bhaskar, *Reclaiming Reality*

I. INTRODUCTION

This paper offers a materialist feminist framework for making sense of the impact of agricultural modernization—also called the green revolution[2]—on the lives of peasant women in Third World countries. The perspective offered here emerges through a critical engagement with the leading Third World ecofeminists, notably Vandana Shiva and Maria Mies, who represent the current thinking of intellectuals and activists broadly engaged in "overcoming" the project of modernization in Third World countries and moving into a "post-developmental" era.[3] Many critiques of "western" science and modernity that are fashionable in the postmodern academy in the West find a concrete expression in these intellectuals' opposition to the project of development in the Third World.

Two highly influential ecofeminist texts, Vandana Shiva's *Staying Alive: Women, Ecology and Survival in India* and the more recent *Ecofeminism* co-authored by Shiva with Maria Mies, condemn the green revolution as a species of "western patriarchal violence" against women and nature in the "colonies." They ground their sweeping and totalizing indictment of the green revolution in the claim that it forces Third World women out of their "embeddedness in nature" (Shiva 1988, 47), something they value and want to protect. They locate the source of this violence against nature and women in the Third World in the very rationality of science and the underlying "western cosmology," against which they wish to defend the holism and interconnectedness they believe characterizes women's work in subsistence agriculture in the Third World.

This paper will argue against both the ecofeminist diagnosis of the problems that women face as a result of modernization and the ecofeminist prescriptions regarding what needs to be done. I will argue that the alleged violence of the green revolution follows directly from the ecofeminists' ahistorical and idealistic understanding of the causes and nature of Third World women's purported "embeddedness" in nature. Women's work in subsistence agriculture cannot be read as a material instance of a special non-western rationality, which ecofeminists hold up as all that western science supposedly lacks: non-dualist, feminine, whole. Rather, as I will show, it is more useful to understand women's work as embedded in a complex ensemble of social relations in which class, gender, and caste interact in culturally sanctified ways to appropriate women's unpaid labor. This kind of analysis can provide a much more complex and nuanced explanation of the available empirical findings about the changing nature of women's entitlements to social goods under the impact of the green revolution. In this paper I will juxtapose a materialist analysis against the ecofeminist analysis of empirical findings regarding three indices of women's well-being—their claims to life, livelihood, and productive assets—and will argue for the superior explanatory power of the former.

Theoretically, I will argue against the kind of uncritical acceptance and celebration of women's purported embeddedness in nature that abounds in ecofeminist literature. Indeed, celebration of women's connection to nature constitutes the central dogma of ecofeminism itself.[4] I will argue that the ecofeminists' uncritical embrace of what in fact is a source of extreme and unremunerated labor and material deprivation for peasant women in Third World makes their eco*feminism* a misnomer. Shiva, Mies, and their sympathizers have offered eco*feminine*[5] support of the status quo, couched as a critique of the green revolution. Their "critique" only succeeds in glorifying the "splendid underdogs" and the "splendid system" that produces them, as the statement by Adorno cited at the beginning of this paper suggests. Their attempt to portray the fundamentally unjust and anti-female social order that forces Third World peasant women into a life of stupefying drudgery and deprivation as a source of revolutionary ideas and practices can hardly be expected to lead to an emancipatory transformation of that social order. Theoretically confused and factually erroneous though their work is, it requires a critical engagement for it has lately begun to assert a powerful influence over the agenda for women's role and place in development. To cite one instance: influence of the Shiva-Mies brand of ecofeminism was evident at the 1992 Earth Summit, where the basic ecofeminist assumptions about women being more "caring, non-violent, concerned with local and practical issues," set the framework for future directions of Third World development (Braidotti 1994).

I will counter the ecofeminist interpretation of both the sources of women's "embeddedness" in nature and how modernization affects women's lives as it "disembeds" them from their subsistence work. Contrary to ecofeminists, my aim is not to celebrate the apparent harmony between women and nature in peasant cultures, but rather to bring to light the systemic logic of global capitalism and local patriarchal traditions—and their deadly antifemale biases—that hides behind the surface of the perceived harmony. In other words, I refuse to accept women's experiences of nature as I find them, but instead try to understand their historical origin and their place in the totality of relationships. Furthermore, I see modernization not in terms of a confrontation between western patriarchal science/rationality etc. and some purported non-western wisdom, but rather as a contradictory development that erodes the hold of local patriarchal relations even while it integrates women into the circuits of global capitalism. A methodological note is in order here. Since Shiva and Mies base their critique mostly on the findings from the northwestern states of Punjab and Haryana in India, the original site of green revolution in India, I too will limit myself to empirical data about women's work and their well-being from these states only. Punjab and Haryana and northwestern India generally are well-known examples of classical patriarchy. Finally and not incidentally, Punjab also happens to be where I was born and where I grew up.

Apart from an attempt to understand the changing forces and relations of production in the Indian countryside, one of the major goals of this paper is to combat the reactionary Third Worldism that masquerades as a celebration of cultural "difference" and "identity" in Third World ecofeminism and most of the post-developmentalist literature. I believe that the politics that follow from valorizing cultural difference are disastrous for Third World women. In reifying the traditional Third World woman, this argument erases the fact that development has meant some loosening of the bonds of classical patriarchy. In my opinion, the entire enterprise of making the economic and cultural divide between the predatory "West" and the innocent "non-West" as the central axis of division in the late-twentieth-century global order is highly dubious. Capitalism close to the end of the millennium is much more fluid culturally, politically, and economically than the Eurocentric capitalism that led to colonialism of the eighteenth and nineteenth centuries.

While its inherently exploitative logic of extraction of surplus value from labor has remained unchanged, the dynamic of new global capitalism cannot be understood in terms of the existing model of dependency and neo-colonialism. The qualitatively new technologies based on flexible automation and the relative autonomy of developmentalist states in adopting these technologies to improve their bargaining position and the (relative) skills and wage level of workers are eroding the basis of the so-called new international division of labor, which was supposed to underlie the top-down relationship between the First and the Third World (Nanda forthcoming; Castells 1989).[6] Similarly in the cultural sphere, the McDonaldization of the world is no top-down westernization: the apparent homogenization hides the cultural *hybridity* that follows from the indigenization of western ideas in nonwestern countries, and the flow of nonwestern ideas and life-styles with the historically high rates of immigration of peoples from and to all parts of the world (Appadurai 1990; Gilroy 1992).[7] One crucial consequence of transnationalization of capital, production, and culture that is completely lost on Third Worldists of all stripes is the emergence of capitalism as the "authentically global abstraction," which is no longer an exclusive part of the "narrative of the history of Europe; non-European capitalist societies can now make their own claims on the history of capitalism" (Dirlik 1994, 350).

The total rejection of modernity by Shiva, Mies, and most post-developmentalists represents a lament against this globalization of the capitalist mode of production and indicates their desire to hold on to the local narratives in some imagined authentic form. This kind of assertion of difference, however, is not very incompatible with the cultural logic of global capitalism, which can easily sell any such cultural difference as ethnic chic or cannibalize it in order to better market commodities. The celebrity status that Shiva has acquired in the West cannot be understood apart from the surge of multiculturalism in the West, which, as Dirlik points out, serves the interests of transnationalized capital. (In India itself, however, Shiva's work has been received a lot more critically [Braidotti et al. 1994, 94].)

Simply decrying the new global environment in the name of cultural difference, as post-developmentalists tend to, amounts to nothing more than a gesture of futile defiance, defending nothing more than the right of non-Western "others" to be exploited by their own local overlords. A more appropriate response is to hold the claim of universalism of the new global order—that is, the claim of global capitalism to advance human rights globally—to a critical and systematic scrutiny in order to understand what it can deliver and what it is structurally incapable of delivering. A critical understanding of the systematic logic of global capitalism must be motivated by advancing the "conditions that would have to prevail in order for a universalism really worthy of the name, a horizon extended to all the world, to ground itself" (Lazarus et al. 1995, 89). In other words, equality, justice, and autonomy extended to "all the world," and all the people therein, are the true and as yet unrealized universals of modernity which capitalism makes false claims to but cannot actually deliver. We need a theory of "critical universalism," as Martha Nussbaum (1995) has recently suggested, that can speak not in the name of the tribe or a false new world order, but in the name of a flourishing of the human potential of all.

My case against Third World ecofeminism proceeds by first laying out the main theoretical differences that distinguish my materialist position from that of the ecofeminists. The next section describes the ecofeminist case against the green revolution and is followed by a juxtaposition of materialist and ecofeminist readings of three sets of empirical data from green revolution areas in India. The final section anticipates and answers some possible objections to my treatment of the environmental problems and wage labor in the Third World.

II. "THIRD WORLD DIFFERENCE": MATERIALIST VERSUS ECOFEMINIST APPROACHES

The materialist feminist perspective on the lives of Third World peasant women and the impact of the green revolution on their lives offered in this paper differs from the ecofeminist perspective in at least three significant ways.

First, instead of accepting as a given that Third World women are more intimately embedded in nature in their daily lives, I will instead ask *why* it is so. Why do women and not men belonging to the same socioeconomic group get this "privileged access to nature," which allows them to do the "invisible work"[8] that goes into keeping the family farm in good health—work that, ecofeminists forget to mention, is also unpaid and unrecognized as valuable? Contrary to Third World ecofeminism, which *begins* with an assumption of a gendered relationship between women, nature, and subsistence activities in the Third World, I will treat the gendering of subsistence work as an empirical question that must be answered by studying the logic of the larger structure in which it exists.

In contrast to ecofeminism, my starting assumption will be free from any gender bias. I will assume only that *both men and women, in Third World just as everywhere else, relate to nature in their search for a livelihood and survival.* This struggle for livelihood and survival shapes (and is shaped by) the relationship between the sexes. But the concrete forms the social institutions and gender relations will take in any given historical era cannot simply be deduced from some a priori assumptions regarding the nature of these relations and institutions. Introduction of new technology, for instance, does not have any singular, pre-determined impact upon women and men in different classes, but depends crucially upon the pre-existing sexual division of labor in a society. Likewise, the outcome of social change is not given either to the essence of being female or male, or to western versus non-western ways of thinking or doing. It is the structural and historically contingent junctures of technologies, social relations of production, and gender relations that decide who will do what and with what rewards and control.

By invoking the notion that "history is what hurts" in the title of my essay, I intended to emphasize the *historical genesis* of Third World women's place in the sexual division of labor in the traditional farm economy. Together social institutions, property relations, cultural narratives, and gender ideologies interact to make some aspects of farm work appear as "women's work" and thus natural, just, and meaningful to the women themselves. Any cultural singularity of these practices or feminine meaning women may derive from these practices has to be understood as a result of a constant interplay between the meaning and the structure.

The goal of this kind of historicizing is, as Teresa Ebert puts it, to help us

> understand the ways in which meanings are materially formed and social reality is constructed in relation to various strategies of power [and to acquire] historical knowledge of social totalities and the relations of power, profit and labor rendering certain forms of daily practices legitimate ("meaningful") and marking others as meaningless. (1993, 13)

This understanding of meanings and subjective experiences in relation to the social totalities of capitalism and patriarchy is the core of materialist feminism. However, given the emphasis of much current materialist feminism on cultural studies, it tends to emphasize subjectivity over the possibility of the experience itself. I will, however, try to understand how men and women are allowed different sets of experiences through the "strategies of power" coded into the relations of men and women to each other, to productive assets, to socially valued work, and to cultural resources. The gender-based differences in access to all these resources sets distinct limits to the range of activities and experiences that women can experience as legitimate and meaningful.

My second major disagreement with ecofeminists lies in how to morally, ethically, and politically *evaluate* the purported "privileged access" Third World women have to nature, and the culturally sanctified experiences this "privilege" is supposed to rest upon. Here, I start with Rosemary Hennessy's insight that emancipatory movements require "normative grounds and closures" that aim at "redefining the system of values, the divisions of labor and the allocation of resources the social construction of difference helps determine" (1993a, 3).

Third World ecofeminists are not devoid of normative concerns: they are, indeed, vocal about their concerns for ecological sustainability and a more equitable and just development. However, they believe that the cooperative, family- and community-oriented and ecologically sensitive practices of Third World peasant women can lead the way to fulfilling these normative goals. Thus one finds constant reference to a couple of examples of women's activism on behalf of nature and subsistence, especially the much abused example of Chipko[9] in the foothills of the Himalayas, where women prevented trees from being felled by private contractors by hugging them. Both Shiva and Mies, for somewhat different reasons, want to *encourage* the kind of lifestyle and work that gives Third World women their supposedly superior cooperative and ecological sensibilities. For Shiva, this project seems to stem more from her need to assert the superiority of the Indian worldview, which she simply equates with Brahminical and Hindu philosophy, over what she repeatedly refers to derisively as "western patriarchal reductionist science." Mies fully shares Shiva's denigration of the West and goes beyond it: her "White Man" is all-powerful and omniscient; the Third World and women and nature everywhere are his colonies, for him to plunder and control (Mies and Shiva 1993, 56 and passim). One finds here an insidious process at work which I will return to later: zealous anti-imperialists making imperialism the only motor of history, giving it powers that imperialists themselves could have only dreamt of, including the power to create the other entirely to suit their own ends. But Mies goes even further. She declares as impossible and undesirable any attempt to level the difference between the living standards and freedoms that the "White Man" enjoys (as a result of his "loot," as Mies would have it) and the rest of the world. Her message to the women of the "colonies" is that "equality for all is a logical and material impossibility" (1993, 59) and in any case undesirable, for the White Man's ideas of emancipation are the flip side of colonialism.

Clearly, ecofeminists wish to encourage rather than reduce the difference between women's ways of life in the West and in the Third World. The reason lies in the way ecofeminists read the experiences of Third World women. They understand Third World women's place in the sexual division of labor and the rather limited range of experiences their position allows them, not as a part of the material relations of production, but rather as symbols of *cultural essences of civilizations*. For all their gesturing toward a materialist understanding of subsistence work and colonialism, the real force driving social relations in ecofeminist accounts has the all the features of fixed, ahistorical essences: the "White Man's" essence to colonize women's bodies, nature, and the Third World, and the non-western people's essence as noble victims, seeking nothing but harmony and unity. Once such fixed essences are given a leading role in understanding economic and social relations between the First and Third Worlds, any potential of convergence between the two easily raises the specter of a loss of cultural authenticity. Thus cultural essences make it hard, if not impossible, to see how ecofeminists hope to ever achieve the kind of redefinition in the "system of values, division of labor and the allocation of resources" that Hennessy, correctly, singles out as the desired objective of all emancipatory movements.

Shiva and Mies seek to legitimize their claim that Third World women have a distinctive and holistic understanding of nature by grounding that understanding in the everyday subsistence work women do in the farms and forests. In keeping with the work of Sandra Harding and other feminist critics of empiricism in science, they present Third World ecofeminism as the standpoint epistemology of women of the Third World. However, the relationship ecofeminists posit between the knowledge Third World women may have and the everyday subsistence work that allows them to have that knowledge suffers from two problems, one due to the ecofeminists' misreading of standpoint epistemology and the other due to a theoretical problem with standpoint epistemology itself.

The first lies in the way Shiva and Mies simply equate women's raw experience with their eco-*feminist* "standpoint." This is completely contrary to the many denials by Sandra Harding and other standpoint theorists that experience itself does not constitute a feminist standpoint, but rather emerges through a *critical, feminist reflection* on the experience. Critical reflection on experience is sadly lacking in the ecofeminist texts under consideration here. Shiva and Mies follow this line of reasoning: because Third World women work with nature, they have a special knowledge of their own environment, their farm, their forests, etc. And because of this work that lets them participate in the rhythms and productivity of nature in a certain way, they have a special interest in protecting nature. Third World women's experience *becomes* their standpoint. Indeed, one of the reasons ecofeminists oppose green revolution is that they believe that the new technologies devalue the understanding and knowledge of Third World women, which is supposed to follow directly from the fact that they do certain kinds of work bringing them in a more intimate contact with the elements.

The complete lack of historicization of the kind of the work women do and the knowledge they can derive from that work stems from a problem central to standpoint epistemology itself. While standpoint theories draw attention to how what a person can know depends crucially on her position in the society and her concrete everyday practices, they neglect to show how these epistemically relevant practices are causally related to the social relations created by capitalism and their intersection with patriarchy. As Hennessy has pointed out in her trenchant critique of standpoint epistemologies (1993b), this systemic understanding of practices and knowledges has become a "limit term in feminist thinking," always gestured toward in theory but neglected in practice in favor of a more discursive deconstruction of women's conscious awareness of their social positions as workers, wives, and mothers. Without a systemic theory that connects women's knowledge to women's lives, the door is thrown wide open for the kind of romantic celebration of women's knowledge that pervades ecofeminist accounts. Third World women's special standpoint is justified in terms of their material practices, but these material practices are themselves understood as ahistorical "ways of life" embodying some essence of a nation, a people, or even a whole civilization. The carriers of these ways of life, in turn, emerge as voluntarist subjects who, regardless of the limits set by the nature of capitalism and patriarchy, will lead the world toward ecological recovery.

I believe that materialist feminism can serve as a useful corrective to this problem. Here I appropriate Hennessy's critique of standpoint epistemology and rephrase it to fit the context of ecofeminism: starting thought from Third World women's lives can expose the ways they are oppressed and exploited and how they resist and often consent *only* if this project issues from a perspective that understands social relations in systemic terms. "Systemic," furthermore, need not be read as economic in any reductionist manner. The consciousness of women themselves—that is, the narratives they tell of their own lives and the knowledge they derive about the natural and social world from their position in the social order—can be understood as a material force, for it "reproduces what gets to count as 'reality' and at the same time shapes other material forces both economic and political" (Hennessy 1993b, 21). Thus, what is supposed to be seen as purely cultural "ways of being" have productive and distributive effects. In the case of Third World peasant women, cultural narratives about what is appropriate and just for women and what they "deserve" can, literally, make the difference between life and death.

This brings me to my second theoretical corrective to the cultural nationalism of ecofeminists, namely, Amartya Sen's and Martha Nussbaum's influential "capabilities ethic," which understands the process of international and national development as the expansion of human capabilities and the promotion of valuable human functionings.[10] Sen, an Indian-born economist-philosopher, has asked one seemingly simple question: what do economic goods do for human beings? This question and Sen's answer to it are extremely significant for they break the commodity fetishism that prevails in mainstream economics and development. For Sen, economic goods and the social arrangements that make these goods possible have no inherent value but are valuable only to the extent they enhance a person's "functioning and capabilities." Sen defines these simply as "what he or she is able to do or be, [including] the ability to be well-nourished, to avoid escapable morbidity or mortality, to read and write and communicate, to take part in the life of the community, to appear in public without shame" (Sen 1990a, 126). Using this basic definition of capability, Sen and Nussbaum arrive at a criteria of evaluating the state of development across nations and cultures, namely, "What are the people of the country in question actually able to do and to be?" (Nussbaum and Grover 1995, 5).

I don't believe that ecofeminists (or most postmodernists, more generally) would have any disagreement with Sen in that economic goods should not be valued for themselves. A large part of their dissent from development theory is motivated precisely by the worship at the alter of economic growth regardless of any questioning of its ends. Both Shiva and Mies are very emphatic in their rejection of the concept of development that, as Shiva puts it, "equated improved well-being of all . . . with the westernization of economic categories of needs, of productivity, of growth" (1988, 1). But Shiva, Mies, and their fellow post-developmentalists may disagree rather vehemently with how Sen and Nussbaum use capabilities to critique social structures and cultural traditions, *both western and non-western,* that keep their members from achieving their full potential.[11]

Contrary to the ecofeminist and other postmodern-minded critics who tend to relativize the criteria for evaluating well-being with respect to the cultural context, the capabilities ethics is based upon a "critical universalism" that holds a set of basic human capabilities as *intrinsically* worthwhile for a flourishing of human life, while admitting that these capabilities may be expressed differently in different cultures and different historical epochs. Amartya Sen holds—and I agree—that "personal interests and welfare are not just matters of perception; *there are objective aspects of these concepts that command attention, even when the corresponding self-perception does not exist*" (1990, 126; emphasis added). Two levels of human capabilities serve as the objective criteria for judging whether or not any society can be said to be developing or regressing. The first level sets the ground floor for a life suitable for humans as a species distinct from other animals and includes bodily capacities like avoiding hunger and thirst, and the distinctively human traits like humor and play and the ability to reason and make moral judgments. The next level describes capabilities that make a human life a *good* life, that is, in the absence of these second set of capabilities, though we may judge the form of life a human one, we will not think of it as a *good* human life. These capabilities include, for instance, the ability to "imagine, to think and to reason," and the ability for critical reflection and, crucially for women, the ability to "live one's own life and nobody else's."[12]

Again, contrary to Shiva and Mies, Nussbaum and Sen believe that it is both possible and desirable to move *all* people, everywhere, above the threshold for a good life defined in terms of capabilities. This reflects their commitment that "all persons are equal bearers of human claims, no matter where they are starting from in terms of circumstance, special talents, wealth, gender, or race" (Nussbaum 1995, 86). By holding these capabilities to be universally valid (because grounded in our species characteristics) Nussbaum and Sen are not seeking to homogenize all cultures, sub-cultures, and traditions. Rather, they have identified components that are fundamental to *any* human life. These components can and do find expression in culturally and linguistically specific local ways. What Sen and Nussbaum are suggesting is that there is a sufficient overlap between different traditions and cultures so that they can be evaluated on the same metrics of capabilities. If some cultures fail to allow all or some of their members (based on their gender, class, caste, race, or sexual orientation) access to a good life, they cannot hide behind the irrelevance of these capabilities to their culturally sanctioned idea of a good life, because, as Nussbaum puts it, "human capabilities exert a moral claim that they should be developed. Human beings are creatures such that, provided with the right educational and material support, they can become fully capable of major human functions, . . . their very being makes reference to functioning" (1995, 88).

I believe this interplay between universal capabilities and their culturally and historically specific expressions is useful to counter the ecofeminists' blanket indictment of agricultural modernization (and modernity in general) as imperialistic imposition of western criteria of good life. These criteria themselves, ecofeminists assert, are foreign to Third World people. Shiva (1988), for instance, believes that subsistence economies were the "original affluent societies," for they took care of the basic vital needs of their members (1988, 12). But the problem is that she defines the nature of these needs, the level at which they could be assumed to be satisfied, and the social relations of satisfying them as determined by the prevalent cultural norms alone. By so relativizing needs, Shiva is able to gloss over some grim facts behind her much celebrated "affluence" of non-western agricultural systems: the fact that subsistence economies did not (and still do not) supply all the nutritional needs of all their members at a level that is biologically adequate for maintaining basic capabilities; the fact that social practices that go into meeting even that minimal level of culturally defined needs include back-breaking work of poor women—who by Shiva's own admission work harder than farm animals (1988, 109)—as well as other forms of degrading work like gleaning the farms to collect grain that would otherwise be eaten by birds (1988, 111); or the fact that the culturally defined needs did not include access to education, personal autonomy, freedom of thought, and a host of other higher-level cultural capabilities identified by Sen and Nussbaum. A similar problem crops up with Maria Mies's assertion that Third World women reject western ideas of self-determination and autonomy for they value their connections with the community (Mies and Shiva 1993, 220). Again, behind this totally amazing assertion lies the impulse to reaffirm local traditions as regulative ideals of social life for Third World.

By making local cultures the final arbiters of what is just and worth preserving, ecofeminists and like-minded critics of development end up justifying the status quo, which has been anything but just or fair to women. In this context, it is important to heed Sen's caution against mistaking the pleasure some deprived people may take in "small mercies" as a sign of contentment:

> It can be a serious error to take the absence of protest and questioning of inequality as evidence of the absence of that inequality or the nonviability of that question. . . . Deprived groups may be habituated to inequality, may be unaware of possibilities of social change, may be hopeless about upliftment of objective circumstances of misery, may be resigned to fate and may well be willing to accept the legitimacy of the established order. . . . But the real deprivations are not just washed away by the mere fact that in the particular utilitarian metrics of happiness and desire fulfillment such a deprived person may not seem particularly disadvantaged. (Sen 1990, 127)

How the deprived get to accept their lot plays an important role in Sen's concept of "entitlements," which comes very close to Hennessy's idea of the materiality of discourse. Entitlements refer to sociocultural consensus about resource allocation: Who deserves what? Who is worthy of what and how much? Who is perceived to be entitled to a good and who can be deemed unworthy is decided by a society's larger cultural beliefs about distributional justice, beliefs causally related to the ensemble of social relationships, including the relationship between owning and working classes and male and female genders. On Sen's account, women end up poorer than their male counterparts in all socioeconomic groups not because of poverty as such, but because of culturally determined consensus about their "worth" that determines their relative access to the available goods and resources, both material (food, health care, etc.) and cultural (education). Like Hennessy, who believes that cultural narratives are a part of the material reality ("what we know shapes what we do," [1993a, 37]), the concept of entitlement makes the cultural repertoire containing ideas about the relative value of categories of persons (women, lower castes) inseparable from what the members of these categories actually get and do. An important mechanism that ensures a lower entitlement of women to capability-enhancing resources enlists women themselves in their own deprivation, through a process that Hanna Papanek (1990, 162) has aptly described as "socialization for inequality."

In the later sections of this paper, I will critically examine the ecofeminists' evaluation of how the green revolution is changing Indian peasant women's entitlements to life, to livelihood, and to productive assets. I will argue that because they miss the connection between the cultural construction of women's worth and resource allocation to them, ecofeminists fail entirely to see how the displacements caused by the modernization of forces of production has in fact changed the cultural perception of worth of women, and thus has improved their future access to resources they need for developing their capabilities.

The above description of the theoretical blind spots in Shiva's and Mies's work makes it clear why I believe their work cannot be rightfully called *feminist*. Above all, feminism is a discourse of emancipation, but Shiva and Mies are willing to sacrifice the emancipation of Third World women at the altar of "Third World difference." So keen are they on establishing the difference in the lives and experiences of women—of all women from all men, and of Third World women from First World women—that they do not stop to investigate the systemic, political-economic, and cultural genesis of the differences they want to affirm. Without understanding the social relations that give rise to these differences, these critics deprive themselves of any objective bases to distinguish *legitimate diversity from illegitimate inequities.* Once the cover of culture is thrown over the material inequities, preservation of culture begins to take priority over the elimination of inequality.

For a feminist—that is, emancipatory—understanding of the lives of women in the Third World, it is crucial that we learn to distinguish between legitimate and illegitimate differences. If some differences are born out of unjust relationships, then justice requires that we try to eliminate these differences.[13] This project requires lifting the cover of culture from material relationships and seeing cultural differences in their materiality, that is, in the way they socialize Third World women for inequality of entitlements.

If difference is not to be reified and stabilized in the face of change, then technological modernization in general and green revolution in particular lose the univocal imperialistic connotations (of imposing their rationality on other cultures) they have been given in the "radical" critiques. The materialist perspective developed here will see technological modernization, including the capitalist labor relations it introduces in the traditional division of labor, as a *contradictory* process that simultaneously challenges and erodes the classic patriarchal structures even as it integrates women into capitalist relations of exploitation. This simultaneous presence of contradictory tendencies is important to remember if one wants to avoid a reductive culturalism that abounds in Third World ecofeminist literature.

This culturalism has a contradictory form. On the one hand, ecofeminists denounce the very idea of modernization as universalizing white, upper-class ideas of a good life. But then, ecofeminists want the entire world to live by another set of universals, this time based on Third World women's "privileged" experience and understanding of nature. This new universalism even bears an appropriately feminine and Third World-ish name: *Prakriti* (Shiva 1988). Moreover, even though they set out to give agency and voice to Third World women against the hegemonic discourses of western feminism, "Third World women" are structurally in the same position in ecofeminist writings that they have been traditionally assigned in some First World accounts: they are reduced to a composite, singular category without any attention to the complexity of their social positions in terms of class, race/caste, and other traditional determinants like age, marital status, number of sons, independent access to productive assets, and wage earnings. Thus, western feminists are not alone in colonizing the life world of Third World women and reduce them to a singular, monolithic subjects (Mohanty 1988, 60). Third World ecofeminists are capable of exactly the same move.

III. THE ECOFEMINIST CASE AGAINST THE GREEN REVOLUTION: "WESTERN PATRIARCHAL VIOLENCE"

What is ecofeminism's special brief against the green revolution? Shiva, Mies, and their postcolonials have offered the most devastating and totalizing critique of the green revolution to date. The central theme of their critique is also the most damning: the green revolution has committed "violence" against Third World people. While all Third World people are supposed to be the victims of this violence, the situation is worse for women. The surplus violence against women follows directly from the logic of common domination on which ecofeminism is founded: because women are closer to nature, anything that hurts nature hurts women more than it hurts the men in the same socio-economic strata. This violence, furthermore, is supposed to be inherent in the western way of knowing (i.e., modern science). As Shiva puts it, "the violence against nature and women is built into the very mode of perceiving both and forms the basis of the current development paradigm. . . . modern science and development are the latest and most brutal expression of a patriarchal ideology which is threatening to annihilate nature and the entire human species" (1988, xvi). This theme of "western science as violence" is not limited to ecofeminists but appears as an article of faith among most feminist critiques of science and among most post-developmentalists.[14]

Three related themes recur in Shiva and Mies's critique of the green revolution. These themes have become the staple of most "post"-marked critiques of science.

First of all, modern science and the modern social order is understood as constituted through the opposition between incommensurate binaries, each of which is defined as the absence of the other. Maria Mies and Vandana Shiva state in their recent book:

> Capitalism is based upon a cosmology that structurally dichotomizes reality: the one always considered superior, always thriving, and progressing *at the expense of the other*. Thus nature is subordinated to man, women to men, consumption to production and the local to the global. (Mies and Shiva 1993, 5)

In order to explain the green revolution through this logic of dualism, Shiva and Mies add more binary categories to the list: First World/Third World, urban/rural, western/indigenous, rationality/ irrationality. In all these cases, they associate the green revolution as imposing the first and the more powerful category over the second, less powerful, non-western category in the pair. Thus, the green revolution is charged with imposing the interests of the First World over the Third World, the urban over the rural, the western over the indigenous, culture over nature, and of course, men over women.

These dualisms lack any historical movement and resolution. Dualisms also exist in historical materialism, which understands the relationship between nature and culture and production and consumption as contradictory under capitalism. But these contradictions are the motor of history: class struggle leads to a resolution of these contradictions and the generation of new contradictions. In Mies and Shiva, any such movement is missing. They believe these dualisms are rooted not in the social relations of production in capitalism, but in the scientific worldview—the "cosmology"—that gave birth to the modern age. Thus, the only way to end the contradictions between nature and culture, between women and men, between Third World and the First World, is to deny, destroy, or otherwise step out of the modern cosmology itself.

In critiquing the green revolution for its dualism, Shiva and Mies use a handed-down and warmed-over deconstruction. The indictment of western metaphysics as dualistic lies at the heart of Derrida's deconstruction. Derrida has claimed that western metaphysics understands the world using binary oppositions, one of which is assumed to be superior to the other. With Foucault and poststructuralism, these dualisms have come to be seen as discursive effects of power. This trajectory of social theory, as Aijaz Ahamad shows, has made deep inroads among Third World intellectuals, primarily through Edward Said's influential book *Orientalism,* which claims that the representation of the Orient as inferior and irrational was essential for the West's understanding of itself as the rational and superior. This thinking places a dualistic rationality at the very core of colonialism itself. This intellectual trajectory has also shaped postdevelopmentalist critiques of science and technology.

The problem with the ecofeminist zero-sum appropriation of this logic is that it does not leave any room for any mutation in the aforementioned binary categories themselves, as a result of their coming together due to historical forces. No hybridity between western and non-western knowledge systems, technologies, and worldviews is allowed. These categories remain immutable and defined by the absence of the bipolar other. Caught between these unchanging binaries, women in the Third World do not have the option to use the discourses of modernity to critically question the assumptions of their natal social order.[15] The only role ecofeminism allows them is as the carriers/preservers of the supposedly unsullied "authentic" episteme—Shiva's concept of "Prakriti," for instance—of the cultures they are born into.

For all their critique of dualistic thinking, Shiva and Mies happily fall into a rather crass dualism themselves when they portray the non-West as the binary opposite of what they take to be the West. If the cultural essence of the modern West is dualistic thinking, the non-West is presented at the polar opposite: guided by a cosmology of harmony. As Shiva asserts:

> Contemporary western views of nature are fraught with the dichotomy or duality between man and woman, and person and nature. In Indian cosmology, by contrast, person and nature (Purusha [literally, man]-Prakriti) are a duality in unity. They are inseparable complements of one another in nature. . . . Every form of creation bears the sign of this dialectical unity, of diversity within a unifying principle, and this dialectical harmony between the male and female principles and between nature and man becomes the basis of ecological thought and action in India. (Shiva 1988, 40)

Anyone with any experience of living in India will attest that the social life in India is anything but this "dialectical duality in unity." The caste system and the practice of untouchability are as far away as one can go from the notion of unity. If nature was indeed considered an inseparable complement of human life, why is it that the upper-caste Hindus treat those who work with nature—plowing the fields (owned mostly by upper castes), handling human and animal waste, coming in contact with bodies—as untouchables? Or if men, women, and nature were in "dialectical harmony," as Shiva claims, why don't upper-caste Hindus allow menstruating women—when they are at their most "natural"—even to enter the kitchen or other clean places? As Aijaz Ahmad points out (1992, 184), Indians regularly posit a Hindu spirituality against western materialism and Muslim barbarity; and Hindu holy texts like the *Mahabharta* abound in making the foreigners, the lower orders, and women into dangerous inferior others.

Complementing Shiva's metaphysical, Brahminical idea of *Prakriti* is Mies's adulation for the subsistence labor of housewives. In her earlier work, Mies had posited that women in the West were domesticated—turned into housewives who were supported by the male breadwinners—only because women, peasants, and other subsistence workers in the "colonies" were superexploited through colonialism (Mies 1986). Mies now believes that the same category of exploited workers who supplied the unpaid, invisible labor that made housewifization of western women possible under colonialism will now lead the way to liberation of women everywhere. Does that mean the position of these workers has improved with the passing of colonialism? That is not the case. Subsistence work is still carried out by women, peasants, and other small producers in the hidden unpaid and poorly paid informal sector, as Mies admits (1986, 297). What has changed is that Mies has now found a use of this sector of exploited workers for her ecofeminism. Mies believes that the work of subsistence producers is "life producing and life-preserving work . . . the bulk of which is done by women" (1986, 298) who apparently understand better than men that "a subsistence perspective is the only guarantee of the survival at all, even of the poorest, and not integration into and continuation of the industrial growth system" (1993, 303). That Mies should have arrived at this position is not surprising, for her much celebrated analysis of colonialism and patriarchy was premised on an unchanging male desire to dominate women. Though it took a while for a full-fledged ecofeminism to emerge from her premises, it is not surprising that it finally did.[16] Mies believes rather naively and unrealistically that this hidden underground of capitalist market economy can show the way out of the many impasses of "this destructive system called industrial society, market economy or capitalist patriarchy [toward] self-reliance, self-provisioning, re-ruralization, participatory democracy, inter-regional cooperation. . . . A subsistence perspective, which would not be based upon the colonization of women, nature and other people, can show the way forward for Africa and other countries of the South, as well for the North" (1993, 302).

As an example of what such a "subsistence perspective" would involve, Mies finds hope in the current economic and energy crisis in Cuba, which has forced the Castro government to replace tractors with oxen and buses and cars with bikes. She believes that this "compulsory retreat to subsistence production [should be] seen as chance rather than a defeat" and it may offer a new model for the new nation-states born out of the collapse of the Soviet Union and the struggling nations of Africa. Thus, while Mies has ruled out material equality between the Third and the First World as a "logical impossibility," which is "not even desirable" (1986, 300), she suggests that the rest of the world lower its expectations to the bare survival that subsistence economy delivers.

Subsistence perspective has a natural affinity with Shiva's "feminine principle" or *prakriti*. Shiva interprets the ecological crisis as a symptom of the "death of *prakriti*, symbolically as well as in everyday work of rural women in survival and sustenance" due to forces of industrialization and market relations—all unleashed by "patriarchal maldevelopment," of which she holds green revolution to be a prime example. Like Mies, Shiva indeed finds in the subsistence work of rural women in India a paradigm for a "non-dualistic science" which she believes offers an alternative to Cartesian, that is, modern science. *Prakriti* is based upon "an ontological continuity between society and nature" which "excludes possibilities of exploitation and domination" (1988, 41) and which brings women and nature together *"not in passivity but in creativity and in the maintenance of life"* (1988, 47; emphasis in original). Clearly, Shiva's *prakriti* and Mies's "subsistence perspective" both serve as models for ecofeminist resistance to green revolution and western technology in general.

But why these ideas are "feminist" is hard to understand, for they change nothing. There are political economic reasons precapitalist peasant societies tend to be compatible with a more non-dualistic thinking, and none of them is even remotely egalitarian. The political and the economic spheres are not separate in these societies and surplus value is extracted through extra-economic means including political, juridical, and military domination of the producers. These kinds of social relations require a non-dualism between society and nature, the economic and the political (Wood 1988). As far as women are concerned, the traditional Indian ideologies of women as mothers and wives served to maintain not just class purity but also the purity of caste (Chakravarti 1993). Moreover, the traditional peasant agriculture has always rationalized its exploitation of women's work by claiming that women are more "natural" and ought to extend loving care to cows and plants and children and not worry themselves with men's concerns about property and ownership and the like. That is the essence of the patriarchal bargain, especially in the areas of classical patriarchy in India: for their motherhood and mothering, submissiveness, and propriety, women are promised "protection" from other men and subsistence (Kandiyoti 1988). Ecofeminists, in effect, accept the patriarchal bargain as moral and just and exhort Third World women to keep their end of it. Their critique of the green revolution can be read as a conservative response to the threat modern technology poses to classical patriarchy.

Neither, indeed, will the new transnational agribusiness have any problem with the ecofeminist ideas of *prakriti:* as long as women continue with their "loving interactions" with mother nature, the transnational agribusiness can continue to use their unpaid labor to increase their profits. As I have argued elsewhere (Nanda 1995), without independent rights of ownership of land, access to credit and new technologies, and equal, legally enforced wages for their labor, peasant women in the Third World face a bleak future under the transnationalization of agriculture. This new phase of transnationalization no longer depends on plantations but on small peasants who produce export crops on contract with transnational agribusiness (e.g., Pepsi Corporation in India). The ecofeminist celebration of women's invisible work can only serve to extract more unpaid labor from women in peasant households. This awareness in not lost on the sponsors of these giant food producers. As Cecile Jackson (1993b) has shown, the British Overseas Development Administration and the World Bank have lost no time in jumping on the ecofeminist bandwagon. Even the state-sponsored and voluntary development agencies, which often operate on anti-feminist and culturally conservative ideas (as documented recently by Mayoux 1995), often find the ecofeminist logic quite useful, for they can consign low-budget, low-priority, low-skill conservation and other appropriate technology projects to women and get credit for "pro-women" policies.[17]

Shiva's concept of *prakriti* has been criticized by feminist and progressive scholars who are not unsympathetic to the overall project of making development more woman- and environment-friendly. Many, including Nanda (1991) and more recently Bina Agarwal (1992a), Cecile Jackson (1995, 1993a,b), and Rosi Braidotti et al. (1994) have criticized Shiva's tendency to essentialize the woman-nature connection, to idealize the subsistence-based peasant societies, and to place the entire burden of women's "illfare" in developing societies on modernity and western influences while completely overlooking the traditionally sanctioned patterns of patriarchy and class/caste injustices that prevail with exceptional severity in most of India's peasant cultures. Most of these critiques can be leveled against Mies's work as well.

Shiva and Mies have found the theories of feminist standpoint very useful to deflect any such criticism. *Prakriti* or subsistence perspectives are not explicitly referred to as standpoint epistemologies, but that is clearly intended by their celebration of the knowledge Third World women have acquired through their specific material position in the social order. *Prakriti* is nothing more than standpoint understood as a "way of conceptualizing reality from the vantage point of women's lives" (Hennessy 1993a, 14). Moreover, the case for *prakriti* over western science is built on the logic of standpoint epistemology that is "starting thought from the lives of the oppressed [which] decreases the partiality and distortion of our images of nature and social relations" (Harding 1992, 181).

But like standpoint epistemology in general, ecofeminism takes the fact of Third World women's work in subsistence agriculture at its face value, without connecting their over-representation in this sector as compared to the men in the same class and caste, to the larger social structures of the society. Nor do they seem to be concerned about how the knowledge women have of the natural and social world *limits* their expectations and self-worth. While they valorize the fact of women's work in subsistence and also celebrate the consciousness and knowledge women seem to develop through this work, Mies and Shiva simply fail to see their connection to the sexual division of labor and the patriarchal ideologies that legitimize these relations. This blindness is evident in the way they see the role of the green revolution in changing women's entitlements to vital social goods: life, livelihood, and productive assets.

IV. WOMEN'S ENTITLEMENTS AND GREEN REVOLUTION AGRICULTURE

Entitlement to Life, or the Case of the "Missing Women"

"More than 100 Million Women Are Missing around the World," the title of a 1990 paper by Amartya Sen reminds us. As he goes on to demonstrate, if women in the developing world, covering most of Asia and North Africa and to a lesser extent Latin America, were provided with the same level of care—in terms of food, medical care, and other basic necessities—as men receive, nearly 100 million more women would still be alive today.

Despite the biological advantage in survival that women have compared to men, the number of women falls far short of men in Asia and North Africa, though not in sub-Saharan Africa. If we take the European and North American sex ratios as standards (where there are about 106 women for every 100 men), the disparity in sex ratio becomes apparent: there are only 97 women for every 100 men in the Third World as a whole. The deficit in women is most marked in parts of Asia—India, China, Bangladesh—with roughly 94 for 100 men, and in Pakistan only 90 women for every 100 men (1990b). Even if one takes the sub-Saharan African ratio of females to males (102 for every 100 males), Sen calculates (1995) the number of missing women would be more than 44 million in China and 37 million in India (which is close to 10 percent of the total female population there), with the total exceeding 100 million worldwide.[18] There are regional variations inside these countries. In India, Punjab and Haryana, the richest states of the country and also the seat of the green revolution, have only about 86 women per 100 men, while the much poorer southern state of Kerela has a sex ratio (103 women for 100 men) similar to that in industrialized countries. The most recent census (1991) reported in *The Economist* (March 11, 1995) shows a declining sex ratio in India, with only 93 women for every 100 men in 1991, as compared to 93.3 in 1981. In northwestern India, there were only 87 women for every 100 men in 1991.

If the very survival of female persons is not on par with males born in the same socio-economic-cultural space, discrimination against them in access to all other pro-motive entitlements—to food, health, and education—is only to be expected. Countless micro-level studies from India (reviewed most recently by Agarwal 1992b, Harriss 1992, and Agarwal 1988a) show that women in India, on average, fall behind men in life expectancy (though the gap is closing); nutrition (in Punjab, discrimination in food is seen only among the poorest families, while studies in other areas of India indicate protein and caloric intake is lower for females as compared to males in all socioeconomic groups); and health care (with fewer numbers of girls and women seek-ing medical treatment as compared to boys and men for similar ailments). Not surprisingly, girls lag behind in schooling, with the gap wider among the poor agricul-tural laborers and the lower-caste women, who are "a century behind caste Hindu women in their schooling" (Harriss 1992, 350).

Why are these women missing? Why did they not get to live and thrive? Shiva is most explicit in her answer: the green revolution killed them. Shiva reads the fact that the green revolution areas are also the areas with the lowest sex ratio as a sign of the "violence" of the green revolution. But worse, she believes that the frightening rise in the practice of selective abortions of female fetuses—a practice widespread in Punjab and Haryana, as in most parts of India—is also caused by the green revolution. Underlying this and other forms of female infanticide, Shiva claims, is dowry, and underlying dowry is the green revolution (Shiva 1988, 119).

Shiva explains these damning charges through her overall critique of modernity, of which the green revolution is only an agent. Thus, following the basic ecofeminist tenet of women's closeness with nature, Shiva valorizes "precisely those links in farm opera-tions which involve a partnership with nature and are crucial for maintaining the food cycle." With the green revolution, women are "dispossessed" as they are forced out of the "ecological work" of soil builders into the "economic work" of wage earners (1988, 114). Or, in another formulation, Shiva claims that commercialization of labor and farm inputs devalues the survival work women do without wages (1988, 117). Commerce, wages, and capitalist agriculture in general—promoted by the green revolu-tion—are seen as men's work, which stands in total opposition to the non-commercial "survival economy" of women. As we will show in the next section, Shiva's correlation of wage work with devaluation of women is entirely at odds with what empirical evi-dence shows. But let us first see if her claim that the green revolution is a cause of lower sex ratio holds.

Shiva can only sustain her charge if she ignores history. Far from an introduction of modern farming techniques, female infanticide has a long tradition in northwestern India. British records dating back to 1901, when British annexed Punjab to the empire, show that female infanticide had been widely prevalent among dominant castes in that region. Indeed, the historical investigation of the British documents done by Indian anthropologist Prem Chowdhry (1989) shows that at that time, the British officials believed (as a part of their "civilizing mission," perhaps) that female infanticide had actually come *down* from the pre-colonial levels. The 1931 Census of India done under the British shows that Punjab had only 831 women for each 1,000 men, even then the lowest ratio in all of India.

Most geographers and demographers agree with Bina Agarwal's summary of the extent and causes of female infanticide:

> Historically, female infanticide was practiced widely in the northern and western (Gujrat upwards) belts, especially in the states of Rajasthan, Punjab and Haryana, with very few and scattered instances noted elsewhere. It was most common among the upper castes and is attributed to factors such as hypergamy, heavy dowry expenditure, prevention of excessive land fragmentation etc. (Agarwal 1988a, 91)

Any understanding of the changes in women's lives as India modernizes will have to start from this grim history. This is especially true of technological change and new innovations, which are typically fed through pre-existing sexual division of labor and family relations (Whitehead 1985). In Shiva's account, these pre-existing, lethal biases find only a passing reference, and in Mies's celebration of subsistence none at all. The green revolution is made to carry the weight not just of its own biases and inequities, but of these historical injustices as well.

Female infanticide is only the most extreme and brutal sign of the devaluation of female life in northwestern India. Most missing women are not actually killed directly but are casualties of persistent neglect in nutrition, health care, and other entitlements necessary for survival. Here, one meets another dimension of inequality completely missing in the ecofeminist romance—the family as the site of gender inequality, or the fact that all members of even the poorest family are not equally poor. Village level studies have shown beyond doubt the gender discrimination in intrahousehold food allocation and health care (Agarwal 1992b). None of these findings is mentioned in the ecofeminist celebration of peasant life.

These pre-existing gender inequities in survival are not just a result of poverty. Empirical studies have established beyond doubt that female infanticide is an upper-caste and upper-class phenomenon (motivated by a son preference and the cultural pressures to withdraw women from visible work), while female neglect persists across classes and is more acute among the very poor. How a group or society distributes available resources among members reflects not only economic power and authority relations, but also the moral basis of that group, its consensus about distributive justice, and its implicit priorities. The long history of gender biases, dating into India's most remote history (see Chakravarti), shows that contrary to the claims of ecofeminists, the so-called moral economy of the peasant did not value the work women have always done in the agricultural economy. Despite their contribution to the family's wealth through their work in the farms and forests and where the culture of seclusion kept them home-bound—work in processing food and fuel—the premodern and even the pre-British peasant economy in India did not consider women as *deserving* of resources as men. Peasant economy has always placed more value on visible work, work that brings in *earnings*. Thus an economic logic that values life in terms of a hierarchy of material returns on labor is no western import but rather an integral part of the "moral economy" of the peasant. In the light of history, it is simply factually incorrect to equate peasant economies with some nonwestern, nondualistic ethic of care and cooperation and modern technology with a "western patriarchal" dualistic exploitation of nature and women.

Many cultural discourses, including folk tales and popular proverbs which are sanctioned by religious texts (especially Hinduism) in the Indian Northwest, show that devaluation of female lives is not a pathology of modernity but an integral part of the traditional cultural order. Prem Chowdhry (1989) has collected many of these common proverbs and folk discourses:

> The son of an unfortunate dies,
> The daughter of a fortunate dies.
> Who can be satisfied without rain and sons;
> for cultivation of both are necessary.

These folk traditions serve to "socialize women for inequality," in Papanek's apt phrase. They reflect and simultaneously construct the collective consciousness regarding what the differently sexed members of the family and the community are entitled to or deserve. It is through these discourses that mothers come to believe their daughters do not "need" as much food or as good an education as their sons, and it is through these discourses that daughters come to accept their share as fair and just.

From a materialist perspective, the lower sex ratio and the spread of female foeticide in green revolution areas appear as existing *despite* and not because of the green revolution. Given the long and culturally entrenched bias against females that prevails in the green revolution enclaves, all one can defensibly claim is that three decades of rapid agricultural modernization have not been able to reverse or even weaken the culture of female sacrifice—at least, not yet. Even though in Punjab women are increasingly participating in wage labor, which, as we shall see in the next section, is linked to improvement in female survival and well-being, the practice is largely "distress driven" and therefore limited to women from poor and low-caste families. But because women's withdrawal from fieldwork is associated with higher social status, most small and/or lower-caste peasants tend to follow the norms of their social superiors and withdraw their women from farm work as soon as they can afford to—a process aptly described as "sanskritization" by most development scholars. Confined to home, where they continue to work in the "invisible" farm economy, women are not perceived as making an economic contribution. The consensus is that Punjab, the state with the lowest sex ratio, is also the state with the lowest rural female labor participation rate in the entire country (Chowdhry 1993, 139; Agarwal 1992a). Thus *withdrawal* from visible work, rather than an increase in it, as Shiva believes, is the reason women are seen as burdens. So many women are missing in green revolution areas because of culturally enforced withdrawal to the invisibility of work done in the private space of the home, without any remuneration and recognition.

Access to "Visible Work"

A striking feature of women's work in rural India, writes Indian feminist economist Kalpana Bardhan, is that "while women's overall workforce participation rate is low, and decreasing over the last two decades, the proportion of wage-laborers among those working is high and increasing" (Bardhan 1989, A33). In other words, more rural women who work in the farms are doing it for wages, and the proportion of all women wage laborers active in farm labor is increasing. In 1971 and in 1981, half of the total women in the job market in India were agricultural workers, as compared to only a fifth of the male workers (Bardhan 1989). Bina Agarwal (1992b) and Hanumantha Rao (1994) both provide figures supporting this assertion.

But it appears that apart from the situation in Punjab and Haryana, where an increase in female wages is drawing some women from small-farmer/upper-to-middle-caste households into wage labor (Chowdhry 1993), women's presence in the wage market is "distress driven." This is indicated from the fact that outside of Punjab and Haryana, most women who work for wages are from lower-income classes/castes and tribal groups. (Upper castes and richer farm households tend to withdraw women from farm labor altogether once their economic status begins to improve.) As a general rule, it appears that those regions which have seen a sustained economic growth accompanied with an increase in irrigation and multiple crops have also seen a decrease in the disparity between male and female wages. In these areas there has been some improvement in the bargaining power of female workers as a result of the increased demand for their work in transplanting and interculturing, both considered female jobs (Rao 1995, 43; Bardhan 1989).[19] But apart from these areas, the wages for female agricultural workers remain much lower than the minimum wage and lower than men's wages for similar work. The lower-caste status of most female farm workers along with cultural biases against women in general are the major reasons for their lower wages. Thus while the increase in female proletarianization is a fact supported by census data, its causes and its effects on women's well-being are not as clear cut. They are open to varying interpretations, depending upon the starting assumptions about the causes of women's poor access to life and other promotive entitlements.

As expected, Shiva and Mies read the increasing proletarianization of women as a cause of women's oppression and hold women's work for wages as a sign of devaluation of their work. Again, in a logic similar to that deployed to link the green revolution with female infanticide and neglect, Shiva sees all commodity relations, including work for wages, as leading to increased devaluation of women in green revolution areas. There are two parts of her argument against wage work: first, modernization favors production for profits instead of needs, and this "masculinist equation of economic value and cash flows creates a split between the market economy controlled by men, and the survival economy supported by women. Commercialization leads to increased burdens on women for producing survival and decreased valuation of their work on the market" (1988, 117). Second, Shiva believes that with wage labor, women's work shifts from "ecological work" to "economic work," which she describes as "subsidiary workers and wage earners on an agricultural assembly line" (1988, 114).

The first part of Shiva's argument hinges on a neat and a near-complete split between a cash-mediated, masculine farming sector and a non-commercial, nonmarket, not-for-profit female sector: any change that gives more power to the former—as the green revolution supposedly does—is considered by definition a loss for women. The problem with this logic is that the male and female spheres of agriculture are nowhere as clearly distinct, not even in Africa, on which Shiva seems to be basing her analysis of India. In the case of Africa, it has been argued persuasively by Anne Whitehead (1990) that development scholars from Ester Boserup onward have overstated the extent of female labor in subsistence farming and underestimated the involvement of women in the modern sector of the economy. Furthermore, evidence from village studies simply does not confirm that production for market actually is inimical to women's position in the family. Indeed, the phenomenal success of

Bangladesh's Grameen Bank and other community banks is based upon enabling women to start micro-enterprises that enable them to produce products (from milk to baskets) for the market or to simply retail products (cosmetics, clothes) that other women may need or desire. In her aversion to market relations, Shiva simply shares the generalized anti-market attitude that is quite widespread among the activists who organize around politics of food production. The problem, as Maureen Mackintosh (1990) has pointed out, is not with markets as such, but with the terms on which people come to the market, which are shaped both by gender and class. The real problem for women is not producing for the market, but the lack of independent ownership of assets that make their entry into the market difficult.

The second part of the argument—that women's work ceases to be ecological and becomes economic—is also problematic. It is true that with the green revolution, many of the inputs that women provided through their free labor (weeding, making organic manure, etc.) are being replaced by chemicals or hired labor. But what is not clear is whether this shift implies a devaluation of women's work. Shiva seems to assume that the ecological work women did was valued by their families in the first place. The available evidence suggests that because women's ecological work was naturalized to such an extent—that is, considered simply what women do because that's what is appropriate for their womanly natures—that work was (and still is) rendered invisible. Shiva valorizes the invisibility of women's work for the value it has for the environment—although it is debatable whether only women in traditional societies were involved in ecological work, or whether all of women's work was ecologically beneficial to nature,[20] or for that matter whether the green revolution has been as unremittingly disastrous for the environment as critics have made it out to be. What Shiva misses entirely is that *women's subsistence work is not only invisible ecologically, it is also invisible socially.* And this social invisibility did not start with the "ecological disruption rooted in the arrogance of the west and those that ape it" (1988, 44). All available signs from history, mythology, and folk narratives indicate that the lot of all those who worked with the elements in traditional agriculture was not a happy one.

The ecofeminist denigration of wage labor flies in the face of the evidence accumulated from myriad village level studies linking women's entitlements and well-being to their participation in wage work. Indeed, a *positive relation between female labor participation and entitlements* is one of the few guiding principles of development studies that enjoys a consensus. This principle is stated firmly and simply by Barbara Miller (quoted by Papanek 1990, 167): "Where female labor force participation (FLP) is high, there will *always* be high preservation of female life, but where FLP is low, female children may *or* may not be preserved" (emphasis in original).

It is important to note that the simple fact that women labor is not sufficient to translate that labor into well-being for women. For labor to lead to "preservation of female life," it has to be *visible* or what Amartya Sen calls "gainful" labor, as compared to unpaid and unhonored work as a part of the family either inside the house or on the family farm. There is no denying that women's ecological work has a substantial economic worth, but given the repertoire of cultural and religious narratives of caste and class purity and the female propriety required for maintaining both, traditional Indian culture does not recognize this work as valuable. The kind of gainful labor most positively related with improvements in women's entitlements is "working outside the home for a wage or in such productive occupations as farming" (Sen 1990). Agarwal

(1992b, 403) has ranked on the scale of visibility agricultural work that is physically more visible over home-based work, and work that brings in earnings over the "free" collection of fuelwood, fodder, or water. Although women have always worked on their family farms (except where they observe the purdah, as in Muslim and some upper-caste communities), because of cultural prohibitions and gender stereotypes they are assigned to tasks that are not valued as productive.

This positive correlation between visible or gainful employment and lower gender disparities in female survival and well-being is strong enough to explain the variations of sex ratios across different regions of India, and indeed, the world. Pranab Bardhan's work (quoted by Agarwal 1988a) shows that the relatively better survival rate and status of women in southern India is related to the greater demand for female labor generated under rice cultivation in these states, rather than under wheat cultivation that prevails in most of northern India.[21] Similarly, Amartya Sen finds a positive correlation between employment and survival in different parts of the world: countries where cultural norms permitted women to work for wages outside the home were also the countries where fewer women were missing. Thus despite higher absolute poverty, women in sub-Saharan Africa have fared much better than women in southern Asia (1990b).

It is important to realize that the increase in wage labor in green revolution areas is affecting different women differently depending upon their class and caste status. The increase in wage labor may improve the perception of worth of women workers who bring in wages, and thus may make them appear more deserving of entitlements to nutrition and health care. But these women who work for wages are for the most part drawn from lower classes and lower castes. They face numerous problems (ranging from sexual assault and low wages), and their social location simply does not give them the power to set new cultural norms. In fact, as their families move up the economic ladder, they tend to withdraw these women from wage labor, following the custom of upper castes. Moreover, female farm laborers replace the work the farmers' wives, daughters, and daughters-in-law did gratis—converting these relatively privileged women into economic liabilities and raising the rates of dowry. The pre-existing cultural norms that associate upper-caste status with women's withdrawal from visible work tend to dampen the other improvements in women's status generally supposed to follow from economic growth. This is evident in a recent study from Maharashtra (Vlassoff 1994), which shows that women who have withdrawn from farm work have gained more education and more leisure time, but have actually become more conservative in terms of marriage and dowry. Another study from Haryana (Chowdhry 1993) shows that even though there is an increased involvement of women—even from the middle-class and -caste status—in wage labor, this has not led to any change in the evaluation of women's work[22] or loosened the controls of the family over their life choices. Indeed as Chowdhry points out, a new kind of semi-proletarianization seems to be in the making, under which men continue to work on their own farms, where they retain full control, while they send women to work for wages.

Thus Shiva is not entirely off the mark when she claims that women are becoming economic liabilities as wage labor associated with the green revolution replaces the work they did for free. But she fails to see how wage labor affects different classes of women differently. Furthermore, Shiva fails to appreciate how the new relations of production are powerfully shaped by pre-existing cultural norms and social relations. It is simply not the case that the peasant societies valued the work women did for free.

The devaluation of women is not "inherent" or built into the "western patriarchal ways of knowing" that have produced the high-yielding seeds of the green revolution. Instead, their effect on women's lives in the Third World is shaped, at every step of the way, by local cultural mores that define female and caste propriety along with the existing inequities in social and economic power. Shiva makes it appear that the pre-existing social relations were devoid of an economic rationality and operated only to satisfy need. But as I have tried to show, any attempt to portray traditional subsistence economy as driven by logic of cooperation and altruism simply does not match the historical data.

V. ACCESS TO LAND AND OTHER PRODUCTIVE ASSETS

The "poverty literature" supports the commonsense idea that ownership of land, however small in size, serves as a hedge against absolute poverty and destitution. However, as Agarwal's (1988b) detailed study shows, women in India are not allowed by custom and religion (especially Hinduism) to inherit land, plow it, or self-manage it. Although after Independence the Hindu civic law was revised to allow women the right to individually own, use, and dispose of land, strong cultural and ideological sanctions prevent most women from exercising this right. Lack of independent ownership further constrains women's access to credit, extension services, and new technologies.

Women still have the customary entitlement to the forests and the village commons, which provide especially the poorest among them essential items for personal use and sale. But most village commons and forests are shrinking as a result of environmental degradation (chiefly due to deforestation, water logging, and salinity) and population pressures and privatization (caused in part by the government's land redistribution programs), causing disproportionate hardships for women and children who have the primary responsibility for collection of firewood, fodder, and water (Shiva 1988, passim).

While ecofeminists have done a service in highlighting the deterioration of the commons and the resulting hardships for women, they have characteristically turned a blind eye to women's independent ownership of farm land and other productive assets. Both Shiva and Mies are explicit and generous in their praise of Third World women who

> appropriate nature, yet their appropriation does not constitute a relationship of dominance or a property relationship. Women are not owners of their own bodies or of the earth, but they cooperate with their bodies and with the earth in order to grow and make grow. (Shiva 1988, 43)

In a similar vein, Maria Mies holds up women's work in subsistence agriculture as a critique of the prevailing capitalist-, profit-, and growth-oriented development paradigm. Both hold the example of Chipko to affirm that Third World women "expect nothing from 'development' or the money economy. They want only to preserve their autonomous control over their subsistence base, their common property resources: the land, forests, hills" (Mies and Shiva 1993, 303).

These claims about women's lack of interest in ownership of land or material benefit from development appear to be ideological interpretations ascribed to rural women by ecofeminists. The evidence of economic studies and social movements suggests that

Agarwal (1994, 1455) has it right when she claims that "the gender gap in ownership and control of property is the single most critical contributor to the gender gap in economic well-being, social status and empowerment."

One major problem is that ecofeminists tend to overuse the Chipko movement to explain all aspects of the problems of rural women. Indeed, some (e.g., Jackson 1993) have suggested with some merit that Shiva's valorization of Chipko as an exemplar of women's spontaneous environmental and community commitments of women is self-serving and biased. Historical and ethnographic studies have shown that Chipko is an essentially conservative, anti-change movement led by populist peasant leaders who are patriarchal in their way of life and leadership. Be that as it may, an overemphasis on Chipko shifts the attention away from women's movements fighting to win the right to own and manage land in their own names, rather than as family or community property. The problem with not paying attention to these other movements is that it diverts attention from the material causes that make independent ownership of land so vital to women's interests.

Contrary to the ecofeminist claim that Third World women organize spontaneously on the behalf of embattled mother nature, Indian women have shown an equal zeal in organizing to win the right to own and manage land in their own name. One such struggle is described by Agarwal (1988b), namely the Bodhgaya movement that emerged in Bihar in the mid-1970s, in which men and women of landless households jointly participated in an extended struggle for the ownership of the plots they cultivated, held illegally by a local religious body (a *Math*). During the struggle, women raised the demand for independent land rights. Their demand was based on their understanding that ownership in their husbands' names might improve the welfare of the family but would not automatically improve their position in the family. Similar demands for independent land rights are a part of many of the other women's movements in India (see Agarwal 1994 and 1988b for more details), none of which are mentioned in ecofeminist literature.

Defending the commons against environmental decay and fragmentation through government's land redistribution and privatization is important, and ecofeminists are right in bringing this issue to the forefront. But so is women's private ownership of land. One may be ideologically opposed to private ownership and wish for women to lead the quest for a new way of living. But the fact remains that rural women in India labor under a regime of property laws which has been privatized since time immemorial—the justification for private ownership of land dates back to the early Vedic literature (Bandyopadhyay 1993). Nearly 86 percent of India's arable land is in private hands, with only a very small and shrinking area serving as village commons (Agarwal 1994). In this context, to expect women to concern themselves only with the commons is tantamount to ignoring the real problems they might be experiencing in their families and communities as a result of their being denied the right to own and inherit land in their own names.

Under the current regime of property relations in India, the right to own and sell land is a matter of justice and empowerment for women. It is important to remember that there are tremendous religious and cultural strictures against women's independent ownership of land in South Asia (see Agarwal 1988b for a detailed examination of Hindu and Muslim personal laws). Without these rights, women are at a clear disadvantage. As numerous studies have shown, land serves as a defense against absolute poverty. Not having ownership of land but only the right to use it puts women at the mercy of their husbands and their families. In the case of the death of their husbands, women are reduced to the status of dependents. In many cases, widows or the wives of farmers who have migrated to the cities manage land without a title to it, and that implies that they cannot mortgage it or use it as a collateral to borrow money for improvements in productivity. Last but not the least, lack of independent access to land worsens women's bargaining position in the family (Agarwal 1994).

The same problems arise in the traditional taboos against women using—or even touching—certain technologies of production. Taboos against women plowing hold across all communities in India: men have complete monopoly over the plow, while women are allowed to use the hoe only. Different communities have different religious justifications for why women should not use the plow. In the hilly parts of the North, women are simply told that God decreed that they should not plow. These strictures are followed quite strictly, with communal punishments for women who out of desperation might try to plow the field themselves (Agarwal 1988b). Similar strictures also apply to other technologies, like the potters' wheel or the loom in some communities. To understand the relationship between women and nature in Third World, these cultural taboos must be taken into consideration.

VI. ANSWERING CRITICISM:
THE ENVIRONMENT, WAGE LABOR, AND WOMEN

Two sets of objections are most often made against the materialist understanding of the green revolution presented here. First, critics claim that a materialist analysis ignores or minimizes the problems the green revolution (and modernization in general) has caused for the environment. Second, it is objected that the analysis offered here valorizes wage relations and overlooks the plight of wage workers in capitalist sectors of the economy.

First the question of the environment: It is true that the materialist perspective offered here is not eco-centric; that is, it does not treat the new stresses introduced by the green revolution as central to understanding its impact on the lives of women and the rural population at large. This is consistent with the overall theoretical framework of historical materialism: environmental effects cannot be understood apart from the totality of social relations, and the history of the relationship between nature and the livelihood systems of any social formation. Thus, while I am not unsympathetic to the problems of soil erosion, salination, and loss of diversity that ecofeminists have raised, I don't think these problems are inherent in the nature of modern science or technology, and neither do I believe that these problems are created, *ab initio*, by the new technology. Environmental problems, like anything else, have a history and must be understood historically.

As an illustration, take the ecofeminist charge that the green revolution is responsible for deforestation and soil erosion. Critics arrive at this conclusion by a purely empiricist examination of the situation: they see that the forests are diminishing and the soils are decaying, and that farmers are adopting new farming techniques, and they quickly conclude that the new techniques have caused the sad state of affairs. But in fact, if one keeps in mind the long history of low productivity, extensive agriculture and the combined pressures of the subsistence needs of the growing population, and the profits of timber industries both under colonialism and today, a different picture emerges. The historically low productivity of Indian agriculture even as compared to its neighbors China and Japan is a well-established historical fact. For a variety of reasons—the oppressive social relations, those based on caste chief among them[23]—the traditional agricultural system was primarily an extensive farming system, that is, it could only increase the total output by extension of farming to new areas rather than increasing the yield per unit of land. This feature of the traditional farming system has played a historic role in the environmental crisis India faces today; it has been estimated that out of the total forest lost in this century, nearly half was cleared in order to put it under food production (Rao 1994, 161). Increase in the land area under the plow brought with it a proportionate increase in the livestock population, which played a big role in the erosion of the grazing lands. These were not the only factors: colonial use of timber for the railways played a role as well. But if the history of deforestation and soil erosion is kept firmly in the background, it becomes totally unjustified to hold the green revolution alone accountable for India's ecological crisis. In fact, it becomes reasonable to think that the yield-increasing, land-saving nature of the green revolution has *reduced* the pressure to put more land under the plow. Indeed, the recent data bear out this interpretation: Indian food-grain output has continued to grow at a healthy rate of around 3 percent annually through the last decade (1981–1991) while the land brought under cultivation has actually *decreased* annually by about 0.3 percent (Sawant and Achuthan 1995; Rao 1994).

The ecofeminist complaints against chemicalization of agriculture are similarly overblown and abstracted out of the totality. That fertilizers and pesticides are often misused and over-applied is true, but it is not something that cannot be corrected through proper training and extension services. To ascribe all use of chemical inputs to imperialistic interests or to the reductionism of modern science is simply going too far. There is another far more basic problem: the way ecocentric critics of the green revolution have portrayed the green revolution seeds as necessarily dependent on chemical inputs. It is simply not true, as charged *ad nauseam* by Shiva and her sympathizers, that the high-yielding varieties of seeds "inherently" need chemical fertilizers and pesticides in order to produce higher yields. Modern seed varieties are designed to produce more grain (and less stem and leaves) by making better use of nitrogen and other nutrients in the soil, *irrespective of the source of the nutrients*. The claim that green revolution seeds are some kind of package deal made by seed and chemical companies so that they can sell more chemicals to unsuspecting farmers is simply not true. There are many studies showing that high-yielding seeds continue to produce high yields even when supplied with organic manure or other organically derived inputs (see Nanda 1991 for more details).

Thus the needs of the environment, when understood in their ecological and social complexity and history, can be accommodated in materialist analysis of technological change. But if the demand is to accommodate overblown and unscientific critiques in the name of environmentalism, the problem lies with these claims and not with the analysis presented here. Intellectual responsibility demands that these claims should not be uncritically accepted and made to appear true simply by repetition.

Let us turn now to the vexed issue of the role of wage work in women's emancipation. The way I have tried to resolve the issue of wage work in the agricultural economy does give the impression of simply turning the ecofeminist negative assessment of wage work on its head: they decry it, and materialist feminists, I argue, should celebrate it. This impression is regrettable and unintended. I am by no means suggesting that wage labor in itself will liberate women or that Third World societies must simply embrace capitalism and call it progress. All I am suggesting is that wage labor moves the struggle for gender equality from the family to the public sphere, where it can connect with the larger struggles of other workers locally and globally to challenge the dominance of capital and patriarchy. I see increased opportunities for wage labor for women as a point of departure rather than the endpoint of Third World feminism.

I firmly believe that the role of wage relations in women's lives has to be understood historically and in the context of the ensemble of social relations, all of which set distinct limits on human relations and autonomy. That the green revolution is replacing the relationships based on kinship, family, patronage with relationships decided largely by calculations of profits, productivity, and the demand and supply of labor as a commodity is not in dispute.[24] The question is the relative assessment of these changes.

I strongly urge all those who believe that wage relations are more oppressive for Third World women today than the work relationships based on family and kinship to read a recent account by Martha Chen (1995) of the struggle of poor and widowed women in Bangladesh and India to win the right to work for wages in the face of pressures to continue to work as a part of the family economy. The Bangladeshi and Indian women in Chen's account had to struggle against the culturally sanctioned norms of purdah and upper-caste seclusion respectively so that they could sell their labor in order to survive and raise their families in the absence of the male members of the family. What becomes very clear from Chen's account is that the existing institutions of the civil society are no longer meeting the basic subsistence needs of these women without denuding them of all personal dignity. As Chen concludes, these struggles are not just for survival but for *justice* as well. I concur with Chen and will try to show in what sense wage labor—which is premised on the fundamental injustice of surplus extraction—can be said to be a means for survival with justice in today's Third World.

First, there is simply the matter of the collapse of the traditional patriarchal bargain. The traditional bargain, especially in the region of India under consideration here, promised women survival and protection against other men in return for women's fulfillment of her culturally defined "womanly" duties, including production of sons, sexual chastity, and deference to the elders. There has been an erosion of this classical patriarchal bargain under the impact of modernization. To expect women to live by the same norms of femininity and domesticity when men and the extended family are no longer able or willing to keep their end of the bargain is simply unjust. Wage work allows women to survive in the face of the loss of the traditional support structures.

Indeed, now we come to the crux of the matter. The ecofeminist (and post-developmentalist) critique of modernization is a lament over the erosion of the classical patriarchal bargain, while the analysis I have offered does not consider the prospect of the erosion of classical patriarchy as something feminists should grieve about. Thus I contend that Third World women need wage labor, not simply as matter of strategy to tide over the turbulence caused by modernization, but as a *welcome means to break out of the classical patriarchal bargain altogether.*

To say that is obviously not to claim the end of patriarchy or class and caste inequities. As the experience of women in the West shows, wage labor under capitalism only changes the private patriarchy regulated by the household and headed by the husband/father to a public patriarchy guided by relations of markets and non-kin men (Walby 1992). The personal liberties and autonomy that this change from private to public patriarchy affords women are limited when compared to the degree of autonomy truly human societies are capable of. But, limited though they might seem against an as yet unborn future, *these liberties are by no means insignificant* when compared to the far more oppressive limits that the classical, private forms of patriarchy have imposed on women in Third World societies.

It is important to remember both the potential and the limits of emancipation possible under capitalism. By converting the process of extracting surplus value from labor from extra-economic means (of feudal lords, slave owners, or family) into an economic exchange (wages for labor), capitalism devalues extra-economic powers. The extra-economic powers in peasant societies, as Wood (1988) has argued, have a disposition to male dominance. The data presented in this paper regarding female survival and well-being bears out the cost of male dominance in peasant societies for women: it is amply clear that women in the largely peasant society of northwestern India have not fared at all well in terms of even basic survival needs. Modernization can erode the very material bases of the male dominance of peasant societies, and for that reason feminists cannot afford to turn their backs on it.

Wage work is fundamentally exploitative, and I don't for a moment wish to deny that fact. But I don't want to lose sight of the fact that the nature of exploitation of wage work is such that it is amenable to collective action. When I argue for wage work, I am simultaneously arguing for a strong labor movement that can link the poorest landless farm workers to their sisters and brothers throughout the nation and the world.[25] Indeed, one of the biggest problems with ecofeminists and other critics of modernity is that they have diverted attention from the real struggles of farm laborers for enforcement of labor laws and minimum wages. The pressing issues of gender equity in wages, opportunities for education, and training have all been sidelined in the shrill rhetoric of critics aligned against modernization itself. Rather than decry modernity, it is time to consolidate the opportunities it has opened up for the struggles that lie ahead—the struggle for deeper and more substantive equality, and the struggle for socialism.

VII. CONCLUSION

By extolling the traditional order and making modernization look like a conspiracy on the part of an unchanging, congenitally imperialistic West, Shiva, Mies, and all who share their animus against modernity are asking women in the Third World to forgo their opportunity to cut loose from the ties that have kept them subservient to men for so long. And this brings us to where we started: the feminism of this brand of ecofeminism is a misnomer. For a *feminist* analysis, one has to start from an understanding that enables a "transformation of structures, rather than just the amelioration of the state of affairs." The materialist understanding of the historic changes taking place in the countryside of Third World countries presented here is an attempt toward that transformation.

Author's note

An abridged version of this paper was presented at the Women, Gender and Science Question conference held at the University of Minnesota in May 1995. The conference paper was coauthored with Kim Laughlin from the Department of Science and Technology Studies at Rensselaer Polytechnic Institute. I appreciate Kim's many insights. Rosemary Hennessy's critique of an earlier draft of helped me rethink some of my earlier positions.

NOTES

1. "History is what hurts, it is what refuses desire and sets inexorable limits to individual as well as collective praxis" Jameson (1981, 102).

2. "Green revolution" is the name given to the agricultural modernization that started around the mid-1960s and aimed at increasing the yield of food grains in the Third World through the introduction of high-yielding varieties, primarily of rice and wheat. The high-yielding seeds have now spread to most of the Third World and include many other crops.

3. As Arturo Escobar (1992) has recently christened this intellectual trajectory. Other notable intellectuals include the neo-Gandhian critics of science and technology like Ashis Nandy, Shiv Vishwanath, and their colleagues at the Center for Study of Developing Societies in New Delhi; feminists who subscribe to the WED philosophy (Women, Environment and sustainable Development), especially the UK-based Women's Environmental Network; and anthropologists and geographers in the West as well as in the Third World who use postmodern ideas to critique development in the Third World. Notable among the last category are Arturo Escobar and Stephen and Frederique Marglin.

4. Ecofeminism holds that the same logic that dominates/liberates women also dominates/liberates nature. That women and nonhuman nature are dominated together and the practices that will liberate one will also liberate the other is what gives ecofeminism its claim for being both ecological and feminist. See the recent anthology edited by Karen Warren (1994) for many restatements of this basic connection between women and nature.

5. For a similar concern over whether certain strands of ecofeminist thinking can be called feminist, see Davion (1994).

6. This is not to say that the transnational corporations do not seek lower-wage *skilled* work in the Third World (e.g., the Indian software engineers and the Mexican and Chinese engineers working in highly automated offshore auto plants and the like)—they obviously do. The difference is that these developments are led by Third World countries' internal class dynamic, policies, and prior development efforts in education and training. Some of these countries (especially in East Asia), which started out as junior partners of American capitalism, have improved their competitive advantage, rapidly moved up the ladder of the international division of labor, and are in a better position to negotiate the terms of transnational investment in their countries. See Castells (1989) for a good discussion of the logic behind this "new" international division of labor.

7. "The globalization of culture is not the same as its homogenization, but globalization involves the use of a variety of instruments of homogenization (armaments, advertising, language hegemonies and clothing styles) which are absorbed into local political and cultural economies, only to be repatriated as . . . *difference*" (Appadurai 1990, 16).

8. "The woman peasant works invisibly with the earthworm in building soil fertility . . . women have a major productive role in maintaining the food cycle. In feeding animals from trees or crop byproducts, in nurturing cows and animals, in composting and fertilizing fields with organic manure, in managing mixed and rotation cropping, this critical work of maintaining ecological cycles was done by women, in partnership with the land, with trees, with animals and with men" (Shiva 1988, 109).

9. Various movements have claimed Chipko for their own agendas. Shiva, aligned with one of the (male) leaders of the movement, Sundarlal Bahuguna, has been instrumental in making Chipko the *cause célèbre* of ecofeminism. But the hill women's agency on behalf of either the environment or their families is not that clear. See Jackson (1993).

10. For a recent collection of papers that attempt to understand a concrete struggle of Indian and Bangladeshi women using capabilities approach, see Nussbaum and Glover (1995). See David Crocker (1992) for an exposition of Sen and Nussbaum's capability ethics.

11. Nussbaum reports a sharp exchange between herself, Sen, and the stars of postdevelopmentalism, Stephen and Frederique Apffel Marglin. The latter have defended the Indian practices of isolating menstruating women and have critiqued the eradication of smallpox as an affront to the local Indian practice of goddess worship as a cure for smallpox (Marglin and Marglin 1992). The Marglins attacked Sen and Nussbaum for imposing western values on other cultures, while Sen and Nussbaum faulted them for celebrating values and traditions in other cultures which they would never accept for themselves. See Nussbaum (1992, 1995).

12. Capabilities like "living one's own life" often serve as the reminders of the "limits against which we press" instead of being included in the "capabilities through which we aspire" (Nussbaum 1995, 75). Whether a capability has become a part of the already available repertoire of capabilities of a group of people, or is still a dimly perceived desire beyond the limits of the possible, depends upon the historical context. But the point the critical universalists would hold onto is that some capabilities, even those which may not be attainable under certain contexts, are part of any life we will count as a human life. Nussbaum lists eleven capabilities in the first level and ten in the second level. See Nussbaum (1995) for a complete description.

13. I am indebted to a paper by Sypnowich (1993) for this formulation.

14. There is vast and growing postdevelopmentalist literature that equates development and modernity with "violence." For the most recent statement of this style of thinking, see Ashis Nandy (1994, 11) who claims that "development stinks . . . because . . . it is *fundamentally* incompatible with social justice, human rights, autonomy and cultural survival. Development in *all its forms* is contaminated by its origins in the structure of repression implicit in the social sensitivities produced by colonial exploitation and by the systematic scientization and desacralization of life and living nature" (emphases added).

15. This internal critique of traditions using modern western science is possible. See Nanda (forthcoming).

16. For a short but sharp critique of Mies's prioritization of patriarchy and the West over class relations, see Kabeer (1994) and Walby (1992).

17. That is the reason the stress on economic rights in the 1995 International Conference on women in Beijing was so heartening. The Beijing conference's "Platform for Action" demanded "equal access to economic resources including land, credit, science and technology, vocational training, information, communication and markets as a means to further the advancement and empowerment of women and girls" (*New York Times,* Sept. 15, 1995). At one point in the conference, Mohammed Yunus, the director of Bangladesh 's Grameen Bank, declared access to credit was a human right. I couldn't agree more.

18. On translating these figures of the total women who are missing into ratios of the number of missing women to the number of actual women in a country, for Pakistan we get 12.9 percent, for India 9.5 percent, for Bangladesh 8.7 percent, for China 8.6 percent, for Iran 8.5 percent, for North Africa 3.9 percent, for Latin America 2.2 percent, and for Southeast Asia 1.2 percent (Nussbaum 1995, 3).

19. This contradicts Agarwal's claim that the absolute differentials in female/male wages are the highest in Punjab (Agarwal 1992b, 399). The problem with Agarwal's study is that it relies solely on figures that are more than two decades old (1974–75). Rao and Bardhan are basing their claim about improvement in women's wages on statistics from the 1980s leading up to the 1990s.

20. Cecile Jackson cites many instances from her experience in Africa of men, because of ownership interest, making an investment in conservation.

21. The difference in female participation in rice versus wheat cultivation does not explain all the differences. There are considerable variations between rice regions in female participation, with women's participation in rice-growing eastern India being low as compared to their participation in the rice-growing south (Agarwal 1988a).

22. Jobs like transplanting, weeding, and sowing, requiring less skills and generally stereotyped as female tasks, have come to be reserved for females. Some other household tasks like handling cow dung, etc., are still considered women's work. See Chowdhry (1993).

23. The causal relationship between degraded, low-caste farm labor and low productivity of Indian agriculture has been well established by both Indian and western historians. See the classic works of Irfan Habib and Barrington Moore Jr.

24. Though not entirely. As Kalpana Bardhan has shown, the rural labor markets continue to use traditional gender, caste, and kinship norms to decide the level of wages for different categories of workers.

25. Agricultural modernization has indeed sparked a vigorous farmers' movement in India. Some groups of this movement (e.g., the Shetkari Sanghatan in Maharashtra) are emerging as important forces in secular, democratic, and feminist struggles. See Omvedt (1993) and Lindberg (1995) for recent works.

33

Feminism and the Ends of Postmodernism

Carol A. Stabile

I. The relationship to the social world is not the mechanical causality between a "milieu" and a consciousness, but rather a sort of ontological complicity. When the same history inhabits both habitus and habitat, both dispositions and position, the king and his court, the employer and his firm, the bishop and his see, history in a sense communicates with itself, is reflected in its image. (Bourdieu 1981, 306)

This essay deals with constellations of relationships that have largely been overlooked during the process of feminism's arduous trek into the university. In what follows, I trace a set of homologies that exist among and between postmodernism, feminism, and the larger political context to illustrate what Bourdieu describes as "ontological complicity" (but what might also be defined as "ideology" in Marx's sense of a distortion of real contradictions). The main tendency I will discuss is a correspondence among postmodernist social theory, the postmodernist turn in feminism, and the wider sphere of political debate.

Because the terms I use in this argument have been unnecessarily complicated and mystified, I want to briefly define the following at the outset: socialism, historical materialism, and postmodernist social theory. In the first, socialism describes an organized political movement at the center of which is the concept that the relations of production structure social life, that the exploitative character of capitalism is the root of social and political oppression, and that the proletariat will serve as the agent of revolutionary social change. In terms of class, under capitalism, society is divided antagonistically into a ruling class, which owns the means of production, and a working class, those who must sell their labor power in order to survive. The middle class in the U.S. are those workers who do not own the means of production, but for whom certain advantages (i.e., economic, institutional, cultural) do exist. Gramsci's theory of hegemony—primarily concerned with the issue of consent—mainly addresses such a middle class, for in order to give consent, one must be convinced that one will receive certain rewards, however slight. While in the more prosperous Cold War era university professors occupied a privileged, solidly middle-class position, the profession is presently much more divided. A class of more privileged workers—those with tenure or tenure-stream positions who have modest teaching loads and institutional privileges—still exists, but the number of part-time, adjunct, and contingent workers with heavy teaching loads, no job security (many of them have only annual contracts), and very little institutional privilege is increasing.

By postmodernist social theory, I mean the work of those theorists who subscribe to the belief that, in the last portion of the twentieth century, politics can exist only through the necessarily fragmented, divided, and contentious identities through which people think themselves; and that the only similarity among such groups is their struggle—from very different positions and in isolation from one another—against an amorphous and ill-defined category known as "power." For example, against the Marxist centrality of class struggle and in an ironic if unintentional mirroring of the mercurial nature of capitalism, Michel Foucault argues: "But if it is against *power* that one struggles, then all those who acknowledge it as intolerable can begin the struggle wherever they find themselves and in terms of their own activity (or passivity)" (1977, 216). Following Neil Lazarus (1991) and Christopher Norris (1990, 1992), I use the term "postmodernist social theory" to designate those critical theories that rely upon an uncritical and idealist focus on the discursive constitution of the "real," a positivistic approach to the notion of "difference" (one that does not consider the divisiveness of such differences), and a marked lack of critical attention to the context of capitalism and academics' locations within capitalist processes of production and reproduction.[1]

Unless one resorts to reified notions of objectivity and intellectual autonomy, it is difficult to see how postmodernist social theorists and feminists could make arguments about the discursive constitution of reality, the primacy of discourse, and the possibilities of fragmentation at a time in which conditions in the U.S. were growing more repressive in all too material ways. A grim irony inheres in the fact that as capitalism's attacks on the working class, the poor, and social programs intensify, at a time when the division of wealth is deepening, intellectuals discover that identity is actually fluid and discursive, that the economy is really discursively constructed, and that class position no longer matters. Why, at this point in history, did postmodernist social theory become popular within the academy? Why did arguments against class as a category of analysis emerge at a point when class divisions were growing?

In order to address these questions, we must first acknowledge that intellectuals are not autonomous from larger political, ideological, and economic contexts. In other words, we receive much of our information about the world in the same way others do: through the mass media. Issues and topics in academic fields do not emerge fully formed from our heads, but frequently emerge from conflicts within academic fields produced and structured by larger fields of cultural and political production. Second, we must understand that the ways in which we process this information are structured by institutional training and position. Feminists have criticized educational institutions such as law and medicine for their powerful ability to shape subjects' attitudes, investments, and behaviors. Indeed, it is easier to see how scientific institutions function in oppressive ways, since the material effects of scientific theories are more visible than the ideological effects of philosophical or social theories. But like any institution, those educated in the humanities—if they are to succeed in the field—must also internalize the rules of the game as well as certain received categories of thought and behavior. In short, we inherit and reproduce certain classificatory schema that in turn delineate the contours of our own understandings.

> II. In order to exist or develop, this society not only needs certain relationships of pro-
> duction, exchange, and communication, but it also creates a certain set of intellectual
> relations within the framework of contradictory class interests. (Luxemburg 1976, 253)

In France, postmodernist social theory responded to the perceived hegemony of Marxist political analysis. Imported into the U.S., it gained a different material context while maintaining the original outline of its anti-Marxist critique. Both postmodernism and, as we shall see, feminism, entered into intellectual debates specific to European contexts, thus obscuring the historical and material conditions that produced these debates. In a kind of phantom-limb syndrome, a backlash against economic analyses was appropriated by a society whose history of class struggle has been consistently repressed.[2]

Although U.S. feminists remain suspicious of the work of French postmodernists such as Jean-François Lyotard and Jean Baudrillard, the postmodernist social theory of Ernesto Laclau and Chantal Mouffe in *Hegemony and Socialist Strategy* (1985) has had a profound—if frequently unacknowledged—impact on theory in the U.S. Lyotard and Baudrillard's visions tend toward the more fatal—John Clarke claims that the conclusion to Lyotard's *The Postmodern Condition* contains one of "the saddest passages in postmodernist writing" (33), and one can only read Baudrillard's reference to the oppositional potential of the "silent apathy of the masses" as just short of overt despair. In contrast, the popularity of Laclau and Mouffe in the U.S. results at least in part from their optimism about the political potential of "radical democracy."

The postmodernist social theory laid out in Ernesto Laclau and Chantal Mouffe's *Hegemony and Socialist Strategy* (1985) has had a major influence on feminist arguments in the U.S., heightening tendencies toward abstraction within feminist theory and legitimizing already existing arguments against historical materialism as a method and class as a category of analysis. In *Hegemony and Socialist Strategy*, Laclau and Mouffe argue that the Marxist concept of class is essentialist. Calling for radical democracy based on reformist premises, they view the main impediment to "radical democratic politics" as "essentialist apriorism, the conviction that the social is sutured at some point, from which it is possible to fix the meaning of any event independently of any articulatory practice" (1990, 17).[3] In place of the "essentialist apriorism" of the proletariat as the class that "has to bear all the burdens of society without enjoying its advantages" (Marx and Engels 1976, 94)—and in opposition to any conceptualization of capitalism as a system—Laclau and Mouffe argue for the practice of "articulation." Articulation, they claim, is

> the construction of nodal points which partially fix meaning . . . the partial character of
> this fixation proceeds from the openness of the social, a result, in its turn, of the constant
> overflowing of every discourse by the infinitude of the field of discursivity. (1985, 113)

Articulatory practices, which "take place not only *within* given social and political spaces, but *between* them" (140), thus replace alliances previously forged with subordinated classes and through political struggle.

Laclau and Mouffe wish to dispense with the Marxist premise that the proletariat will form the agency for revolutionary social change. However, they do not dispense with the notion of agency altogether; rather, they perform a bait-and-switch act. In place of the revolutionary proletariat and indeed any notion of revolution, Laclau and Mouffe smuggle in a new agent for reformist struggles.[4] Laclau and Mouffe conclude:

> To the extent that the resistance of traditional systems of difference is broken, and inde-
> terminacy and ambiguity turn more elements of society into "floating signifiers," the
> possibility arises of attempting to institute a centre which radically eliminates the logic
> of autonomy and reconstitutes around itself the totality of the social body. (1985, 186)

Thus, despite their insistence that the centrality of class in Marxist analyses is essential-ist, they recognize the need for some form of centrality, some "new" center. Within the context of Laclau and Mouffe's argument, it seems clear that—however implicit the claim—articulation and articulatory practices can best be done by those trained in the nuances of discourse and discursivity: namely, intellectuals. "Social relations," Laclau and Mouffe tell us, "are discursively constructed":

> Synonymy, metonymy, metaphor are not forms of thought that add a second sense to
> a primary, constitutive literality of social relations; instead, they are part of the prima-
> ry terrain itself in which the social is constituted. (110)

In place of the so-called privileging of class (and here it seems revealing that in the United States, the only place where class may be said to be centralized is within margin-alized Marxist analyses in the academy and even more marginalized socialist organizations), we find the privileging of intellectuals and intellectual activity. This is, of course, a convenient move for intellectuals since it means that (a) since the concept is intrinsically essentialist, we can jettison the category of class and the contradictions it introduces into our own work; (b) we do not need to concern ourselves with our own class positions, since oppressions are, within the discursive field, necessarily unfixed and somehow equivalent; and (c) we do not have to participate in class struggle since, as Ellen Meiksins Wood puts it, we have put "intellectual activity *in place of* class strug-gle" (1995, 10).

Laclau and Mouffe are consistent in their argument that Marxism "privileges" class in ways that marginalize or ignore the oppression of social groups not constituted eco-nomically: predominantly middle-class movements, such as feminism, environmen-talism, antinuclear activism, and lesbian and gay rights. In the U.S., the category of race presents the main challenge to Laclau and Mouffe's theory of discursive equivalences and antieconomism—a category about which they are noticeably silent. For one cannot consider race in the U.S. without confronting the increasing immiseration of African Americans, Latinos, and immigrants in the U.S., the overt state repression against com-munities of color and immigrants, and the racist rhetoric used to legitimize such atrocities. Further, when race and (necessarily) class are introduced into the analysis, it becomes difficult to make arguments for the "openness of the social."[5]

Michèle Barrett, a recent convert to postmodernist social theory, does not offer an uncritical endorsement of Laclau and Mouffe in *The Politics of Truth,* but she does claim that:

An obvious explanation of the enormous current interest in their work is that it speaks to a problem—the weight to be attached to social class as opposed to other salient divisions such as gender, ethnicity or age, for example—that has exercised a major hold on both academic analyses and on practical political activity across the traditional right/left spectrum. (1991, 68)

Barrett mentions that this "radical new theorisation of politics, in which the iconic factor of class is dramatically shifted from its privileged position" would be attractive "to many people," but she stops short of theorizing why this radical new theorization is so attractive, as well as who it would attract. In addition, her categorizations—"gender, ethnicity, or age"—reproduce Laclau and Mouffe's elision of race and class.

Barrett's admittedly partial solution, in keeping with Foucault, is to replace the Marxist concept of "the economics of untruth" with "the politics of truth" (1991, 140). Ironically, her central critique of Laclau and Mouffe is that they are too Marxist. She would prefer a more Foucauldian, and even less deterministic model of power relations, suggesting that issues of determinism and materiality can be shelved. Barrett asks, "It remains to be seen, however, how far *Hegemony and Socialist Strategy* really does carry though its iconoclastic project of the complete dismantling of class privilege" (74). This "iconoclastic project of the complete dismantling of class privilege" does pose an important, if unintentional, question. Where Barrett means the privileging of class within Marxist political analyses, I want to read this question against her grain. Whose class privilege is "dismantled" by Laclau and Mouffe's argument? When transplanted onto a U.S. context, what does it mean to dismantle a category whose very existence has been routinely denied? Finally, isn't this dismantling of class privilege itself an effect of class position and consequently enabled by many academics' distance from economic necessity?

> III. The class that has the means of material production at its disposal has control at the same time over the means of mental production, so that thereby, generally speaking, the ideas of those who lack the means of mental production are subject to it. (Marx and Engels 1976, 64)

The idealist turn in postmodernist social theory finds its counterpart within anti-essentialist feminist theory.[6] Just as postmodernists argue that "the real" no longer refers to concrete, objective reality, the anti-essentialist critique within feminism has dissolved the political category of women (and however problematic this category was, it was at least a political one) into a "discursive" construct. At a time when feminists of color had begun to criticize the use of women as a category of analysis, the important questions raised by their critiques of the invisibility of race and class were deferred by the anti-essentialist claim that identity was discursively constructed, bodies were discursively produced, and class was a totalizing fiction. Intersections between anti-essentialist feminism and postmodernist social theory run throughout much feminist theory in the 1980s, but are abundantly evident in the influential work of Judith Butler. In order to illustrate this relationship, I want to look at Butler's "Contingent Foundations: Feminism and the Question of 'Postmodernism,'" published in *Feminists Theorize the Political,* because it more explicitly elaborates theoretical investments that are otherwise implicit in her work.

Defending a theory of the social as contingent and foundations as a hegemonic fiction, the essay is a critique of critiques of postmodernism. According to Butler, "The chant of antipostmodernism runs, if everything is discourse, then is there no reality to bodies?" (1992, 17). Following Laclau and Mouffe, Butler proposes

> a distinction between the constitution of a political field that produces and *naturalizes* that constitutive outside and a political field that produces and *renders contingent* the specific parameters of that constitutive outside. (20; original emphases)

Like most defenses of an a priori, discursive realm, Butler does not identify those forces intent on toppling critiques of the subject, although her references to foundationalism, totality, and universalizing make it clear that at least one of these antipostmodernist critiques issues from a Marxist perspective. Criticisms of postmodernist social theories are accordingly dismissed as gestures of "conceptual mastery" (5), "an authoritarian ruse by which political contest . . . is summarily silenced" (4), and "paternalistic disdain" (3).

The theory that Butler advances promotes a belief that discourse precedes, structures, and limits subject formation. The point, she claims, most powerfully made by postmodernists and poststructuralists (and since Butler does not identify the first, it is to be assumed that critiques of postmodernist social theories are identical with critiques of poststructuralism) is "that recourse to a position that places itself beyond the play of power, and which seeks to establish the metapolitical basis for a negotiation of power relations is perhaps the most insidious ruse of power" (Butler 1992, 6). That the first does not necessarily follow from the second is inconsequential to Butler's argument, because the establishment of any organized material basis for politics is precisely the object of her critique.

Since the subject is constructed by politics and power prior to its material constitution, or rather its "intelligibility" (Butler 1992, 17) as material, the political goal for Butler is to intervene at the level of this discursive construction by "reworking that very matrix of power by which we are constituted, of reconstituting the legacy of that constitution, and of working against each other those processes of regulation that can destabilize existing power regimes" (13). It is, Butler claims, "only through releasing the category of women from a fixed referent that something like 'agency' becomes possible" (16).

While Butler does not provide examples of antipostmodernist critiques, she does offer an example of what happens when unquestioned foundations are accepted: the Persian Gulf War, which served "not merely to destroy Iraqi military installations, but also to champion a masculinized Western subject" (Butler 1992, 10). This is a curious example indeed, for it implies that a social and political theory committed to contesting economic injustice (Marxism)—a theory that explicitly positions itself against capitalism—performs the same authoritarian operations as a war waged in the interests of capitalism itself. Moreover, it flattens out very real power differentials and constitutes, as Wood puts it, "a kind of self-promotion of intellectuals as world-historic forces" (1995, 10).

The consideration of discourse as constitutive of materiality, the conflation of "discursive ordering" and "material violence" (Butler 1992, 17), and the belief that contingent signifying acts produce material bodies simply are not viable strategies for oppositional politics. In the end, Butler's theory of "politics as such" (4) runs aground on the usual Foucauldian reef. Stuart Hall observes of Foucault that he "saves for himself 'the political' with his insistence on power, but he denies himself *a politics* because he has no idea of the 'relations of force'" (1986, 49). Similarly, Butler's text ignores that the institutions productive of subjects and the history of these institutions are based on relations of force and ideologies that maintain and reproduce antagonistic class relations. Ultimately, Butler's theory of the political precludes political action, because the site for intervention is purely discursive:

> To deconstruct the concept of matter or that of bodies is not to negate or refuse either term. To deconstruct these terms means, rather, to continue to use them, to repeat them, to repeat them subversively, and to displace them from the contexts in which they have been deployed as instruments of oppressive power. (1992, 17)

In this way, Butler's work enacts the very authoritarian and authoritative ruse that she seeks to avoid: society (now replaced by "the social") is unfixed, and politics (now replaced by "the political") are of necessity limited to idealist and discursive interventions performed by intellectuals.

Consequently, Butler's jettisoning of materiality and her inattention to class position and historical context prioritizes the political interests of particular constituencies (namely, academics), while others (whose interests are not so easily represented within this context) are again marginalized. A related problem appears in a "conversation" in *Conflicts in Feminism* (1990) among Jane Gallop, Marianne Hirsch, and Nancy Miller. The primary topic, and to a minor degree the source of dissension, involves the participants' feelings about critiques of feminism made by feminists. Particularly salient to my argument is their identification of certain conflicts within feminism and the way such identifications work to isolate feminism in terms of race and class.

Gallop, Hirsch, and Miller see the central conflict within feminism as a discursive one that operates in relative isolation from economic or historical contexts. As a result, feminism exists only within the institutional boundaries of the academy, and feminist interests are reducible to questions of "power" and tenure. The sole form of power to which they lay claim is power over female graduate students and untenured female professors. Yet their claim to being "women" permits them to stress their alleged marginality. As Hirsch puts it, "we never really *feel* in power. It is important for tenured feminists to articulate that, as difficult as it may be for younger feminists to hear" (Gallop et al. 1990, 355). What their feelings have to do with the all-too-real power differentials between tenured and untenured faculty (be they female or male) goes unacknowledged.

At one point, Gallop raises the context of the conservative political climate only to rein it back into the limited sphere of the academy: "In the world, women are not powerful and feminism isn't doing well and abortion is about to become illegal, etc. There is all this stuff to support one's sense that one is still simply oppressed" (Gallop et al. 1990, 355). Gallop, who tends to be precise elsewhere, becomes vague around the relationship between "the world" (where feminism isn't doing well, etc.) and "her world" (where there is all this stuff). In other words, her argument lapses into vagueness around the very issues that would challenge her "sense that one is still *simply* oppressed."

Ellipses caused by the absence of economic context, or any concession to the belief that "society does not consist of individuals, but expresses the sum of interrelations, the relations within which these individuals stand" (Marx 1978, 247), become even more dramatic when the conversation turns to race. Here the tendency is to address a lengthy and complicated history of racism through a pluralist logic of "inclusion." One of the issues raised is the fact that *The Poetics of Gender* (1986), an anthology edited by Miller, did not include writings by women of color; another is that women of color were not invited to a particular conference. Speaking of the addition of a chapter on "race" to her most recent book, Miller observed:

> As powerful as my fear of not finishing [the book] is, it was not as strong as my wish for McDowell's approval. For McDowell, whom I do not know, read black feminist critic. I realize that the set of feelings that I used to have about French men I now have about African-American women. Those are the people I feel inadequate in relation to and try to please in my writing. (1986, 363–64)

The displacement of French men by African American women is problematic enough on its own; but then Miller proceeds to attribute the larger problem to "political correctness" because, she asserts, her experience of writing about race suggested that "it created more problems than it solved." Among the disturbing aspects of this conversation—and I would argue that it is a problem that follows from tendencies existing within postmodernist social theory—is the way in which class and race are replaced by reference to more "fluid" categories of identity. Although this text departs from the stylistic vagaries and more esoteric level of argumentation characteristic of postmodernist social theory, it ultimately enacts similarly abstract moves: a preoccupation with intellectual production that excludes historical and economic contexts, recourse to vaguely defined relations of power that exclude material relations of force, and a resultant narrowing of the field of intellectual vision.

> IV. One of the great advantages of America is that Americans have no memory. The reason I left Europe was because there's such a long memory that you can't initiate change. But Americans have no memory at all. I'm convinced an American workforce can come into work on Monday morning and find the whole production line has changed and by coffee break they're used to the new environment. Americans, unlike, say, the Japanese, are used to change. Most other countries are not. Americans are uniquely adapted to change. Change is the way we can win. (Wilf Corrigan, Executive, LSI Logic, in Davidow and Malone, 1992)

In order to clarify the relationship between intellectual production and the larger political and economic context, I want to examine an incident that garnered enormous media attention during the 1992 presidential campaign: Dan Quayle's speech on "family values." I turn to this speech because of the ways in which it deflected attention from the current economic crisis to another crisis, discursive and abstract, a rhetorical practice also at work in Robert Dole's recent critiques of mainstream Hollywood films. Quayle's speech, excerpts of which were published in newspapers nationwide and repeatedly highlighted on television, was made in response to the Los Angeles uprising and played a part in Republicans' attempts to efface problems of racism and economic injustice (a move to which the Democrats implicitly consented). Quayle rendered the crisis in these terms:

> Right now the failure of our families is hurting America deeply. When families fail, society fails. The anarchy and lack of structure in our inner cities are testament to how quickly civilization falls apart when the family foundation cracks.[7]

Quayle's speech began by referring to the "terrible problem" of racism in the United States, but claimed that the "landmark civil rights bill of the 1960s removed legal barriers to allow full participation by blacks in the economic, social and political life of the nation." According to Quayle, "By any measure the America of 1992 is more egalitarian, more integrated and offers more opportunities to black Americans and all other minority group members than the America of 1964." The rhetoric that Quayle mobilized has a lengthy racist history. Despite his claims to progress and among a series of blatant lies, Quayle resorted to a conservative rhetoric dating back at least to Daniel Moynihan's 1965 report, *The Negro Family*. In that report, Moynihan claimed that the problems plaguing inner-city residents could be reduced to a single, isolated factor: a family structure "which, because it is so out of line with the rest of American society, seriously retards the progress of the group as a whole."[8]

In 1986, CBS aired Bill Moyers's special, *The Vanishing Family: Crisis in Black America,* which reworked the message contained in Moynihan's earlier report: economic problems in America's inner cities have been solely caused by single mothers and absent or otherwise irresponsible fathers. Moyers's purpose resembles both Moynihan's and Quayle's: to duck the question of how people can support themselves and their communities in the absence of an economic base. In 1992, Quayle's appeal to this discursive crisis surgically removed attention from the material circumstances in which people struggle to survive. Families, he pontificates, have failed. It is never a matter of how—in terms of health care, day care, employment, housing—the system has abandoned and failed its constituents. In the aftermath of the Los Angeles uprising, this is precisely the sort of diversionary tactic so urgently sought by both conservatives and liberals to disguise their incapacity and lack of will concerning issues of race.

Both television and newspaper coverage of Quayle's speech originally contextualized the speech, quoting Quayle as claiming that a "poverty of values" caused the Los Angeles uprising. The day after Quayle's speech, in fact, the *New York Times* ran a front-page story entitled "Quayle Says Riots Sprang from Lack of Family Values." On the following day, the *New York Times* reported that

> Thailand is in turmoil, the Federal deficit is ballooning and hot embers of racial resentment still smolder in the ruins of inner-city Los Angeles. But today the high councils of government were preoccupied with a truly vexing question: Is Murphy Brown a tramp? (Wines 1992, A1)

Why did subsequent attention to Quayle's argument center around this single sentence referring to a fictional television character? "It doesn't help matters when prime time TV has Murphy Brown—a character who supposedly epitomizes today's intelligent, highly paid, professional woman—mocking the importance of fathers by bearing a child alone and calling it just another 'life style choice'" (Quayle 1992, A20).

The logic that links the Los Angeles uprising, Dan Quayle's speech, and intellectual production lies in the emphasis on language and abstract definitions or categories and how this emphasis is used to displace attention from material concerns. In the aftermath of Quayle's speech, many feminists took on the task of defending a sitcom character's right to parent, winding up in a much publicized squabble over definitions of what counts as a family.[9] In this case, feminism seems to function dangerously like trickle-down economics, since how these representations of family values affect women

in socioeconomic positions other than those of the more privileged and educated middle classes was ignored during the *Murphy Brown* controversy. When writer/producer
Diane English accepted an Emmy award for the show, she thanked "all the single parents out there who, either by choice or necessity, are raising their kids alone. Don't let
anybody tell you you're not a family." On the season premiere of *Murphy Brown*
(September 1992), Murphy paraphrased English's earlier remark. Surrounded by "families," she said: "Perhaps it's time for the Vice President to expand his definition and
recognize that whether by choice or circumstance families come in all shapes and sizes."

Two points are worth drawing attention to in these statements. First, there's the
underlying belief in a particularly American form of pluralism, which resembles arguments made by postmodernist social theorists. Here, Laclau and Mouffe's argument
about pluralism has followed a politically reactionary trajectory, for—as Elizabeth
Spelman (1988) has pointed out—pluralism always has a center defined by dominant
economic interests. Thus, the solution to conservative appeals to "traditional" family
values is merely to expand the definition of what constitutes a family without addressing the manner in which this highly particularized and racist version of "family" serves
as a scapegoat for an economic crisis.

The second point concerns the equivalence of the terms "choice" and "circumstance," and the underlying notion that those who can afford to choose single
parenthood and those who have no choice but to parent alone confront the same or
similar problems. The rhetoric of choice, as in "whether by choice or necessity,"
implies that such choices are uniformly available to women. The choices afforded
Murphy and the constituency she represents are choices enabled by economic advantage and cultural capital. The reality is that a vast majority of single parents in the
United States—most of them are women—raise their children in a society that has in
effect abandoned them. Unlike more privileged women, these women cannot afford
day care (not to mention in-home day care), nor can many afford health care.[10] The
belief that the solution to the problem is to adjust or expand the definition of what
counts as a family—to intervene at the level of discursive constructions—without
working toward material changes as well, operates through a very abstract and ultimately ineffectual form of politics.

By not discussing the intertwined contexts of race and economics, the response to
Quayle's speech further ceded any discussion of class privilege to the right. The program and its producers, Quayle could claim, are "out there in the world of comfort.
They ought to come with me out to where the real America is." White House
spokesman Marlin Fitzwater endorsed Quayle's comments about the "poverty of values," saying, "The glorification of the life of an unwed mother does not do good service
to most unwed mothers who are not highly paid, glamorous anchorwomen." The claim
that feminists were "glamorizing" single parenthood is not far from the mark, given the
economic circumstances enjoyed by the fictitious Murphy Brown. In the end, the erasure of the Los Angeles uprising in the *Murphy Brown* incident moved the debate away
from issues of race, the plight of inner cities, and the deteriorating economic base in the
United States, to a much safer, symbolic ground. By shifting the debate from the material conditions of inner cities to the discursive field of "family values," both parties
occupied a familiar and comfortable terrain for debate.

Why has this particular context been erased? Why should it matter to feminism? To
answer these questions, we need to return to the reasons postmodernism and anti-

essentialist feminism converged to spawn in the fertile ground of U.S. academic production, where the fragmentation celebrated by postmodernist social theorists and the
retreat from an understanding of the economic structuring of various debates continue
to work in specifically divisive ways. I want to briefly sketch out four sites where the
ideology of postmodernism converges with dominant ideologies in the United States:
(1) anti-empiricist tendencies within the humanities; (2) the logic of consumerism and
consumer capitalism; (3) postmodernism and the legacy of anti-communism; and
(4) anti-organizational bias and individualism.

In terms of the first, postmodernism gave added momentum to a strong social con-
structionist version of reality already implicit in the largely qualitative, interpretive
methods of humanities research. I am not endorsing a strong empiricist position, but
rather suggesting that the postmodernist rejection of foundations, representation,
empirical research, and any attempt at working toward objective understandings of
political reality undermined our ability to speak on behalf of progressive issues and
causes, much less to speak intelligibly about political issues. To a large extent, this led
to a mystification of the very political issues that most desperately needed to be demys-
tified for ourselves, our communities, our colleagues, and our students. In fact,
postmodernism replicates the workings of contemporary political debate in the U.S.:
both refuse to confront political realities and both operate at a level of abstraction that
bears little relation to the realities experienced by ordinary people on a daily basis.

Second, consumer capitalism itself has produced what postmodernist social theorists view as the potentially liberating proliferation of identities in contemporary
culture—the marketing of feminist, environmentalist, and lesbian or gay lifestyles bears
out this point. To speak about "identity" politics is to buy into consumerist ideologies
and to suggest that identities (not to mention politics) can be as easily adopted and discarded as clothes off the rack.[11] Rather than viewing the fragmentation and proliferation
of identities as a symptom of the failure of Marxism or as cause for political optimism,
we need to consider how the globalization of capitalism as a world system and shifts in
the flow of capital have in fact produced the very effects (market segmentation, niche
marketing, narrowcasting, and the commodification of lifestyles) we wish to claim as
oppositional strategies.

Third, Neil Larsen has suggested that "postmodern philosophy and political theory
becomes objectively, albeit perhaps obliquely, a variation of anti-communism" (1990,
15). In the wake of the Cold War, postmodernism has replaced right-wing anti-communist ideologies.[12] The very language used by postmodernist social theory and
feminism to dismiss Marxism suggests this connection: "totalitarian," "authoritarian,"
and "a ruse of power." While intellectuals might fancy themselves beyond the reach of
such ideologies, it remains the case that those intellectuals who identify themselves as
members of an explicitly socialist organization are subject to red-baiting (i.e., they
teach politics rather than intellectual matter, they use classrooms as recruiting sites,
and so on), intellectual suspicion and disdain, and frequently marginalization within
their discipline. For those with no experience within Marxist or socialist organizations
(and even for some with a certain amount of such experience), anti-communist ideologies continue to permeate understandings of how these organizations function.

The fourth point is a byproduct of these anti-communist tendencies. In the U.S.,
people are socialized as passive consumers of organizations rather than active participants in the building and democratic functioning of institutions. I think it's accurate to

say that most people in the U.S. view political organizations with suspicion and distrust. Although suspicion is in order with regard to mainstream political organizations, political organizations outside the mainstream bear the brunt of hostility. They are perceived as "cults" or sites of brainwashing, conversion, or ideological indoctrination (ostensibly, the university system is outside such processes). To join an explicitly socialist organization is to lose one's precious individuality and to be viewed as the Borg of *Star Trek: The Next Generation*—as part of a mindless hive, incapable of uttering anything but the chilling words—"You will be assimilated."[13] Ironically, postmodernist social theorists and feminists are willing to find resistance in the most banal and inconsequential media texts, but when it comes to socialist organizations, they see no agency, but only mindless conformity.

Anti-organizational bias is part and parcel of the postmodernist package. To organize any but the most provisional and spontaneous coalitions is, for postmodernist social theorists and feminists alike, to reproduce oppression, hierarchies, and forms of intractable dominance. The fact that capitalism is extremely organized makes little difference, because one resists against a multivalent, diffuse form of power. Nor, as Joreen pointed out over two decades ago, does it seem to matter that structurelessness produces its own forms of tyranny. Thus, in place of any organized politics, postmodernist social theory offers us variations on pluralism, individualism, individualized agency, and ultimately individualized solutions that have never—and will never—be capable of resolving (much less addressing) structural problems. But this is, precisely, postmodernism's telos. As Neil Larsen observes, it is the "perfect 'radical' argument for a capitalist politics of pure irrationalist spontaneity. And we know who wins on the battlefield of the spontaneous" (1990, 13–14).

These four sites of convergence culminate in deepening depoliticization and apathy among academics. Postmodernist social theory teaches us to make peace with the fragmentation, deterioration, and devastation that surround us. Revolution, we are told, is impossible despite the fact that the ongoing consolidation of capital at the top of society constitutes, according to most pundits, a revolution. Revolution, moreover, is undesirable—we need to be considering the discursive constitution of the social and the political—seeking those contingent and ephemeral moments of rupture, rather than doing the more difficult, frustrating, and time-consuming work of building organized opposition.

Certainly these forms of thought offer a complex rationale for avoiding the very questions we need to be raising at this historical moment, not to mention convenient alibis for our lack of engagement with politics and political issues. It is time to put a stop to this discursive channel surfing. A change, in fact, is taking place across the humanities in a renewed interest in historical materialism and political activism among graduate students and faculty. This change is taking place not because of fissures in discourse or a rejection of the alleged essentialist fixity of class analysis, but because academics are beginning to feel the material pressures of downsizing, deregulation, outsourcing, and speed-ups in production. As Louis Menand has written,

> The university's external enemies are real and they have attained a position of power over us unknown since the 1950s. These enemies could care less about distinguishing classic liberals and neo-Victorians from critical pedagogues. They loathe the very idea of public subsidy for independent thought, and they would happily put us all out in the cold if they could. (in Perlstein 1995, 795)

Changes are taking place, in short, not because we have successfully intervened in any discursive formations, but because our distance from economic necessity is dwindling.[14]

We face important challenges in the coming years as intellectuals and as members of society. In order to confront these challenges, we need better strategies for understanding the correspondences that exist between our own work and the work of capitalist ideologies. And—this point is crucial—we need tactics for transforming that understanding into action. As levels of repression and immiseration grow in the U.S., so does the necessity for making connections across class and race lines: for building solidarity both inside and outside the academy. Instead of disavowing the authority conferred upon us by our institutional positions—instead of condemning representations—we might learn how to wield what power remains to us more strategically, collectively, and effectively.[15] Of course, such a project depends on whether academics' interest in "the political" and "the social" has any substance beyond an apologia for learning to live with the status quo.

A draft of this paper appeared as "Feminism without Guarantees" in Rethinking Marxism. *I want to thank Rosemary Hennessy for the extensive and generous comments that provoked a complete rethinking of the original essay, as well as those who commented on earlier versions: Anthony Arnove, Carol Biewener, Julian Halliday, Thomas Kane, Elizabeth Terzakis, and Mark Unger.*

NOTES

1. Although there are certainly distinctions that can be made between the categories "postmodernist" and "poststructuralist," my purpose in this paper is to chart tendencies that cut through these terms.

2. Edward Said (1984) argues that when theories travel (historically and culturally), what may once have been an effective mode of analysis can become an ideological trap. The point I am making here is similar, although more focused on the synchronic rather than the diachronic elements of this process.

3. Of course, Marx did not argue for an essentialism based on an authentic working-class "identity." Although "the consciousness of the necessity of a fundamental revolution" emanates from the subordinated classes, it "may, of course, arise among the other classes too through the contemplation of the situation of this class" (Marx and Engels 1976, 95). It is also worth recalling the following distinction from *The Eighteenth Brumaire:* "In so far as millions of families live under economic conditions of existence that separate their mode of life, their interests and their culture from those of the other classes, and put them in hostile opposition to the latter, they form a class. In so far as there is merely a local interconnection among these small-holding peasants, and the identity of their interests begets no community, no national bond and no political organization among them, they do not form a class" (Marx 1963, 172).

4. See Paul Smith's "Laclau's and Mouffe's Secret Agent" (1991) for a much more thorough and incisive analysis of this point.

5. I realize that this is more a moral than a descriptive statement: one *shouldn't* be able to speak about race and racism without speaking about class. The abstract nature of postmodernist social theory, however, has made it possible to do just that.

6. To the extent that few feminists would identify themselves as "essentialist," anti-essentialism within feminist theory has more the characteristics of a rigid, dogmatic position than a debate.

7. "Excerpts from Vice President's Speech on Cities and Poverty," *New York Times*, 20 May 1992. All further references to Quayle's speech are from this article.

8. For detailed discussions of the deployment of this argument by politicians and the media, see *The Nation*'s special issue, "Scapegoating the Black Family," July 24/31 1989. See also Maude

Lavin's "The Feminization of Poverty and the Media," *Global Television,* ed. Cynthia Schneider and Brian Wallis (New York: Wedge Press, 1988).

9. In regard to another variant of rights rhetoric, Rosa Luxemburg argued, "In a word, the formula, 'the right of nations to self-determination,' is essentially not a political and problematic guideline in the nationality question, but only a means of *avoiding that question*" (1976, 110). Her point here, which has immediacy today, is that such abstract, eternal calls for rights offer no practical guidelines for action. Thus, to demand the "right to parent" or "women's right to abortion," without at the same time demanding the material conditions that would make these rights possible, is in fact a way of avoiding the question.

10. An example of a similar displacement occurred during the debates over President Clinton's appointment of Zoe Baird for Attorney General and the revelations about the hiring of illegal aliens. Many claimed that such scrutiny only applied because of Baird's gender. There was, however, absolutely no attention in the mainstream media as to why privileged women and men hire illegal aliens—namely, the issue of wages. Barbara Katz Rothman offers an excellent analysis of the entry of women's unpaid labor into the marketplace and its implications for feminist theory in *Recreating Motherhood: Ideology and Technology in a Patriarchal Society* (New York: W.W. Norton and Company, 1989).

11. To speak about "identity" politics, moreover, is to run together a number of politically, ideologically, and historically different categories and/or movements.

12. Of course, anti-communist ideologies have a history that pre-dates the Cold War in the U.S. To adequately understand the roots of this ideology, one would have to look at the response to the Bolshevik Revolution in U.S. culture.

13. Those who have participated in attempts to organize faculty at universities will attest to the fact that objections to unionization all too frequently boil down to an anti-organizational bias held in place by individualism.

14. In no way do I mean to suggest that revolutionary agency is on the rise in the academy; nor do I mean to suggest that intellectuals will be the agents of revolutionary social change. Marx had valid reasons for suggesting that workers would be the agents of the revolution: they could shut down production and, more important for the purpose of this essay, having the least to gain from the status quo, they had the most to gain by changing it.

15. I hope that my argument throughout this paper has underscored the need for collective action rather than individual academics speaking out as "public intellectuals" for some non-existent constituency.

Bibliography

Editors' note: This bibliography includes both the references used by the various authors in this anthology and key works on materialist feminism, provided as an additional resource.

Abbott, Pamela. 1992. Feminist perspectives in sociology: The challenge to "Mainstream" Orthodoxy. In *Revolutions in knowledge: Feminism in the social sciences,* edited by S. R. Zalk and J. Gordon-Kelter. Boulder, CO: Westview Press.

Acker, Joan. 1973. Women and social stratification: A case of intellectual sexism. *American Journal of Sociology* 78: 936–45.

Ackroyd, Peter R. 1979. *Goddesses, women and Jezebel.* In *Images of women in antiquity,* edited by Averill Cameron and Amelie Kuhrt. London: Routledge.

Adams, Parveen. 1979. A note on the distinction between sexual division and sexual differences. *m/f* 3: 52.

——— and Beverly Brown. 1979. The feminine body and feminist politics. *m/f* 3: 35–50.

——— and Jeff Minson. 1978. The "subject" of feminism. *m/f* 2.

——— and Elizabeth Cowie, eds. 1990. *The Woman in question.* Cambridge, MA: MIT Press.

Adorno, Theodor, et al. 1969. *Der positivismusstreit in der leuschen soziologie.* Darmstadt: Suhrkamp.

Agarwal, Bina. 1994. Gender, resistance and land: Interlinked struggles over resources and meanings in South Asia. *Journal of Peasant Studies* 22 (1): 81–125.

———. 1992a. The gender and environmental debate: Lessons from India. *Feminist Studies* 18 (1): 119–58.

———. 1992b. Rural women, poverty and natural resources: Sustenance, sustainability and struggle for change. In *Poverty in India: Research and policy,* edited by Barbara Harris, S. Guhan, and R. H. Cassen. Bombay: Oxford University Press.

———. 1988a. Neither sustenance nor sustainability: Agricultural strategies, ecological degradation and Indian women in poverty. In *Structures of patriarchy: The state, community and household in modernizing Asia,* edited by Bina Agarwal. London: Zed Press.

———. 1988b. Who sows? Who reaps? Women and land rights in India. *Journal of Peasant Studies* 15: 531–81.

Agger, Ben. 1992. *Cultural studies as critical theory.* London: Falmer.

Agosin, Marjorie. 1987. Metaphors of female political ideology: The cases of Chile and Argentina. *Women's International Studies Forum* 10: 571–77.

Ahmad, Aijaz. 1992. *In theory: Classes, nations, literatures.* London: Verso.

Al-Hibri, Azizah. 1983. Reproduction, mothering, and the origins of patriachy. In *Mothering and the oppression of women: Towards a unitary theory,* edited by Joyce Trebilcot. Totowa, NJ: Rowman and Allenheld.

Allen, Jeffner. 1983. Motherhood: The annihilation of women. In *Mothering and the oppression of women: Towards a unitary theory,* edited by Joyce Trebilcot. Totowa, NJ: Rowman and Allenheld.

Althusser, Louis. 1976. *Essays in self-criticism.* Atlantic Highlands, NJ: Humanities Press.

———. 1971. *Lenin and philosophy and other essays,* translated by Ben Brewster. New York: Monthly Review.

———. 1970. *For Marx,* translated by Ben Brewster. London: NLB.

——— and Etienne Balibar. 1968. *Reading* Capital, translated by Ben Brewster. London: NLB.

Alvarez, Sonia E. 1991. *Engendering democracy in Brazil: Women's movement in transition politics.* Princeton, NJ: Princeton University Press.

———. 1989. Women's movements and gender politics in the Brazilian transition. In *The women's movement in Latin America,* edited by Jane Jacquette. Boston: Unwin Hyman.

———. 1988. Women's participation in the "people's church": A critical appraisal. Paper presented at the Fourteenth International Congress of the Latin American Studies Association, New Orleans, LA, March 17–19.

Amadiume, L. 1988. *Male daughters, female husbands.* London: Zed Books.

American Fertility Society. 1986. Ethical considerations of the new reproductive technologies. *Fertility and Society,* supplement 1 (46): 3 (September).

Andersen, Margaret. 1993. *Thinking about women.* New York: St. Martin's Press.

Anderson, Perry. 1976. *Considerations on western Marxism.* London: Routledge.

Andrews, Lori B. 1986. My body, my property. *Hastings Center Report* (October), 28–38.

Anzaldúa, Gloria, ed. 1990. *Making face, making soul/Haciendo caras: creative and critical perspectives by women of color.* San Francisco: Aunt Lute Books.

Appadurai, Arjun. 1990. Disjuncture and difference in the global cultural economy. *Public Culture* 2 (2): 1–24.

———. 1986. Introduction: Commodities and the politics of value. In *The Social life of things.* Cambridge: Cambridge University Press.

Apter, Emily. 1991. *Feminizing the fetish: Psychoanalysis and narrative obsession in turn-of-the-century France.* Ithaca, NY: Cornell University Press.

Arditti, Rita, Renate Duelli Klein, and Shelly Minden, eds. 1984. *Test tube women: What future for motherhood?* London: Pandora Press.

Arizpe, Lourdes. 1990. Democracy for a small two-gender planet. In *Women and social change in Latin America,* edited by Elizabeth Jelin. Atlantic Highlands, NJ: Humanities Press.

Armstrong, Pat. 1972a. SUNY Conference paper.

———. 1972b. Racism and feminism: Division among the oppressed. Unpublished paper.

Arnott, Theresa, and Matthaei, Judith. 1991. *Race, gender and work.* Boston: South End Press.

Aronowitz, Stanley. 1992. *The politics of identity: Class culture, social movements.* New York: Columbia University Press.

Arthur, Chris. 1979. Dialectics and labour. In *Issues in Marxist philosophy I: Dialectics and method,* edited by John Mepham and D. H. Ruben. New York: Humanities Press.

Asian Women's Liberation. 1980. Good news for women. *Asian Women's Liberation,* no. 2 (April).

Atwood, Margaret. 1985. *The Handmaid's Tale.* New York: Fawcett Crest Books.

Bachofen, Johann. 1861. *Das mutterecht.* Berlin: Bauhaus-Archiv.

Badinter, E. 1980. *L'amour en plus.* Paris: Flammarion.

Bahro, Rudolf. 1978. *The alternative in eastern Europe.* London: New Left Books and Verso Editions.

Bandyopadhyay, Rekha. 1993. Land system in India: A historical review. *Economic and Political Weekly,* December 25.

Bardhan, Kalpana. 1989. Poverty, growth and rural labor markets in India. *Economic and Political Weekly,* March 25: A21–A38.

Baron, Harold. 1971. The demand for black labor: Historical notes on the political economy of racism. *Radical America* (March–April).

Barrett, Michèle. 1991. *The politics of truth: From Marx to Foucault.* Stanford: University of California Press.

———. 1982. *The anti-social family.* London: Verso.

———. 1980. *Women's oppression today: Problems in marxist feminist analysis.* London: Verso.

Barrett, Michèle, and Mary McIntosh. 1985. Ethnocentrism and socialist feminist theory. *Feminist Review* 20: 23–47.

———. 1979. Christine Delphy: Toward a materialist feminism? *Feminist Review* (January): 95–106.

Barrios de Chungara, Domitila (with Moema Viezzer). 1978. *Let me speak!* New York: Monthly Review Press.

Barros, Robert. 1986. The left and democracy: Recent debates in Latin America. *Telos* 68: 49–70.

Bart, Pauline. 1971. Sexism in social science: From the iron cage to the gilded cage—The perils of Pauline. *Journal of Marriage and the Family* 33 (November): 742–50.

Baudrillard, Jean. 1983. *Simulations.* New York: Semiotext(e).

Beechey, V. 1979. On patriarchy. *Feminist Review* 3: 66–82.

———. 1971. Female wage labour in capitalist production. *Capital and Class* 3: 45–66.

Begley, Sharon. 1993. Cures from the womb. *Newsweek* (February 22).

Belsey, Catherine. 1985. *The subject of tragedy: Identity and difference in Renaissance drama.* London: Methuen.

———. 1980. *Critical practice.* New York: Methuen.

Benhabib, Seyla. 1986. *Critique, norm, utopia: A study of the foundations of critical theory.* New York: Columbia University Press.

Benhabib, Seyla, and Drucilla Cornell, eds. 1987. *Feminism as critique.* Minneapolis: University of Minnesota Press.

Benston, Margaret. 1987. *Work and new technologies: Other perspectives.* Toronto: Between the Lines.

———. 1969. The political economy of women's liberation. *Monthly Review* (September) 21: 13–25.

Bernard, Jessie. 1973. My four revolutions: An autobiographical history of the ASA. In *Changing women in a changing society,* edited by J. Huber. Chicago: University of Chicago Press.

Beverly, Creigs C., and Howard J. Stanback. 1986. The black underclass: Theory and reality. *The Black Scholar* 17: 24–32.

Bhaskar, Roy. 1989. *Reclaiming reality: A critical introduction to contemporary philosophy.* London: Verso.

Bhavhani, Kum-Kum, and ·Margaret Coulson. 1986. Transforming socialist feminism: The challenge of racism. *Feminist Review* 23 (Summer).

Birnbaum, Lucia Chiavola. 1986. *Liberazione della donna: Feminism in Italy.* Middletown, CT: Wesleyan University Press.

Bluestone, Barry, and Bennett Harrison. 1982. *The deindustrialization of America.* New York: Basic Books.

Bobbio, Norberto. 1989. *Democracy and dictatorship.* Minneapolis: University of Minnesota Press.

Bonancich, Edna. 1976. Advanced capitalism and black/white relations. *American Sociological Review* 41: 34–51.

Bonder, Gloria. 1989. Women's organizations in Argentina's transition to democracy. In *Women and counter-power,* edited by Yolande Cohen. Montreal: Black Rose Books.

Bongie, Chris. 1991. *Exotic memories: literature, colonialism, and the fin de siecle.* Stanford: Stanford University Press.

Bordo, Susan. 1993. *Unbearable weight: Feminism, western culture, and the body.* Berkeley: University of California Press.

———. 1988. Anorexia nervosa: Psychopathology as the crystallization of culture. In *Feminism and Foucault: Reflections on resistance,* edited by Irene Diamond and Lee Quinby. Boston: Northeastern University Press.

Bottomore, Tom, et al., eds. 1983. *A dictionary of Marxist thought.* Cambridge, MA: Harvard University Press.

Bourdieu, Pierre. 1990. *In other words: Essays towards a reflective sociology.* Stanford, CA: University of Stanford Press.

———. 1988. *Homo academicus.* Stanford: Stanford University Press.

Bourdieu, Pierre, and Jean Claude Passeron. 1990. *Reproduction in education, society and culture.* London: Sage Publications.

Brah, Avtar. 1992. Difference, diversity and differentiation. In *"Race," culture and difference,* edited by James Donald and Ali Rattansi. London: Sage Publications.

Braidotti, Rosi. 1994. *Nomadic subjects: Embodiment and sexual difference in contemporary feminist theory.* New York: Columbia University Press.

Braidotti, Rosi, et al. 1994. *Women, the environment and sustainable development: Towards a theoretical synthesis.* London: Zed Books and INSTRAW.

Braverman, Harry. 1974. *Labor and monopoly capital: The degradation of labor in the twentieth century.* New York and London: Monthly Review Press.

Brecht, Bertolt. 1964. *Kleines Organon für das Theater. Schriften zum Theater vol. 7, 1948–56.* Frankfurt am Main: Suhrkamp.

Breitman, George, ed. 1990. *Malcolm X speaks.* New York: Pathfinder.

Brenner, Johanna, and Nancy Holmstrom. 1983. "Women's self-organization: Theory and strategy." *Monthly Review* 34.11.

Brenner, Johanna, and Maria Ramas. 1984. Rethinking women's oppression. *New Left Review* 144: 33–80.

Brewer, Rose. 1993. Theorizing race, class, and gender. In *Theorizing black feminisms: The visionary pragmatism of black women,* edited by Stanlie M. James and Abenda P.A. Busia. New York: Routledge.

———. 1989. Black women and feminist sociology: The emerging perspective. *American Sociologist* 20 (1): 57–70.

———. 1983. Black workers and corporate flight. *Third World Socialists* 1: 9–13.

Bristow, Edward J. 1977. *Vice and Vigilance: Purity movement in Britain since 1700.* Dublin: Gill and Macmillan.

Brooks, G. E. 1976. The Signares of Saint-Louis and Gorée: Women entrepreneurs in eighteenth-century Senegal. In *Women in Africa,* edited by N. J. Hafkin and E. B. Bay. Stanford: Stanford University Press.

Brown, Doug. 1990. Sandinismo and the problem of democratic hegemony. *Latin American Perspectives* 17: 39–61.

Brown, Elsa Barkley. 1989. Womanist consciousness: Maggie Lena Walker and the independent order of St. Luke. *Signs* 14: 610–33.

Brown, Rita Mae. 1976. *Plain brown rapper.* Baltimore: Diana Press.

Bruegel, Irene. 1978. What keeps the family going? *International Socialism* 2.1 (Summer).

Brunt, Rosalind. 1989. The politics of identity. In *New times,* edited by Stuart Hall and Martin Jacques. London: Verso.

Bunch, Charlotte. 1995. *Paying the price: Women and the politics of international economic strategy.* London: Zed.

———. 1994. *Demanding accountability: The global campaign and Vienna tribunal for women's human rights.* New Brunswick, NJ: Rutgers University Press.

———. 1987. *Passionate politics: Feminist theory in action.* New York: St. Martin's Press.

———. 1975. Not for lesbians only. *Quest: A Feminist Quarterly* (Fall).

Burbach, Roger, and Orlando Nuñez. 1987. *Fire in the Americas: Forging a revolutionary agenda.* New York: Verso.

Burnham, Linda, and Miriam Louie. 1985. The impossible marriage: A Marxist critique of socialist feminism. *Line of March,* no. 17 (Spring).

Burris, Val. 1982. The dialectic of women's oppression: Notes on the relation between capitalism and patriarchy. *Berkeley Journal of Sociology* 27: 51–74.

Butler, Judith. 1994. *Bodies that matter: On the discursive limits of "sex."* New York: Routledge.

———. 1992. Contingent foundations: Feminism and the question of "postmodernism." In *Feminists theorize the political,* edited by Judith Butler and Joan W. Scott. New York: Routledge.

———. 1990. *Gender trouble: Feminism and the subversion of identity.* New York: Routledge.

Butler, Judith, and Joan Scott, eds. 1992. *Feminists theorize the political.* New York: Routledge.

Calhoun, Craig, Donald Light, and Suzanne Keller. 1994. *Sociology.* New York: McGraw-Hill.

Callinicos, Alex. 1993. *Race and class.* London: Bookmarks.

Campbell, Beatrix. 1984. *Wigan Pier revisited: Poverty and politics in the 80s.* London: Virago Press.

———. 1982. Women: Not what they bargained for. *Marxism Today* (March).

Campbell, Beatrix, and Anna Coote. 1982. *Sweet freedom: The struggle for women's liberation.* Oxford: Blackwell.

Capital Gay. 1993. (February 5).

Carby, Hazel V. 1987. *Reconstructing Womanhood: The Emergence of the Afro-American woman novelist.* New York: Oxford University Press.

———. 1982. White woman listen!: Black feminism and the boundaries of sisterhood. In *The empire strikes back: Race and racism in Britain,* edited by the Centre for Contemporary Cultural Studies. London: Hutchinson.

Carlson, Marifran. 1988. *Feminismo! The women's movement in Argentina from its beginnings to Eva Peron.* Chicago: Academy Chicago.

Carter, Angela. 1985. Black Venus. In *Saints and strangers.* New York: Penguin Books.

Castells, Manuel. 1989. High technology and the new international division of labor. *Labour and Society* 14: 7–41.

Caulfield, Mina Davis. 1977. Universal sex oppression?—A critique from Marxist anthropology. *Catalyst* 10–11 (Summer): 60–77.

Chakravarti, Uma. 1993. Conceptualizing brahminical patriarchy in early India: Gender, caste, class and state. *Economic and Political Weekly* (April): 579–85.

Chapkis, Wendy, and Cynthia Enloe, eds. 1983. *Of common cloth: Women In the global textiles industry.* Amsterdam: Transnational Institute, and London: Pluto Press.

Chavez, Cesar. 1993. Farm workers at risk. In *Toxic struggles: The theory and practice of environmental justice,* edited by Richard Hofrichter. Philadelphia and Gabriola Island, BC: New Society Publishers.

Chen, Martha. 1995. A matter of survival: Women's right to employment in India and Bangladesh. In *Women, culture and development,* edited by Martha Nussbaum and Jonathan Glover. Oxford: Clarendon Press.

Chester, Silvia. 1986. The women's movement in Argentina: Balances and strategies. In *The Latin American women's movement,* edited by ISIS International. Santiago, Chile: ISIS International.

Chinchilla, Norma Stoltz. 1993. Women's movements in the Americas: Feminism's second wave. *Report on the Americas* 27(1) (July).

———. 1990. Revolutionary popular feminism in Nicaragua: Articulating class, gender and national sovereignty. *Gender and Society* 4.3 (September): 370–97.

———. 1985–86. Women in the Nicaraguan revolution. *Nicaraguan Perspectives* 11: 18–26.

———. 1980. Ideologies of feminism: Liberal, radical, marxist. *Social Science Research Reports* 61 (February)

———. 1977. Mobilizing women: Revolution in the revolution. *Latin American Perspectives* 4: 83–102.

Chinchilla, Norma Stoltz, and James Lowell Dietz. 1982. Towards a new understanding of development and underdevelopment. In *Dependency and Marxism: Toward a resolution of the debate,* edited by Ronald Chilcote. Boulder, CO: Westview Press.

Chinchilla, Norma Stoltz, and Martha Gimenez, eds. 1991. Special issue on Marxist feminist theory. *Gender & Society* 5.

Chodorow, Nancy. 1978. *The reproduction of mothering.* Berkeley: University of California Press.

Chowdhry, Prem. 1993. High participation, low evaluation: Women and work in rural Haryana. *Economic and Political Weekly* (Dec. 25): A135–A148.

———. 1989. Customs in a peasant economy: Women in colonial Haryana. In *Recasting women: Essays in colonial history,* edited by Kumkum Sangari and Sudesh Vaid. New Delhi: Kali for Women.

Christophe, Marc-A. 1990. Jeanne Duval: Baudelaire's Black Venus or Baudelaire's Demon? *CLA Journal* 33: 428–39.

Chuchryk, Patricia M. 1989. Feminist anti-authoritarian politics: The role of women's organizations in the Chilean transition to democracy. In *The women's movement in Latin America: Feminism and the transition to democracy,* edited by Jane Jacquette. Boston: Unwin Hyman.

———. 1984. *Protest, politics and personal life: The emergence of feminism in a military dictatorship, Chile 1973–1983.* Ph.D. diss., York University, Toronto, Canada.

Clarke, John. 1991. *New times and old enemies: Essays on cultural studies and America.* London: Harper Collins Academic.

Clavell, Pierre, John Forester, and William Goldsmith, eds. 1980. *Urban and regional planning in an age of austerity.* New York: Pergamon Press.

Coates, Ken. 1985. A new internationalism. *New Socialist* (September): 38.

Cochrane, Allan. 1986. What's a strategy? The London industrial strategy and municipal socialism. *Capitalism and Class* 28 (Spring).

Cohen, Derek. 1994. Full Marx. *Rouge* 15.

Collier, Andrew. 1979. In defense of epistemology. In *Issues in marxist philosophy,* edited by John Mepham and David Hillel-Ruben, editors. Brighton.

Collins, Patricia Hill. 1990. *Black feminist thought: Knowledge, conciousness, and the politics of the women's movement.* Boston, MA: Unwin Hyman.

———. 1989. Toward a new vision: Race, class and gender as categories of analysis and connection. Keynote address, delivered at Integrating Race and Gender into the College Curriculum: A Workshop Sponsored by the Center for Research on Women, Memphis State University, Memphis, TN, May 24.

———. 1986. Learning from the outsider within: The sociological significance of black feminist thought. *Social Problems* 33 (6) (December): 14–32.

Combahee River Collective. 1983. A black feminist statement. In *This bridge called my back: Writings of radical women of color,* edited by Gloria Anzaldúa and Cherrie Moraga. New York: Kitchen Table Press.

Connexions. 1982. Change our working conditions. *Connexions: An International Women's Quarterly,* no. 6 (Fall).

Cook, Katsi. 1993. Update: First environment project. *Indigenous woman* 1.3: 39–41.

———. 1985. A community health project: Breastfeeding and toxic contaminants. *Indian studies* (Spring): 14–16.

Coole, Diana. 1996. Is class a difference that makes a difference? *Radical Philosophy* (May–June): 17–25.

Cooper, Anna Julia. 1892. *A voice from the south by a black woman of the south.* Ohio: Aldine Scott and Smith.

Cordero, Margarita. 1986. Latin American and Caribbean feminism: A multiple challenge (an interview with Magaly Pieda). In *The Latin American women's movement,* edited by ISIS International. Santiago, Chile: ISIS International.

Corliss, Richard. 1992. Having it all. *Time Magazine* (September 21).

Cornell, Drucilla. 1991. *Beyond accommodation: Ethical feminism, deconstruction, and the law.* New York: Routledge.

Corrigan, Phillip, and Derek Sayer. 1978. Hindess and Hirst: A critical review. *The Socialist Register.*

Coulson, Margaret, et al. 1975. The housewife and her labor under capitalism: A critique. *New Left Review* 89 (January–February): 59–71.

Coward, Rosalind. 1983. *Patriarchal precedents: Sexuality and social relations.* London: Routledge.

Cowasjee, Saros, ed. *Stories from the Raj from Kipling to independence.* London: Triad Granada.

Criquillon, Ana, and Olga Espinoza. 1987. Mujeres en transcisión: de lo especifico a lo integral. In ISIS International, *Mujeres, crisis y movimiento en America Latina.* Ediciones de las mujeres, no. 9 (June).

Crocker, David. 1992. Functioning and capability: The foundation of Sen's and Nussbaum's development ethic. *Political Theory* 20 (4): 584–612.

Cueva, Augustin. 1987. *La teoria Marxista: Categorias de base y problemas actuales.* Mexico City, Mexico: Planeta.

Currie, Elliott, and Jerome H. Skolnick. 1984. *America's problem.* Boston: Little, Brown.

Cvetkovich, Ann. 1992. *Mixed feelings: Feminism, mass culture and Victorian sensationalism.* New Brunswick, NJ: Rutgers University Press.

Dalla Costa, Mariarosa, and Selma James. 1972. *The power of women and the subversion of the community.* Bristol, England: Falling Wall Press.

Daly, Mary. 1978. *Gyn/Ecology.* Boston: Beacon.

Davidow, William H., and Michael S. Malone. 1992. *The virtual corporation: Structuring and revitalizing the corporation for the 21st Century.* New York: Harper Collins Publishers.

Davin, Anna. 1978. Imperialism and motherhood. *History Workshop Journal* 5.

Davion, Victoria. 1994. Is ecofeminism feminist? In *Ecological feminism,* edited by Karen Warren. New York: Routledge.

Davis, Angela. 1996. Gender, class, and multiculturalism: Rethinking "race" politics. In *Mapping multiculturalism,* edited by Avery Gordon and Christopher Newfield. Minneapolis, MN: University of Minnesota Press.

———. 1983. *Women, culture, and politics.* New York: Vintage.

———. 1981. *Women, race and class.* New York: Random House.

———. 1971. Reflections on the black woman's role in the community of slaves. *The Black Scholar* 3 (4) (December).

de Barbieri, Teresita, and Orlandina de Oliveira. 1986. Nuevos sujetos sociales: La presencia politica de las mujeres en America Latina. *Nueva Anthropogia* 8 (30): 5–29.

D'Emilio, John. 1984. Capitalism and gay identity. In *Powers of desire,* edited by A. Snitow et al. New York: Monthly Review Press.

de Beauvoir, Simone. 1952. *The second sex.* New York: Alfred A. Knopf.

Deegan, Mary Jo. 1978. Early women sociologists and the American Sociological Society: The patterns of exclusion and participation. *American Sociologist* 16: 14–24.

Deere, Carmen Diane. 1979. Rural women's subsistence production. In *Peasants and proletarians: The struggles of third world women workers,* edited by Robin Cohen et al. New York: Monthly Review Press.

de Lauretis, Teresa. 1987. *Technologies of gender: Essays on theory, film, and fiction.* Bloomington: Indiana University Press.

———. 1984. *Alice doesn't: Feminism, semiotics, cinema.* Bloomington: Indiana University Press.

Delphy, Christine. 1992. *Familiar exploitation: New analysis of marriage in contemporary western societies.* London: Polity Press.

———. 1984. *Close to home: A materialist analysis of women's oppression.* London: Hutchinson.

———. 1981. For a materialist feminism. *Feminist Issues* 1 (2) (Winter).

———. 1980. *The main enemy.* London: Women's Research and Resource Centre.

Derrida, Jacques. 1992. *Given time: 1. Counterfeit money.* Translated by Peggy Kamuf. Chicago: University of Chicago Press.

Deutsch, Sandra McGee. 1988. Feminism. In *Latinas of the Americas: A sourcebook,* edited by K. Lynn Stoner. New York: Garland.

Devault, Marjorie L. 1991. *Feeding the family: The social organization of caring as gendered work.* Chicago: University of Chicago Press.

Diamond, Irene, and Lee Quinby, eds. 1988. *Feminism and Foucault: Reflections on resistance.* Boston: Northeastern University.

Dickinson, James, and Bob Russell. 1986. *Family, economy and state: The social reproduction process under capitalism.* New York: St. Martin's Press.

Dill, Bonnie. 1979. The dialectics of black womanhood. *Signs: Journal of Women in Culture and Society* 3: 543–55.

Dirlik, Arif. 1994. The postcolonial aura: Third world criticism in the age of global capitalism. *Critical Inquiry* 20 (Winter): 328–56.

Dixon, Marlene. 1979. *Secondary social status of women.* Chicago: U.S. Voice of Women's Liberation Movement.

———. 1979. *Women in class struggle.* San Francisco: Synthesis Publications.

DN. 1990. Women and forests. *Economic and political weekly.* (April 14): 795–797.

Doyle, Sir Arthur Conan. 1986. *The complete Sherlock Holmes.* Ware, Herts: Omega.

Duchen, Claire, ed. 1987. *French connections: Voices from the women's movement in France.* London: Routledge and Kegan Paul.

———. 1986. *Feminism in France: From May '68 to Mitterand.* London: Routledge and Kegan Paul.

Dunayevskaya, Raya. 1985. *Women's liberation and the dialectics of revolution: reaching for the future.* Atlantic Highlands, NJ: Humanities Press.

Eagleton, Terry. 1976. *Criticism and ideology.* London: Verso.

———. 1980. Ideology, fiction, narrative. *Social Text.*

Eastman, Crystal. 1978. Feminism, In *On Women and Revolution,* edited by Blanche Wiesen Cook. New York: Oxford University Press.

Ebert, Teresa. 1996. *Ludic feminism.* Ann Arbor: University of Michigan Press.

———. 1996. Postal politics and red feminism. *Rethinking Marxism* 8 (2) (Summer).

———. 1993. Ludic feminism, the body, performance, and labor: Bringing materialism back into feminist cultural studies. *Cultural Critique* (Winter): 5–50.

———. 1991. The "difference" of postmodern feminism. *College English* 53 (8): 886–904.

Echols, Alice. 1989. *Daring to be bad: Radical feminism in America 1967–75.* Minneapolis: University of Minnesota Press.

Ehrenreich, Barbara, et al. 1986. *Remaking love: The feminization of sex.* New York: Anchor Books.

———. 1984. Life without father: Reconsidering socialist feminist theory. *Socialist Review* 14 (1): 48–57.

———. 1976. What is socialist feminism? *The Nation.*

——— and Dierdre English. 1979. *For her own good: 150 years of experts' advice to women.* London: Pluto Press.

———. and Annette Fuentes. 1983. *Women in the global factory.* Boston: South End Press.

Eisenstein, Zillah, ed. 1979. *Capitalist patriarchy and the case for socialist feminism.* New York: Monthly Review Press.

Elam, Diane. 1994. *Feminism and deconstruction.* New York: Routledge.

Elson, Diane, and Ruth Pearson. 1981. Nimble fingers make cheap workers: an analysis of women's employment in third world export manufacturing. *Feminist Review* 7 (spring).

EMAS (Equipo de Accion Sindical) (and six other groups). 1987. *Feminismo y sectores populares en America Latina.* Mexico City, Mexico: Editorial Electrocomp.

Emecheta, Buchi. 1985. White sisters listen. *New Internationalist* (August).

Engels, Dagmar. 1983. The Age of Consent Act of 1891: Colonial ideology in Bengal. *South Asia Research* 3: 107–34.

Engels, Frederick. 1942. *The origin of the family, private property, and the state in the light of the researches of Lewis H. Morgan.* New York: International.

Enloe, Cynthia. 1993. *The morning after: Sexual politics and the end of the Cold War.* Berkeley: University of California Press.

———. 1989. *Bananas, beaches and bases: Making feminist sense of international politics.* Berkeley: University of California Press.

Escobar, Arturo. 1992. Imagining a post-development era? Critical thought, development and social movements. *Social Text* 31/32: 20–56.

Evans, David T. 1993. *Sexual citizenship: The material construction of sexualities.* New York: Routledge.

Evans, Sara. 1979. *Personal politics: The roots of women's liberation in the civil rights movement and the new left.* New York: Vintage.

Feijo, Maria del Carmen. 1989. The challenge of constructing civilian peace: Women and democracy in Argentina. In *The women's movement in Latin America,* edited by Jane Jacquette. Boston: Unwin Hyman.

Feinberg, Leslie. 1996. *Transgender warriors: Making history from Joan of Arc to RuPaul.* Boston: Beacon.

Ferguson, Ann. 1991. *Sexual democracy: Women, oppression and revolution.* Sydney: Allen and Unwin.

———. 1989. *Blood at the root: Motherhood, sexuality, and male dominance.* London: Pandora.

———. 1979. Women as a new revolutionary class. In *Between Labor and Capital,* edited by Pat Walker. Boston: South End.

Fernandez-Kelly, Maria Patricia. 1983. *For we are sold.* Albany: State University of New York Press.

Field, Nicola. 1995. Identity and the lifestyle market. In *Over the rainbow: Money, class and homophobia.* London: Pluto Press

Fields, Barbara. 1990. Slavery, race and the ideology in the United States of America. *New Left Review* 18 (1).

Firestone, Shulamith. 1970. *The dialectic of sex: The case for the feminist revolution.* New York: Morrow.

Flandrin, J. L. 1980. *Families in former times: Kinship, household, and sexuality.* Cambridge: Cambridge University Press.

Flax, Jane. 1990. Postmodernism and gender relations in feminist theory. In *Feminism/Postmodernism,* edited by Linda Nicholson. New York: Routledge.

———. 1976. "Do feminists need Marxism?" *Quest* 3.1 (Summer).

Flora, Cornelia Butler. 1984. Socialist feminism in Latin America. *Women and Politics* 4 (Winter): 69–93.

Foley, Barbara. 1985. The politics of deconstruction. In *Deconstruction at Yale,* edited by Robert Con Davis and Ronald Schleifer. Norman: University of Oklahoma Press.

Foreman, Ann. 1977. *Femininity as alienation: Women and the family in Marxism and psychoanalysis.* London: Pluto Press.

Fortunati, Leopoldina. 1995. *The arcane of reproduction,* translated by Hilary Creek. Brooklyn: Autonomedia.

Foucault, Michel. 1980. *The History of Sexuality, Vol. 1: An Introduction,* translated by Robert Hurley. New York: Vintage.

———. 1977. *Language, counter-memory, practice: Selected essays and interviews.* Ithaca: Cornell University Press.

Fraad, Harriet, Stephen Resnick, and Richard Wolff. 1990. Class, patriarchy, and power: A reply. *Rethinking Marxism* 3 (2): 124–44.

———. 1989. For every knight in shining armor, there's a castle waiting to be cleaned: A Marxist-feminist analysis of the household. *Rethinking Marxism* 2 (4): 9–69.

Fraser, Nancy. 1983. Foucault's body language: A post-humanist political rhetoric? *Salmagundi* 61: 55–70.

———. 1981. Foucault on modern power: Empirical insights and normative confusions. *Praxis International* (October): 272–87.

———. 1985. Michel Foucault: A young conservative? *Ethics* (October): 165–84.

———. 1990. The uses and abuses of French discourse theories for feminist politics. *boundary* 2 (17.2) (Summer): 82–101.

Fraser, Nancy, and Linda Nicholson. 1990. Social criticism without philosophy: An encounter between feminism and postmodernism. In *Feminism/Postmodernism,* edited by Linda Nicholson, 19–38. New York: Routledge.

Fuentes, Ann, and Ehrenreich, Barbara. 1983. *Women in the global factory.* Boston: South End Press.

Fuss, Diana. 1989. *Essentially speaking: Feminism, nature, and difference.* New York: Routledge.

———. 1991. *Inside/Out.* New York: Routledge.

Gallop, Jane, et al. 1990. Criticizing feminist criticism. In *Conflicts in feminism,* edited by Marianne Hirsch and Evelyn Fox Keller. New York: Routledge.

Garber, Marjorie. 1992. *Vested interests: Cross-dressing & cultural anxiety.* New York: Routledge.

Gardiner, Jean. 1976. Political economy of domestic labor in capitalist society. In *Dependence and exploitation in work and marriage,* edited by Diana Leonard Barker and Sheila Allen. London: Longman.

———. 1975. Women's domestic labor. *New Left Review* (January–February) 89: 47–58.

Gargallo, Francesca. 1987. La relación entre participación política y conciéncia feminista en las militantes salvadoreñas. *Cuadernos Americanos.* Nueva Epoca 2 (April–May): 58–76.

Gay Times. 1993. (August).

Geertz, Clifford. 1973. *The interpretation of cultures.* New York: Basic Books.

Geras, Norman. 1987. Post-Marxism? *New Left Review* 163: 40–82.

German, Lindsey. 1989. *Sex, class and socialism.* London: Bookmarks.

———. 1983. *The socialist case against theories of patriarchy.* Toronto: Workers' Action Books.

Gerstein, Ira. 1973. Domestic work and capitalism. *Radical America* 7(4–5) (July–October): 101–28.

Giddings, Paula. 1984. *When and where I enter: The impact of black women on race and sex in America.* New York: Bantam Books.

Gilroy, Paul. 1993. *The black Atlantic: Modernity and double consciousness.* Cambridge, MA: Harvard University Press.

Gimenez, Martha. 1978. Structuralist marxism on "the woman question." *Science and Society* (Fall) 42: 301–23.

Glazer, Nona. 1987. Questioning eclectic practice in curriculum change: A Marxist perspective. *Signs* 12 (2): 293–304.

Glenn, Evelyn Nakano. 1985. Racial ethnic women's labor: The intersection of race, gender and class oppression. *Review of Radical Political Economics* 17 (3): 86–108.

Godelier, Maurice. 1978. *Perspectives in marxist anthropology.* New York: Cambridge University Press.

———. 1970. System, structure and contradiction in *Das kapital.* In *Introduction to structuralism,* edited by Michael Lane. New York: Basic Books.

Gonzalez, Maruja, S. Cecilia Loria, and Itziar Lozano. 1988. *Utopia y lucha: Feminista en America Latina y el Caribe.* Mexico City, Mexico: Comunicación Intercambio y Desarrollo Humano en America Latina (CID-HAL), Equipo de Mujeres en Accion Solidaria (EMAS), and Grupo de Educación Popular con Mujeres (GEM).

Good News for Women. 1980. *Asian Women's Liberation* 2 (April).

Gordon, David, Richard Edwards, and Michael Reich. 1982. *Segmented work, divided workers.* Cambridge: Cambridge Unversity Press.

Gordon, Linda. 1976. *Woman's body, woman's right: A social history of birth control in America.* New York: Grossman Publishers.

Gorham, Deborah. 1978. The maiden tribute of modern Babylon re-examined: Child prostitution and the idea of childhood in late Victorian England. *Victorian Studies* 21: 353–379.

Gorz, André. 1982. *Farewell to the working class: An essay on post-industrial socialism.* London: Pluto Press.

———. 1980. *Abschied vom Proletariat. Jenseits des Sozialismus.* Frankfurt am Main.

Gough, Ian. 1981. *The political economy of the welfare state.* New York: Macmillan.

Gould, Meredith, and Rochelle Kern Daniels. 1977. Toward a sociological theory of gender and sex. *American Sociologist* 12: 182–89.

Gould, Stephen Jay. 1981. *The mismeasure of man.* New York: Norton.

Gramsci, Antonio. 1971. *Selections from the prison notebooks,* translated by Quentin Hoare and Geoffrey Nowell Smith. Newark: International.

Granby, Moses. 1844. *Narrative of the life of Moses Granby: Late a slave in the United States of America.* Boston.

Greater London Council. 1986. *Report of the National Homeworking Conference of 1984.* London.

Greenberg, David. 1988. *The construction of homosexuality.* Chicago: University of Chicago Press.

Guillaumin, Colette. 1995. *Racism, sexism, power and ideology.* New York: Routledge.

Guy-Sheftall, Beverly, and Patricia Bell-Scott. 1989. Black women's studies: A view from the margin. In *Educating the majority: Women challenge tradition in higher education*, edited by C. Pearson, J. S. Touchton, and D. C. Shavlik. New York: Macmillan.

Hacker, Helen. 1969. Women as a minority group in higher academics. *The American Sociologist* 4: 95–99.

Hall, Fielding. 1915. *A people at school*. London: Constable.

Hall, Stuart. 1986. On postmodernism and articulation: An interview with Stuart Hall. *Journal of communication inquiry* 10: 2 (Summer).

———. 1978. Some problems with ideology/subject couplet. *Ideology and Consciousness* 3: 116.

Hamilton, Cynthia. 1993. Coping with industrial exploitation. In *Confronting environmental racism: Voices from the grassroots*, edited by Robert D. Bullard. Boston: South End Press.

Hamilton, Roberta. 1978. *The liberation of women: A study of patriarchy and capitalism*. London: Allen and Unwin.

Hamilton, Roberta, and Michèle Barrett, eds. 1986. *The politics of diversity: Feminism, marxism and nationalism*. London: Verso.

Hansen, Karen, and Ilene Philipson, eds. 1990. *Women, class, and the feminist imagination: A socialist-feminist reader*. Philadelphia: Temple University Press.

Haraway, Donna. 1991. *Simians, cyborgs, and women: The reinvention of nature*. New York: Routledge.

———. 1985. A manifesto for cyborgs: Science, technology, and socialist feminism in the 1980s. *Socialist Review* 80: 65–105.

Harding, Sandra. 1993. *The "racial" economy of science: Toward a democratic future*. Bloomington: Indiana University Press.

———. 1991. *Whose science? Whose knowledge? Thinking from women's lives*. Ithaca, NY: Cornell University Press.

Harley, Sharon, and Rosalyn Terborg-Penn. 1970. *The Afro-American woman: Struggles and images*. Port Washington, NY: Kennikat Press.

Harman, Chris. 1986. Base and superstructure. *International Socialism* 2.32 (Summer).

Harman, Moses. 1901. *Institutional marriage*. Chicago: Lucifer.

Harris, Laurence. 1978. The science of the economy. *Economy and Society* 7(3).

Harriss, Barbara. 1992. Rural poverty in India: Micro level evidence. In *Poverty in India: Research and policy*, edited by Barbara Harriss, S. Guhan, and R. H. Cassen. Bombay: Oxford University Press.

Hartmann, Heidi. 1981. The unhappy marriage of Marxism and feminism: Towards a more progressive union. In *Women and revolution: A discussion of the unhappy marriage of Marxism and feminism*, edited by Lydia Sargent. Boston: South End Press.

Hartsock, Nancy. 1985. *Money, sex and power: Toward a feminist historical materialism*. Boston: Northeastern University Press.

Haug, Frigga. 1992. *Beyond female masochism: Memory-work and politics*, translated by Rodney Livingstone. New York: Verso.

———. 1987. Erinnerungsarbeit. In *Sexualiserung der Körper, Argument Sonderband* 90, West Berlin 1983.

———. 1987. *Female sexualization: A collective work of memory*. London: Verso.

———. 1983. The women's question and the class question. In *Rethinking ideology*, edited by S. Hanninen and L. Paldan. New York: Verso.

———. 1982. Frauen und theorie. *Das Argument* 132 (3/4).

———. 1981. Erfahrungen in die Krise führen. *Die Werifrage in der Erziehung, Argument-Sonderband* 58, West Berlin 1981.

———. 1981. Männergeschichte, frauenbefreiung, sozialismus. *das argument* 129 (9/10).

———. 1978. Dialektische theorie und empirische Methodik. *Das Argument* 11 (1): 9–10.

———, ed. 1980. *Frauenformen: alliagsgeschichien und entwurf einer theorie weibhcher sozialisation*. Argument-Sonderband 45, West Berlin.

Heinsohn, G., and R. Knieper. 1976. *Theorie des familenrechts, geschlechts rollenaufhebung, kindesvernachlässigung, geburtenrückgang*. Frankfurt: Suhrkamp.

Hennessy, Rosemary. 1996. Lesbians in late capitalism: Queer subjects, class acts. *Das Argument* (Fall).

———. 1996. Ambivalence as alibi: On the materiality of late capitalist myth in *The crying game* and cultural theory. *Genders* 24 (Summer).

———. 1995. Subjects, knowledges . . . And all the rest: Speaking for what? In *Who can speak? Authority and critical identity*, edited by Judith Roof and Robyn Wiegman. Urbana: University of Illinois Press.

———. 1994–95. Queer visibility in commodity culture. *Cultural Critique* 29 (Winter).

———. 1994. Incorporating queer theory on the left. In *Marxism in the postmodern age,* edited by Antonio Callari, Stephen Cullenberg, Carole Beweiner. New York: Guilford. 1994.

———. 1993a. *Materialist feminism and the politics of discourse.* New York: Routledge.

———. 1993b. Women's lives/Feminist knowledge: Feminist standpoint as ideology critique. *Hypatia* 8 (1): 14–34.

Hennessy, Rosemary, and Chrys Ingraham. 1992. Putting the heterosexual order in crisis. *Mediations* 16 (2): 17–23.

Hennessy, Rosemary, and Rajeswari Mohan. 1989. The construction of woman in three popular texts of empire: Towards a critique of materialist feminism. *Textual Practice* 3 (3): 323–59.

Hess, Beth, J. Markson, and J. Stein. 1989. *Sociology.* New York: Macmillan.

Higginbotham, Evelyn Brooks. 1992. African-American women's history and the metalanguage of race. *Signs: Journal of Women in Culture and Society* 17 (2): 253–54.

Hill, Monica. 1984. Patriarchy, class and the left. (Speech) *Discussion Bulletin* (of Freedom Socialist party, Los Angeles, California) 1, no. 1 (February): 19–21.

Himmelfarb, Gertrude. 1983. *The idea of poverty: England in the early industrial age.* New York: Alfred A. Knopf.

Himmelweit, S., M. McKenzie, and A. Tomlin. 1976. Why theory? In *Papers on patriarchy,* edited by the Women's Publishing Collective. Lewes. London: Women's Press.

Hirst, Paul. 1979. Althusser and the theory of ideology. *Economy and Society* 5 (4): 395.

———. 1979. *On law and ideology.* Atlantic Highlands, NJ: Humanities Press.

Hodges, Donald C. 1974. *The Latin American revolution.* New York: William Morris.

Holcombe, Lee. 1973. *Victorian ladies at work: middle-class working women in England and Wales, 1850–1914.* Hamden, CT: Archon.

Holland, Stuart, ed. 1983. *Out of crisis: A project for European recovery.* Nottingham: Spokesman.

Holter, Harriet. 1973. *Sex roles and social structure.* Oslo: Universitetsforiaget.

hooks, bell. 1992. *Black looks: Race and representation.* Boston: South End Press.

———. 1990. *Yearning: Race, gender and cultural politics.* Boston: South End Press.

———. 1984. *Feminist theory: From margin to center.* Boston: South End Press.

———. 1981. *Ain't I a woman?* Boston: South End Press.

Howard, Jean E. 1986. The new historicism in renaissance studies. *English Literary Renaissance* 16: 13–43.

Hughes, Helen MacGill. 1975. Women in academic sociology, 1925–1975. *Sociological Focus* 8 (3): 215–22.

Hull, Gloria T., Patricia Bell-Scott, and Barbara Smith. 1982. *All the women are white, all the blacks are men, but some of us are brave.* Old Westbury, NY: Feminist Press.

Hull, Richard. 1990. *Ethical issues in the new reproductive technologies.* Belmont, CA: Wadsworth.

Humphries, Jane. 1977. Class struggle and the persistence of the working class family. *Cambridge Journal of Economics* 1: 241–58.

Hussein, Shirley-Ann. 1981. "Four views on women in the struggle." In *Caribbean women in the struggle.* New York: Random House.

Illych, Ivan. 1983. *Gender.* London: Marion Boyers.

Ingraham, Chrys. 1996. Systemic pedagogy: Activating sociological thinking. *International Journal of Sociology and Social Policy* (Fall).

———. 1994. The heterosexual imaginary: Feminist sociology and theories of gender. *Sociological Theory* 12 (2) (July): 203–19.

———. 1992. *Out of print, Out of mind: Toward a materialist feminist theory of censorship and suppression.* Dissertation. Syracuse University.

Irigaray, Luce. 1980. *Speculum of the other woman,* translated by Gillian G. Gill. Frankfurt am Main.

ISIS. 1983. *International Women and New Technology Conference.* Women's International Bulletin, Geneva, no. 28.10.

Jackson, Cecile. 1993a. Doing what comes naturally? Women and environment in development. *World development* 21 (12): 1947–63.

Jackson, Cecile. 1993b. Women/nature or gender/history? A critique of ecofeminist "development." *Journal of Peasant Studies* 20 (3): 389–419.

Jackson, Stevi. 1992. Towards a historical sociology of housework—A materialist feminist analysis. *Women's Studies International Forum*. 15 (2): 153–72.

Jacquette, Jane. 1989. *The women's movement in Latin America: Feminism and the transition to democracy*. Boston: Unwin Hyman.

Jaggar, Allison. 1983. *Feminist politics and human nature*. Sussex: Harvester.

Jameson, Fredric. 1981. *The political unconscious: The narrative as a socially symbolic act*. Ithaca: Cornell University Press.

James, Selma. 1971. The American family: Decay and rebirth. Reprinted in *From feminism to liberation,* collected by Edith Hoshino Altback, Schenkman, Cambridge, MA, 1971, pp. 197–8.

Janiewski, Dolores E. 1985. *Sisterhood denied*. Philadelphia, PA: Temple University Press.

Jayawardena, Kumari. 1986. *Feminism and nationalism in the third world*. London: Zed.

Jeffreys, Sheila. 1990. *Anticlimax*. London: Women's Press.

Jelin, Elizabeth, ed. 1990. *Women and social change in Latin America*. London: Zed.

Johnson, Richard. 1979. Histories of culture/theories of ideology. In *Ideology and Cultural Production,* edited by Michele Barrett and Phillip Corrigan; reprinted in *From feminism to liberation,* collected by Edith Hoshino Altback. Schenkman, Cambridge, MA, 1971.

Jones, Gayle. 1975. *Corregidora*. New York: Random House.

Jones, Jacqueline. 1985. *Labor of love, labor of sorrow*. New York: Basic Books.

Jordon, Winthrop. 1969. *White over black*. New York: Penguin.

Joreen. 1973. The tyranny of structurelessness. *Radical feminism,* edited by Anne Koedt, Ellen Levine, and Anita Rapone. New York: Quadrangle.

Joseph, Gloria. 1987. *Common differences: Conflicts in black and white feminist perspectives*. Boston: South End Press.

———. 1981. The incompatible ménage à trois: Marxism, feminism and racism. In *Women and revolution: A discussion of the unhappy marriage of marxism and feminism,* edited by Lydia Sargent, 91–107. Boston: South End Press.

Kabeer, Naila. 1994. *Reversed realities: Gender hierarchies in development thought*. London: Verso.

Kandiyoti, Deniz. 1988. Bargaining with patriarchy. *Gender and Society* 2 (3): 274–90.

Kaplan, Cora. 1987. *Sea changes: culture and feminism*. London: Verso.

———. 1979. Radical feminism and literature: Rethinking Millett's *Sexual Politics*. *Red Letters* 9:7.

Katz, Jonathan. 1976. *Gay American history: Lesbians and gay men in the U.S.A.: A documentary*. New York: Crowell.

Kelly, Joan. 1979. The doubled vision of feminist theory: A postscript to "The Women and Power" conference. *Feminist Studies* 5 (1): 216–27.

Kelly, Patricia Fernandez. 1994. *The political economy of gender in Latin America: The emerging dilemmas*. Washington, DC: Woodrow Wilson International Center for Scholars.

Kimbrell, Andrew. 1993. *The human body shop*. New York: Harper and Row.

King, Deborah K. 1988. Multiple jeopardy, multiple consciousness: The context of a black feminist ideology. *Signs: Journal of Women in Culture and Society* 14 (1) (August): 42–72.

Kipnis, Laura. 1988. Feminism: The political conscience of postmodernism? In *Universal abandon?* edited by Andrew Ross. Minneapolis: University of Minnesota Press.

Kirkwood, Julieta. 1987. *Feminarios*. Santiago, Chile: Ediciones Documentas.

———. 1986. *Ser politica en Chile: Las feministas y los partidos*. Santiago, Chile: Facultad Latinoamericana de Ciencias Sociales.

———. 1983. El feminismo como negación del autoritarismo. Santiago, Chile: Programa FLACSO, Materia de discusion, no. 52.

Kittay, Eva Feder. 1983. *Womb envy: An explanatory concept*. In *Mothering: Essays in feminist theory,* edited by Joyce Trebilcot. Totowa, NJ: Rowman and Allenfield.

Kollontai, Alexandra. 1984. *Sexual revolution and the class struggle*. London: Socialist Workers Party.

———. 1984. *Selected articles and speeches,* translated by Cynthia Carlile. New York: International Publishers.

———. 1978. *Love of worker bees*. Chicago: Academy Press.

———. 1973. *Red love*. Westport, CT: Hyperion Press.

Kramer, Laura. 1991. *The Sociology of gender*. New York: St. Martin's Press.

Kruks, Sonia, Rayna Rapp, and Marilyn B. Young, eds. 1989. *Promissory notes: Women in the transition to socialism.* New York: Monthly Review Press.

Kuhn, Annette. 1987. *Women's pictures: Feminism and cinema.* London: Routledge and Kegan Paul.

Kuhn, Annette, and Ann Marie Wolpe, eds. 1978. *Feminism and materialism: Women and modes of production.* London: Routledge.

Kulikoff, Allan. 1986. *Tobacco and slaves: The development of southern cultures in the Chesapeake 1680–1800.* Chapel Hill: University of North Carolina Press.

Laclau, Ernesto, and Chantal Mouffe. 1990. *Hegemony and socialist strategy: Towards a radical democratic politics.* New York: Verso.

Lamas, Marta, ed. 1990. Debate feminista. *Ano 1,* vol. 1. Mexico City: n.p.

Landry, Donna, and Gerald MacLean. 1993. *Materialist feminisms.* Cambridge, MA: Blackwell Press.

Lau Jaiven, Ana. 1987. *La nueva ola del feminismo en Mexico.* Mexico City, Mexico: Planeta.

Lazarus, Neil. 1991. Doubting the new world order: Marxism, realism, and the claims of postmodernist social theory. *Differences* 3: 3.

Lazarus, Neil, Steven Evans, Anthony Arnove, and Anne Menke. 1995. The necessity of universalism. *differences: A Journal of Feminist Cultural Studies* 7 (1): 75–145.

Leacock, Eleanor, and Safa, Helen. 1986. *Women's work: Development and the division of work by gender.* South Hadley, MA: Bergin & Garvey.

———. 1981a. *Myths of male dominance: Collected articles on women cross-culturally.* New York: Monthly Review Press.

———. 1981b. History, development, and the division of labor by sex: Implications for organization. *Signs: Journal of Women in Culture and Society* 7:2 (Winter).

———. 1978. The study of women: Ideological issues. Unpublished.

Lechner, Norbert. 1990. De la revolución a la democracia. In *Debate feminista,* edited by Marta Lamas. *Ano 1,* vol. 1, Mexico City: n.p.

Leghorn, Lisa, and Katherine Parker. 1981. *Women's worth, sexual economics and the world of women.* London: Routledge and Kegan Paul.

Lengermann, Patricia, and Jill Niebrugge-Brantley. 1990. Feminist sociological theory: The near-future prospects. In *Frontiers in social theory,* edited by George Ritzer. New York: Columbia University Press.

Lengermann, Patricia, and Ruth A. Wallace. 1985. *Gender in America.* Englewood Cliffs, NJ: Prentice-Hall.

Lenin, V. I. 1966. *The emancipation of women.* New York: International.

Lessing, Doris. 1990. *The Summer before the dark.* London: Paladin.

Lewis, Jane. 1984. *Women in England, 1870–1950: Sexual divisions and social change.* Sussex: Wheatsheaf.

Lindberg, Steffan. 1995. Farmers' movements and cultural nationalism in India: An ambiguous relationship. *Theory and Society* 24: 837–68.

Loewenberg, J., and R. Bogin, eds. 1978. *Black women in nineteenth-century American life.* State College, PA: Pennsylvania State University Press.

Long Laws, Judith. 1979. Patriarchy and feminism: Competing ways of doing social science. *Resources in Education* (June): 101–20.

Lorde, Audre. 1981. An open letter to Mary Daly. In *This bridge called my back: Writings by radical women of color,* edited by Gloria Anzaldúa and Cherrie Moraga. Watertown, MA: Persephone Press.

———. 1983. Age, race, class, and sex: Women redefining difference. In *Sister outsider, essays and speeches.* New York: Crossing Press.

Lovell, Terry, ed. 1990. *British feminist thought: A reader.* Oxford: Blackwell.

———. 1987. *Consuming fiction.* London: Verso.

Lowy, Michael. 1986. Mass organization, party and state: Democracy in the transition to socialism. In *Transition and development: Problems of Third World socialism,* edited by Richard T. Fagen, Carmen Diana Deere, and Jose Luis Coraggio. New York: Monthly Review Press.

Lozano, Itziar, and Maruja Gonzales. 1986. *Feminismo y movimiento popular: Desencuentro or relación historica?* Mexico City, Mexico: Equipo de Mujeres Solidarias.

Lugones, Maria. 1989. On the logic of pluralist feminism. Lecture, Syracuse University, Fall.

Luxemburg, Rosa. 1986. *The mass strike.* London, Chicago, and Melbourne: Bookmarks.

———. 1976. *The national question: Selected writings.* New York: Monthly Review Press.

———. 1972. *The accumulation of capital: An anti-critique.* New York: Monthly Review Press.

Macherey, Pierre. 1979. In defense of epistemology. In *Issues in Marxist Philosophy*, edited by John Mepham and David-Hillel-Ruben. Atlantic Highlands, NJ: Humanities Press.

———. 1978. *A theory of literary production.* London: Routledge.

MacDonald, George. 1972. *Fifty years of free thought.* New York: Arno.

Macionis, John J. 1993. *Sociology.* Englewood Cliffs, NJ: Prentice-Hall.

MacKinnon, Catharine A. 1981. Feminism, Marxism, method and the state: An agenda for theory. In *Feminist theory: A critique of ideology,* edited by N. Keohane, M. Rosaldo, and B. Gelpi. Chicago: University of Chicago Press.

Mackintosh, Maureen. 1990. Abstract markets and real needs. In *The food question: Profits vs. people?* edited by Henry Bernstein et al. New York: Monthly Review Press.

———. 1989. *Toward a feminist theory of the state.* Cambridge: Harvard University Press.

———. 1981. Gender and economics: The sexual division of labor and the subordination of women. In *Of marriage and market,* edited by Kate Young et al. London: CSE.

Mandel, Ernest. 1972. *Late capitalism,* translated by Joris de Bres. London: Verso.

———. 1967. *An introduction to Marxist economic theory.* New York: Merit.

———. nd. "Workers Under Neocapitalism." Paper delivered at Simon Fraser University. Burnaby, B.C., Canada.

Manthey, Jürgen, ed. 1979. *Literaturmagazin 11, Schreiben oder Literatur.* Reinbek bei Hamburg.

Marcuse, Herbert. 1964. *One dimensional Man.* Boston: Beacon.

Marglin, Stephen, and F. Marglin, eds. 1990. *Dominating knowledge: Development, culture and resistance.* Oxford: Clarendon Press.

Marx, Karl. 1977. *Capital,* translated by Ben Fowkes. New York: Vintage.

———. 1967. Critique of Hegel's philosophy of the state. In *Writings of the young Marx on philosophy and society,* edited by Loyd D. Easton and Kurt H. Guddat. New York: Doubleday.

———. 1972. *The grundisse,* edited by David McLellan. New York: Harper & Row.

———. 1970a. *A contribution to the critique of political economy.* New York: International Publishers.

———. 1970b. *Capital, vol. 1.* New York: International Publishers.

———. 1963. *The eighteenth brumaire of Louis Bonaparte.* New York: International.

Marx, Karl, and Frederick Engels. 1988. *The communist manifesto.* New York: Norton.

Marx, Karl, and Frederick Engels. 1976. *Collected works.* New York: International.

Marx, Karl, and Frederick Engels. 1976. *The German ideology.* New York: International.

Mauss, Marcel. 1967. *The gift,* translated by Ian Cunnison. New York: W. W. Norton.

Maynard, Mary. 1990. The re-shaping of sociology? Trends in the study of gender. *Sociology* 24 (2): 269–90.

McDonough, Roisin, and Rachel Harrison. 1978. Patriarchy and relations of production. In *Feminism and Materialism,* edited by Annette Kuhn and Ann Marie Wolpe. London: Routledge.

Meillassoux, Claude. 1975. *Femmes, greniers, et capitaux.* Paris: F. Maspero.

Mies, Maria. 1993. *Ecofeminism.* Melbourne: Spinifex.

———. 1988. From the individual to the dividual: In the supermarket of "reproductive alternatives." *Reproductive and Genetic Engineering* 1 (3): 225–37.

———. 1986. *Patriarchy and accumulation on a world scale: Women in the international division of labor.* London: Zed.

———. 1980. *Housewives produce for the world market: The lace makers of Narsapur.* Geneva: International Labor Office.

Mies, Maria, Veronika Bennholdt-Tomsen, and Claudia Von Werhof. 1988. *Women: The last colony.* London: Zed Books.

Milkman, Ruth. 1985. *Women, work, and protest: A century of women's labor history.* New York: Routledge.

Miller, Nancy K. 1986. *The poetics of gender.* New York: Columbia University Press.

Millett, Kate. 1971. *Sexual politics.* New York: Doubleday.

Millman, Marcia, and Rosabeth Moss Kanter. 1975. *Another voice: Feminist perspectives on social life and social science.* New York: Anchor.

Minh-Ha, Trinh. 1989. *Woman, native, other.* Bloomington: Indiana University Press.

Mitchell, Juliet. 1974. *Psychoanalysis and feminism.* New York: Random House.

———. 1971. *Woman's estate.* New York: Pantheon.

―――. 1966. Women: The longest revolution. *New Left Review* (December).

Mitter, Partha. 1986. Should artificial intelligence take culture into consideration? In *Artificial intelligence for society,* edited by K. S. Gill. London: John Wiley.

Mitter, Swasti. 1995. *Women encounter technology: Changing patterns of employment in the Third World.* London: Routledge.

―――. 1994a. *Dignity and daily bread: New forms of organizing among poor women in the Third World and the First.* New York: Routledge.

―――. 1994b. *Women in the trade unions: Organizing the unorganized.* Geneva: International Labor Office.

―――. 1986. *Common fate, common bond: Women in the global economy.* London: Pluto Press.

Mohan, Rajeswari. 1990. *Modernity and imperialism: A critique of literary modernism.* Dissertation. Syracuse University.

―――. 1989. Review of *The political forms of modern society* by Claude Lefort. *Rethinking Marxism* 2 (1): 141–57.

Mohanty, Chandra. 1995. *Feminist genealogies, colonial legacies, democratic futures.* New York: Routledge.

―――. 1991. Introduction: Cartographies of struggle. In *Third World women and the politics of feminism,* edited by Chandra Talpade Mohanty, Ann Russo, and Lourdes Torres. Bloomington: Indiana University Press.

―――. 1988. Under western eyes: Feminist scholarship and colonial discourses. *Feminist Review* 30: 61–88.

Moi, Toril, and Janice Radway, eds. 1994. Materialist feminism. Special Issue. *South Atlantic Quarterly* 93.4 (Fall).

―――. 1988. Feminism, postmodernism, and style: Recent feminist criticism in the United States. *Cultural Critique* 9 (Spring): 3–24.

―――. 1987. *French feminist thought: A reader.* New York: Blackwell.

Molina, Natacha. 1986. *Lo femino y lo democratico en el Chile de hoy.* Santiago, Chile: Vector, Centro de Estudios Economicos y Sociales.

Molyneux, Maxine. 1986. Mobilization with emancipation? Women's interests, state and revolution. In *Transition and development: Problems of Third World socialism,* edited by Richard R. Fagen, Carmen Diana Deere, and Jose Luis Coraggio. New York: Monthly Review Press.

―――. 1982. Socialist societies old and new: Progress toward emancipation? *Monthly Review* 34: 56–100.

―――. 1979. Beyond the domestic labor debate. *New Left Review* 116 (July August): 3–27.

Monroy Limon, Lilia. 1987. *Memorias de Taller: Mujer, Centroamericana, violencia y guerra.* IV Encuentro Feminista Latinoamericano y del Caribe. Taxco, Guerrero, Mexico.

Moraga, Cherrie. 1986. From a long line of vendidas: Chicanas and feminism. In *Feminist studies/critical studies,* edited by Teresa de Lauretis. Bloomington: Indiana University Press.

Moraga, Cherrie, and Gloria Anzuldúa, eds. 1981. *This bridge called my back: Writings by radical women of color.* Watertown, MA: Persephone Press.

Morgan, Lewis Henry. 1877. *Ancient society.* Cambridge: Belknap Press.

Morisse, Inge, et al. 1982. Unsicherheit in der Politik—Gewerkschafterinnentagebuch. *das argument* 135: 9/10.

Morrell, Frances. 1985. AES: The Alternative European Strategy. *New Socialist* (October): 9.

Mort, Frank. 1989. The politics of consumption. In *New times,* edited by Stuart Hall and Martin Jacques. London: Verso.

Morton, Donald. 1996a. *Material queer.* Denver: Westview.

―――. 1996b. The class politics of queer theory. *College English* 58.4 (April):471–82.

―――, ed. 1991. *Theory/pedagogy/politics: Texts for change.* Urbana: University of Illinois Press.

Morton, Donald, and Mas'ud Zavarzadeh. 1987. The nostalgia for law and order and the policing of knowledge: The politics of contemporary literary theory. *Syracuse Scholar Supplement* (Spring): 25–71.

Morton, Peggy. 1971. A woman's work is never done. In *From feminism to liberation,* edited by Edith Altbach. Cambridge, MA: Schenkman.

Moser, Carolyn O.N. 1991. Gender planning in the Third World: Meeting practical and strategic needs. In *Gender and international relations,* edited by Rebecca Grant and Kathleen Newland. Bloomington: Indiana University Press.

Mouffe, Chantal. 1983. The sex-gender system and the discursive construction of women's subordination. In *Rethinking ideology: A Marxist debate,* edited by Sakari Hanninen and Leena Paldan. New York: International.

Moulián, Tomas. 1982. Evolución de la izquierda Chilena: La influencia del Marxismo. In *Que significa hacer politica,* edited by Norbert Lechner. Lima, Peru: DESCO.

Moynihan, D.P. 1965. *The negro family: The case for national action.* Washington, D.C.: U.S. Department of Labor, Office of Policy Research.

Munck, Ronaldo. 1990. Farewell to socialism? A comment on recent debates. *Latin American Perspectives* 17: 113–21.

Murguialday, Clara. 1990. *Nicaragua, revolución y feminismo, 1977–89.* Madrid: Editorial Revolucion.

———. 1989. Una brecha en el muro del machismo: Diez años de lucha de las mujeres nicaraguenses. *Terra Nuova Forum* 13: 9–65.

Naiman, Joanne. 1996. Left feminism and the return to class. *Monthly Review* 42 (8) (June): 12–28.

Nanda, Meera. 1996. Post-Fordist technology and the changing geography of production: Challenges for Third World women. *Gender and Society* (forthcoming).

———. 1996. The science question in post-colonial feminism. *Economic and Political Weekly* 31 (16–17).

———. 1995. Transnationalization of the Third World state and the undoing of the Green Revolution. *Economic and Political Weekly* (January 28).

———. 1994. Is modern science a western, patriarchal myth? A critique of the neo-populist orthodoxy. *South Asia bulletin* XI: 1–2: 32–61.

Nandy, Ashis. 1994. Culture, voice and development: A primer for the unsuspecting. *Thesis Eleven* 39: 1–18.

———. 1988. The Human Factor. *The Illustrated Weekly of India* January 17: 20–23.

Nash, June, and Maria Patricia Fernandez Kelly, eds. 1983. *Women, men, and the international division of labor.* Albany: SUNY Press.

———. 1980. *Sex and class in Latin America: Women's perspectives on politics, economics and the family in the Third World.* New York: Bergin and Garvey.

Newton, Judith. 1994. *Starting over: Feminism and the politics of cultural critique.* Ann Arbor: University of Michigan Press.

Newton, Judith, and Deborah Rosenfelt, eds. 1985. *Feminist criticism and social change: Sex, class and race in literature and culture.* New York: Methuen.

Newton, Judith, Mary P. Ryan, and Judith R. Walkowitz, eds. 1983. *Sex and class in women's history.* London: Routledge.

Nicholson, Linda J. 1986. *Gender in history: The limits of social theory in the age of the family.* New York: Columbia University Press.

Nicolini, Marta. 1982. Idea: Investiamo nei servizi. *Noidonne* (November).

Nnadi, Joseph E. 1980. *Visions de l'Afrique dans l'oeuvre de Baudelaire.* Yaoundé, Cameroon: Éditions CLE.

Noble, Charles. 1993. Work: The most dangerous environment. In *Toxic struggles: The theory and practice of environmental justice,* edited by Richard Hofrichter. Philadelphia and Gabriola Island, BC: New Society Publishers.

Norris, Christopher. 1992. *Uncritical theory: Postmodernism, intellectuals, and the gulf war.* Amherst: University of Massachusetts Press.

———. 1990. *What's wrong with postmodernism? Critical theory and the ends of philosophy.* Baltimore: Johns Hopkins Press.

Noyelle, Thierry, and Stanback, Thomas M., Jr. 1983. *The economic transformation of American cities.* Totowa, NJ: Rowman & Littlefield.

Nun, Jose. 1989. *La rebelión del coro: Estudio sobre la racionalidad politica y el sentido coman.* Buenos Aires: Editorial Nueva Vision.

Nussbaum, Martha. 1992. Human functioning and social justice: In defense of Aristotelian essentialism. *Political Theory* 20 (2): 202–46.

Nussbaum, Martha, and Jonathan Glover. 1995. *Women, culture and development: A study of human capabilities.* Oxford: Clarendon Press.

Oakley, Ann. 1975. *Sociology of housework.* New York: Pantheon.

———. 1972. *Sex, gender, and society.* London: Harper.

O'Brien, Mary. 1982. *The politics of reproduction.* Boston: Routledge and Kegan Paul.

Off Our Backs. 1989. Compañeras, solidarity, movement: Women talk about the Encuentro. March.

O'Gara, Debra, and Guerry Hoddersen. 1986. Dine elders resist eviction from Big Mountain. *The Freedom Socialist* 9 (3): 2.

Ollman, Bertell. 1971. *Alienation: Marx's conception of man in capitalist society.* New York: Cambridge University Press.

Omi, Michael, and Winant, Howard. 1987. *Racial formation in the United States.* New York:

Omvedt, Gail. 1993. *Reinventing revolution: New social movements and the socialist tradition in India.* Armonk, NY: M. E. Sharpe.

———. 1986. Patriarchy: The analysis of women's oppression. *Insurgent Sociologist* 13.3: 30–50.

———. 1980. *We will smash this prison.* London: Zed.

———. 1974. *The sociology of housework.* London: Martin Robertson.

Outshorn, Joyce. 1984. The dual heritage. In *A creative tension: Explorations in socialist feminism,* edited by Anja Meulenbelt et al. and translated by Della Couling. Boston: South End Press.

OWAAD. 1979. *Fowaad,* no. 2.

Pala, Achola O. 1977. Definitions of women and development: An African perspective. *Signs* 3.1 (Fall).

Palmer, John. 1983. New vision of a socialist Europe. *New Socialist* 9: 15–19.

Papanek, Hanna. 1990. To each less than she needs, from each more than she can do: Allocations, entitlements and value. In *Persistent inequalities: Women and world development,* edited by Irene Tinker. New York: Oxford University Press.

Parker, Andrew, Mary Russo, Doris Sommer, and Patricia Yaeger. 1992. *Nationalisms and sexualities.* New York: Routledge.

Parmar, Pratibha. 1982. Gender, race and class: Asian women in resistance. In *The empire strikes back: Race and racism in 70s Britain.* London: Hutchinson.

Parmar, Pratibha, and Nadira Mirza. 1981. Growing angry, growing strong. *Spare Rib,* no. iii (October).

Perkins, T. E. 1977. Rethinking stereotypes. In *Ideology and cultural production,* edited by David Perry and Alfred Watkins. New York.

Perlstein, Rick. 1995. Criticism vs. citizenship. *The nation* 261: 21 (December 18).

Perry, David, and Alfred Watkins. 1977. *The rise of sunbelt cities.* Beverly Hills, CA: Sage.

Petchesky, Rosalind. 1979. Dissolving the hyphen: A report on Marxist-feminist groups. In *Capitalist patriarchy and the case for socialist feminism,* edited by Zillah R. Eisenstein. New York: Monthly Review Press.

Petras, James. 1981. *Class, state, and power in the Third World with case studies on class conflict in Latin America.* London: Zed.

Phelps, Linda. 1975. "Patriarchy and Capitalism" *Quest* 2.2 (Fall).

Phillips, Anne. 1984. *Hidden hands: Women and economic policies.* London: Pluto Press.

Phoenix, Janet. 1993. Getting the lead out of the community. In *Confronting environmental racism: Voices from the grassroots,* edited by Robert D. Bullard. Boston: South End Press.

Plummer, Kenneth. 1992. *Modern homosexualities.* New York: Routledge.

Pollitt, Katha. 1990. A new assault on feminism. *The Nation* (March 26).

Pollock, Griselda. 1977. What's wrong with images of women? *Screen Education* 24.

Poovey, Mary. 1988. *Uneven developments: The ideological work of gender in mid-Victorian England.* Chicago: University of Chicago Press.

Porché, François. 1928. *Charles Baudelaire,* translated by John Mavin. New York: Horace Liveright.

Portantiero, Juan Carlos. 1982. Socialismos y politica en America Latina: Notas para una revision. In *Que significa hacer politica?* edited by Norbert Lechner. Lima, Peru: DESCO.

Portes, Alejandro. 1985. Latin American class structures: Their composition and change during the last decades. *Latin American Research Review* 20: 7–10.

Portugal, Ana Maria. 1986. On being a feminist in Latin America. Santiago, Chile: ISIS International Women's Information and Communication Service, ISIS International.

Prescod-Roberts, Margaret, and Norma Steele. 1980. *Black women: Bringing it all back home.* Bristol, UK: Falling Wall Press.

Projeki-Ideologie-Theorie: Theorien fiber Ideologie. 1979. Argument-Sonderband 40, West Berlin.

Projekt Frauengrundstudium: Frauengrundstudium. 1982. Argument-Studienheft 44, West Berlin.

Radical Women. *Radical Women Manifesto.* Seattle, WA: Radical Women Publications.

Ramazanoglu, Caroline. 1986. Ethnocentrism and socialist feminist theory. *Feminist Review* 22 (February): 83–97.

Randall, Margaret. 1981. *Sandino's daughters: Testimonies of Nicaraguan women in struggle.* Seattle, WA: Left Bank.

Rao, Hanumantha C.H. 1994. *Agricultural growth, rural poverty and environmental degradation in India.* New Delhi: Oxford University Press.

Rascón, Maria Antonietta. 1975. La mujer y la lucha social. In *Imagen y realidad de la mujer,* edited by Elena Urrutia. Mexico City, Mexico: Sep Setentas.

Rauter, E. A. 1978. *Vom Umgang mit Wörtern.* Munich.

Reddock, Rhoda. 1984. *Women, labor and struggle in 20th century Trinidad and Tobago 1898–1960.* The Hague: Institute of Social Studies.

Redstockings Collective. 1975. *Feminist revolution.* New York: Random House.

Reed, Evelyn. 1970. *Problems of women's liberation: A Marxist approach.* New York: Pathfinder.

Reinharz, Shulamit. 1984. *On Becoming a social scientist.* New York: Transaction Books.

———. 1983. Experiential analysis: A contribution to feminist research. In *Theories of women's studies,* edited by Gloria Bowles and Renate Duelli Klein. London: Routledge.

Renzetti, Claire, and Daniel Curran. 1989. *Women, men and society.* Boston: Allyn and Bacon.

Rich, Adrienne. 1980. Compulsory heterosexuality and lesbian existence. *Signs* 5 (Summer): 631–60.

———. 1979. Disloyal to civilization: Feminism, racism and gynephobia. *Chrysalis,* no. 7.

Richardson, Colin. 1991. Porn again. In *High risk lives,* edited by Tara Kaufmann and Paul Lincoln. Bridgeport: Prism.

Richardson, Laurel. 1981. *The dynamics of sex and gender.* Boston: Houghton Mifflin.

Ritzer, George. 1990. *Frontiers in social theory.* New York: Columbia University Press.

Robinson, Lillian. 1994. Touring Thailand's sex industry. *The Nation.* (July 5).

———. 1978. *Sex, class, and culture.* New York: Methuen.

Robinson, Lillian, and Lise Vogel. 1971. Modernism and history. *New Literary History* 3: 177–99.

Romero, Mary. 1992. *Maid in the U.S.A.* New York: Routledge.

Rosaldo, M. Z. 1980. The use and abuse of anthropology: Reflections on feminism and cross-cultural understanding. *Signs* (Spring) 5: 389–417.

Rothman, Barbara Katz. 1989. *Recreating motherhood: Ideology and technology in a patriarchal society.* New York: W.W. Norton and Company.

Rowbotham, Sheila. 1995. *Women encounter technology: Changing patterns of employment in the Third World.* London: Routledge.

———. 1994. *Dignity and daily bread: New forms of economic organizing among poor women in the Third World and the First.* London: Routledge.

———. 1993. *Homeworkers worldwide.* London: Merlin Press.

———. 1992. *Women in movement: Feminism and social action.* New York: Routledge.

———. 1989. *The past is before us: Feminism in action since the 1960s.* Boston: Beacon.

———. 1973. *Women's consciousness, man's world.* Harmondsworth: Penguin.

———. 1972. *Women, resistance and revolution in the modern world.* New York: Random House.

Rowbotham, Sheila, Lynne Segal, and Hilary Wainwright. 1979. *Beyond the fragments: Feminism and the making of socialism.* Boston: Alyson.

Rowntree, Mickey, and John. 1969. Notes on the political economy of women's liberation. *Monthly Review* 21 (7) (December): 26–32.

Rowntree, Mickey, and John, Lynne Segal, and Hilary Wainwright. 1979. *Beyond the fragments: feminism and the making of socialism.* London: Merlin Press.

Rubin, Gail. 1975. The traffic in women: Notes on the "political economy" of sex. In *Toward an anthropology of women,* edited by Rayna Reiter. New York: Monthly Review Press.

Rubin, Isaak Illich. 1972. *Essays on Marx's theory of value.* Detroit: Black and Red.

Russell, Kathryn. 1984. The internal relations between production and reproduction: Reflections on the manipulations of family life in South Africa. *Journal of Social Philosophy* 15 (2) (Summer): 14–25.

Sachs, Abie, and Joan Hoff Wilson. 1978. *Sexism and the law: A study of male beliefs and legal bias in Britain and the United States.* New York: Free Press.

Sacks, Karen. 1989. Toward a unified theory of class, race, and gender. *American Ethnologist* 16 (3).

———. 1984. *My troubles are going to have trouble with me.* New Brunswick, NJ: Rutgers University Press.

———. 1975. Engels revisited: Women, the organization of production and private property. In *Women, culture, and society,* edited by Michele Rosaldo and Louise Lamphere. Stanford, CA: Stanford University Press.

Safa, Helen. 1983. Women, production and reproduction in industrial capitalism. In *Women, men, and the international division of labor,* edited by June Nash and Maria Patricia Fernandez Kelly. Albany: SUNY Press.

Said, Edward. 1984. *The world, the text, and the critic.* Cambridge, MA: Harvard University Press.

Sandoval, Cheyla. 1991. U.S. Third World feminism: The theory and method of oppositional consciousness in the postmodern world. *Genders* 10 (Spring): 1–24.

Sargent, Lydia, ed. 1981. *Women and revolution: A discussion of the unhappy marriage of marxism and feminism.* Boston: South End Press.

Sawant, S. D., and C. V. Achuthan. 1995. Agricultural growth across crops and regions: Emerging trends and patterns. *Economic and Political Weekly* (March 25).

Sawers, Larry, and William K. Tabb. 1984. *Sunbelt/snowbelt.* New York: Oxford University Press.

Sayers, Janet, Mary Evans, and Nanneke Redclift, eds. 1987. *Engels revisited: New feminist essays.* London: Tavistock.

Schwendinger, J., and H. Schwendinger. 1971. The subjection of women: Ideological views and solutions. In *Sociologists of the chair: A radical analysis of the formative years of North American sociology.* New York: Basic.

Scott, Joan Wallach. 1988. *Gender and the politics of history.* New York: Columbia University Press.

Seabrook, Jeremy. 1985. Sewa plants the seeds of women's rights. *The Guardian* (12 April): 14.

Seager, Joni, and Ann Olson, eds. 1986. *Women in the world: An international atlas.* New York: Pan Books.

Sears, Hal D. 1977. *The sex radicals: Free love in high victorian America.* Lawrence: Regents Press of Kansas.

Secombe, Wally. 1974. The housewife and her labor under capitalism. *New Left Review* (January–February) 83: 3–24.

Sedgwick, Eve Kosofsky. 1990. *Epistemology of the closet.* Berkeley: University of California Press.

Seidman, Steven. 1993. Identity and politics in a postmodern gay culture: Some conceptual and historical notes. In *Fear of a queer planet,* edited by Michael Warner. Minneapolis: University of Minnesota Press.

———. 1992. *Embattled eros.* New York: Routledge.

———. 1991. *Romantic longings.* New York: Routledge.

Self-Employed Women's Association (SEWA). 1983. *We, the self-employed: Voice of the self-employed worker.* Ahmedabad: SEWA.

Sen, A. 1995. Gender inequality and theories of justice. In *Women, culture and development: A study of human capabilities,* edited by Martha Nussbaum and J. Glover. Oxford: Clarendon Press.

———. 1990a. Gender and cooperative conflicts. In *Persistent inequalities: Women and world development,* edited by Irene Tinker. New York: Oxford University Press.

———. 1990b. More than 100 million women are missing. *New York Review of Books* (December 20).

Shaikh, Anwar. 1990. Abstract and concrete labor. In *Marxian economics,* edited by John Eatwell, Murray Milgate, and Peter Newman. New York: W. W. Norton.

Shiva, Vandana. 1988. *Staying alive: Women, ecology and survival in India.* New Delhi: Kali For Women.

Sidel, Ruth. 1986. *Women and children last.* New York: Viking Press.

Simms, Margaret C., and Julianne M. Malveaux, eds. 1986. *Slippng through the cracks: The status of black women.* New Brunswick, NJ: Transaction Publishers.

Sinha, Mrinilini. 1996. Nationalism and respectable sexuality in India. *Genders* 21.

Sivard, Ruth. 1993. *World military and social expenditures, 1992–93.* 17th ed. Washington, DC: World Priorities.

Smith, Barbara. 1993. Where's the revolution. *The Nation* (July 5).

———, ed. 1983. *Home girls: A black feminist anthology.* Albany, NY: Kitchen Table Women of Color Press.

Smith, Dorothy. 1990. *The conceptual practices of power: A feminist sociology of knowledge.* Boston: Northeastern Press.

———. 1990. *Texts, facts, and femininity.* New York: Routledge.

———. 1987. *The everyday world as problematic: Toward a feminist sociology.* Boston: Northeastern University Press.

———. 1975. An analysis of ideological structures and how women are excluded: considerations for academic women. *Canadian Review of Sociology and Anthropology* 12 (4): 131–54.

———. 1974. Women's perspective as a radical critique of sociology. *Sociological Inquiry* 44: 73–90.

Smith, George W. 1991. The ideology of "fag": Barriers to education for gay students. Paper presented at Meetings of the Canadian Sociology and Anthropology Association, Kingston, Ontario.

———. 1990. Political activist as ethnographer. *Social Problems* 37 (4): 87–98.

———. 1988. Policing the gay community: An inquiry into textually mediated social relations. *International Journal of the Sociology of Law* 16: 163–83.

Smith, Joan. 1977. Women and the family, part 1. *International Socialism* 1 (July): 100.

Smith, Paul. 1991. Laclau's and Mouffe's secret agent. In *Community at loose ends,* edited by Miami Theory Collective. Minneapolis: University of Minnesota Press.

———. 1978. Domestic labour and Marx's theory of value. In *Feminism and materialism: Women and modes of production,* edited by Annette Kuhn and Annemarie Wolpe. Boston: Routledge and Kegan Paul.

Smith, Sharon. 1994. Mistaken identity. *International socialism* 62 (March): 4.

Sojo, Ana. 1985. *Mujer y politica.* San Jose, Costa Rica: DEI.

Sölle, Dorothee. 1981. Feministische Theologie. *Das Argument* 129: 9/10.

Sombart, Werner. 1922. *Liebe, luxus und Kapitalismus: uber die Eatstehung der modernen welt aus dem geist der verschwendung.* Berlin: Wagenbachs.

Spelman, Elizabeth V. 1989. *Inessential woman: Problems of exclusion in feminist thought.* Boston: Beacon Press.

Spender, Dale. 1985. *Man made language.* London: Routledge & Kegan Paul.

Spivak, Gayatri. 1988. Can the subaltern speak? In *Marxism and the Interpretation of Culture,* edited by Cary Nelson and Lawrence Grossberg. Chicago: University of Illinois Press.

———. 1987. *In other worlds: Essays in cultural politics.* New York and London: Methuen.

———. 1985. Feminism and critical theory. In *For alma mater,* edited by Paula Treichler, Chris Kramarae, and Beth Stafford. Chicago: University of Illinois Press.

Stabile, Carol A. 1994. *Feminism and the technological fix.* New York: St. Martin's Press.

Stacey, Judith, and Barrie Thorne. 1985. The missing feminist revolution in sociology. *Social Problems* 32: 301–16.

———. 1983. *Patriarchy and socialist revolution in China.* Berkeley: University of California Press.

Stanley, Liz, and Sue Wise. 1983. *Breaking out: Feminist consciousness and feminist research.* London: Routledge.

Staples, Robert. 1991. The political economy of black family life. In *The Black Family.* Belmont, CA: Wadsworth.

Steel, Flora Annie. 1982. Mussumat Kirpo's doll. In *Stories from the Raj from Kipling to independence,* edited by Saros Cowasjee. London: Triad Granada.

Sternbach, Nancy Saporta, et al. Forthcoming. Feminisms in Latin America: From Bogata to Taxco. *Signs.*

Stetson, Dorothy M. 1982. *The politics of family law reform in England.* Westport, CT: Greenwood Press.

Stoehr, Taylor. 1979. *Free love in America: A documentary history.* New York: AMS Press.

Sumner, Colin. 1979. *Reading ideologies: An investigation into the marxist theory of ideology and law.* London: Academic Press.

Sypnowich, Christine. 1993. Some disquiet about "difference." *Praxis International* 13 (2): 99–112.

Takaki, Ronald. 1990. *Iron cages: Race and culture in nineteenth-century America.* New York: Oxford University Press.

Tanganqco, Luz. 1982. The family in western science and ideology: A critique from the periphery. Masters thesis. Institute of Social Studies, The Hague.

Tatchell, Peter. 1994. Realising your potential. *Pink paper* 18 (February).

———. 1993. Self reliance: The x-factor in queer politics. *Gay times.* (April).

Tax, Meredith. 1980. *The rising of the women: Feminist solidarity and class Conflict, 1880–1917.* New York: Monthly Review Press.

Teague, Paul. 1985. The alternative economic strategy: A time to go European. *Capital and Class* 26 (Summer): 58–69.

Terborg-Penn, Rosalyn. 1990. Historical treatment of black women in the women's movement. In *Black women in United States,* edited by Darlene Clark Hine. Brooklyn: Carolson Publishing Co.

Trebilcot, Joyce, ed. 1983. *Mothering: Essays in feminist theory.* Totowa, NJ: Rowman and Allenheld.

Truong, Thanh-dam. 1990. *Sex, money and morality: Prostitution and tourism in Southeast Asia.* London: Zed Books.

U.S. Bureau of the Census. 1995. *Statistical abstracts of the U.S.: 1995.* 115th ed. Washington, DC: Government Printing Office.

van Allen, Judith. 1976. Aba riots or Igbo "Women's War"? Ideology, stratification and the invisibility of women. In *Women in Africa Studies in Social and Economic Change,* edited by Nancy Hafkin and Edna Bay. Stanford, CA: Stanford University Press.

Van Beck, Steve. 1992. *Insight guide to Thailand.* New York: Random House.

Vargas, Virginia. 1989. *El aporte de la rebeldia de las mujeres.* Lima, Peru: Ediciones Flora Tristan.

———. 1988. The feminist movement in Peru: Inventory and perspectives. In *Women's struggles and strate-gies,* edited by Saskia Wieringa. Brookfield, VT: Gower.

Vasconi, Tomas A. 1990. Democracy and socialism in South America. *Latin American Perspectives* 17: 25–38.

Vilas, Carlos. 1986. *The Sandinista revolution: National liberation and social transformation in Central America.* New York: Monthly Review Press.

Vlassoff, Carol. 1994. From rags to riches: The impact of rural development on women's status in an Indian village. *World Development* 22 (5): 707–19.

Vogel, Lise. 1995. *Woman questions: Essays for a materialist feminism.* New York: Routledge.

———. 1993. *Mothers on the job: Maternity policy in the U.S. workplace.* New Brunswick, NJ: Rutgers University Press.

———. 1984. Response to Brenner and Holmstrom. *Contemporary Sociology* 13: 601.

———. 1983. *Marxism and the oppression of women: Toward a unitary theory.* New Brunswick, NJ: Rutgers University Press.

———. 1979. Questions on the woman question. *Monthly Review* 31 (June): 39–59.

———. 1973. The earthly family. *Radical America* 7 (4, 5) (July–October): 9–50.

Wainwright, Hilary. 1994. *Arguments for a new left: answering the free market right.* Oxford, UK: Blackwell.

Walby, Sylvia. 1992. Post-post-modernism? Theorizing social complexity. In *Destabilizing theory: Contemporary feminist debates,* edited by Michèle Barrett and Anne Phillips. Stanford, CA: Stanford University Press.

———. 1989. *Theorizing patriarchy.* London: Blackwell.

———. 1987. *Patriarchy at work.* Minneapolis: University of Minnesota Press.

Walker, Pat, ed. 1979. *Between labor and capital.* Boston: South End Press.

Walkowitz, Judith R. 1983. *Prostitution and Victorian sexuality: Women, class, and the state.* Cambridge: Cambridge University Press.

Wallace, Phyllis 1984. *Pathways to work.* Cambridge, MA: MIT Press.

———. 1980. *Black women in the labor force.* Cambridge, MA: MIT Press.

Wallerstein, Immanuel. 1974. *The Modern World System.* New York: Academic Press.

Warner, Michael. 1993. *Fear of a queer planet: Queer politics and social theory.* Minneapolis: University of Minnesota Press.

Warren, Karen. 1994. *Ecological feminism.* New York: Routledge.

Waters, Mary Alice. 1970. *The politics of women's liberation today.* London: Pathfinder Press.

Weber, M. 1947. *Theory of social and economic organization.* New York: Oxford University Press.

Weeks, Jeffrey. 1985. *Sexuality and its discontents.* London: Routledge.

Weinbaum, Batya, and Amy Bridges. 1979. The other side of the paycheck: Monopoly capitalism and the structure of consumption. In *Capitalist Patriarchy and the Case for Socialist Feminism,* edited by Zillah Eisenstein. New York: Monthly Review Press.

Wells, Ida B. 1977. Lynching and rape: An exchange of views. Occasional papers series no. 25, San Jose State University.

West, Candace, and Don H. Zimmerman. 1987. Doing gender. *Gender and Society* 1 (2): 125–51.

White, E. Frances. 1984. Listening to the voices of black feminism. *Radical America* 7–25.

Whitehead, Anne. 1990. Food crisis and gender conflict in the African countryside. In *The food question: Profits vs. people?* edited by Henry Bernstein et al. New York: Monthly Review Press.

———. 1985. Effects of technological change on rural women: A review of analysis and concepts. In *Technology and rural women,* edited by Iftikhar Ahmed. London: Allen and Unwin.

Williams, Frances. 1994. Dykes mean business, gay lifestyles. *Gay to Z Business Directory.*

Williams, Raymond. 1977. *Marxism and literature.* Oxford: Oxford University Press.

Williams, Rhonda. 1985. Competition, class location and discrimination: black workers and the new growth dynamic. Unpublished paper presented at the Current Economic Revolution in Black America Conference, University of Texas, Austin, Tex.

Willis, Ellen. 1992. *No more nice girls: Countercultural essays.* Hanover, NH: Wesleyan University Press.

Willis, Paul. 1979. *Spass am Widerstand.* Frankfurt am Main.

Wilson, Amrit. 1978. *Finding a voice: Asian women in Britain.* London: Virago.

Wilson, Elizabeth. 1980. *Only halfway to paradise: Women in Postwar Britain 1945–1968.* London: Tavistock.

Wilson, William J. 1987. *The truly disadvantaged.* Chicago: University of Chicago Press.

———. 1980. *The declining significance of race.* Chicago: University of Chicago Press.

Wines, Michael. 1992. Views on single motherhood are multiple at White House. *New York Times* (21 May).

Winn, Peter. 1989. Socialism fades out of fashion. *The Nation* (26 June): 882–86.

Wittig, Monique. 1992. *The straight mind.* Boston: Beacon Press.

Women's Collective. 1977. Women's domestic labor. In *On the political economy of women.* London: Women's Press.

Wong, Nellie. 1991. Socialist feminism: Our bridge to freedom. In *Third World women and the politics of feminism,* edited by Chandra Talpadz Mohanty, Ann Russo, and Lourdes Torres. Bloomington: Indiana University Press.

Wood, Ellen Mieskins. 1995. *Why not capitalism?* London: Merlin Press.

———. 1995. *Democracy against capitalism.* London: Cambridge University Press.

———. 1992. *The pristine culture of capitalism.* London: Verso.

———. 1988. Capitalism and human emancipation. *New Left Review* 167: 3–20.

———. 1986. *The retreat from class: A new "true" socialism.* London: Verso.

Woody, Bette, and Michelene Malson. 1984. In crisis: Low income black employed women in the U.S. workplace. Working Paper no. 131. Wellesley Center for Research on Women, Wellesley, MA.

World Bank. 1994. *Infrastructure for development.* New York: Oxford University Press.

Wright, Erik Olin. 1985. *Classes.* London: Verso.

———. 1977. *Class crisis and the state.* London: New Left Books.

Young, Iris M. 1994. "Gender as seriality: Thinking about women as a social collective." *Signs* 18 (Spring): 713–38.

———. 1981. Beyond the unhappy marriage: A critique of the dual systems theory. In *Women and revolution: A discussion of the unhappy marriage of Marxism and feminism,* edited by Lydia Sargent. Boston: South End Press.

———. 1980. Socialist feminism and the limits of dual systems theory. *Socialist Review* 50/51: 169–88.

Yuval-Davis. 1992. Fundamentalism, multiculturalism and women in Britain. In *"Race," culture and difference,* edited by James Donald and Ali Rattansi. London: Sage.

Zaretsky, Eli. 1973. Capitalism, the family, and personal Life. *Socialist Revolution* 13–14 (January–April): 69–125.

Zetkin, Klara. 1934. *Reminiscences of Lenin.* New York: International.

———. 1934. *The toilers against war.* New York: Workers Library.

Zimmerman, Matilde. 1987. 1500 women attend Latin American feminist conference in Mexico. *The Militant* (20 November).